Stanley's Despatches to the *New York Herald,*
1871–1872, 1874–1877

Boston University African Research Studies Number 10

Stanley's Despatches to the *New York Herald*

1871-1872, 1874-1877

Edited by Norman R. Bennett

Boston University Press   1970

To Robert E. Moody

Preface

Stanley's despatches first came to my attention in 1960 when I was checking materials for the study of nineteenth-century East African history. The despatches contained material that was worthy of publication and had not been incorporated in Stanley's published volumes. Since the despatches are not readily available, it was suggested by Robert E. Moody that the whole collection be published. Further research demonstrated that an edited and annotated collection would be useful both to those interested in African history and in Stanley's life, especially since the African aspects of Stanley's career have not yet been well treated. William O. Brown and A. A. Castagno, past and present directors of the African Studies Center, gave the project their full support. It could not have been completed without their continuing interest.

The documents are presented in their original form (as they appeared in the *Herald*), with only minor changes in punctuation for the sake of clarity. Most of the despatches were taken from photocopies of the *Herald* supplied by the Library of Congress. The Boston Athenaeum kindly allowed the use of their issues of the *Herald* for consultation during the final typing of the manuscript. Additional materials—part of Stanley's diary, a sketch by Stanley of Livingstone at Ujiji, and a photograph of Stanley—were discovered in the Peabody Museum of Salem, Massachusetts; they are published with the kind permission of its directors.

Svend Holsoe, Carl Haywood, Barbara Dubins, Marguerite Ylvisaker, and Shams Bahloo gave vital aid in preparing the documents; Israel Katoke supplied valuable information on Swahili terminology and on the Lake Victoria region. Charles F. Holmes also supplied helpful information on the Lake Victoria region. Several of my colleagues made useful comments on the introduction to this volume; my especial thanks go to George E. Brooks, Jr., and Roy C.

Bridges for their penetrating remarks. Suzanne Marcus, with the aid of Cynthia Heinonen and Shirley McNerney, performed the laborious task of typing the manuscript. Ruth Bennett drew the maps. My thanks go also to Fathers Frits Versteynen and J. van Hensbergen of the Holy Ghost Mission at Bagamoyo for aid concerning Stanley's visit to their mission. A special measure of appreciation goes to Alyce Havey for ensuring that all went smoothly, especially during my absence from Boston.

The Tanzania Society and Philip Gulliver kindly allowed me to adapt a map appearing in *Tanganyika Notes and Records*, 54(1960), as did Brian K. Taylor and the International African Institute for a map appearing in Taylor's *The Western Lacustrine Bantu* (London: International African Institute, 1962). They serve as the bases for Maps I and III respectively.

My first acquaintance with Stanley's despatches came while I was studying the history of East Africa with the aid of a Foreign Area Training Fellowship from the Ford Foundation. Support from the African Studies Center allowed the project to continue over the years. A fellowship from the American Philosophical Society for study of related East African problems provided an opportunity to check works of relevance both to Stanley and to East Africa. Finally my thanks go to the universities of Hamburg and St. Andrews for allowing me the use of their resources.

Norman R. Bennett

St. Andrews, Scotland
Boston, Massachusetts
August and December 1966
March 1968

Contents

Appendices

Illustrations

Maps

Introduction

Stanley remains one of the most controversial of the major European explorers of Africa. His often turbulent career and the internal stresses of his personality help to explain this fact. Nonetheless, there is no apparent reason why, more than three-quarters of a century after his last venture, Stanley should continue to be singled out for his supposed excesses in Africa, while other Europeans, of greater or lesser note in Africa—often responsible for far more loss of African life than Stanley—receive sympathetic treatment.[1] Much of the problem comes from the lack of an adequate biographical study of Stanley, one well-grounded in the multitudinous sources necessary to the understanding of a life spent in traveling and working in widely different parts of Africa (and of Europe, Asia, and North America), leaving information in the oral and written records of numerous countries.[2]

Instead of carrying out the necessary research, Stanley's biographers—with one partial exception[3]—have concentrated on his personality, advancing analyses to explain his career that reveal more of the authors' dexterity of interpretation than of their capacity for the research essential to an understanding of a man and his epoch. Important data about Stanley's early life have been uncovered in recent

1. At a recent historical conference he was described by one participant as "that horror."
2. The most useful source of information concerning Stanley is Dorothy Stanley, ed., *The Autobiography of Sir Henry Morton Stanley*. There are, however, many lacunae in Mrs. Stanley's edited work. Hird, *H. M. Stanley. The Authorized Life*, builds on the previous source. Both Anstruther, *I Presume: Stanley's Triumph and Disaster*, and Farwell, *The Man Who Presumed: A Biography of Henry M. Stanley*, offer new materials on Stanley's early life, and on some aspects of his career in Britain and America; they are of limited use for his African experiences, however. Luwel, *Stanley* offers a sound and reliable, although brief, account of Stanley and is by far the best source for the explorer's life. Luwel also lists the essential bibliographical works concerning Stanley.
3. Luwel, *Stanley*.

years, but the mature years, the years of his major impact upon Africa, have not been satisfactorily treated as yet.

One of the most serious defects of the recent interpretations of Stanley is their almost total lack of concern with the African milieu in which he carved out his career. Stanley's own descriptions—almost always written in haste—are cited with little or no analysis and without reference to the considerable body of scholarship available on the peoples and areas through which the explorer passed. Thus, African names which no longer have any meaning are used; errors of location that Stanley understandably perpetrated are continued; and legends about his career long ago disproven are transmitted as fact.[4]

This edition of Stanley's despatches to the *New York Herald,* with some related documents, is designed then to serve two purposes. The original reports are of considerable historical value because Stanley, after his return from the two expeditions dealt with (those of 1871–1872 and 1874–1877), rewrote the despatches—written during the heat of his explorations—for publication in book form. In *How I Found Livingstone* the differences are no greater than one would expect,[5] but in *Through the Dark Continent* Stanley, influenced by criticism of his literary style, used outside help in preparing his published account.[6] More significantly, the many tumultuous encounters with Africans described in Stanley's despatches had roused the ire of humanitarians in Europe and the United States;[7] consequently, he felt compelled to rewrite some of the battle descriptions to place himself

4. For example, Farwell, *Man Who Presumed,* especially 184, 219, demonstrates a sense of ethnocentric superiority that mars his interpretation of Stanley in Africa.

5. Some writers refer to *How I Found Livingstone* as Stanley's "Diary." See Jackson, *Meteor Out of Africa,* 40, or Macdonald, *The Story of Stanley,* viii. Macdonald wrote: "The real Stanley is to be found, not in the newspaper reports, but in his books, which are for the most part faithful diaries of the thoughts, acts, and experiences of his adventurous life." But Stanley did rearrange his original notes for publication. He said: "I have adopted the narrative form of relating the story of the search, on account of the greater interest it appears to possess over the diary form, and I think that in this manner I avoid the great fault of repetition for which some travellers have been severely criticised." *HIFL,* xxiii. Compare the section of Stanley's diary given in document 11 with the relevant *HIFL* section.

6. *TDC,* X, viii. Stanley perhaps reacted to a feeling expressed by Burton: "The letters are evidently written in haste, and after much weariness of mind and body; and more mature reflection combined with further experience, may introduce important modifications into the more permanent record of travel." Burton's letter of Oct. 19, 1875, in *Geographical Magazine* 2(1875), 354.

7. See documents 24 and 25.

in a better light. There are several important descrepancies between the accounts given in the despatches and those presented in *Through the Dark Continent*. Even the accounts in the unsatisfactory edition of Stanley's diary of the 1874–1877 trip differ from the original reports.[8] For this reason, all the despatches written during these two expeditions are presented here exactly as they appeared in the *Herald*.[9]

My second purpose has been to annotate the letters so that the information Stanley remitted from Africa will be more useful to those concerned with his life, his two most important African ventures, and Africa in general. All of the problems the texts present have not been solved, but hopefully a useful beginning has been made to supplying the needed context of understanding for what Stanley heard, saw, and reported from an Africa that was then first coming into contact with European culture—of which Stanley was often the first representative.

Stanley's Early Life

John Rowlands, illegitimate son of John Rowland and Elizabeth Parry, was born at Denbigh, Wales, on January 28, 1841.[10] A more unlikely beginning for the later prominent reporter, explorer, colonial administrator, member of Parliament, and holder of the Grand Cross of the Bath is difficult to conceive; and it was a beginning that Stanley never forgot. Abandoned by his mother, young Rowlands lived for a time with his maternal grandfather; but early in life the latter's death caused him to be boarded with a neighboring couple at an uncle's expense. Eventually the cost became more than his relatives were willing to bear. In 1847 the unwanted child was delivered to St. Asaph Union Workhouse to be confined and educated in the manner thought proper for children of his class. Stanley later said of St. Asaph, "to the young it is a house of torture," and he called himself "a British outcast."[11]

But young Rowlands managed to survive the inherent dangers of this example of nineteenth-century benevolence; he absorbed, during a nine-year stay, a reasonably good education—he was a leading stu-

8. Stanley and Neame, eds., *The Exploration Diaries of H. M. Stanley*.

9. Some of Stanley's despatches as originally published have been printed in book-form. See the anonymous *Life & Finding of Dr. Livingstone*; Heudebert, *La Découverte du Congo*; Bellenger, *Lettres de H. M. Stanley*. None of these collections are complete and none are annotated.

10. The general information on Stanley's life is drawn from the sources mentioned in note 2 unless otherwise indicated.

11. *Autobiography*, 10–11.

dent of the institution—and a lasting, if narrow, belief in a Calvinist God. Finally, when the excesses of a brutal headmaster became too great, the growing orphan, in what can only be described as a proper Victorian reaction to injustice, thrashed him, after receiving an undeserved beating, and fled St. Asaph.

The fifteen-year-old refugee, pudgy and unprepossessing, attempted life with various relatives in Wales, but he had the not-uncommon tribulations of a poor and unwanted relation. The gate to a wider world then opened with the opportunity for the boy to reside with relatives in Liverpool, where he had hopes of successful employment. But success escaped the young Welshman, and he remained a poor relation employed in menial positions until one day on the busy docks of Liverpool, the master of a vessel asked him if he wanted to become a cabin boy. The dissatisfied errand boy reacted quickly and in December 1858, he left Britain for New Orleans.

Thus occurred the major break with Stanley's Nonconformist and restrictive past. Arriving, in February 1859, in that bustling port of the south, young Rowlands deserted, as the captain, who pocketed his wages, had intended. The youth joined the quest for position and advancement offered by the fluid society of a developing America. By pure chance the new arrival asked his famous question—"Do you want a boy, Sir?"—to a receptive, and childless, commission merchant, Henry Stanley.[12] The result was moderately well-paid employment and, more important, a gradually developing intimacy with the older man.

Later in the year Mrs. Stanley died, and soon a virtual father-and-son relationship developed between the American merchant and the Welsh immigrant, leading to the youth's eventual informal adoption and the assumption of the name Henry Stanley. Young Stanley was groomed in that peculiarly American combination of religion and business, and until the intendedly temporary departure of his mentor for Cuba in the fall of 1860, he spent what he described as one of the happiest periods of his life. While the elder Stanley was absent—he died in Cuba in 1861—the younger Stanley was left to work in the frontier region of Arkansas. There he acquired an appropriate frontier familiarity with firearms that would stand him in good stead in Africa; there also Stanley had his first experiences with malarial fevers.

Then came the Civil War to wrench Stanley from what might have been the undistinguished life of a frontier merchant. Incongruously, the later self-appointed redeemer of the African now went to war to preserve Negro slavery in the South. But Stanley, as most men, natur-

12. *Ibid.*, 87.

ally took on the views of his immediate environment; and after being shamed by being sent a chemise and petticoat, he enlisted in an Arkansas volunteer regiment. Here, as a man of twenty—a photograph shows him slim and manly—Stanley learned the discipline and harshness of camp life. In April 1862, Stanley had his baptism of fire at Shiloh where he was taken prisoner; he was sent to Camp Douglas, near Chicago. The unhealthy life of confinement soon led him to abandon a cause for which he had no great commitment, and to secure freedom by enlisting in the Union army in June 1862. But the stay in Camp Douglas had undermined his health, and in the same month he was discharged, a very sick man, from army life.

Once recovered, the veteran of the armies of North and South worked his way back to Liverpool and to his family in Wales. But his reception, even by his mother, was no better than in earlier years—he was still a poor relation, after all. A short period of service in the merchant navy, which included a visit to Cuba, followed; there Stanley learned of the elder Stanley's death. Returning to the United States in 1863, he reentered military service in 1864 by joining the Union Navy.

Stanley was present at the two attacks on Fort Fisher in North Carolina. These battles signaled the beginning of Stanley's rise to eminence, for he wrote accounts of the actions that were published later in the press. At last he had found his vocation. With the war's end approaching, he deserted from the Navy in February 1865. After perhaps attempting employment in a lawyer's office, he began to make his living as a free-lance reporter.[13] The character of the man was now apparent: Stanley was ready for adventure. He began in 1865 a career of twenty-five years' travel and exploration that would take him from the American West to the Middle East and Central Asia, and to Africa.

During 1866, Stanley traveled in western America. For a time he was based in Omaha, Nebraska. Here his boisterous nature demonstrated itself in a minor affair over a traveling actress. According to one account, the young reporter fell in love with one Annie Ward. Another reporter "made sport" of the affair and was assaulted by Stanley, but in a resulting court case Stanley was acquitted "on the ground of justifiable cause." A second version has it that Stanley was not the aggrieved lover, but the individual who twitted the captive of Annie Ward's charms. A fight ensued, and Stanley was acquitted of assault

13. See Appendix C.

charges.[14] The affair was minor and the facts are unclear, but it demonstrated that Stanley had developed the rough temper of the American frontier, a trait that would show itself again during his African travels.

Stanley capped his western experiences by descending the dangerous Platte River with a new acquaintance, W. H. Cook. Stanley and Cook resolved to continue their adventures by travel in Asia, so, accompanied by Lewis Noe, they left Boston for Turkey in July 1866. But the venture was a failure, and it returned to plague Stanley in later life.[15] (See Appendices A–I.)

In 1867, Stanley traveled to the West again, to report on the efforts of the Army to resolve the Indian problem. He wrote for the *Missouri Democrat* and other newspapers, including the *New York Herald*.[16]

With the earnings from this busy year, the ambitious Stanley decided to visit New York and attempt to secure a more important position with a major newspaper. He approached James Gordon Bennett, Jr. of the *Herald* and offered to report on the British expedition against Emperor Theodore of Ethiopia. Bennett was unenthusiastic —he judged American interest in Africa to be minimal—but decided that Stanley could cover the campaign for the *Herald* at his own expense; he was promised a permanent post if his efforts were successful. Because of a fortuitous agreement with the telegraph operator at Suez to forward his despatches before all others, Stanley scooped the field. Even more fortuitously, the telegraph cable broke after Stanley's message had been sent so that his story reached Europe before all other accounts, including the official reports of the British staff. Bennett was as good as his word, and Stanley entered into the busy life of a leading correspondent for the *Herald* in 1868.

Stanley, Livingstone and the New York Herald

While Stanley was making his way as a reporter, the European exploration of Africa had been increasing in momentum until it had captured the attention of the European and American press. The most popular of the explorers opening Africa to the outside world was the tenacious and troublesome Scot, David Livingstone.[17] Born in Blan-

14. *Autobiography*, 221–22, gives only an oblique reference to the affair. Farwell, *Man Who Presumed*, 30, and Hird, *Stanley*, 45, merely incorporate the same description. For the affair, Alfred Sorenson, *Story of Omaha*, 242–44; see also Appendix H.

15. For details on this period of Stanley's life, see Appendix E.

16. Excerpts from Stanley's letters for this period are given in Wheeler, "Henry M. Stanley's Letters to the *Missouri Democrat*," 269–86.

17. There is no satisfactory biography of Livingstone; Seaver, *David Livingstone*, offers the latest significant account.

tyre, near Glasgow, in 1813, of poor parents, Livingstone managed
to secure an education and to go on to medical training and a career
as a missionary for the London Missionary Society. He did not find the
daily and difficult routine of evangelization congenial, however, and
soon began a series of explorations that he regarded as necessary to
the proper conversion of Africa. In doing so Livingstone became the
greatest propagandist for Africa the European world had yet known.
His explorations were significant; but more important was the way
in which they were carried out. Lacking both extensive resources for
organizing expeditions and the talent to keep large groups of men in
order—either Europeans or Africans—the Scots missionary set about
penetrating Africa in a manner that captured the imagination of his
contemporaries. Accompanied by only a few African companions, he
traveled during 1854–1856 from Luanda on the West coast across the
breadth of the continent to Quelimane. His account of the journey,
enlivened by his curiosity for all things animate and inanimate, became an immediate best seller.[18] Livingstone had gained a secure niche
as Africa's most famous explorer.

In 1858, with government support, Livingstone led a large expedition of Europeans in exploring the Zambezi and Shire rivers and
Lake Nyasa. Although significant results were accomplished for the
future development of the Nyasa region, Livingstone's inability to
work with his European subordinates left him with a feeling of
frustration, and he resolved to avoid large expeditions in the future.[19]

The Scotsman's final venture into Africa, less important for actual
discoveries—which were nonetheless significant—than for the influence it had on the course of events in Africa, began in 1866.
Livingstone left the eastern African coast for the interior to inquire
into the imperfectly understood problems of the watershed of central
Africa and the sources of the Nile. The course of his travels was slow
and irregular, and communications were non-existent. By the end of
the 1860's popular interest in the missionary's fate turned toward
him the attention of James Gordon Bennett, Jr.[20]

18. The trip is described in Livingstone, *Missionary Travels and Researches in
South Africa*. For this early period of his life, see also the following volumes
edited by Schapera: *David Livingstone. Family Letters 1841–1856; Livingstone's
Private Journals 1851–1853; Livingstone's Missionary Correspondence 1841–1856;
Livingstone's African Journal 1853–1856*.

19. See [David and Charles] Livingstone, *Narrative of an Expedition to the
Zambesi*; Wallis, ed., *Zambezi Expedition of David Livingstone 1858–1863*;
Shepperson, ed., *David Livingstone and the Rovuma*; Foskett, ed., *Zambesi
Journals and Letters of Dr. John Kirk 1858–63*.

20. Livingstone's account is given in Waller, ed., *Last Journals of David
Livingstone*. See also documents 4 and 7.

Bennett first became interested in the news possibilities of Livingstone in 1868, when rumors were circulating that Livingstone might
emerge from inland Africa at Zanzibar, or that he might return down
the Nile. Stanley was summoned to London from an assignment in
Spain. The *Herald's* representative, Finlay Anderson, sent the rising
young reporter to Aden to seek information, with the option of proceeding to Zanzibar if necessary.[21] Stanley visited Aden from November
1868, to February 1869, without gaining news of Livingstone; the
rumors of his return proved groundless. But Stanley made a valuable
contact for the future by writing to the American representative in
Zanzibar, Francis R. Webb, for information.[22] With no word from
Livingstone, Stanley left Aden and returned to reporting in Spain.[23]

Popular interest in Livingstone remained acute, and when the missionary continued in the interior, Bennett called Stanley to Paris in
October 1869 for the interview that led to Stanley's undertaking the
famous expedition. The assignment would lead him from Egypt
through Central Asia to India, whence, if Livingstone yet remained in
Africa, he was to proceed to Zanzibar and then inland to interview
the long-absent missionary explorer.[24] Stanley fulfilled the first part
of the instructions with his usual talent,[25] arriving in Zanzibar in
January 1871, to begin the quest after Livingstone described in the
letters given in Part I of this volume.

Stanley's expedition was to surpass whatever Bennett had had in
mind for his star reporter. Zanzibar sources informed Stanley that
Livingstone would at some time be at Ujiji; Stanley, seizing the initiative, set out to meet the missionary there, or elsewhere in the interior
if necessary. Bennett, however, as was his custom, said little of the
venture in his columns. A first reference came when news from London reported: "A Party of Americans is hurrying into the interior
with the object of rescuing the doctor from his perilous position."[26]
No doubt, if the news had not been circulating in Britain, Bennett
would not have published even this brief note.

21. Anderson has been given credit for first suggesting the *Herald* idea of a
meeting of one of their reporters with Livingstone. Seitz, *The James Gordon
Bennetts*, 303.
22. See document 1, note 24.
23. Stanley had also checked in Egypt for information concerning Livingstone.
See Macgregor, *Rob Roy on the Jordan*, 53–54; Balch, "American Explorers of
Africa," 278–79.
24. Stanley later said about the early section of this trip that he set off
"with a budget of instructions which I look upon even to this day with dismay."
Stanley, *My African Travels*, 3.
25. See document 1.
26. *NYH*, Sept. 19, 1871.

The *Herald's* columns kept attention focused on eastern Africa from then on by publishing, for example, letters about Livingstone from a British official in Zanzibar, John Kirk.[27] Stanley's first despatch was published in the *Herald* of December 22, 1871. Following Bennett's policy, Stanley was described only as the "HERALD Commissioner," and his name was not given. But the affair was now public and Bennett played the news for its full impact on an interested public. One theme that emerged was the new role of the American press: "An African exploring expedition is a new thing in the enterprises of modern journalism, and in this, as in many other great achievements of the 'third estate,' to the NEW YORK HERALD will belong the credit of the first bold adventure in the cause of humanity, civilization and science." *Herald* writers advanced the view that Stanley, though unnamed, had given promise of being able to succeed in reaching Livingstone from his earlier Ethiopian trip, and that the *Herald* was "thus encouraged in the hope that this expedition will settle all doubts in reference to Dr. Livingstone, and we hope too, that it will accomplish something more than the solution of the Livingstone mystery." The something more was the unfinished exploration of central Africa; the final result would be to join forever the *Herald* with "the names of Bruce and Speke and Grant, and of Baker and Burton and Livingstone" in the development of African exploration. Another theme was the attack on Britain for leaving the task of reaching Livingstone to an American newspaper. Britain had been "too slow and too penurious," and the *Herald* would now show how decisive action could succeed.[28]

While waiting for more news from Stanley, the *Herald* columns ran series of articles under such titles as "The HERALD and Dr. Livingstone," or quoted appreciative excerpts from other newspapers—one described Stanley's venture as "the most extraordinary newspaper enterprize ever dreamed of." [29]

Sensing the great public interest in this developing story, Bennett went deeper into African reporting. The explorer and Egyptian administrator, Samuel Baker, was then acting in the Sudan in the service of Khedive Ismail.[30] It was decided to send a "HERALD special exploring expedition in quest of Sir Samuel Baker." Alvan S. South-

27. *Ibid.*, Dec. 11, 1871.
28. *Ibid.*, Dec. 23, 1871. A further elaboration on the theme of the role of the American press came in a Feb. 13, 1872, editorial: "When the HERALD equipped an expedition to explore Africa . . . it marked a new era in journalism as the ripest phase of modern civilization."
29. *Ibid.*, Dec. 27, 1871, quoting the *Buffalo Express*.
30. See document 6, note 5.

worth—his name was not mentioned until July 5, 1872—went south in January 1872, with the "longest streamer ever floated from a Nile dahabeah" bearing the name of the *Herald* in black letters, adding yet another gun to the *Herald's* African reporting.[31] It also supplied another opportunity to "twist the lion's tail"; Southworth wrote of Baker's expedition: "it has been conducted too much after the fashion of the British tourist, and too many theodolytes, barometers, sextants and artificial horizons have replaced canned meats and desiccated necessities. I am of the opinion (hastily formed, perhaps) that twelve energetic, live, I might say reckless Americans, each with his special mental and physical gifts, could bare this whole Continent to the view of an anxious mankind. The British are good, hardy, stubborn travellers, but they are like their journalism and ideas—slower than the wrath of the Grecian gods." [32]

Bennett had further material for his news venture when the Royal Geographical Society decided to send out a relief expedition after Livingstone.[33] The proprietor of the *Herald* let it be known that this action was due only to the stimulation of the *Herald* expedition.[34] The rivalry only heightened interest in the Livingstone story, and articles now came forth ridiculing the Geographical Society and Britain for their tardy effort, particularly as the British group was not optimistic that Stanley would reach Livingstone.[35]

On May 2, 1872, came the "Grand Triumph of American Enterprize" when the news of the meeting with Livingstone reached London, a triumph made even sweeter by letters from John Kirk predicting that Stanley would not reach Livingstone.[36] The dramatic story was stressed for its full impact and the columns of the *Herald* were replete

31. *NYH,* Jan. 19, 1872, Jan. 30, 1872. Southworth went south from Khartoum until blocked by the sudd of the Nile; he returned to Khartoum and left the Sudan by traveling overland to Suakin. In addition to his *Herald* despatches, Southworth wrote *Four Thousand Miles of African Travel.* His report to the American Geographical Society is given in *NYH,* March 26, 1873. For the "dahabeah," see document 1, note 15.

32. *Ibid.,* Dec. 28, 1871.

33. See document 11, note 5.

34. *NYH,* Jan. 7, 1872. The *Herald's* London correspondent wrote: "British munificence at times presents queer aspects. No sum is thought too large to devote to Christianizing the Fiji islanders, or for the purpose of carrying Bibles and warming pans to the benighted heathen of Central Africa or Nova Zembla, but for furthering in comparatively the greatest work of the nineteenth century— that of the discovery and exploration—the British Government manifests an apathy and infirmity of purpose singularly at variance with both past policy and with present interest." *Ibid.,* Jan. 30, 1872.

35. See *ibid.,* Feb. 14, 1872, Feb. 17, 1872.

36. Kirk's letters are in *ibid.,* May 5, 1872.

with the praises of admiring newspapers and with anti-British sentiments.[37]

Then, certainly much to Bennett's delight, several prominent British
individuals publicly expressed doubts about the veracity of Stanley's
accounts.[38] These doubts were matched against the information that
continued to come from the yet-unnamed *Herald* reporter[39] and with
continuing encomiums on the role of the American press, then and
in the future.[40] To further feed the fires of interest, the Southworth
party was kept in the news, and the *Herald* optimistically predicted:
"This exploring party will, probably, proceed south over Lake [Vic-
toria] Nyanza, and after reaching Ujiji, go to the east by the caravan
track and come out at Zanzibar." A hope was expressed that this
group too would meet Livingstone.[41]

In the midst of these triumphs for the *Herald,* along came an enemy
of Stanley, with the backing of a rival New York newspaper, *The Sun*
of Charles A. Dana, to challenge Stanley's accomplishment.[42] *The
Sun* would call Stanley's claimed exploits "the most gigantic hoax
ever attempted on the credulity of mankind." [43] *The Sun,* through
Lewis Noe, who had accompanied Stanley on his trip to Turkey in
1866, now both attacked Stanley's character and brought information
forward concerning his Welsh childhood.[44] But the *Herald* did not
avoid the issue; it exploited the quarrel for its full circulation value.[45]

37. The Elkton *Democrat* said: "The cause of science, British pride and the
British Treasury, African wilds and jungles and savage beasts and scarcely less
savage men, fever and famine and Egyptian darkness have alike succumbed
before the invincible powers and peerless enterprize of the great untamed, un-
tamable, unconvinced and unconvincible Scotch-American octogenarian prince
of journalists. Three cheers for the HERALD and a tiger for Bennett." *Ibid.,* May
5, 1872. The *Herald* demonstrated a touch of humor by publishing in this issue
of the *Herald* a letter from a reader asking, "Can't you 'let up' a little on Livingstone? Has he relatives 'on' the HERALD that expect to become his heirs?"

38. See *ibid.,* May 20, 1872, where the *Herald's* London correspondent reported:
"From what appears in the daily papers it would seem to be the earnest desire of
all persons here interested in geographical science that the recent good news
from Zanzibar may prove not true." For the British reaction to Stanley's reports,
Coupland, *Livingstone's Last Journey,* 197 ff.; Anstruther, *I Presume,* 117 ff.

39. See *NYH,* July 2, 1872.

40. *Ibid.,* July 3, 1872, where it was stated: "Henceforth the great discoveries
of the world, scientific and geographical, are to be heralded, not by the slow and
ineffectual means of books and through the ordinary agencies of publication,
but by the press of the land."

41. *Ibid.,* July 5, 1872.

42. See Wilson, *Life of Charles A. Dana,* 380 ff.

43. Quoted in *NYH,* Aug. 29, 1872.

44. See the Noe letters and other evidence, given in Appendices A through I.

45. Some of the New York press was not impressed with the sincerity of this
journalistic quarrel. The *New York Evening Mail,* Aug. 29, 1872, wrote: "We are

It printed a letter on Stanley's Welsh past, containing much correct information about the former John Rowlands, but upheld Stanley, stating he was "simply a native American. Missouri and not Wales is his birthplace." [46]

The quarrel continued, but by July 1872, it was apparent that Stanley had really met Livingstone; the *Herald* called it "no myth, but a sober, substantial and somewhat expensive fact." [47] Letters from Livingstone to Bennett arrived to be published,[48] and *The Sun's* and Noe's contention that Stanley had forged them did not convince many.[49] But even if Stanley had met Livingstone, there remained issues to exploit, particularly Stanley's charges that John Kirk had not served Livingstone well in his efforts to send supplies to the missionary;[50] further recriminations came from the break-up of the Royal Geographical Society expedition which had been sent to Zanzibar to relieve Livingstone before the news of Stanley's triumph.[51]

Stanley's arrival in Europe gave new life to the *Herald's* continuing story. His receptions in France and Britain brought only honor to the *Herald,* while the remaining episodes connected with disbelief in Stanley's achievements only made his, and the *Herald's,* eventual tri-

---

not to get through with this Livingstone-Stanley-Noe business in a hurry. The *Herald* and the *Sun* have enlisted for a protracted campaign, and each generously supplies the other with ammunition. Yesterday the *Sun* borrowed the *Herald's* plates to show that Livingstone's letters were written by Stanley. Today the *Herald* . . . uses the *Sun's* plates . . . If the controversy can be kept up with such an economy of materials there is no knowing how long it may last."

46. *NYH,* July 6, 1872, July 25, 1872. A generally correct version of Stanley's youth became known and was published in several accounts before the end of the nineteenth century. See for example, Ker, "Africa's Cortez," in Keltie, ed., *Story of Emin's Rescue as Told in Stanley's Letters,* 171; Reichard, *Stanley,* 3ff.; Kerfyser, *Henry M. Stanley,* 3–14. There were many conflicting stories, however, with Stanley often disseminating conflicting information. See Hoffmann, *With Stanley in Africa,* 11–12. A close acquaintance of his later added: "No one doubted his nationality, for he spoke in those days with a decided American accent." Johnston, "Stanley: A Biographical Note," 451.

47. *NYH,* July 16, 1872. For Bennett's initial reluctance to pay Stanley's large bills, see document 1, note 7.

48. *Ibid.,* July 26, 1872, July 27, 1872. Livingstone's letter to Bennett, dated Nov. 1871, was reproduced in the *Herald* of Aug. 27, 1872, to answer *The Sun's* charges that Stanley had forged it. The *Herald* added that if there were still doubters of Stanley, it would advance one-half the funds for an expedition to seek out Livingstone to have him settle the affair. The other newspapers were to pay the other one-half, and all could send correspondents along.

49. See the issues of *The Sun* from Aug. 27, 1872, through Oct. 21, 1872, for the campaign against Stanley.

50. *NYH,* Aug. 4, 1872, Aug. 5, 1872, Aug. 23, 1872. See also the references in note 38.

51. *NYH,* Aug. 10, 1872, Nov. 16, 1872. See also document 11, note 5.

umph all the more convincing.[52] The *Herald's* columns remained full of news about this most successful of journalistic ventures.[53]

The *Herald* was also quick to advance to itself credit for the new moves Britain and others were taking against the slave trade in eastern Africa.[54] The events leading to the Bartle Frere mission to Zanzibar were connected with the meeting of Stanley and Livingstone, and thus the new British policy was attributed to the *Herald's* influence. The *Herald* announced the hope that Frere's forthcoming mission would succeed; if it did "it will be a source of thankful pride to the HERALD that its journalistic enterprize struck the first blow against the slave trade of the Nile basin." [55] To demonstrate its serious view of the slave trade, the *Herald,* reacting to a letter to the editor, put forward a proposal for an international crusade against the slave trade. The un-named letter writer had sent $25 to begin a fund to equip the proposed force, and the *Herald* added $1000 to the venture.[56] Nothing came of the suggestion.

Loaded with honors gained in Britain, including an audience with, and a gift from, Queen Victoria, Stanley returned to New York on November 20, 1872.[57] He immediately became the sensation of the day and was honored at numerous receptions.[58]

Stanley had agreed while in Britain upon an American lecture tour

52. See the reports on Stanley at Paris and Brighton, *ibid.*, Aug. 18, 1872, Aug. 19, 1872, Aug. 27, 1872. The *Herald* of July 29, 1872, reported Stanley had been offered $10,000 for a book on his expedition.

53. Included in the *Herald* during this period were the following letters from Livingstone: Aug. 14, 1872—to Waller, Nov. 1871 and Feb. 19, 1872; Aug. 17, 1872—to Lord Stanley, Nov. 15, 1870, to Clarendon, Nov. 1, 1871, to Granville, Nov. 14, 1871, Dec. 18, 1871, and Feb. 20, 1872, and to Kirk, Oct. 3, 1871; Aug. 22, 1872—to John Livingstone, Nov. 16, 1871; to Braithwaithe, Nov. 1870; Aug. 29, 1872—to Stearns, Feb. 2, 1866, Feb. 15, 1866, and Feb. 19, 1866; Sept. 7, 1872—to John Livingstone, Jan. 12, 1866; Sept. 21, 1872—to Stearns, March 13, 1872; Nov. 4, 1872—to Granville, July 1, 1872, to Frere, July 1, 1872.

Other items of interest included an interview with John Livingstone, Sept. 2, 1872, and the following letters from Stanley: Sept. 2, 1872—to the *Times;* Sept. 15, 1872—to the *Herald,* Sept. 1, 1872; Sept. 26, 1872—to the *Times,* Sept. 28, 1872.

54. See document 16, note 22.

55. *NYH,* April 13, 1872, Aug. 13, 1872, Nov. 5, 1872, Jan. 2, 1873. When the treaty was signed, the *Herald* also took the credit. *Ibid.*, June 18, 1873. See also the report of Stanley's participation in an anti-slave trade meeting described in *ibid.,* Nov. 17, 1872.

56. *Ibid.,* Oct. 18, 1872.

57. See *ibid.,* Nov. 21, 1872.

58. Stanley increased the popular interest by appearing with Kalulu (see document 3, note 41) who was "clothed . . . after the manner of an English page." *Ibid.,* Nov. 22, 1872. Details of Stanley's attendance at various receptions are given in *ibid.,* Nov. 23, 1872, Nov. 25, 1872, Nov. 27, 1872, Nov. 28, 1872, Jan. 14, 1873, and Jan. 15, 1873.

to recount his African adventures; the fee reported was £10,000 plus all expenses.[59] A series of lectures began in New York in December 1872, but they failed drastically.[60] The *Herald* reported that the first lecture was given to a crowded audience,[61] but other reporters commented on an unfilled house.[62] Stanley turned out to be a poor lecturer. The *Herald* reporter said: "Mr. Stanley still betrays some of the vices which are the necessary blunders of the tyro. He speaks too fast in his eagerness not to bore his hearers, the consequence is that they sometimes fail to understand the force of what he has said." [63] Stanley began with a background summary of African exploration, beginning with the career of Diaz, going on to prove Mr. Darwin "insane," and concluding "by drawing a glowing Christian future for Central Africa." [64] The lecture was held to be "a trifle abstruse for his public." [65] "The audience was remarkably quiet during the entire course of the lecture, not one single sound of approbation greeted Mr. Stanley's remarks." [66]

The second lecture, in which he spoke about Livingstone and his own mission, although an improvement—the *Times* reporter said: "Mr. Stanley retired amid much applause"—was also disappointing as the hall was only one-third filled.[67] When a few individuals came for the third lecture, they were turned away, the hall's janitor being quoted as saying: "Stanley's played out; there will be no lecture to-

59. *Ibid.*, Oct. 6, 1872.

60. The brochure advertising the lectures gave the following misinformation, no doubt supplied by Stanley, on the explorer's youth. It was stated that Stanley was born in New York city in 1843; after running away from school he went to sea and had various adventures until the Civil War began. Then he returned to enlist in the Union army for a period of active service, followed by a period as a war correspondent. The rest of the details given agree generally with the accepted facts of Stanley's life. The brochure, however, made an amusing error; it said Stanley greeted Livingstone in Ujiji with the words, "Dr. Livingstone, I Believe." *Henry M. Stanley's American Lectures on the Discovery of Dr. Livingstone.*

61. *NYH*, Dec. 4, 1872. Anstruther, *I Presume*, 175, supports this, with apparent stylistic exaggerations.

62. *New York Evening Mail*, Dec. 4, 1872; *New York Tribune*, Dec. 4, 1872; *New York Times*, Dec. 4, 1872.

63. *NYH*, Dec. 4, 1872.

64. *New York Times*, Dec. 4, 1872.

65. *NYH*, Dec. 4, 1872.

66. *New York Times*, Dec. 4, 1872. Farwell, *Man Who Presumed*, 91–92, and Anstruther, *I Presume*, 175–77, make much of the fact that a *Herald* reporter commented unfavorably on this and the following lecture in order to win Bennett's favor; it is claimed that the *Herald* owner was upset over the great public acclaim Stanley received. But the *Herald* articles on the lectures, in the Dec. 4 and Dec. 5, 1872, issues, were not unduly severe; they matched the general comment given in the other New York papers.

67. *New York Times*, Dec. 5, 1872; *NYH*, Dec. 5, 1872.

night or any other night, as Mr. Stanley's receipts do not meet expenses." [68] *The Sunday Mercury's* evaluation of these disappointing events was perhaps the fairest: "the tones of the lecturer were distinct, and his delivery was fair. As nobody cares anything about Africa, he labored with an unattractive subject, which he failed to present in the most interesting light." [69]

Stanley, the New York Herald, *and the Expedition across Africa*

Despite this minor failure, and the other problems Stanley had in New York and Washington,[70] The *Herald* reporter had nevertheless attained a reputation as one of the eminent journalists of his day. He was given a new African assignment, to cover the British campaign against the Ashanti in 1873–1874. In the company of other well-known correspondents, Stanley performed in his usual efficient manner but without any opportunity to gain undue distinction.[71]

Meanwhile Livingstone had continued his travels with the aid provided by Stanley. In 1873, his long travels came to an end near Lake Bangweulu in a manner that would do more for the future of Africa than all his previous exploits. Livingstone's men, devoted to their leader and understandably reluctant to return to Zanzibar without proof of his death, carried his remains—after burying his heart beneath a tree—to the coast. There the full propaganda machine of humanitarian Britain took over, both as a measure of devotion to Livingstone himself and as a stimulant for the anti-slavery and pro-Christian work the humanitarians promoted. Livingstone's remains were interred with moving ceremony in Westminster Abbey. Stanley held an honored position as a pallbearer at the funeral.

Then came a decision to exploit the great interest in Africa evoked by Livingstone; its successful outcome was to make Stanley the most famous explorer of his age. The young journalist proposed to complete Livingstone's explorations, and many other tasks as well, in

---

68. *The Sun,* Dec. 7, 1872. See also *New York Evening Mail,* Dec. 7, 1872. The *Mail* of Dec. 6 reported that at this time a false Stanley arrived in Pittsburgh, where he was treated for two days as the guest of the city.

69. *Sunday Mercury,* Dec. 8, 1872. The *Mercury* added a sarcastic note: "A New Mission for Stanley—the discoverer of Livingstone is reported to have been dispatched by the *Herald* at an immense expense in search of an audience. 'On! Stanley, on!'"

70. See Anstruther, *I Presume,* 173–81.

71. Ward, "H. M. Stanley's View of the Sixth Ashanti War through His Dispatches to *The New York Herald,*" covers this aspect of his career. Stanley collected his material, as well as that on the earlier Ethiopian campaign in his *Coomassie and Magdala.* Despite his fame, the *Herald* did not mention Stanley by name in its columns until Feb. 4, 1874.

central Africa. The scheme was accepted by the *Herald* and the British
Daily Telegraph; Stanley's despatches from this 1874–1877 venture
form Part II of the present volume.

The *Herald* had been following the activities of Livingstone since
Stanley's meeting with him at Ujiji in 1871. The dramatic details of
the explorer's death—given three and a half-columns in the *Herald*[72]
—immediately revived popular interest in Africa.[73] Stanley's participation in the funeral services was fully covered,[74] while readers were
further reminded of Livingstone's connections with the *Herald* by
the publication of letters sent by Livingstone to Stanley and Bennett.[75]

On July 17, 1874, the *Herald* announced the joint *Herald-Telegraph*
expedition. The public statement was made only because the news
was known in Britain, since "the policy of the HERALD has always
been to do things and then say what is proper to be said after they
have been done." But since the news was out, the *Herald* did drop its
"reserve and modesty" to announce that Stanley would now proceed
into Africa as "the ambassador of two great powers, representing the
journalism of England and America, and in command of an expedition more numerous and better appointed than any that has ever
entered Africa." Moreover, this expedition would serve as an example
for nations to follow; they sent armies to conquer, the press sent
"armies of peace and light." [76]

The *Herald* coverage of this expedition was quite different in character from that of the Livingstone search. Stanley's first despatches
were given immoderate praise; his minor trip to the Rufiji was described in this fashion: "No more important discovery than this has
been made for years." [77] But one *Herald* prophecy was to come true:
"It would not surprize us if Mr. Stanley's achievements in Africa
would surpass what he has already done in that strange land, impossible as this may seem." [78]

Stanley's despatches soon began to show that the *Herald's* statements were not unfounded. But a joint journalistic venture had its

---

72. *NYH*, Jan. 24, 1874.

73. See Stanley's letter concerning Livingstone in *ibid.*, April 4, 1874.

74. For accounts of the funeral, *ibid.*, April 16, 1874, April 19, 1874, April 20,
1874, April 29, 1874, April 30, 1874, May 1, 1874.

75. *Ibid.*, April 20, 1874, for Livingstone to Stanley; April 25, 1874, for
Livingstone to Bennett. A quotation from the latter letter would appear, in part, on
Livingstone's memorial stone in Westminster Abbey: "All I can add in my loneli-
ness is, may Heaven's rich blessing come down on every one—American,
English or Turk—who will help to heal this open sore of the world [the slave
trade]."

76. *Ibid.*, July 26, 1874.

77. *Ibid.*, Nov. 17, 1874.

78. *Ibid.*, Nov. 30, 1874.

problems; a minor quarrel occurred between the *Herald* and *Telegraph* in the fall of 1875. The agreement between the two papers required the British journal to hold publication of despatches until copies reached the *Herald;* then both were to publish simultaneously.[79] But the *Telegraph* did not wait and on October 10, 1875, in a two-column attack, the *Herald* blasted "The Premature Synopsis," presented in the *Telegraph.* The New York paper announced that "we cannot characterize the singular course of our ally in this matter as anything short of a breach of faith," adding that in the future the American paper should follow the rules of American diplomacy—"Avoid all entangling alliances." [80] The editor of the *Telegraph* managed to explain the breach, however, and harmony was restored.[81]

Stanley's progress around Lake Victoria and his encounter with the Africans of Bumbire Island created the human interest and controversy that the second expedition had theretofore lacked.[82] While in Buganda in 1875, Stanley met a French representative of Gordon, Linant de Bellefonds.[83] The two Europeans quickly became friends, and when Stanley left Buganda he gave De Bellefonds several despatches to deliver on his return to the Sudan. The French officer delivered Stanley's letters safely but was soon after killed in an encounter with Africans. A story spread that the despatches had been recovered from his body—a *Herald* sub-heading read "A Blood-Stained Mail." [84] The story would soon be disproven but would become an enduring myth long associated with Stanley's adventures.[85]

Between November 1875 and August 1876 there was a long period without news as Stanley went on to Lake Tanganyika and the Congo.[86]

---

79. *Ibid.,* Nov. 30, 1874.

80. *Ibid.,* Oct. 17, 1875. A sufficient reason for the joint venture was the cost; Stanley estimated this expedition cost around £12,000. H. M. Stanley, "Central Africa and the Congo Basin," 22.

81. *NYH.,* Oct. 20, 1875.

82. See documents 24 and 25.

83. See document 20, note 33 for De Bellefonds and for the sources on the "blood-stained" letter episode.

84. *NYH,* Nov. 10, 1875. The *Herald* added that the French officer's fate "may well intensify the notion that the correspondent [Stanley] bears a charmed life," and that "through revolt and war and treacherous assault and an atmosphere saturated with the fever poison Stanley always goes safely."

85. See the sources referred to in note 83. A letter of E. Marston of May 16, 1876, in *NYH,* May 28, 1876, gave the correct information concerning De Bellefonds. The old story was however retold as fact in Farwell, *Man Who Presumed,* 108–09.

86. The *New York Times* had not been optimistic on Stanley's aiming for the Congo: "It is, however, earnestly to be hoped that he will not undertake an enterprise so certain to end in irretrievable disaster." Quoted in *NYH,* Nov. 19, 1875.

The *Herald* announced that it was not worried: "For our own part, we have no doubt of Stanley's safety. His courage, coolness, energy and judgment have been so signally displayed that he merits supreme confidence. Such a man will triumph when any other explorer would be baffled and defeated." [87] Letters from Stanley finally arrived to be published in August 1876; those detailing the Bumbire Island affair were to trigger one of the more important conflicts about Stanley's career in Africa.

The details Stanley supplied of his punishment expedition to Bumbire[88] led humanitarian and other groups in Britain to attack the explorer. The Anti-Slavery Society and the Aborigines Protection Society memorialized the British government to act against Stanley and his "act of blind and ruthless vengeance." It was suggested that Stanley be returned to the scene of the attack under the British flag and there "be hanged with impartial justice as other murderers are," with the goods of the caravan being auctioned off for the benefit of the injured population. The government replied that they could not interfere in the dispute since Stanley was held to be an American citizen; their only course of action was to attempt to inform Stanley that he had no authority to fly the British flag.[89] This decision amounted to little; the American representative in Zanzibar merely promised to forward the message to Stanley.[90] There was little else the American diplomat could do; it is doubtful if the British message ever reached Stanley in the African interior.

The affair did not, however, end there. At the November 13, 1876, meeting of the Royal Geographical Society, H. M. Hyndman attempted to introduce a resolution censuring Stanley for his deeds.[91] He was ruled against, since the council judged the censure outside the proper business of the Society. When the Society met on November 27, 1876, Hyndman, through the aid of the influential Henry Yule,[92] was finally permitted to speak. He asked if he could read some of Stanley's words and wished the organization to express its opinion of them. Yule felt this proper as, even though the group had no connection with Stanley, they had praised his African work in the past.

87. *Ibid.*, July 11, 1876.
88. See document 25.
89. Lister to Kirk, Oct. 21, 1876, with enclosures, Q-15, ZA.
90. Bennett, "Stanley and the American Consuls at Zanzibar," 48.
91. Henry M. Hyndman (1842–1921), then employed by the *Pall Mall Gazette*. He later became an important British socialist leader. *DNB 1912–1921*, 280–82. Hyndman gives the justification for his moves in his *Record of an Adventurous Life*, 151–52.
92. Henry Yule (1820–1889), the well-known geographer and scholar. *DNB.*, XXI, 1,320–22.

The proposal met with no better success than the previous one, and no action was taken.[93]

The affair went on, however, without the Royal Geographical Society; the American press joined in. The *Herald* was perfectly willing to use the conflict for its own interests and to print the anti-Stanley articles of other newspapers. [94] Still, Stanley was the *Herald's* man, and he was defended. One strong editorial entitled "Stanley and the Philanthropists" struck out at those it called the "howling dervishes of civilization" who while "safe in London" could attack Stanley.[95] Other articles dealt with the Royal Geographical Society in a similar tone.[96] All in all, the *Herald* had found an issue similar to those raised after the Livingstone expedition—enabling it to praise American vigor and enterprise while stimulating the latent anti-British sentiments of the American people.[97]

Finally, in September 1877, came news of Stanley's arrival at the mouth of the Congo River. The *Herald* sealed "Stanley's Triumph" in this fashion: "This will greatly distress the philanthropists of London, who will again appeal to the British government to declare him a pirate. Their humane but rather impractical view is that a leader in such a position should permit his men to be slaughtered by the natives and should be slaughtered himself and let discovery go to the dogs, but should never pull a trigger against this species of human vermin that puts its uncompromising savagery in the way of all progress and all increase of knowledge." [98]

The "philanthropists" did try to strike at Stanley, but they had little chance of success in view of his great discoveries. An earlier writer had suggested that such "knowledge is dearly bought at the cost of piratical proceedings of this nature," [99] but this viewpoint was soon lost in the triumphal return given to Stanley in Europe. Yule and

93. *PRGS* 21 (1876–1877), 6, 59–63; Yule and Hyndman, *Mr. Henry M. Stanley and the Royal Geographical Society, passim;* see also Grant, "On Mr. H. M. Stanley's Exploration of the Victoria Nyanza," 25–26, for additional moderate criticisms read to the Society.

94. See, for example, *NYH,* Aug. 19, 1876.

95. *Ibid.,* Nov. 7, 1876.

96. *Ibid.,* Nov. 25, 1876, Nov. 29, 1876.

97. See *ibid.,* Jan. 1, 1877, March 14, 1877. In the latter issue it was advanced that " to explore the sources of the Nile and settle the problem of the Congo needs a man of bold and soldierly instincts. These Stanley evidently possesses. If the truly good members of the Royal Geographical Society believe that the difficulties of the task can be overcome by the distribution of tracts and taffy we see no good reason why they should not go at once to Ujiji or Uganda and start business as missionary . . . traders."

98. *Ibid.,* Sept. 17, 1877.

99. "Mr. Stanley's Proceedings in the Lake Regions of Central Africa," 3(1876), 247.

Hyndman did attempt to prevent the Royal Geographical Society from hearing Stanley speak about his exploits; they failed, however, and both resigned from the Society.[100] All other proposals for action against Stanley met a similar fate.[101]

Stanley's Later Years

Stanley's journey was a magnificent one, full of consequence for the future. Lakes Victoria and Tanganyika had been circumnavigated; the state of Buganda would soon receive Christian missionaries because of an appeal from Stanley. Finally, the greatest result of all, a great navigable river had been revealed to an interested Europe. The reporting of this epic voyage colored European and American attitudes to Africa for long years—the Africa Stanley called the Dark Continent.

And, while Stanley was making his troubled way through Africa, events in Europe were preparing the way for a full utilization of his discoveries. Missionary societies, boosted by funds and by enthusiasm resulting from the reaction to Livingstone's death and Stanley's reporting, were ready for new work. Soon Protestant and Catholic groups were following in his footsteps to begin a work that, for better or worse, would permanently change the character of the African life Stanley had found.[102] In Brussels a monarch, too ambitious for his role as the constitutional sovereign of a small state, would soon be ready to use Stanley's discoveries for his own ends.[103] In 1876 Leopold II of Belgium had called a conference at Brussels to discuss the opening of Africa to European civilization—and to his own energies. Leopold's plans were flexible and at first were directed to the eastern side of the continent; but with the revelation of the Congo as a magnificent waterway into the center of Africa, his interest turned to take advantage of the newly-known region.

Stanley too had plans for developing the Congo area, plans that he hoped Britain would carry forward. But there was little interest, com-

---

100. Mill, *Record of the Royal Geographical Society 1830–1930*, 119; Yule and Hyndman, *Stanley and the Royal Geographical Society*, 27ff.

101. A missionary, Farler, suggested a commission of inquiry into the expedition since he had learned from Stanley's men "dreadful accounts" of their proceedings. No action was taken. Pauncefote to Kirk, Feb. 28, 1878, enclosing a Farler extract of Dec. 28, 1877, Q-19, ZA. See also Bennett, "Stanley and the American Consuls at Zanzibar," 48–49.

102. See Oliver, *The Missionary Factor in East Africa*; Slade, *English-Speaking Missions in the Congo Independent State (1878–1908)*.

103. See Roeykens, *Léopold II et l'Afrique 1855–1880* and Anstey, *Britain and the Congo in the Nineteenth Century*, 57ff., for accounts of Leopold's early plans. For the later period, Slade, *King Leopold's Congo*.

mercial or political, in such schemes in Britain; inevitably, Leopold and Stanley came together. Thus in 1879, Stanley left for Africa again, this time to direct operations for Leopold that would lead to the founding of the Congo Independent State. He remained in Africa until 1884, except for a brief visit to Europe in 1882, laying the groundwork for a political entity stretching along the Congo River from the Atlantic to Stanley Falls.[104] The work was well done, and it showed Stanley in a new role—no longer as a journalist, but as a colonial administrator attempting to resolve the complex problems resulting from the introduction of European ideas and methods into an African territory.

Even after his retirement from the direction of Congo affairs in 1884, Stanley's interest in Africa remained constant. He served as a technical adviser to the American delegation at the Berlin Conference of 1884–1885—an expedient to make his knowledge available to the newly-formed Congo Independent State and to the American interests involved in it.[105] But he was denied any more active participation in the affairs of the Congo state. Although he remained under contract to Leopold until 1895, the Belgian monarch would not return him to Africa because Stanley's rivalry with Pierre Savorgnan de Brazza, founder of the French Congo, had alienated the French government. Leopold needed French support; Stanley, therefore, was kept on the shelf.[106]

Stanley was called, however, to yet one more major task of exploration. In the area of the present-day southern regions of the Sudan, an enigmatic European, Eduard Schnitzer, or Emin Pasha,[107] was maintaining the remnants of the former Egyptian administration of the Sudan against the forces of the Mahdi, Muhammad ibn Abdullah. The position of this able administrator and scholar, who in the contemporary European view was holding the torch of civilization against the hordes of African darkness, soon made Emin a focal point of European interest. At the same time, more practical ends could be served by winning over the man and his territory, a matter

104. Stanley's version is given in his *Congo and the Founding of its Free State.*
105. There is some discussion of Stanley's role at Berlin in Bontinck, *Aux Origines de l'Etat Indépendant du Congo. Documents Tirés d'Archives Américaines* and in Clendenen, Collins, and Duignan, *Americans in Africa 1865–1900,* 52 ff. The latter study also deals with Stanley's career, but the authors commit several major errors in describing his explorations. See the present writer's review in *Southwestern Social Science Quarterly* 48 (1968), 652–53.
106. Luwel, *Stanley,* 25–26. For Savorgnan-de Brazza, Brunschwig, *L'Avènement de l'Afrique Noire du XIXᵉ siècle à nos jours,* 133–69.
107. For Emin's career in Africa, Stuhlmann, ed., *Die Tagebücher von Dr. Emin Pascha;* see also Simpson, "A Bibliography of Emin Pasha," 138–65.

of concern to both Leopold and the Imperial British East African Company (IBEA). So in 1887 Stanley set out on an Emin Pasha Relief Expedition financed by British and Egyptian funds (the latter to evacuate Emin and his garrison), but heavily influenced by Leopold to whom Stanley was still under contract. Stanley carried conflicting offers of service to Emin from Leopold and the IBEA, but circumstances made them of little value. The expedition, after a tortuous march through the great Congo forest, arrived at Emin's territory to upset an equilibrium between Emin and his troops. Emin's men did not want to leave the region—it was home to many of them—and their resultant mutiny against Emin's authority made Stanley's mission futile. Stanley never realized this fact and instead blamed everything on Emin's vacillating and weak character. To cover his political failure, Emin had to be rescued, distressingly like a trophy for Stanley to display to a waiting world; and rescued he was. But the expedition, despite Stanley's reporting of much new African territory —including the Ruwenzori Mountains—would be the least satisfying of his African ventures. Recriminations from the relatives of staff members who died during the expedition and arguments between the various backers of Emin or Stanley filled many pages of print. Certainly they did much to cement Stanley's reputation as the most ruthless explorer of his age.[108]

This reputation of ruthlessness was the one mark on the otherwise phenomenal career of Stanley. There was some justice in the criticisms, but Stanley has certainly received an undue share of recrimination for his acts. His own code of ethics—Calvinist based—was clear. He believed in the redemption of Africa. How could a disciple of Livingstone believe otherwise? Stanley also, in contrast to many other Europeans then active in Africa, viewed the individual African in a favorable light. His feeling of European superiority, natural to a man of his epoch, was clear, but so was his belief that Africans were possessed of all the attributes of other humans. The African in his view needed only long and careful guidance to reach what secure Europeans of his generation regarded as perfection.[109] Stanley cannot be compared to Samuel Baker, who regarded central Africa

---

108. For the expedition and the diplomatic background, Sanderson, *England, Europe and the Upper Nile 1882–1899*, 27–46; Ceulemans, *La question arabe et le Congo (1883–1892)*, 86ff. Stanley's account is given in his *In Darkest Africa*.

109. There are many indications of Stanley's attitude in his works. See his fictional *My Kalulu*, 231, where he said in one instance: "women are the same all over the world, whether they are white or black, and . . . human love and kindness belong as much to the black as to the white, and are as often practised." See also, for example, *TDC*, II, 73.

as "peopled by a hopeless race of savages, for whom there is no prospect of civilization";[110] nor to Richard Burton who could say that the African "would appear rather a degeneracy from the civilized man than a savage rising to the first step, were it not for his apparent incapacity for improvement . . . He seems to belong to one of those childish races which, never rising to man's estate, fall like worn-out links from the great chain of animated nature." [111] Any comparison can only reflect favorably on Stanley's outlook.

But if Stanley was willing to treat the African as a rational being and to work for the eventual raising of the African to a level acceptable to nineteenth-century Europeans, he was not willing to brook opposition to his efforts. Africans who met him in peace were received in a similar fashion; Africans who worked loyally for him were treated in a way that won him a devotion given to few African explorers.[112] There was no turning of the other cheek, however. Stanley was certain he represented the correct path of development, whether as explorer or administrator, and his hard early years had not prepared him to accept opposition unanswered. Thus, Africans who attacked him, however justly in their own view, were punished, and punished with vigor.[113] When observers—often safely residing in Europe—rose to criticize his acts, Stanley really could not understand them. He met their charges with ridicule and contempt.[114] He may not convince us; but if we can understand Stanley's actions we can perhaps understand the man and not condemn him more than other Europeans of his era who were guilty of similar, or even more serious, excesses.[115]

Finally, it might be noted, that critics of Stanley drew much of their ammunition from his own honest reporting, as well as his lack of awareness that he was doing anything open to rebuke. Gordon, for example, who had reasons of his own for feeling guilty about his

110. Baker, *Exploration of the Nile Tributaries of Abyssinia,* x; see also the frequent similar references in his *Albert N'yanza,* especially I, 288–94.

11. Burton, "The Lake Regions of Central Africa," 328ff.

112. See, for example, the statement of Holmwood quoted in Farwell, *Man Who Presumed,* 204. The original is in Holmwood to FO, Feb. 25, 1887, E-99, ZA.

113. In a letter after the Bumbire and Ituru episodes (see documents 18 and 25) Stanley wrote: "I am prudent enough not to seek a quarrel with great or small tribes, if anything but bullets will answer. But with such people as the Wanyaturu and Bumbireh what can a man do, for they will listen to no overtures of peace or amnity?" Stanley to Levy, Aug. 13, 1875, given in Depage, "Notes au sujet de Documents inédits à deux expéditions de H. M. Stanley," 135.

114. See document 5, note 4.

115. He certainly cannot be described as one who took a "lustful pleasure" in beating his men. See Cairns, *Prelude to Imperialism. British Reactions to Central African Society 1840–1890,* 44.

treatment of Africans in the southern Sudan, wrote: "He is to blame for *writing* what he did (as Baker was). These things may be done, but not advertised." [116] It was a hard age, and Stanley's youthful experiences had done nothing to soften his feelings. He represented, perhaps all too well, the civilization Europeans liked to preach they were bringing to Africa. But we have observed enough brutality to Africans, then and since, not to single out Stanley unjustly as representative of the worst that Europe had to offer Africa.

Following the Emin Pasha expedition, Stanley entered into a new phase of his life. In 1890, he married Dorothy Tennant, a well-known British artist and social figure, and began to acquire a position of standing in British society—a position unusual to one of his origins. The rounds of society at times grated upon the former adventurer; but his damaged health, and Leopold's continued failure to call upon him, plus concern for his wife's fears, prevented any return to African adventures.

In an effort to keep her restless spouse occupied, Dorothy Stanley encouraged Stanley to stand for the House of Commons in 1892. He was defeated, but he stood again and was elected in 1895. The experience was not a happy one. Stanley, insecure because of his origins, could not enter into the heat of parliamentary debate as he could into battle in Africa. His constant references to his "dignity," both in the election campaigns and during his time in the House, make this abundantly clear. And, like other new parliamentarians who have first made their reputations in fields outside of politics, he was not prepared for the lack of attention given new members, especially on the African questions about which he felt so knowledgeable. Thus the explorer who had survived all the hardships Africa put before him did not stand for reelection in 1900, using the heat and hours of parliamentary attendance, plus the unsatisfactory ways of parliamentary life, to justify his decision.

Meanwhile Stanley, who was often ill, was living a full life—a very full one for a "graduate" of St. Asaph. In 1896, he and his wife adopted a son, Denzil, for whom no affection was too great. In 1898 a country estate was purchased in Surrey, and from 1899 Stanley devoted his energies to perfecting it. An award of the Grand Cross of the Bath came in 1899 as a rather belated recognition of his career. These years of happiness, however, did not last long. In 1903 Stanley

116. Gordon to Burton, Oct. 19, 1877, quoted in Wilkins, *Romance of Isabel Lady Burton*, II, 661. See also Gray, *History of the Southern Sudan*, 110–12, for Gordon's raiding of the Bari. Baker had earlier said: "All must be struck with Mr. Stanley's candour in the letters which he had sent home. It was not at all necessary for him to write about the fights and the bloodshed that occurred between him and the natives." *PRGS* 20(1875–1876), 47.

suffered a stroke; he never completely recovered. Stanley died on
May 10, 1904.

Stanley and Africa

Perhaps the best evaluation of Stanley's work to date was given
by the noted German geographer, A. Petermann, who characterized
Stanley as the "Bismarck" of African exploration in the complimen-
tary German sense as one who had resolved all of the major problems
of his age—in Stanley's case of African exploration.[117] During the
two expeditions covered in the despatches in this volume Stanley
certainly accomplished major work for Africa. The meeting with
Livingstone, besides turning the attention of the outside world to
Africa, allowed the Scots missionary-explorer to obtain the supplies
he needed to attempt to fulfill his quest. Livingstone's death while
on this quest gave Africa yet another boost of interest in the European
mind, while his influence on Stanley helped to lead that young reporter to attempt to finish the older man's work. This he did, and
more. With or without respect to the criticisms of his personal qualities, we must give Stanley his due as a major figure in pushing
together the cultures of Europe and Africa. That many find so much
to dislike in what Stanley did in Africa is less a reflection upon
Stanley himself than upon the society he represented. Western society
prefers to see its qualities in a man of the character of a Livingstone
while forgetting those often unpleasant attributes reflected in a Stanley.

Note on the Despatches

The despatches from Stanley are given in this volume as they
appeared in the columns of the *New York Herald* except for minor
alterations needed to correct errors. Stanley often wrote in haste and
on his return from the Livingstone venture said that his published
letters had "some curious typographical errors, especially in figures
and African names. I suppose my writing was wretched, owing to
my weakness." [118] Corrections have been made where necessary to
agree with the forms Stanley used in *How I Found Livingstone* and
Through the Dark Continent. The despatches are arranged by the date
of Stanley's writing and not by their order of publication.[119]

117. Petermann, "Henry M. Stanley's Reise durch Afrika," 467.
118. *HIFL*, 649–50, 680.
119. For the original order of publication of Stanley's despatches in the
Herald, see Appendix V. A contemporary account affirmed that Stanley prepared
more extended versions of the African despatches when he returned to Europe.
Life & Finding of Dr. Livingstone, 41. Stanley arrived in Marseilles on March 2,
1872.

All non-English words explained in the footnotes are from Swahili unless otherwise indicated and are taken from *A Standard Swahili-English Dictionary* (Oxford, 1955).

An effort has been made to indicate differences between Stanley's despatches, his published accounts, and his diary of the 1874–1877 expedition. The fullest use of this edition of despatches, therefore, requires the scholar to utilize all of the above sources for comparison. Most of the differences can be attributed to haste of writing, etc., but some demonstrate considerable rewriting—and often a rewriting that altered the truth of the materials presented. Individuals, peoples and places are identified, when possible, on their first appearance. The works of Gulliver[120] and Murdock,[121] particularly because of their tribal maps, were of great use in this process.[122]

120. Gulliver, "A Tribal Map of Tanganyika," 61–74.
121. Murdock, *Africa. Its Peoples and Their Culture History.*
122. The map in Boone, "Carte Ethnique du Congo Belge et du Ruanda-Urundi," was also of great use.

Abbreviations

Autobi-ography	Dorothy Stanley, ed., *The Autobiography of Sir Henry Morton Stanley*, Boston and New York, 1909.
BCB	*Biographie Coloniale Belge*, 5 vols., Bruxelles, 1948–1958.
CCZ	Correspondance Commerciale, Zanzibar, Archives des Affaires Etrangères, Paris.
CMS	Church Missionary Society Archives, London.
DAB	Allen Johnson and Dumas Malone, eds., *Dictionary of American Biography*, 22 vols., New York, 1928–1958.
Diary	Richard Stanley and Alan Neame, eds., *The Exploration Diaries of H. M. Stanley*, London, 1961.
DKB	*Deutsches Kolonialblatt.*
DKZ	*Deutsche Kolonialzeitung.*
DNB	Leslie Stephens and Sidney Lee, eds., *Dictionary of National Biography*, 28 vols., London, 1921–1959.
EIHC	Essex Institute *Historical Collections.*
FO	Foreign Office.
GJ	*The Geographical Journal.*
HIFL	Henry M. Stanley, *How I Found Livingstone*, London, 1872.
JAH	*The Journal of African History.*
JAS	*Journal of the African Society.*
JRAI	*Journal of the Royal Anthropological Institute of Great Britain and Ireland.*
JRGS	*The Journal of the Royal Geographical Society.*
LLJ	Horace Waller, ed., *The Last Journals of David Livingstone*, 2 vols., London, 1874.
LMS	London Missionary Society Archives, London.
MAC	Musée de l'Afrique Centrale, Tervuren, Belgium.
MAE	Ministère des Affaires Etrangères.
MFGDS	*Mitteilungen von Forschungsreisenden und Gelehrten aus den Deutschen Schutzgebieten.*

NYH   The *New York Herald.*
  PM   Peabody Museum, Salem, Mass.
  PM   *Mittheilungen aus Justus Perthes' Geographischer Anstalt ... von Dr. A. Petermann.*
 PRGS *Proceedings of the Royal Geographical Society.*
 PRO   Public Record Office, London.
  PZ   Politique, Zanzibar, Archives des Affaires Etrangères, Paris.
 SLRB Enclosures to Secret Letters Received from Bombay, India Office Archives, London.
 TDC   Henry M. Stanley, *Through the Dark Continent*, 2 vols., New York, 1878.
 TNR   *Tanganyika Notes and Records* (since No. 65, *Tanzania Notes and Records*).
  UJ   *Uganda Journal.*
UMCA   Universities Mission to Central Africa Archives, Archives of the United Society for the Propagation of the Gospel, London.
 USZ   Despatches from United States Consuls in Zanzibar (microfilm), National Archives, Washington, D.C.
VGEB   *Verhandlungen der Gesellschaft für Erdkunde zu Berlin.*
  ZA   Zanzibar Archives.
ZGEB   *Zeitschrift der Gesellschaft für Erdkunde zu Berlin.*

Part I   In Search of Livingstone

Stanley was well fitted for African exploration. He possessed an immense fund of nervous energy, accompanied by a cool courage, which sustained him undismayed in the face of danger, and by a dogged resolution, which left him undeterred by the most stupendous difficulties. He was a born leader of men.

—William Garstin, "Fifty Years of Nile Exploration and Some of Its Results," *GJ* 23 (1909), 128

1

Kwihara, District of Unyanyembe
July 4, 1871[1]

Your[2] expedition, sent out under me, has arrived in Unyanyembe.[3]
Were you living at Zanzibar or on the East African coast you would
have a much better idea what the above few words meant than you
have now. You would know, without any explanation, that it had
travelled $525\frac{1}{2}$ miles, and if you heard that we had travelled that
great distance within eighty-two days—a little under three months
—you would at once know that we had marched it in a very short
time; but since you and your readers live in America I must return
to the island of Zanzibar, close to the coast of East Africa, whence
we started, and give you a brief summary of the incidents and misfortunes which befell us throughout the march.

The instructions which I received from you close on two years ago
were given with the usual brevity of the HERALD. They were, "Find
out Livingstone, and get what news you can relating to his discoveries."
But before seeking Livingstone in the unknown wilds of Africa I had
other orders to fulfil which you had given me. I had to be present at
the inaguration of the Suez Canal; I had to ascend the Nile to the first
cataract; I had to write full accounts of what I had seen and what
was done—a guide to Lower and Upper Egypt. From Egypt I was
instructed to go to Jerusalem, write up what Warren was discovering
under that famous city;[4] thence I had to proceed to the Crimea,
whence I was to send you descriptions of Sebastopol as it stands
to-day, of the graveyards in and about it, of the battle-fields where
England and France met Russia in the shock of war. This done, I
had to travel through the Caucasus, visit Turkestan, find out what
Stoletoff and the Russians were doing towards the conquest of the
Oxus valley,[5] and then advance towards India. Next I had to travel
through the length of Persia, and write about the Euphrates valley,

1. *NYH*, Dec. 22, 1871.
2. James Gordon Bennett (1841–1918), owner of the *New York Herald*. His
turbulent life is described by Seitz, *The James Gordon Bennetts;* see also *DAB*, II,
199–202.
3. Present-day Tabora. Kwihara, one of the settlements in this Nyamwezi
chiefdom, was located three miles south of Tabora. Longland, "A Note on the
Tembe at Kwihara, Tabora," 84.
4. Charles Warren (1840–1927), then a lieutenant in the Royal Corps of
Engineers, worked for the Palestine Exploration Fund in Palestine from 1867 to
1870. Williams, *The Life of General Sir Charles Williams; GJ* 69 (1927), 382–83.
5. Colonel N. G. Stoletov was then leading a Russian expedition in the area of
the southern shore of the Caspian Sea. Pierce, *Russian Central Asia*, 37.

the railroad that has been on the tapis so long, and its prospects. Lastly, I had to sail to the African coast, and, according as circumstances guided me, seek out Livingstone and ascertain from him what discoveries he had made—only such facts as he would be pleased to give to one who had made such efforts to reach him. Quickly and briefly as the instructions were given by you their performance required time and a large expenditure of money. What I have already accomplished has required nineteen months.[6]

I arrived at Zanzibar on the 6th of January of this year, and at once set about making the necessary inquiries from parties who ought to know about the whereabouts of Dr. Livingstone. The most that I could glean was that he was in the neighborhood of Ujiji, which was a little over 900 miles from the coast. It would never do to return to Bombay or Aden with such scanty and vague news after the time and money expended in reaching Zanzibar. Why, all the world knew or supposed such to be the fact. What was I to do? Go by all means, and never to return unless I could better such information. Go I did.

It occupied me a month to purchase such things as were necessary and to organize an expedition to collect such information as would be useful to me on the long march and would guide me in the new sphere in which I found myself. The expense which you were incurring frightened me considerably; but then "obey orders if you break owners" is a proverb among sailors, and one which I adopted. Besides, I was too far from the telegraph to notify you of such an expense or to receive further orders from you; the preparations for the expedition therefore went on. Eight thousand dollars were expended in purchasing the cloth, beads and wire necessary in my dealings with the savages of the territories through which I would have to traverse.[7] As each tribe has its peculiar choice of cloth, beads and wire, much care was to be bestowed in the selection and arrangement of these things; also one had to be careful that an over great quantity of any one kind of cloth or beads should not be purchased, otherwise such things

6. This entire journey is described in Stanley, *My Early Travels in America and Asia*, II, *passim*. Stanley went to Zanzibar on the American whaler, *Falcon*. The captain reported: "I have taken a man as pasenger to Zanzibar that is travlin to central Africa for the New York Herald . . ." Richmond to Osgood, Dec. 14, 1870, John C. Osgood Papers, PM. My thanks to Carl Haywood for this reference.

7. Stanley, who found no letter of credit from the *Herald* awaiting him in Zanzibar, raised the necessary funds through the aid of the American consul. Bennett, however, delayed on covering the heavy debts until the news of his reporter's success in meeting Livingstone. Bouveignes, "Deux lettres inédites de Stanley sur le façon dont il découvert Livingstone dans l'Afrique Centrale," 9–10; Bennett, "Stanley and the American Consuls at Zanzibar," 42–43.

would soon become a mere impediment of travel and cause a waste of money. The various kinds of beads required great time to learn, for the women of Africa are as fastidious in their tastes for beads as the women of New York are for jewelry. The measures also had to be mastered, which, seeing that it was an entirely new business in which I was engaged, were rather complicated, and perplexed me considerably for a time.

These things having been purchased, arranged and adjusted in bales and packages, there remained for me to raise a small company of faithful men, who should act as soldiers, guards to the caravan and servants when necessary. Some of Speke's[8] faithfuls and Burton's[9] soldiers yet lived in Zanzibar. These were found out by Johari, the American Consul's dragoman,[10] and, as they were willing to accompany me, were immediately engaged. Bombay,[11] the honestest of black men who served with Burton, and subsequently with Speke, was commissioned captain and ordered to collect a company of twenty men, in which he succeeded most admirably. All these men are with me to-day. I could not have been better served by any set of men than I have by these faithful people. By twos and threes I sent them out with the carriers as they were collected, and entrusted to them my bales of cloth, bags of beads and coils of wire, which you must recol-

8. John H. Speke (1827–1864) accompanied Burton on his 1857–1859 expedition from Zanzibar to Lake Tanganyika. On the return from Tanganyika, while Burton remained in Tabora, Speke in 1858 visited the southern shore of Lake Victoria. With Grant, in an 1860–1863 exploration, he partially explored the connection of the Nile with Lake Victoria. Speke's death in 1864 left problems concerning the Nile and Lake Victoria that Stanley would later attempt to resolve. *DNB*, XIII, 732–35. For the best account of the various British explorers of eastern Africa, see Bridges, "The British Exploration of East Africa, 1788–1885, with Special Reference to the Activities of the Royal Geographical Society."

9. Richard F. Burton (1821–1890), the brilliant and irreverent linguist, traveler and scholar, did not return to eastern Africa after his successful Lake Tanganyika venture. His opinions, however, on Speke's Lake Victoria finds would help frame the objectives for Stanley's 1874–1877 African expedition. Burton yet requires an adequate biography; see Brodie, *The Devil Drives*, for the latest attempt at presenting his complex career. See also the able account of Burton's period as consul in West Africa (1861–1864) in Newbury's introduction to *A Mission to Gelele King of Dahome by Sir Richard Burton* and Waterfield's introduction to *First Footsteps in East Africa by Sir Richard Burton*.

10. Johari bin Saif served the Salem firm of John Bertram, and its successor Ropes, Emmerton and Co., as interpreter for over forty years. He died in 1887. Bennett, "Edward D. Ropes, Jr., Salem Merchant at Zanzibar."

11. Mbarak Bombay, a Yao and a former slave, served with the Burton-Speke and Speke-Grant expeditions. After accompanying Stanley he traveled with Cameron and with the Church Missionary Society in 1876. Bombay then retired from caravan life; he died around 1886. Speke, *What Led to the Discovery of the Source of the Nile*, 186, 210–12, 264–65; Smith to Wright, Aug. 22, 1876, C.A6/M2, CMS; Johnston, *The Nile Quest*, 169.

lect are as gold, silver and copper money in Africa. Three months afterward I found every bale, every bag of beads, every coil of wire in Unyanyembe, 525½ miles from Bagamoyo, their initial point on the African coast. Arms were purchased for these men who were to be my soldiers; a musket, a hatchet, a knife, a shot pouch and powder flask, flints, bullets and powder were to be served out to each man. Then there were cooking utensils and dishes, tents to cover the property during the rainy season, which was fast approaching, to be required. In order to guard against such contingencies as might very possibly arise—viz: lack of carriers on the coast, one very grave one —I was obliged to purchase twenty-five donkeys, in which task I had to be careful lest any worthless animals might be passed on me. Twenty-five saddles for the donkeys had to be manufactured by myself, or by such men as could understand what kind of saddles I needed, for there were nothing of the kind obtainable at Zanzibar.

To assist me in such work, and in tasks of similar nature, I hired two white men, sailors, who had been mates of ships—one an Englishman and the other a Scotchman[12]—and having cut the canvas for the saddles and cloth for the tents, gave to these practical men the task to sew them up. After they had finished their work I re-engaged them to accompany me to Africa, to fill the respective duties of first and second mates. As I had the success of the NEW YORK HERALD Expedition near and dear to my heart, constant thinking about it and the contingencies that might arise to prevent its success, over and over I had long sketched its march from the sea coast to Ujiji, and knew almost as well as if I had been there before what kind of difficulties I should meet. The following is one of my sketches made on board ship while coming to Zanzibar:

"One hundred pagazis[13] will be required to convey cloth, beads and wire enough to keep me and my soldiers for one year and to pay expenses, such as hire of fresh pagazis, &c.; twenty men, to act as guards or soldiers; fifty bales of cloth, ten bags of beads and five loads of wire, for food and pagazi hire. In three months I will try to reach Unyanyembe. Shall stop in Unyanyembe two weeks probably. From Unyanyembe is one month's march to Ujiji, on the Tanganyika Lake. And after!—where is Livingstone? If Livingstone is at Ujiji my work is easy. I will get what information I can and return to Unyanyembe. The race is now for the telegraph. It is three months to Zanzibar, and from Zanzibar, as I was three months coming to Zanzi-

12. John W. Shaw of London, a recently discharged third-mate of the ship *Nevada*, and William L. Farquhar, former first-mate of the bark *Polly*. Shaw and Farquhar left no defense to help evaluate the subsequent criticisms of Stanley, but a fair discussion concerning the two men is given in Jackson, *Meteor Out of Africa*, 134, 181–83, 351–53.

13. *Mpagazi*, a caravan porter.

bar from Bombay, I may be three months going from Zanzibar to Bombay. That will not do. We will try another road. To Lake Victoria N'Yanza from Unyanyembe is twenty-six days. By boat to Uganda would be fifteen days. From Uganda to Gondokoro[14] twenty days. From Gondokoro by Dahabeah[15] down the Nile to Cairo forty or fifty days. I have then the telegraph from Unyanyembe to Bombay from five to six months, from Unyanyembe three to four months. The latter route is the best by far.

"Again: I have reached Ujiji. Where is Livingstone? He may be in Marungu,[16] Ubembe,[17] Uguhha,[18] Usige,[19] Urundi[20] or somewhere else on the other side of the Lake Tanganyika. Shall I expose my mission, which requires speed, to the caprice of a King Kannena[21] or a Hamed Bin Sulayyam?[22] No. I shall take my own boat from Zanzibar, carry it with me to Ujiji, and with it search its coast from Ujiji to Marungu,

14. An administrative post in the southern Sudan then serving as a base for Samuel Baker, representative of the Khedive of Egypt. Baker, *Ismaïlia*, I, 220ff.

15. A Nile sailing vessel. See C. A. M., "Sketches from Egypt. No. I. The Dahabiah," for a description.

16. The area of the Tabwa, or Marungu, along the southwestern coast of Lake Tanganyika. The Arabs of central Arica would later take advantage of the lack of central authority in Marungu, and of its inter-tribal strife, to make the region a principal arena of their raids for slaves. Maes and Boone, *Les Peuplades du Congo Belge*, 178–80; Hore, "On the Twelve Tribes of Tanganyika," 16; Vansina, *Introduction à l'Ethographie du Congo*, chap. 13.

17. The Bemba occupied the plateau between the lakes Tanganyika, Nyasa, Bangweulu and Mweru. Equipped with firearms gained from the Arabs and under the leadership of their powerful chief, the Citimukulu, they formed a society that lived largely on the profits derived from their extensive raids on neighboring Africans. Richards, "The Bemba of North-Eastern Rhodesia"; Whitely, *Bemba and Related Peoples of Northern Rhodesia*, 7–32; Tweedie, "Towards a History of the Bemba from Oral Tradition."

18. The Holoholo, or Guha, occupying "the gateway from Tanganyika to the West," lived along the shores of Lake Tanganyika between 5°30' south latitude and the mouth of the Lufuko River. Their then flourishing port of Mtowa was on the main caravan route from the east African coast into the Congo. Schmitz, *Les Baholoholo*; Hore's letter of April 16, 1879, *The Chronicle of the London Missionary Society* (1880) 13; Maes and Boone, *Peuplades du Congo Belge*, 64–67; Vansina, *Introduction à l'Ethnographie du Congo*, chap. 13.

19. One of the few districts of Burundi with active trading relations with outsiders—here the Arabs of Ujiji. Bennett, "Mwinyi Kheri," 139–64.

20. Burundi. See d'Hertefeldt, Trouwborst, Scherer, *Les Anciens Royaumes de la Zone Interlacustrine Meridionale*, 119ff.

21. The *umutware munini*, or chief, in the Ha state of Bujiji. Burton and Speke had difficulties with Kannena, Speke bitterly characterizing him as " a very ill-disposed chief . . . tyrannical, and, as such savages invariably are, utterly unreasonable." Speke, "Journal of a Cruise on the Tanganyika Lake, Central Africa," 342. See also Burton, "Lake Regions of Central Equatorial Africa . . . ," 224–26.

22. A prominent Arab trader of Lake Tanganyika at the time of the visit of Burton and Speke. They attempted to hire his dhow, but without success. Hamed was later killed while trading to the west of the lake. *Ibid.*, 215–16, 238, 246; Speke, *What Led to the Discovery*, 229–33, 239–42; Burton, *Zanzibar*, II, 301.

Marungu to Usige, Usige to Ujiji, for the long absent Livingstone, and the same boat shall carry me from Muanza, at the southern extremity of the lake, to the Ripon Falls,[23] the point where the Nile issues out of the N'Yanza."

This was one of many sketches I made, and the one I adopted for my guidance. I purchased two boats in Zanzibar—one twenty-five feet long and six feet wide, the other ten feet long and four and a half feet wide. I stripped them of their boards, and packed up the timbers, or ribs, with a few of the boards, keel, stem and stern pieces, thwarts and knees, which should be screwed together as the boat was required, and covered with double canvas skins well tarred. These were my boats, and having such men as sailors with me I doubted not but they could be made to answer. In the absence of anything better they must be made to answer.

Before leaving Zanzibar Captain Francis R. Webb,[24] United States Consul, introduced me to Syed Barghash, Sultan of Zanzibar and Pemba.[25] After a very kind reception, besides furnishing me with letters to Said Bin Salim (formerly Ras Cafilah to Burton), now Governor of Unyanyembe,[26] and Sheikh Bin Nasib[27] and to all his Arab subjects, he presented me with an Arab horse. Mr. Goodhue,[28] an

23. Named by Speke in 1862 after the Earl of Ripon (1827–1909), president of the Royal Geographical Society when Speke's expedition was organized. Speke, *Journal of the Discovery of the Source of the Nile,* 466–70; DNB, *Twentieth Century, 1901–1911,* 216–21.

24. Francis R. Webb (1833–1892) of Salem, after serving as master of Salem vessels in the Zanzibar trade, acted as resident agent for John Bertram in Aden and Zanzibar. He was American consul in Zanzibar, and later held a similar office in New Zealand. Stanley later affirmed that Webb was the only person then in Zanzibar who knew the real aim of his expedition. Putnam, "Salem Vessels and their Voyages," 22–23; Ropes to Seward, Jan. 7, 1867, USZ, V; Stanley, *My African Travels,* 5.

25. Barghash bin Said (c. 1840–1888), ruler of Zanzibar from 1870, was generally regarded by Europeans as "able and enlightened." The best account of his career remains Coupland, *The Exploitation of East Africa 1856–1890, passim.* See also Holmwood, "The Trade between India and the East Coast of Africa," 420.

26. After participating in the Burton-Speke expedition, Said bin Salim joined the Speke and Grant venture, but was left at Tabora in 1861 because of illness. He became governor of the Arab community of Tabora shortly thereafter, holding the position until Arab rivals drove him from office in 1878. He died at nearby Uyuwi in 1879. Speke, *Journal of the Discovery,* 99; A. M. *Mackay* (by his sister), 66; Bennett, *Studies in East African History,* 5–15.

27. Shaykh bin Nasibu, brother of Abdulla bin Nasibu, one of the most influential Arabs of the interior, resided at Tabora. He died in 1882, allegedly poisoned by Barghash. Reichard, *Deutsch-Ostafrika,* 101; Reichard, "Die Unruhen in Unjanjembe."

28. William Goodhue of Salem, a merchant, was long resident in Zanzibar. He served as American diplomatic resident in 1862–1863. Goodhue's Zanzibar career apparently closed in 1873 when his business failed. Bennett and Brooks, eds.,

American gentleman, residing at Zanzibar, also made me a present of a blooded horse, imported from the Cape of Good Hope. To the other American gentlemen—Mr. Spalding,[29] Mr. Morse[30] and Mr. Sparhawk[31]—I am indebted for many courtesies, but more particularly to Captain Webb and Mrs. Webb, whose many kindnesses were innumerable. It was at Captain Webb's house I lived for a month, and during that time his forbearance knew no bounds; for, as you may imagine, I littered his house with tons upon tons of bulky material of cloth, beads, wire, tar, canvas, tents, utensils and a thousand other things.

On the morning of the 5th of February, one month after arrival at Zanzibar, a fleet of dhows bore the expedition and its effects from the Island of Zanzibar to Bagamoyo, on the main land, distant about twenty-five miles from the island. We were detained at Bagamoyo nearly two months for lack of sufficient pagazis; but as fast as they were obtained a small number was at once fitted out and despatched to the interior under guard of two or three soldiers. But despite the utmost efforts and double prices which I paid in order to induce the pagazis or carriers the collecting together of over a hundred men proceeded but slowly. The reason of this was that the cholera, which last year desolated Zanzibar and the coast, had frightened the Wanyamuezi[32] from coming to a place where they were almost certain to meet their fate.[33] They were but just recovering from the effects of their fear when the expedition disembarked at Bagamoyo.

New England Merchants in Africa, 521; Webb to Seward, March 31, 1862, USZ, IV; Webb to Ropes, May 11, 1873, Ropes Papers, PM.

29. Henry Spalding was Zanzibar agent for the American firm of Arnold, Hines and Co., the successor to Rufus Greene of Providence. He was recognized as a very able competitor by his Salem rivals, while his influence with the Indian merchants of Zanzibar secured valuable information for Christie's important study of the spread of cholera in East Africa. Burton, *Zanzibar*, I, 318; J. Webb to Ropes, May 29, 1871, June 21, 1871, Ropes Papers, PM; Christie, *Cholera Epidemics in East Africa*, xi, 108.

30. Morse was a coworker in Spalding's agency. He left Zanzibar in 1871 after a three-year stay. J. Webb to Ropes, March 10, 1871, May 17, 1871, Ropes Papers, PM.

31. Augustus Sparhawk was Zanzibar agent for the firm of John Bertram. In 1879 he left commercial life to serve with Stanley in the Congo, where he became commander of the Vivi station. Sparhawk left Africa because of illness in Dec. 1881. *BCB*, I, 859–60; Bennett, "Stanley and the American Consuls at Zanzibar," 50.

32. The Nyamwezi of central Tanzania, divided politically into numerous states—many of a very limited territorial extent—played a major role as carriers in East African caravan organizations. See Abrahams, *The People of Greater Unyamwezi, Tanzania,* and *The Political Organization of Unyamwezi.*

33. A useful discussion of the recurring cholera epidemics is given by Christie, *Cholera Epidemics in East Africa.*

As I must employ the word pagazi often in this letter I had best explain what the word means. A pagazi is a Kinyamuezi word for "carrier" [34]—one who carries ivory or any other goods on his shoulders. This useful person is the camel, the horse, the mule, the ass, the train, the wagon and the cart of East and Central Africa. Without him Salem would not obtain her ivory, Boston and New York their African ebony, their frankincense, myrrh and gum copal.[35] He travels regions where the camel could not enter and where the horse and the ass could not live. He carries the maximum weight of seventy pounds on his shoulders from Bagamoyo to Unyanyembe, where he belongs, for which he charges from fifteen doti to twenty-five doti of American sheeting[36] or Indian calico, dyed blue, called kaniki, mixed with other cloths, imported from Muscat and Cutch, equal to from $7.50 to $12.50. He is therefore very expensive to a traveller. For the carriage of my goods I had to disburse nearly two thousand dollars' worth of cloth. The pagazi belongs to Unyamwezi (Land of the Moon), an extensive country in Central Africa, in which Unyanyembe, the central depot of the Arabs, is situated, and which all caravans for the interior must reach, and where they must obtain fresh relays of carriers before they can proceed further. The doti in which he is paid, and which is equivalent to his dollar, measures four yards. A shukka is half a doti, or two yards. The proprietor of a caravan purchases his cloth by the bale, or gorah. A gorah of Merikani (a corrupted name for American sheeting) means a piece of Merikani of thirty yards, into which they are folded up by the mills of Salem and Nashua, N.H. The gorah, therefore, contains seven and a half doti, or fifteen shukka.

During the two months we were halted at Bagamoyo there was plenty of work for us. The eight thousand yards of American sheeting which I had purchased had to be made into bales for the pagazis. A bale is a package of cloth weighing not more than seventy pounds, wherein pieces of American sheeting must be laid in layers alternately with the cloths of India, Cutch and Muscat; so that if one bale or two are lost you do not lose too much of one thing, which might by and by prove fatal to your enterprise. When the cloths are thus laid in alternate layers and the scale indicates the maximum weight a doti of cloth spread out receives them, and after being tied or pinned

---

34. *Mupagasi,* or porter. Dahl, *Nyamwezi-Wörterbuch,* 230.

35. For a general account of the porter in East Africa, Lamden, "Some Aspects of Porterage in East Africa."

36. Sheeting was brought to East Africa in pieces of thirty yards in length and from thirty-six to thirty-eight inches in breadth. Burton, "Lake Regions," 422. For the *doti,* see below.

over it neatly it is then bound as firmly as possible with coir rope and pounded by two men until the bale is one solid roll, three and a half feet long, a foot wide and a foot deep. It is then taken and put in a makanda, or a mat bag, until the pagazi coming for his load and hire cradles it in three long sticks arranged in a fork to receive it, and binds the fork firmly on the bale, for the purpose of protecting the bale from injury from wet, moisture and white ants and for the convenience of lifting it on his shoulder and stacking it when his day's march is over. Beads are placed in long narrow bags of domestics, and not more than sixty-two pounds are put in the bag, as the bead load is not so flexible as the cloth bale. Wire is conveyed in coils—six coils generally considered a handsome load—averaging sixty pounds. It is arranged for carriage, in three coils, at each end of a five-foot pole.

My life at Zanzibar I thought hard, but my two months at Bagamoyo a convict at Sing Sing would not have envied. It was work all day, thinking all night; not an hour could I call my own. It was a steady grind on body and brain this work of starting. I state with truth, now resting at Unyanyembe, after the fatigues of the long march, after the dangers and vexations we have suffered, that I would prefer the three months' march, with all its horrors, anxieties, swamps and fevers, to the two months' preparation for the expedition I had at Bagamoyo. The greatest trouble of all that I endured at Bagamoyo—I am sure you will smile at the thought—was with my agent, who obtained me my pagazis, without whom I could not have started even to this day, probably never; for had I stayed so long I would have thrown up the job as impracticable and would have committed suicide by putting my head in a barrel of sand, which I thought to be a most easy death, and one I gratuitously recommend to all would-be suicides. Smile now, please, when I tell you that his name was Soor Hadji Palloo, and his age nineteen.[37] During my whole stay at Bagamoyo this young ——— gave me more trouble than all the scoundrelism of the city of New York gives to its Chief of Police. Half a dozen times a day I found him in dishonesty, yet the boy was in no way abashed by it; otherwise there had been hopes for him. Each day he conceived a new system of roguery. Every instant of his time seemed to be devoted to devising how to plunder

37. Sewa Haji Paru (1851–1897); he rose from a street peddler in Zanzibar to become one of the most important, and wealthy, of East Africa's Indians. In 1895 he became head of the East African Khoja community and local representative of the Agha Khan. "Sewa Hadji"; Clyde, *History of the Medical Services of Tanganyika,* 5–11; Heudebert, *Vers les Grands Lacs de l'Afrique Orientale,* 86; Matson, "Sewa Haji: A Note."

me, until I was at my wits' end how to thwart or check him. Exposure before the people brought no shame to his cheeks. A mere shrug of the shoulders, which I was to interpret any way I pleased, was the only proof he gave that he heard me. A threat to reduce his present had no effect on him—"a bird in the hand was worth two in the bush;" so $10 worth of goods stolen from me was worth a promise of $20 when his work should be finished. Several times a day the young Hindoo[38] dog escaped a sound thrashing because I knew his equal for collecting pagazis was not to be found. Will you believe it, that after the most incomparable rascality, at the end of two months he had escaped a flogging and received a present of money for his services? The reason was, at last he had released me from torment and I was free to go.

The convict free to go after a protracted imprisonment—the condemned man on the scaffold, with the awful cord dangling before his eyes, the executioners of the dread sentence of the law ready to perform their duties, when told he was at liberty to depart, could not feel keener pleasure than I felt when my business was concluded with Soor Hadji Palloo and I felt myself at liberty to depart on my mission. Five caravans had already been despatched—four under the protection of soldiers, the fifth under the Scotchman who acted as my first mate. The sixth and last was to be led by myself.[39] Burton and Speke arrived at Zanzibar in 1857, in January—the same month that I, fourteen years later, had arrived. But as the masika, or rainy season, which lasts for forty days, was then drawing near, they preferred to wait on the coast and defer their departure until after the masika. It was not until the 16th June that they left Zanzibar for Kaole (three miles below Bagamoyo), and not until the 27th of the same month that they made the great start, the pagazis, soldiers and donkeys having been collected for them by Ladha Danyée,[40] the most influential man in Zanzibar, second only to the Sultan of the island. But my mission was one that required speed; any delay would render it valueless; immediate departure was essential to success—departure from the coast—after which my movements would depend in a great measure on my own energy. Forty days' rain and a 200 mile

38. In East Africa, Muslim Indians were designated as *Wahindi*; non-Muslim Indians were called Banyans. Baumann, *Usambara und seine Nachbargebiete*, 67.
39. In *HIFL*, 70, Stanley asserts he led the fifth caravan.
40. Ladha Damji was the customs master of Zanzibar. See Bennett and Brooks, *New England Merchants*, 409. He was the recipient of some bitter strictures from Livingstone for advancing credit to Arab slave and ivory traders. Livingstone to Kirk, Oct. 30, 1871, Zanzibar Museum; Chamberlin, ed., *Some Letters from Livingstone 1840–1872*, 272–74.

swamp must not prevent the NEW YORK HERALD correspondent
from marching, now that the caravan is ready.

On Saturday, the 1st of April, exactly eighty-three days after arrival at Zanzibar,[41] the sixth caravan, led by myself, left the town of
Bagamoyo for our first journey westward, with "Forward" for its
mot de guet and the American flag borne aloft by the Kirangozi or
guide of the caravan. As it defiled out of the town we bid a long
farewell to the *dolce far niente* of civilization, to the blue sea and its
open road to home and to the hundreds of dusky spectators who
were gathered to witness our departure with repeated salvos of musketry.

The caravan which I led consisted of ten pagazis, carrying the
boats; nine soldiers, under Captain Bombay, in charge of seventeen
donkeys and their loads; Selim, my boy interpreter, a Christian Arab
from Jerusalem, who had been with me through Persia; one cook
and sub from Malabar, and Shaw, the English sailor, now transformed
into a rear guard and overseer, mounted on a good riding donkey;
one dog from Bombay, called Omar, from his Turkish origin, who
was to guard my tent at night and bark at insolent Wagogo,[42] if not
to bite their legs—a thing he is very likely to do—and, lastly, myself,
mounted on the splendid bay horse given me by Mr. Goodhue, the
mtongi[43] leader, the thinker and reporter of the expedition. Altogether the expedition numbers three white men, twenty-two soldiers,
four supernumeraries, with a transport train of eighty-two pagazis,
twenty-seven donkeys and two horses, conveying fifty-two bales of
cloth, seven man-loads of wire, sixteen man-loads of beads, twenty
loads of boat fixtures, three loads of tents, four loads of clothes and
personal baggage, two loads of cooking utensils and dishes, one load
of medicines, three of powder, five of bullets, small shot and metallic
cartridges; three of instruments and small necessaries, such as soap,
sugar, tea, coffee, Liebig's extract of meat, pemmican, candles, &c.,

41. In *HIFL*, 70, Stanley notes that he left on March 21, seventy-three days
after his arrival.

42. The Gogo, politically divided into small and independent groups, profited
from their strategic location, between areas subject to raids from such predatory
groups as the Masai and Hehe, and from their control of scarce water supplies, to
levy a tax on passing caravans. Although excessive rates at times led to friction,
most travelers bowed to necessity and accepted the system, many recognizing the
work required to provision passing caravans justified some recompense. Claus, *Die
Wagogo*; Schweinitz, *Deutsch-Ost-Afrika in Krieg und Frieden*, 203; see also the
studies by Rigby, "Dual Symbolic Classification among the Gogo of Central
Tanzania" and "Sociological Factors in the Contact of the Gogo of Central
Tanzania with Islam."

43. Probably *mtunga*, the arranger.

which make a total of 116 loads—equal to eight and a half tons of material.[44] The weapons of defence which the expedition possesses consist of one double-barrelled smooth bore No. 12, two American Winchester rifles or "sixteen shooters," two Starr's breech-loading carbines, one Jocelyn breech-loader, one elephant rifle, carrying balls eight to the pound; two breech-loading revolvers, twenty-four flint-lock muskets, six single-barrelled pistols, one battle axe, two swords, two daggers, one boar spear, two American axes, twenty-four hatchets and twenty-four long knives.

The expedition has been fitted up with care; whatever was needed for its success was not stinted; everything was provided; nothing was done too hurriedly, yet everything was purchased, collected, manufactured and compounded with the utmost despatch consistent with efficiency and means.[45] Should it fail of success in its errand, of rapid marching to Ujiji and back, it must simply happen from an accident which could not be controlled. So much for the *personnel* of the expedition and its purpose.

We left Bagamoyo, the attraction of all the curious, with noisy *eclat,* and defiled up a narrow lane shaded to twilight by the dense umbrage of two parallel hedges of mimosas. We were all in the highest spirits—the soldiers sang extempore, the Kirangozi lifted his voice into a loud, bellowing note, and fluttered the American flag, which told all on-lookers, "Lo, a musungre's[46] (white man) caravan," and my heart, I thought, palpitated much too quickly for the sobriety of a leader. But I could not help it. The enthusiasm of youth still clung to me despite my travelled years, my pulses bounded with the full glow of staple health; behind me were the troubles, which had harassed me for over two months; with Soor Hadji Palloo I had said my last word; with the blatant rabble of Banyans, Arabs and Beloochees[47] I had taken my last look, and before me beamed the sun of promise as he sped toward the Occident. Loveliness glowed around me as I

44. In *HIFL,* 68, 70, 72, there are slightly different totals for the men and equipment of the expedition.

45. Other travelers and writers would comment, often with envy, at Stanley's well-equipped and well-financed expeditions. They became a standard for comparison to demonstrate that a particular explorer had achieved good results, even if he had not had the resources available to Stanley. For example, Burton, *The Life of Captain Sir Richd F. Burton,* I, 304; Jackson, *Early Days in East Africa,* 142–43; Schmidt, "Die Bedeutung Hermann von Wissmann's in der Entdeckungsgeschichte Afrikas und in Deutschlands Kolonialgeschichte," 357–58.

46. *Mzungu,* a European.

47. Baluchis, from the Makran coast. Many had come to the Zanzibar region for service in the army of Barghash's father, Said bin Sultan. Baumann, *Der Sansibar-Archipel. II. Die Insel Sansibar und ihre Kleineren Nachbarinseln,* 24.

looked at the fertile fields of manioc, the riant vegetation of the tropics, the beautiful, strange trees and flowers, plants and herbs, and heard the cry of pee-wit and cricket and the noisy sibilance of many insects; methought each and all whispered to me, "At last you are started." At such a time what more appropriate could I do than lift up my face toward the pure, glassy dome of heaven and cry "God be thanked?"

We camped that night on the banks of the Kingani, our dreams being sadly disturbed by the sportive hippopotami, which emerged at night for their nocturnal feed on the tall, high grass that grows on the savannahs to the westward of the Kingani River.

"Sofari, Sofari, leo—a journey, a journey to-day," shouted the Kirangozi as he prepared to blow his kudu horn—the usual signal for a march. "Set out, set out," rang the cheery voice of Captain Bombay, echoed by that of my drum major, servant, general help and interpreter, Selim. As I hurried my men to their work, lent a hand with energy to drop the tents, I mentally resolved that if my caravans ahead gave me clear room for travel I should be in Unyanyembe before that day three months. By six o'clock A.M. our early breakfast was despatched, and the pagazis and donkeys were *en route* for Kikoka. Even at this early hour there were quite a collection of curious natives to whom we gave the parting "quahary" [48] with sincerity. My bay horse was found to be invaluable for the service of a quartermaster of a transport train, for as such was I compelled to compare myself. I could stay behind until the last straggler had left camp, and by a few moments' gallop put myself at the head of the caravan, leaving the white man Shaw to bring up the rear.

The road, as it is, throughout Africa, was a mere footpath, leading over a sandy soil of surprising fertility—producing grain a hundred fold, though the sowing of it might be done in the most unskilful manner. In their fields, at heedless labor, were men and women in the scantiest costumes, compared to which the fig-leaf apparel of our first parents must have been *en grande tenue*. Nor were they at all abashed by the devouring gaze of men who were strangers to clotheless living men and women; nor did they seem to understand why their inordinate curiosity should be returned with more than interest. They left their work as the Wasungu drew near—such hybrids were they in white flannels, solar topees and horse boots! But were the Wasungu desirous of studying the principles of comparative anatomy and physiology, what a rich field for study! We passed them with

48. *Kwa heri*, good-by.

serious faces enough, while they giggled and laughed outright, pointing with their index fingers at this or that thing in our dress which
to them seemed so strange and bizarre.

The western side of the Kingani was a considerable improvement
upon the eastern. We were travelling over a forest-clad and jungly
plain, which heaved upward as smoothly as the beach of a watering
place, culminating at intervals in rounded ridges, whence fair views
might be obtained of the new and strange land. The scenery was as
beautiful as that which many an English nobleman is proud to call his
"park." On the whole it was lawn and sward, with boscage sufficient to
agreeably diversify it.

Passing Kikoka we traversed on the next day a young forest of
ebony trees, where guinea fowl were seen, besides pigeons, jays, ibis
sacra, golden pheasants, quails, moorhens florican, hawks, eagles,
and now and then a solitary pelican winged its way to the distance.
As we advanced further into the interior antelopes bounded away to
our right and left, the steinbok and noble kudu fled in terror, giraffes
rushed away from us like moving forests and zebra galloped frantic
toward the far horizon at the sound of the strange noises which the
caravan made.

By Sunday, the 23d of April, we had travelled 125 miles, and had
reached Simbawenni, situated in longitude 37°42′ east, latitude 6°20′
south.[49] We had experienced no trouble on the road up to this place.
The country was like that above described—park-like—abounding in
large and noble game. Not until we had left Simbawenni did we
experience any trouble.

The first which we experienced was from the Sultana of Simbawenni,[50] in Usagara,[51] which we found to be a large and well built

49. In *HIFL*, 115, Stanley gives an earlier date. Kisabengo, a Zigula leader of
fugitive slaves from the East African coast, raided among the Kami and founded
near present-day Morogoro the strongly fortified center that Stanley called
Simbawenni. Kisabengo died around 1867. Baur and Le Roy, *A Travers le
Zanguebar*, 200–04; Burton, "Lake Regions," 45, 76; Heudebert, *Vers les Grands
Lacs*, 159–60; Young and Fosbrooke, *Smoke in the Hills*, chap. 2.

50. Kisabengo was succeeded by a daughter, who was known as Simbawenni
(lion-like). She had especially close relations with the Zanzibar authorities
during her long reign and even visited the island in 1884. Her town declined
somewhat after Stanley's visit because of a natural disaster, but it remained an
important station on the route to the interior. In her later years effective power
appears to have passed to her relative, Kingo of Morogoro. Heudebert, *Vers les
Grands Lacs*, 150–53; *A l'Assaut des Pays Nègres. Journal des Missionaires d'Alger
dans l'Afrique Equatoriale*, 100–01; Ledoulx to MAE, Oct. 11, 1884, PZ, I;
Ledoulx to MAE, Oct. 23, 1884, CCZ, I; Spring, *Selbsterlebtes in Ostafrika*, 22–23,
177; Winans, *Shambala*, 23, 80–81.

51. Simbawenni was located in the territory of the Luguru, not among the
Sagara. Beidelman, *Matrilineal Peoples of Eastern Tanzania*, 26–34, describes
them. The designation Sagara was often extended to other peoples. See the ex-

town, fortified by four towers and a stone wall, having considerable pretensions to architectural skill. The Sultana sent her ambassadors to demand tribute from me. I refused to pay, though she possessed 300 muskets and 500 slaves, on the ground that as my caravans had paid already I was exempted from it according to her custom. The ambassadors retired with a "Ngema"—very well. Soon after passing the town we arrived at Simbo Khombi, and here I was compelled to order my cook to be flogged for his incorrigible dishonesty and waste. Upon leaving Simbo for the wilderness and swamp of Makata I was made aware that the cook had deserted. I despatched three soldiers in pursuit, who, in the ardor of following his tracks, fell into the hands of the Sultana of Simbawenni, who robbed them of their guns and put them in chains. Some Arabs happening to see them in this condition, and knowing they were my men, made haste to inform the Sultana that she did not know what white people were capable of doing if they were angered; that I had guns with me that would kill her in her house at the distance of half a mile. This extraordinary announcement caused her to mitigate her anger against me and to release my soldiers, returning one gun and retaining two as just and equitable tribute. The cook was afterward reported to me to be murdered.[52]

From Simbo to Rehenneko in Usagara extends the terrible Makata swamp, a distance of forty-five miles. It is knee deep of water and black mire, and for five days we marched through this cataclysm. From here commenced the list of calamities which afterwards overtook me. First the white man Shaw caught the terrible fever of East Africa, then the Arab boy Selim, then myself, then the soldiers one by one, and smallpox and dysentery raged among us. As soon as I had recovered from the effects of the fever I was attacked with dysentery, which brought me to the verge of the grave. From a stout and fleshy person, weighing 170 pounds, I was reduced to a skeleton, a mere frame of bone and skin, weighing 130 pounds. Two pagazis fell victims to this dysentery.[53] Even the dog "Omar" was attacked by it, and presently died. At Rehenneko we experienced the last of the rainy season. It had rained almost every day since we had left Bagamoyo, but until we had arrived at the verge of the Makata swamp we did not experience much inconvenience from it.

amples given in Beidelman, "Hyena and Rabbit: A Kaguru Representation of Matrilineal Relations," 73.

52. In *HIFL*, 126–29, Stanley asserts that after the flogging he gave the cook his kit and told him to leave the expedition. Stanley claimed that he did not really mean this, but the cook did leave and Stanley was unsuccessful in his efforts to recall him.

53. *Ibid.*, 141, says one porter died.

Two days beyond Rehenneko we caught up with the fourth caravan, which had been sent out under the leadership of the Scotchman.
I found the white man in a most miserable plight. All the donkeys
—numbering nine—that I had sent out with him were dead and he
was attacked by dropsy or elephantiasis—a disease of which he has
since died. He had wasted upward of six bales of cloth, five of which
had been entrusted to him to convey to Unyanyembe. An Arab proprietor would have slaughtered him for his extravagance and im-
becility; but I—I had no other course but to relieve him of all charge
of such goods. Had I not foreseen some such mismanagement and
provided plenty of cloth against such loss I should have been compelled to return to the coast for more bales to replace them.

By the 24th May we had travelled 278 miles, and had entered the
dangerous land of the Wagogo. We had passed through the territories
of the Wakami,[54] Wakwere,[55] Wadoe,[56] Wasegura,[57] Wasagara[58]

54. The Kami are now held to be Luguru and not a separate people. Beidelman,
Matrilineal Peoples of Eastern Tanzania, 26. Nineteenth century observers located
them in an upland district near the seventh parallel of latitude and in the midst
of the Zigula. They had earlier suffered much from slave traders. Last, *Polyglotta
Africana Orientalis,* 11; *A l'Assaut des Pays Nègres,* 93; Ricklin, *La Mission
Catholique du Zanguebar. Travaux et Voyages du R. P. Horner,* 160ff., for a full
contemporary account.

55. The Kwere were bordered by the Luguru on the west, the Zaramu on the
east, and the Zigula to the north. They were a peaceful people whose largest
political unit was the lineage, and have many similarities with the Luguru and
Sagara. *Ibid.,* 129–30; Brain, "The Kwere of the Eastern Province"; Beidelman,
Matrilineal Peoples of Eastern Tanzania, 22–25.

56. The Doe, a small group living not far from Bagamoyo, have the reputation
of being East Africa's only cannibals and at times are discussed in a rather
sensational manner—as in Bojarski, "The Last of the Cannibals in Tanganyika."
For examples of their activity, on both Europeans and Africans, Schynse, *A
Travers l'Afrique avec Stanley et Emin-Pacha,* 290; *Central Africa* 2(1884), 9.
For explanations of their practices, Baumann and Westermann, *Les Peuplades
et les Civilisations de l'Afrique,* 233; J. Brain, Letter on the Doe. The dangers of
adopting European reports of cannibalism are presented in Evans-Pritchard,
"Zande Cannibalism."

57. The Zigula were a warlike but not centrally organized people inhabiting an
area behind the coast between the Ruvu and Wami rivers. They suffered heavily in
the early nineteenth century from slave raids and were famous for some particularly serious risings against their Arab owners. Last, *Polyglotta Africana
Orientalis,* 8; Baumann, *Der Sansibar-Archipel. III. Die Insel Pemba und Ihre
Kleineren Nachbarinseln,* 97. For a full contemporary account, Picarda, "Autour
de Mandéra"; Beidelman, *Matrilineal Peoples of Eastern Tanzania,* 66–72.

58. For a general account of the Sagara region, Meyer, *Das Deutsche Kolonialreich,* 192–99. European visitors were generally much impressed with the lands of
the Sagara; Stanley's favorable descriptions were credited with stimulating the
decision of the later German empire-builders to begin their efforts in East Africa.
Pfeil, *Die Erwerbung von Deutsch-Ostafrika,* 56–57; Peters, *Wie Deutsch-
Ostafrika entstand!,* 25; for the Sagara, Beidelman, *Matrilineal Peoples of Eastern
Tanzania,* 51–53.

and Wahehe.[59] We had crossed the rivers Kingani, Ungerengeri, Little Makata, Great Makata, Rudewa and Mukondokwa. We had discovered the sources of the Kingani, Wami and Mukondokwa rivers[60] and the Lake of Ugombo,[61] three miles long by two and a half miles wide. Our losses up to this date were seventeen donkeys dead, one coil of wire stolen, one tent eaten up by white ants, one tent lost, also one axe, one pistol, twenty pounds of bullets, and Captain Bombay's stock of uniform clothes, all of which losses I ascribe to the fatigues experienced during the transit of the Makata swamp. Three pagazis had deserted, two were dead; also one white man[62] and two natives of Malabar had died. The two horses died on the third day after leaving Bagamoyo, for so fatal is this land to both men and animals.

In entering Ugogo we were entering a new land, to meet with different dangers, different accidents from those we had now left behind us. We had ascended a plateau 3,700 to 4,200 feet above the level of the sea; the extraordinary fertility and rivers of the maritime region we should not see in Ugogo, but a bare and sterile plateau, though cultivated by the Wagogo.

The Wagogo are the Irish of Africa—clanish and full of fight. To the Wagogo all caravans must pay tribute, the refusal of which is met by an immediate declaration of hostilities.[63] The tribute which

59. The Hehe, inhabiting the area around present-day Iringa, were one of the most militant groups in East Africa. In the 1870's they were infiltrating some of the areas on the caravan route to Tabora where such people as the Kaguru welcomed their settlement in return for the military support they provided. Beidelman, "A History of Ukaguru: 1857–1916," 14, 30; Beidelman, "The Baraguyu," 255. For the organization and history of the Hehe, Brown and Hutt, *Anthropology in Action;* Nigmann, *Die Wahehe.*

60. Stanley had crossed the river systems of the Ruvu and the Wami. The Ngerengere is part of the Ruvu system. (The Ruvu is known as the Kingani near the ocean). The Mkata, Rudewa, and Mkondoa are part of the Wami system. Later ventures proved both systems of little use for navigation. For the Kingani, or Ruvu, Holmwood, "On the River Kingani in East Africa"; Mackay to Wright, July 25, 1876, C.A6/M1, CMS; Behr, *Kriegsbilder aus dem Araberaufstand in Deutsch-Ostafrika,* 141–43; Ricklin, *Mission Catholique du Zanguebar,* 221. For the exploration of the Wami, see document 12, note 4.

61. Because of the variations in the size of Lake Ugombo, due to the state of the rains, Cameron asserted that Stanley "must have been dreaming" when he gave its extent. Hore, with more understanding, and after visiting the lake in the dry season, said such conditions were "a reminder that one ought to have charitable considerations for apparently conflicting accounts of different travellers." Cameron's letter of June 16, 1873, *PRGS* 18(1873–1874), 70; Hore, *Tanganyika,* 58.

62. W. L. Farquhar.

63. Velten, *Schilderungen der Suaheli,* 1ff., provides an interesting account on the problems of a caravan moving through this and other areas.

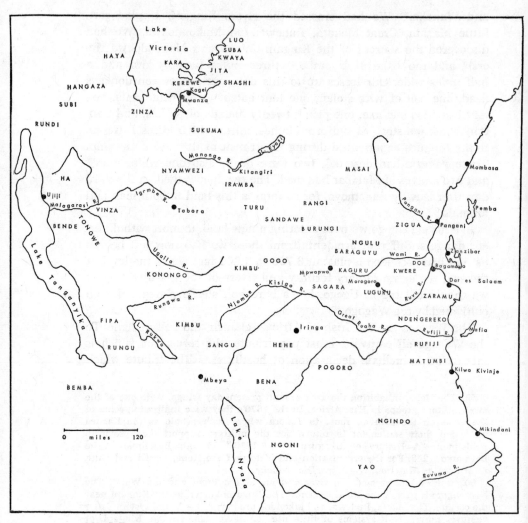

Map I. Tanzania

I alone paid to these people amounted to 170 doti ($170 in gold), for the mere privilege of travelling through their country to Unyanyembe beyond.

On the thirtieth day after entering Ugogo we arrived in Unyanyembe, at the Arab village of Kwihara—so called from the plain of Kwihara, in which it is situated. The march of this last month had been very rapid, we having travelled 247½ miles, while the previous march of 278 miles, viz., from Bagamoyo to Ugogo had occupied fifty-four days. Altogether we had travelled 525½ miles in eighty-four days, including halts, which makes our rate of marching per day six and a quarter miles. Burton and Speke in travelling the same distance from Kaole to Unyanyembe in 134 days, which is at the rate of three and one-sixth miles per day. You must not imagine that I am stating this in order to make an invidious comparison, but simply to show you how expeditiously we have travelled. The Arabs travel the distance from two months and twelve days to four months. On the second visit of Speke with Grant[64] to Unyanyembe he made the march in 115 days.

I should like to enter into more minute details respecting this new land, which is almost unknown, but the very nature of my mission, requiring speed and all my energy, precludes it. Some day, perhaps, the HERALD will permit me to describe more minutely the experiences of the long march, with all its vicissitudes and pleasures, in its columns, and I can assure your readers beforehand that they will not be quite devoid of interest. But now my whole time is occupied in the march, and the direction of the expedition, the neglect of which in any one point would be productive of disastrous results.

I shall here proceed to relate what I have heard of Livingstone *verbatum*.

On the 12th of April I met at Moussoudi, on the Ungerengeri River, four marches from Simbawenni, Salim bin Rasheed,[65] who gave me the following intelligence respecting Livingstone:

"I saw the musungu who came up from the Nyassa a long time ago, at Ujiji last year. He lived in the next tembe to me. He has a long, white mustache and beard, and was very fat. He was then about going to Marungu and Manyema." [66]

On the 18th of May Sheikh Abdullah bin Nasib[67] found me encamped at Mpwapwa and gave me the following:

64. James A. Grant (1827–1892). After his return from exploring with Speke, Grant remained an active member of the Royal Geographical Society, where he always commented fully on the relation of new discoveries to those of Speke. *DNB*, XXII, 764–66; Gray, "Speke and Grant," 154–59.

65. Salim bin Rashid al Manzuri was a well-known Arab of Zanzibar; his travels included a visit to the area of Lake Victoria. He supplied Burton with information of his expeditions. Burton, "Lake Regions," 260, 270, 275, 346.

66. The region of the eastern Congo bordered roughly by the Lualaba River on the west, by the mountains west of Lake Tanganyika on the east, by a line one degree north of the Lukuga River on the south, and by a line parallel with the southern extremity of Lake Edward on the north. Manyema is inhabited by diverse tribal groups. For the area and its peoples, Stuart, "Manyema Culture and History prior to 1894"; Vansina, *Introduction à l'Ethnographie du Congo*, chap 7.

67. Abdulla bin Nasibu, Arab governor of Tabora from 1878 to 1881, was noted for his successful raids upon Africans. He was recalled to Zanzibar by Barghash and was poisoned allegedly by his orders in 1882. Bennett, *Studies in East African History*, 5–15; Becker, *La Troisième Expédition Belge*, 89; Reichard, *Deutsche-Ostafrika*, 93–96, 101; Reichard, "Die Unruhen in Unjanjembe."

The musungu (white man) has gone to Maniema, a month's march from Ujiji. He has met with a bad accident, having shot himself in the thigh while out hunting buffalo. When he gets well he will return to Ujiji. There are many lakes on the other side of the Tanganyika. Lake Ujiji is very great; Lake Uruwa is also great, Lake Bangweolo is great, but Lake Maniema is great, exceedingly great.[68]

At Kusuri, in Mgunda Mkhali, or the land of the Wayanzi,[69] on the 13th of June, I met Sheik Thani bin Massoud, who imparted the following:

"You are asking me about the musungu whom people call 'Dochter Fellusteen' (Dr. Livingstone). Yes; I lived near him about three months at Ujiji. His men have all deserted him, except three slaves, whom he was obliged to buy."

"Why?"

"He used to beat his men very hard if they did not do instantly what he told them. At last they all ran away; no one would stop with him. He had nothing with him, no cloth nor beads, to buy food for a long time; so he had to go out and hunt buffalo every day. He is a very old man and very fat, too; has a long white beard. He is a great eater, Mashallah! He would eat a pot of ghee and a big plateful of rice three or four times a day. Mashallah! but you see this thing (pointing to a tea saucer)?"

"Yes."

"Well he would eat that full of butter, with a potful of ugali (porridge)."

On the 16th of June I met Hassan, a Balooch soldier of Sheikh Said bin Salim, of Unyanyembe, who gave news about Livingstone to this effect:

"He is a very old man, with a beard nearly white. His left shoulder is out of joint from a fight he had with a *suriba* (lion). He has gone to Maniema with some Arabs. Maniema is three months' march from Ujiji. He is about returning to Ujiji soon, owing to a letter he received from the 'Balyuz' (Consul).[70] They say that although he has been out here so long he has done nothing. He has fifteen bales of cloth at Unyanyembe, not yet sent to him."

68. See document 4, note 25.

69. The Mgunda Mkali, or Itigi thicket, "a dense, fully closed thicket of coppicing shrubs, 8 to 15 feet high, covering over 2,000 square miles," was a major hindrance to travelers. Moffett, ed., *Handbook of Tanganyika*, 153–54. The Yanzi were the first Nyamwezi group on the caravan route after it left Ugogo. Blohm, *Die Nyamwezi. Land und Wirtschaft*, 9; Burton, "Lake Regions," 153–55.

70. *Balozi*, a consul or political agent; specifically, the British representative at Zanzibar.

On the 20th, at Kubuga, three days from Unyanyembe, Sheikh Amir bin Sultan[71] informed me as follows:

"Yes, there is a musungu, a very old man, who came to Ujiji by the way of Lake Nyassa and Cazembe.[72] After coming to Ujiji he went to Marungu, and then returned to Ujiji. About a year ago he crossed the Tanganyika Lake, and accompanied some Arabs to Lake Maniema, which, I am told, is a very great lake, much larger than Tanganyika. Lately a caravan coming from Ukonongo[73] brought the news that he was dead. I don't know whether the news be true or not."

At this place I have received the following additional information: He is on the road to Ujiji from Lake Maniema, which is west of Uguhha. The lake is fifteen camps from the Tanganyika, in a south-southwest direction. With me are going to Ujiji for him fifteen loads of cloth, eight loads of beads and twelve boxes, containing wine, provisions—such as sugar, tea, salt, pepper, spices and such little luxuries—besides clothes, books and newspapers. If at Ujiji in one month more I shall see him, the race for home shall begin. Until I hear more of him or see the long absent old man face to face I bid you a farewell; but wherever he is be sure I shall not give up the chase. If alive you shall hear what he has to say; if dead I will find and bring his bones to you.

2

Kwihara, Unyanyembe
September 20, 1871[1]

The African expedition of the NEW YORK HERALD arrived at Unyanyembe on June 23, 1871. It had suffered considerably in its *personnel* and transport. One of the white men has died, he but lived to reach half-way here; two of the armed escort as well as eight pagazis

71. Amir bin Sultan al Harthi, a long-time resident of Tabora, was later sent by Barghash in command of a Zanzibari army against the Nyamwezi leader Mirambo. Amir bin Sultan was a member of the Arab group that drove Said bin Salim from office. Bennett, *Studies in East African History*, 5–6; Mackay to Wigram, May 25, 1878, CMS. See also *HIFL*, 219–20.

72. The Kazembe was the ruler of the important Lunda state centered around the valley of the Luapula River. See Cunnison, *The Luapula Peoples of Northern Rhodesia*; Vansina, *Kingdoms of the Savanna*, 78ff. The ruler Livingstone visited was Kazembe VII, Muonga Sunkutu. Cunnison, "The Reigns of the Kazembes," 135.

73. The Konongo are members of the southern Nyamwezi. Moffett, *Handbook of Tanganyika*, 272; Broyon-Mirambo, "Note sur l'Ouniamouézi," 255.

1. *NYH*, July 15, 1872.

died also from dysentery and smallpox. Two horses and twenty-seven asses have also perished. On arriving at Unyanyembe your correspondent wrote two letters and entrusted them to Said Ben Salim (Burton and Speke's former Ras cafilah), now Governor of Unyanyembe. One gave an account of our journey from the coast here; the other of our battle with Mirambo,[2] who occupied the country lying between the HERALD expedition and the object of its search. I then prepared for the second stage, viz: the journey to Ujiji and Manyema.

But difficulties had been on the increase for about a month before our arrival here. Mirambo, King of Uyowa, in western Unyamwezi, had been levying blackmail to an unconscionable amount upon all caravans bound westward to Ujiji, the lake and the regions lying behind; to Urundi, to Karagwah,[3] Uganda[4] and Unyoro.[5] The road to these countries led through his country, a serious misfortune not only to the expedition but to all caravans bound anywhere westward. About the time the expedition arrived Mirambo capped his arbitrary course by taking from a caravan five bales of cloth, five guns and five kegs of powder, and then refusing it permission to pass, declaring that none should pass any more except over his body. This, of course, led to a declaration of war on the part of the Arabs, which was given after I had secured new carriers and was almost ready for the journey.

The Arabs were so confident of easy victory over the African King, declaring that fifteen days at the most would suffice to settle him, that I was tempted in an unlucky moment to promise them my aid, hoping that by this means I would be enabled to reach Livingstone sooner than by stopping at Unyanyembe awaiting the turn of events. Mirambo was but twenty-seven hours' march from Unyanyembe.

On the first day we burned three of his villages, captured, killed or

2. Mirambo (*c.* 1830/40–1884), the most important of all Nyamwezi leaders. For his life, Bennett, *Studies in East African History*, 1–30. Kabeya, *Mtemi Mirambo*, has valuable oral information on Mirambo.

3. The Haya state of Karagwe, through which led the trade route to Buganda, was one of the more important African states of the Lake Victoria region during the first two-thirds of the nineteenth century. Taylor, *The Western Lacustrine Bantu*, 132–44; Cory, *History of the Bukoba District*, 17–34.

4. Buganda, on the northwestern side of Lake Victoria, one of the most highly centralized states in Africa, was the dominant power on the lake during this period. Fallers, *The Eastern Lacustrine Bantu (Ganda and Soga)*; Fallers, ed., *The King's Men*, for an excellent collection of studies on the Baganda state.

5. Bunyoro, to the north of Buganda, was losing during the nineteenth century its former dominance of the region to the rising state of Buganda. Taylor, *Western Lacustrine Bantu*, 17–41; Beattie, "Bunyoro: An African Feudality?"; Beattie, *Bunyoro: An African Kingdom*.

drove away the inhabitants. On the second I was taken down with the ever-remitting fever of the country. On the third a detachment was sent out and audaciously attacked the fenced village where the King was, and after an hour's fighting entered it at one gate while Mirambo left it by another.

In returning to our camp this detachment was waylaid by Mirambo and his men and a great slaughter of the Arabs took place. Seventeen Arab commanders were slain, among them one or two personal friends of mine, who had travelled with me from the coast. Five of the soldiers of the HERALD expedition were killed. The fourth day was a frightful retreat, from the simple cause of seeing smoke in the distance, which was believed to be caused by Mirambo's advance or Ruga-Ruga[6] freebooters. Without informing each other the Arabs, followed by their slaves, rushed out of their village, and I was left in my tembe alone, in a fever. My own men, frightened by their isolation, lost courage and ran, all but six, my Arab boy, Selim, and the Englishman Shaw. With these I reached Mfuto, half-way to Unyanyembe, at midnight. After this graceless retreat it became evident to me that it was going to be a long affair between Arab and African. Livingstone's caravan, which had gone to its first camp preparatory for the journey, had been ordered back, and the goods had been safely lodged in my house.

The Arabs' cowardly retreat invited Mirambo to follow them to their homes. While I was debating what to do (knowing that speed was a necessity with the expedition) Mirambo entered Tabora, the Arab capital of Central Africa, with his ferocious allies, the Watuta.[7] Tabora is one mile from Kwihara, the place where I date this telegram. The Kazeh of Speke and Burton[8] is not known here except

6. The *ruga-ruga* were the professional fighting men of the area. Descriptions of them can be found in Storms, "L'Esclavage entre le Tanganika et la Côte Est," 14–15; Reichard, "Die Wanjamuesi," 307–309.

7. The Ngoni, who, moving up from southern Africa, spread destruction through much of Tanganyika in the nineteenth century. The group Stanley met were settled to the northwest of Tabora under the leader, Mtambalika. Hatchell, "The Angoni of Tanganyika Territory." See also Barnes, *Politics in a Changing Society. A Political History of the Fort Jameson Ngoni*.

8. The future Tabora was then made up of a complex of settlements, each with its own name. See the list in Velten, *Schilderungen der Suaheli*, 9. Speke and Burton had used the name, and despite Stanley's opinion, later visitors would also. Cameron added, "By the way, Kazeh and Taborah turn out to be one and the same place, and the name Kazeh is well known to all the Arabs here. They laugh at Stanley's idea of Kazeh meaning a kingdom." Cameron's letter of Oct. 16, 1873, in *PRGS* 18 (1873–74), 178; see also Burdo, *Les Belges dans l'Afrique Centrale. De Zanzibar au Lac Tanganika*, 305. See document 3.

as the fenced residence of an old Arab. Tabora includes all the Arab residences.[9] The Arabs of Kwihara were in great alarm and their thorough selfishness came out strongly. The Governor and others were for running to the coast at once, declaring Central Africa forever closed to travel and trade.

About one-fourth of Tabora was burned; five eminent Arabs were killed; cattle, ivory and slaves carried away. Expecting attack I turned the Governor's house into a little fort, in order to defend the property of the expedition and that of Livingstone from the Watuta. All fugitives from Tabora who were armed were invited in, until I had 150 armed men within the tembe. Provisions and water were brought to last five days. At the end of that time Mirambo and his allies retired with great booty. During the state of siege the American flag was hoisted.

After this event I informed the Arabs that I could not assist them any more, for if they ran away once they would run away again, and declared my intention to travel at once to Ujiji by another road. They all advised me to wait until the war was over; that I was going straight to death by travelling during war time. But I was obstinate, and they looked on me as a lost man. I engaged thirty men of Zanzibar at treble prices. The effects of the expedition were reduced to the smallest scale consistent with the actual necessities of the journey. As the day drew near the restlessness of the men increased and Bombay (Burton and Speke's handy man, but always my stumbling block), did his utmost to slacken the courage of the armed escort— the Englishman Shaw even became so smitten with fear that he could not assist in my preparations. The Arab reports of the wars along our road were influencing the men of the expedition.

3

Kwihara, Unyanyembe
Sept. 21, 1871[1]

How can I describe my feelings to you, that you may comprehend exactly the condition that I am in, the condition that I have been in, and the extremely wretched condition that the Arabs and slave trad-

9. Kabeya, *Mirambo*, 16, derives the name, Tabora, from the Kinyamwezi word, *matobolwa*, or sweet potato.
1. *NYH*, Aug. 9, 1872.

ing people of the Mrima[2]—the hill land or the coast—would fain keep me in? For the last two months I have been debating in my own mind as to my best course. Resolves have not been wanting, but up to to-day they have failed. I am no nearer the object of my search apparently than I was two years ago, when you gave me the instructions at the hotel in Paris called the "Grand Hotel." This object of my search you know is Livingstone—Dr. David Livingstone— F.R.G.S., LL.D., &c. Is this Dr. David Livingstone a myth? Is there any such person living? If so, where is he? I ask everybody—Omani, Arab-half-cast, Wamrima-pagazis—but no man knows. I lift up my head, shake off day dreams and ask the silent plains around and the still dome of azure upheaving to infinity above, where can he be? No answer. The attitude of my people, the asinine obstinacy of Bombay, the evidently determined opposition of the principal Arabs to my departure from here, the war with Mirambo, the other unknown road to Central Lake, the impossibility of obtaining pagazis, all combine, or seem to, to say: "Thou shalt never find him. Thou shalt neither hear of him. Thou shalt die here."

Sheikh, the son of Nasib, one of the ruling Powers, here declares it an impossibility to reach Ujiji. Daily he vexes me with "There is no road; all roads are closed; the Wakonongo, the Wagara[3] and the Wawendi[4] are coming from the south to help Mirambo; if you go to the north, Usukuma[5] is the country of Mirambo's mother; if you take the Wildjankuru road,[6] that is Mirambo's own country. You see, then, sir, the impossibility of reaching the Tanganyika. My advice is that you wait until Mirambo is killed, then, inshallah (please God), the road will be open, or go back." And oftentimes I explode, and cry out: "What! wait here until Mirambo is killed? You were five years

2. The coast opposite Zanzibar.

3. Ugala, a southeastern district of the Nyamwezi. Burton, "Lake Regions," 165. A later traveler reported that the aggressive acts of Abdulla bin Nasibu had made the Gala very hostile to the Arabs. Reichard, "Das afrikanische Elfenbein und sein Handel," 165.

4. The Bende, occupying the territory known as Ukawendi, lived along Lake Tanganyika's shores from the area of Karema to the Malagarasi River. Hore, "Twelve Tribes of Tanganyika," 18; Avon, "Vie sociale des Wabende au Tanganika."

5. The Sukuma lived to the north of their close relations, the Nyamwezi. They were divided into numerous independent political entities. See the sources given above for the Nyamwezi, and Malcolm, *Sukumaland*. Stanley later said of their territory: "It was while traversing through Usukuma that I first awoke to the bare possibility that some portions of Equatorial Africa might really be worth serious attention from Europe." Stanley, *My African Travels*, 15.

6. Bulyankulu, a Nyamwezi chiefdom. See Bennett, *Studies in East African History*, 83; Spellig, "Die Wanjamwesi," 205.

fighting Manua Sera![7] Go back! after spending $20,000! O Sheikh, the son of Nasib, no Arab can fathom the soul of a muzungu (white man)! I go on and will not wait until you kill Mirambo; I go on, and will not go back until I shall have seen the Tanganyika," and this morning I added, "and the day after to-morrow I start."

"Well, master," he replied, "be it as you say; but put down the words of Sheikh, the son of Nasib, for they are worthy to be remembered."

He has only just parted from me, and to comfort myself after the ominous words I write to you. I wish I could write as fast as the thoughts crowd my mind. Then what a wild, chaotic and incoherent letter you would have! But my pen is stiff, the paper is abominable, and before a sentence is framed the troubled mind gets somewhat calmer. I am spiteful, I candidly confess, just now; I am cynical—I do not care who knows it. Fever has made me so. My whining white servant contributes toward it. The stubbornness of Bombay—"incarnation of honesty" Burton calls him—is enough to make one cynical. The false tongues of these false-hearted Arabs drive me on to spitefulness; the cowardice of my soldiers is a proverb with me. The rock daily, hourly growing larger and more formidable against which the ship of the expedition must split—so says everybody, and what everybody says must be true—makes me fierce and savage-hearted. Yet I say that the day after to-morrow every man Jack of us who can walk shall march.

But before the expedition tries the hard road again—before it commences the weary, weary march once more—can I not gain some information about Livingstone from the scraps of newspapers I have been industriously clipping for some time back? May they not with the more mature knowledge I have obtained of the interior since I went on this venture give me a hint which I might advantageously adopt? Here they are, a dozen of them, fifteen, twenty, over thirty bits of paper. Here is one. Ah, dolor of heart, where art thou? This mirth-provoking bit of newspaper is almost a physician to me. I read: ["]Zanzibar, Feb. 6, 1870. I am also told by Ludha Damjee that a large caravan, laden with ivory, and coming from Nayamweze, has completely perished from this disease in Ujiji.["] To you who stay

7. Mnywa Sere, former Nyamwezi ruler of Tabora, who was deposed by the Arab community when he sought to secure a larger share of the profits of the trade passing through his chiefdom. After several years of warfare, Mnywa Sere was killed by the Arabs in 1865. Tippu Tip, *Maisha ya Hamed bin Muhammed el Murjebi Yaani Tippu Tip*, 8, 41, 43.

at home in America may be accorded forgiveness if you do not quite understand where "Nayamweze" or "Ujiji" is; but to the British politico and Her Britannic Majesty's Consul, Dr. John Kirk,[8] a former companion of Livingstone, a man of science, a member of the Royal Geographical Society, and one who is said to be in constant communication with Livingstone, forgiveness for such gross ignorance is impossible. A parallel case of ignorance would be in a New York editor writing, "I am also told by Mr. So and So that a large wagon train, bringing silver bricks from Montana, has perished in Alaska." Ujiji, you must remember, is about a month's march westward of Unyamwezi—not "Nayamweze"—and to me it is inconceivable how a person in the habit of writing weekly to his government about Livingstone should have conceived Ujiji to be somewhere between the coast and "Nayamweze," as he calls it. But then I am spiteful this morning of September 21, and there is nothing loveable under the sun at this present time except the memory of my poor little dog "Omar," who fell a victim to the Makata Swamp. Poor Omar!

Amid these many scraps or clippings all about Livingstone there are many more which contain as ludicrous mistakes, mostly all of them having emanated from the same scientific pen as the above. I find one wherein Sir R. Murchison,[9] President of the Royal Geographical Society, stoutly maintains that Livingstone's tenacity of purpose, undying resolution and herculean frame will overcome every obstacle. Through several scraps runs a vein of doubt and unbelief in the existence of the explorer. The writers seem to incline that he has at last succumbed. But to the very latest date Sir Roderick rides triumphant over all doubts and fears. At the very nick of time he has always a letter from Livingstone himself, or a despatch from

8. John Kirk (1832–1922), who served for over twenty years in Zanzibar, was the dominant political figure on the island from the early 1870's until the declaration of the German protectorate on the East African mainland in 1885. For his career, Coupland, *Exploitation of East Africa, passim.* Kirk and Stanley were to have a famous feud (see document 7, notes 3 and 14); it can largely be blamed on the interaction of two overbearing personalities. As one Zanzibar resident said of Kirk: "He is a great hand at contradicting you flat, and aims at being *the* authority on all points under debate." Tozer to Steere, Sept. 30, 1869, A.1.I, UMCA.

9. Roderick I. Murchison (1792–1871), described by Livingstone as "the best friend I ever had—true, warm, and abiding," was the influential president of the Royal Geographical Society for most of the years that Livingstone was exploring in Africa. Seaver, *David Livingstone,* 316; Geikie, *Life of Sir Roderick I. Murchison,* especially II, 294–99. For Murchison's role as a stimulator of East African exploration, Bridges, "John Hanning Speke and the Royal Geographical Society."

Livingstone to Lord Clarendon,[10] or a private note from Dr. Livingstone to his friend Kirk at Zanzibar. Happy Sir Roderick! Good, Sir Roderick! a healthy, soul-inspiring faith is thine.

Well, I am to tell you the outspoken truth, tormented by the same doubts and fears that people in America and England are—to-day uncommonly so. I blame the fever. Yet, though I have heard nothing that would lead me to believe Livingstone is alive, I derive much comfort in reading Sir Roderick's speech to the society of which he is President.

But though he has tenacity of purpose and is the most resolute of travellers, he is but a man, who, if alive, is old in years. I have but to send for Said bin Habib,[11] who claims to be the Doctor's best friend, and who lives but a rifle shot from the camp of the HERALD and Livingstone expeditions, and he will tell me how he found him so sick with fever that it seemed as if the tired spirit was about to take its eternal rest. I have but to ask Suliman Dowa, or Thomas, how he found "old Daoud Fellasteen"—David Livingstone—and he will tell me he saw a very old man, with very gray beard and mustache, who ought to be home now instead of wandering among those wild cannibals of Manyema.

What made me to-day give way to fears for Livingstone's life was that a letter had reached Unyanyembe, from a man called Sherif,[12] who is in charge of Livingstone's goods at Ujiji, wherein he asked permission from Said bin Salim, the Governor here, to sell Livingstone's goods for ivory, wherein he states further that Sherif had sent his slaves to Manyema to look for the white man, and that these slaves had returned without hearing any news of him. He (Sherif) was therefore tired of waiting, and it would be much better if he were to receive orders to dispose of the white man's cloth and beads for ivory.

It is strange that these goods, which were sent to Ujiji over a year

10. George Villiers, Earl of Clarendon (1800–1870), was foreign secretary at times after 1853 and thus in contact with Livingstone, who held an appointment from the Foreign Office during his later explorations. *DNB*, XX, 347–50.

11. Said bin Habib, one of the most enterprising of Zanzibari Arabs, had returned to Zanzibar in 1860 after a sixteen-year stay in Africa. During this period he had traveled across the continent to Luanda. Said bin Habib returned to the interior to become one of the Arab leaders around Lake Tanganyika and in the Congo. He died in 1889 while returning to Zanzibar. "Narrative of Said bin Habeeb, an Arab Inhabitant of Zanzibar"; Rigby to Anderson, March 20, 1860, E-27, ZA; Ceulemans, *La question arabe et le Congo (1883–1892)*, 50–51, 147; Muxworthy to LMS, Aug. 2, 1889, LMS.

12. Sherif Bashaykh bin Ahmed; he reached Ujiji on Nov. 10, 1870. See his letter to Kirk of Nov. 15, 1870, *PRGS* 15 (1870–1871), 206. See also Livingstone to Kirk, Oct. 20, 1871, in *HIFL*, 704–07, for Livingstone's complaints.

ago, have not yet been touched, and the fact that Livingstone has not been in Ujiji to receive his last year's supplies puzzles also Said bin Salim, Governor of Unyanyembe, or, rather, of Tabora and Kwihara, as well as it puzzles Sheikh, the son of Nasib, accredited Consul of Syed Barghash, Sultan of Zanzibar and Pemba at the Courts of Rumanika[13] and Mtesa,[14] Kings respectively of Karagwah and Uganda.[15]

In the storeroom where the cumbersome moneys of the NEW YORK HERALD Expedition lie piled up bale upon bale, sack after sack, coil after coil, and the two boats, are this year's supplies sent by Dr. Kirk to Dr. Livingstone—seventeen bales of cloth, twelve boxes of wine, provisions, and little luxuries such as tea and coffee. When I came up with my last caravan to Unyanyembe I found Livingstone's had arrived but four weeks before, or about May 23 last, and had put itself under charge of a half-caste called Thani Kati-Kati, or Thani, "in the middle," or "between." Before he could get carriers he died of dysentery. He was succeeded in charge by a man from Johanna, who, in something like a week, died of small-pox; then Mirambo's war broke out, and here we all are, September 21, both expeditions halted. But not for long, let us hope, for the third time I will make a start the day after to-morrow.

To the statement that the man Sherif makes, that he has sent slaves to Manyema to search for Dr. Livingstone, I pay not the slightest attention. Sherif, I am told, is a half-caste. Half Arab, half negro. Happy amalgamation! All Arabs and all half-castes, especially when it is in their interest to lie, lie without stint. What and who is this man Sherif, that he should, unasked, send his slaves twenty days off to search for a white man? It was not for his interest to send out men, but it was policy to say that he had done so, and that his slaves had returned without hearing of him. He is, therefore, in a hurry to sell off and make money at the expense of Livingstone. This man has treated the old traveller shamefully—like some other men I know of, who, if I live, will be exposed through your columns. But why should

13. Rumanika, ruler of Karagwe from the 1850's until his death in 1878; he is considered by the Haya as "the wisest and one of the cleverest Kings of Karagwe" since he brought their state to the height of its power. Wilson to Wigram, May 23, 1878—addenda of July 3, 1878, C.A6/025, CMS; Berger, "Oral Traditions in Karagwe," 6–7; Cory, *History of Bukoba*, 23ff.

14. Mutesa I, *kabaka* of Buganda from 1856 until his death in 1884. Stanley would meet him on his next expedition. For Mutesa's reign, Low, "The Northern Interior, 1840–84," 333ff.

15. Shaykh bin Nasibu was perhaps acting in this office when he wrote to Livingstone in 1871; the Arab leader was then proceeding to Karagwe. *LLJ*, II, 102.

I not do so now? What better time is there than the present? Well, here it is—cooly, calmly and deliberately. I have studied the whole thing since I came here, and cannot do better than give you the results of the searching inquiries instituted.

It is the case of the British Public vs. Dr. John Kirk, Acting Political Agent and Her Britannic Majesty's Consul at Zanzibar, as I understand it. The case is briefly this: Some time in October, 1870, Henry Adrian Churchill, Esq., was Political Agent and Her Britannic Majesty's Consul at Zanzibar.[16] He fitted out during that month a small expedition to carry supplies to Dr. Livingstone, under the escort of seven or eight men, who were to act as armed soldiers, porters or servants. They arrived at Bagamoyo, on the mainland, during the latter part of October. About the latter part of October or the early part of November Mr. Churchill left Zanzibar for England, and Dr. John Kirk, the present occupant of the consular chair, succeeded him as "acting" in the capacity Mr. Churchill heretofore had done. A letter bag, containing letters to Dr. Livingstone, was sealed up by Dr. John Kirk at Zanzibar, on which was written "November 1, 1870— Registered letters for Dr. David Livingstone, Ujiji," from which it appears that the letter bag was closed on the 1st November, 1870. On the 6th January, 1871, your correspondent in charge of the NEW YORK HERALD Expedition arrived at Zanzibar, and then and there heard of a caravan being at Bagamoyo, bound for the interior with supplies for Dr. Livingstone. On the 4th of February, 1871, your correspondent in charge of the HERALD Expedition arrived at Bagamoyo and found this caravan of Dr. Livingstone's still at Bagamoyo. On or about the 18th February, 1871, appeared off Bagamoyo Her Britannic Majesty's gunboat *Columbine*, Captain Tucker,[17] having on board Dr. John Kirk, acting Her Britannic Majesty's Consul. Three days before Dr. John Kirk arrived at Bagamoyo Livingstone's caravan started for the interior, hurried, no doubt, by the report that the English Consul was coming. That evening about the hour of seven P.M. your correspondent dined at the French mission[18] in company

16. Henry A. Churchill was British representative at Zanzibar from 1867 to 1870. See Coupland, *Exploitation of East Africa*, 58ff.; Gavin, "The Bartle Frere Mission to Zanzibar," 126ff., for aspects of his work there.

17. John C. Tucker, captain of H.M.S. *Columbine;* he was especially active against the slave trade in 1871. There are reports on some of this activity in E-61, ZA. See also Clowes *et al., The Royal Navy,* VII, 234.

18. The Holy Ghost Mission, a French order established in Zanzibar since 1860 and in Bagamoyo since 1868. Bennett, *Studies in East African History,* 54–75. Stanley was received at the mission with great hospitality—including a bottle of champagne left by the French consul. On p. 44 of *HIFL* Stanley painted such special treatment as the normal course of living at the mission,

with the pères, Dr. Kirk and Captain Tucker of the *Columbine*. The next morning Dr. Kirk and Captain Tucker and another gentleman from the *Columbine*, and Père Horner,[19] Superior of the French mission, left for Kikoko, first camp on the Unyanyembe road beyond the Kingani River; or, in other words, the second camp for the up caravans from Bagamoyo. Père Horner returned to Bagamoyo the evening of that same day; but Messrs. Kirk and Tucker, the French Consul, M. Diviane,[20] and, I believe, the surgeon of the *Columbine*, remained behind that they might enjoy the sport which the left bank of the Kingani offered them.

A good deal of ammunition was wasted, I heard, by the naval officers, because, "you know, they have only pea rifles," so said Dr. Kirk to me. But Dr. Kirk, the companion of Livingstone and something of a sportsman, I am told bagged one hartbeest and one giraffe only in the four or five days the party was out. M. Diviane, or Divien, hurried back to Bagamoyo and Zanzibar with a piece of the aforesaid hartbeest, that the white people on that island might enjoy the sight and hear how the wondrous animal fell before the unerring rifle of that learned showman of wild beasts, Dr. John Kirk. Showman of wild beasts did I say? Yes. Well I adhere to it and repeat it. But to proceed. At the end of a week or thereabouts the party were said to have arrived at the French mission again. I rode up from the camp of the HERALD Expedition to see them. They were sitting down to dinner, and we all heard the graphic yarn about the death of the hartbeest. It was a fine animal they all agreed.

"But, Doctor, did you not have something else?" (Question by leader of HERALD Expedition.)

"No! we saw lots of game, you know—giraffe, zebra, wild boar,

---

thus leading an irate missionary to write on p. 44 of the mission's copy of *HIFL:* "Yes!! a gift of the French Consul—an honour fr Stl. Very nice and thankful from the Yankee!" When Stanley returned to the mission in 1874 the fathers made sure that he received their normal fare. See LeRoy's letter of Oct. 1, 1883, in *Annales de la Propagation de la Foi* 56 (1884), 58; *Bulletin Général de la Congrégation du St. Esprit et du l'Imé. Coeur de Marie*, XI, 722–23.

19. Anton Horner (1827–1880); he arrived in Zanzibar in 1863 to lead the Holy Ghost Mission, a task he performed with great efficiency until ill health caused his permanent return to France in 1879. *Ibid.*, 796–808; Bennett, *Studies in East African History*, 54ff.

20. Charles de Vienne, French representative at Zanzibar at different intervals between 1869 and 1874. He was actively interested in Africa and once traveled inland to Ukami. Ricklin, *La Mission Catholique*, 24–25, 147–48; De Vienne, "De Zanzibar à l'Oukami." For his controversial role during the Bartle Frere mission to Zanzibar, Bennett, "Charles de Vienne and the Frere Mission to Zanzibar."

&c.—but they were made so wild, you know, by the firing of pea rifles by the officers, that immediately one began to stalk them off they went. I would not have got the hartbeest if I had not gone alone."

Well, next morning Dr. Kirk and a reverend padre came to visit the camp of the HERALD Expedition, partook of a cup of tea in my tent, then went to see Moussoud [21] about Dr. Livingstone's things. They were told that the caravan had gone several days before. Satisfied that nothing more could be done, after a déjeuner at the French Mission, Dr. Kirk about eleven A.M. went on board the *Columbine*. About half-past three P.M. the *Columbine* steamed for Zanzibar.

On the 15th of March your correspondent returned to Zanzibar to settle up the last accounts connected with the expedition. While at Zanzibar your correspondent heard that the report had industriously been spread among those interested in Livingstone, the traveller, that Dr. Kirk had hurried off the Livingstone caravan at once, and that he had accompanied the said caravan beyond the Kingani, and that your correspondent could not possibly get any pagazis whatever, as he (Dr. Kirk) had secured them all. I wondered, but said nothing. Really the whole were marvellous, were it not opposed to fact. Livingstone's caravan needed but thirty-three men; the HERALD Expedition required 140 men, all told. Before the Livingstone caravan had started the first caravan of the HERALD Expedition had preceded them by four days. By the 15th of March 111 men were secured for the HERALD Expedition, and for the remainder donkeys were substituted.

June 23 saw us at Unyanyembe, and there I heard the reports of the chiefs of the several caravans of the HERALD Expedition. Livingstone's caravan was also there, and the men in charge were interrogated by me with the following questions:

Q. When did you see Dr. Kirk last?

A. 1st of November, 1870.

Q. Where?

A. At Zanzibar.

Q. Did you not see him at Bagamoyo?

A. No; but we heard that he had been at Bagamoyo.

Q. Is this true; quite, quite true?

A. Quite true, Wallah (by God).

The story is told. This is the case—a case, as I understand it to be, of the British Public vs. John Kirk. Does it not appear to you that

21. See *HIFL*, 272. He apparently died while leading the caravan.

Dr. John Kirk never had a word to say, never had a word to write to his old friend Dr. Livingstone all the time from 1st November, 1870, to about the 15th February, 1871; that during all this period of three and a half months Dr. John Kirk showed great unkindness, unfriendliness towards the old traveller, his former companion, in not pushing the caravan carrying supplies to the man with whom all who have read of him sympathize so much? Does it not seem to you, as it does to me, that had Dr. John Kirk bestirred himself in his grand character of English "Balyuz"—a noble name and great title out here in these lands—that that small caravan of thirty-three men might have been despatched within a week or so after their arrival at Bagamoyo, by which it would have arrived here in Unyanyembe long before Mirambo's war broke out? This war broke out June 15, 1871.

Well, I leave the case in your hands, assured that your intelligence, your natural power of discrimination, your fine sense of justice, will enable you to decide whether this man Dr. John Kirk, professed friend of Livingstone, has shown his friendship for Livingstone in leaving his caravan three and a half months at Bagamoyo; whether, when he went over to Bagamoyo in the character of showman of wild beasts to gratify the sporting instincts of the officers of Her Britannic Majesty's ship *Columbine,* did he show any very kindly feeling to the hero traveller when he left the duty of looking up that caravan of the Doctor's till the last thing on the programme.

Unyamwezi is a romantic name. It is "Land of the Moon" rendered into English—as romantic and sweet in Kinyamwezi as any that Stamboul or Ispahan can boast is to a Turk or a Persian.[22] The attraction, however, to a European lies only in the name. There is nothing of the mystic, nothing of the poetical, nothing of the romantic, in the country of Unyamwezi. I shudder at the sound of the name. It is pregnant in its every syllable to me. Whenever I think of the word immediately come thoughts of colycinth, rhubarb, calomel, tartar emetic, ipecacuanha and quinine into my head, and I feel qualmish about the gastric regions and I wish I were a thousand miles away from it. If I look abroad over the country I see the most inane and the most prosaic country one could ever imagine. It is the most unlikely country to a European for settlement; it is so repulsive owing to the notoriety it has gained for its fevers. A white missionary would shrink back with horror at the thought of settling in

22. The question of the derivation of the word Unyamwezi is discussed in Blohm, *Die Nyamwezi. Land und Wirtschaft,* 8–10; Bösch, *Les Banyamwezi,* 3–9. The term appears to be derived from the Nyamwezi word for the west.

it.[23] An agriculturist might be tempted; but then there are so many better countries where he could do so much better he would be a madman if he ignored those to settle in this. And, supposing it were necessary to send an expedition such as that which boldly entered Abyssinia[24] to Unyamwezi, the results would be worse than the retreat of Napoleon from Moscow. No, an ordinary English soldier could never live here. Yet you must not think of Unyamwezi as you would of an American swamp; you must not imagine Unyamwezi to have deep morasses, slushy beds of mud, infested with all abominable reptiles, or a jungle where the lion and the leopard have their dens. Nothing of the kind. Unyamwezi is a different kind of country altogether from that. To know the general outline and physical features of Unyamwezi you must take a look around from one of the noble coigns of vantage offered by any of those hills of syenite, in the debatable ground of Mgunda Makali, in Uyanzi.

From the summit of one of those natural fortresses, if you look west, you will see Unyamwezi recede into the far, blue, mysterious distance in a succession of blue waves of noble forest, rising and subsiding like the blue waters of an ocean. Such a view of Unyamwezi is inspiring; and, were it possible for you to wing yourself westward on to another vantage coign, again and again the land undulates after the same fashion, and still afar off is the same azure, mystic horizon. As you approach Unyanyembe the scene is slightly changed. Hills of syenite are seen dotting the vast prospect, like islands in a sea, presenting in their external appearance, to an imaginative eye, rude imitations of castellated fortresses and embattled towers. A nearer view of these hills discloses the denuded rock, disintegrated masses standing on end, boulder resting upon boulder, or an immense towering rock, tinted with the sombre color age paints in these lands. Around these rocky hills stretch the cultivated fields of the Wanyamwezi—fields of tall maize, of holcus sorghum, of millet, of vetches, &c.—among which you may discern the patches devoted to the cultivation of sweet potatoes and manioc, and pasture lands where browse the hump-shouldered cattle of Africa, flocks of goats and sheep. This is the scene which attracts the eye, and is accepted as promising relief after the wearisome marching through the

23. The Roman Catholic White Fathers established a mission there in 1881. Its troubled progress is given in *Bulletin des Missions d'Afrique (d'Alger)* (1879–1882), 466–69, and in subsequent issues.

24. The British expedition against Theodore. See the account in Marston, *Britain's Imperial Role in the Red Sea Area, 1800–1878*, 271ff. Stanley's account is given in his *Coomassie and Magdala*, 265ff.

thorny jungle plains of Ugogo, the primeval forests of Uyanzi, the dim plains of Tura[25] and Rubuga,[26] and when we have emerged from the twilight shades of Kigwa.[27] No caravan or expedition views it unwelcomed by song and tumultuous chorus, for rest is at hand.

It is only after a long halt that one begins to weary of Unyanyembe, the principal district of Unyamwezi. It is only when one has been stricken down almost to the grave by the fatal chilly winds which blow from the heights of the mountains of Usagara, that one begins to criticize the beauty which at first captivated. It is found, then, that though the land is fair to look upon; that though we rejoiced at the sight of its grand plains, at its fertile and glowing fields, at sight of the roving herds, which promised us abundance of milk and cream —that it is one of the most deadly countries in Africa; that its fevers, remittent and intermittent, are unequalled in their severity.

Unyamwezi, or the Land of the Moon—from U (country) nya (of the) mwezi (moon)—extends over three degrees of latitude in length and about two and a half degrees of longitude in breadth. Its principle districts are Unyanyembe, Ugunda,[28] Ugara, Tura, Rubuga, Kigwa, Usagozi[29] and Uyoweh.[30] Each district has its own chief prince, king, or *mtemi*,[31] as he is called in Kinyamwezi. Unyanyembe, however, is the principle district, and its king, Mkasiwa,[32] is generally considered to be the most important person in Unyamwezi. The other kings often go to war against him, and Mkasiwa

25. Tula, or Tura, an eastern Nyamwezi district; it was often the first Nyamwezi area visited by travelers coming from the coast. Burton, "Lake Regions," 159, 178; Guillet's letter of March 8, 1882, in *Annales de la Propagation de la Foi* 55 (1883), 62–63.

26. The Nyamwezi area to the west of Tura. Burton, "Lake Regions," 164, 178; Stuhlmann, *Mit Emin Pascha ins Herz von Afrika*, 57.

27. The Nyamwezi district to the west of Tura and Rubuga. Burton, "Lake Regions," 179.

28. Ugunda, one of the more important Nyamwezi chiefdoms, was located south of Tabora. Many European travelers visited it; the volumes of the *Mittheilungen der Afrikanischen Gesellschaft in Deutschland* have the fullest contemporary accounts because of the Gesellschaft's stations located there.

29. Usaguzi, one of the western regions of Nyamwezi. Burton, "Lake Regions," 168–69, 191–92.

30. Uyowa, a small Nyamwezi chiefdom; Mirambo was a member of its ruling family. Bennett, *Studies in East African History*, 1, 84; Kabeya, *Mtemi Mirambo*, 1.

31. See Oliver, "Discernible Developments in the Interior, c. 1500–1840," 191–92, for a brief discussion of the significance of this office.

32. Mkasiwa was made the ruler of Unyanyembe after Mnywa Sere had been deposed. He ruled in close agreement with his Arab allies until his death, apparently during the latter part of 1876. Speke, *Journal of the Discovery*, 77–78; Shorter, "Nyungu-Ya-Mawe."

often gets the worst of it; as, for instance, in the present war between the King of Uyoweh (Mirambo) and Mkasiwa.

All this vast country is drained by two rivers—the Northern and Southern Gombe,[33] which empty into the Malagarazi River, and thence into Lake Tanganyika. On the east Unyamwezi is bounded by the wilderness of Mgunda Makali and Ukimbu,[34] on the south by Urori[35] and Ukonongo, on the west by Ukawendi and Uvinza,[36] on the north by several small countries and the Ukereweh Lake.[37] Were one to ascend by a balloon and scan the whole of Unyamwezi he would have a view of one great forest, broken here and there by the little clearings around the villages, especially in and around Unyanyembe.

The forests of Southern Unyamwezi contain a large variety of game and wild beasts. In these may be found herds of elephants, buffaloes, giraffes, zebras, elands, hartbeests, zebras, springboks, pallahs, black bucks and a score of other kinds. In the neighborhood of the Gombe (Southern) may be seen any number of wild boars and hogs, lions and leopards. The Gombe itself is remarkable for the number of hippopotami and crocodiles to be found in it.

I have been in Unyanyembe close on to three months now. By and by I shall tell you why; but first I should like to give you a glimpse of our life here. The HERALD Expedition has its quarters in a large,

33. The Southern Gombe is the Ugalla River. The German explorer Böhm corrected Stanley's error in 1881. Böhm, *Von Sansibar zum Tanganjika*, 56, 63. The Northern Gombe is the Igombe River.

34. The Kimbu, a group closely allied to the Nyamwezi, were then pushing into the Mgunda Mkali, and were bringing parts of it under cultivation. They had migrated into Nyamwezi territory from the south due to pressure from the Sangu. Mirambo's wars destroyed much of their work in the Mgunda Mkali, but they remained around the area. Moffett, *Handbook of Tanganyika*, 240; Burton, "Lake Regions," 155, 165, 195–96; Cameron, *Across Africa*, I, 127–28 and II, 295–96; *A l'Assaut des Pays Nègres*, 157; Reichard, "Die Wanjamuezi," 229; Shorter, "Nyungu-Ya-Mawe."

35. The Sangu, or Rori, lived to the west of the Hehe and Bena. Under their leader, Merere, they played an important role in this region from the 1870's. Meyer, *Deutsches Kolonialreich*, 190–92; Oliver, "Discernible Developments in the Interior," 210; Mumford, "The Hehe-Bena-Sangu Peoples of East Africa," 203–22; Heese, "Sitte und Brauch der Sango."

36. The Vinza, a people with similarities to the Ha, controlled a main ferry across the Malagarasi River. They were generally regarded as unfriendly to visitors, and in 1881–1882 suffered heavily in a war with Tippu Tip. The Vinza maintained their reputation, however, despite their losses. Moffett, *Handbook of Tanganyika*, 271; Burton, "Lake Regions," 193, 207; Hutley to LMS, Feb. 28, 1881, Griffith to LMS, Jan. 15, 1882, Hore to LMS, Feb. 11, 1883, LMS; Leue, *Dar-es-Salaam*, 249ff.

37. Lake Victoria; it here took its name from the island of Ukerewe. For a description of the island and its people, Chacker, "The Kerewe. Aspects of their Nineteenth Century History."

strong house, build of mud, with walls three feet thick.[38] It is of one
story, with a broad mud veranda in front and a broad flat roof. The
great door is situated directly in the centre of the front, and is the
only one possible means of ingress and egress. Entering in at this
door we find a roomy hallway; on our right is the strong storeroom,
where the goods of the HERALD Expedition and Livingstone's caravan are kept well padlocked up to guard against burglars. Soldiers at
night occupy this hallway with loaded guns, and during the day there
are always two men on guard, besides Burton's bull-headed Mabrouki,[39] who acts as my porter or policeman. On our left is a room
open to the hallway, on the floor of which are spread straw mats and
two or three Persian carpets, where the Arab sheikhs squat when
they come to visit me. Passing through the hallway we come to the
courtyard, a large quadrangle, fenced in and built around with houses.
There are about a dozen pomegranate trees planted in the yard, more
for their shade than for their fruit. The houses around consist, first,
of the granary, where we keep the rice, the matama, the Indian corn,
the sweet potatoes, &c.; next comes the very much besmoked kitchen,
a primitive affair, merely a few stones on which the pots are placed.
The cook and his youthful subs are protected from the influences of
the weather by a shed. Next to the kitchen is the stable, where the
few remaining animals of the expedition are housed at night. These
are two donkeys, one milch cow and six milch goats. The cow and
the goats furnish me with milk for my gruel, my puddings, my
sauces and my tea. (I was obliged to attend to my comfort and make
use of the best Africa offers). Next to the stable is another large
shed, which serves as barracks for the soldiers. Here they stow themselves and their wives, their pots and beds, and find it pretty comfortable. Next to this is the house of the white man, my nautical help,
where he can be just as exclusive as he likes, has his own bedroom
veranda, bathroom, &c.; his tent serves him for a curtain, and, in
English phrase, he has often declared it to be "jolly and no mistake."
Occupying the half of one side of the house are my quarters, said
quarters consisting of two well-plastered and neat rooms. My table

38. This *tembe* became the usual staying place for European visitors to Tabora. See the list in Thomson, *To the Central African Lakes and Back*, II, 249–51.
For the *tembe* type, Huntingford, "The Distribution of Certain Culture Elements in East Africa"; Bösch, *Les Banyamwezi*, 324ff.

39. Mabruki served on expeditions with Burton, Speke, Grant, von der Decken,
Livingstone, and New. Gray, "Livingstone's Muganda Servant," 128; Speke,
What Led to the Discovery, 264–65; New, "Journey from the Pangani, viâ
Usambara to Mombasa," 414. See also Burdo, *Les Belges dans l'Afrique Cen-
trale*, 166.

is an oxhide stretched over a wooden frame. Two portmanteaus, one on top of the other, serve for a chair. My bedspread is only a duplicate of my table, over which I spread my bearskin and Persian carpet.

When the very greatest and most important of the Arab sheikhs visit me Selim, my invaluable adjunct, is always told to fetch the bearskin and Persian carpet from the bed. Recesses in the solid wall answer for shelves and cupboards, where I deposit my cream pots and butter and cheese (which I make myself) and my one bottle of Worcestershire sauce and my tin candlestick. Behind this room, which is the bed, reception, sitting, drawing room, office, pantry, &c., is my bathroom, where are my saddle, my guns and ammunition always ready, my tools and the one hundred little things which an expedition into the country must have. Adjoining my quarters is the jail of the fortlet, called "tembe" here—a small room, eight by six feet, lit up by a small air hole just large enough to put a rifle through—where my incorrigibles are kept for forty hours, without food, in solitary confinement. This solitary confinement answers admirably, about as well as being chained when on the road, and much better than brutal flogging.

In the early morning, generally about half-past five or six o'clock, I begin to stir the soldiers up, sometimes with a long bamboo, for you know they are such hard sleepers they require a good deal of poking. Bombay has his orders given him, and Feragji,[40] the cook, who, long ago warned by the noise I make when I rouse up, is told in unmistakable tones to bring "chai" (tea), for I am like an old woman, I love tea very much, and can take a quart and a half without any inconvenience. Kalulu,[41] a boy of seven, all the way from Cazembe's country, is my waiter and chief butler. He understands my ways and mode of life exactly. Some weeks ago he ousted Selim from the post of chief butler by sheer diligence and smartness. Selim, the Arab boy, cannot wait at table. Kalulu—young antelope—is frisky. I have but to express a wish and it is gratified. He is a perfect Mer-

40. Feraji had served on the Speke-Grant expedition. Speke, *Journal of the Discovery*, 614; *HIFL*, 351. A Feraji accompanied Stanley on his 1874–1877 journey; he drowned in the Congo River in 1877. *TDC*, II, 340. But see Maurice, *H. M. Stanley: Unpublished Letters*, 141, for a Feraji serving under Stanley in 1882, and Gibbons, "British East African Plateau Land and its Economic Conditions," 243, for another Feraji who claimed he had crossed Africa with Stanley.

41. Kalulu, a Lunda youth, was given to Stanley by a Tabora Arab in 1871. Kalulu caught Stanley's fancy and accompanied the explorer to Britain and the United States after the close of the Livingstone expedition. He drowned in the Congo in 1877 while again accompanying Stanley. Bennett, "Some Notes on Two Early Novels concerning Tanzania."

cury, though a marvellously black one. Tea over, Kalulu clears the dishes and retires under the kitchen shed, where, if I have a curiosity to know what he is doing, he may be seen with his tongue in the tea cup licking up the sugar that was left in it and looking very much as if he would like to eat the cup for the sake of the divine element it has so often contained.

If I have any calls to make this is generally the hour; if there are none to make I go on the piazza and subside quietly on my bearskin to dream, may be, of that far off land I call my own or to gaze towards Tabora, the Kaze of Burton and Speke, though why they should have called it Kaze as yet I have not been able to find out (I have never seen the Arab or Msawahili who had ever heard of Kaze. Said bin Salim, who has been traveling in this country with Burton, Speke and Grant, declares he never heard of it); or to look towards lofty Zimbili and wonder why the Arabs, at such a crisis as the present, do not remove their goods and chattels to the summit of that natural fortress. But dreaming and wondering and thinking and marvelling are too hard for me; this constitution of mine is not able to stand it; so I make some ethnological notes and polish up a little my geographical knowledge of Central Africa.

I have to greet about 499 people of all sorts with the salutation "Yambo." This "Yambo" is a great word. It may mean "How do you do?" "How are you?" "Thy health?" The answer to it is "Yambo!" or "Yambo Sana!" (How are you; quite well?) The Kinyamwezi—the language of the Wanyamwezi—of it is "Moholo," and the answer is "Moholo." The Arabs, when they call, if they do not give the Arabic "Spal-kher," give you the greeting "Yambo;" and I have to say "Yambo." And, in order to show my gratitude to them, I emphasize it with "Yambo Sana! Sana! Sana?" (Are you well? Quite well, quite, quite well?) [42] And if they repeat the words I am more than doubly grateful, and invite them to a seat on the bearskin. This bearskin of mine is the evidence of my respectability, and if we are short of commonplace topics we invariably refer to the bearskin, where there is room for much discussion. If I go to visit the Arabs, as I sometimes do, I find their best Persian carpets, their silk counterpanes and kitandas[43] gorgeously decorated in my honor. One of the principal Arabs here is famous for this kind of honor-doing. No sooner did I show my face than I heard the order given to a slave to produce the Kitanda, that the Muzunga—white man—might lie thereon, and that

42. *Mhola,* good news. Dahl, *Nyamwesi-Wörterbuch,* 180. *Sabalkheri*—good morning (from Arabic).
43. Swahili—a bedstead.

the populous village of Maroro might behold. The silk counterpane was spread over a cotton-stuffed bed; the enormously fat pillows, covered with a vari-colored stuff, invited the weary head; the rich carpet of Ajim spread alongside of the Kitanda was a great temptation, but I was not to be tempted; I could not afford to be so effeminate as lie down while four hundred or five hundred looked on to see how I went through the operation.

Having disposed of my usual number of "Yambos" for the morning I begin to feel "peckish," as the sea skipper says, and Feragji, the cook, and youthful Kalulu, the chief butler, are again called and told to bring "chukula"—food. This is the breakfast put down on the table at the hour of ten punctually every morning: Tea, Ugali, a native porridge made out of the flour of dourra, holcus sorghum, or matama, as it is called here; a dish of rice and curry—Unyanyembe is famous for its rice;[44] fried goat's meat, stewed goat's meat, roast goat's meat, a dish of sweet potatoes, a few "slapjacks" or specimens of the abortive efforts of Feragji to make dampers or pancakes, to be eaten with honey. But neither Feragji's culinary skill nor Kalulu's readiness to wait on me can tempt me to eat. I have long ago eschewed food, and only drink tea, milk and yaourt—Turkish word for "clabber" or clotted milk. Plenty of time to eat goat meat when we shall be on the march; but just now—no, thank you.

After breakfast the soldiers are called, and together we begin to pack the bales of cloth, string beads and apportion the several loads which the escort must carry to Ujiji some way or another. Carriers come to test the weight of the loads and to inquire about the inducements offered by the "Muzungu." The inducements are in the shape of so many pieces of cloth, four yards long, and I offer double what any Arab ever offered. Some are engaged at once, others say they will call again, but they never do, and it is of no use to expect them when there is war, for they are the cowardliest people under the sun.

Since we are going to make forced marches I must not overload my armed escort, or we shall be in a pretty mess two or three days after we start; so I am obliged to reduce all loads by twenty pounds, to examine my kit and personal baggage carefully, and put aside anything that is not actually and pressingly needed. As I examine my fine lot of cooking utensils, and consider the fearfully long distance to Ujiji, I begin to see that most of them are superfluous, and I vow that one saucepan and kettle for tea shall suffice. I must leave

44. For comments on the extensive cultivations of the Tabora Arabs, Burdo, *Les Arabes dans l'Afrique Centrale,* 14–15.

half my bed and half my clothes behind; all my personal baggage is not to weigh over sixty-four pounds. Then there are the ammunition boxes to be looked to. Ah, me! When I started from the coast I remember how ardently I pursued the game; how I dived into the tall, wet grass; how I lost myself in the jungles; how I trudged over the open plains in search of vert and venison. And what did it all amount to? Killing a few inoffensive animals the meat of which was not worth the trouble. And shall I waste my strength and energies in chasing game? No, and the man who would do so at such a crisis as the present is a ———. But I have my private opinion of him, and I know whereof I speak. Very well; all the ammunition is to be left behind except 100 rounds to each man. No one must fire a shot without permission, nor waste his ammunition in any way, under penalty of a heavy fine for every charge of powder wasted. These things require time and thought, for the HERALD Expedition has a long and far journey to make. It intends to take a new road—a road with which few Arabs are acquainted—despite all that Sheikh, the son of Nasib, can say against the project.

It is now the dinner hour, seven P.M. Ferrajji has spread himself out, as they say. He has all sorts of little fixings ready, such as indigestible dampers, the everlasting ugali, or porridge, the sweet potatoes, chicken and roast quarter of a goat; and lastly, a custard, or something just as good, made out of plantains.

At eight P.M. the table is cleared, the candles are lit, pipes are brought out, and Shaw, my white man, is invited to talk. But poor Shaw is sick and has not a grain of spirit or energy left in him. All I can do or say does not cheer him up in the least. He hangs down his head, and with many a sigh declares his inability to proceed with me to Ujiji.

"Not if you have a donkey to ride?" I ask.

"Perhaps in that way I may be able," says Shaw in a most melancholy tone.

"Well, my dear Shaw," I begin, "you shall have a donkey to ride and you shall have all the attendance you require. I believe you are sick, but what is this sickness of yours I cannot make out. It is not fever, for I could have cured you by this, as I have cured myself and as I have cured Selim; besides, this fever is a contemptible disease, though dangerous sometimes. I think if you were to exert your will —and say you will go, say you will live—there would be less chance of your being unable to reach the coast again. To be left behind, ignorant of how much medicine to take or when to take it, is to die.

Remember my words—if you stop behind in Unyanyembe I fear for you. Why, how can you pass the many months that must elapse before I can return to Unyanyembe? No man knows where Livingstone is. He may be at Ujiji, he may be in Manyema, he may be going down the Congo River for the West Coast, and if I go down the Congo River after him I cannot return to Unyanyembe, and in that event where would you be?"

"It is very true, Mr. Stanley. I shall go with you, but I feel very bad here (and he put his hand over his liver); but, as you say, it is a great deal better to go on than stop behind."

But the truth is that like many others starting from the coast with superabundant health Shaw, soon after realizing what travel in Africa was, lost courage and heart. The ever-present danger from the natives and the monotony of the country, the fatigue one endures from the constant marches which every day take you further into the uninteresting country, all these combined had their effect on him, and when he arrived in Unyanyembe he was laid up. Then his intercourse with the females of Unyanyembe put the last finishing touch to his enfeebled frame, and I fear if the medicines I have sent for do not arrive in time that he will die. It is a sad fate. Yet I feel sure that if another expedition fitted out with all the care that the HERALD Expedition was, regardless of expense, if the members composing it are actuated by no higher motives than to get shooting or to indulge their lust, it would meet with the same fate which has overtaken my white man Farquhar, and which seems likely will overtake Shaw. If on the day I depart from here this man is unwilling or unable to accompany me I shall leave him here under charge of two of my soldiers, with everything that can tend to promote his comfort.

It was on the 23d day of June that the expedition arrived here, and after resting ten days or thereabouts I intended to have continued the journey to Ujiji. But a higher power ordained that we should not leave without serious trouble first. On the 6th of July we heard in Unyanyembe that Mirambo, a chief of Unyamwezi, had, after taking very heavy tribute from a caravan bound to Ujiji, turned it back, declaring that no Arab caravan should pass through his country while he was alive. The cause of it was this: Mirambo, chief of Uyoweh, and Wilyankuru had a long grudge against Mkasiwa, King of Unyanyembe, with whom the Arabs lived on extremely friendly terms. Mirambo proposed to the Arabs that they should side with him against Mkasiwa. The Arabs replied that they could not possibly do so, as Mkasiwa was their friend, with whom they lived on peaceable terms.

Mirambo then sent to them to say: "For many years I have fought against the Washenzi[45] (the natives), but this year is a great year with me. I intend to fight all the Arabs, as well as Mkasiwa, King of Unyanyembe."

On the 15th July war was declared between Mirambo and the Arabs. Such being the case, my position was as follows: Mirambo occupies the country which lies between the object of my search and Unyanyembe. I cannot possibly reach Livingstone unless this man is out of the way—or peace is declared—nor can Livingstone reach Unyanyembe unless Mirambo is killed. The Arabs have plenty of guns if they will only fight, and as their success will help me forward on my journey, I will go and help them.

On the 20th July[46] a force of 2,000 men, the slaves and soldiers of the Arabs, marched from Unyanyembe to fight Mirambo. The soldiers of the HERALD Expedition to the number of forty,[47] under my leadership, accompanied them. Of the Arabs' mode of fighting I was totally ignorant, but I intended to be governed by circumstances. We made a most imposing show, as you may imagine. Every slave and soldier was decorated with a crown of feathers, and had a lengthy crimson cloak flowing from his shoulders and trailing on the ground. Each was armed with either a flintlock or percussion gun—the Balooches with matchlocks, profusely decorated with silver bands. Our progress was noisy in the extreme—as if noise would avail much in the expected battle. While traversing the Unyanyembe plains the column was very irregular, owing to the extravagant show of wild fight which they indulged in as we advanced. On the second day we arrived at Mfuto, where we all feasted on meat freely slaughtered for the braves. Here I was attacked with a severe fever, but as the army was for advancing I had myself carried in my hammock almost delirious. On the fourth day we arrived at the village of Zimbizo, which was taken without much trouble. We had arrived in the enemy's country. I was still suffering from fever, and while conscious had given strict orders that unless all the Arabs went together that none of my men should go to fight with any small detachment.

On the morning of the fifth day a small detachment went out to reconnoitre, and while out captured a spy, who was thrown on the

45. Singular, *mshenzi*, a barbarian. The Muslim Africans of the coast used the term to show contempt for Africans of the interior.

46. In *HIFL*, 274–75, Stanley explains that the forces left on July 29. Fever had caused him to lose a week in his dating.

47. *Ibid.*, 275, 279, lists fifty soldiers.

ground and had his head cut off immediately. Growing valiant over this little feat a body of Arabs under Soud, son of Said bin Majid,[48] volunteered to go and capture Wilyankuru, where Mirambo was just then with several of his principal chiefs. They were 500 in number and very ardent for the fight. I had suggested to the Governor, Said bin Salim, that Soud bin Said, the leader of the 500 volunteers, should deploy his men and fire the long dry grass before they went, that they might rout all the forest thieves out and have a clean field for action. But an Arab will never take advice, and they marched out of Zimbizo without having taken this precaution. They arrived before Wilyankuru, and, after firing a few volleys into the village, rushed in at the gate and entered the village.

While they entered by one gate Mirambo took 400 of his men out by another gate and instructed them to lie down close to the road that led from Wilyankuru to Zimbizo, and when the Arabs would return to get up at a given signal, and each to stab his man. The Arabs found a good deal of ivory and captured a large number of slaves, and, having loaded themselves with everything they thought valuable, prepared to return by the same road they had gone. When they had arrived opposite to where the ambush party was lying on each side the road Mirambo gave the signal, and the forest thieves rose as one man. Each taking hold of his man, speared him and cut off his head.[49]

Not an Arab escaped, but some of their slaves managed to escape and bring the news to us at Zimbizo. There was great consternation at Zimbizo when the news was brought, and some of the principal Arabs were loud for a retreat, but Khamis bin Abdullah [50] and myself did our utmost to prevent a disgraceful retreat. Next morning, however, when again incapacitated by fever from moving about, the Governor came and told me the Arabs were going to leave for Un-

48. Said bin Majid was one of the leading Arabs of Tabora and Ujiji; Stanley also noted that he was a relative of the Sultan of Zanzibar. Said bin Majid had traveled widely in the interior and had met Livingstone who described him as "a good man." He later left Ujiji to become one of the Arab leaders in the war against Mirambo. Burton, *The Lake Regions of Central Africa*, I, 323; *Autobiography*, 265; LLJ, II, 155, 176; Bennett, *Studies in East African History*, 87; Kirk to FO, April 10, 1872, FO 84/1357, PRO.

49. The French representative at Zanzibar reported an Arab version of this defeat; they claimed they were attacked at night and not as Stanley stated. De Vienne to MAE, Oct. 20, 1871, CCZ, II.

50. Khamis bin Abdulla al Barwani, one of the leaders in the struggle with Mirambo; he was killed during the conflict. Khamis bin Abdulla had been active in the difficulties with Mnywa Sere and had also traded to Buganda. Speke, *Journal of the Discovery*, 107; Welbourn, "Speke and Stanley at the Court of Mutesa," 223; Brode, *Tippoo Tib*, 136.

yanyembe. I advised him not to think of such a thing, as Mirambo would then follow them to Unyanyembe and fight them at their own doors. As he retired I could hear a great noise outside. The Arabs and Wanyamwezi auxiliaries were already running away, and the Governor, without saying another word, mounted his donkey and put himself at their head and was the first to reach the strong village of Mfuto, having accomplished a nine hours' march in four hours, which shows how fast a man can travel when in a hurry.

One of my men came to tell me there was not one soldier left; they had all run away. With difficulty I got up and I then saw the dangerous position I had placed myself in through my faith in Arab chivalry and bravery. I was deserted except by one Khamis bin Abdullah, and he was going. I saw one of my soldiers leaving without taking my tent, which lay on the ground. Seizing a pistol, I aimed it at him and compelled him to take up the tent. The white man, Shaw, as well as Bombay, had lost their heads. Shaw had saddled his donkey with my saddle and was about leaving his chief to the tender mercies of Mirambo, when Selim, the Arab boy, sprung on him, and pushing him aside, took the saddle off, and told Bombay to saddle my donkey. Bombay I believe would have stood by me, as well as three or four others, but he was incapable of collecting his senses. He was seen viewing the flight of the Arabs with an angelic smile and with an insouciance of manner which can only be accounted for by the charitable supposition that his senses had entirely gone. With bitter feelings toward the Arabs for having deserted me I gave the order to march, and in company with Selim, the brave Arab boy; Shaw, who was now penitent; Bombay, who had now regained his wits; Mabruki Speke, Chanda, Sarmeen[51] and Uredi Manu-a-Sera[52] arrived at Mfuto at midnight. Four of my men had been slain by Mirambo's men.

The next day was but a continuation of the retreat to Unyanyembe with the Arabs; but I ordered a halt, and on the third day went on leisurely. The Arabs had become demoralized; in their hurry they had left their tents and ammunition for Mirambo.

Ten days after this, and what I had forewarned the Arabs of, came to pass. Mirambo, with 1,000 guns, and 1,500 Watuta, his allies,

51. Sarmean also accompanied Stanley on his 1874–1877 expedition. In Manyema he received the lasting nickname of Kacheche, or "the weasel," for his qualities as a detective. Kacheche perhaps led an embassy to Buganda in 1879 with a message from Kirk to Mutesa; later he served on Thomson's journey into Masailand. *TDC*, II, 69, 89, 379; Yule, *Mackay of Uganda*, 127; Thomson, *Through Masailand*, 21.

52. Apparently the Uledi Pagani whose adventures are given in Ward, *A Voice from the Congo*, 193–200.

invaded Unyanyembe, and pitched their camp insolently within view of the Arab capital of Tabora. Tabora is a large collection of Arab settlements, or tembes, as they are called here. Each Arab house is isolated by the fence which surrounds it. Not one is more than two hundred yards off from the other, and each has its own name, known, however, to but few outsiders. Thus the house of Amram bin Mousoud [53] is called by him the "Two Seas," yet to outsiders it is only known as the "tembe of Amram bin Mousoud," in Tabora, and the name of Kaze, by which Burton and Speke have designated Tabora, may have sprung from the name of the enclosed grounds and settlement wherein they were quartered. South by west from Tabora, at the distance of a mile and a half, and in view of Tabora is Kwihara, where the HERALD Expedition has its quarters. Kwihara is a Kinyamwezi word, meaning the middle of the cultivation. There is quite a large settlement of Arabs here—second only to Tabora.

But it was Tabora and not Kwihara that Mirambo, his forest thieves and the Watuta came to attack. Khamis bin Abdallah, the bravest Trojan of them all—of all the Arabs—went out to meet Mirambo with eighty armed slaves and five Arabs, one of whom was his little son, Khamis.[54] As Khamis bin Abdallah's party came in sight of Mirambo's people Khamis' slaves deserted him, and Mirambo then gave the order to surround the Arabs and press on them. This little group in this manner became the targets for about one thousand guns, and of course in a second or so were all dead—not, however, without having exhibited remarkable traits of character.

They had barely died before the medicine men came up, and with their scalpels had skinned their faces and abdominal portions, and had extracted what they call "mafuta," or fat, and their genital organs. With this matter which they had extracted from the dead bodies the native doctors or waganga made a powerful medicine, by boiling it in large earthen pots for many hours, with many incantations and shakings of the wonderful gourd that was only filled with pebbles. This medicine was drunk that evening with great ceremony, with dances, drum beating and general fervor of heart.

Khamis bin Abdallah dead, Mirambo gave his orders to plunder, kill, burn and destroy, and they went at with a will. When I saw the fugitives from Tabora coming by the hundred to our quiet valley of

53. Amrani bin Masudi was subsequently killed in Usangu. He had earlier traded there profitably; then he returned to raid. According to information gained by a missionary, Amrani bin Masudi was ordered by Barghash to return to Zanzibar; when he refused Barghash sent aid to the Sangu and Amrani was killed in the fighting. Last to Wigram, Jan. 20, 1879, C.A6/014, CMS; Brode, *Tippoo Tib*, 29; Frere to Granville, May 7, 1873, F0 84/1391, PRO; *LLJ*, II, 194.

54. In *HIFL*, 293–94, Stanley calls him the "son of a dead friend."

Kwihara, I began to think the matter serious and began my operations for defence. First of all, however, a lofty bamboo pole was procured and planted on the top of the roof of our fortlet, and the American flag was run up, where it waved joyously and grandly, an omen to all fugitives and their hunters.

Then began the work of ditch making and rifle pits all around the court or enclosure. The strong clay walls were pierced in two rows for the muskets. The great door was kept open, with material close at hand to barricade it when the enemy came in sight, watchmen were posted on top of the house, every pot in the house was filled with water, provisions were collected, enough to stand a siege of a month's duration, the ammunition boxes were unscrewed, and when I saw the 3,000 bright metallic cartridges for the American carbines I laughed within myself at the idea that, after all, Mirambo might be settled with American lead, and all this furor of war be ended without much trouble. Before six P.M. I had 125 muskets and stout fellows who had enlisted from the fugitives, and the house, which only looked like a fortlet at first, became a fortlet in reality—impregnable and untakable.

All night we stood guard; the suburbs of Tabora were in flames; all the Wanyamwezi and Wanguana[55] houses were destroyed, and the fine house of Abid bin Sulemian[56] had been ransacked and then committed to the flames, and Mirambo boasted that "to-morrow" Kwihara should share the fate of Tabora, and there was a rumor that that night the Arabs were going to start for the coast.

But the morning came, and Mirambo departed, with the ivory and cattle he had captured, and the people of Kwihara and Tabora breathed freer.

And now I am going to say farewell to Unyanyembe for a while. I shall never help an Arab again. He is no fighting man, or, I should say, does not know how to fight, but knows, personally, how to die. They will not conquer Mirambo within a year, and I cannot stop to see that play out. There is a good old man waiting for me somewhere, and that impels me on. There is a journal afar off which expects me to do my duty, and I must do it. Goodby; I am off the day after to-morrow for Ujiji; then, perhaps, the Congo River.

---

55. *Mwungwana,* freeman. The term was applied generally to men from the coast and Zanzibar (even though their original homes might have been in the interior). See Burton, "Lake Regions," 115; Wilson and Felkin, *Uganda and the Egyptian Sudan,* I, 14–17.

56. Abid bin Suliman was a rich Arab trader of Tabora and Ujiji. He later proved a friend to the missionaries of the London Missionary Society at Ujiji. Hore to Kirk, April 15, 1879, Q-22, ZA.

4

Ujiji, Lake Tanganyika
November 10, 1871[1]

The HERALD expedition, upon leaving Unyanyembe, intended to make Ujiji the end of the second stage, then to march to Manyema, whither Livingstone had gone in 1869; then, if he had gone down the Congo, to go after and overtake him, or, if he was dead, as was often reported to me, to seek his grave and satisfy myself of its identity, and to take the bones home in proper cases. Fortunately, as this telegram will prove, the expedition has no such mournful task to perform, but what it did perform was far more meritorious, in my opinion.

Instead of going west along a well known road the NEW YORK HERALD expedition struck into regions very little known and travelled by Arabs. For ten days it journeyed south as if bound for Western Urori, during which time many deserted and the Englishman had been sent back as perfectly useless. Crossing Ukonongo westward we travelled until we entered Kawendi, an entirely new country. After supplying the men of the expedition with ten days' provisions we plunged into the wilderness and went north, from which we did not emerge until we had sighted the Malagarazi River. Here, after already dodging and escaping from four wars, which make the country dangerous to travellers, we were confronted with hostilities waged by Sultan Nzogera[2] against Lokanda Mira, another Sultan of Uvinza, which was a most serious inconvenience to me—nay, it well nigh ruined the expedition. After paying heavy tribute to Nzogera and crossing the Malagarazi River, we might have reached Ujiji without further trouble had there been no war. But this war compelled me to adopt the Uhha[3] route—one always avoided by Arabs. It was almost as bad as if I had gone straight into the middle of their battlefield. While not yet half-way through Uhha, which in its entire

1. *NYH*, July 15, 1872.
2. Burton had found a Mzogera, perhaps the same chief, in control of the ferry in 1858. Mzogera died before Feb. 1874, when Cameron arrived to find his heirs quarreling over the succession. Burton, "Lake Regions," 193; "Journal of Lieutenant V. L. Cameron," 149.
3. The Ha were divided into six independent chiefdoms during the nineteenth century; Stanley went through the Luguru chiefdom. Scherer, "The Ha of Tanganyika." Ha hostility to outsiders was marked, especially to Arabs. One traveler remarked: "In fact an Arab would dare not enter the country except with a large force of armed men." Griffith to LMS, May 15, 1882, LMS.

length is only two good-days' journey, I had been mulcted of half the available property of the expedition, and had, as often as the tribute was imposed, been in danger of open rupture owing to the insolence of the Uhha chiefs. Had I continued on this road the expedition might possibly have arrived at Ujiji with a month's provisions left.

Our resolve was taken. At midnight we left the Mutware's[4] village, with guns loaded, and left the road, plunging into the low jungle, and, travelling parallel to the road westward, marched twenty-five miles without halting. We then cooked and rested, and at night again marched all night until we had crossed Uhha and had arrived in Ukaranga[5] safely. Two marches more, and we were entering the suburbs of Ujiji, firing away our guns as only exuberant heroes do, to the intense astonishment of the Arabs of Ujiji, who turned out *en masse* to know what it meant.

Among those who came to question us were the servants of Dr. Livingstone, who shortly ran ahead in haste to inform him that an Englishman was coming; "Sure, sure," he was an Englishman, they said, though the American flag was in the front, held aloft by the stout arms of my gigantic Kirangoze. We entered slowly, the immense number of people who had collected about us impeding rapid progress. As we advanced the crowd became larger and more mingled with the chief Arabs, and the noise of firing and shouting became deafening. Suddenly the firing and hubbub ceased; the van of the expedition had halted.

Passing from the rear of it to the front I saw a knot of Arabs, and, in the centre, in striking contrast to their sunburnt faces, was a pale-looking and gray-bearded white man, in a navy cap, with a faded gold band about it, and red woollen jacket. This white man was Dr. David Livingstone, the hero traveller, the object of the search.

It was the dignity that a white man and leader of an expedition ought to possess that prevented me from running to shake hands with the venerable traveller; but when I first caught sight of him— the man with whose book on Africa I was first made acquainted when a boy—so far away from civilization, it was very tempting. False pride and the presence of the grave-looking Arab dignitaries of

4. The *umutware munini*, or sub chief, was subordinate to the *umwami*, or chief, of a Ha state. Scherer, "The Ha," 880–84.

5. Ukaranga was located between the Ha state of Bujiji and Ukawendi. The people were part of the Bende group. Avon, "Vie sociale des Wabende," 109; Burton, "Lake Regions," 213–14, 218.

Ujiji restrained me and suggested to me to say, with a shake of the hand,

"Dr. Livingstone, I presume?" [6]

"Yes," was the answer, with a kind smile.

Together we turned toward his house. We took seats on goatskins spread over the mud floor of his veranda. Conversation began, it would be difficult to say about what—the topics changed so rapidly; but shortly I found myself acting the part of a newspaper—I had five years of news to give him.

Our first day was passed in eating so voraciously and talking so fast, and about such manifold subjects, that it is difficult to say which we did most. But it is certain that, before retiring, he asserted his belief that I had brought new life to him; he already felt stronger and better. That night he read the packet of letters which I had brought him, the reading of which he had deferred for that time. Some days after my arrival at Ujiji I elicited from him the following story of his travels and sufferings and discoveries for the last five years:

Dr. Livingstone's expedition left Zanzibar in March, 1866.[7] On the 7th of April he left the sea coast with an expedition consisting of twelve Sepoys, nine Johanna men, seven liberated slaves and two Zambezi men—in all thirty men. He also had with him six camels, three buffaloes, two mules and three donkeys. The expedition travelled up the left bank of the Rovuma River, a route teeming with difficulties. The dense jungles which barred their way required great labor with the axes before they could proceed, which retarded very much the progress of the expedition. Soon after leaving the coast Dr. Livingstone was made aware of the unwillingness of the Sepoys and Johanna men to march into the interior. Their murmurings and complaints grew louder day by day. Hoping that he might be induced to return the Sepoys and Johanna men so abused the animals that in a short time not one was left alive. This plan not succeeding they

6. This rather unfortunate remark has provided abundant fodder for biographers of Stanley when they attempt analyses of his character. See in particular, Anstruther, *I Presume*. To a scholar with broader interests, the statement is also of importance since it "reflected the psychology of racial superiority" —*i.e.*, of how Europeans felt they should maintain their dignity in the presence of Africans. Cairns, *Prelude to Imperialism*, 38. In any case, the greeting was soon so well known that it was only natural when one explorer met another that he "came forward, and according to the African salutation *à la mode* he touched his hat, and said, 'Mr. Thomson, I presume?'" Thomson, *Central African Lakes*, II, 4.

7. Livingstone's version is given in *LLJ*. See also Coupland, *Livingstone's Last Journey*; Debenham, *The Way to Ilala*, 214ff.

set about poisoning the minds of the simple natives towards the Doctor by circulating the most mischievous and false reports concerning his character and intentions. As this might possibly become dangerous the Doctor resolved to discharge the Sepoys, and accordingly sent them back to the sea coast, with a sufficiency of cloth to purchase food on their return.

The first of his troubles began with these men. A more worthless crew as escort it would be impossible to conceive. After suffering considerably from hunger during the transit of a wide extent of unoccupied country after leaving the Rovuma River, the Doctor and his party arrived in the country of a Mhiyow[8] chief on the 18th of July, 1866. Desertion of faithless men, in the meanwhile, had greatly thinned his party. Early in August, 1866, Dr. Livingstone and what remained of his expedition arrived at Mponda's,[9] a chief of a tribe of Wahiyow, living near the Nyassa lake.

Here Wakotani[10]—one of the "nice honorable fellows" of Mr. Horace Waller[11]—a *protégé* of the Doctor, insisted upon his discharge, alleging as an excuse, which the Doctor subsequently found to be false, that he had seen his brother. He also claimed Mponda's chief wife as his sister. After delivering himself of many more falsehoods Wakotani was given by the Doctor in charge of Mponda until his "big brother" should call for him.

This ingrate—released from slavery and educated at the Nassick School,[12] Bombay, at the sole charge of the Doctor—perceiving his

8. The Yao; see Mitchell, "The Yao of Southern Nyasaland," 292–353; Tew, *Peoples of the Lake Nyasa Region*, 2–22.

9. Mponda, whose center was near the Shire outlet of Lake Nyasa, remained, through his contacts with Arab traders, one of the most important exporters of ivory and slaves of the Lake Nyasa region until his death in 1886. Moir, "Eastern Route to Central Africa," 104; Hawes to FO, June 3, 1886, FO 84/1751, PRO; Young, *Nyassa*, 61ff.

10. Wakotani, a Yao, had been freed from slavers by Livingstone and others in 1861. When the Universities Mission to Central Africa left the Nyasa region Wakotani was brought to India and put in the care of the Scots missionary, Wilson, until Livingstone prepared his next expedition. After leaving Livingstone, Wakotani apparently held a position of trust with Mponda. *LLJ*, I, 108–09; Smith, *The Life of John Wilson*, 583–85; Laws to Mitchell, March 18, 1878, in *Home and Foreign Missionary Record of the Free Church of Scotland* (1878), 165.

11. Horace Waller (1833–1896) had been a member of the abortive 1861–1864 venture of the Universities Mission to Central Africa to the Nyasa region. On his return to Britain he became an influential worker in the movement against the slave trade. *DNB*, XX, 586.

12. An establishment near Nasik, in India, for the training of Africans rescued from slavery. Stock, *The History of the Church Missionary Society*, II, 173, 432. Neither Wakotani nor Chuma (see below) attended the Nasik institution.

application for a discharge to be successful, endeavored to persuade Chumah,[13] another *protégé*, to go with him, in order, as the Doctor believes, to enslave him. Upon Chumah consulting the Doctor, he was strongly advised not to put himself in the power of Wakotani.

From Mponda's the Doctor proceeded to the heel of the Nyassa, to the village of a Babisa[14] chief, who required medicine for a skin disease. To treat the malady he stopped at this place two days. While stopping here a half-caste Arab arrived at the same place from the western shore of Lake Nyassa, who reported that he had been plundered by a band of the Ma Zitu[15] at a place which the Doctor and Musa,[16] the chief of his Johanna men, knew perfectly was at least one hundred and fifty miles north-northwest, or twenty days' march from the village. This Musa is he who manufactured that wonderful tale of murder which so startled all friends of the Doctor. During the Zambezi expedition Musa had visited this place, where the Arab reported himself robbed, in company of the Doctor. To the news which the Arab imparted Musa was an eager listener, and lost no time in conveying it to the Doctor. The Doctor cooly asked him if he believed, to which Musa answered that he did believe every word, for the Arab had told "true, true." The Doctor said he did not; and after explaining to him his reasons, he suggested to Musa that they should go and consult the Babisa chief, for if any one should know if the story was true, he should. The Babisa chief denounced the Arab as "a liar" when consulted. But Musa broke out with, "No, no, Doctor, I no want to go to Ma Zitu; I no want Ma Zitu to kill me; I want to see my father, my mother, my child in Johanna. I no want Ma Zitu kill me." Musa's words are here reported *ipsissima verba*. To this

13. James Chuma, a Yao, liberated by Livingstone and the Universities Mission, was left by Livingstone with Wilson in Bombay. He was among the group of Africans that returned Livingstone's body to Zanzibar, and he went to Britain for the missionary's funeral. Chuma served the Universities Mission on his return to Africa; he also accompanied the explorer Thomson. Chuma died in Zanzibar in 1882. *LLJ*, I, 9; Smith, *Wilson*, 583–85; Thomson, *Central African Lakes*, especially II, 30–34, 202; *Central Africa* 1 (1883), 13.

14. The Bisa live to the west of Lake Nyasa; Livingstone was then in Yao territory. In *LLJ*, I, 113, Livingstone describes the village as of Bisa origin. For the Bisa, Whiteley, *Bemba and Related Peoples of Northern Rhodesia*, 7–32.

15. The Ngoni.

16. Musa of Johanna, or Anjouan, had served in Livingstone's Zambezi expedition. His conduct confirmed to the nineteenth-century prejudice against the men from his island: to Kirk they were "the most untrustworthy and cunning of all the people of this region." *LLJ*, I, 9; Kirk to Seward, Dec. 20, 1866, in *PRGS* 11 (1866–67), 130; Kirk to FO, Jan. 1, 1873, FO 84/1374, PRO. For his punishment, Coupland, *Livingstone's Last Journey*, 261.

outburst the Doctor replied, "I don't want the Ma Zitu to kill me either, but since you are afraid of them, I promise to go west until we are far past the beat of the Ma Zitu." Musa was not satisfied with this promise of the Doctor, for he said in the same dolorous tone: "If we had 200 guns with us I would go; but our small party, they will come by night and kill us all." The Doctor repeated his promise, but to no purpose. When he turned his face westward, Musa and the Johanna escort heartlessly deserted him. Hence the fabrication of the Livingstone murder tale to hide the fact of their desertion and to obtain their wages. Livingstone's party was very small now; he had sent back the worthless and maudlin Sepoys; the Johanna men had deserted him in a body, and Wakotani had been discharged. He was obliged to seek aid from the natives. He engaged them as carriers, and as they had never been tampered with or betrayed by the slave traders he managed exceedingly well. From this country, which he left in the beginning of December, 1866, he entered on a northern course, where the Ma Zitu had swept the land clean of provisions, and where the expedition suffered the most pinching hunger.

Added to this, desertions continued, which in one or two instances caused a loss of almost all his clothes and cooking utensils and dishes. Though misfortunes constantly dogged the footsteps of the expedition, it struggled on and traversed the countries of the Babisa, Bobemba,[17] Banlungu,[18] Barungu,[19] besides the country of Londa, where lives the famous King Cazembe.

Cazembe and his Queen received him kindly and showed every disposition to assist him, and it was he who gave the information about Lake Bangweolo (which he called "Large Water") to the Doctor. Near Cazembe's the Doctor had crossed a fine stream called the Chambezi. But he relied too much upon the correctness of Portuguese information, and paid not much attention to it at the time, believing it to be, as Portuguese travellers stated, but the headwaters of the great Zambezi, and having no connection with the great river of Egypt, of which he was now in search. This excessive reliance upon the veracity of Portuguese travellers and traders misled him very much, and caused him double work, plunging him into a labyrinth

17. The Bemba.
18. The Lungu; they lived around the southeastern shores of Lake Tanganyika. The Lungu lack of a powerful central authority aided the Arabs in making extensive raids upon them for slaves. Willis, *The Fipa and Related Peoples of the South-West Tanzania and North-East Zambia*, 39–46; Storms Ms. Notes, Storms Papers, MAC.
19. The Marungu.

of errors and discoveries, making the whole country and intricate system of rivers and lakes clear to him only after repeating his journeys many times.[20]

From the beginning of 1867 to the middle of March, 1869, he says he was mostly engaged in correcting the errors of Portuguese travellers. The Portuguese when writing or speaking of the Chambezi invariably called it "our own Zambezi," or the Zambezi that flows through the Portuguese possessions of the Mozambique. Over and over again he had to traverse the countries around Londa like an uneasy spirit; over and over again he asked the same questions from the different people whom he met, until he was obliged to desist lest they might say—"The man is mad; he has water on the brain."

These tedious travels have established, first, that the Chambezi is a totally distinct river from the Portuguese Zambezi; second, that the Chambezi, starting from about latitude 11° south, is none other than the headwaters of the Nile itself, thus giving the wonderful river a length of over 2,600 miles of direct latitude.[21]

During this series of journeys which he made in these latitudes he came to a lake lying northeast from Cazembe's. The natives called it Liemba, or Luwemba, from a country of that name which bordered it on the southeast.[22] Livingstone discovered it to be an extensive heel, or rather foot, of the Tanganyika. By his map the southern part of the Tanganyika resembles the southern part of Italy in configuration. The extremity of the Tanganyika south reaches to 8 deg. 42 sec. south latitude, thus giving the lake a length of 323 geographical miles,[23] or seventy-three miles longer than Captains Burton and Speke described it.

From the Tanganyika he crossed Marungu and came in sight of Lake Moero. Tracing this lake, which is about sixty miles in length, to its southern extremity he found a river entering it from that direction. Following the Luapula north, as this river was called, he found it issued from the great lake of Bangweolo, which is as large in superficial area as the Tanganyika. The most important feeder of this lake is the Chambezi. He had traced the Chambezi running north through three degrees of latitude. It could not, then, be the Zambezi.

20. Livingstone, who was largely unfamiliar with the previous Portuguese explorations, was here unfair to his Lusitanian predecessors. This question, and the extent of former Portuguese ventures, are treated in Duffy, *Portuguese Africa*, 174ff.; Bridges, "British Exploration of East Africa," 23–29, 246–50; Price, "Portuguese Relations with David Livingstone."

21. See the map in *HIFL*, 448, for the projection of this theory.

22. Lake Tanganyika. A missionary later reported that Liemba was the Lungu word for a lake. Hore, "Lake Tanganyika," 16.

23. In *HIFL*, 360, Stanley gives the length as 360 miles. Lake Tanganyika is 420 miles long.

He returned to King Cazembe, thence to Ujiji, whence he dated those letters to the London Geographical Society, under whose auspices he travels, which, though the outside world still doubted that the traveller was alive, fully satisfied the minds of the members of that society. The way in which Musa left the Doctor and what the Doctor was doing all the time the world thought him dead has now been told as Dr. Livingstone told your correspondent. But his experiences, his troubles, his sufferings in mind, body and estate—how Arabs conspired against him, his men robbed him, false Moslems betrayed him—how he was detained by inundations, by scanty means to cross rivers and lagoons, by wars between Arabs and natives from the beginning of 1867 to the middle of March, 1869, when he arrived at Ujiji—no one will be better able to relate than himself.

After resting at Ujiji he thought of exploring the head of the Tanganyika and ascertaining whether this lake had any connection, or whether the river Rusizi was an influent or an affluent; but the avarice of the Wajiji,[24] which would have deprived him of most of his cloth, prevented him. At the end of June, 1869, he set off by way of Uguhha for his last series of explorations.

Fifteen days' march brought him to Manyema, a virgin country, but lately known to the Arabs even. On the threshold of great discoveries he was laid up six months from ulcers in the feet. When recovered he set off northerly, and came to a broad lacustrine river called Lualaba, which flowed northward, westward, and in some places southward in a most confusing way. The river was from one to three miles broad. Following it northerly he discovered Lake Kamolondo,[25] in latitude 6 deg. 30 min. south. He traced the river southward to Lake Moero, where he saw it issue out of this lake through an enormous and deep chasm in the mountains. Satisfied that this Lualaba was the Chambezi which entered Bangweolo, or the Luapula which entered Moero, he retraced his steps northward, to Lake Kamolondo. He came to a river flowing from the west called the Locki, or Lomami, which issued from a large lake called Chebungo, situated to the south-southwest from Kamolondo. To this Lake Chebungo Dr. Livingstone gave the name Lake Lincoln,[26] after President Abraham Lincoln, whose sad fate the civilized world lamented.

24. For the inhabitants of Ujiji, Bennett, "Mwinyi Kheri," 144–46.
25. A section of the Congo-Lualaba system to the north of Lake Mweru. See Colle, Les Baluba, I, 17–18. The extreme breadth of the river in places, and the imprecise words for bodies of water in African languages, caused these false reports of lakes along the course of the Congo.
26. The river "flowing from the west" might be the Lualaba. The Luvua River issues from Lake Mweru and eventually joins the Lualaba. There was no Lake Chebungo. See the remarks of the German explorer, Von Wissmann, in PRGS 5 (1883), 99.

To the memory of the American President, whose labors in behalf of the black race won his entire sympathy and approval, the great traveller has contributed a monument more durable than brass, iron, or stone.

Still working his way north, bit by bit, against several and varied difficulties, along the Lualaba's crooked course as far as latitude 4° south, he heard of another large lake situated to the north, in the same central line of drainage as the four other lakes; but here he was compelled to turn back to Ujiji. Against this compulsion his iron will and indomitable energy fought in vain; his men had mutinied and absolutely refused to budge a step, and to Ujiji he was obliged to return, a baffled, sick and weary and destitute man. It was in this state your correspondent met him only eighteen days after his arrival. So far had the traveller gone north that he was at the beginning of the final and certain end. Six hundred miles of watershed had been examined carefully. At the beginning of the seventh hundred the false slaves sent to him from the British Consul at Zanzibar, and who were to him as escort, rose up against him, saying in their determined actions, "Thus far you shall go, and not one step further."

That this remarkable river (the Lualaba) is the Nile and none other no one doubts, but this one little blank—this one little link—who will fill it up? How will imagination fill up the void? In this blank, north of latitude four degrees south, is a lake, it was reported to Dr. Livingstone—may it not be Piaggia's lake? [27]—out of which Petherick's branch [28] issues into the Bahr Ghazal and the White Nile. He has followed this river from eleven degrees south to four degrees south—that is, through seven degrees of latitude, or 420 geographical miles. It only wanted 180 miles more—this is the length of the undiscovered link—and the Nile, which had baffled oracles and sages, kings and emperors, had been revealed throughout its length.

According to Livingstone two things yet remain before the Nile sources can be said to be discovered. First—He has heard of the existence of four fountains, two of which give birth to a river flowing

27. Carlo Piaggia (1830–1882), an Italian trader and explorer, arrived in the Sudan in 1856. On one of his journeys he reported hearing of a large lake on the equator and extending to the south. Hill, *A Biographical Dictionary of the Anglo-Egyptian Sudan*, 306; *PRGS* 13 (1868–1869), 8. The supposed position of this lake is given in the map in *HIFL*, 448.

28. John Petherick (1813–1882), British official, trader, and explorer in the Sudan. During his travels in the years between 1848 and 1863 he penetrated to the region of the upper Uele River. Hill, *Biographical Dictionary*, 305–06; Mr. and Mrs. Petherick, *Travels in Central Africa and Explorations of the Western Nile Tributaries*, especially, II, 137; Langlands, "Concepts of the Nile," 19.

north, which is the Lualaba, and two to a river flowing south into
inner Ethiopia, which is the Zambezi, thus verifying the statement
which the Secretary of the Goddess Minerva at Sais made to Herodotus over two thousand years ago.[29] He has heard of them repeatedly and has been several times within a fortnight's march from
them, but something always interposed to prevent him going to see
them. These fountains require to be seen. Second—Remains the link
above described to be explored. The stories which the Doctor relates
of the two immense countries through which the great river runs
read like fable. The most southerly is called Rua; [30] the northern is
called Manyema by the Arabs and Manuema by the natives, who
are cannibals. He tells of ivory being so cheap that twenty-five cents'
worth of copper will purchase a large tusk, worth $120 at Zanzibar.
He tells of ivory being turned into doorposts and eave stanchions
by the cannibals; of skilful manufactures of fine grass cloth, rivaling
that of India; of a people so nearly approaching to white people and
so extremely handsome that they eclipse anything ever seen in Africa;
and from this fact supposes them to be descendants of the ancient
Egyptians, or of some of the lost tribes of Israel; [31] he tells of copper
mines at Katanga which have been worked for ages,[32] of docile and
friendly peoples who up to this time have lived buried in the lap of
barbarism, ignorant that there lived on earth a race so cruel and
callous as the Arabs who have come among them, rudely awaking
them out of their sleep with the thunder of gunpowder, to kidnap,
rob and murder them without restraint,[33] and of many other things
he tells, some details of which will follow this telegram.

The Doctor arrived at Ujiji on the 16th of October, the HERALD
expedition on the 3d of November,[34] eighteen days later, and, as if
guided by the hand of Providence, not a month too late nor a month

29. Herodotus, *The Histories*, 112–15; HIFL, 455–59, also has a translation.
Herodotus doubted the story; see Langlands, "Concepts of the Nile," 2–3. See
also Debenham, *Way to Ilala*, 269–72.

30. The country of the Luba, extending roughly from the area to the west
of Lake Tanganyika to the Lualaba River. A later explorer, Cameron, would
be so impressed with his visit that he described the Luba as having "the most
important state of Africa." Cameron, "On the Anthropology of Africa," 172.
See also Verhulpen, *Baluba et Balubaïsés du Katanga*; Maes et Boone, *Peuplades du Congo Belge*, 107–13, 347–48; Vansina, *Kingdoms of the Savanna*,
70ff.; Vansina, *Introduction à l'Ethnographie du Congo*, chap. 11.

31. See document 26, note 12.

32. For Katanga and its copper: Vansina, *Kingdoms of the Savanna*, 11,
227–35; Clark, *The Prehistory of Southern Africa*, 307–09.

33. An account of the Arabs of the Congo is given in Ceulemans, *La question arabe et le Congo*.

34. The date was Nov. 10; see document 3, note 46.

too soon. He was sick and he was destitute, and help came in time. He had returned to Ujiji only to find himself robbed of everything by the very man to whom the British Consulate had entrusted his goods. This man, called Shereef, had sold them all off for ivory, and had feasted on the little stock of luxuries sent to the Doctor by his friends.

5

Bunder, Ujiji, on Lake Tanganyika, Central Africa
November 23, 1871[1]

Only two months gone, and what a change in my feelings! But two months ago, what a peevish, fretful soul was mine! What a hopeless prospect presented itself before your correspondent! Arabs vowing that I would never behold the Tanganyika; Sheikh, the son of Nasib, declaring me a madman to his fellows because I would not heed his words. My men deserting, my servants whining day by day, and my white man endeavoring to impress me with the belief that we were all doomed men! And the only answer to it all is, Livingstone, the hero traveller, is alongside of me, writing as hard as he can to his friends in England, India and America, and I am quite safe and sound in health and limb. Wonderful, is it not, that such a thing should be, when the seers had foretold that it would be otherwise— that all my schemes, that all my determination would avail me nothing? But probably you are in as much of a hurry to know how it all took place as I am to relate. So, to the recital.

September 23 I left Unyamyembe, driving before me fifty well-armed black men, loaded with the goods of the expedition, and dragging after me one white man.[2] Several Arabs stood by my late residence to see the last of me and mine, as they felt assured there was not the least hope of their ever seeing me again. Shaw, the white man, was pale as death, and would willingly have received the order to stop behind in Unyamyembe, only he had not quite the courage to ask permission, from the fact that only the night before he had ex-

1. *NYH*, Aug. 10, 1872. Bunder, or Bandar—a port. Hava, *Arabic-English Dictionary*, 47. Stanley in this document covers in more detail the incidents described in document 2 and 4. See Introduction, note 119, for the possible explanation of the repetition.
2. In *HIFL*, 310, Stanley says September 20.

pressed a hope that I would not leave him behind, and I had promised to give him a good riding donkey and to walk after him until he recovered perfect health. However, as I gave the order to march, some of the men, in a hurry to obey the order, managed to push by him suddenly, and down he went like a dead man. The Arabs, thinking, doubtless, that I would not go now because my white subordinate seemed so ill, hurried in a body to the fallen man, loudly crying at what they were pleased to term my cruelty and obstinacy; but, pushing them back, I mounted Shaw on his donkey, and told them that I must see the Tanganyika first, as I had sworn to go on. Putting two soldiers, one on each side of him, I ordered Shaw to move on and not to play the fool before the Arabs, lest they should triumph over us. Three or four black laggards loth to go (Bombay was one of them) received my dog whip across their shoulders as a gentle intimation that I was not to be baulked after having fed them so long and paid them so much. And it was thus we left Unyanyembe. Not in the best humor, was it? However, where there is will there is a way.

Once away from the hateful valley of Kwihara, once out of sight of the obnoxious fields my enthusiasm for my work rose as newborn as when I left the coast. But my enthusiasm was shortlived for before reaching camp I was almost delirious with fever. Long before I reached the camp I saw from a ridge overlooking a fair valley, dotted with villages and green with groves of plantains and fields of young rice, my tent and from its tall pole the American flag waving gaily before the strong breeze which blew from the eastward. When I had arrived at the camp, burning with fever, my pulse bounding many degrees too fast and my temper made more acrimonious by my sufferings, I found the camp almost deserted.

The men as soon as they had arrived at Mkwenkwe, the village agreed upon, had hurried back to Kwihara. Livingstone's letter carrier had not made his appearance—it was an abandoned camp. I instantly despatched six of the best of those who had refused to return to ask Sheikh, the son of Nasib, to lend or sell me the longest slave chain he had, then to hunt up the runaways and bring them back to camp bound, and promised them that for every head captured they should have a brand new cloth. I also did not forget to tell my trusty men to tell Livingstone's messenger that if he did not come to camp before night I would return to Unyanyembe—or Kwihara rather, for I was yet in Unyanyembe—catch him and put him in chains and never release him until his master saw him. My men went off in high glee, and I went off to bed passing long hours groaning and tossing about for the deadly sickness that had overtaken me.

Next morning fourteen out of twenty of those who had deserted back to their wives and huts (as is generally the custom) had reappeared, and, as the fever had left me, I only lectured them, and they gave me their promise not to desert me again under any circumstances. Livingstone's messenger had passed the night in bonds, because he had resolutely refused to come. I unloosed him and gave him a paternal lecture, painting in glowing colors the benefits he would receive if he came along quietly and the horrible punishment of being chained up until I reached Ujiji if he was still resolved not to come. "Kaif Halleck" (Arabic for "How do you do?") melted, and readily gave me his promise to come and obey me as he would his own master—Livingstone—until we should see him, "which Inshallah we shall! Please God, please God, we shall," I replied, "and you will be no loser."

During the day my soldiers had captured the others, and as they all promised obedience and fidelity in future they escaped punishment. But I was well aware that so long as I remained in such close proximity the temptation to revisit the fat pasture grounds of Unyanyembe, where they had luxuriated so long, would be too strong, and to enable them to resist I ordered a march towards evening, and two hours after dark we arrived at the village of Kasegera.

It is possible for any of your readers so disposed to construct a map of the road on which the HERALD expedition was now journeying, if they draw a line 150 miles long south by west from Unyanyembe, then 150 miles west northwest, then ninety miles north, half east, then seventy miles west by north, and that will take them to Ujiji.

Before taking up the narrative of the march I must tell you that during the night after reaching Kasegera two deserted, and on calling the men to fall in for the road I detected two more trying to steal away behind some of the huts of the village wherein we were encamped. An order quietly given to Chowpereh [3] and Bombay soon brought them back, and without hesitation I had them tied up and flogged, and then adorned their stubborn necks with the chain kindly lent by Sheikh bin Nasib. I had good cause to chuckle complacently for the bright idea that suggested the chain as a means to check the tendency of the bounty jumpers to desert; for these men were as

---

3. Chowpereh, from Bagamoyo, was held in high regard by Stanley. He became one of the small group of Africans that remained with Livingstone until his death. Later Chowpereh did good service for Stanley on his 1874–1877 expedition across Africa; he served also with Stanley in the Congo after 1879. *HIFL*, 312, 348; *LLJ*, II, 299ff.; Maurice, *Stanley's Unpublished Letters*, 115.

much bounty jumpers as our refractory roughs during the war, who pocketed their thousands and then cooly deserted. These men, imitating their white prototypes, had received double pay of cloth and double rations, and, imagining they could do with me as they could with the other good white men, whom tradition kept faithfully in memory, who had preceded your correspondent in this country, waited for opportunities to decamp; but I was determined to try a new method, not having the fear of Exeter Hall before my eyes, and I am happy to say to-day, for the benefit of all future travellers, that it is the best method yet adopted, and that I will never travel in Africa again without a good long chain.[4] Chowpereh and Bombay returned to Unyanyembe and the "HERALD Expedition" kept on its way south, for I desired to put as many miles as possible between that district and ourselves, for I perceived that few were inclined for the road, my white man, I am sorry to say, least of all. The village of Kigandu was reached after four hours' march from Kasegera.

As we entered the camp Shaw, the Englishman, fell from his donkey, and, despite all endeavors to raise him up, refused to stand. When his tent was pitched I had him carried in from the sun, and after tea was made I persuaded him to swallow a cup, which seemed to revive him. He then said to me, "Mr. Stanley, I don't believe I can go further with you. I feel very much worse, and I beg of you to let me go back." This was just what I expected. I knew perfectly well what was coming while he was drinking his tea, and, with the illustrious example of Livingstone travelling by himself before me, I was asking myself, Would it not be just as well for me to try to do the same thing, instead of dragging an unwilling man with me who would, if I refused to send him back, be only a hindrance? So I told

4. Exeter Hall, built by the supporters of the evangelical movement in Britain, was the usual meeting place for humanitarian groups; it occupied the location where the Strand Palace Hotel now stands. The more "practical" African explorers used the term to refer to the attitude of the humanitarians—and not usually in a complementary fashion. When Stanley heard of complaints against his treatment of Africans on a later trip, he had this to say: "He only wished he could get every member of Exeter Hall to explore by the same route he had gone from the Atlantic to longitude 23°. He would undertake to provide them with seven tons of Bibles, any number of surplices, and a church organ into the bargain, and if they reached as far as longitude 23° without chucking some of the Bibles at some of the negroes' heads, he would _____." The reporter added that laughter cut off the sentence. Sanderson, *England, Europe & the Upper Nile*, 12; Bourne, *The Other Side of the Emin Pasha Relief Expedition*, 19. Stanley did, however, pay attention to such strictures. On his 1874–1877 expedition he did use chains, but he did not mention them in his published account. *Diary*, 37; *TDC*, I, 104. Stanley was not of course the only European to use them. See for example Perham, ed., *The Diaries of Lord Lugard*, I, 159, 278.

him, "Well, my dear Shaw, I have come to the conclusion that it is best you should return, and I will hire some carriers to take you back in a cot which I will have made immediately to carry you in. In the meanwhile, for your own sake, I would advise you to keep yourself as busy as possible and follow the instructions as to diet and medicine which I will write out for you. You shall have the key to the storeroom, and you can help yourself to anything you may fancy." These were the words with which I parted from him—as next morning I only bade him goodby, besides enjoining on him to be of good hope, as, if I was successful, not more than five months would elapse before I would return to Unyanyembe.[5] Chowpereh and Bombay returned before I started from Kigandu, with the runaways, and after administering to them a sound flogging I chained them, and the expedition was once more on its way.

We were about entering the immense forest that separates Unyanyembe from the district of Ugunda. In lengthy undulating waves the land stretches before us—the new land which no European knew, the unknown, mystic land. The view which the eyes hurry to embrace as we ascend some ridge higher than another is one of the most disheartening that can be conceived. Away, one beyond another, wave the lengthy rectilinear ridges, clad in the same garb of color. Woods, woods, woods, forests, leafy branches, green and sere, yellow and dark red and purple, then an indefinable ocean, bluer than the bluest sky. The horizon all around shows the same scene—a sky dropping into the depths of the endless forest, with but two or three tall giants of the forest higher than their neighbors, which are conspicuous in their outlines, to break the monotony of the scene. On no one point do our eyes rest with pleasure; they have viewed the same outlines, the same forest and the same horizon day after day, week after week; and again, like Noah's dove from wandering over a world without a halting place, return wearied with the search.

Mukunguru, or fever, is very plentiful in these forests, owing to their density preventing free circulation of air, as well as want of drainage. As we proceed on our journey, in the dry season as it is with us now, we see nothing very offensive to the sight. If the trees are dense, impeding fresh air, we are shaded from the sun, and may often walk long stretches with the hat off. Numbers of trees lie about in the last stages of decay, and working with might and main are numberless ants of various species to clear the encumbered ground, and thus they do such a country as this great service. Im-

5. In *HIFL,* 320–21, Stanley gives a different version, caused no doubt by his knowledge of the subsequent death of Shaw.

palpably, however, the poison of the dead and corrupting vegetation is inhaled into the system with often as fatal result as that which is said to arise from the vicinity of the upas tree.[6] The first evil results experienced from the presence of malaria are confined bowels, an oppressive languor, excessive drowsiness and a constant disposition to yawn. The tongue has a sickly yellow hue, or is colored almost to blackness; even the teeth assume a yellow color and become coated with an offensive matter. The eyes sparkle with a lustre which is an unmistakable symptom of the fever in its incipient state, which presently will rage through the system and lay the sufferer prostrate quivering with agony. This fever is sometimes preceded by a violent shaking fit, during which period blankets may be heaped upon the sufferer with but little amelioration of his state. It is then succeeded by an unusually severe headache, with excessive pains about the loins and spinal column, spreading gradually over the shoulder blades, and which, running up the nape of the neck, finally find a lodgment in the posterior and front parts of the head. This kind is generally of the intermittent type, and is not considered dangerous. The remittent form—the most dangerous—is not preceded by a shaking fit, but the patient is at once seized with excessive heat, throbbing temples, loin and spinal aches: a raging thirst takes possession of him, and the brain becomes crowded with strange fancies, which sometimes assume most hideous shapes. Before the darkened vision float in a seething atmosphere figures of created and uncreated, possible and impossible figures, which are metamorphosed every instant into stranger shapes and designs, growing every instant more confused, more complicated, hideous and terrible until the sufferer, unable to bear longer the distracting scene, with an effort opens his eyes and dissolves it, only to glide again unconsciously into another dreamland, where a similar unreal inferno is dioramically revealed.

It takes seven hours to traverse the forest between Kigandu and Ugunda, when we come to the capital of the new district, wherein one may laugh at Mirambo and his forest thieves. At least the Sultan, or Lord of Ugunda,[7] feels in a laughing mood while in his strong stockade, should one but hint to him that Mirambo might come to settle up the long debt that Chieftain owes him, for defeating him the last time—a year ago—he attempted to storm his place. And

6. *Antiaris toxicaria;* it is also known as the false mvule (see below) because of its "superficial resemblance to Mvule." Dale and Greenway, *Kenya Trees & Shrubs,* 308.

7. Muli-manombe, the ruler of the Nyamwezi chiefdom of Ugunda. He died in 1881. Blohm, *Die Nyamwezi. Land und Wirtschaft,* 3; Böhm, *Von Sansibar zum Tanganjika,* 33ff.

well may the Sultan laugh at him, and all others which the hospitable
Chief may permit to reside within, for it is the strongest place—
except Simba-Moeni and Kwikuru, in Unyanyembe—I have as yet
seen in Africa. The defences of the capital consist of a strong stockade surrounding it, or tall thick poles planted deep in the earth, and
so close to each other in some places that a spear head could not be
driven between. At intervals also rise wooden towers above the pali-
sade, where the best marksmen, known for their skill with the musket,
are posted to pick out the foremost or most prominent of the as-
sailants. Against such forces as the African chiefs could bring against
such palisaded villages Ugunda may be considered impregnable,
though a few white men with a two-pounder might soon effect an
entrance. Having arrived safely at Ugunda we may now proceed on
our journey fearless of Mirambo, though he has attacked places four
days south of this; but as he has already at a former time felt the
power of the Wanyamwezi of Ugunda he will not venture again in
a hurry. On the sixth day of our departure from Unyanyembe we
continued our journey south.

Three long marches, under a hot sun, through jungly plains, heat-
cracked expanses of prairie land, through young forests, haunted by
the tseetse and sword flies, considered fatal to cattle, brought us to
the gates of a village called Manyara, whose chief was determined
not to let us in nor sell us a grain of corn, because he had never
seen a white man before, and he must know all about this wonderful
specimen of humanity before he would allow us to pass through his
country.[8] My men were immediately dismayed at this, and the guide,
whom I had already marked as a coward, and one I mistrusted,
quaked as if he had the ague. The chief, however, expressed his belief that we should find a suitable camping place near some pools of
water distant half a mile to the right of his village.

Having arrived at the khambi, or camp, I despatched Bombay
with a propitiating gift of cloth to the Chief—a gift at once so handsome and so munificent, consisting of no less than two royal cloths
and three common dotis, that the Chief surrendered at once, declaring that the white man was a superior being to any he had ever seen.
"Surely," said he, "he must have a friend; otherwise how came he
to send me such fine cloths? Tell the white man that I shall come
and see him." Permission was at once given to his people to sell us

8. Manyara was in Ukonongo. In *HIFL*, 331, Stanley blames the delay on
a local war. Livingstone met the chief in 1872 and described him as "a kind
old man." *LLJ*, II, 167, 233.

as much corn as we needed. We had barely finished distributing five days' rations to each man when the Chief was announced.[9]

Gunbearers, twenty in number, preceded him, and thirty spearmen[10] followed him, and behind these came eight or ten men loaded with gifts of honey, native beer, holcus sorghum, beans and maize. I at once advanced and invited the Chief to my tent, which had undergone some alterations, that I might honor him as much as lay in my power. Ma-manyara was a tall, stalwart man, with a very pleasing face. He carried in his hand a couple of spears, and, with the exception of a well-worn barsati[11] around his loins, he was naked. Three of his principal men and himself were invited to seat themselves on my Persian carpet. They began to admire it excessively, and asked if it came from my country? Where was my country? Was it large? How many days to it? Was I a king? Had I many soldiers? were questions quickly asked, and as quickly answered, and the ice being broken, the chief being equally candid as I was myself, he grasped my fore and middle fingers and vowed we were friends. The revolvers and Winchester's repeating rifles were things so wonderful that to attempt to give you any idea of how awe-struck he and his men were would task my powers.

The Chief roared with laughter; he tickled his men in the ribs with his forefinger, he clasped their fore and middle fingers, vowed that the Muzungu was a wonder, a marvel, and no mistake. Did they ever see anything like it? "No," his men solemnly said. Did they ever hear anything like it before? "No," as solemnly as before. "Is he not a wonder? Quite a wonder—positively a wonder!"

My medicine chest was opened next, and I uncorked a small phial of medicinal brandy and gave each a teaspoonful. The men all gazed at their Chief and he gazed at them; they were questioning each other with their eyes. What was it? Pombe was my reply. Pombe kisungu. (The white man's pombe.) "Surely this is also wonderful, as all things belonging to him are," said the Chief. "Wonderful," they echoed; and then all burst into another series of cachinations, ear-splitting almost. Smelling at the ammonia bottle was a thing all must have; but some were fearful, owing to the effects produced on each man's eyes and the facial contortions which followed the ol-

9. In *HIFL*, 332–33, the chief refused the original gift mentioned here and Stanley had to offer more to secure permission to get food.

10. The numbers are reversed in *ibid.*, 333.

11. ". . . a blue cotton cloth, with a broad red stripe extending along one quarter of the depth, the other three-quarters being dark blue." Burton, "Lake Regions," 429–30.

factory effort. The Chief smelt three or four times, after which he declared his headache vanished and that I must be a great and good white man. Suffice it that I made myself so popular with Ma-ma-nyara and his people that they will not forget me in a hurry.

Leaving kind and hospitable Ma-manyara, after a four hours' march we came to the banks of the Gombe Nullah, not the one which Burton, Speke and Grant have described, for the Gombe which I mean is about one hundred and twenty-five miles south of the Northern Gombe.[12] The glorious park land spreading out north and south of the Southern Gombe is a hunter's paradise. It is full of game of all kinds—herds of buffalo, giraffe, zebra, pallah, water buck, spring-bok, gemsbok, blackbuck and kudu, besides several eland, warthog, or wild boar, and hundreds of the smaller antelope. We saw all these in one day, and at night heard the lions roar and the low of the hippopotamus. I halted here three days to shoot, and there is no occasion to boast of what I shot, considering the myriads of game I saw at every step I took. Not half the animals shot here by myself and men were made use of. Two buffaloes and one kudu were brought to camp the first day, besides a wild boar, which my mess finished up in one night. My boy gun-bearers sat up the whole night eating boar meat, and until I went to sleep I could hear the buffalo meat sizzling over the fires as the Islamized soldiers prepared it for the road.

The second day of the halt I took the Winchester rifle or the fif-teen-shooter to prey on the populous plain, but I only bagged a tiny blue buck by shooting it through the head. I had expected great things of this rifle, and am sorry I was disappointed. The Winchester rifle cartridges might as well have been filled up with sawdust as with the powder the New York Ammunition Company put in them. Only two out of ten would fire, which so spoiled my aim that nothing could be done with the rifle. The cartridges of all the English rifles always went off, and I commend Eley, of London, to everybody in need of cartridges to explode. The third day, arming myself with a double-barrelled English smooth-bore, I reaped a bountiful harvest of meat, and having marched over a larger space saw a much larger variety of game than on any preceding day. The Gombe Nullah dur-ing the dry season is but a system of long, narrow pools, full of crocodiles and hippopotami. In the wet season it overflows its banks and is a swift, broad stream, emptying into the Malagarazi, thence into the Lake Tanganyika.

12. See document 3, note 33.

From Manyara to Marefu, in Ukonongo, are five days' marches. It is an uninhabited forest now and is about eighty miles in length. Clumps of forest and dense islets of jungle dot plains which separate the forests proper. It is monotonous owing to the sameness of the scenes. And throughout this length of eighty miles there is nothing to catch a man's eye in search of the picturesque or novel save the Gombe's pools, with their amphibious inhabitants, and the variety of noble game which inhabit the forests and plain. A travelling band of Wakonongo, bound to Ukonongo from Manyara, prayed to have our escort, which was readily granted. They were famous foresters, who knew the various fruits fit to eat; who knew the cry of the honey bird,[13] and could follow it to the treasure of honey which it wished to show its human friends. It is a pretty bird, not much larger than a wren, and, "tweet-tweet," it immediately cries when it sees a human being. It becomes very busy all at once, hops and skips, and flies from branch to branch with marvellous celerity. The traveller lifts up his eyes, beholds the tiny little bird, hopping about, and hears its sweet call—"tweet-tweet-tweet." If he is a Mkonongo he follows it. Away flies the bird on to another tree, springs to another branch nearer to the lagging man as if to say, "Shall I, must I come and fetch you?" but assured by his advance, away again to another tree, coquets about, and tweets his call rapidly; sometimes more earnest and loud, as if chiding him for being so slow; then off again, until at last the treasure is found and secured. And as he is a very busy little bird, while the man secures his treasure of honey, he plumes himself, ready for another flight and to discover another treasure. Every evening the Makonongo brought us stores of beautiful red and white honey, which is only to be secured in the dry season. Over pancakes and fritters the honey is very excellent; but as it is apt to disturb the stomach, I seldom rejoiced in its sweetness without suffering some indisposition afterwards.

As we were leaving the banks of the Gombe at one time, near a desolate looking place, fit scene for a tragedy, occurred an incident which I shall not readily forget.[14] I had given three days' rest to the soldiers, and their clothloads were furnished with bountiful sup-

13. *Indicator indicator*, the Greater Honey-guide, "has developed a most remarkable habit of guiding human beings to the nests of wild bees in order to feed upon the honeycomb and grubs when the nest is chopped out." Williams, *A Field Guide to the Birds of East and Central Africa*, 170. For some other interesting habits, Jackson, "On Honey Guides"; Culwick, "Ngindo Honey-Hunters," 73.

14. Compare *HIFL*, 343–46. The guide was named Asmani; his companion was Mabruki.

plies of meat, which told how well they had enjoyed themselves during the halt; but the guide, a stubborn fellow, one inclined to be impertinent whenever he had the chance, wished for another day's hunting. He selected Bombay as his mouthpiece, and I scolded Bombay for being the bearer of such an unreasonable demand, when he knew very well I could not possibly allow it after halting already three days. Bombay became sulky, said it was not his fault, and that he could do nothing more than come and tell me, which I denied in toto, and said to him that he could have done much, very much more, and better, by telling the guide that another day's halt was impossible; that we had not come to hunt, but to march and find the white man, Livingstone; that if he had spoken to the guide against it, as it was his duty, he being captain, instead of to me, it would have been much better. I ordered the horn to sound, and the expedition had gone but three miles when I found they had come to a dead stand. As I was walking up to see what was the matter I saw the guide and his brother sitting on an ant hill, apart from the other people, fingering their guns in what appeared to me a most suspicious manner. Calling Salim, I took the double-barrelled smooth-bore and slipped in two charges of buckshot and then walked on to my people, keeping an eye, however, upon the guide and his brother. I asked Bombay to give me an explanation of the stoppage. He would not answer, though he mumbled something sullenly, which was unintelligible to me. I looked to the other people, and perceived that they acted in an irresolute manner, as if they feared to take my part or were of the same mind as the party on the ant hill. I was but thirty paces from the guide, and throwing the barrel of the gun into the hollow of my left hand, I presented it, cocked at the guide and called out to him if he did not come to me at once I would shoot him, giving him and his companion to understand that I had twenty-four small bullets in the gun and that I could blow them to pieces.

In a very reluctant manner they advanced toward me. When they were sufficiently near I ordered them to halt; but the guide, as he did so, brought his gun to the present, with his finger on the trigger, and, with a treacherous and cunning smile which I perfectly understood, he asked what I wanted of him. His companion, while he was speaking, was sidling to my rear and was imprudently engaged in filling the pan of his musket with powder; but a threat to finish him if he did not go back to his companion and there stand until I gave him permission to move compelled this villanous Thersites to execute the "right about" with a promptitude which earned commendation from me. Then, facing my Ajax of a guide with my gun, I next requested him to lower his gun if he did not wish to receive the contents of mine in his head; and I do not know but what the terrible catastrophe warranted by stern necessity had occurred then and there if Mabrouki ("bull-headed" Mabrouki, but my faithful porter and faithful soldier) had not dashed the man's gun aside asking him how he dared level his gun at his master, and then thrown himself at my feet, praying me to forgive him. Mabrouki's action and subsequent conduct somewhat disconcerted myself as well as the murderous-looking guide, but I felt thankful that I had been spared shedding blood, though there was great provocation. Few cases of homicide could have been more justified than this, and I felt certain that this man had been seducing my soldiers from their duties to me, and was the cause principally of Bombay remaining in the background during this interesting episode of a march through the wilderness, instead of acting the part which Mabrouki so readily undertook to do. When Mabrouki's prayer for forgiveness was seconded by that of the principal culprit, that I would overlook his act, I was enabled to act as became a prudent commander, though I felt some remorse that I had not availed myself of the opportunity to punish the guide and his companion as they eminently deserved. But perhaps had I proceeded to extremities my people—fickle enough at all times—would have taken the act as justifying them for deserting in a body, and the search after Livingstone had ended there and then, which would have been as unwelcome to the HERALD as unhappy to myself.

However, as Bombay could not bend himself to ask forgiveness, I came to the conclusion that it were best he should be made to feel the penalty for stirring dissensions in the expedition and be brought to look with a more amiable face upon the scheme of proceeding to Ujiji through Ukonongo and Ukawendi, and I at once proceeded about it with such vigor that Bombay's back will for as long a time bear traces of the punishment which I administered to him as his front teeth do of that which Speke rightfully bestowed on him some eleven years ago.[15] And here I may as well interpolate by way of parenthesis that I am not at all obliged to Captain Burton for a recommendation of a man who so ill deserved it as Bombay.

Arriving at Marefu, we overtook an embassy from the Arabs at Unyanyembe to the Chief of the ferocious Watuta, who live a month's march southwest of this frontier village of Ukonongo. Old Hassan, the Mseguhha, was the person who held the honorable post of Chief of the embassy, who had volunteered to conduct the negotiations

15. See Speke, *Journal of the Discovery*, 270–71.

which were to secure the Watuta's services against Mirambo, the dreaded Chief of Uyoweh. Assured by the Arabs that there was no danger, and having received the sum of $40 for his services, he had gone on, sanguine of success, and had arrived at Marefu, where we overtook him. But old Hassan was not the man for the position, as I perceived when, after visiting me in my tent, he began to unfold the woes which already had befallen him, which were as nothing, however, to those sure to happen to him if he went on much farther. There were only two roads by which he might hope to reach the Watuta, and these ran through countries where the people of Mbogo of Ukonongo were at war with Niongo,[16] the brother of Manua Sera (the chief who disturbed Unyanyembe during Speke's residence there), and the Wasavira contended against Simba,[17] son of King Mkasiva. He was eloquent in endeavoring to dissuade me from the attempt to pass through the country of the Wasavira, and advised me as an old man who knew well whereof he was speaking not to proceed farther, but wait at Marefu until better times; and, sure enough, on my return from Ujiji with Livingstone, I heard that old Hassan was still encamped at Marefu, waiting patiently for the better times he hoped to see.

We left old Hassan—after earnestly commending him to the care of "Allah"—the next day, for the prosecution of the work of the expedition, feeling much happier than we had felt for many a day. Desertions had now ceased, and there remained in chains but one incorrigible, whom I had apprehended twice after twice deserting. Bombay and his sympathizers were now beginning to perceive that after all there was not much danger—at least not as much as the Arabs desired us to believe—and he was heard expressing his belief in his broken English that I would "catch the Tanganyika after all," and the standing joke was now that we could smell the fish of the Tanganyika Lake, and that we could not be far from it. New scenes also met the eye. Here and there were upheaved above the tree tops sugar-loaf hills, and, darkly blue, west of us loomed up a noble ridge of hills which formed the boundary between Kamirambo's territory

16. Nyungu ya Mawe, a member of the ruling family of Unyanyembe, was one of the most noted warrior leaders of the interior; he died in 1884. For a most able account of his career, Shorter, "Nyungu-Ya-Mawe."

17. Simba was also a member of Tabora's ruling family; he eventually seized power in Usavira. Simba remained a rival of Isike, the successor to Mkasiwa, but he was not able to return to Tabora until Isike was defeated and killed by the Germans in 1893. Association Internationale Africaine, *Rapports sur les Marches de la Première Expédition*, 67, 71, 79; Becker, *La Vie en Afrique*, I, 245ff., II, 78ff.; Burdo, *Les Belges dans l'Afrique Centrale*, 53–55; von Prince's letter of Jan. 28, 1893, *DKZ* 6 (1893), 65.

and that of Utende.[18] Elephant tracks became numerous, and buffalo met the delighted eyes everywhere. Crossing the mountainous
ridge of Mwaru, with its lengthy slope slowly descending westward,
the vegetation became more varied and the outlines of the land
before us became more picturesque. We became sated with the varieties of novel fruit which we saw hanging thickly on trees. There
was the mbembu, with the taste of an overripe peach; the tamarind
pod and beans, with their grateful acidity, resembling somewhat the
lemon in its flavor. The matonga, or *nux vomica*, was welcome, and
the luscious singwe, the plum of Africa, was the most delicious of
all. There were wild plums like our own, and grapes unpicked long
past their season, and beyond eating.[19] Guinea fowls, the moorhen,
ptarmigans and ducks supplied our table; and often the lump of a
buffalo or an extravagant piece of venison filled our camp kettles.
My health was firmly established. The faster we prosecuted our journey the better I felt. I had long bidden adieu to the nauseous calomel
and rhubarb compounds, and had become quite a stranger to quinine.
There was only one drawback to it all, and that was the feeble health
of the Arab boy Selim, who was suffering from an attack of acute
dysentery, caused by inordinate drinking of the bad water of the
pools at which we had camped between Manyara and Mrera. But
judicious attendance and Dover's powders brought the boy around
again.[20]

Mrera, in Ukonongo, nine days southwest of the Gombe Nullah,
brought to our minds the jungle habitats of the Wakwere on the
coast, and an ominous sight to travellers were the bleached skulls of
men which adorned the tops of tall poles before the gates of the
village. The Sultan of Mrera and myself became fast friends after
he had tasted of my liberality.

After a halt of three days at this village, for the benefit of the
Arab boy, we proceeded westerly, with the understanding that we
should behold the waters of the Tanganyika within ten days. Traversing a dense forest of young trees, we came to a plain dotted with
scores of ant hills. Their uniform height (about seven feet high above
the plain) leads me to believe that they were constructed during an

18. Stanley was still in Ukonongo; Utende was a village. *HIFL*, 356–57.
19. The *mbura*, Stanley's mbembu—*Parinari curatellaefolium;* the tamarind
—*Tamarindus indica; mtonga—Strychnos spinosa;* the singwe is perhaps the
mzambarau—Syzygium jambolanum. Standard Swahili-English Dictionary, 270,
310, 324; Dale and Greenway, *Kenya Trees,* 109, 256; Burton, "Lake Regions,"
63–64, 143.
20. Compare this solicitous treatment of Selim with that of the Englishman,
Shaw.

unusually wet season, and when the country was inundated for a long time in consequence. The surface of the plain also bore the appearance of being subject to such inundations. Beyond this plain about four miles we came to a running stream of purest water—a most welcome sight after so many months spent by brackish pools and nauseous swamps. Crossing the stream, which ran northwest, we immediately ascended a steep and lofty ridge, whence we obtained a view of grand and imposing mountains, of isolated hills, rising sheer to great heights from a plain stretching far into the heart of Ufipa, cut up by numerous streams flowing into the Rungwa River, which during the rainy season overflows this plain and forms the lagoon set down by Speke as the Rikwa.[21] The sight was encouraging in the extreme, for it was not to be doubted now that we were near the Tanganyika. We continued still westward, crossing many a broad stretch of marsh and oozy bed of nullahs, whence rose the streams that formed the Rungwa some forty miles south.

At a camping place beyond Mrera we heard enough from some natives who visited us to assure us that we were rushing to our destruction if we still kept westward. After receiving hints of how to evade the war-stricken country in our front, we took a road leading north-northwest. While continuing on this course we crossed streams running to the Rungwa south and others running directly north to the Malagarazi, from either side of a lengthy ridge which served to separate the country of Unyamwezi from Ukawendi. We were also attracted for the first time by the lofty and tapering mvule tree,[22] used on the Tanganyika Lake for the canoes of the natives, who dwell on its shores. The banks of the numerous streams were lined with dense growths of these shapely trees, as well as of sycamore, and gigantic tamarinds, which rivalled the largest sycamore in their breadth of shade. The undergrowth of bushes and tall grass dense and impenetrable, likely resorts of leopard and lion and wild boar, were enough to appal the stoutest heart. One of my donkeys, while being driven to water along a narrow path, hedged by the awesome brake on either side, was attacked by a leopard, which fastened its fangs in the poor animal's neck, and it would have made short work of it had not its companions set up such a braying chorus as might well have terrified a score of leopards. And that same night,

21. Burton and Speke heard the first reports of Lake Rukwa, a lake with no outlet and of varying area according to the season. It was not visited by a European until 1882 when E. Kaiser arrived. Fuchs, "The Lake Rukwa Expedition"; Gunn, "A History of Lake Rukwa and the Red Locust"; Moffett, *Handbook of Tanganyika*, 266.

22. *Chlorophora excelsa.* Dale and Greenway, *Kenya Trees*, 309–11.

while encamped contiguous to that limpid stream of Mtambu, with that lofty line of enormous trees rising dark and awful above us, the lions issued from the brakes beneath and prowled about the well-set bush defence of our camp, venting their fearful clamor without intermission until morning. Towards daylight they retreated to their leafy caverns, for

> There the lion dwells, the monarch,
> Mightiest among the brutes.
> There his right to reign supremest
> Never one his claim disputes.
> There he layeth down to slumber,
> Having slain and ta'en his fill,
> There he roameth, there he croucheth,
> As it suits his lordly will.[23]

And few, I believe, would venture therein to dispute it; not I, "i'-faith" when searching after Livingstone.

Our camps by these thick belts of timber, peopled as they were with the wild beasts, my men never fancied. But Southern Ukawendi, with its fair, lovely valleys and pellucid streams nourishing vegetation to extravagant growth, density and height, is infested with troubles of this kind. And it is probable, from the spread of this report among the natives, that this is the cause of the scant population of one of the loveliest countries Africa can boast. The fairest of California scenery cannot excel, though it may equal, such scenes as Ukawendi can boast of, and yet a land as large as the State of New York is almost uninhabited. Days and days one may travel through primeval forests, now ascending ridges overlooking broad, well watered valleys, with belts of valuable timber crowning the banks of the rivers, and behold exquisite bits of scenery—wild, fantastic, picturesque and pretty—all within the scope of vision whichever way one may turn. And to crown the glories of this lovely portion of earth, underneath the surface but a few feet is one mass of iron ore, extending across three degrees of longitude and nearly four of latitude, cropping out at intervals, so that the traveller cannot remain ignorant of the wealth lying beneath.[24]

Ah, me! What wild and ambitious projects fill a man's brain as he

23. From a poem by Hermann Ferdinand Freiligrath (1810–1876). *HIFL*, 368; *Allgemeine Deutsche Biographie,* VII, 343–47.

24. Statements of this type drew forth the ire of the explorer and geologist, Thomson; he called them the "unrestrained exercise of fancy." Thomson, *Central African Lakes,* II, 281.

looks over the forgotten and unpeopled country, containing in its bosom such store of wealth, and with such an expanse of fertile soil, capable of sustaining millions! What a settlement one could have in this valley! See, it is broad enough to support a large population! Fancy a church spire rising where that tamarind rears its dark crown of foliage, and think how well a score or so of pretty cottages would look instead of those thorn clumps and gum trees! Fancy this lovely valley teeming with herds of cattle and fields of corn, spreading to the right and left of this stream! How much better would such a state become this valley, rather than its present deserted and wild aspect! But be hopeful. The day will come and a future year will see it, when happier lands have become crowded and nations have become so overgrown that they have no room to turn about. It only needs an Abraham or a Lot, an Alaric or an Attila to lead their hosts to this land, which, perhaps, has been wisely reserved for such a time.

After the warning so kindly given by the natives soon after leaving Mrera, in Ukonongo, five days' [25] marches brought us to Mrera, in the district of Rusawa, in Ukawendi. Arriving here we questioned the natives as to the best course to pursue—should we make direct for the Tanganyika or go north to the Malagarazi River? They advised us to the latter course, though no Arab had ever taken it. Two days through the forest, they said, would enable us to reach the Malagarazi. The guide, who had by this forgotten our disagreement, endorsed this opinion, as beyond the Malagarazi he was sufficiently qualified to show the way. We laid in a stock of four days' provisions against contingencies, and bidding farewell to the hospitable people of Rusawa, continued our journey northward. After finding a pass to the wooded plateau above Mrera, through the arc of mountains which environed it on the north and west, the soldiers improved another occasion to make themselves disagreeable.

One of their number had shot a buffalo towards night, and the approaching darkness had prevented him from following it up to a clump of jungle, whither it had gone to die, and the black soldiers, ever on the lookout for meat, came to me in a body to request a day's halt to eat meat and make themselves strong for the forest road, to which I gave a point-blank refusal, as I vowed I would not halt again until I did it on the banks of the Malagarazi, where I would give them as much meat as their hearts could desire. There was an evident disposition to resist, but I held up a warning finger as an indication

25. In *HIFL*, three days is given.

that I would not suffer any grumbling, and told them I had business at Ujiji, which the Wasungu expected I would attend to, and that if I failed to perform it they would take no excuse, but condemn me at once. I saw that they were in an excellent mood to rebel, and the guide, who seemed to be ever on the lookout to revenge his humiliation on the Gombe, was a fit man to lead them; but they knew I had more than a dozen men upon whom I could rely at a crisis, and besides, as no harsh word or offensive epithet challenged them to commence an outbreak, the order to march, though received with much peevishness, was obeyed. This peevishness may always be expected when on a long march. It is much the result of fatigue and monotony, every day being but a repetition of previous days, and a prudent man will not pay much attention to mere growling and surliness of temper, but keep himself prepared for an emergency which might possibly arise. By the time we had arrived at camp we were all in excellent humor with one another, and confidently laughed and shouted until the deep woods rang again.

The scenery was getting more sublime every day as we advanced northward, even approaching the terrible. We seemed to have left the monotony of a desert for the wild, picturesque scenery of Abyssinia and the terrible mountains of the Sierra Nevadas. I named one tabular mountain, which recalled memories of the Abyssinian campaign, Magdala, and as I gave it a place on my chart it became of great use to me, as it rose so prominently into view that I was enabled to lay down our route pretty accurately.[26] The four days' provisions we had taken with us were soon consumed, and still we were far from the Malagarazi River. Though we eked out my own stores with great care, as ship-wrecked men at sea, these also gave out on the sixth day, and still the Malagarazi was not in sight. The country was getting more difficult for travel, owing to the numerous ascents and descents we had to make in the course of a day's march. Bleached and bare, it was cut up by a thousand deep ravines and intersected by a thousand dry water courses whose beds were filled with immense sandstone rocks and boulders washed away from the great heights which rose above us on every side. We were not protected now by the shades of the forest, and the heat became excessive and water became scarce. But we still held on our way, as a halt would be death to us, hoping that each day's march would bring us in sight of the long-looked for and much-desired Malagarazi. Fortunately we had filled our bags and baskets with the forest peaches

26. Jackson, *Meteor Out of Africa*, 317, suggests this is the present Makoma peak.

with which the forests of Rusawa had supplied us, and these sustained us in this extremity.

On the seventh day, after a six hours' march, during which we
had descended more than a thousand feet, through rocky ravines,
and over miles of rocky plateaus, above which protruded masses of
hematite of iron, we arrived at a happy camping place, situated in a
valley which was seductively pretty and a hidden garden. Deserted
bomas told us that it had once been occupied, and that at a recent
date, which we took to be a sign that we were not far from habited
districts. Before retiring to sleep the soldiers indulged themselves
in prayer to Allah for relief. Indeed, our position was most desperate and unenviable; yet since leaving the coast when had it been
enviable, and when had travelling in Africa ever been enviable?

Proceeding on our road on the eighth day everything we saw
tended to confirm us in the belief that food was at hand. Rhinoceros
tracks abounded, and the *bois de vache*, or buffalo droppings, were
frequent, and the presence of a river or a body of water was known
in the humidity of the atmoshpere. After travelling two hours, still
descending rapidly towards a deep basin which we saw, the foremost
of the expedition halted, attracted by the sight of a village situated
on a table-topped mountain on our right. The guide told us it must
be that of the Son of Nzogera, of Uvinza.[27] We followed a road
leading to the foot of the mountain, and camped on the edge of an
extensive morass.

Though we fired guns to announce our arrival, it was unnecessary,
for the people were already hurrying to our camps to inquire about
our intentions. The explanation was satisfactory, but they said that
they had taken us to be enemies, few friends having ever come along
our road. In a few minutes there was an abundance of meat and
grain in the camp, and the men's jaws were busy in the process of
mastication.

During the whole of the afternoon we were engaged upon the
terms Nzogera's son exacted for the privilege of passing through his
country. We found him to be the first of a tribute-taking tribe which
subsequently made much havoc in the bales of the expedition. Seven
and a half doti of cloth were what we were compelled to pay, whether
we returned or proceeded on our way. After a day's halt we proceeded under the guidance of two men granted to me as qualified to
show the way to the Malagarazi River. We had to go east-northeast
for a considerable time in order to avoid the morass that lay directly

27. Perhaps the son, Rusunzu, met by Stanley in 1876; he had then succeeded to his father's position in Uvinza. *TDC*, I, 506–08.

across the country that intervened between the triangular mountain
on whose top Nzogera's son dwelt. This marsh drains three extensive
ranges of mountains which, starting from the westward, separated
only by two deep chasms from each other, run at wide angles—one
southeast, one northeast and the other northwest. From a distance
this marsh looks fair enough; stately trees at intervals rise seemingly from its bosom, and between them one catches glimpses
of a lovely champaign, bounded by perpendicular mountains, in the
far distance. After a wide detour we struck straight for this marsh,
which presented to us another novelty in the water shed of the Tanganyika.

Fancy a river broad as the Hudson at Albany, though not near so
deep or swift, covered over by water plants and grasses, which had
become so interwoven and netted together as to form a bridge covering its entire length and breadth, under which the river flowed calm
and deep below. It was over this natural bridge we were expected to
cross. Adding to the tremor which one naturally felt at having to
cross this frail bridge was the tradition that only a few yards higher
up an Arab and his donkey, thirty-five slaves and sixteen tusks of
ivory had suddenly sunk forever out of sight. As one-half of our little
column had already arrived at the centre we on the shore could see
the network of grass waving on either side and between each man,
in one place like to the swell of a sea after a storm and in another like
a small lake violently ruffled by a squall. Hundreds of yards away
from them it ruffled, and undulated one wave after another. As we
all got on it we perceived it to sink about a foot, forcing the water
on which it rested into the grassy channel formed by our footsteps.
One of my donkeys broke through and it required the united strength
of ten men to extricate him. The aggregate weight of the donkey and
men caused that portion of the bridge on which they stood to sink
about two feet and a circular pool of water was formed, and I expected every minute to see them suddenly sink out of sight. Fortunately we managed to cross the treacherous bridge without accident.

Arriving on the other side, we struck north, passing through a delightful country, in every way suitable for agricultural settlements or
happy mission stations. The primitive rock began to show itself anew
in eccentric clusters, as a flat-topped rock, on which the villages of
the Wavinza were seen and where the natives prided themselves on
their security and conducted themselves accordingly, ever insolent
and forward, though I believe that with forty good rifles I could have
made the vain fellows desert their country *en masse*. But a white
traveller's motto in their lands is, "Do, dare and endure," and those

who come out of Africa alive have generally to thank themselves for their prudence rather than their temerity. We were halted every two or three miles by the demand for tribute, which we did not, because we could not, pay, as they did not press it overmuch, though we had black looks enough.[28]

On the second day after leaving Nzogera's son we commenced a series of descents, the deep valleys on each side of us astonishing us by their profundity, and the dark gloom prevailing below, amid their wonderful dense forests of tall trees, and glimpses of plains beyond, invited sincere admiration. In about a couple of hours we discovered the river we were looking for below, at the distance of a mile, running like a silver vein through a broad valley. Halting at Kiala's, eldest son of Nzogera, the principal Sultan of Uvinza, we waited an hour to see on what terms he would ferry us over the Malagarazi. As we could not come to a definite conclusion respecting them we were obliged to camp in his village. Late in the afternoon Kiala sent his chiefs to our camp with a bundle of short sticks, fifty-six in number. Each stick, we were soon informed, represented a doti, or four yards of cloth, which were to consist of best, good, bad and indifferent. Only one bale of cloth was the amount of the tribute to be exacted of us! Bombay and the guide were told by me to inform Kiala's ambassadors that I would pay ten doti. The gentlemen delegated by Kiala to receive the tribute soon made us aware what thoughts they entertained of us by stating that if we ran away from Mirambo we could not run away from them. Indeed, such was the general opinion of the natives of Uvinza; for they lived directly west of Uyoweh, Mirambo's country, and news travels fast enough in these regions, though there are no established post offices or telegraph stations. In two hours, however, we reduced the demand of fifty-six doti to twenty-three, and the latter number was sent and received, not for crossing the Malagarazi, but for the privilege of passing through Kiala's country in peace. Of these twenty-three cloths thirteen were sent to Nzogera, the Sultan, while his affectionate son retained ten for himself. Towards midnight, about retiring for the night after such an eventful day, while congratulating ourselves that Nzogera, and Kiala were both rather moderate in their demands, considering the circumstances, came another demand for four more cloths, with a promise that we might depart in the morning, or when we pleased; but as poor Bombay said, from sheer weariness, that if we had to

28. Stanley later advised a newcomer to Africa: "one golden rule which you should remember is, 'Do not fire the first shot,' whatever may be the provocation." Maurice, *Stanley's Unpublished Letters*, 21–22.

talk longer he would be driven mad, I told him he might pay them, after a little haggling, least they, imagining that they had asked too little, would make another demand in the morning.

Until three o'clock P.M. the following day continued the negotiations for ferrying us across the Malagarazi, consisting of arguments, threats, quarrels, loud shouting and stormy debate on both sides. Finally, six doti and ten fundo of sami-sami beads[29] were agreed upon. After which we marched to the ferry, distant half a mile from the scene of so much contention. The river at this place was not more than thirty yards broad, sluggish and deep; yet I would prefer attempting to cross the Mississippi by swimming rather than the Malagarazi. Such another river for the crocodiles, cruel as death, I cannot conceive. Their long, tapering heads dotted the river everywhere, and though I amused myself, pelting them with two-ounce balls, I made no effect on their numbers. Two canoes had discharged their live cargo on the other side of the river when the story of Captain Burton's passage across the Malagarazi higher up was brought vividly to my mind by the extortions which the Mutware now commenced.[30] About twenty or so of his men had collected, and, backed by these, he became insolent. If it were worth while to commence a struggle for two or three more doti of cloth the mere firing of one revolver at such close quarters would have settled the day, but I could not induce myself to believe that it was the best way of proceeding, taking in view the object of our expedition, and accordingly this extra demand was settled at once with as much amiability as I could muster, but I warned him not to repeat it, and to prevent him from doing so ordered a man to each canoe, and to be seated there with a loaded gun in each man's hands. After this little episode we got on very well until all the men excepting two besides Bombay and myself were safe on the other side.

We then drove a donkey into the river, having first tied a strong halter to his neck; but he had barely reached the middle of the river when a crocodile, darting beneath, seized him by the neck and dragged him under, after several frantic but ineffectual endeavors to draw him ashore. A sadness stole over all after witnessing this scene, and as the shades of night had now drawn around us, and had tinged the river to a black, dismal color, it was with a feeling of relief that

29. ". . . the small coral bead, a scarlet enamelled upon a white ground." Burton, "Lake Regions," 425. It was a popular bead in eastern Africa and was used as a currency as far inland as Burundi. See Coulbois, *Dix Années au Tanganyka*, 79–80. For a general study see Harding, "Nineteenth-Century Trade Beads in Tanganyika."

30. See Burton, *Lake Regions*, I, 408–12.

the fatal river was crossed, that we all set foot ashore. In the morning the other donkey swam the river safe enough, the natives firmly declaring that they had so covered him with medicine that though the crocodiles swarmed around him they did not dare attack the animal, so potent was the medicine—for which I had to give a present, such as became a kindness. I rather incline to the belief, however, that the remaining donkey owed his safety to the desertion of the river for the banks, where they love to bask in the sun undisturbed, and as the neighborhood of the ferry was constantly disturbed they could not possibly be in the neighborhood, and the donkey consequently escaped the jaws of the crocodiles.

The notes in my journal of what occurred on the following day read as follows: November 3, Friday, 1871.

Katalambula, N.N.W., 1¼ hours.

What talk! What excitement, so grotesque, yet so frenzied! Withal what anxiety have we suffered since we came to Uvinza! These people are worse than the Wagogo, and their greed is immeasurable. They are more noisy and intolerable, especially those who dwell close to the river. Their pride, the guide says, is because they have possession of the river, and all men have to speak them fair, pay high tribute, &c. On the northern side, though, I find the Wavinza, more amiable and more favorably disposed toward caravans, because they bring terms, and might in a pinch help them against their cruel neighbors, the Watuta. Before crossing the river a native guide, procured from the son of Nzogera, who lives on the frontier, was recognized as a spy in the service of Lokandamira, who is at war against King Nzogera. The cry for rope to bind him was quickly responded to, for every tree in their vicinity was furnished with enough strong bark to tie a dozen spies. They afterwards conveyed him to Kwi-Kuru, or the capital of Nzogera, which is situated a few miles below here, on an island well guarded by crocodiles. Lokandamira is at war with Nzogera about certain salt-pans, which must, of course, belong to the strongest party, for might is right in this world.

We set out from the banks of the river with two new guides, furnished us by the old man (Usenge is his name) of the ferry. Arriving at Isinga after traversing a saline plain, which, as we advanced into the interior, grew wonderfully fertile, we were told by the native Kirangozi that to-morrow's march would have to be made with great caution, for Makumbi, a great warrior chief of Nzogera, was returning triumphantly from war, and it was his custom to leave nothing behind him at such times. Intoxicated with victory he attacked villages and caravans, and of whatever live stock, slaves or bales he met, he took what he liked. The results of a month's campaign against Lokandamira were two villages captured, several men and a son of Nzogera's enemy being killed, while Makumbi only lost three men in battle and two from bowel explosion from drinking too much water. So the Kirangozi says.

"Near Isinga met a caravan of eighty Waguhha direct from Ujiji, bearing oil,[31] and bound for Unyanyembe. They report that a white man was left by them five days ago at Ujiji.[32] He had the same color as I have, wears the same shoes, the same clothes, and has hair on his face like I have, only his is white. This is Livingstone. Hurrah for Ujiji! My men share my joy, for we shall be coming back now directly; and, being so happy at the prospect, I buy three goats and five gallons of native beer, which will be eaten and drank directly."

Two marches from Malagarazi brought us to Uhha. Kawanga was the first place in Uhha where we halted. It is the village where resides the first mutware, or chief, to whom caravans have to pay tribute. To this man we paid twelve and a half doti, upon the understanding that we would have to pay no more between here and Ujiji. Next morning, buoyed up by the hope that we should soon come to our journey's end, we had arranged to make a long march of it that day. We left Kawanga cheerfully enough. The country undulated gently before us like the prairie of Nebraska, as devoid of trees almost as our own plains. The top of every wave of land enabled us to see the scores of villages which dotted its surface, though it required keen eyes to detect at a distance the beehive and straw-thatched huts from the bleached grass of the plain. We had marched an hour, probably, and were passing a large village, with populous suburbs about it, when we saw a large party pursuing us, who, when they had come up to us, asked us how we dared pass by without paying the tribute to the King of Uhha.[33]

"We have paid it!" we said, quite astonished.

"To whom?"

"To the Chief of Kawanga."

"How much?"

"Twelve and a half doti."

"Oh, but that is only for himself. However, you had better stop and rest at our village until we find all about it."

But we halted in the middle of the road until the messengers they sent came back. Seeing our reluctance to halt at their village,

31. From the wild oil palm—*Elaeis guineensis*. Dale and Greenway, *Kenya Trees & Shrubs*, 11–12.

32. *HIFL*, 384, says eight days.

33. See document 4, notes 3 and 4.

they sent men also to Mionvu, living an arrow's flight from where
we were halted, to warn him of our contumacy. Mionvu came to us,
robed most royally, after the fashion of Central Africa, in a crimson
cloth, arranged toga-like over his shoulder and descending to his
ankles, and a brand new piece of Massachusetts sheeting folded
around his head. He greeted us graciously—he was the prince of
politeness—shook hands first with myself, then with my head men,
and cast a keen glance around, in order, as I thought, to measure our
strength. Then seating himself, he spoke with deliberation something
in this style: [34]

Why does the white man stand in the road? The sun is hot;
let him seek the shelter of my village, where we can arrange this
little matter between us. Does he not know that there is a king in
Uhha, and that I, Mionvu, am his servant? It is a custom with us
to make friends with great men, such as the white man. All Arabs
and Wanguana stop here and give us cloth. Does the white man
mean to go on without paying? Why should he desire war? I know
he is stronger than we are here, his men have guns, and we have
but spears and arrows; but Uhha is large, and has plenty of people.
The children of the king are many. If he comes to be a friend to
us he will come to our village, give us something, and then go on
his way.

The armed warriors around applauded the very commonplace
speech of Mionvu because it spoke the feelings with which they
viewed our bales. Certain am I, though, that one portion of his speech
—that which related to our being stronger than the Wahha—was
an untruth, and that he knew it, and that he only wished us to start
hostilities in order that he might have good reason for seizing the
whole. But it is not new to you, of course, if you have read this letter
through, that the representative of the HERALD was held of small
account here, and never one did I see who would care a bead for
anything that you would ever publish against him. So the next time
you wish me to enter Africa I only hope you will think it worth while
to send with me 100 good men from the HERALD office to punish
this audacious Mionvu, who fears neither the NEW YORK HERALD
nor the "Star Spangled Banner," be the latter ever so much spangled
with stars.

I submitted to Mionvu's proposition, and went with him to his village, where he fleeced me to his heart's content. His demand, which

34. In *HIFL*, 389–90, Stanley presents a slightly different account.

he adhered to like a man who knew what he was about, was sixty doti for the King, twelve doti for himself, three for his wife, three each to three makko, or subchiefs,[35] one to Mibruri's little boy: total, eighty-five doti, or one good bale of cloth. Not one doti did he abate, though I talked until six P.M. from ten A.M. I went to bed that night like a man on the verge of ruin. However, Mionvu said that we would have to pay no more in Uhha.[36]

Pursuing our way next day, after a four hours' march, we came to Kahirigi, and quartered ourselves in a large village, governed over by Mionvu's brother, who had already been advised by Mionvu of the windfall in store for him.[37] This man, as soon as we had set the tent, put in a claim for thirty doti, which I was able to reduce after much eloquence, lasting over five hours, to twenty-six doti. I am short enough in relating it because I am tired of the theme; but there lives not a man in the whole United States with whom I would not gladly have exchanged positions had it been possible. I saw my fine array of bales being reduced fast. Four more such demands as Mionvu's would leave me, in unclassic phrase, "cleaned out."

After paying this last tribute, as it was night, I closed my tent and, lighting my pipe, began to think seriously upon my position and how to reach Ujiji without paying more tribute. It was high time to resort either to battle or to a strategy of some kind, possibly to striking into the jungle; but there was no jungle in Uhha, and a man might be seen miles off on its naked plains. At least this last was the plan most likely to succeed without endangering the prospects almost within reach of the expedition. Calling the guide, I questioned him as to its feasibility, first scolding him for leading me to such a strait. He said there was a Mguana, a slave of Thani Bin Abdullah,[38] in the Boma,[39] with whom I might consult. Sending for him, he presently came, and I began to ask him for how much he would guide us out of Uhha without being compelled to pay any more Muhongo. He replied that it was a hard thing to do, unless I had complete control over my men and they could be got to do exactly as I told them. When satisfied on this point he entered into an agreement to show me a road—or rather to lead me to it—that might be clear of all

35. See d'Hertefeldt, Trouwborst, Scherer, *Les Anciens Royaumes*, 208–11, for Ha political organization.

36. Compare the differences in *HIFL*, 393–94.

37. *Ibid.*, 395, calls him instead "the King of Uhha's brother."

38. Thani bin Abdulla was an Arab settled at Tabora; he had lived in the Comoro Islands and spoke French. Mackay's Journal, May 1878, C.A6/016B, CMS; Guillet's Journal, in *Les Missions Catholiques* 15 (1883), 165–66.

39. Stockade, fort.

habitations as far as Ujiji for twelve doti, paid beforehand. The cloth was paid to him at once.[40]

At half-past two A.M. the men were ready, and, stealing silently past the huts, the guide opened the gates, and we filed out one by one as quickly as possible.[41] The moon was bright, and by it we perceived that we were striking across a burned plain in a southerly direction, and then turned westward, parallel with the high road, at the distance of four miles, sometimes lessening or increasing that distance as circumstances compelled us. At dawn we crossed the swift Rusizi,[42] which flowed southward into the Malagarizi, after which we took a northwesterly direction through a thick jungle of bamboo. There was no road, and behind us we left but little trail on the hard, dry ground. At eight A.M. we halted for breakfast, having marched nearly six hours, within the jungle which stretched for miles around us.

We were only once on the point of being discovered through the mad freak of a weak-brained woman, who was the wife of one of the black soldiers. We were crossing the knee-deep Rusizi, when this woman, suddenly and without cause, took it into her head to shriek and shout as if a crocodile had bitten her. The guide implored me to stop her shrieking, or she would alarm the whole country, and we would have hundreds of angry Wahha about us. The men were already preparing to bolt—several being on the run with their loads. At my order to stop her noise, she launched into another fit of hysterical shrieking, and I was compelled to stop her cries with three or four smart cuts across her shoulders, though I felt rather ashamed of myself; but our lives and the success of the expedition was worth more, in my opinion, than a hundred of such women. As a further precaution she was gagged and her arms tied behind her, and a cord led from her waist to that of her liege lord's, who gladly took upon himself the task of looking after her, and who threatened to cut her head off if she attempted to make another outcry.[43]

At 10 A.M. we resumed our journey, and after three hours camped at Lake Musuma,[44] a body of water which during the rainy season has a length of three miles and a breadth of two miles. It is one of

40. Compare *HIFL*, 396.

41. *Ibid.* says in gangs of four.

42. The text reads Rusizi, but *HIFL*, 397, indicates the Rusugi (Stanley's spelling).

43. Compare this account with that of *HIFL*, 398–99. In the third edition of *HIFL*, Stanley cut out almost all reference to this episode. Coupland, *Livingstone's Last Journey*, 212.

44. *HIFL*, 399, has Lake Musunya. One observer considers the lake was "only one of the depressions of the Sabaga swamp which is seasonally filled with water." Jackson, *Meteor Out of Africa*, 332.

a group of lakes which fill deep hollows in the plain of Uhha. They swarm with hippopotami, and their shores are favorite resorts of large herds of buffalo and game. The eland and buffalo especially are in large numbers here, and the elephant and rhinoceros are exceedingly numerous. We saw several of these, but did not dare to fire.

On the second morning after crossing the Sunuzzi and Rugufu Rivers, we had just started from our camp, and as there was no moonlight the head of the column came to a village, whose inhabitants, as we heard a few voices, were about starting. We were all struck with consternation, but, consulting with the guide, we despatched our goats and chickens, and leaving them in the road faced about, retraced our steps, and after a quarter of an hour struck up a ravine, and descending several precipitous places, about half-past six o'clock found ourselves in Ukaranga—safe and free from all tribute taking Wahha.

Exultant shouts were given—equivalent to the Anglo-Saxon hurrah —upon our success. Addressing the men, I asked them, "Why should we halt when but a few hours from Ujiji? Let us march a few hours more and to-morrow we shall see the white man at Ujiji, and who knows but this may be the man we are seeking? Let us go on, and after to-morrow we shall have fish for dinner and many days' rest afterwards, every day eating the fish of the Tanganyika. Stop; I think I smell the Tanganyika fish even now." This speech was hailed with what the newspapers call "loud applause; great cheering," and "Ngema —very well, master;" "Hyah Barak-Allah—Onward, and the blessing of God be on you."

We strode from the frontier at the rate of four miles an hour, and, after six hours' march the tired caravan entered the woods which separate the residence of the Chief of Ukaranga from the villages on the Mkuti River. As we drew near the village we went slower, unfurled the American and Zanzibar flags, presenting quite an imposing array. When we came in sight of Nyamtaga, the name of the Sultan's residence, and our flags and numerous guns were seen, the Wakaranga and their Sultan deserted the village *en masse,* and rushed into the woods, believing that we were Mirambo's robbers, who, after destroying Unyanyembe, were come to destroy the Arabs and bunder of Ujiji; but he and his people were soon reassured, and came forward to welcome us with presents of goats and beer, all of which were very welcome after the exceedingly lengthy marches we had recently undertaken.[45]

45. Cameron visited this chief in 1874 and found him unfriendly. Cameron, *Across Africa,* I, 236.

Rising at early dawn our new clothes were brought forth again that we might present as decent an appearance as possible before the Arabs of Ujiji, and my helmet was well chalked and a new puggeree folded around it, my boots were well oiled and my white flannels put on, and altogether, without joking, I might have paraded the streets of Bombay without attracting any very great attention.

A couple of hours brought us to the base of a hill, from the top of which the Kirangozi said we could obtain a view of the great Tanganyika Lake. Heedless of the rough path or of the toilsome steep, spurred onward by the cheery promise, the ascent was performed in a short time. On arriving at the top we beheld it at last from the spot whence, probably, Burton and Speke looked at it—"the one in a half paralyzed state, the other almost blind." Indeed, I was pleased at the sight; and, as we descended, it opened more and more into view until it was revealed at last into a grand inland sea, bounded westward by an appalling and black-blue range of mountains, and stretching north and south without bounds, a gray expanse of water.

From the western base of the hill was a three hours' march, though no march ever passed off so quickly. The hours seemed to have been quarters, we had seen so much that was novel and rare to us who had been travelling so long on the highlands. The mountains bounding the lake on the eastward receded and the lake advanced. We had crossed the Ruche, or Liuche, and its thick belt of tall matete grass.[46] We had plunged into a perfect forest of them, and had entered into the cultivated fields which supply the port of Ujiji with vegetables, &c., and we stood at last on the summit of the last hill of the myriads we had crossed, and the port of Ujiji, embowered in palms, with the tiny waves of the silver waters of the Tanganyika rolling at its feet, was directly below us.

We are now about descending—in a few minutes we shall have reached the spot where we imagine the object of our search—our fate will soon be decided. No one in that town knows we are coming; least of all do they know we are so close to them. If any of them ever heard of the white man at Unyanyembe they must believe we are there yet. We shall take them all by surprise, for no other but a white man would dare leave Unyanyembe for Ujiji with the country in such a distracted state—no other but a crazy white man, whom Sheik, the son of Nasib, is going to report to Syed or Prince Burghash for not taking his advice.

46. The Luiche River. *Matete*, or elephant grass—*Pennisetum cf. Benthami.* For a good description of *matete*, Mecklenburg, *In the Heart of Africa*, 210-11.

Stanley "Gray haired"
35 years old. CAPE TOWN.

Henry M. Stanley, 1877

Stanley's pencil sketch of Livingston, Ujiji, 1872

Well, we are but a mile from Ujiji now, and it is high time we should let them know a caravan is coming; so "Commence firing" is the word passed along the length of the column, and gladly do they begin. They have loaded their muskets half full, and they roar like the broadside of a line-of-battle ship. Down go the ramrods, sending huge charges home to the breech, and volley after volley is fired. The flags are fluttered; the banner of America is in front waving joyfully; the guide is in the zenith of his glory. The former residents of Zanzibar will know it directly, and will wonder—as well they may —as to what it means. Never were the Stars and Stripes so beautiful to my mind—the breeze of the Tanganyika has such an effect on them. The guide blows his horn, and the shrill, wild clangor of it is far and near; and still the cannon muskets tell the noisy seconds. By this time the Arabs are fully alarmed; the natives of Ujiji, Waguhha, Warundi, Wanguana, and I know not whom, hurry up by the hundreds to ask what it all means—this fusilading, shouting and blowing of horns and flag-flying. There are Yambos shouted out to me by the dozen, and delighted Arabs have run up breathlessly to shake my hands and ask anxiously where I came from. But I have no patience with them. The expedition goes far too slow. I should like to settle the vexed question by one personal view. Where is he? Has he fled?

Suddenly a man—a black man—at my elbow shouts in English, "How do you, sir?"

"Hello! who the deuce are you?"

"I am the servant of Dr. Livingstone," he says; but before I can ask any more questions he is running like a madman towards the town.

We have at last entered the town. There are hundreds of people around me—I might say thousands without exaggeration, it seems to me. It is a grand triumphal procession. As we move they move. All eyes are drawn towards us. The expedition at last comes to a halt; the journey is ended for a time; but I alone have a few more steps to make.

There is a group of the most respectable Arabs, and as I come nearer I see the white face of an old man among them. He has a cap with a gold band around it, his dress is a short jacket of red blanket cloth, and his pants—well, I didn't observe. I am shaking hands with him. We raise our hats, and I say:

"Dr. Livingstone, I presume?"

And he says, "Yes."

Finis coronat opus.

6

Ujiji, Lake Tanganyika
December 23, 1871[1]

A few days after the arrival of the HERALD expedition at Ujiji, I asked the Doctor if he had explored the head of the Tanganyika. He said he had not, "he had not thought it of so much importance as the central line of drainage; besides, when he had proposed to do it, before leaving for Manyema, the Wajiji had shown such a disposition to fleece him that he had desisted from the attempt."

Your correspondent then explained to him what great importance was attached to the lake by geographers, as stated in the newspapers, and suggested to him that it were better, seeing that he was about to leave for Unyanyembe, and that something might occur in the meanwhile to hinder him from ever visiting it, to take advantage of the offer I made of putting myself, men and effects of the expedition at his service for the purpose of exploring the northern head of the Tanganyika.[2] He at once accepted the offer, and, like a hero, lost no time in starting.

On the 20th of November Dr. Livingstone and your correspondent, with twenty picked men of the HERALD Expedition Corps, started. Despite the assertion of Arabs that the Warundi were dangerous and would not let us pass,[3] we hugged their coast closely, and when fatigued boldly encamped in their country. Once only were we obliged to fly—and this was at dead of night—from a large party which we knew to be surrounding us on the landside. We got to the boat safely, and we might have punished them severely had the Doctor been so disposed. Once also we were stoned, but we paid no heed to them and kept on our way along their coast until we arrived at Mokamba's,[4] one of the chiefs of Usige.

Mokamba was at war with a neighboring chief, who lived on the left bank of the Rusizi. That did not deter us, and we crossed the head of the Tanganyika to Mugihewah, governed by Ruhinga, brother of Mokamba.

Mugihewah is a tract of country on the right bank of the Rusizi,

1. *NYH*, July 15, 1872.
2. The trip is discussed in Leroy, "Stanley et Livingstone en Urundi."
3. Mukamba of Usige in Burundi had earlier defeated the Arabs. *LLJ*, II, 13–16.
4. Mukamba died after the visit. His successor, Mvuruma, was hostile to some later European visitors because of this. Hutley to LMS, Oct. 19, 1879, LMS.

extending to the lake. With Mokamba and Ruhinga we became most intimate; they proved to be sociable, good-natured chiefs, and gave most valuable information concerning the countries lying to the north of Usige; and if their information is correct, Sir Samuel Baker will be obliged to curtail the ambitious dimensions of his lake by one degree, if not more.[5] A Mgwana, living at Mokamba's, on the eastern shore of the lake, had informed us that the River Rusizi certainly flowed out of the lake, and after joining the Kitangule[6] emptied into the Lake N'yanza (Victoria).

When we entered Ruhinga's territory of Mugihewah, we found ourselves but 300 yards from the river about which a great deal has been said and written. At Unanyembe I was told that the Rusizi was an affluent. At Ujiji all Arabs but one united in saying the same thing, and within ten miles of the Rusizi a freedman of Zanzibar swore it was an affluent.

On the morning of the eleventh day of our departure from Ujiji, we were rowed towards the river. We came to a long narrow bay, fringed on all sides with tall, dense reeds and swarming with crocodiles, and soon came to the mouth of the Rusizi. As soon as we had entered the river all doubt vanished before the strong, turbid flood against which we had to contend in the ascent. After about ten minutes we entered what seemed a lagoon, but which was the result of a late inundation. About an hour higher up the river began to be confined to its proper banks, and is about thirty yards broad, but very shallow.

Two days higher up Ruhinga told us the Rusizi was joined by the Loanda, coming from the northwest. There could be no mistake then. Dr. Livingstone and myself had ascended it, had felt the force of the strong inflowing current—the Rusizi was an influent, as much so as the Malagarazi, the Liuche and Rugufu, but with its banks full it can only be considered as ranking third among the rivers flowing into the Tanganyika. Though rapid it is extremely shallow; it has three mouths, up which an ordinary ship's boat loaded might in vain attempt to ascend. Burton and Speke, though they ascended to within six hours' journey by canoe from the Rusizi, were compelled to turn back by the cowardice of the boatmen.[7] Had they ascended to Mreuta's

5. Samuel W. Baker (1821–1893) was the first European to visit Lake Albert (1864). From African reports Baker believed the lake to extend southward a great distance. See Baker, *The Albert N'yanza*, II, 94ff. For his life, *DNB*, XXII, 101–05; *GJ* 3 (1894), 152–56. See document 15, note 23.

6. The Kagera River. See document 30, note 14.

7. See Burton, "Lake Regions," 17, 254; Speke, *What Led to the Discovery*, 246–47.

capital,[8] they could easily have seen the head of the lake. Usige is but a district of Urundi, governed by several small chiefs, who owe obedience to Mwezi, the great King of Urundi.[9]

We spent nine days at the head of the Tanganyika exploring the islands and many bays that indent its shores. In returning to Ujiji we coasted along the west side of the Tanganyika, as far as the country of the Wasansi,[10] whom we had to leave on no amicable terms, owing to their hostility to Arabs, and arrived at Ujiji on the 18th of December,[11] having been absent twenty-eight days.

Though the Rusizi River can no longer be a subject of curiosity to geographers—and we are certain that there is no connection between the Tanganyika and Baker's Lake, or the Albert N'yanza—it is not yet certain that there is no connection between the Tanganyika and the Nile River. The western coast has not all been explored; and there is reason to suppose that a river runs out of the Tanganyika through the deep caverns of Kabogo Mountain, far under ground and out on the western side of Kabogo into the Lualaba, or the Nile. Livingstone has seen the river about forty miles or so west of Kabogo (about forty yards broad at that place), but he does not know that it runs out of the mountain. This is one of the many things which he has yet to examine.[12]

7

Bunder Ujiji, on Lake Tanganyika
December 26, 1871 [1]

The goal was won. *Finis coronat opus.* I might here stop very well —for Livingstone was found—only the HERALD I know will not be satisfied with one story, so I will sit down to another; a story so inter-

8. The ruler of Uvira. *HIFL*, 507.
9. Mwezi IV Kissabo (*c.* 1860–1908). For his reign, Bourgeois, *Banyarwanda et Burundi*, I, 196–200; Louis, *Ruanda-Urundi*, 114–30; Vansina, "Notes sur l'Histoire du Burundi," 3–7.
10. The territory on the Lake Tanganyika coast south of Uvira. An English visitor later gave them a reputation for "morose hospitality." Hore, "Twelve Tribes of Tanganyika," 13. See also *Près des Grands Lacs* (anon.), 57ff.; Vansina, *Introduction à l'Ethnographie du Congo*, chap. 7.
11. Dec. 12, in *HIFL*, 514.
12. See *LLJ*, II, 154, and the map accompanying the volume.
1. *NYH*, Aug. 15, 1872. There is some duplication in this despatch and Stanley's despatch of Nov. 10, 1871, given above. The letters should be read jointly. See Introduction, note 119.

esting, because he, the great traveller, the hero Livingstone, tells most of it himself.

We were met at last. The HERALD's special correspondent had seen Dr. Livingstone, whom more than three-fourths of all who had ever heard of him believed to be dead. Yet at noon on the 10th of November of this year I first shook hands with him, and said to him, "Doctor, I thank God I have been permitted to shake hands with you." I said it all very soberly and with due dignity, because there were so many Arabs about us, and the circumstances under which I appeared did not warrant me to do anything else. I was as much a stranger to Livingstone as I was to any Arab there. And, if Arabs do not like to see any irregularity, indeed I think that Englishmen must be placed in the same category.

But what does all this preface and what may this prolixity mean? Well, it means this, that I looked upon Livingstone as an Englishman, and I feared that if I showed any unusual joy at meeting with him he might conduct himself very much like another Englishman did once whom I met in the interior of another foreign and strange land wherein we two were the only English-speaking people to be found within the area of two hundred miles square, and who, upon my greeting him with a cordial "Good morning," would not answer me, but screwed on a large eye-glass in a manner which must have been as painful to him as it was to me, and then deliberately viewed my horse and myself for the space of about thirty seconds, and passed on his way with as much *insouciance* as if he had seen me a thousand times and there was nothing at all in the meeting to justify him coming out of that shell of imperturbability with which he had covered himself.[2]

Besides, I had heard all sorts of things from a quondam companion[3] of his about him. He was eccentric, I was told; nay, almost a misanthrope, who hated the sight of Europeans; who, if Burton, Speke, Grant or anybody of that kind were coming to see him, would make haste to put as many miles as possible between himself and such a person. He was a man also whom no one could get along with —it was almost impossible to please him; he was a man who kept no journal, whose discoveries would certainly perish with him unless he himself came back. This was the man I was shaking hands with whom I had done my utmost to surprise, lest he should run away.

2. Compare with Hird, *Stanley*, 88–90.
3. John Kirk. This hostile feeling and the subsequent quarrel between Stanley and Kirk are discussed in Coupland, *Livingstone's Last Journey* and Anstruther, *I Presume*. See also Bennett, "Stanley and the American Consuls at Zanzibar," 43-44.

Consequently you may know why I did not dare manifest any extraordinary joy upon my success. But, really, had there been no one present—none of those cynical-minded Arabs I mean—I think I should have betrayed the emotions which possessed me, instead of which I only said, "Doctor, I thank God I have been permitted to shake hands with you." Which he returned with a grateful and welcome smile.

Together we turned our faces towards his tembe. He pointed to the veranda of his house, which was an unrailed platform, built of mud, covered by wide overhanging eaves. He pointed to his own particular seat, on a carpet of goatskins spread over a thick mat of palm leaf. I protested against taking this seat, but he insisted, and I yielded. We were seated, the Doctor and I, with our backs to the wall, the Arabs to our right and left and in front, the natives forming a dark perspective beyond. Then began conversation; I forget what about; possibly about the road I took from Unyanyembe, but I am not sure. I know the Doctor was talking, and I was answering mechanically. I was conning the indomitable, energetic, patient and persevering traveller, at whose side I now sat in central Africa. Every hair of his head and beard, every line and wrinkle of his face, the wan face, the fatigued form, were all imparting the intelligence to me which so many men so much desired. It was deeply interesting intelligence and unvarnished truths these mute but certain witnesses gave. They told me of the real nature of the work in which he was engaged. Then his lips began to give me the details—lips that cannot lie. I could not repeat what he said. He had so much to say that he began at the end, seemingly oblivious of the fact that nearly six years had to be accounted for. But the story came out bit by bit, unreservedly—as unreservedly as if he was conversing with Sir R. Murchison, his true friend and best on earth. The man's heart was gushing out, not in hurried sentences, in rapid utterances, in quick relation—but in still and deep words.

His quondam companion must have been a sad student of human nature or a most malicious person—a man whose judgment was distorted by an oblique glance at his own inner image, and was thus rendered incapable of knowing the great heart of Livingstone—for after several weeks' life with him in the same tent and in the same hut I am utterly unable to perceive what angle of Livingstone's nature that gentleman took to base a judgment upon. A happier companion, a truer friend than the traveller thus slandered I could not wish for. He was always polite—with a politeness of the genuine kind —and this politeness never forsook him for an instant, even in the midst of the most rugged scenes and greatest difficulties.

Upon my first introduction to him Livingstone was to me like a huge tome, with a most unpretending binding. Within the book might contain much valuable lore and wisdom, but its exterior gave no promise of what was within. Thus outside Livingstone gave no token —except of being rudely dealt with by the wilderness—of what element of power or talent lay within. He is a man of unpretending appearance enough, has quiet, composed features, from which the freshness of youth has quite departed, but which retains the mobility of prime age just enough to show that there yet lives much endurance and vigor within his frame. The eyes, which are hazel, are remarkably bright, not dimmed in the least, though the whiskers and mustache are very gray. The hair, originally brown, is streaked here and there with gray over the temples, otherwise it might belong to a man of thirty. The teeth above show indications of being worn out. The hard fare of Londa and Manyema have made havoc in their ranks. His form is stoutish, a little over the ordinary in height, with slightly bowed shoulders. When walking he has the heavy step of an overworked and fatigued man. On his head he wears the naval cap, with a round vizor with which he has been identified throughout Africa. His dress shows that at times he has had to resort to the needle to repair and replace what travel has worn. Such is Livingstone externally.

Of the inner man much more may be said than of the outer. As he reveals himself, bit by bit, to the stranger, a great many favorable points present themselves, any of which taken singly might well dispose you toward him. I had brought him a packet of letters, and though I urged him again and again to defer conversation with me until he had read the news from home and children, he said he would defer reading until night; for the time he would enjoy being astonished by the European and any general world news I could communicate. He had acquired the art of being patient long ago, he said, and he had waited so long for letters that he could well afford to wait a few hours more. So we sat and talked on that humble veranda of one of the poorest houses in Ujiji. Talked quite oblivious of the large concourse of Arabs, Wanguana and Wajiji, who had crowded around to see the new comer.

There was much to talk about on both sides. On his side he had to tell me what had happened to him, of where he had been, and of what he had seen during the five years the world believed him to be dead. On my side I had to tell him very old, old news, of the Suez Canal and the royal extravagance of Ismail Pacha; of the termination of the Cretan insurrection; of the Spanish revolution; of the flight of Isabella; of the new King, Amadeus, and of the assassination of

Prim; of the completion of the Pacific Railroad across the American Continent; of the election of General Grant as President; of the French and Prussian war; of the capture of Napoleon, the flight of Eugénie and of the complete humiliation of France. Scores of eminent persons—some personal friends of his—had died. So that the news had a deep interest to him, and I had a most attentive auditor.

By and by the Arabs retired, understanding well the position, though they were also anxious to hear from me about Mirambo, but I sent my head men with them to give them such news as they wanted.

The hours of that afternoon passed most pleasantly—few afternoons of my life more so. It seemed to me as if I had met an old, old friend. There was a friendly or good-natured *abandon* about Livingstone which was not lost on me. As host, welcoming one who spoke his language, he did his duties with a spirit and style I have never seen elsewhere. He had not much to offer, to be sure, but what he had was mine and his. The wan features which I had thought shocked me at first meeting, the heavy step which told of age and hard travel, the gray beard and stooping shoulders belied the man. Underneath that aged and well spent exterior lay an endless fund of high spirits, which now and then broke out in peals of hearty laughter—the rugged frame enclosed a very young and exuberant soul. The meal—I am not sure but what we ate three meals that afternoon— was seasoned with innumerable jokes and pleasant anecdotes, interesting hunting stories, of which his friends Webb,[4] Oswell,[5] Vardon[6] and Cumming (Gordon Cumming) [7] were always the chief actors.

"You have brought me new life," he said several times, so that I was not sure but that there was some little hysteria in this joviality and abundant animal spirits, but as I found it continued during sev-

4. William F. Webb (1829–1899) had been a companion of Livingstone in southern Africa. Livingstone wrote the account of his Zambezi expedition while staying at his estate in 1864. Fraser, *Livingstone and Newstead; GJ* 13 (1899), 440.

5. William C. Oswell (1818–1893) had accompanied Livingstone on some of his southern African explorations. Oswell, *William Cotton Oswell.* For Oswell's modesty concerning his role in these explorations, Lacy, "A Century of Exploration in South Africa," 221–22.

6. Frank Vardon of the Indian army had been a companion of Oswell in southern Africa. During 1846–1847 they hunted along the Limpopo River where they encountered the tsetse fly. Vardon brought the first specimens back to Britain. Schapera, *Livingstone's Private Journals 1851–1853,* 64; Johnston, *Livingstone and the Exploration of Central Africa,* 47, 107.

7. R. Gordon Cumming (1820–1866), the hunter, had met Livingstone during his travels in southern Africa in the late 1840's. Schapera, *Livingstone's Missionary Correspondence 1841–1856,* 114.

eral weeks I am now disposed to think it natural. Another thing which specially attracted my attention was his wonderfully retentive memory. When we remember the thirty years and more he has spent in Africa, deprived of books, we may well think it an uncommon memory that can recite whole poems of Burns, Byron, Tennyson and Longfellow. Even the poets Whittier and Lowell were far better known to him than to me. He knew an endless number of facts and names of persons connected with America much better than I, though it was my peculiar province as a journalist to have known them. One reason, perhaps, for this fact may be that the Doctor never smokes, so that his brain is never befogged, even temporarily, by the fumes of the insidious weed. Besides, he has lived all his life almost, we may say, within himself—in a world of thought which revolved inwardly, seldom awaking out of it except to attend to the immediate practical necessities of himself and his expedition. The immediate necessities disposed of, he must have relapsed into his own inner world, into which he must have conjured memories of his home, relations, friends, acquaintances, familiar readings, ideas and associations, so that wherever he might be, or by whatsoever he was surrounded, his own world had attractions far superior to that which the external world by which he was surrounded had.

Dr. Livingstone is a truly pious man—a man deeply imbued with real religious instincts. The study of the man would not be complete if we did not take the religious side of his character into consideration. His religion, any more than his business, is not of the theoretical kind—simply contenting itself with avowing its peculiar creed and ignoring all other religions as wrong or weak. It is of the true, practical kind, never losing a chance to manifest itself in a quiet, practical way—never demonstrative or loud. It is always at work, if not in deed, by shining example. It is not aggressive, which sometimes is troublesome and often impertinent. In him religion exhibits its loveliest features. It governs his conduct towards his servants, towards the natives and towards the bigoted Mussulmans—even all who come in contact with him. Without religion Livingstone, with his ardent temperament, his enthusiastic nature, his high spirit and courage, might have been an uncompanionable man and a hard master. Religion has tamed all these characteristics; nay, if he was ever possessed of them, they have been thoroughly eradicated. Whatever was crude or wilful religion has refined, and made him, to speak the earnest, sober truth, the most agreeable of companions and indulgent of masters.

I have been frequently ashamed of my impatience while listening to his mild rebuke to a dishonest or lazy servant, whereas had he been of mine his dishonesty or laziness had surely been visited with prompt punishment. I have often heard our servants discuss our respective merits. "Your master," say my servants to those of Livingstone, "is a good man—a very good man. He does not beat you, for he has a kind heart; but ours—oh! he is sharp, hot as fire—*mkali sana-kana moto.*" From being hated and thwarted in every possible way by the Arabs and half castes upon first arrival in Ujiji, through his uniform kindness and mild, pleasant temper he has now won all hearts. I perceived that universal respect was paid to him by all.

Every Sunday morning he gathers his little flock around him and has prayers read, not in the stereotyped tone of an English High Church clergyman, which always sounds in my ears insincerely, but in the tone recommended by Archbishop Whately[8]—viz., natural, unaffected and sincere. Following them he delivers a short address in the Kisawahili language about what he has been reading from the Bible to them, which is listened to with great attention.

There is another point in Livingstone's character about which we, as readers of his books and students of his travels, would naturally wish to know something—viz., his ability to withstand the rigors of an African climate, and the consistent energy with which he follows the exploration of Central Africa. Those who may have read Burton's *Lake Regions of Central Africa* cannot have failed to perceive that Captain Burton, the author, was very well tired of Africa long before he reached Ujiji, and that when he had reached Ujiji he was too much worn out to be able to go any farther, or do anything but proceed by boat to Uvira, near the northern head of the Tanganyika —a task he performed, we must admit, in no enviable humor. We also know how Speke looked and felt when Baker met him at Gondokoro; how, after merely glancing at the outflow of Lake Victoria into the Victoria Nile, he was unable or indisposed to go a little farther west to discover the lake which has made Baker famous and given him a knighthood. Also, do we not all know the account of Baker's discovery of that lake, and what resolutions he made after his return to civilization from his visit to the Albert Lake? [9]

When I first met the Doctor I asked him if he did not feel a desire to visit his country and take a little rest. He had then been absent about six years, and the answer he gave me freely shows what kind

8. Richard Whately (1783–1863), the often controversial Archbishop of Dublin. *DNB*, LX, 423–29.

9. In *HIFL*, 435, Stanley omits these critical statements about Burton, Speke, and Baker.

of man he is, and how differently constituted he is from Burton, Speke or Baker. Said he: "I would like very much to go home and see my children once again, but I cannot bring my heart to abandon the task I have undertaken when it is so nearly completed. It only requires six or seven months more to trace the true source that I have discovered with Petherick's branch of the White Nile, or with the Albert Nyanza of Sir Samuel Baker.[10] Why should I go before my task is ended, to have to come back again to do what I can very well do now?"

"And why," I asked, "did you come so far back without finishing the short task which you say you have yet to do?"

"Simply because I was forced; my men would not budge a step forward. They mutinied and formed a secret resolution that if I still insisted on going on to raise a disturbance in the country, and after they had effected it to abandon me, in which case I should be killed. It was dangerous to go any farther. I had explored six hundred miles of the watershed, had traced all the principal streams which discharged their waters into the central line of drainage, and when about starting to explore the last one hundred miles the hearts of my people failed, and they set about frustrating me in every possible way. Now, having returned seven hundred miles to get a new supply of stores and another escort, I find myself destitute of even the means to live but for a few weeks, and sick in mind and body."

Let any reader study the spirit of the above remark, and compare it with those which animated a Burton, a Speke or a Baker. How would those gentlemen have comported themselves in such a crisis, unprepared, as we all know they were, for the terrible fevers of Central Africa?

Again, about a week after I had arrived in Ujiji, I asked Livingstone if he had examined the northern head of the Tanganyika. He answered immediately he had not, and then asked if people expected he had. I then informed him that great curiosity was felt about the connection that was supposed to exist between the Tanganyika and Lake Albert. One party said that a river flowed out of the Tanganyika into the Albert; another party held that it was impossible, since the Tanganyika was, according to Burton and Speke, much lower than the Albert. Others were inclined to let the subject alone until they should hear from him, the only one capable at the present time to set the matter at rest forever.

The Doctor replied to these remarks that he was not aware so

10. See documents 4, note 28, and 15, note 23.

much importance was attached to the Tanganyika, as his friends at home, instead of writing to him, contented themselves with speculating as to where he should come out of Africa, and thus he had been kept ignorant of many things of which those who took any interest in him should have informed him.

"I did try before setting out for Manyema to engage canoes and proceed northward, but I soon saw that the people were all confederating to fleece me as they had Burton, and had I gone under such circumstances I should not have been able to proceed to Manyema to explore the central line of drainage, and of course the most important line—far more important than the line of the Tanganyika; for whatever connection there may be between the Tanganyika and the Albert the true sources of the Nile are those emptying into the central line of drainage. In my own mind I have not the least doubt that the Rusizi River flows from this lake into the Albert. For three months steadily I observed a current setting northward. I verified it by means of water plants.

"When Speke gives the altitude of the Tanganyika at only 1,880 feet above the sea I imagine he must have fallen into the error by frequently writing the Anno Domini, and thus made a slip of the pen; for the altitude is over two thousand eight hundred feet by boiling point, though I make it a little over three thousand feet by barometers.[11] Thus you see that there are no very great natural difficulties on the score of altitude, and nothing to prevent the reasonable supposition that there may be a water connection by means of the Rusizi or some other river between the two lakes. Besides, the Arabs here are divided in their statements. Some swear that the river goes out of the Tanganyika, others that it flows into the Tanganyika."

"Well, Doctor," said I, "if I were you, before leaving this part of the country for Unyanyembe, perhaps never to return here—for one knows not what may occur in the meantime—I would go up and see, and if you like I will accompany you. You say you have no cloth and only five men. I have enough cloth and men for all your purposes. Suppose you go up and settle this vexed question, for so far as I see by the newspapers everybody expects it of you."[12]

Many a traveller, as I have shown, would have pleaded fatigue and utter weariness of mind and body, but Livingstone did not. That very instant the resolve was made; that very instant he started to execute it. He sent a man to Said Ben Majid to request the loan of his canoe, and his baggage was got ready for the voyage. Not yet

11. Speke gave the altitude as 1,840 feet. Speke, "The Upper Basin of the Nile, from Inspection and Information," 323. The actual altitude is 2,534 feet.
12. Compare with Hird, *Stanley*, 95–97.

recovered from the sore effects of his return from his unsuccessful and lengthy journey to accomplish the object that lay so near his heart; yet suffering from an attack of diarrhoea and the consequent weakness it induced, the brave spirit was up again, eager as a high-spirited boy, for the path of duty pointed out.

The above is but a slight sketch of the main points in the great traveller's character, whose personal story I am about to relate. It was necessary that the reader should know what sort of man this Dr. Livingstone was, after whom the NEW YORK HERALD thought proper to despatch a special correspondent, with an expedition, at no matter what cost.[13] After this study of him I cannot better sum up his character than by using the words of one of my own men: "He is a good man, an extremely good and kind man." Is it not true, then, that his quondam companion did not know the nature of the man with whom he lived and travelled, who said that Livingstone would run away from any other white man who would come after him; and, is it likely that the intellect of the facetious gentleman who stated his belief that "Livingstone had married an African princess, and had settled down for good," [14] could fathom the single-minded traveller and upright man, David Livingstone?

Dr. David Livingstone left the island of Zanzibar in March, 1866. On the 7th of the following month he departed from Mikindini Bay for the interior, with an expedition consisting of twelve Sepoys from Bombay, nine men from Johanna, of the Comoro Isles, seven liberated slaves and two Zambezi men (taking them as an experiment), six camels, three buffaloes, two mules and three donkeys. He thus had thirty men, twelve of whom—viz., the Sepoys—were to act as guards for the expedition. They were mostly armed with the Enfield rifles presented to the Doctor by the Bombay government. The baggage of the expedition consisted of ten bales of cloth and two bags of beads, which were to serve as currency by which they would be enabled to purchase the necessaries of life in the countries the Doctor intended to visit. Besides the cumbrous moneys they carried several boxes of instruments, such as chronometers, air thermometers, sextant and artificial horizon, boxes containing clothes, medicines and personal necessaries.[15]

The expedition travelled up the left bank of the Rovuma River, a

13. Anstruther, *I Presume*, 197, gives the cost as £9,000. See document 1, note 7.

14. Stanley later attributed the "wife" story to Burton. Stanley, "Twenty-Five Years' Progress in Equatorial Africa," 472. John Kirk, the "quondam companion," it might be noted, had a reputation with some in Zanzibar for telling "what Americans call tall tales." Tozer to Steere, Sept. 30, 1869, A.1.I, UMCA.

15. See Letroye, "Traces des itinéraires des premiers explorateurs en Afrique centrale," for the instruments and necessary skills of African explorers.

route as full of difficulties as any that could be chosen. For miles Livingstone and his party had to cut their way with their axes through the dense and almost impenetrable jungles which lined the river's banks. The road was a mere footpath, leading, in the most erratic fashion, in and through the dense vegetation, seeking the easiest outlet from it without any regard to the course it ran. The pagazis were able to proceed easily enough, but the camels, on account of their enormous height, could not advance a step without the axes of the party first clearing the way. These tools of foresters were almost always required, but the advance of the expedition was often retarded by the unwillingness of the Sepoys and Johanna men to work.

Soon after the departure of the expedition from the coast the murmurings and complaints of these men began, and upon every occasion and at every opportunity they evinced a decided hostility to an advance. In order to prevent the progress of the Doctor, in hopes that it would compel him to return to the coast, these men so cruelly treated the animals that before long there was not one left alive. Failing in this they set about instigating the natives against the white man, whom they accused most wantonly of strange practices. As this plan was most likely to succeed, and as it was dangerous to have such men with him, the Doctor arrived at the conclusion that it was best to discharge them and accordingly sent the Sepoys back to the coast, but not without having first furnished them with the means of subsistence on their journey to the coast. These men were such a disreputable set that the natives talked of them as the Doctor's slaves. One of the worst sins was their custom to give their guns and ammunition to carry to the first woman or boy they met, whom they impressed for that purpose by either threats or promises which they were totally unable to perform and unwarranted in making. An hour's march was sufficient to fatigue them, after which they lay down on the road to bewail their hard fate and concoct new schemes to frustrate their leader's purposes. Towards night they generally made their appearance at the camping ground with the looks of half dead men. Such men naturally made but a poor escort, for had the party been attacked by a wandering tribe of natives of any strength the Doctor could have made no defence, and no other alternative would be left to him but to surrender and be ruined. The Doctor and his little party arrived on the 18th July, 1866, at a village belonging to a chief of the Mahiyaw, situated eight days' march south of the Rovuma and overlooking the watershed of the Lake Nyassa. The territory lying between the Rovuma River and this Mahiyaw chieftain was an uninhabited wilderness, during the transit of which Livingstone and the expedition suffered considerably from hunger and desertion of men.

Early in August, 1866, the Doctor came to Mponda's country, a chief who dwelt near the Lake Nyassa. On the road thither two of the liberated slaves deserted him. Here, also, Wakotani (not Wiko-tani) a *protégé* of the Doctor, insisted upon his discharge, alleging as an excuse, which the Doctor subsequently found to be untrue, that he had found his brother. He further stated that his family lived on the east side of the Nyassa Lake. He further said that Mponda's favorite wife was his sister. Perceiving that Wakotani was unwilling to go with him further the Doctor took him to Mponda, who now saw and heard of him for the first time, and, having furnished the ungrateful boy with enough cloth and beads to keep him until his "big brother" should call for him, left him with the chief, after first assuring himself that he would have honorable treatment from that chief. The Doctor also gave Wakotani writing paper (as he could read and write, being some of the accomplishments acquired at Bombay, where he had been put to school) that should he at any time feel so disposed he might write to Mr. Horace Waller or to himself. The Doctor further enjoined on him not to join any slave raid usually made by his countrymen, the men of Nyassa, on their neighbors. Upon finding that his application for a discharge was successful, Wakotani endeavored to induce Chumah, another *protégé* of the Doctor's, and a companion or chum of Wakotani, to leave the Doctor's service and proceed with them, promising as a bribe a wife and plenty of pombe from his "big brother." Chumah, upon referring the matter to the Doctor, was advised not to go, as he (the Doctor) strongly suspected that Wakotani wanted only to make him his slave. Chumah wisely withdrew from his tempter.

From Mponda's the Doctor proceeded to the heel of the Nyassa, to the village of a Babisa chief, who required medicine for a skin disease. With his usual kindness he stayed at this chief's village to treat his malady. While here a half-caste Arab arrived from the western shore of the lake, who reported that he had been plundered by a band of Ma-Zitu at a place the Doctor and Musa, chief of the Johanna men, were very well aware was at least a hundred and fifty miles north-northwest of where they were then stopping. Musa, however, for his own reasons—which will appear presently—eagerly listened to the Arab's tale, and gave full credence to it. Having well digested its horrifying contents, he came to the Doctor to give him the full benefit of what he had heard with such willing ears. The traveller patiently listened to the narrative—which lost none of its portentous significance through his relation, such as he believed it bore for himself and master—and then asked Musa if he believed it.

"Yes," answered Musa, readily; "he tell me true, true. I ask him good, and he tell me true, true."

The Doctor, however, said he did not believe it, for the Ma-Zitu would not have been satisfied with simply plundering a man; they would have murdered him; but suggested, in order to allay the fears of his Moslem subordinate, that they should both proceed to the chief with whom they were staying, who, being a sensible man, would be able to advise them as to the probability or improbability of the tale being correct. Together they proceeded to the Babisa chief, who, when he had heard the Arab's story, unhesitatingly denounced the Arab as a liar and his story without the least foundation in fact, giving as a reason that if the Ma-Zitu had been lately in that vicinity he would have heard of it soon enough. But Musa broke out with "No, no, Doctor; no, no, no. I no want to go to Ma-Zitu. I no want Ma-Zitu to kill me. I want see my father, my mother, my child in Johanna. I no want Ma-Zitu kill me." *Ipsissima verba*. These are Musa's words.

To which the Doctor replied, "I don't want Ma-Zitu to kill me either; but, as you are afraid of them, I promise to go straight west until we get far past the beat of the Ma-Zitu."

Musa was not satisfied, but kept moaning and sorrowing, saying, "If we had 200 guns with us I would go, but our small party they will attack by night and kill all."

The Doctor repeated his promise, "But I will not go near them; I will go west."

As soon as he turned his face westward Musa and the Johanna men ran away in a body. The Doctor says, in commenting upon Musa's conduct, that he felt strongly tempted to shoot Musa and another ringleader, but was nevertheless glad that he did not soil his hands with their vile blood. A day or two afterwards another of his men—Simon Price[16] by name—came to the Doctor with the same tale about the Ma-Zitu, but, compelled by the scant number of his people to repress all such tendencies to desertion and faint-heartedness, the Doctor "shut him up" at once and forbade him to utter the name of the Ma-Zitu any more. Had the natives not assisted him he must have despaired of ever being able to penetrate the wild and unexplored interior which he was now about to tread.

"Fortunately," as the Doctor says with unction, "I was in a country

16. One of the Africans from Nasik; he left Livingstone in June 1870 and joined an Arab group. Thomas, "The Death of Dr. Livingstone: Cyrus Farrar's Narrative," 126.

now, after leaving the shores of the Nyassa, where the feet of the
slave trader had not trodden. It was a new and virgin land, and of
course, as I have always found it in such cases, the natives were
really good and hospitable, and for very small portions of cloth my
baggage was conveyed from village to village by them." In many
other ways the traveller in his extremity was kindly treated by the
undefiled and unspoiled natives.

On leaving this hospitable region in the early part of December,
1866, the Doctor entered a country where the Mazitu had exercised
their customary spoilating propensities. The land was swept clean of
all provisions and cattle, and the people had emigrated to other countries beyond the bounds of these ferocious plunderers. Again the expedition was besieged by famine and was reduced to great extremity.
To satisfy the pinching hunger it suffered it had recourse to the wild
fruits which some parts of the country furnished. At intervals the
condition of the hard-pressed band was made worse by the heartless
desertion of some of its members, who more than once departed with
the Doctor's personal kit—changes of clothes and linen, &c. With
more or less misfortunes constantly dogging his footsteps, he traversed in safety the countries of the Babisa, Bobemba, Barungu, Bau-
lungu and Londa.

In the country of Londa lives the famous Cazembe—made known
to Europeans first by Dr. Lacerda,[17] the Portuguese traveller. Cazembe is a most intelligent prince; is a tall, stalwart man, who wears
a peculiar kind of dress, made of crimson print, in the form of a
prodigious kilt. The mode of arranging it is most ludicrous. All the
folds of this enormous kilt are massed in front, which causes him
to look as if the peculiarities of the human body were reversed in his
case. The abdominal parts are thus covered with a balloon-like
expansion of cloth, while the lumbar region, which is by us jealously
clothed, with him is only half draped by a narrow curtain which by
no means suffices to obscure its naturally fine proportions.[18] In this
State dress King Cazembe received Dr. Livingstone, surrounded by
his chiefs and body guards. A chief, who had been deputed by the
King and elders to find out all about the white man, then stood up
before the assembly and in a loud voice gave the result of the inquiry
he had instituted. He had heard the white man had come to look for
waters, for rivers and seas. Though he did not understand what the

17. Francisco J. M. de Lacerda e Almeida (c. 1750–1798), Brazilian scholar
and explorer, who died in 1798 while on an expedition in the Kazembe's territory. Cunnison, "Kazembe and the Portuguese, 1798–1832," 61–70; Duffy, Portuguese Africa, 190–91.
18. The three preceding sentences are omitted from HIFL, 444.

white man could want with such things he had no doubt that the object was good. Then Cazembe asked what the Doctor proposed doing and where he thought of going. The Doctor replied that he had thought of going south, as he had heard of lakes and rivers being in that direction. Cazembe asked: "What can you want to go there for? The water is close here. There is plenty of large water in this neighborhood." Before breaking up the assembly Cazembe gave orders to let the white man go where he would through his country undisturbed and unmolested. He was the first Englishman he had seen, he said, and he liked him.

Shortly after his introduction to the King the Queen entered the large house surrounded by a body guard of Amazons armed with spears. She was a fine, tall, handsome young woman, and evidently thought she was about to make a great impression upon the rustic white man, for she had clothed herself after a most royal fashion, and was armed with a ponderous spear. But her appearance, so different from what the Doctor had imagined, caused him to laugh, which entirely spoiled the effect intended, for the laugh of the Doctor was so contagious that she herself was the first who imitated, and the Amazons, courtier-like, followed suit. Much disconcerted by this, the Queen ran back, followed by her obedient damsels—a retreat most undignified and unqueenlike compared to her majestic advent into the Doctor's presence. But Livingstone will have much to say about his reception at this Court and about this interesting King and Queen; and who can so well relate the scenes he witnessed, and which belong exclusively to him as he himself?

Soon after his arrival in the country of Londa, or Lunda, and before he had entered the district of Cazembe, he had crossed a river called the Chambezi, which was quite an important stream. The similarity of the name with that large and noble river south, which will be forever connected with his name, misled Livingstone at that time, and he accordingly did not pay it the attention it deserved, believing that the Chambezi was but the headwaters of the Zambezi, and consequently had no bearing or connection with the sources of the river of Egypt, of which he was in search. His fault was in relying too implicitly upon the correctness of Portuguese information. This error cost him many months of tedious labor and travel. From the beginning of 1867—the time of his arrival at Cazembe—to the middle of March, 1869—the time of his arrival in Ujiji—he was mostly engaged in correcting the errors and corruptions of the Portuguese travellers. The Portuguese, in speaking of the River Chambezi, invariably spoke of it as "our own Zambezi"—that is, the Zambezi which flows through the Portuguese possessions of the Mozambique. "In going to Cazembis from Nyassa," said they, "you will cross our own Zambezi." Such positive and reiterated information like this not only orally, but in their books and maps was naturally confusing. When the Doctor perceived that what he saw and what they described was at variance, out of a sincere wish to be correct, and, lest he might have been mistaken himself, he started to retravel the ground he had travelled before; over and over again he traversed the several countries watered by the several rivers of the complicated water system like an uneasy spirit; over and over again he asked the same questions from the different peoples he met until he was obliged to desist, lest they might say, "The man is mad; he has got water on the brain."

But these travels and tedious labors of his in Londa and the adjacent countries have established beyond doubt first, that the Chambezi is a totally distinct river from the Zambezi of the Portuguese, and secondly, that the Chambezi, starting from about latitude eleven degrees south, is none other than the most southerly feeder of the great Nile, thus giving this famous river a length of over two thousand six hundred miles of direct latitude, making it second to the Mississippi, the longest river in the world.[19] The real and true name of the Zambezi is Dombazi. When Lacerda and his Portuguese successors came to Cazembe, crossed the Chambezi and heard its name, they very naturally set it down as "our own Zambezi," and without further inquiry sketched it as running in that direction.

During his researches in that region, so pregnant in discoveries, Livingstone came to a lake lying northeast of Cazembe, which the natives called Liemba, from the country of that name, which bordered it on the east and south. In tracing the lake north he found it to be none other than the Tanganyika, or the southeastern extremity of it, which looks on the Doctor's map very much like an outline of Italy. The latitude of the southern end of this great body of water is about nine degrees south, which gives it thus a length, from north to south, of 360 geographical miles.[20]

From the southern extremity of the Tanganyika he crossed Marungu and came in sight of Lake Moero. Tracing this lake, which is about sixty miles in length, to its southern head, he found a river called the Luapula entering it from that direction. Following the Lua-

19. The Nile, even without this mistaken extension to the south, is 4,160 miles long, measured from its remotest source. It is certainly the second longest river in the world, and perhaps even the first. Hurst, The Nile, 4–5.

20. See document 4, note 23.

pula south he found it issue from the large lake of Bangweolo, which is as large in superficial area as the Tanganyika.[21] In exploring for the waters which emptied into the lake he found by far the most important of these feeders was the Chambezi. So that he had thus traced the Chambezi from its source to Lake Bangweolo, and issue from its northern head under the name of Luapula, and found it entered Lake Moero. Again he returned to Cazembis, well satisfied that the river running north through three degrees of latitude could not be the river running south under the name of the Zambezi, though there might be a remarkable resemblance in their names.

At Cazembis he found an old white-bearded half-caste named Mohammed ben Salih,[22] who was kept as a kind of prisoner at large by the King because of certain suspicious circumstances attending his advent and stay in his country. Through Livingstone's influence Mohammed ben Salih obtained his release. On the road to Ujiji he had bitter cause to regret having exerted himself in the half-caste's behalf. He turned out to be a most ungrateful wretch, who poisoned the minds of the Doctor's few followers and ingratiated himself in their favor by selling the favors of his concubines to them, thus reducing them to a kind of bondage under him. From the day he had the vile old man in his company manifold and bitter misfortunes followed the Doctor up to his arrival in Ujiji, in March, 1869.

From the date of his arrival until the end of June (1869) he remained in Ujiji, whence he dated those letters which, though the outside world still doubted his being alive, satisfied the minds of the Royal Geographical people and his intimate friends that he was alive, and Musa's tale an ingenious but false fabrication of a cowardly deserter. It was during this time that the thought occurred to him of sailing around the Lake Tanganyika, but the Arabs and natives were so bent upon fleecing him that, had he undertaken it the remainder of his goods would not have enabled him to explore the central line of drainage, the initial point of which he found far south of Cazembis, in about latitude 11 degrees, in the river Chambezi. In the days when tired Captain Burton was resting in Ujiji, after his march from the coast near Zanzibar, the land to which Livingstone, on his departure from Ujiji, bent his steps, was unknown to the Arabs save

21. The area of Lake Tanganyika is 12,700 square miles; that of Lake Bangweulu, 3,800 square miles. Seltzer, ed., *The Columbia Lippincott Gazetteer of the World*, 157, 1,874.

22. Muhammed bin Salih, after the experiences related here, remained in Ujiji as head of the Arab community until his death in the early 1870's. Bennett, "Mwinyi Kheri," 151; Cunnison, "Kazembe and the Arabs to 1870," 228.

by vague report. Messrs. Burton and Speke never heard of it, it seems. Speke, who was the geographer of Burton's expedition, heard of a place called Uruwa, which he placed on his map according to the general direction indicated by the Arabs; but the most enterprising of the Arabs, in their search after ivory, only touched the frontiers of Rua, as the natives and Livingstone called it; for Rua is an immense country, with a length of six degrees of latitude and as yet an undefined breadth from east to west.[23]

At the end of June, 1869, Livingstone took *dhow* at Ujiji and crossed over to Uguhha, on the western shore, for his last and greatest series of explorations, the results of which was the discovery of a series of lakes of great magnitude connected together by a large river called by different names as it left one lake to flow to another.[24] From the port of Uguhha he set off in company with a body of traders, in an almost direct westerly course, through the lake country of Uguhha. Fifteen days march brought them to Bambarre,[25] the first important ivory depot in Manyema, or, as the natives pronounce it Manuyema.

For nearly six months he was detained at Bambarre from ulcers in the feet, with copious discharges of bloody ichor oozing from the sores as soon as he set his feet on the ground. When well, he set off in a northerly direction, and, after several days, came to a broad, lacustrine river, called the Lualaba, flowing northward and westward, and, in some places southward, in a most confusing way. The river was from one to three miles broad. By exceeding pertinacity he contrived to follow its erratic course until he saw the Lualaba enter the narrow but lengthy Lake of Kamolondo, in about latitude 6 deg. 30 min. south. Retracing it south he came to the point where he had seen the Luapula enter Lake Moero.

One feels quite enthusiastic when listening to Livingstone's description of the beauties of Moero scenery. Pent in on all sides by high mountains clothed to their tips with the richest vegetation of the tropics, Moero discharges its superfluous waters through a deep rent in the bosom of the mountains. The impetuous and grand river roars through the chasm with the thunder of a cataract; but soon after leaving its confined and deep bed it expands into the calm and broad Lualaba—expanding over miles of ground, making great bends

23. Burton had collected a few remarks from the Arabs about Urua. Burton, "Lake Regions," 255–56.
24. *HIFL*, 449, mentions only one lake.
25. In the area of the Bangobango. Maes and Boone, *Peuplades du Congo Belge*, 136–37; Vansina, *Introduction à l'Ethnographie du Congo*, chap. 11.

west and southwest, then, curving northward, enters Kamalondo. By the natives it is called the Lualaba, but the Doctor, in order to distinguish it from other rivers of the same name, has given it the name of Webb's River, after Mr. Webb, the wealthy proprietor of Newstead Abbey, whom the Doctor distinguishes as one of his oldest and most consistent friends.[26] Away to the southwest from Kamolondo is another large lake, which discharges its waters by the important river Loki, or Lomani, into the great Lualaba. To this lake, known as Chebungo by the natives, Dr. Livingstone has given the name of Lincoln, to be hereafter distinguished on maps and in books as Lake Lincoln, in memory of Abraham Lincoln, our murdered President. This was done from the vivid impression produced on his mind by hearing a portion of his inauguration speech read from an English pulpit, which related to the causes that induced him to issue his emancipation proclamation, by which memorable deed 4,000,000 of slaves were forever freed. To the memory of the man whose labors in behalf of the negro race deserved the commendation of all good men Livingstone has contributed a monument more durable than brass or stone.

Entering Webb's River from the south-southwest, a little north of Kamolondo, is a large river called the Lufira, but the streams that discharge themselves from the watershed into the Lualaba are so numerous that the Doctor's map would not contain them, so he has left all out except the most important. Continuing his way north, tracing the Lualaba through its manifold and crooked curves as far as latitude four degrees south, he came to another large lake called the Unknown Lake; but here you may come to a dead halt, and read it thus: * * * * * * Here was the furthermost point. From here he was compelled to return on the weary road to Ujiji, a distance of 600 miles.[27]

In this brief sketch of Doctor Livingstone's wonderful travels it is to be hoped that the most superficial reader, as well as the student of geography, comprehends this grand system of lakes connected together by Webb's River. To assist him, let him procure a map of Africa, by Keith Johnston,[28] embracing the latest discoveries. Two degrees south of the Tanganyika, and two degrees west, let him draw

26. William F. Webb.

27. *HIFL*, 451, gives 700 miles.

28. Alexander Keith Johnston (1844–1879), recently described as "one of the most thoroughly trained and active geographers in Britain," died near the East African coast while leading an expedition for the African Exploration Fund. *PRGS* 1 (1879), 598–600; Bridges, "The R. G. S. and the African Exploration Fund, 1876–80," 32.

the outlines of a lake, its greatest length from east to west, and let him call it Bangweolo. One degree or thereabout to the northwest let him sketch the outlines of another but smaller lake and call it Moero; a degree again north of Moero another lake of similar size, and call it Kamolondo, and still a degree north of Kamolondo another lake, large and as yet undefined limits, which, in the absence of any specific term, we will call the Nameless Lake. Then let him connect these several lakes by a river called after different names. Thus, the main feeder of Bangweolo, the Chambezi; the river which issues out of Bangweolo and runs into Moero, the Luapula; the river connecting Moero with Kamolondo, Webb's River; that which runs from Kamolondo into the Nameless Lake northward, the Lualaba; and let him write in bold letters over the rivers Chambezi, Luapula, Webb's River and the Lualaba the "Nile," for these are all one and the same river. Again, west of Moero Lake, about one degree or thereabouts, another large lake may be placed on his map, with a river running diagonally across to meet the Lualaba north of Lake Kamolondo. This new lake is Lake Lincoln, and the river is the Lomami River, the confluence of which with the Lualaba is between Kamolondo and the Nameless Lake. Taken altogether, the reader may be said to have a very fair idea of what Doctor Livingstone has been doing these long years, and what additions he has made to the study of African geography.[29] That this river, distinguished under several titles, flowing from one lake into another in a northerly direction, with all its great crooked bends and sinuosities, is the Nile, the true Nile, the Doctor has not the least doubt. For a long time he did doubt, because of its deep bends and curves—west, and southwest even—but having traced it from its headwaters, the Chambezi, through seven degrees of latitude —that is, from latitude eleven degrees south to a little north of latitude four degrees south—he has been compelled to come to the conclusion that it can be no other river than the Nile. He had thought it was the Congo, but he has discovered the sources of the Congo to be the Kasai and the Quango, two rivers which rise on the western side of the Nile watershed in about the latitude of Bangweolo; and he was told of another river called the Lubilash, which rose from the north and ran west.[30] But the Lualaba the Doctor thinks cannot be the Congo, from its great size and body and from its steady and continual flow northward through a broad and extensive valley,

29. The scheme is given map form in *HIFL*, 449.
30. Livingstone had crossed the Kasai river system during his trans-Africa expedition. Livingstone, *Missionary Travels and Researches in South Africa*, 355, 494–95.

bounded by enormous mountains, westerly and easterly. The altitude
of the most northerly point to which the Doctor traced the wonderful
river was a little over two thousand feet, so that though Baker
makes out his lake to be 2,700 feet above the sea, yet the Bahr Ghazal,
through which Petherick's branch of the White Nile issues into the
Nile, is only a little over two thousand feet, in which case there is a
possibility that the Lualaba may be none other than Petherick's
branch. It is well known that trading stations for ivory have been
established for about five hundred miles up Petherick's branch. We
must remember this fact when told that Gondokoro, in latitude four
degrees north, is 2,000 feet above the sea, and latitude four degrees
south, where the Doctor was halted, is only a little over 2,000 feet
above the sea. That two rivers, said to be 2,000 feet above the sea,
separated from each other by eight degrees of latitude, are the same
stream may, among some men, be regarded as a startling statement.
But we must restrain mere expressions of surprise and take into
consideration that this mighty and broad Lualaba is a lacustrine
river—broader than the Mississippi—and think of our own rivers,
which, though shallow, are exceedingly broad—instance our Platte
River[31] flowing across the prairies of Colorado and Nebraska into
the Missouri. We must wait also until the altitude of the two rivers
—the Lualaba, where the Doctor halted, and the southern point
on the Bahr Ghazal, where Petherick has been—are known with perfect accuracy.

Webb's River, or the Lualaba, from Bangweolo is a lacustrine river,
expanding from one to three miles in breadth. At intervals it forms
extensive lakes, then contracting into a broad river it again forms a
lake, and so on to latitude four degrees north, and beyond this point
the Doctor heard of a large lake again north. Now, for the sake of
argument, suppose we give this nameless lake a length of four degrees of latitude,[32] as it may be the one discovered by Piaggia, the
Italian traveller, from which Petherick's branch of the White Nile
issues out through reeds, marshes and the Bahr Ghazal into the
White Nile south of Gondokoro. By this method we can suppose the
rivers one—for the lakes extending over so many degrees of latitude
would obviate the necessity of explaining the differences of altitude
that must naturally exist between the points of a river eight degrees
of latitude apart. Also, that Livingstone's instruments for observation and taking altitude may have been in error, and this is very
likely to have been the case, subjected as they have been to rough
handling during nearly six years of travel.

31. Stanley knew the Platte from his own experience; see Appendix E.
32. *HIFL*, 453, gives six degrees.

Despite the apparent difficulty about the altitude, there is another strong reason for believing Webb's River, or the Lualaba, to be the Nile. The watershed of this river, 600 miles of which Livingstone has travelled, is drained by a valley which lies north and south between the eastern and western ranges of the watershed. This valley or line of drainage, while it does not receive the Kasai and the Quango, receives rivers flowing from a great distance west—for instance, the important tributaries Lufira and Lomami, and large rivers from the east, such as the Lindi and Luamo; and while the most intelligent Portuguese travellers and traders state that the Kasai, the Quango and Lubilash are the head waters of the Congo river, no one as yet has started the supposition that the grand river flowing north, and known to the natives as the Lualaba, was the Congo. If this river is not the Nile where, then, are the head waters of the Nile? The small river running out of the Victoria Nyanza and the river flowing out of the little lake Albert have not sufficient water to form the great river of Egypt. As you glide down the Nile and note the Asua, the Geraffe, the Sobat, the Blue Nile and Atbara, and follow the river down to Egypt, it cannot fail to impress you that it requires many more streams, or one large river, larger than all yet discovered, to influence its inundations and replace the waste of its flow through a thousand miles of desert. Perhaps a more critical survey of the Bahr Ghazal would prove that the Nile is influenced by the waters that pour through "the small piece of water resembling a duck pond buried in a sea of rushes," as Speke describes the Bahr Ghazal. Livingstone's discovery answers the question and satisfies the intelligent hundreds, who, though Bruce[33] and Speke and Baker, each in his turn had declared he had found the Nile, the only and true Nile sources, yet doubted and hesitated to accept the enthusiastic assertions as a final solution of the Nile problem. Even yet, according to Livingstone, the Nile sources have not been found; though he has traced the Lualaba through seven degrees of latitude flowing north, and though neither he nor I have a particle of doubt of its being the Nile,[34] not yet can the Nile question be said to be resolved and ended. For three reasons:

First—He has heard of the existence of four fountains,[35] two of which give birth to a river flowing north—Webb's River, or the

33. James Bruce (1730–1794). He visited the source of the Blue Nile in 1770. Ullendorf, "James Bruce of Kinnaird"; Beckingham, ed., *Travels to Discover the Source of the Nile by James Bruce,* are two recent accounts of his explorations.

34. In *HIFL*, 454-55, Stanley disassociates himself from this positive statement and leaves its resolution to the further explorations of Livingstone.

35. See document 4, note 29.

Lualaba; two to a river flowing south, which is the Zambezi. He has heard of these fountains repeatedly from the natives. Several times he has been within one hundred and two hundred miles from them, but something always interposed to prevent him going to see them. According to those who have seen them, they rise on either side of a mound or hill which contains no stones. Some have even called it an ant hill. One of these fountains is said to be so large that a man standing on one side cannot be seen from the other. These fountains must be discovered, and their position taken. The Doctor does not suppose them to lie south of the feeders of Lake Bangweolo.

Second—Webb's River must be traced to its connection with some portion of the old Nile.

Third—The connection between the Tanganyika and the Albert Nyanza must be ascertained.[36]

When these three things have been accomplished, then, and not till then, can the mystery of the Nile be explained. The two countries through which this marvellous lacustrine river—the Lualaba—flows, with its manifold lakes and broad expanses of water, are Rua —the Uruwa of Speke—and Manyema. For the first time Europe is made aware that between the Tanganyika and the known sources of the Congo there exist teeming millions of the negro race who never saw or heard of the white peoples who make such noisy and busy stir outside of Africa. Upon the minds of those who had the good fortune to see the first specimen of these remarkable white races Livingstone seems to have made a favorable impression, though, through misunderstanding his object and coupling him with the Arabs who make horrible work there, his life has been sought after more than once.

These two extensive countries, Rua and Manyema, are populated by true heathens—governed not as the sovereignties of Karagwah, Urundi and Uganda by despotic kings, but each village by its own sultan or lord. Thirty miles outside of their own immediate settlements the most intelligent of those small chiefs seem to know nothing. Thirty miles from the Lualaba there were but few people who had ever heard of the great river. Such ignorance among the natives of their own countries, of course, increased the labors of Livingstone. Compared with these all tribes and nations in Africa with whom Livingstone came in contact may be deemed civilized. Yet in the arts of home manufacture these wild people of Manyema are

36. *HIFL*, 459, omits the third reason.

far superior to any he had seen. When other tribes and nations contented themselves with hides and skins of animals thrown negligently over their shoulders the people of Manyema manufactured a cloth from fine grass which may favorably compare with the finest grass cloth of India. They also know the art of dyeing them in various colors—black, yellow, and purple. The Wanguana or freed men of Zanzibar, struck with the beauty of this fine grass fabric, eagerly exchange their cotton cloths for fine grass cloth, and on almost every black man returned from Manyema I have seen this native cloth converted into elegantly made *damirs* (Arabic)—short jackets.

These countries are also very rich in ivory. The fever for going to Manyema to exchange their tawdry beads for the precious tusks of Manyema is of the same kind as that which impelled men to the gulches and placers of California, Colorado, Montana and Idaho; after nuggets to Australia, and diamonds to Cape Colony. Manyema is at present the El Dorado of the Arabs and the Wamrima tribes. It is only about four years since the first Arab returned from Manyema with such wealth of ivory and reports about the fabulous quantities found there that ever since the old beaten tracks of Karagwah, Uganda, Ufipa[37] and Marungu have been comparatively deserted. The people of Manyema, ignorant of the value of the precious article, reared their huts upon ivory stanchions. Ivory pillars and doors were common sights in Manyema, and hearing of these one can no longer wonder at the ivory palace of Solomon. For generations they had used ivory tusks as doorposts and eave stanchions, until they had become perfectly rotten and worthless. But the advent of the Arabs soon taught them the value of the article. It has now risen considerably in price, though yet fabulously cheap. At Zanzibar the value of ivory per frarsilah of thirty-five pounds weight is from fifty dollars to sixty dollars, according to its quality.[38] In Unyanyembe it is about one dollar and ten cents per pound; but in Manyema it may be purchased for from half a cent to one and a quarter cent's worth of copper per pound of ivory.

The Arabs, however, have the knack of spoiling markets by their rapacity and wanton cruelty. With muskets a small party of Arabs are invincible against such people as those of Manyema, who until lately never heard the sound of a gun. The report of a musket inspires mortal terror in them, and it is almost impossible to induce

37. The Fipa occupy the plateau between lakes Tanganyika and Rukwa. Willis, *The Fipa and Related Peoples of South-West Tanzania and North-East Zambia,* 17–32.

38. See the ivory price list in Bennett, *Studies in East African History,* 89.

them to face the muzzle of a gun. They believe that the Arabs have stolen the lightning, and that against such people the bow and arrow can have but little effect. They are by no means devoid of courage, and they have often declared that were it not for the guns not one Arab would leave the country alive, which tends to prove that they would willingly engage in fight with the strangers, who have made themselves so detestable, were it not that the startling explosion of gunpowder inspires them with such terror.

Into whichever country the Arabs enter they contrive to render their name and race abominated. But the mainspring of it all is not the Arab's nature, color or name, but simply the slave trade. So long as the slave trade is permitted to be kept up at Zanzibar so long will these otherwise enterprising people, the Arabs, kindle against them throughout Africa the hatred of the natives. On the main lines of travel from Zanzibar into the interior of Africa none of these acts of cruelty are seen, for the very good reason that they have armed the natives with guns and taught them how to use weapons, which they are by no means loath to do whenever an opportunity presents itself. When too late, when they have perceived their folly in selling guns to the natives, the Arabs repent and begin to vow signal vengeance on the person who will in future sell a gun to a native.[39] But they are all guilty of the same folly, and it is strange they did not perceive that it was folly when they were doing so. In former days the Arab, protected by his slave escort armed with guns, could travel through Useguhha, Urori, Ukonongo, Ufipa, Karagwah, Unyoro and Uganda, with only a stick in his hand; now, however, it is impossible for him or any one else to do so. Every step he takes, armed or unarmed, is fraught with danger. The Waseguhha near the coast halt him, and demand the tribute or give him the option of war; entering Ugogo he is subjected every day to the same oppressive demand, or to the other fearful alternative. The Wanyamwezi also show their readiness to take the same advantage; the road to Karagwah is besieged with difficulties; the terrible Mirambo stands in the way, defeats their combined forces with ease and makes raids even to the doors of their houses in Unyanyembe, and, should they succeed in passing Mirambo, a chief [40] stands before them who demands tribute by the bale, against whom it is useless to contend. These remarks have reference to the slave trade inaugurated in Manyema

39. Some discussion of the arms trade is given in Beachey, "The Arms Trade in East Africa in the Late Nineteenth Century."

40. Rwesarura of Rusubi. *HIFL*, 462, 296; Low, "The Northern Interior," 331.

by the Arabs. Harassed on the road between Zanzibar and Unyanyembe, minatory natives with bloody hands on all sides ready to
avenge the slightest affront, the Arabs have refrained from kidnapping between the Tanganyika and the sea; but in Manyema, where
the natives are timid, irresolute and divided into small, weak tribes,
the Arabs recover their audacity and exercise their kidnapping propensities unchecked. The accounts which the Doctor brings from
that new region are most deplorable.

He was an unwilling spectator of a horrible deed—a massacre
committed on the inhabitants of a populous district—who had assembled in the market place, on the banks of the Lualaba, as they
had been accustomed to for ages. It seems the Wa-Manyema are
very fond of marketing, believing it to be the *summum bonum* of
human enjoyment. They find unceasing pleasure in chaffering with
might and main for the least mite of their currency—the last bead
—and when they gain the point to which their peculiar talents are
devoted they feel intensely happy. The women are excessively fond
of their marketing, and as they are very beautiful, the market place
must possess considerable attractions for the male sex.[41] It was on
such a day, with just such a scene, that Tagomoyo,[42] a half-caste
Arab, with his armed slave escort, commenced an indiscriminate
massacre by firing volley after volley into the dense mass of human
beings. It is supposed that there were about two thousand present,
and at the first sound of the firing these poor people all made a rush
for their canoes. In the fearful hurry to avoid being shot the canoes
were paddled away by the first fortunate few who got possession of
them. Those that were not so fortunate sprang into the deep waters
of the Lualaba, and, though many of them became an easy prey to
the voracious crocodiles that swarmed to the scene, the majority
received their deaths from the bullets of the merciless Tagomoyo
and his villainous band. The Doctor believes, as do the Arabs themselves, that about four hundred people, mostly women and children,
lost their lives, while many more were made slaves. This scene is

41. Livingstone must have passed on his high opinion of the females of
Manyema. See *Autobiography*, 273; LLJ, II, 105–06.
42. Mwinyi Mtagamoyo bin Sultani, or Mwinyi Mohara; he became the
leading Arab of Nyangwe and one of the most powerful of the Arabs of the
Congo. Mwinyi Mohara remained a warrior to the end; he died in battle,
while in his seventies, in 1893 as he led his men against the forces of the
Congo Independent State. Ceulemans, *La Question arabe et le Congo*, 51; "Les
Arabes du Haut Congo," 130; "Les Chefs Arabes du Haut Congo," 18–19; Stuhlmann, *Mit Emin Pascha*, 599.

only one of many such which he has unwillingly witnessed, and he is utterly unable to describe the loathing he feels for the inhuman perpetrators.

Slaves from Manyema command a higher price than those of any other country, because of their fine forms and general docility. The women, the Doctor says repeatedly, are remarkably pretty creatures, and have nothing except their hair in common with the negroids of the West Coast. They are of very light color, have fine noses, well-cut and not over full-lips, and a prognathous jaw is uncommon. These women are eagerly sought after for wives by the half-castes of the East Coast, and even the pure Amani Arabs do not disdain connection with them. To the north of Manyema Livingstone came to a light-complexioned race of the color of Portuguese, or our own Louisiana quadroons, who are very fine people, and singularly remarkable for commercial "cuteness" and sagacity. The women are expert divers for oysters, which are found in great abundance in the Lualaba.

Rua, at a place called Katanga, is rich in copper. The copper mines of this place have been worked for ages. In the bed of a stream gold has been found washed down in pencil-shaped lumps, or particles as large as split peas. Two Arabs have gone thither to prospect for this metal, but as they are ignorant of the art of gulch mining it is scarcely possible that they will succeed.

From these highly important and interesting discoveries Dr. Livingstone was turned back when almost on the threshold of success by the positive refusal of his men to accompany him further. They were afraid to go unless accompanied by a large force of men, and as these were not procurable in Manyema the Doctor reluctantly turned his face toward Ujiji.

It was a long and weary road back. The journey had now no interest for him. He had travelled it before when going westward, full of high hopes and aspirations, impatient to reach the goal which promised him rest from his labors; now returning unsuccessful, baffled and thwarted when almost in sight of the end, and having to travel the same road back on foot, with disappointed expectations and defeated hopes preying on his mind, no wonder that the brave old spirit almost succumbed and the strong constitution almost wrecked. He arrived at Ujiji October 26, almost at death's door. On the way he had been trying to cheer himself up, since he had found it impossible to contend against the obstinacy of his men, with "it won't take long, five or six months more; it matters not, since it can't be helped. I have got my goods in Ujiji and can hire other people and make a new start." These are the words and hopes with which he tried to delude himself into the idea that all would be right yet; but imagine, if you can, the shock he must have suffered when he found that the man to whom was entrusted his goods for safe keeping had sold every bale for ivory.

The evening of the day Livingstone had returned to Ujiji Susi and Chuma, two of his most faithful men, were seen crying bitterly. The Doctor asked them what ailed them, and was then informed for the first time of the evil tidings that awaited him. Said they: "All our things are sold, sir. Shereef has sold everything for ivory."

Later in the evening Shereef came to see him and shamelessly offered his hand, with a salutatory "Yambo." Livingstone refused his hand, saying he could not shake hands with a thief. As an excuse Shereef said he had divined on the Koran and that had told him the Hakim (Arabic for Doctor) was dead. Livingstone was now destitute. He had just enough to keep him and his men alive for about a month, after which he would be forced to beg from the Arabs. He had arrived in Ujiji October 26. The HERALD Expedition arrived November 10 from the coast—only sixteen days difference. Had I not been delayed at Unyanyembe by the war with Mirambo I should have gone on to Manyema, and very likely have been travelling by one road, while he would have been coming by another to Ujiji. Had I gone on two years ago, when I first received the instructions, I should have lost him without doubt. But I am detained by a series of circumstances, which chafed and fretted me considerably at the time, only to permit him to reach Ujiji sixteen days before I appeared. It was as if we were marching to meet together at an appointed rendezvous—the one from the west, the other from the east.

The Doctor had heard of a white man being at Unyanyembe, who was said to have boats with him, and he had thought he was another traveller sent by the French government to replace Lieutenant Le Sainte, who died from fever a few miles above Gondokoro.[43] I had not written to him because I believed him to be dead, and of course my sudden entrance into Ujiji was as great a surprise to him as it was to the Arabs. But the sight of the American flag, which he saw waving in the van of the expedition, indicated that one was coming who could speak his own language, and you know already how the leader was received.

43. Joseph F. M. Le Saint (1833–1868); he planned to explore the area between the upper White Nile and the West African coast. Hill, *Biographical Dictionary*, 212.

8

Kwihara, Unyanyembe
February 21, 1872 [1]

After spending Christmas at Ujiji Dr. Livingstone, escorted by the NEW YORK HERALD Expedition, composed of forty Wanguana soldiers, well armed, left for Unyanyembe on the 26th of December, 1871.[2]

In order to arrive safely, untroubled by wars and avaricious tribes, we sketched out a road to Unyanyembe, thus:

Seven days by water south to Urimba.[3]

Ten days across the uninhabited forests of Kawendi.

Twenty days through Unkonongo, direct east.

Twelve days north through Unkonongo.

Thence five days into Unyanyembe, where we arrived without adventure of any kind, except killing zebras, buffaloes and giraffes, after fifty-four days' travel.

The expedition suffered considerably from famine, and your correspondent from fever, but these are incidental to the march in this country.

The Doctor tramped it on foot like a man of iron. On arrival at Unyanyembe I found that the Englishman, Shaw, whom I had turned back as useless, had about a month after his return succumbed to the climate of the interior and had died, as well as two Wanguana of the expedition who had been left behind sick.[4] Thus during less than twelve months William Lawrence Farquhar, of Leith, Scotland, and John William Shaw, of London, England, the two white men I had engaged to assist me, had died; also eight baggage carriers and eight soldiers of the expedition had died.

I was bold enough to advise the Doctor to permit the expedition to escort him to Unyanyembe, through the country it was made acquainted with while going to Ujiji, for the reason that were he to sit down at Ujiji until Mirambo was disposed of he might remain a year there, a prey to high expectations, ending always in bitter disappointment. I told him, as the Arabs of Unyanyembe were not equal to the task of conquering Mirambo, that it were better he should accompany the HERALD expedition to Unyanyembe, and

1. *NYH*, July 15, 1872.
2. *HIFL*, 566, gives Dec. 27.
3. "A large district of Kawendi." *Ibid.*, 574.
4. In *ibid.*, 596–97, Stanley recounts how he learned this while in Ukonongo on the way to Tabora.

there take possession of the last lot of goods brought to him by a caravan which left the seacoast simultaneously with our expedition.

The Doctor consented, and thus it was that he came so far back as Unyanyembe.

9

Kwihara, Unyanyembe
March 1, 1872 [1]

It is erroneously supposed by his friends that Doctor Livingstone is most industriously attended to, that he receives annually, if not semi-annually, large supplies of cloth, beads and necessaries. Your correspondent begs to inform his friends that the HERALD Expedition found him turned back from his explorations when on the eve of being terminated thoroughly by the very men sent to him by the British Consulate; that the expedition found him sitting down at Ujiji utterly destitute, robbed by the very men sent by the British Consulate at Zanzibar with his caravan; that the HERALD Expedition escorted him to Unyanyembe only in time to save his last stock of goods, for they were rapidly being made away with by the very men entrusted by the British Consulate with the last lot of goods; that it was only by an accident that your correspondent saw a packet of letters addressed to Livingstone, and so, forcibly, took one of Livingstone's men to carry the letters to his employer.

When we arrived at Unyanyembe two bales of cloth, two bags of beads[2] and one case of brandy had already disappeared out of the last lot.

Neither are the supplies or letters hurried up to him. He might have waited long at Ujiji waiting for goods and letters that never would come, if the HERALD Expedition had not informed him.

Though the distance from Zanzibar to Unyanyembe is but three months for a loaded caravan, yet the Consulate's trusty men stopped on the seacoast, within a stone's throw (figuratively speaking) of the consulate, over three and a half months, and Livingstone got his goods thirteen and a half months after they left the seacoast, and only at three months from the coast. Livingstone had to come for them himself, a distance of 350 miles.

1. *NYH*, July 15, 1872.
2. *HIFL*, 610, lists four bags.

Within the time that the British Consul's men took to convey Livingstone's goods and letters a distance of only 525 miles, the HERALD Expedition was formed, and marched 2,059 English statute miles, and before the fourteenth month of its departure from the seacoast the HERALD Expedition will have arrived at the seacoast, be paid off and disbanded.

In the matter of supplies, then, being sent to Livingstone semiannually or annually there is no truth whatever. The cause is extreme apathy at Zanzibar and the reckless character of the men sent. Where English gentlemen are so liberal and money so plentiful it should be otherwise.

When preparing to return to the coast your correspondent, in command of your expedition, turned over to Dr. Livingstone nine bales of mixed cloths, 980 pounds of assorted beads, well adapted for Rua and Manyema, and 350 pounds of brass wire, besides one portable boat to cross rivers, a supply of carpenter's tools, revolvers, carbines and several hundred pounds of ammunition.[3]

10

Kwihara, Unyanyembe
March 12, 1872 [1]

The day after to-morrow the HERALD expedition will leave the Land of the Moon—Unyamwezi—for the sea coast.

Your correspondent has been commissioned by Dr. Livingstone, if there is time before the first ship leaves Zanzibar, to send him fifty well-armed men from Zanzibar, to act as soldiers and servants for a new expedition which he is about to organize for rapid exploration of a few doubtful points before returning home to declare to those concerned that he has finished his work.

He will leave Unyanyembe for Ufipa, thence to Liemba and Marungu, and crossing the Luapula River at Chicumbi's[2] will make his way to the copper mines of Katanga, in Rua; then eight days south, to discover the fountains of Herodotus; then return by

3. *Ibid.*, 613, has a fuller and slightly different list.
1. *NYH*, July 15, 1872.
2. See *LLJ*, I, 308–10. Chikumbi was a Bemba chief. See also Debenham, *Way to Ilala*, 250.

Katanga to the underground houses of Rua,[3] ten days northeast of Katanga; thence to Lake Kamolondo, and by river Lufira to Lake Lincoln; thence back to Lualaba, to explore the lake north of Kamolondo;[4] thence return by Uguhha to Ujiji, or by Marungu, through Urori, to the coast, and England.

This is his present programme, which he thinks will only take him eighteen months, but, as I have told him, I think it will take two years.

Though he is now going on sixty years of age, he looks but forty-five or fifty—quite hale and hearty. He has an enormous appetite, which has abated nothing of its powers since I have known him. He is in need of no rest; he needed supplies; he has got them now and everything he needs. Though sick and thin when I saw him at Ujiji, he is now fleshy and stoutish, and must weigh about one hundred and eighty pounds. Though I have hung my balance scales temptingly before his eyes, I have never been able to get him to weigh himself. I have not the slightest fears about his health or of any danger coming to him from the natives.

11

April 29 to May 4, 1872, Stanley's Journal[1]

29*th* April Halfway between Kisemo & Msuwa—6 hours. In Forest. Shot a young Boa. 4 feet long. 3 inch diameter—9 inch girth measured. The Wangwana call the Boa Chatto.[2] Plenty in these jungles, some 12 or 15 ft long.

30*th* Ap. Imbiki 6h—30m. Passed Msuwa, and came on hurriedly through the horrid jungles which saw such hard work with us in going to Unyanyembe. What dreadful smells—what horrors the very odor of the jungle suggests—so dense that a tiger could not plunge through because of its impenetrable thorns & spear headed cactus

3. See Cerckel, "Les Galeries Souterraines de Mokana (Monts Mitumba)"; *LLJ*, I, 274, 287–88.
4. The rest of this sentence is omitted in *HIFL*, 626.
1. The journal, which includes only the entries given here, is in the Peabody Museum, Salem, Mass. It covers the events in *HIFL*, 646–53. Stanley, hurrying towards the coast as fast as any messenger, wrote no despatches for this part of the return trip.
2. *Chatu.*

. . . Could a bottle full of concentrated miasma be used what deadly & unknown poison—undiscoverable—would it make. I think act quicker than chloroform & more fatal than prussic acid. Boas in the woods above our heads, and snakes on the ground as well as Scorpions & crabs, land terrapins & iguanas. Malaria in the air we breathe, the road infested with "hot water" ants which bite you mad until you dance & squirm as if you had the St. Vitus. Yet somehow we are fortunate enough to escape death & destruction, and you might also, but not the effects—the effects remain in the System. Here are the ten plagues of Egypt, through which one must run the gauntlet.

1 Plague of Boas.
2   "   Red-Ants. Hot water
3   "   Scorpions
4   "   Thorns & Spear Cactus
5   "   Impediments
6   "   Black mud knee-deep
7   "   Suffocation
8   "   Stench
9   "   Thorns on the road
10   "   Malaria

1st May 1872, Kingaru Hera—6h. 45m. Storm as far as Simbo—the mountains West of Simbamwenni acting as a barrier against it. Here we have news of a storm having raged on the coast destroying every ship except one Steamer belonging to the Wasungu.[3] The trees are laid prostrate here in several places across the road impeding a rapid march especially have the [?porters] suffered from the stiff branches & the loam soil. The Kingani was like a sea—I can very well believe that, having seen the traces of the mighty floods of some of its headwaters. Rivers all calm from Msuwa to [journal breaks off here] . . .

If I buy a goat I take what I want & give the rest away. If the Wangwana, they do the same. Though they give plenty of trouble an Expedition of white men would give 50 times more.

2nd May. Rosako. 6h. 15m. After this long march I went to this village & had hardly sat down to rest before Sarmeen with his comrades came bringing with them from the Am. Consul a few bottles of wine, a few pots of jam & 2 boxes of crackers very much welcomed. Inside one of these boxes carefully put up by the Consul were four numbers of the New York Herald, one of which contains one of my letters which I had written from Unyanyembe. In another

3. The hurricane of April 15, 1872, is described in Coupland, *Exploitation of East Africa*, 55–57.

several Extracts containing views of the American & Canadian press upon this Expedition. One extract especially attracted my attention for the singular expressions contained in it. This was from an American paper published in Nashville Tennessee. The animus which prevailed throughout the article was hostile to the Expedition from what cause I know not, nor can guess but its closing paragraph provoked a most hearty laugh. We were two days only from the coast. It read thus. I quote it.[4]

I also learned from a letter that there was an Expedition being formed at Bagamoyo—called the "Livingstone Expedition"[5] for what purpose the letter did not state but I guessed that its business was for the same purpose which I had accomplished as successfully as could be desired as will be seen by those who have read this letter.

3d. Kikoka. 5h. 50m.

4th. Gongoni—on the low ridge overlooking the Kingani river & plain came to river—fired several shots to attract canoe men to us. 2 Canoes came in the afternoon & after much chaffing about the fare by the parties [journal breaks off here] . . . Kingwere[6] must be a descendant of some dusky king Log, for I never saw in any man the attributes of that royal personage so faithfully depicted as in Kingwere, movements which in this respect was not a whit behind any of his white relatives.

Happy me after finishing our work. after the hurry & vexation of the march—after the storm of fractious tribes, after tramping for the last 3 days through water & mire—we are nearing Beulahs peace & rest.[7] Can we do otherwise than vent our joy in firing away gunpowder until our horns are emptied, than shout our hurrahs until we are hoarse, than with hearty Yambos greet every soul fresh from the sea. Not so thinks the Wangwana Soldiers—so sympathizing with their longing I let them act their maddest—without censure. "More pilgrims are come to town" were the words heard in the streets of Beulah. The Musungu has come were the words heard in Bagamoyo. "And another would answer saying—And so many went over the water, and were let in at the golden gates to day." And in like manner did we hear, "he will cross the water to morrow and will arrive at Zanzibar about midday." Then also like Bunyans pilgrims —we shall see nothing smell nothing taste nothing that is offensive

4. Stanley quoted an extract in *HIFL,* 650.
5. For the abortive Livingstone Search and Relief Expedition, Bridges, "British Exploration of East Africa," 294–306.
6. Kingwere of Gongoni owned the canoes. *HIFL,* 651.
7. See John Bunyan, *The Pilgrim's Progress,* 153–54, 303–04.

to our stomachs. And with many conjectures as to the good things I shall eat at the American Consul's house to morrow I fall asleep.

Farewell Oh Wagogo with their wild effrontery & nosy curiosity. Farewell to the Wahha's Mutware Mionvu—chief of tribute takers & prince of blackmailers. Farewell Wavinza to your turbulent [?nature] & your troubled river. You Warundi & your unreasonable hostility. A farewell to you Arabs with your sinful work—your lying tongues & black hearts. Farewell to fevers remittent & intermittent, to Makata Swamps & crocodiles—to brakish waters and howling thorny plains—to worse than Egypts plagues—& Pluto's realm. & a Farewell to you my dusky friends—& faithful soldiers. Farewell to all, & welcome—thrice welcome—happy land—great & free America until I see thee again. Above all fare thee well Oh Livingstone true Hero & christian—be thou healthy & prosperous wheresoever thou goest. Thy work is holy—thy mission sacred—& when thy work is ended return to receive the reward [?] of thy lengthened labors, to receive the plaudits of all—for thy name is blessed with men.

The kirangozi blows his horn & gives forth blasts as powerful as Astolpho on this happy day.

And that bright flag whose stars have waved over Inner Africa & which promised relief to the harrassed Livingstone when in distress in Ujiji—which though not so rich yet vied in beauty with Azzel's flag—return once more to the Sea, its proper domain—torn it is true but not dishonored, tattered but not disgraced—as we all are.

Part II   The Expedition across Africa

The "finding" of Livingstone had won Stanley popularity; his next expedition was to gain for him a foremost position among African pioneer explorers, not only of the nineteenth century, but of all times.

—E. G. Ravenstein, "Henry M. Stanley," *GJ* 24 (1904), 104

12

Zanzibar, East Coast of Africa
October 19, 1874 [1]

As I sit down to the table and take up the writing implements to record my experiences of the last few weeks a wish darts to my mind that the art of writing was never invented. It is true. Writing to me is such a labor at this moment. I have but the day before yesterday returned from the exploration of the Rufiji River and its delta[2]—returned only in time to be compelled to write to you of what I have seen, because if I do not take advantage of the four days of grace given me by the stay of the mail steamer in port you and your readers would have to wait another month before information could be received by you of the movements of your "Commissioner." Yet would I gladly avail myself of some excuse—a reasonable excuse—to postpone writing to you for various reasons. One main reason is that it is exceedingly hot and the perspiration is unrestrainable, and a feeling of lassitude and *ennui* which has succeeded the return to Zanzibar from our exploration of the Rufiji is inimical to physical exertion or mental thought. Besides, every few moments I am troubled by the arrival of volunteers for the expedition into the interior, the rumor of its intended departure having stirred up an heroic desire in the minds of the able-bodied and poor people, residents of this town, to visit the distant regions of Africa, where the tribes are called pagans; where elephants—and consequently ivory —are numerous; where there are vast extents of level country "covered" with game of all kinds. These volunteers came to make "shauri" —to hold a palaver or talk—to question me respecting the amount of pay I can afford to give them, the probable duration of the journey I propose to make, the countries I propose to visit, and other things of like nature. These volunteers are not to be despised; they are not to be told to depart without words of a conciliatory and friendly kind, for out of this class the members of the expedition must be selected, without whom its objects could never be consummated. The palaver requires, therefore, time, tact and patience; and though I am inwardly fuming and storming at these several interruptions I

1. *NYH*, Dec. 2, 1874. The trip to the Rufiji here described is not included in *TDC*.
2. The Rufiji, the largest river system in East Africa, has tributaries reaching almost as far as Mbeya; it drains an area of some 68,500 square miles and has a fifty-mile wide delta. Moffett, *Handbook of Tanganyika*, 166; Barker, "The Rufiji River."

endeavor to commend myself cheerfully to my fate, hoping that my apparent placable disposition will invite confidence on the part of the volunteers, and that my excuses, which I humbly tender, may conciliate the editors of the *Daily Telegraph* and the NEW YORK HERALD for the brevity of this letter or the sterility of its information.

Ever since my march to Ujiji in search of Dr. Livingstone I have entertained a desire that I might be permitted to explore that most promising of all East African rivers—the Rufiji. Burton, my heroic predecessor in Africa, had, with his usual industry, collected much valuable information respecting this river;[3] and when, subsequently, I heard from the natives that all the small streams to the south of that country were received by the Rwaha, or Rufiji—that the Kisigo, an important river in Urori, which is south of Ugogo, also emptied into the Rwaha—I mentally placed the Rufiji among the list of those rivers whose navigation benefits commerce and the world. I entertained the opinion that the Rufiji was a river worthy of exploration; that it was a river likely to benefit East and that portion of Central Africa contiguous to it; that by its means the Gospel might find readier and more feasible access into the interior than by any other route, not even excluding the Wami River,[4] whose utmost limit of navigation I place at Mbumi-Usagara at the foot of the Usagara mountains; that by means of this noble stream the white merchants of Europe and America might exchange their cottons and beads for the valuable products of the interior. I say this was my opinion, until I saw in some geographical publication two several accounts of explorations of the Rufiji. The first purported to be an account of an exploration made by Dr. John Kirk and Captain Wharton, of the surveying ship *Shearwater*, in a steam launch;[5] the second

3. He called it "a counterpart of the Zambesi . . . and a waterway that appears destined to become the high-road of nations into Eastern Africa." Burton also called for its exploration. Burton, "Lake Regions," 18, 44–45.

4. Stanley had optimistic hopes about the navigability of the Wami from information secured during his Livingstone expedition. British visitors in 1873 and 1876 proved his hopes unfounded. Stanley confirmed this himself in 1879. *HIFL*, 233–34; Hill, "Boat Journey up the Wami River"; "Der ostafrikanischen Fluss Wami. Aus einem Briefe des Capt. Malcolm, Commander des Briton, Brit. R.N., d. d. Zanzibar, 13. Februar 1873"; Smith to Wright, June 26, 1876, C.A6/MI, CMS; Kirk to FO, May 1, 1879, Q–22, ZA. For the Wami system, Meyer, *Deutsche Kolonialreich*, 166–67, 193–94.

5. William J. L. Wharton (1843–1905) became hydrographer of the Admiralty in 1884 after an active career of surveying, particularly on the East African coast. He visited the Rufiji in 1873 and 1877. *The Nautical Magazine* 66 (1897), 279–81; *GJ* 26 (1905), 684–86; Kirk, "Examination of the Lufigi River Delta, East Africa"; Kirk, "On Recent Surveys of the East Coast of Africa."

was made by Captain Elton,[6] first assistant to the Political Agent at Zanzibar, who proceeded inland from Sumanga, on the north side of the Kikunia mouth of the Rufiji.

Messrs. Kirk and Wharton proceeded as far as Fuguha, which I presume to be the same as that which the natives call Agunia, or near it. Captain Elton reached Mpenbeno, ten miles higher up the river. All these gentlemen expressed themselves emphatically against the possibility of utilizing the Rufiji River. Of course, after such emphatic expressions of opinion I dared not hope that I would return from the Rufiji with any better opinion of it. The following letter will show what my impressions of the navigable utility of the Rufiji are, with which I venture to say that nine-tenths of American river steamboat captains would at once agree if they were called upon to examine and report upon the river.

At half-past three P.M. of the 30th September I sailed from Zanzibar in the Yarmouth yawl *Wave*, bound south. The yawl was purchased for the purpose of exploring the portion of East Africa which I considered to be of most interest to the philanthropic and commercial public of England and America. Through the courtesy and kindness of the gentlemen of the Peninsular and Oriental office, on Leadenhall street, and those of the British India Steam Navigation office—more especially Captain Bayley,[7] of the former, and Messrs. Mackinnon and Dawes,[8] of the latter—I was enabled to have her safely shipped and landed at Zanzibar without damage, though she was a large and heavy boat. Her dimensions were 41 feet length and

6. James F. Elton (1840–1877), after service in Zanzibar, became British consul in Mozambique. He died while traveling from Lake Nyasa to the East African coast. Elton, *Travels and Researches among the Lakes and Mountains of Eastern and Central Africa*, v–x (a biographical sketch by H. Waller). Elton's report of the Rufiji is included in his "On the Coast Country of East Africa, South of Zanzibar."

7. Henry Bayley (c. 1826–1887), then one of the managing directors of the Peninsular and Oriental Steam Navigation Company. See Cable [Ernest Andrew Ewart], *A Hundred Year History of the P. & O.*, 170, 175; Divine, *These Splendid Ships. The Story of the Peninsula and Oriental Line*, 139; PRGS 10 (1888), 423; see also *The P. & O. Pocket Book* (London, 1926), 1–13, for a historical sketch of the company.

8. William Mackinnon (1823–1893), one of the founders of what became in 1863 the British India Steam Navigation Company. In 1872 the company opened, from Aden, the first regular steam service to Zanzibar. BCB, I, 627–30; *P. & O. Pocket Book*, 14–27. Mackinnon's later important role in Africa is discussed in de Kiewiet, "History of the Imperial British East African Company 1876–1895," 17ff.; Anstey, *Britain and the Congo in the Nineteenth Century*, 67ff. Edwyn Dawes belonged to the firm of Gray, Dawes and Co. They were close associates of Mackinnon and would be of service to Stanley in the future. Stanley, *In Darkest Africa*, I, 35, 48; *History of Smith, Mackenzie and Co.*, 11.

9 feet beam; with her deep rudder shipped she drew five feet, which we afterward found to be a disadvantage.[9] Had I been wiser I should have ordered a second rudder, specially for river navigation, to be exchanged on entering the river for the sea rudder.

The crew of the *Wave* mustered, beside myself, two efficient, industrious and willing young Englishmen, Francis and Edward Pocock,[10] twenty-four Wangwana or freemen of Zanzibar, armed with Snider rifles, two black cabin boys and a cabin passenger in the shape of a thoroughbred English bull terrier, Jack, who for his fare and passage was to make himself useful at night while on the Rufiji to warn off midnight plunderers. If you add as stores two casks of water, a thousand pounds of rice and some cabin provisions for the whites, it will be seen that she was a boat of some capacity. Several officers of the cruising fleet at Zanzibar who had seen her at anchor in port had spoken highly of her, and some had said that she was just the kind of boat Her Majesty's cruisers on the East Coast of Africa ought to be supplied with for slave dhow catching in shallow waters. After a three weeks' trial of this kind of boat I am inclined to the same opinion. With a moderate monsoon breeze she travels faster than any steam launch that ever came to Zanzibar could. As an instance of her sailing qualities it is worth mention that on a run from Bagamoyo to Zanzibar, a distance of about twenty-five miles, the *Wave* beat a large dhow by two hours.

After rounding Shangani Point we were favored with a stiff breeze from the southeast and steered for Mbwenni, on the mainland. The natives yelled their approbation of the speed at which the *Wave* dashed past the dhows bound for the coast of the mainland. Owing to the head wind we were compelled to pay close attention to our course and keep a good lookout to avoid the numerous reefs and sand patches which make the navigation of the sea in the vicinity a difficult and perplexing task to a novice. No sooner had we passed by the pale green waters of the South Lackbrey bank than the Northern Harps indicated their presence by their gleaming tops of sand and a thousand short snow-crested waves, which tumbled tumultuously over their low sloping shores; while on our starboard side the Hamisa bank and its dangerous neighbors showed current enough by many an angry looking wave. A short half hour of swift sailing brought us in the neighborhood of the ugly dark coral reefs, strangely

9. The *Wave* was later acquired by the Universities Mission; see Steere to Festing, May 6, 1876, A.1.III, UMCA.

10. Francis Pocock (*c.* 1850–1877) and Edward Pocock (*c.* 1852–1875), two brothers from Kent, had signed on as Stanley's assistants. *BCB*, II, 775–78; Arnold, *Giants in a Dressing Gown*, 98–99; *NYH*, Nov. 29, 1875. For their letters on the Rufiji trip, see Appendices N–P.

called the "Cow Reefs," which cover an area of about three square miles. The helm was pressed hard down, and the *Wave* was forced almost in the very teeth of the rising gale. Not until the last white crest over the reefs had disappeared were we relieved from the anxiety and able to share in the general enthusiasm of the crew at the perfect behavior of the tiny vessel.[11]

Shortly after dark we anchored at a point a few miles north of Mbwenni and disposed ourselves to sleep as best we could, the surf sounding drearily monotonous in our ears, and a faint rumor of the noises of the night which are caused by the myriad insects of tropical Africa reaching us only during the pauses of the heavy surf-beats.

At dawn we were wakened, thoroughly damp and cold from the night dew, and one of the young Englishmen was soon obliged to lie down again from his first attack of fever. It struck me at this moment that we were engaged in rather a foolish trip if we intended to tramp into the interior, and that to brave the malaria of the Rufiji delta just as we ought to be sparing of the health and energy we brought from Europe was not a wise proceeding. This thought, however, was but the consequence of the misery in which we had passed the night and the damp cold we then experienced. It was soon stilled, however, by the genial warmth of the rising sun and by the bright green appearance of the palms and patches of forest which lined the shore.

With a favorable land breeze we sailed southward, clinging to the shore as closely as possible that we might lose nothing of the riant beauty of the varied and interesting bits of land scenery.

Some people may, perhaps, object to the term "interesting," applied to East African scenery, but I maintain that a cluster of palms, over-topping an humble little fishing village, with a background of dense jungle, swathed in deep dark green, and a foreground of a white, sandy beach, laved with ocean waves, deserved to be termed interesting. The palms and sea contribute that which makes the picture one of interest. Without the palms the background would become a mere jungle; without the sea before it the sandy beach would represent nothing but sterility.

Taken in this sense, then, in coasting southward numbers of such scenes are revealed, becoming only more interesting when a more important town comes to view, with numbers of square white houses, like so many white painted blocks of wood under the ever beautiful palm groves. Such a town is Mbwenni, near Cape Thomas.

From Mbwenni southward to Dar Salaam the coast retains the

11. Contemporary knowledge of the coast is given in De Horsey, *The African Pilot*, 97ff.; Horsburgh, *The India Directory*, 162ff.

characteristics already spoken of. Small dark brown huts, clustered under the shade of a tree of ample foliage and enormous girth, are frequent, separated by jungle, through which a narrow footpath runs, serving as the commercial highway along the seaboard.

Soon after passing Konduchi, at a distance of forty-one miles south of Zanzibar, we come to Dar Salaam. This town possesses some interest as the creation of the late Seyyid Majid, Sultan of Zanzibar.[12] As we round Condogo Point a group of islands make their appearance, consisting of Sinda and its neighboring islets, and westward of these a ridge of tall trees is seen. The tall trees are cocoa palms, and the presence of such a large plantation indicates in East Africa a town of some importance and magnitude. This is precisely what Dar Salaam was intended to be by Seyyid Majid. He found a fishing village of a few humble huts the possessor of an ample harbor where three times the number of his naval and mercantile fleet might lie at anchor secure from the dangers of wind and a boisterous sea, and he at once conceived the project of making this fishing village a seaport and the depot for his Central African trade. He sent his laborers and slaves to clear the neighborhood of the jungle, which had voraciously swallowed every portion of cultivable ground close to the water's edge. He then caused 200,000 cocoa palms to be planted, which in time, if carefully looked after and nourished, would bring him in a revenue of from $150,000 to $200,000. A palace was built as a residence for him, and a fort or barracks for his officers and soldiers. Influential Arabs engaged in commerce were also invited to follow his example, and take lots for building purposes. Several chose to do so, and about a dozen imposing edifices, compared to the former humble fishing huts, gleamed white and large in contrast to the green fronds of the palms. To those of sanguine disposition such a scene must have assured them that commercial progress was begun in earnest in East Africa, and that Seyyid Majid was a wise and energetic prince.

In reality, the Sultan of Zanzibar had inaugurated a work which all Europeans who look beyond home could heartily commend. The trade with Central Africa was being rapidly developed; large consignments of ivory from new regions were constantly arriving at Zanzibar. New copal diggings were discovered near Dar Salaam, and to the westward and southward. What the Sultan's dominions lacked was a proper port for trade, and in the harbor of Dar Salaam he

12. Majid bin Said, Sultan of Zanzibar from 1856 to 1870. He began to build a settlement at Dar es Salaam in 1866. Coupland, *Exploitation of East Africa*, 14ff.

had found deep water and roomy anchorage, easy of access from Zanzibar and centrally located for the southern and northern towns. The seacoast towns whence the caravans departed for the interior in search of ivory labored under various disadvantages. Mombasa, to the north, though possessing a moderately good harbor, was limited to the west by the vast hunting and marauding grounds of the Masai;[13] to the north by the intractable Gallas,[14] while to the south other towns claimed to be as good starting-points for Africa as Mombasa. Saadani, Whindi, and Bagamoyo were dangerous ports for vessels, the approaches to each infested with reefs and sand banks. Mboamaji, to the south of Dar Salaam, had a similar disadvantage, while Kilwa was too far removed from Zanzibar.

Everything promised fairly well for the success of Dar Salaam as a future rival to Zanzibar until Seyyid Majid died. Then all the fine schemes relating to its prosperity perished as it became known that Seyyid Burghash, his successor, did not share in the views of his predecessor. The palace, the barracks, the houses, the palm grove, the fine harbor, with its deep, still, green water are here to this day as Seyyid Majid's last effort left them, silent and comparatively deserted. Not one house has been built here since his death. The Arabs who did build houses preferred to remain in Zanzibar.[15]

A few months ago the question was agitated in England as to what could be done with the freed slaves, and I remember that some suggested Dar Salaam as the most eligible place where they might be settled and instructed in useful arts of industry, with which, after a visit to the port, I agree. Here are good, roomy houses already built, but uninhabited. A large area of ground already cleared of jungle, but comparatively uncultivated, a capacious and deep harbor, likely to suffice for the harboring of all vessels which may engage in East African commerce for the next hundred years, above which at present not a single flag waves.

I am informed that about 600 slaves have been captured within the last six months in the Mozambique Channel by British cruisers. Now the question may be asked, What has been done with those

13. For the Masai of Kenya and Tanzania, Huntingford, *The Southern Nilo-Hamites;* Low, "The Northern Interior," 300–08.

14. The Galla, then occupying territory as far south as the Tana River, were held in high repute by nineteenth-century Europeans; one missionary described them as "the finest race of men in Africa." Wakefield's statement at a meeting of May 18, 1888, in *Journal of the Manchester Geographical Society* 4 (1888), 166. For an extended treatment, Haberland, *Galla Süd-Äthiopiens.*

15. For the future development of the city, Schneider, *Dar Es Salaam. Stadtentwicklung unter Einfluss der Araber und Inder.*

slaves? Have they been, as usual, leased out to Mauritius sugar planters at so many dollars a head to remunerate the government for the expense it undertook to fit their men-of-war for these slave-hunting expeditions? Let us hope not, but we may as well be told what becomes of the freed slaves.[16]

From the silent harbor of Dar Salaam we sailed next day, with the same stubborn headwind against us. We tacked and retacked for twelve mortal hours, sometimes dashing the spray over our bows with long lines of reefs close to our lee, and sometimes plunging in the deep blue of the ocean; and at night we anchored under the shadows which the palms of Kimbigi Head threw across the sea.

13

Zanzibar, Coast of Africa
Oct. 21, 1874[1]

The next day, delayed by calms and head wind, we cast anchor in the harbor of Kwale Island. The people are Wangwana, subjects of the Zanzibar Sultan, and may possibly number 300 souls, all told. The one village which it boasts is on the western side, close to the port. The island is situated in latitude 7 deg. 25 min., south. The mouth of the Dendeni River, on the mainland, is to be seen nearly northwest of Kwale.[2]

The first thing that struck me as remarkable on this island was the large number of gigantic baobab trees. It seemed to me, when well screened from view of the sea by foliage, that I had suddenly stepped into a portion of Ugogo. The next things that caused me surprise were the very large and very small hens' eggs that were profered to me for sale. The large eggs were of the size of geese eggs, while the small eggs did not much exceed in size pheasant eggs.

16. There was much criticism of this system of disposal of liberated slaves, Steere describing the system as operated in the Seychelles as "little if anything less than slavery." Non-British observers were particularly harsh critics and used its workings to discredit the entire British antislave-trade policy. Steere to West, Oct. 22, 1874, A. 1. III, UMCA; de Mahy, *Autour de l'île Bourbon et Madagascar*, 280; "Einige Worte über den augenblicklichen Stand der Sklaverei in Ostafrika. Brieflich an Dr. Reichenow von Dr. med. G. Fischer in Zanzibar." For one attempted solution of the problem, Bennett, "The Church Missionary Society at Mombasa, 1873–1894."

1. *NYH*, Dec. 3, 1874.
2. Villiers, *Sons of Sinbad*, 227–36, gives a description of Kwale Island.

Goats were numerous and cheap; two were purchased by us at a dollar each. The people seemed not to have much occupation. Those who owned land possessed domestic slaves to cultivate it, while they themselves chat and sleep, sleep and chat from morning until night, and through the night till morning.

From Kwale we sailed, after a night's anchorage in the port, past the islands of Pembagu and Koma, the latter of which is inhabited by a few people who obtain a precarious living by planting millet and holcus and by fishing, and steered south straight for a broad opening in the dense foliage which lined the mainland. Arriving before this opening, which we took to be one of the mouths of the Rufiji River, we were favored with a stiff nine-knot breeze from the southeast, and as the water appeared dark green, indicating considerable depth, we sailed boldly in with all sail set. When quite within this mouth we observed one broad avenue of water, leading south-southwest, and another south-southeast, equally wide, but, being ignorant of the exact course of the true river, we anchored at the distance of a mile and a half from the sea, close to that part of the land near which the two branches conflowed. When we had communicated with this shore, which we ascertained to be the island of Saninga, we learned that, led by accident, we had halted but a few yards from the spot where the steam launch of the *Shearwater* had anchored in 1873 prior to her departure up stream in 1873.[3]

We had not been at our anchorage ten minutes before a colored gentleman of stoutish build and cleanly, good-natured face was seen paddling alongside our vessel, who introduced himself as Moeni Bana-Kombo ben Ahad, which rendered into English, means Lord and Master Kombo, the son of Ahad, chief of Saninga Island. Probably according to a previous generous act, he had brought with him a weighty chicken and three fresh eggs, which we reciprocated with a gift of royal Dabwani cloth.[4]

Kombo, the son of Ahad, chief of Saninga Island—who, though the Wangwana of his village styled him "Jimrie," I prefer shall remain as he designated himself—was wise and learned respecting the geography of the Rufiji River, and volunteered, for the information of the curious white people of the white people's country, "Ulyah," [5] several interesting facts. The two white men of the "smoke

3. H.M.S. *Shearwater*, the vessel which brought Kirk and Wharton to the Rufiji; see document 12, note 7. See also *PRGS* 11 (1889), 738–40.

4. ". . . a kind of small blue and white check made at Maskat; one fourth of its breadth is a red stripe, edged with white and yellow." Burton, "Lake Regions," 430.

5. *Ulaya*—Europe.

boat," Dr. Kirk and Captain Wharton, he remembered perfectly. They asked him endless questions, until he was quite tired—"choka sana"—and put down ever so many things in a little book that he, Kombo, the son of Ahad, had told them.

"Very good. Is there much water in the Rufiji River?"

"Plenty," answered Kombo, confidently.

"What do you call plenty?"

"Deep water—very deep."

"Good! How many pima?" (fathoms).

"Sometimes five pima, sometimes four, sometimes three; but always plenty."

"Do you know this river from what you yourself have seen?"

"No; I have never been up."

"Ah! then how do you know there is plenty of water in the river?"

"Huh! have I not my people who go up and come down?"

"Why do your people go up and come down?"

"To trade, of course."

"What do they trade?"

"They take up salt and cloth and bring me msan-durusi (gum copal), which I send to Zanzibar to sell." [6]

"Very good. Perhaps you can lend me one of your men who know this river to show me the way and to talk for me to the people in the interior?"

"Yes; I can let you have two, one of whom showed the way to the white men of the 'smoke-boat.' "

We had entered the Simbooranga mouth of the Rufiji River, and we were told this was not the largest debouchure of the river. Its noble breadth of surface, its depth of clear green water promised well to us. In the center of the stream an ocean steamer might float in perfect security, though there is a fall of ten feet at lowest ebb in the water.

Saninga Island possesses one village and its position before the mouth of the river is indicated by the presence of a few tall palm trees, which rear their graceful leafage above the surrounding vegetation. Looking westward, southward and northward we note that the two branches of the broad stream which conflow near the Simbooranga mouth are bounded by "league beyond league of gigantic foliage, by lofty summits of resounding mangrove woods, which grasp the depths and grapple with the floods."

6. *Msandarusi*, or the gum copal tree (*Trachylobium verrucosum*). Dale and Greenway, *Kenya Trees*, 110–11.

Dingoti Island forms the southern boundary and Simbooranga Island the northern boundary of this noble entrance to the Rufiji delta.[7] Near the shore of Saninga there were two small dhows, which are employed in conveying wood for building purposes to Zanzibar.[8] Sometimes they also convey rice and gum copal to that Arabian port.

A few Banians live on Dingoti Island, who keep cows and cultivate the ground, and sometimes trade with the villages up the Rufiji for rice, which is of a most superior quality.

Early next morning after our arrival in the Simbooranga, we sailed up the right branch, which came from the southwest. Our two promised guides accompanied us. That the reader may understand our experience of the navigable utility of the stream we were about to ascend, to save needless repetition it must be borne in mind that our deep rudder, common to Yarmouth yawls, caused our vessel to draw five feet of water. It being the southeast monsoon, we were fortunately favored with a strong breeze from that direction. The *Wave* fairly flew against the ebb up stream. Contrary to what we had anticipated, the scenes which each bend and curve of the river, as we ascended, disclosed were of exceeding beauty. Both banks of the river were clothed with dense foliage of varied green of a uniform height, which gave it an appearance of a broad canal, with a tall, green hedge on each side. We had ascended some five or six miles before the water, despite the ebb tide, began to be discolored. Then it gradually changed from its clear pale green to a muddy gray, and became rather sweet to the taste.

A large number of creeks were seen on each side of the river. Some of considerable size on the right side, we were informed, connected the Simbooranga with the Kikunia mouth of the Rufiji. Others on the left side joined the Simbooranga with the more southern and larger mouth of the Rufiji, the Magambu, each of which I promised myself I should explore. As I noted these internal channels of this great maritime delta, I became more and more interested, as its exploration promised to disclose something different from the reports sent to England by my predecessors. Every few moments

7. Villiers, *Sons of Sinbad,* 238, 337–56, gives a twentieth-century description of the delta. He concludes: "If in all this world there is a worse place than the Rufiji Delta, I hope I may never find it."

8. The mangrove tree, most commonly *Rhizophora mucronata,* was extensively used for building purposes in African, Arabian, and Persian Gulf areas. Its high tanin content gave termite resistance. Dale and Greenway, *Kenya Trees,* 399; Grant, "Mangrove Woods of Tanganyika Territory, their Silviculture and Dependent Industries."

when doubtful of the depth of the river, I caused one of the young
Englishmen to sound with a long boathook, over nine feet in length,
and eight times out of ten I heard the cheery cry of "No bottom."
Sometimes I felt anxiety, going at the rate we did up an unknown
river, when the cry was "Just touched, sir," or "Getting shoalier;"
but a movement of the tiller after consultation with the guide was
almost invariably followed by the cry of "No bottom" again.

In this manner we proceeded for two hours, until we came abreast
of a large creek which separates Salati Island from Surveni Island,
when, through inattention and a feeling of oversecurity, we missed
the channel and in a short time were aground, which sprung the
iron pintles. The halliards were let fall, the rudder unshipped, and
we proceeded to straighten matters by straightening the pintles and
cutting out a portion of the rudder. A few moments later damage
was repaired and sail was hoisted again, and the center of the stream
was tried, only, however, to run aground again. We labored with sail
and oars to find a feasible channel for some time, but failed, and
I began to think that my predecessors must be correct in their estimate of the commercial utility of the Rufiji until, hugging closely
the northern bank, we heard the cry of "No bottom," and proceeded
on our way as smoothly as though the Rufiji River was many fathoms
deep.

Five miles from this place we came to where the Kikunia mouth
of the Rufiji branched from the Simbooranga in a northeasterly direction, apparently a much more insignificant stream than the latter;
but the guide said that, though the Kikunia was narrow, it was deep.

Two miles higher up we arrived at a broad, lake-like expanse of
water, out of which branched to the southeast a much mightier
stream than the Simbooranga. This was the Magambu, the principal
mouth of the Rufiji River. It was studded with beautiful islands. Its
lengthy, straight, broad reaches of water were banked by enormous
and lofty globes of foliage; its islands and banks were the homes of
vast numbers of aquatic birds; hippopotami sported in its depths;
and on the gray spits of sand numbers of crocodiles basked in the
hot glowing sunshine. Altogether it was a grand picture, and most
alluring to the explorer. Over the mighty expanse of water blew the
freshening breeze of the monsoon, urging our good little vessel at
a quickened speed, and waving the topmost boughs of the forest,
exposing the sheen and glister of their leaves, besides cooling our
bodies and renewing vigor within us, until we laughed in mockery
of the malaria of the extensive delta, and our healthy appetite began
to rage for food.

An hour later the thick, tall forest, which had hitherto covered every space save that occupied by the watery channels of the delta, began to thin sensibly, and vestiges of former cultivation appeared. Now and then a tall, dark cluster of trees, overgrown with convolvuli, was seen, at the dark shadow and gloom of which one or two of my men, new to such tropical density of vegetation, shuddered.

By noon we had passed the most easterly feeder of the Rufiji—the Mbumi River—and were opposite Miehweh. The Mbumi issues from the northwest, and is about sixty yards wide at its mouth. Canoes ascend even this tributary a considerable distance.

Miehweh is the name of a small colony of villages and a district which may extend about four miles along the northern banks of the Rufiji. The inhabitants cultivate rice fields, the products of which they exchange with the Banians of Kikunia and Pemba, Bagamoyo, &c., for cotton, cloth and pice.

In order to illustrate the disposition of the natives,[9] I will describe an incident which occurred near an island called Surveni, opposite Miehweh. A large flock of birds, kingfishers and whydahs, were shot at with a rifle ball, which, piercing the flock, was seen to ricochet a considerable distance beyond along the surface of the river. After we had proceeded a mile, we detected several canoes close to the Miehweh bank, trying to outstrip us. Four continued their way, while one canoe separated from the others, which, taking advantage of the dead water along the lee of some islets, was soon able to overtake us.

One of our guides hailed the solitary canoeman and asked him what he wanted. He answered that he had come to inquire who we were, and for what purpose we came to the Rufiji, and why we fired bullets, to the imminent risk of people fishing in the river. His reply and questions were given with that force, volubility and rasping harshness I remembered so well were the characteristics of the voices of the Wagogo when angered.

The guide replied mildly that we had come to "see, that's all"— *Tembea tou.*

"To see? See what?"

"To see the river?"

"What for?"

"To see. Why? God knows! The white men do such strange things.

9. The population of the Rufiji area is a mixed one. At present the area is mostly inhabited by the Rufiji and Ndengereko. Meyer, *Deutsche Kolonial-reich*, 151; Moffett, *Handbook of Tanganyika*, 171. See also von Behr, "Am Rufigi."

They put it down in a book, and that is all I know that ever comes of it."

"Huh! How far do they intend to go?"

"As far as there is plenty of water for the boat in the Rufiji."

"Inside?"

"Yes, inside."

"Huh! The Rufiji extends far—many days' journey—and there is always water in the Rufiji."

"The white men intend to go and see for themselves how far there is plenty of water."

"How much do they intend to give me for shooting on the river?"

"Nothing."

The breeze came down over the tops of the trees, bellied the sails out full and large, and the *Wave* passed by the prurient native irresistibly.

Half an hour later the Pamloumeh district west of Miehweh was reached, with the tide and wind now strong in our favor, and soon after we came to Bumba, the remaining mouth of the Rufiji, which relieves the channel of the river proper of its volume of water. Bumba, accordingly, is also an insignificant stream compared to either the Magambu, Simbooranga, or the Kikunia. Its appearance and breadth corroborated the guides' report. Lower down the Bumba divides its waters among the Nguruweh, Otikiti, Simaya, Mtote, Njemjia, and Mdwana mouths.

At Kisembea, situated at the head of a long reach of the Rufiji, whose course here came from the southeast, large numbers of people flocked to the banks of the river to observe the strange phenomenon of a large boat towing another one and going fast up stream by means of sails. They had heard of a "smoke boat" having ascended as far as Agunia, lower down, but they had not seen it, though they marvelled much that such things should be. They were exceedingly inquisitive, and wondered that white men should come so far to "see" only water. Long after we had passed them we noted that the strange incident was being discussed by the interested groups, who had greedily fastened their eyes upon the boats and their belongings as they glided by them.

Beyond Kisembea, the Rufiji's course has a straight three-mile reach from the south-southwest. It has a breadth varying from 400 to 250 yards, and the channel is deep and easily found by observing the banks of the river. At no place could we find soundings with the boat-hook. Any river steamboat man in America could, so far, have found no fault with the stream. It was marked by every characteristic of a navigable river. From the sea up to Kisembea, a distance of twenty-two miles as I made it, the largest steamer that floats on the Mississippi River—which I believe has a tonnage of over 5,000 tons —might ascend and descend without impediment. The *Wave* ran aground twice in that distance, but it was our own fault—we had missed the proper channel. When we had ascertained it we found plenty of water, and no difficulty.[10]

Marenda district, which succeeds Kisembea as we ascend, is very populous, and small villages are found in clusters. The plain is exceedingly fertile, and produces rice, holcus sorghum, Indian corn, sweet potatoes, vegetables in abundance; cocoanut trees are frequently seen, while the plaintain is most prolific.

At sunset we anchored in midstream opposite Jumbe, at a distance of forty miles by river from Sininga Island, congratulating ourselves that we had done a good day's work and at having ascended at least twenty miles higher up the Rufiji than any other white man, and with a conviction strong in our minds that my predecessors had libelled the noble river without sufficient cause.

I despatched men on shore as soon as we anchored to convey my most respectful salaams to the chief Jumbe,[11] and to inform him that I should be delighted to make friends with him, which message was cordially received by him, at the same time that he took occasion to send tokens of his regard in the shape of five cocoanuts and one chicken.

Had I not done the diplomatic thing, our guides informed us that we would very likely have been visited by "river thieves" during the night.

Next morning Jumbe came, bringing with him more substantial tokens of friendship, and quite a retinue of chiefs, until our boat, already well loaded, had her gunwales but a foot above water.

After reciprocating Jumbe's acts of friendship, the first questions I naturally asked were relative to the length, breadth and depth of the Rufiji River; the countries round about him and the slave trade; its land route, and what the prospects of opening legitimate commerce between him, his people and neighbors with white people. What information may be embodied in the following remarks have been gleaned from him, the Chief of Saninga, the guides and Hasson bin Salim el Shaksi, whom I met next day on the Rufiji River.

First as regards the Rufiji River, its length and value to European merchants.

10. The Rufiji is in reality navigable for some 60 to 100 miles, but only for small vessels. Moffett, *Handbook of Tanganyika,* 4; Barker, "Some Rivers of Southern Tanganyika."
11. *Jumbe* means chief or headman.

All parties united in informing us that the Rufiji River rises in Gangeh-Ugangeh[12] according to Arabic and Swahili traders, which, as near as I can make out, with a desire to be as accurate as possible, is south by west of Unyanyembe. The main branch, known in the far interior as the Rwaha, comes from south of west from Jumbe; the lesser branch, but an important one, is called Kienga, and comes from the southwest, from possibly the same range of mountains as the northwestern branch of the Rovuma takes its rise. On traversing Ugangeh, the Rufiji, as yet an insignificant stream, flows eastward through Northern Ubena,[13] then the country of Sango or Usango,[14] when, arriving in Urori it gains power and volume by an accession of many small streams which drain the pastoral lands of Urori.

The Warori, or people of Urori, use this stream greatly. They fish in its waters; they hunt hippopotamus for the sake of its teeth,[15] and hides to make their shields; they convey butter and fat long distances up and down in canoes to trade for salt; they voyage on it for important hunting excursions; from all of which I gather that at a distance of 240 geographical miles from the sea the Rufiji is of magnitude sufficient to be utilized by the natives; and from Hasson bin Salim el Shaksi, who has crossed it several times in Urori, I believe that it is about forty or fifty yards wide, with numerous fords in it, where the water only comes up to the hips—say about three feet deep.

14

Zanzibar, Coast of Africa
Oct. 23, 1874[1]

It is well known to travellers who have been in Central Africa that Urori is a large country situate south of Ugogo. Along the southerly frontier of Ugogo rise several streams, the principal of

12. The area of the Pogoro. See Last, *Polyglotta Africana Orientalis*, viii, 14; Beardall, "Exploration of the Rufiji River under the Orders of the Sultan of Zanzibar," 653; Johnston, *A Comparative Study of the Bantu and Semi-Bantu Languages*, I, 168, II, 47.
13. The Bena lived to the south of the Hehe. See Culwick and Culwick, *Ubena of the Rivers*.
14. See document 3, note 35.
15. Used for the making of false teeth due to "the superior hardness of its enamel." "Captain J. H. Speke's Discovery of the Victoria Nyanza Lake, the Supposed Source of the Nile. From his Journal," 569.
1. *NYH*, Dec. 4, 1874.

which is the Kisigo, abounding with hippopotami and crocodiles. East of Urori commences Kasungu,[2] through which the Kisigo and its sister streams flow into the Rwaha, which soon becomes known as the Rufiji.

After traversing Kasungu, along a distance which the Arabs designate an eight days' journey, the Rufiji enters Katanga from the southwest, from which may be deduced the inference that the river makes a deep bend before reaching Katanga. From Katanga to Matumbi is ten days' journey. From Jumbe to the Matumbi Mountains[3] is a distance of thirty miles. On the other side of the Matumbi Mountains the Rufiji is joined by the Kienga River, which, as I said before, comes from the southwest.

According to Jumbe and two of his chiefs who had ascended the Rufiji as far as Matumbi the river is deep enough for a boat of the size of the *Wave* (they were not aware that she drew five feet), but there are several bars during low ebb which impede navigation, so that, though we might ascend far, we should find plenty of trouble and hard work. Our gig, they said, might easily ascend as far as Urori if the natives permitted us, but it would require talk and hongo cloth.

The resources of the country around us, of Jumbe and the neighboring tribes, were manifold, according to native report. Jumbe himself could sell me, if I required it, three times as much rice as would fill the *Wave*. The people round about possessed abundance of this grain. On the entire Rufiji plain, between Matumbi and the sea, I might collect as much rice, Indian corn, chickens and eggs as I needed or could take away cheap. Jumbe would sell me fifteen measures of rice for a cloth worth $1 at Zanzibar. Only six measures of rice sell for $1 at Zanzibar. In exchange for their products they were willing to receive silver money, dollars and rupees, umpice,[4] crockery, glassware and cotton cloth, Merikani[5] and Kaniki.

At the base of the mountains of Matumbi is to be found an abundance of gum copal, the fossil gum known here as msan-durusi, from which carriage varnish is made. It is sold by the frasilah, a weight of thirty-five pounds. At the base of the mountains, where there is an inexhaustible supply of it, it can be purchased at from $1.75 to $3 per frasilah, according to the talents and eloquence of

2. Stanley is here giving hearsay information that is very unclear; he does not locate many of the places mentioned in the map accompanying *TDC*, I.

3. South of the Rufiji. See Meyer, *Deutsch Kolonialreich*, 132–33.

4. Pice, a copper currency introduced into Zanzibar by Said bin Sultan in 1840. Burton, *Zanzibar*, II, 405–06.

5. *Amerikani*—unbleached cotton cloth.

the purchaser. At Zanzibar it ranges in price from $7 to $9 per weight of thirty-five pounds. This means, supposing a steam vessel drawing but thirty inches of water, especially constructed for river navigation, with a capacity of thirty tons, were to proceed up the Rufiji to the copal diggings, and purchase thirty tons of this gum at $3 per weight of thirty-five pounds, that at Zanzibar the enterprising merchant could sell his cargo to the first European or American merchant for $8 the frasilah at this very moment; in other words, obtain the handsome sum of $12,500 for an outlay during a few days or weeks of $5,700.

Beyond Matumbi all the countries north, south and west contain ivory in greater or lesser quantities. Urori is rich in this precious article of trade. The same enterprising merchant, having employed the late dry season in the collection of his gum copal cargo, could proceed safely any distance up the Rufiji as far as Urori, where he could have, of course, an agent in advance of him, and collect easily a cargo of thirty tons of ivory. This article is worth in Unyanyembe $1 per pound; in Urori it may be purchased at from sixty cents to ninety cents per pound.

If we make a tabular estimate of the cost and profit to be obtained in this trade your readers will perceive for themselves of what value painstaking geographical research is to the merchant:

To cost at Zanzibar of 30 tons ivory, at $65 the frasilah, free of all duty $124,800

To cost in Urori of 30 tons of ivory, at $31.50 the frasilah 60,480

Clear profit, £11,016,9s.6d, or ....$ 64,320

Ugangeh is richer in ivory than Urori, according to the Arabs; but until my explorations of the Rufiji I admit that I never heard of this country before; but there is such a vast extent of country west of the Rufiji delta so little known that long years must elapse before the geography of Eastern Central Africa can become known. Ugogo at the present time contributes occasionally large supplies of ivory to the coast; but the labor to obtain it by land, the tribute to which the merchant is subjected, the annoyances of which he is the object, are so great and many that, once the river traffic was opened, the proud Wagogo would be compelled to carry their own ivory to the Rufiji for sale.

Katanga and Kasungu are both new countries, now made known for the first time; so also are Korongo, Koni, Toleya, which lie on the north side of the Rufiji, between Kazunga and Matumbi. Descending the river from the Matumbi Mountains, the great plain which lies between them and its maritime delta extends before the eye, bounded to the northeast by the purple lines of the distant hills and ridges of Keecki and Wande; eastward, by the dark, gloomy forests of the delta; southward, by the countries of Muhoro[6] and Kilonga, which, from a distance, present an appearance of unbroken forest.

This great plain of the Rufiji is the creation of the river. The rich deposit it has left during the ages is fathoms deep. On its surface, enriched every rainy season by the dark mould left by the inundations, lies inexhaustible wealth. Sugar, rice, grain of various kinds, thrive wonderfully on the fat soil. It is the most populous district I have seen during four journeys to Africa, and I should estimate that at least 50,000 people inhabit this great plain. The villages stand in knots and clusters along the banks of the river, and from the time we passed Kisimbea until we anchored opposite Jumbe each bank presented troops of curious sightseers, who stood in full view of us without the least fear or distrust, from which one may be pardoned if he concludes that they gained such courage from the knowledge of their numbers. Between Fugalleh and Nyambwa I must certainly have seen some thousands of natives, who, though they chaffed us considerably, showed the very best disposition—such a disposition as may always be looked for in a people with trading instincts.

Almost always the second question propounded to a native by me on this river was, "Do the slaves pass by this way?" They all answered me promptly, "No," following it with the required information. The answer each time was the same, except at Jumbe, where I discovered that I was almost opposite the exact spot where the Arab slave-traders sometimes crossed. The route now mainly adopted by the slave-traders—commencing from Kilwa Kivinjia—crosses the Mgenga River, the Mto-Piani and, arriving at Perereh, passes through Sumanga, Ngumbu, Mamboro, Muhoro, to Mirongegi, which lies close to Jumbe, and, crossing the river at Kisu, sometimes follows the northern bank of the Rufiji to Kikunia, a three days' journey to the slave driver. From Kikunia the main road is that which leads through Kisimeteh, Ngimpia, Sindaji, Kivinjia, Kiviniga, Kisigu, and arrives at Mbuamaji, on the sea; or the slave caravan pushes on to Dar Salaam.[7]

6. For Mohoro, Meyer, *Deutsch Kolonialreich*, 108–09.
7. There was then an argument over the number of slaves being brought over this route. Elton in 1873 and 1874 reported a busy traffic from Kilwa north; Holmwood estimated that 15,000 reached Pemba yearly. Their superior, Prideaux, doubted this total, but a later investigation by Kirk substantially upheld Holmwood's estimate. Elton to Prideaux, Dec. 20, 1873, and other despatches in this file, E-64, ZA; Frederick Holmwood, "Introductory Chapter on Africa and the Slave-Trade," in Elton, *Travels and Researches*, 9–12; Prideaux to Aitchison, March 9, 1875, E-71, ZA; Kirk to Derby, April 20, 1876, FO 84/1453, PRO.

The route adopted by the slave traders mainly in crossing the Rufiji is that which skirts the Matumbi mountains via Ruhingo, on the
river. All the eastern villages along the line of travel through the
Rufiji plain are interested in the slave trade. They keep the slave
traders informed of every item of news concerning the approach of
any foe, particularly the white men, and I discovered that long before we had arrived at Jumbe the natives knew of our coming.
Messengers had been dispatched from Miehweh by river and by
land to herald our advent in the river, and I noted also that as soon
as our boat hove in sight of any village of a principal district a
couple of canoes left well manned with paddlers to inform those
above that the dreaded Wasungu had at last invaded the river with
two boats. On the morrow I was informed by a servant of Jumbe
I should experience different treatment if I persisted in my intention
of ascending the river.

In the morning we prepared to extend our discoveries up stream.
The dew had fallen heavily during the night. The tall reeds which
fringed the river banks dripped huge raindrops, which the morning
sun transformed into the appearance of diamonds. Large crowds of
natives speedily made their appearance and were witnesses of the
preliminary work of getting under way, but they made no demonstration of hostility.

Soon after starting our gig put to shore to convey a man aboard
who expressed a wish to trade with the white men. As the gig rowed
hard after us with him this native took fright at the sound of our
bugle, which was blown to hasten the movements of the rowers,
and took a somerset into the water to the intense merriment of all
on board and the sightseers on shore. We at once dropped anchor
to encourage him and to explain to him that it was a most foolish
thing to be afraid of white men, who would never come up the Rufiji
except as friends to the natives. We had the gratification to see him
come on board again and depart with a profound respect for white
people.

Continuing our journey a few snags made their appearance in the
river for the first time; but they presented no obstacles—the river
was broad and deep enough on either side. Shortly after rounding a
sharp bend of the river, the Matumbi mountains came clear and
distinct into view, from which I surmise that we were not twenty
miles from them. While admiring the scene so suddenly presented
to our view we were approaching the northern bank of the river, on
which a large settlement was visible. The district was called Kisu,

and the people were strong upholders of the slave-trade and hostile
to white men, whom they have been taught to regard as enemies
by the slave traders.

We were compelled by the channel to approach within a few feet
of the bank, and had they been able to decide rapidly upon hostilities
we all should have been exposed to great danger. The friendly breeze,
however, came on strong and fresh at this moment, and we swept by
them in an instant. But we had no sooner passed this than another
large cluster of villages came into view, and a body of about 200
natives were seen at the landing place. As we drew near the chief
stepped out and hailed us, demanding to know what business we
had on the Rufiji. He was answered by one of our armed escort,
a tall, robust, young fellow, black as ink in features, but with an eye
like a hawk and shoulders that in breadth would not have disgraced
the best man in her Majesty's Life Guards.

"We are white men. What do you want with us?"

"I want you to stop for a talk."

"We don't want to talk just yet. We have not gone far enough."

"I want you to stop first before you go up further."

"Cannot do it, master," answered he boldly, and making a certain
sign, which all understand who know East Africans, that he was
wearied.

"I tell you to stop."

"We are sick of stopping, master; cannot do it, master."

"Why have you come up the river?"

"To see."

"To see what?"

"The river."

"What about the river?"

"To know how far it goes and how deep the water is."

"How far do you intend going?"

"As far as we can."

"There are bars (fungo) on the river. You cannot cross those in
that big boat."

"We will try to."

"Well, now, take my advice; stop here, or it will be worse for you."

"Impossible, master."

"I'll make you stop."

"Do so, then, and farewell to you, master."

The chief of Kisu was left fuming on the landing place, and men
were seen running hither and thither in alarm, and the groups were

seen to become small knots of men, violently gesticulating and stamping their feet, and all this time the *Wave* was plunging up river before a spanking breeze.

We were sailing gloriously along, and the Kisu chief and his violent people were left far behind. Bend after bend had been safely rounded, the mountains were seen more distinctly, when we suddenly stopped and half keeled over. Our deep helm was furrowing the sand at the stern, and the bow, though drawing but two feet, was fast. Extricating her from her position, we sought another spot, and, after great difficulty, managed to cross the bar. The sun was fearfully hot, and seemed to burn into our brains. The wind died away, and came only in cats'-paws. The current was not very rapid, as the river was broad at this place; but it was such laborious work with the oars that we had simply become subjects of derision to the jeering and hostile natives. However, we persevered, and, with one sail hoisted, we managed to creep along and make progress, though slow.

Soon we were requested to halt a second time by the shore people, but we paid no heed to them except to answer an occasional question. The excitement was evidently growing along the shore, and our continued progress, despite all threats and commands, seemed to have plunged them into a stupor of rage. At one village, a few miles above the larger settlements of Kisu, a friendly voice shouted out, "You cannot go further with that big boat; there is no water ahead;" to which we answered cheerily that was precisely what we came to know, and we would try, and if not able to go ahead we would return.

About a mile above the village the river widened to about 300 yards. The low shores seemed to be but dried sandbanks, and right across from side to side the water rippled uneasily, with every indication of a stubborn bar. The guides, as they looked at it, said at once that we had come as far as we could go in the large boat. We pushed on, however, and went aground. We unshipped the rudder, hauled down the sail and manned fourteen oars, and, with vociferous chorus to the exhilarating boat song, we plunged forward, one of the young Englishmen sounding ahead. Again and again we tried it, but of no avail; over and over again we ploughed the sands, and stuck fast. Above this sand bar, which is about 200 yards in breadth, the river resumes its usual depth, but the navigation is impeded by sand bars.

After deliberating as to what had best be done I concluded to return and explore the two other principal exits from the delta, the Magambu and the Kikunia, and then visit Mafia Island, opposite the

Rufiji delta, after which I should have expended all the time I could spare before commencing my march into the interior.

On descending the river the natives shouted out to us, "We know why the Wasunga have come up the Rufiji. You came here to find out about the slave trade—to catch the slave traders. Return, and tell the other white people that we will not have the slave traders troubled nor their road crossed."

One chief was so furious that he followed us for half a mile with his men, cursing us and using the most violent language and gesture; but, fortunately for him, he confined himself to this verbal demonstration of hostility.

On the second day we entered the magnificent Magambu, and, eight hours after commencing the descent, arrived at the sea. Then, setting sail, we sailed north again, and two hours later we entered the noble estuary of the Kikunia branch of the delta, and, before a vigorous breeze and an incoming tide, sailed up the river once more, and at night anchored at the mouth of Pemba Creek. At noon the next day we had entered the Simbooranga, and descended that stream to Sanninga, where we were greeted with kindness by the people of that island.

Mafia Island [8] we ascertained to be a most fertile island, abounding in palm groves and shambas, or gardens. It is the third island in size within the Sultan's dominions. Situated opposite the delta of the Rufiji, it seems as if placed by nature at this position as the entrepôt of the main land, which is but ten miles distant. Ships of large tonnage could ride securely at anchor within 500 yards of Kismia Mafia, a place which the Admiralty charts absurdly call Kissomang Point.[9] Were not my letter already of such great length I could easily point out the advantages of securing a portion of Mafia—say the district in the neighborhood of Kismia Mafia—as a place to plant a colony of freed slaves, from which locality, after instruction and preparation, they might emerge as enterprising traders with the interior, via the Rufiji River. But I must leave these remarks for some future letter, for I must now hasten to give an unprejudiced opinion upon the value of our exploration of the Rufiji.

Readers interested in African exploration in new commercial avenues may see for themselves what the Rufiji is after reading this letter. It has lost but little in my estimation because I failed to ascend higher than Kisu in a boat built for ocean sailing. Had

8. See Baumann, *Der Sansibar-Archipel. I. Die Insel Mafia und Ihre Kleineren Nachbarinseln.*

9. De Horsey, *African Pilot*, 186.

I possessed the *Lady Alice,* which Mr. Messenger, of Teddington,[10] was building for me—and which has only arrived by this mail—I could have ascended, I believe, a couple of hundred miles, if not more, with my entire escort of armed men. For exploration, prudence requires that we shall be prepared for all contingencies; that there shall be men sufficient accompanying the explorer to enable him with a few men to make a proper defence if attacked. Our gig would have conveyed eight men and a week's provisions, but she would not have made us independent of the land, nor strong enough to resist attack, which would have endangered the success of our great journey. As I look at the *Lady Alice* I find her a boat of sufficient capacity to convey up any river a force of twenty-five men, with a month's provisions; yet she draws but twelve inches loaded. She is 40 feet in length, 6 feet beam, built of best Spanish cedar, in water-tight compartments. A duplicate of this boat would enable any traveller to proceed up the Rufiji as far as any native canoe, after which the report of such man, on his return, of the navigability of the Rufiji would settle the question for ever.

In the meantime, so far as we ascended, the Rufiji must be classed as a navigable river. Such a steamer as Sir John Glover[11] possessed on the Volta, or one built after the model of an American river steamer, may proceed up the Rufiji with ease, whenever any merchant shall be found bold enough to enter on a promising African venture.

Our work of exploration also clears up the difficulties of annihilating the overland route of the slave trader. Steam launches, properly built for river navigation, commanded by officers familiar with river navigation, assisted by guides procured at Samuga Island, may proceed either up the Magambu or Simbooranga mouth of the Rufiji, and, towing up with them a few light flatboats loaded with coal, could anchor them at Jumbe; and, proceeding lightly loaded, could capture a few slave caravans and bring down their proprietors to be punished at Zanzibar. Any naval officer, acting discreetly and energetically, could strike within four days a most effective and deadly blow at the land slave trade. Such a system of action, at intervals of a few

10. See *TDC,* I, 4. James Messenger also built the *Daisy* for use by the Church Missionary Society on Lake Victoria. Wilson and Felkin, *Uganda and the Egyptian Sudan,* I, 91ff.

11. John Glover (1829–1885) of the Royal Navy had been active in West Africa, both as naval officer and administrator. He participated in the Ashanti war of 1873 where Stanley had reported on his operations. Glover, *Life of Sir John Hawley Glover,* especially 163ff.; McIntyre, "Commander Glover and the Colony of Lagos, 1861–1873."

weeks, could not fail to be followed by results which would gratify and astonish everyone in England. Mafia Island, off Kismia Mafia, offers a capital rendezvous for the man-of-war during the absence of her launches; but if I may suggest anything from my experience of this river, I would advise that those officers charged with this duty should consist of those who have experience and who have volunteered for this important duty; that one man-of-war should be appointed specially for this river work, properly equipped with capacious steam vessel, which might navigate this stream without detriment to the good cause. A small stern-wheeler, which any English Thames shipbuilder could construct, drawing but eighteen inches of water, armed with one mountain steel seven-pounder and a couple of rocket tubes, with a crew of forty men, could forever solve the problem of how to stop the East African slave trade.

Captain Elton, in his official report to Captain Prideaux,[12] acting political agent at Zanzibar, publishes the fact that a grand total of 4,096 slaves were marched by the overland route from Kilwa to Dar Salaam. I know nothing whatever of the accuracy of these figures, but I have already disclosed to you the whereabouts of the slave traders' tracks and have informed you what my exploration of the Rufiji suggests should be done to crush the now established land slave traffic.

I should not have been at such pains to find out what I have given you above if I did not feel from my soul that the government of Great Britain, which has expended such vast sums for the suppression of this slave trade, might, for the small sum of £5,000, begin to hope that her great mission in East Africa was approaching its successful accomplishment, and so enable all men to cry *"Laus Deo!"*

15

Zanzibar
Nov. 12, 1874 [1]

The expedition which bears the above title [the *Herald* and *Telegraph* Expedition for the Exploration of the Nile Sources] is about to commence its long journey into the heart of unexplored Africa,

12. Elton to Prideaux, Jan. 28, 1874, E–64, ZA. William F. Prideaux (1840–1914) of the Indian army and diplomatic service served in Zanzibar as British representative from 1873 to 1875. *Who Was Who 1897–1915,* 576.
1. *NYH,* Dec. 24, 1874.

but before embarking on board the fleet of dhows which are anchored nearby waiting for us, I wish to employ a few hours in giving you some information respecting its organization, present intentions and prospects.

Acquainted but too well with the dangers, the sicknesses, the troubles and annoyances which I shall have presently to encounter, since the burden of responsibility of the conduct of this expedition rests on myself alone, I must confess to a slight feeling of joy at the prospect of immediate departure for the interior. I feel elated at the fact that I have been selected as the commander of this expedition, for the very fact of my selection argues that there is a being in existence something similar to me in form and appearance; and that this being who once was very much doubted has sufficient integrity and honesty to be chosen to repeat his journey to Africa. Though I had very many reasons for not undertaking a second journey to Africa I was conscious that by the acceptance of this command I would compel those who doubted that I had discovered Livingstone at Ujiji to confess themselves in error; and the member of the Royal Geographical Society who called me a "charlatan" to retract the libel. The few months I had spent in Ashantee with the British troops had not materially injured my health; at the same time they had not contributed much to establish that which had been impaired during my search after Livingstone. But without considering the wisdom of the proceeding or my powers to accomplish the duty I was preparing to perform, I sailed from England in command of the *Daily Telegraph* and NEW YORK HERALD expedition, with the paramount idea in me that if I lived to return with good results my unjust enemies would be silenced forever. So much for myself and my hopes.

Soon after the *Daily Telegraph*'s publication of the fact that a new expedition was about to proceed to Africa under my command I became the recipient of some hundreds of letters from volunteers who desired to assist and advise me in my undertaking. It would be no exaggeration to state that these applicants for position in this expedition considerably exceeded 1,200 in number. Probably 700 of them were natives of Great Britain, 300 were natives of America and the balance might be distributed equally between France and Germany. Three of these volunteers were generals, five were colonels, several scores were captains and lieutenants in the army; about fifty applications came from officers in the navy, while the rest were civilians in various professions and walks of life, ranging from the civil engineer high in his profession and proficient in all acquirements, to the Liverpool cotton porter and New York boarding house runner, who desired to see Africa, "having visited almost all parts of the world." The army and navy officers who applied were evidently gentlemen in earnest, far better qualified, perhaps, than I was for the post of commander; but, judging from their letters, I must confess that the majority of the civilians who applied for situations were madmen, and that the rest were fools, who knew nothing of what they boasted they could do. It may be that I use very harsh terms, but I speak the truth; and, as the applicants shall be nameless, I do no harm. The unblushing falsehoods of these nameless applicants naturally disgusted me; there were few of them who did not declare on their honor that they were up to every "dodge," had seen everything and knew everything. One madman proposed that I should take a balloon with me; another a flying ship; another proposed that he and I should go alone, disguised as negroes, and unarmed; another desired me to take a tramway with me and a small locomotive, of which he would be the engineer; another proposed that I should endeavor to establish an empire in Africa, which was a very easy thing to do, as he had read "Kaloolah," "Ned Gray," and "My Kalulu," [2] and knew "all about it;" while one, still more insane than any, suggested to me that, instead of taking guns and ammunition, and paying tribute to "nigger" chiefs, I should poison them off hand. The Frenchmen and Germans were mainly commissioners of hotels, who, like the idiots I imagine them to be by their letters, volunteered to interpret for me at the various hotels I should happen to stop at in Africa. They were rich in recommendations, and could speak seven languages; they were all prime travellers, and the only merit they possessed in my eyes was that they knew how to cook a "bef-tek" on occasion. To all these applicants I was naturally mutely impregnable; but I may as well inform them all though your columns that I have with me three young Englishmen with whom I have every reason to believe I shall be perfectly satisfied, and that I bid them all a regretful farewell.[3]

I never knew how many kind friends I could number until I was about to sail from England. The White Star line treated me in the most princely fashion; gave me free passages to America and back.[4] The Peninsular and Oriental Company and the British India, through

2. *Kaloolah* by William S. Mayo (1811–1895), an adventure story set in Africa. Hart, *The Oxford Companion to American Literature*, 537. For Stanley's novel, *My Kalulu*, see Bennett, "Some Notes on Two Early Novels concerning Tanzania."
3. The Pococks and Frederick Barker (c. 1850–1875). BCB, III, 30–31.
4. See Anderson, *White Star*, for the story of this trans-Atlantic line.

their courteous agents, showered courtesy after courtesy on me. Testimonials from hundreds of gentlemen were thrust on me, and invitations to dinner and parties and to "spend a month or so in the country" were so numerous that if I could have availed myself of them in succession years must elapse before any hotel need charge a penny to my account. But, though my preparations for the journey monopolized my time and prevented me from doing anything more than declining with thanks these manifold kindnesses, my numerous friends must believe that I am none the less grateful. I departed from England August 15, loaded with good wishes, keepsakes, photographs, favors of all kinds, prouder of the knowledge that I had more friends than enemies than any prince or potentate can be of his throne or power.

At Aden I met my white assistants, whom I had despatched from England, via Southampton, in charge of the dogs. The young Englishmen had quite got over all melancholy feelings, and were in prime spirits, though they entertained a doubt that, if Central Africa was as hot as Aden, whether they should enjoy it very much. On my assuring them that they need fear nothing on the score of heat in Africa, they expressed themselves as relieved from their greatest fear. On the British India steamer *Euphrates* I was delighted to find that the Pocock brothers possessed several qualifications beyond those of sobriety, civility and industry. I discovered that they were capital singers and musicians having belonged to some choir in their native town, where they were much esteemed.

The delightful weather we experienced between Aden and Zanzibar was most grateful after the intense heat of Steamer Point, and we consequently arrived at Zanzibar on the 22d of September,[5] almost as fresh and as robust as when we left England. The next morning after I landed some of my old friends of the former expedition heard of my arrival, and it was very gratifying to me to see the pleasure they manifested to one who had been so stern to them on certain occasions, when naught but sternness of the most extreme kind would have enabled me to overmaster a disposition they sometimes betrayed to be sullenly disobedient and mutinous. But they remembered, as well as I did, that though I was merciless when they were disposed to be wicked, I was as kind and as partial to them as Livingstone was when all went fair and well; and they knew that, when the rewards were distributed, that those who had behaved themselves as true men were not forgotten. The report that I had

5. *TDC,* I, 54, gives Sept. 21.

come was soon bruited through the length and breadth of the island, and Livingstone's and my old dusky comrades gathered quickly about my good host, Mr. Sparhawk's, house, to pay their respects to me, and of course to receive heshimeh, or presents, with which, fortunately, I had provided myself before leaving England.

Here was Ulimengo,[6] the incorrigible joker and hunter of the Search Expedition, with his mouth expanding gratefully on this day at the sight of a gold ring which encircled one of his thick black fingers, and a silver chain, which held an ornament, and hung down his broad and superb chest; and Rojab,[7] who narrowly escaped destruction for immersing Livingstone's six years' journal in the muddy waters of the Mukondokwa, with his ebony face lighted up with the most extreme good will towards myself for my munificent gift; and Manwa Sera also, the redoubtable ambassador of Speke and my most faithful messenger, who had once braved a march of 600 miles with his companion Sarmine in my service, and Livingstone's most faithful captain on his last journey; he was speechless with gratitude because I had suspended a splendid jet necklace to his neck and encircled one of his fingers with a huge seal ring, which to his mind was a sight to see and enjoy.

Nor was the now historical Mabruki Speke—styled by Captain Burton "Mabruki the Bull-headed"—who has each time distinguished himself with white men as a hawk-eyed guardian of their property and interests—nor was Mabruki, I say, less enraptured with his presents than his fellows; while the courtly, valiant, faithful Chowpereh—the man of manifold virtues, the indomitable and sturdy Chowpereh—was as pleased as any with the silver dagger and gold bracelet and earrings which fell to his share.

His wife, whom I had purchased from the eternally wandering slave gang, and released from the harsh cold iron collar which encircled her neck, and whom I had bestowed upon Chowpereh as a free woman for wife, was, I discovered the happy mother of a fine little boy, a little tiny Chowpereh, who I hope will grow up to lead future expeditions to Africa, and be as loyal to white men as his good father has proved himself. Besides bestowing presents on the wife and child, Chowpereh, having heard that I had brought a wondrous store of medicine, entreated me that I should secure his son during his absence with me in Africa against any visitation of the smallpox, which I hope I have done by vaccination.

6. Ulimengo had served with Speke; he died at Vinyata in Ituru during this expedition. Gray, "Livingstone's Muganda Servant," 128.
7. See HIFL, 642–43.

Two or three days after my arrival a deputation of the "Faithfuls" came to me to learn my intentions and purposes. I informed them that I was about to make a much longer journey into Africa than formerly, and into very different countries from any that I had ever been into before, and I proceeded to sketch out to the astonished men an outline of the prospective journey. They were all seated on the ground before me, tailor fashion, eyes and ears interested, and keen to see and hear every word of my broken Kisawahili. As country after country was mentioned, of which they had hitherto but dimly heard, and river after river, lake after lake named, all of which I hoped, with their aid, to explore carefully and thoroughly, various ejaculations, expressive of emotions of wonder, joy and a little alarm, broke from their lips, but when I concluded each man drew a long breath, and almost simultaneously they uttered, in their own language, "Ah, fellows, this is a journey worthy to be called a journey!"

"But, master," said they, with some anxiety, "this long journey will take years to travel—six, nine or ten years."

"Nonsense," said I. "Six, nine or ten years! What can you be thinking of? It takes the Arabs nearly three years to go to Ujiji, it is true, but I was only sixteen months from Zanzibar to Ujiji and back to the sea. Is it not true?" [8]

"Ay, true," answered they.

"Very well. And I tell you, further, that there is not enough money in this world to pay me for stopping in Africa ten, nine, or even six years. I have not come here to live in Africa. I have come here simply to see these rivers and lakes, and after I have seen them to return home."

"Ah, but you know the big master (Livingstone) said he was only going for two years, and you know that he was, altogether, nine years." [9]

"That is true enough. Nevertheless, you know what I did before, and what I am likely to do again, if all goes well."

"Yes, we remember that you are very hot, and you did drive us until our feet were sore and we were ready to drop from fatigue. Wallah! but there never was such a journey as that from Unyanyembe home! No Arab or white man came from Unyanyembe in so short a time as you did. It was nothing but throw away this thing and that, and go on, go on, go on, all the time. Aye, master, that is true."

8. In *TDC*, I, 58, Stanley gives a slightly different quotation.
9. Livingstone's last trip lasted from 1866 to 1873.

"Well, is it likely, then, when I marched so quick before that I am likely to be slow now? Am I much older now than I was then? Am I less strong? Do I not know what a journey is now? When I first started from Zanzibar to Ujiji I allowed the guide to show me the way; but when we came back who showed you the way? Was it not I, by means of that little compass which could not lie like the guide?"

"Aye, true master; true, every word."

"Very well, then, finish these foolish words of yours and go and get me 300 good men like yourselves, and when we get away from Bagamoyo I will show you whether I have forgotten how to travel."

"Ay, Wallah, my master;" and, in the words of the Old Testament, "they forthwith arose, and went as they were commanded."

The result of our polite "talk" or "palaver" was witnessed shortly when the doors and gates of the Bertram Agency and former Consulate[10] were thronged by volunteers, who were of all shades of blackness, and who hailed from almost every African tribe known. Wahiyow, Wabena, Wagindo,[11] Wanyamwezi, Wagogo, Waseguhha, Wasagara, Wahehe, Somali,[12] Wagalla, Wanyassa,[13] Wadirigo,[14] and a score of other tribes, had their representatives, and each day added to the number, until I had barely time to do anything more than strive, with calmness and well practised patience, to elicit from them information as to who they were, what they had been doing and whom they had served. The brave fellows who had accompanied Livingstone on his last journey, or myself, of course, had the preference, because they knew me, and fewer words were wanted to strike a bargain. Forty-seven of those who accompanied Livingstone on his last journey answered to their names, and two hundred strangers, in whose fidelity I was willing to risk my reputation as a traveller and nearly £1,000 sterling in advanced wages, were finally enlisted and sworn as escort and servants. Many of them will naturally prove

10. The American representative, Cheney, was an agent of another house. See document 16, note 12.

11. The Ngindo of southeastern Tanzania; they were then "one of the great slave supplying tribes" and were numerous along the coast and in Zanzibar. Steere, *Short Specimens of the Vocabularies of Three Unpublished African Languages (Gindo, Zaramo, and Angazidja)*, 5; see also Cross-Upcott, "Social Aspects of Ngindo Bee-Keeping."

12. See Lewis, *The Modern History of Somaliland*, and the references therein.

13. For the various peoples around Lake Nyasa, Tew, *Peoples of the Lake Nyasa Region*.

14. Cameron met Africans he called Dirigo near Mpwapwa. Cameron, *Across Africa*, I, 88–89. Beidelman, "The Baraguyu," 245–78, suggests they are Baraguyu.

recusants and malcontents, braggarts, cowards and runaways; but it cannot be helped; I have done all that I am able to do in providing against desertion and rascality. Where there is such a large number of wild people it would be absurd to hope that they will all be faithful and loyal to the trust and confidence reposed in them, or, that a large expedition can be conducted thousands of miles without great loss.

The enlistment of the escort and preparations for the expedition were temporarily stopped during our exploration of the Rufiji River, but on our return these were resumed with all vigor and despatch. After the men, the armed escort and porters were secured, I devoted myself to examine the barter goods which were necessary to procure sustenance in the far interior. I discovered, contrary to my expectations (for Mr. Clements Markham,[15] Secretary to the Geographical Society, had published the statement that these goods had risen in price since my departure from Zanzibar), that the barter goods were one per cent and in some instances two per cent cheaper than they were purchasable formerly. Bales of American sheeting that cost me $93.75 in 1871 I was now enabled to buy for $87.50 per bale, while the sami-sami beads, that formerly cost $13 the frahsilah, now cost but $9.75.[16] This was very much in my favor; and after much consultation with the lately returned leaders of caravans upon the present prevailing fashion of beads and cloth among the distant tribes, I ordered the necessary stock of both, which, when piled up in portable bales and sacks, present quite an imposing and somewhat formidable pile.

If cloth and beads and wire are cheaper than they were two years ago the hire of pagazis or porters is double. In 1871 and 1872 I employed Wanyamwezi and Wanguana at the rate of $2.50 per month each man; the same class of persons now obtain $5 per month, and with some people I have had great difficulty to procure them at this pay, for they held out bravely for a week for $7 and $8 per month. There must have been no lack of money, and somewhat inordinate liberality among those English gentlemen of the Cameron Expedition,[17] to have risen the hire of such men to double the

---

15. Clements R. Markham (1830–1916), one of the foremost geographers of his day. He was honorary secretary of the Royal Geographic Society from 1863 to 1888, and its president from 1893 to 1905. Markham, *The Life of Sir Clements R. Markham; GJ* 47 (1916), 161–76.

16. The reduced prices probably were due to the uncertain conditions of trade resulting from the Arab-Nyamwezi difficulties in the interior. See Bennett, *Studies in East African History,* 4ff.

17. Verney L. Cameron (1844–1894) was sent inland by the Royal Geographical Society to aid Livingstone. When he learned of Livingstone's death, Cameron went on to explore Lake Tanganyika and then crossed Africa. Stanley

former rate they were accustomed to. I hear that several of these men engaged with Cameron for $7 and $8 per month, which, if true, only shows too plainly how the money has been expended. If each white traveller who intends penetrating Africa commits himself to such an injudicious proceeding as to double the rate of hire to which the pagazis and Wanguana escort are accustomed, it will soon be impossible for any gentlemen, unless those commissioned by a rich and generous government, to dare the venture. A moment's reflection on the expense which this liberality entails on him would show the traveller the unwisdom of liberality to strange men whom he knows nothing of previous to his journey. The time to be liberal is after the return, when the best men can be discriminated from the worst, the very good from the indifferently good and the steadily loyal fellows from the deserters. At such a time the reward is often considered to be as good as the wages, and should the traveller require them again at some future period his judicious distribution of rewards will be found to have been remembered to his advantage. It has grown to be a custom now for servants, porters and escort to receive at least four months' pay in advance. Before starting from Bagamoyo I expect that the expedition will number 400 men. Each of these men, previous to his marching, will have received £4 pay in advance, either in money or in cloth. The most prudent ask that their advance be given them in cloth. Those who have money require three days to spend it in debauchery and rioting, in purchasing wives, while a few of the staid married men, who have children, will provide stores for their families.

On the morning of the fourth day, when the bugle sounds for the march, I need not be surprised if I find it a difficult task to muster the people together and that hours will be employed in hunting the laggards up and driving them on to our first camp, and very probably I shall find that at least fifteen or so have absented themselves altogether. This, of course, will be annoying, but it is well that I know that it is a probable thing and that I am in a measure prepared for such desertion. On the second day of the march I shall probably find myself minus ten more, which also will be annoying and exceedingly trying to the patience I have bottled up for the emergency. For several days longer there will be constant desertion by twos,

---

would follow parts of his route on the journey he was now preparing. See Cameron, *Across Africa; DNB,* XXIII, 379–81. Cameron was the first African explorer to set out with "a prepared list of queries furnished by the Anthropological Institute." Cameron, "Anthropology of Africa," 167–68; Fox, "Report of the Committee . . . appointed for the purpose of preparing and publishing brief forms of Instructions for Travellers, Ethnologists, and other Anthropological Observers."

threes and fours, but the losses will have to be borne and remedied somehow; and finally disease will break out, the result of their mad three days' debauchery, to be succeeded by smallpox, ulcerous sores, dysentery and fever and other diseases. And about this time, too, the white men will begin to suffer from strange languor of body and feverish pulse, and these, despite the rapidly diminishing force of carriers, will have to be transported on the shoulders of porters or on the backs of such asses as may be strong enough for such work. And the future of the expedition depends upon the way we shall be able to weather this stormy period; for the outlook at about this time will be sad indeed. Just think what a mournful jest a special correspondent of a rival newspaper might make of the *Daily Telegraph* and NEW YORK HERALD expedition at this time, say three short weeks from the coast! The magnificent caravan which started from the sea 400 strong, armed to the teeth, comfortable, well laden and rich, each armed man strong, healthy, well chosen, his skin shining like brown satin, eyes all aglow with pride and excitement, strong in his Snider rifle and twenty rounds of cartridges, his axe and knives; twelve stately, tall guides, tricked out in crimson joho and long plumes, heading the procession, which is nearly a mile long, while brazen trumpets blow and blare through the forest, awakening the deep woods with their sounds and animating every soul to the highest pitch of hope. Ah! this was a scene worth seeing. But three weeks from now how different will be the greatly diminished caravan. Scores will have deserted, the strong will have become weak, the robust sick, the leader will be ready to despair and to wish that he had never ventured a second time into the sea of mishaps and troubles which beset the traveller in Africa! These are my anticipations, which are none of the brightest, you will allow. However, when the soldier has donned his helmet it is too late to deplore the folly which induced him to enlist.

Among other things which I convey with me on this expedition to make our work as thorough as possible is a large pontoon named the *Livingstone*. A traveller having experience of the difficulties which prevent efficient exploration is not likely to enter Africa without being provided with almost every requisite likely to remove the great obstacles which lack of means of ferriage presents. After I had accepted the command of this second expedition I began to devise and invent the most portable kind of floating expedient or vehicle to transport baggage and men across streams and lakes to render me independent of the native chiefs. I thought of everything I had seen likely to suit my purpose. Zinc tubes, such as the Engineer

Department conveyed to the Prah in the late Ashantee war; canvas boats, such as Marcy, in his *Prairie Traveller,* recommends;[18] the devices and expedients suggested in *Art of Travel,* india rubber boats, Irish wicker boats, &c., but everything I thought of that previous travellers had experimented with were objected to by me on account of their weight and insufficient floating power. It is one of the most interesting things in African travel, among chains of lakes and numerous large rivers, to resolve the problem of navigating these waters safely and expeditiously without subjecting an expedition to the caprice and extortion of an ignorant savage chief or entailing upon yourself heavy expense for porterage. As no carts or wagons can be employed in conveying boats or zinc pontoons through the one-foot-wide paths, which are the channels of overland trade in Central Africa, zinc pontoons were not to be thought of. A zinc tube, eighteen inches in diameter and eight feet long, would form a good load for the strongest porter; but fancy the number of tubes of this zinc required to convey across a lake fifty miles wide a force of 300 men and about nine tons of baggage and material of an expedition. And what kind of a boat can transport such a number and weight across a stormy lake, such as we could carry with us, at a moderately rapid rate of travel, a distance of from 1,000 to 2,000 miles?

After much anxious deliberation and ruin of much paper I sketched out a series of inflatable pontoon tubes, to be two feet in diameter and eight feet long, to be laid transversely, resting on three separate keels and securely lashed to them with two separate triangular compartments of the same depth, eight feet at the base, which should form the bow and stern of the inflatable boat. Over these several sections three lengthy poles were to be laid which should be lashed between each transverse tube to the three keels underneath. Above these upper poles laid lengthwise were to be bamboo poles, laid transversely, upon which the passengers and baggage might rest, without danger of foundering. After the design was fully matured the next thing to do was to find a manufacturer intelligent enough to comprehend what was required, and as J. C. Cording of Piccadilly, London, had a good reputation among travellers, I tried him, and after a very few moments' conversation with the foreman of the shop I was delighted to find that he perfectly understood what unusually strong material was requisite, and every part and

18. Randolph B. Marcy (1812–1887), an American army officer; in 1859 he published *The Prairie Traveler* for the War Department to serve as a guide for travelers in the American West. R. F. Burton edited an edition of the volume in 1863. *DAB*, XII, 273–74.

portion of the design. I need only add that within a month I had in my possession the several parts and sections of this peculiar floating craft, beautifully and strongly made, in as complete and efficient order as would please the most fastidious traveller. All these several sections, when put in the scales, weighted 300 pounds, which, divided into portable loads of sixty pounds each, require but five men to carry the entire craft. No material can possibly equal this. If the strong, thick india rubber cloth is punctured or rent Cording has supplied me with the material to repair it, and if all turns out as well with it as I strongly anticipate and hope it will, it must, of course, prove invaluable to me.[19]

But an explorer needs something else, some other form of floatable structure, to be able to produce results worthy of a supreme effort at penetrating the unknown parts of Africa. He must have a boat with him with which he may be enabled to circumnavigate lakes and penetrate long distances up and down rivers with a small and efficient body of men, while the main body is encamped at some suitable and healthy site. And what kind of a boat can be invented for the traveller such as he can carry thousands of miles, through bush and jungle and heat and damp and rain, without impairing its usefulness or causing him to regard it as an incumbrance? After various plans and designs I could think of nothing better than a light cedar boat, something after the manner and style of the Oko-naga (Canada) cedar boat, but larger and of greater capacity. These Canadian boats are generally thirty feet in length and from five to six feet in width. They are extremely light and portable, and when near rapids are taken ashore and easily hoisted on the shoulders of six men and taken to smooth waters again. But a boat of this kind, though portable for short distances in Canada, would have to be constructed differently to be carried along the crooked narrow paths of African jungles. They would require to be built in water-tight sections, each section light enough to be carried by two men without distressing the bearers. Mr. James Messenger, of Teddington, near London, 'has a well-deserved reputation for building superb river boats, and while enjoying a Sunday near Hampton, witnessing the various specimens of his skill and workmanship, I came to the conclusion that Mr. Messenger would suit me. I had an interview with this gentleman, and I laid my plans before him. I soon discovered that I was in the presence of a master workman, by the intelligent way he followed my explanations, though it was evident that he

19. The vessel was not used on the expedition. See *TDC*, I, 4–5.

had not the slightest idea what an African jungle path was like. He understood what I meant by "portability," but his ideas of "portability" of anything naturally suggested it on a broad highway, an English turnpike road, or at the utmost a path over treeless fields or commons. I doubt if even now the gentleman understands the horrors of a jungle path, with its intricate and never-ending crooked curves, beset on each side by a depth and intensity of vegetation through which we must struggle, and twist, and contort our bodies that we may pass through with our burdens, while the perspiration which streams from our brows almost blinds us, and causes us to grope and stumble and halt, like so many blind puppies, in that sickly, dull twilight which reigns there. To convey anything very large, or wide, or high, or long, is out of the question through such a tangle and under such circumstances; and I must assume to myself the credit of having endeavored to describe such a locality as vividly as my powers would enable me to the boat-builder. Mr. Messenger accepted the contract to build a boat of light, well seasoned cedar, 40 feet in length and 6 feet in width, in five sections, each section of which was not to exceed more than 120 pounds in weight.[20] I saw the boat after it was constructed, and before it was sawn up into sections, and her beautiful lines and the skilled workmanship lavished on her elicited at once from me unqualified praise and approbation. Before departing from his yard I suggested to Mr. Messenger that he should weigh her as she stood, and divide her, if he found her of greater weight than he or I anticipated, into sections not exceeding 120 pounds in weight.

This boat, completed and packed with care, followed me to Zanzibar by the next mail. When I opened the packages a perfect marvel of boat architecture was revealed; every bolt and nut worked perfect and free, and every one who saw the sections admired them. In a transport of joy I ordered the weighing scales to be rigged up, and each section weighed carefully. Four of the sections weighed 280 pounds avoirdupois, and one section weighed 310 pounds! The utter impossibility of rectifying this mistake in a place like Zanzibar made me despair at first, and I thought the best thing to do was to ship her back to England, and present her, with my compliments, to Mr. Messenger; but, upon inquiring for a carpenter, a young shipwright called Ferris was introduced to me and recommended for his intelligence. I exhibited the beautiful but totally unmanageable boat, and told him that in her present state she was useless to

20. There is an illustration of the boat in *ibid.*, 4.

me and to everybody else, because she was too heavy and cumbersome and that I could not carry her if I were paid £5 per mile for doing so, and that time was short with me. I desired him to cut her down six inches, and subdivide each section, and to complete the work within two weeks, for that was the utmost time I could give him. To effect these improvements the two after sections had to be condemned, which would curtail the length considerably, and of course, mar her beauty.

I can now congratulate myself (good Mr. Ferris having completed his work to my entire satisfaction) on possessing a boat which I can carry any distance without distressing the porters, with twelve men, rowing ten oars and two short paddles, and able to sail over any lake in Central Africa. I ought to state here that I do not blame Mr. Messenger for the mistake of sending me such unmanageable sections so much as I blame myself for not stopping over another month in England to watch the construction of such a novelty as this kind of boat must necessarily be to a Thames boat builder.

As this expedition is for a different purpose to the former one with which I discovered Livingstone, I am well provided with the usual scientific instruments which travellers who intend to bring home results that will gratify scientific societies take with them. I have chronometers, sextants, artificial horizons, compasses, beam and prismatic; pedometers, aneroid barometers and thermometers; nautical almanacs for three years, hand leads and 1,000 fathoms sounding line, with a very complete little reel, mathematical instruments, a planisphere and a complete and most excellent photographic apparatus, and large stock of dry plates. I have also half a dozen good timepieces, silver and gold, blank charts and every paraphernalia and apparatus necessary to bring home such results as will suit the most captious critic.

The East Coast of Africa, from the mouth of the Juba River to the mouth of the Rovuma, possesses hundreds of good starting points for the unexplored interior; but the best, for many reasons, is Bagamoyo. The present expedition is such a large and costly one, and promises so far to be the best organized and best equipped of any that ever left the seacoast of East Africa for the purpose of exploration, that it would have been a great pity if it were wrecked or ruined just as it began to set out to fulfil its mission. To guard against the possibility of a total collapse I have, after much deliberation, decided to start from Bagamoyo, and proceed some distance along the well known caravan path, so as to give confidence to my men, and withdraw them as much as possible from the temptation to desert, and then plunge northward into the Masai land—a country as yet untrod by white men, and of the state of which the best informed of us are totally ignorant.[21] It will be a risky undertaking, but not half so dangerous as starting for that country from some unknown seaport.

My present intention is, then, to make my way westward to the Victoria Nyanza and ascertain whether Speke's or Livingstone's hypothesis is the correct one—whether the Victoria Nyanza consists of one lake or five lakes. All the most important localities will be fixed by astronomical observations, and whether the Victoria Lake consists of one or many lakes we shall discover by complete circumnavigation. When this work is finished I intend to visit Metesa or Rumanika, and then cross over to the Lake Albert Nyanza, and endeavor to ascertain how far Baker is correct in his bold hypothesis concerning its length and breadth. On this lake I expect to meet Gordon and his party, by whom I hope to be able to send my first reports of my travels and discoveries since leaving the Unyanyembe caravan road.[22]

Beyond this point the whole appears to me so vague and vast that it is impossible to state at this period what I shall try to do next. Whether Gordon circumnavigates the Albert or not, I shall most certainly do so if I reach it, and discover every detail about it to the best of my ability; but what I shall do afterwards will be best told after the circumnavigation of the Albert Nyanza.

What I may discover along this lengthy march I cannot at present imagine. I shall be equally pleased to corroborate either Speke's or Livingstone's hypothesis by actual personal observation and diligent exploration. I confess to you I have no bias either way. I would just as soon have the Victoria Lake one vast sheet of water as I would have it distributed among five insignificant lakelets; and I

21. Stanley overstates the lack of knowledge of the Masai route. In the 1850's a missionary could report that Arab and Swahili caravans were "constantly proceeding to the interior of the Masai country," while in 1870 another missionary collected valuable information of routes from a coast trader. J. L. Krapf's introduction in Erhardt, *Vocabulary of the Enguduk Iloigob*, 3; Wakefield, "Routes of Native Caravans from the Coast to the Interior of Eastern Africa, chiefly from information given by Sádí Bin Ahédi. . . ."

22. Charles Gordon (1833–1885) was then pushing south as governor of the Equatorial Province of the Sudan. His many problems had soured him on exploration. In November, 1875 Gordon wrote: "I declare I do not care whether there are two lakes or a million, or whether the Nile has a source or not . . . I am not paid for exploration. I hope Stanley has done the Lake; if he has not, and will go in the steamer, *when ready*??? I will let him go, if I meet him." Hill, ed., *Colonel Gordon in Central Africa 1874–1879*, 47–48. See also Hill, *Biographical Dictionary*, 138–40.

am quite ready to corroborate Baker's dream of a connection between the Tanganyika and the Albert, as I am to disprove it, if I
find after its exploration that he is incorrect. I have no prejudice
either way. Sir Samuel Baker's grand lake, however, is in more danger
from Gordon than it is from me; for Gordon ought to be able, if all
has gone well with him, to give the results of his decision long,
aye, many months, before I can possibly reach the lake. It is fortunate for me that Gordon will be able to visit the Albert before I
will, for Baker is so tenacious of his opinions that I fear it would
be mere weariness of spirit to attempt to convince him that he was
wrong; for which reason I should much prefer to be enabled to
prove that his hypothetical sketch map of the Albert Nyanza is correct.[23]

You may rest assured that as I journey along I shall avail myself of every opportunity to send my despatches to the coast, but
after I leave the Unyanyembe road the first news you will receive
from me will be, I hope, via the Nile.

16

Zanzibar, East Coast of Africa
Nov. 15, 1874 [1]

For the last four or five years the island and town called Zanzibar
have been very prominent before the public. The rigorous measures
pursued by the British government for the suppression of the slave
trade on this coast and the appeals of Livingstone in behalf of the
aboriginal African have made Zanzibar a well-known name. Previous
to this time it was comparatively unknown—as little known, indeed,
as the polysyllabic name by which it is described in the Periplus of
Arrian.[2] The mention of Zanguebar, Zanji-bar—or, as it is now

23. For Livingstone's hypothesis, see Bridges, "British Exploration of East
Africa," 309, 470–71. Baker postulated a southward extension of Lake Albert
and from African information had decided that lakes Albert and Tanganyika
were "only one vast lake bearing different names according to the localities
through which it passes." Speke believed Lake Victoria to be one vast lake, but
Burton was affirming that there were several lakes, and not one, in the region.
Baker, *Ismaïlia*, II, 263ff.; Baker, "Sir Richard Burton and the Nile Sources."
1. *NYH*, Dec. 26, 1874.
2. The *Periplus of the Erythrean Sea* was formerly wrongly attributed to
Flavius Arrianus, a second-century A.D. Greek soldier, administrator, philosopher
and historian. Cary *et al.*, *The Oxford Classical Dictionary*, 101. For the Periplus,
Mathew, "The East African Coast until the Coming of the Portuguese," 94–97.

called, Zanzibar—produced very little interest. Some few people there were who remembered there was such a name in very large characters on the map of the world, occupying a large strip on the east side of Africa, during their schoolboy days, but what that name indicated or comprehended very few knew or cared. They thought that it might be a very wild land, peopled with cannibals and such like, no doubt; for I remember well, when I first returned from Africa, a great number of those kind who frequent clubs and big societies often asked me, "Where the deuce is Zanzibar?" There were people, however, who prospered and grew rich on the ignorance of their white brothers who were so woefully deficient in elementary geographical knowledge. These were the staid old merchants of London, New York, Salem and Hamburg, who had agents living at Zanzibar,[3] who unobstrusively collected precious cargoes of African productions and shipped them home to their employers, who sold them again quietly and unobtrusively to manufacturers at enormous profits. Great sums of money were made for many many years by these old merchants, until the slave trade question began to be agitated and Livingstone's fate to be a subject of inquiry. When a Committee of the House of Commons held a protracted sitting, sifting every item of information relating to the island and its prospects, its productions and commerce, &c., and the NEW YORK HERALD despatched a special commissioner in search of Livingstone, one result of whose mission was the publication of the name of Zanzibar far and wide. Captain Burton has also written two large volumes, which bear the conspicuous name of "Zanzibar,"[4] in large gold letters, on their backs; but very few of these volumes, I imagine, have found their way among the popular classes. I mean to try in this letter to convey a description of the Island, its prince, and such subjects as have relation to them, as will suit any mind likely to take an interest in reading it. De Horsey's "African Pilot" describes Zanzibar as being an island forty-six miles in length by eighteen miles in width at its greatest breadth, though its average breadth is not more than from nine to twelve miles. The "African Pilot" and None's "Epitome" place the island in south latitude 6 deg. 27 min. 42 sec., and in east longitude 39 deg. 32 min. 57 sec., but the combined navigating

3. For the establishment of these merchants, see Bennett and Brooks, *New England Merchants, passim.*

4. These two volumes, published in London in 1872, rather upset Bishop Steere. He lamented: "Burton's Zanzibar is just what an ill conditioned coarse-minded man with the fever would be likely to write. There is truth at the bottom of it all, but the general result is wholly untruthful." Steere to Ann Steere, July 17, 1872, A. 1. III, UMCA.

talent on board her Britannic Majesty's surveying ship *Nassau* locates
Zanzibar in south latitude 6 deg. 9 min. 36 sec., and east longitude
39 deg. 14 min. 43 sec.[5] Between the island and the mainland runs
a channel from twenty to thirty miles in width, well studded with
coral islands, sand bars, sand banks and coral reefs.

The first view the stranger obtains of Zanzibar is of low land
covered with verdure. If he has been informed much concerning the
fevers which trouble the white traveller in equatorial Africa, he is
very likely to be impressed in his own mind that the low land is
very suggestive of it, but a nearer view is more pleasing and serves
to dispel much of the vague fear or uneasiness with which he
approached the dreaded region of ill-health and sorrow. The wind
is gentle and steady which fills the vessel's sails; the temperature
of the air is moderate, perhaps at 70 deg. or 75 deg. Fahrenheit;
the sky is of one cerulian tint, the sea is not troubled and scarcely
rocks the ship, the shore is a mass of vivid green, the feathery fronds
of palm trees, and the towering globes of foliage of the mangrove
relieve the monotony, while the gleaming white houses of the rich
Arabs heighten the growing pleasure with the thought that the "fever
may not be so bad as people say it is." Proceeding southward
through the channel that separates Zanzibar from the Continent,
and hugging the shore of the island, you will many times be gratified
by most pleasant tropical scenes, and by a strange fragrance which
is borne from the leaf-clad island—a fragrance which may remind
you of "Ceylon's spicey isles." With a good glass you will be able
to make out first the cocoa palm and the deep dark green globe of
foliage which the mango raises above when the tree is in its prime,
the graceful bombax,[6] and the tall tamarind, while numbers of tall
gigantic trees of some kind loom above masses of umbrageous
shrubbery. Bits of cultivated land, clusters of huts, solitary tembes,
gardens and large, square, white houses, succeed each other quickly
until your attention is attracted by the sight of shipping in the distance, and, near-by, growing larger and larger every moment, the
city of Zanzibar, the greatest commercial mart on the east coast of
Africa. Arrived in the harbor you will find the ship anchors about
400 yards from the town, close to a few more European ships, and
perhaps a British man-of-war or two, while a number of queer-looking
vessels, which you will style "native," lie huddled between your own
vessel and the shore. These native vessels are of various tonnage

5. De Horsey, *African Pilot*, 189–203.
6. *Bombax rhodognaphalon*. Dale and Greeenway, *Kenya Trees & Shrubs*, 67.
See also Burton, "Lake Regions," 65.

and size, from the unwieldy Arab trading dhow, with two masts leaning inelegantly and slovenly toward the bows, while the towering after part reminds you of the pictures of ships in the Spanish Armada, to the lengthy, low and swift-looking mtepe, which, when seen going before the wind, seems to be skimming the sea like a huge white seagull.[7] Beyond the native fleet of trading Muscat dhows, Kilwa slavers, Pangani wood carriers and those vessels which carry passengers to the mainland, the town of Zanzibar rises from the beach in a nearly crescent form, white and glaring, and unsymmetrical. The narrow, tall, whitewashed house of the reigning Prince Barghash bin Said rises almost in the centre of the first line of buildings; close to it on the right, as you stand looking at the town from shipboard, is the saluting battery, which numbers some thirty guns or thereabouts; and right behind rises a mere shell of a dingy old Portuguese fort,[8] which might almost be knocked into pieces by a few rounds from Snider muskets. Close to the water battery is the German Consul's[9] house, as neat as clean whitewash can make an Arab building, and next to this house rises the double residence and offices of Her Britannic Majesty's Assistant Political Resident,[10] surmounted by the most ambitious of flagstaffs. Next comes an English merchant's house,[11] and then the buildings occupied by Mr. Augustus Sparhawk, the agent of the great house of John Bertram & Co., of Salem, Mass.; and between the English merchant's house and the Bertram agency, in neighborly proximity, is seen the snow white house of Mr. Frederick M. Cheney, agent of Arnold, Hines & Co., of New York,[12] while beyond all, at the extreme right, on the extreme end of the crescent, on Shangani Point, towers in isolated vastness the English residency, which was formerly the house of Bishop Tozer and his scanty flock of youthful converts.[13] If you

7. For the *mtepe*, the sewn boat of East Africa, Prins, *Sailing from Lamu*, 79, 82–84, 120–28, 296; for dhow types, Villiers, *Sons of Sinbad*, 417–19.

8. It is not a Portuguese fort. *A Guide to Zanzibar*, 35–36.

9. F.H.T. Schultz, agent of the Hamburg house of O'Swald. Coupland, *Exploitation of East Africa*, 95.

10. F. Elton. *Ibid.*, 201.

11. The British firm of Smith, Mackenzie and Co. Ltd. *The History of Smith, Mackenzie and Company, Ltd.*, 10.

12. Frederick M. Cheney of Boston; he spent about twenty years in Zanzibar as a trader and at times acted as American diplomatic representative. Bennett, "Edward D. Ropes, Jr."

13. William G. Tozer (*d.* 1899), missionary bishop of the Universities Mission to Central Africa, had presided over the withdrawal of the mission from the Lake Nyasa region to Zanzibar. There he gained a reputation of being unsuited for his position—largely through his failure to adapt himself to African conditions. His successor, Steere, said: "here he is like a steam engine with

start again from that central and prominent point, the palace of His Highness, and intend to take a searching view of the salient objects of observation along the sea front of the town, you will observe that to the left of the water battery are a number of sheds roofed with palm fronds, and that in front of these is about the only thing resembling a wharf visible along the beach. This you will be told is the Zanzibar Custom House. There may be a native dhow discharging her cargo, and lines of burly strong laborers come and go, go and come, continually, bearing to the Custom House bales, packages, ivory tusks and what not, and returning for fresh burdens; while, on the wharf, turbaned Arabs and long-shirted half-castes either superintend the work or from idle curiosity stand by to look on.

Moving the eye leftward of the Custom House to a building of noble dimensions you will see that mixture of richness of woodwork and unkempt slovenliness and general untidiness or semi-decay which attracts the traveller in almost all large Turkish and Arab houses, whether in Turkey, in Egypt or Arabia. This is the new palace of Prince Barghash. The dark brown veranda, with its open lattice work, interlaced bars of wood, infinitesimal carving—the best work of an Arab artisan—strike one as peculiarly adapted for a glowing climate like this of Zanzibar. But if the eye surmounts this woodwork it will find itself shocked at observing the half-finished roof and the seams of light which fall through it, and the dingy whitewash and the semi-ruinous state of the upper part of the structure. A little left of this stand two palatial buildings which for size dwarf even the British residency. One is the house of Nassur bin Said,[14] the Prime Minister of His Highness; the other is inhabited by the Sultan's harem. Beyond these large buildings are not many. The compact line of solid buildings becomes broken by unsightly sheds with thatched roofs. This is the Melinde quarter, a place devoted to the sale of fish, fruit, &c., to which new European arrivals are banished to seek residences among the few stone houses to be found there.

Beyond Melinde is the shallow Malagash inlet, the cause—I may say the main cause, perhaps the only cause—of the unhealthiness of the town of Zanzibar; and beyond the Malagash inlet extends the

---

the connecting rod broken, he cannot apply his power to any purpose." Ward, ed., *Letters of Bishop Tozer;* Chadwick, *Mackenzie's Grave,* 194ff.; Kirk to FO, Nov. 22, 1872, FO84/1357, PRO; Steere to Festing, Dec. 15, 1872, A.1.III, UMCA.

14. His role in the 1873 treaty negotiations is mentioned in Coupland, *Exploitation of East Africa,* 185–90.

country, like a rich, prolific garden, teeming with tropical plants and trees, sloping gently upward as far as the purpling ridges of Elaysu.[15]

Such is Zanzibar and its suburbs to the new arrival, as he attempts to note down his observations from shipboard. Descending the side ladder he is rowed ashore, and if he has a letter of introduction is welcomed by some "noble specimen of a British merchant," or an American merchant of thirty-five or forty years' standing, or a British official, or by one of those indescribables who has found his way into Zanzibar, and who patiently bides for the good time that is reported and believed to be coming; for I find that Zanzibar, instead of attracting the real merchant, has, since my last visit, but changed its European inutiles. When I was here before I met a living specimen of the happy and sanguine Micawber class. He is gone, but another fills his place. One can scarcely dare say anything good of Zanzibar or of any other place without attracting the wrong class of persons; and as I am on this topic I may as well specify what class of persons can be benefited pecuniarily by immigration to Zanzibar.

To an enterprising man of capital Zanzibar and the entire sea line of the Sultan's dominions offer special advantages. A man with a capital of £5,000 might soon make his £20,000 out of it; but not by bringing his capital and his time and health to compete with great, rich mercantile houses of many year's standing and experience, and, settling at Zanzibar, vainly attempting to obtain the custom of the natives, who are perfectly content with their time-honored white friends, when the entire coast line of the mainland invites his attention, his capital, his shrewdness and industry. The new arrival must do precisely what the old merchants did when they commenced business. He must go where there is no rivalry, no competition, if he expects to have a large business and quick returns for his money. He must bring his river steamer of light draught and penetrate the interior by the Rufiji, the Pangani, the Mtwana, or the Jub, and purchase the native product at first cost and resell to the large mercantile houses of Zanzibar or ship home.[16] The copal of the Rufigi plain, accessible, as I know by experience, to a light draught steamer,

15. For a town plan of Zanzibar and a discussion of the various quarters, Baumann, *Der Sansibar-Archipel. II, passim;* for a stark account of Zanzibar's health conditions, Christie, *Cholera Epidemics, passim.* For "Elaysu," see document 16, note 40.

16. European merchants, except Americans, who did not exercise their rights, were forbidden by treaty to trade for ivory and copal on the *Mrima.* There was little business for Europeans outside this area. Bennett and Brooks, *New England Merchants,* 239ff.

is now carried on the shoulders of natives to Dar Salaam and Mbua-majii, to be sold to the Banians, who reship it to Zanzibar and there resell to the European merchant. The ivory of Unyamwesi is brought down close to Mbumi Usagara, which is accessible by a light draught steamer by the Wami. The ivory trade of Masai and the regions north is carried down through a portion of the Pangani Valley, and the Pangani for a short distance is also navigable and furnishes a means of enabling the white merchant to overreach his more settled white brothers at Zanzibar. The Jub River, next to the Zambezi, is the largest river on the east coast of Africa, while it is comparatively unknown. Arab caravans penetrate the regions south of it and obtain large quantities of ivory and hides. Why should not the white merchant attempt to open legitimate trade in the same articles by means of the river? [17] When John Bertram, of Salem, Mass., came to Zanzibar, some forty years ago, there was not a single European house here. He was an officer of a whaling vessel when he saw this large town, with its splendid opportunities for commencing a mercantile business. On arriving home he invested the results of his venture in chartering a small vessel with goods such as would meet a ready sale in Zanzibar. The speculation turned out to be a good one; he repeated it, and then established an agency at Zanzibar, while he himself resided at Salem to conduct the business at home, to receive the cargoes from Zanzibar and ship cloth and other goods to his agency out here.[18] The business which the young whaler started continued to thrive. Agent succeeded agent as each man went home, after a few years' stay in Zanzibar, to enjoy the fruit of his labors. Boys sent out to Zanzibar to learn the business became responsible clerks, then head agents and subsequently opulent merchants, and so on from year to year, until John Bertram can point with noble pride to his own millions and the long list of noble men whom he taught, encouraged, sustained by his advice and enriched. The moral of all this is, that what John Bertram, of Salem, did at Zanzibar, can be done by any large minded, enterprising Englishman or American on the mainland of Africa. Nay, as there is a larger field on the mainland and as he can profit by the example of Bertram he can do more.

Men experienced in the ways of Oriental life need not be told in

17. The Juba was then little known and Stanley was exaggerating its possibilities. Previous commercial and exploration ventures had had little success there. *Ibid.*, 483, 490; Dundas, "Expedition up the Jub River through Somaliland, East Africa."

18. This is not the usual account of Bertram's first visit. See Bennett, "Stanley and the American Consuls at Zanzibar," 47.

detail how people live in Zanzibar, nor how the town appears within, nor what the Arabs and half-castes and Wangwana know of sanitary laws. Zanzibar is not the best, the cleanest nor the prettiest town I have ever seen; nor, on the other hand, is it the worst, the filthiest nor the ugliest town. While there is but little to praise or gratify in it, there is a good deal to condemn, and, while you condemn it you are very likely to feel the cause for condemnation is irremediable and hopeless. But the European merchants find much that is endurable at Zanzibar. It is not nearly the intolerable place that the smelted rocks of Aden have made Steamer Point, nor has it the parboiling atmosphere of Bushire or Busrah, nor is it cursed by the merciless heat of Ismaila or Port Said. If you expose yourself to the direct rays of the sun of Zanzibar for a considerable time it would be as fatal for you as though you did such an unwise thing on the Aden Isthmus. Within doors, however, life is tolerable—nay, it is luxuriously comfortable. We—I mean Europeans—have numbers of servants to wait on us, to do our smallest bidding. If we need a light for our cigars, or our walking cane, or our hats when we go out, we never think of getting these things for ourselves or of doing anything of which another could relive us of the necessity of doing. We have only the trouble of telling our servants what to do, and even of this trouble we would gladly be relieved. One great comfort to us out here is that there is no society to compel us to imprison our necks within linen collars, or half strangle ourselves with a silken tie, or to be anxious about any part of our dress. The most indolent of us never think of shifting our night pyjamas until nearly midday. Indeed, we could find it in our hearts to live in them altogether, except that we fear a little chaff from our neighbors.

Another luxury, which we enjoy out here, which may be not enjoyed in Europe. What think you of a salt water bath morning, noon and evening just before dinner? Our servants fill our tubs for us, for our residences stand close to the sea, and it is neither trouble nor expense, if we care at all for the luxury, to undress in the cool room and take a few minutes' sleep in the tub. Though we are but a small colony of whites, we resemble, microscopically, society at home. We have our good men and true and sociable men; we have large hearted hospitable men, our pig-giving friends, our hail-fellows well met, and perambulating gossips. Our liquors and wines and cigars are good, if they are not the best in the world. Some of us of course are better connoisseurs in such things than others, and have accordingly contrived to secure the most superior brands. Our houses are large, roomy and cool; we have plenty of servants; we have good fruit on the island; we enjoy health while we have it, and with our tastes, education and national love of refinement, we have contrived to surround ourselves with such luxuries as serve to prolong good health, peace of mind and life, and, inshallah! shall continue to do so while we stay in Zanzibar. The above is but the frank, outspoken description of himself, as as might be given by a dignified and worthy Zanzibar merchant of long standing of European extraction.[19] And your Commissioner will declare that it is as near truth as though the Zanzibar merchant of long standing and experience had written it himself.

Now we have had the Europeans of Zanzibar, their houses and mode and law of life described, let us get into the streets and endeavor to see for ourselves the nature of the native and the Semitic resident, and ascertain how far they differ from the Anglo-Saxon and Anglo-American sublimities.

As we move away toward the Seyid's palace we gradually become conscious that we have left the muddy streets with their small, narrow gutters, and which re-echoed our footsteps so noisily. The tall houses where the Europeans live, separated by but a narrow street, ten feet wide, shut out the heat and dazzling glare which otherwise the clean white-washed walls would have reflected. When we leave these behind we come across the hateful glaring sunlight, and our nostrils become irritated by an amber-colored dust, from the "garbling" of copal and orchilla weed,[20] and we are sensible of two separate smells which affect the senses. One is the sweet fragrance of cloves, the other is the odor which a crowd of slaves bearing clove bags exhale from their perspiring bodies. Shortly we come across an irregular square blank in the buildings which had hemmed us in from the sunlight. A fetid garbage heap, débris of mud houses, sugar-cane leavings, orange and banana peelings, make piles which, festering and rotting in the sun, are unsightly to the eye and offensive to the nostrils. And just by here we see the semi-ruinous Portuguese fort, a most beggarly and dilapidated structure. Several rusty and antique cannon lie strewn along the base of the front wall, and a dozen or so of rusty and beggarly-looking half-castes, armed with long, straight swords and antique Muscat matchlocks, affect to be soldiers and guardians of the gate. Fortunately, however, for

19. A picture of the life of an American merchant in Zanzibar is given in Bennett, "E. D. Ropes, Jr."

20. "Garbling" describes the act of removing refuse from copal, etc. For copal, see Bennett and Brooks, *New England Merchants, passim;* for orchilla (the lichen *Roccella tinctoria*), *ibid.,* 518, 531.

the peace of the town and the reigning Prince, the prisoners whom the soldiers guard are mild-mannered and gentle enough, few of them having committed a worse crime than participating in a bloodless street brawl or being found intoxicated in the street.[21]

Passing the noisy and dusty Custom House, with its hives of singing porters at work, and herds of jabbering busybodies, nobodies and somebodies, we shortly arrive at the palace, where we might as well enter, and see how it fares with His Highness Barghash bin Said, the Prince of Zanzibar and Pemba. As we may have merely made an appointment with him as private citizens of a free and independent foreign country, and are escorted only by a brother citizen of the same rank, etiquette forbids that the Seyyid should descend into the street to receive his visitor. Were we Her Britannic Majesty's Consul or Political Resident His Highness would deem it but due to our official rank to descend into the street and meet us exactly twenty-four steps from the palace door. Were we an Envoy Extraordinary the Prince would meet us some fifty or seventy-five paces from his gate. We are but private citizens, however, and the only honor we get is an exhibition of the guards—Belooches, Persians and half-castes—drawn up on each side of the door, their uniforms consisting of lengthy butternut-colored disdashehs, or shirts which reach from the nape of the neck to the ankles of each.

After we have ascended a flight of steps we discover the Prince, ready to receive us, with his usual cordial and frank smile and good natured greeting, and, during a shower of good natured queries respecting our health, we are escorted to the other end of the barely furnished room, where we are invited to be seated.

I have had (adopting the first person singular again) a long conversation with the Prince of Zanzibar; but, omitting all extraneous matter, I shall only touch upon such portion of our conversation as relates to a subject in which we are all interested, viz.: the slave trade and to the diplomatic mission of Sir Bartle Frere.[22]

We have all read the despatches of Sir Bartle, relating his intercourse officially with the Sultan of Zanzibar; we have also heard from his own lips his views upon East African slavery. But none of

21. Drunkenness was a crime for the local inhabitants under the laws of Zanzibar. Fraser, Tozer, and Christie, *The East African Slave Trade*, 42.
22. H. Bartle E. Frere (1815–1884), a distinguished British Indian official, arrived in Zanzibar in 1873 to negotiate a treaty restricting the limits of the slave trade. British aims were not gained until after the departure of Frere. Martineau, *The Life and Correspondence of Sir Bartle Frere*; Coupland, *Exploitation of East Africa*, 182ff.; PRGS 6 (1884), 403–07; Gavin, "Frere Mission to Zanzibar," 122–48; Bennett, "Charles de Vienne."

your readers have heard the story of the Sultan himself, with his views of slavery and of the mission of Sir Bartle Frere. Without pretence of literal and exact record of what the Sultan said, I yet declare the spirit of what he said will be found embodied in the following:

"During Majid, my brother's time, Speke came here and travelled into Africa, and what he said about us Arabs caused us a little trouble. The consuls, too, have given us great trouble. Some have written home much that is not quite true; but some time ago my brother Majid died, and by the grace of God I succeeded him. The trouble which my brother Majid endured was as nothing compared to that which has been the result of that man, Dr. Livingstone's letters. I maintain that those letters you brought from him and carried to England were the cause of all this great trouble. Indeed, I have had a troublous time of it ever since I came to the throne. First, there came the hurricane of two years ago (April, 1872), which destroyed my entire fleet and all the ships of my people, and devastated the island and the coast. We were well off before that time, and we became suddenly poor. I had seven ships and steamers of war lost, and my people lost about 200 ships, and if you doubt my word respecting the devastation on the land take one of my horses and ride out into the country that you may see for yourself. In the midst of the desolation and ruin which had overtaken us we heard that the former Governor of Bombay, Sir Bartle Frere, was coming out to us to talk to us about the slave trade. Now, you white people must understand that all Arabs trade in slaves, that they have done so from the beginning. Our Koran does not say it is a sin, our priests say nothing against it, the wise men of Mecca say nothing against it; our forefathers traded in slaves, and we followed their footsteps and did likewise. But my father, Said Said,[23] and my brothers, Thouweynee, Majid and Toorkee,[24] were friends with the English and the English gave them advice and got them to sign treaties not to trade in slaves any more. To the treaty that my brothers signed I gave my consent freely when I came to the throne, for I have always been a friend to the English and to Englishmen.

23. Said bin Sultan, ruler of Zanzibar and Masqat from 1804 to 1856. For his rule, Gray, *History of Zanzibar*, 109ff.; Gavin, "Sayyid Sa'id."

24. Thuwayni bin Said, born in 1821, succeeded to the rule in Masqat in 1856; he was murdered by his son, Salim, in 1866. Turki bin Said (1832–1888) became ruler of Masqat with British aid in 1870. Ingrams, *Chronology & Genealogies of Zanzibar Rulers*, 6; Gavin, "Frere Mission to Zanzibar," 124–26; Miles, *The Countries and Tribes of the Persian Gulf*, II, 347ff.; Landen, *Oman since 1856, passim.*

"When Sir Bartle Frere came here we were in sore distress, and very poor. He asked me to sign a treaty that no slave trade should be permitted in my country. When I consulted my chiefs they held their hands out to me and said, 'We have nothing, we are poor, but if the English will give us time—say a year or so—we are quite willing to sign that which they ask us.' I repeated to Sir Bartle what my chiefs were willing to do, and I asked him to give us time such as they gave the Portuguese;[25] but Sir Bartle, in his hurry to get us to sign the treaty, overlooked the distress we were in from the hurricane. Time and time again I asked that he would give us but a few months to consider and prepare for this final stroke of misfortune, but he would not listen, he was deaf to me. Continually, he said to me, 'Sign this treaty.' I was quite willing to sign it, though by signing it I was losing about $20,000 a year revenue; but my people could not understand this haste of Sir Bartle Frere to get the treaty signed without giving us time to think of it. We all knew that the English could do what they wanted to do in Zanzibar; if they took the island we were too poor and weak to resist; if they destroyed us all we could not help it. All we could have done would have been to consign our cause to God, and submit. Sir Bartle Frere went away angry. I cannot help it, but I grieve that he should be angry with me for what I could not help. One of the things he asked me to give my consent to was that I should assist the English in putting down the slave trade. How can I assist the English? I have no ships as I had formerly, or I would willingly do so.

"Soon after Sir Bartle Frere went away an English fleet came to our harbor. The English Admiral (Rear Admiral Arthur Cumming)[26] and Dr. Kirk came to see me about the orders they had received from the Foreign Office to stop the slave trade. They both advised me as friends to sign the treaty. I got my people's consent to do so, and I signed it, not because I was afraid of the English ships, for, if the English came to Zanzibar and said, 'We want this island,' I would not resist them, for I know that they are strong and I am weak—but because the English Admiral and Dr. Kirk advised me as friends, for they knew my poverty and understood my case better than I could have told them."

Such is the story of the Sultan, without embellishment, and I dare

25. See Coupland, *The British Anti-Slavery Movement,* 159–66, for this policy between 1815 and 1842.

26. Arthur Cumming (1817–1893), commander-in-chief of the East Indies Station, 1870–1874. Boase, *Modern English Biography,* IV, 821–22; Clowes, *Royal Navy,* VII, 574.

say that Sir Bartle Frere will indorse most of it, if not all. It was a surprise to Sir Bartle's many admirers that his well known diplomatic talents had failed to secure the Sultan's signature to the treaty for the suppression of the slave trade, but with my knowledge of the method which Sir Bartle adopted to secure the Sultan's signature I may say now that I no longer wonder at his failure. Small and insignificant as Prince Barghash may be in power and influence he is yet an independent chief of an independent State, to whom are due all the little courtesies which skilful diplomats are in the habit of using to persons recognized as rulers, consequently the stern, relentless coercion which Sir Bartle's words and manners embodied could not be met in any other way by a man conscious of his dignity as a sovereign prince than by a refusal to sign the treaty. The mild manners and suavity of Admiral Cumming, together with the tact and friendly entreaties of Dr. Kirk, however, produced the desired result, leaving us nothing to regret save the failure of Sir Bartle to succeed where he ought to have succeeded, and where he might have succeeded had he possessed his soul with patience. Now, however, that the treaty has been signed and England's indignation at the Seyyid's first refusal to concede to her demands been appeased, strict justice requires that the Prince shall in some measure be requited for the concession he made. This is not merely my opinion, nor is it merely my definition of what justice demands in this case; but it is the outspoken and frank declaration of several eminent English gentlemen with whom I have conversed. They say that the Prince should be indemnified, for this concession on his part, with some grant of money or aid, in some form or another, for sacrificing to England's views of what is right and wrong an eighth portion of his revenue; that the plea that England may use, that she guaranteed Prince Barghash release from the annual subsidy of 40,000 crowns to his brother at Muscat, cannot be employed at all, as England herself had imposed this sum on the Zanzibar Sultan in order that her commerce might not be endangered in the fratricidal war which might ensue on Prince Barghash's refusal to pay this heavy subsidy; and that it is doubtful whether Prince Toorkee could ever summon sufficient force to compel Prince Barghash to pay him a single coin.[27] With which views just men will not fail to agree. The beggarly presents which Sir Bartle Frere and his suite brought to Zanzibar for presentation to the Sultan were unworthy of the nation,

27. For the subsidy from Zanzibar to Masqat, the result of the Canning award of 1861, Coupland, *Exploitation of East Africa,* 14, 28–30, 72–74; Gavin, "Frere Mission to Zanzibar," 146.

which no doubt intended to act generously, of the representative of Her Britannic Majesty which conveyed them, and of the prince for whom they were purchased. Well enough, no doubt, for the petty potentate of Johanna, who ultimately received them,[28] but not for the sovereign of Zanzibar and Pemba, and a thousand miles of coast, with whom a British envoy was charged to negotiate. It is not common sense to suppose that any private citizen would look indulgently upon any proposition which required of him to sacrifice £4,000 a year of his income in consideration of a few paltry presents which did not exceed over a few hundred pounds in value at the most, any more than that Prince Barghash should. Yet this is precisely what Sir Bartle Frere was charged to do by the Foreign Office in his late mission to Zanzibar. Owing to the losses incurred by him and his people during the hurricane of 1872, and the sacrifice of a large portion of his revenue by the demands of England, the Prince of Zanzibar suffers from straitness of income and ready money. He has leased the customs to Jewram Sujee, a Banian, for a term of years, for a very insufficient sum.[29] He is sorely troubled with the native war in Unyamwezi, which prevents the ivory from arriving at the sea.[30] His private estates are mere wrecks of what they once were, and the real pecuniary condition of Prince Barghash may be summed up as truly deplorable. Now a present of two condemned gunboats or any two vessels of war, such as the Admiralty has almost always on hand for sale cheap for cash, would be a godsend to the Sultan of Zanzibar, and a round sum of a few thousand pounds given to him as a sign of friendship and good will, might obviate in some measure the necessity of the large expense which England incurs annually in her laudable endeavors to suppress the slave trade.

There are several ways of regarding such a proposition, but it will not appear surprising to the candid reader if he reads the above facts dispassionately and without prejudice. It is a good adage that which advises that we should choose the least evil of two, and everybody will admit that if England could purchase the hearty co-operation of the Zanzibar Sultan with a timely and needful present, in the

28. Abdulla, Sultan of Anjouan, 1855–1891. Frere visited Abdulla and appeared to be somewhat impressed with him, recommending that the sultan receive liberated slaves from the British for settlement on Anjouan. The scheme did not materialize. Kirk to FO, Sept. 20, 1876, Q–17; Sunley to Smith, March 7, 1891, E–131; Frere to Kirk, April 1, 1873, E–63B; Kirk to Smith, March 16, 1873, E–63B: all in ZA.

29. The firm of Jairam Sewji was represented in Zanzibar by Likmidas Ladha. Jairam had died in 1866. Bennett and Brooks, *New England Merchants*, 212.

30. See document 15, note 16.

philanthropic scheme which England has so long attempted to en-
force on the East African Coast, it would be less expensive than
supporting a large squadron at an expense of several thousands of
pounds per annum. And now that the slave trade is carried on inland
it is more necessary than ever that Seyyid Barghash's good will should
be secured. Without the aid that England could give the Prince I
doubt much that however friendly disposed he may be, he can do
anything to assist in suppressing the trade, for the reasons already
given.[31]

Turning again to other topics, I may as well sketch the Prince
before bowing him my adieu. He is now in the prime of life, probably about forty-two years old, of vigorous and manly frame, and
about five feet nine inches in height. He is a frank, cordial and
good natured gentleman, with a friendly brusqueness in his manner
to all whom he has no reason to regard with suspicion. He has an
open, generous and a very undiplomatic face, slightly touched here
and there with traces of the smallpox. He dresses plainly and is not
given to ostentation in any way. He wears the usual linen dress of
the Arabs, with his waist cinctured by a rich belt of plaited gold,
which supports the crooked dagger generally borne by an Arab gentleman. Over his linen dress he wears a long black cloth coat, the
edges of which are covered with a narrow gold braid. His headdress
is the usual ample turban of the Arab, wound about his head, and
completing in his person a somewhat picturesque costume. It would
be difficult to choose a prince with whom diplomatic relations could
be carried on so easily, provided always that the diplomat remembered that the Prince was an Arab and a Moslem gentleman. Politeness will effect more than rudeness, always with Arabian gentlemen. Admiral Cumming, I feel sure, with his gentle, dispassionate
bearing, could effect as much with Seyyid Barghash as Admiral
Yelverton's courteous and calm bearing effected with the menacing
ruffians of Cartagena.[32] In whatever school of deportment these old
British admirals, who, over a steely firmness, wear such courtesy,
are brought up, it might be recommended that diplomats charged
with delicate negotiations might be sent to learn lessons of true
politeness. There is, however, one phase in Prince Barghash's character which presents a difficulty in dealing with him, and that is his

31. For the resolutions of these complaints, real and otherwise, Coupland,
Exploitation of East Africa, 237ff.

32. Hastings R. Yelverton (1808–1878), commander-in-chief, Mediterranean
station, 1870–1875. His conduct when Spanish rebels from Cartagena seized
part of the Spanish fleet in 1871 is given in Clowes, *Royal Navy*, VII, 243–46;
see also Boase, *English Biography*, III, 1562.

fanaticism. Ever since he undertook the journey to Mecca he has shown himself an extremely fervid Moslem, indisposed to do anything or attempt anything not recommended in the Koran.[33] A prince of more liberal religious views might have had an opportunity during the late diplomatic negotiations of permanently bettering himself and people; but Barghash was restrained by his extreme religious scruples from asking any aid of England.

Continuing our journey through the town of Zanzibar, beyond the Sultan's palace, we come to the business quarter of the natives. The spicy smells, intermixed with those of fruit, printed cloth, oils, ghee, peppers, &c., grow stronger as we advance, added to which is the very infragrant odor which is exhaled from the bodies of the naked and unwashed multitude. Flies here congregate in swarms, and settle where they enjoy plentiful repasts. Down into the narrow and crowded alley, flanked by the low palm-roofed sheds where the humble, free and slave populace are engaged in their noisy barter, pours the merciless sunlight, drawing stifling vapors from the filthy and undrained street. Not caring to take more than a hasty glance at anything under such circumstances, we hasten on through the most wretched alleys and streets, by half ruinous houses which only require to be repaired to be made presentable, and only require the superintendence of sanitary police to make them habitable; by low-roofed and square-pillared mosques and verandas, or burzanis, where squat dusky men and yellow men, kinky and straight-haired men, Arabs and Banians, Hindis and half-castes, each of whom we detect by either his garb or his appearance. And so we proceed by ruins and huts and dunghills and garbage heaps and square, dingy white buildings, until we come to the Malagash Inlet, over which a bridge leads to a populous suburb and the evergreen country. If we cross the bridge and skirt the opposite bank by a broad well-trodden path, we will be travelling along the base of a triangle, of which Shangani Point and the British Political Residency may form the apex. A half hour's walk along this path leads us through ill-kept gardens, where mandioca or manioc (the cassava), Indian corn, and holcus, sesame and millet grow half shaded by orange and lime, pomegranate and mangopalm, and jack trees,[34] until we halt before the white and clean buildings of the English Church

33. Barghash had formerly been strongly under the influence of Mutawwa' interpreters of Islam. Gavin, "Frere Mission to Zanzibar," especially 144.

34. *Artocarpus integrifolia.* Naval Staff Intelligence Division, *A Handbook of Kenya Colony (British East Africa) and the Kenya Protectorate (Protectorate of Zanzibar),* 562.

mission.[35] We have noted in our short walk that agricultural skill and industry is at a very low ebb, barely fit to be termed by such names, rather a wretched, burrowing and shiftless, slovenly planting; but the genial soil covers a multitude of defects, sins of indolence and unthriftiness.

As we have arrived at the English Church Mission Buildings, what shall I say about the mission except the honest, truthful facts? The Right Rev. Bishop Tozer, "Bishop of Central Africa," in priestly purple and fine linen, is no more to be seen here, and it really appears as if the mission had begun new life, and had begun to lift its head among the useful societies of the world. As yet I have seen no great increase of converts, but fair promise of future usefulness is· visible everywhere. As a friend to the Church which has sent this mission out, I was formerly restrained from saying much about it, because I knew very little good of it; [36] and had I not seen the erudite but undignified prelate exhibiting himself in such unusual garb to the gaze of the low rabble of Zanzibar I would certainly have passed the Church mission and its pitiful ways of converting the heathen in silence. Now, however, I may speak with candor. The great building now known as the British Residency was, in 1871 and 1872, the episcopal palace and mission house. After its sale to the English government the missionaries removed their school to their country house, a half mile or so beyond the extremity of Malagash Inlet. With the money obtained by the sale of the mission house the Superintendent purchased the old slave market—a vacant area surrounded by mud huts, close to the cattle yards of the Banians and the ooze and stagnant pools of the Malagash. On the site of so much extreme wretchedness and crime the Church missionaries have commenced to erect structures which, when completed, may well be styled superb.

These buildings consist of a fine residence, a school and a church,[37]

35. The Universities Mission to Central Africa.

36. Stanley's restraint was rather limited. See *HIFL*, 19–20. One of Tozer's missionaries noted that the bishop's high church dress had "acted upon the yankee as a red cloth on an insane bull." Alington to Jones, Jan. 16, 1873, A.1.III, UMCA.

37. The church, a future imposing landmark in Zanzibar, was held by some to be a useless extravagance for Muslim Zanzibar. Thomson described it as "a striking illustration of the misapplication of money and energy, which might have been so much more usefully directed into other channels." Steere, its builder, was stung by such criticism—"Do not," he said, "call it a Cathedral. It is the Memorial Church in the Old Slave Market. The fact of the slave-market site and the memorial character are what justify its costliness." Thomson, *Central African Lakes*, I, 18; Steere to Penny, Sept. 20, 1881, A.1.III, UMCA.

which, with another building, just begun by Lacknindoss,[38] the Banian, will surround an irregular square, in which palms and flowers and fruit trees will be planted. A view from one of the windows of the unfinished residence gives us a clearer idea of the locality the missionaries have selected, and suggests grave doubts of the wisdom of its selection. Looking at it from a sentimental point of view, the locality is, no doubt, very appropriate, and a certain fitness is also seen in it. The British government denounced the slave trade, and made a grand effort to crush it; and the market for the sale of slaves in old times was purchased by the mission, on which the missionaries erect a church wherein peace and good will and brotherly love will be preached and taught. The neighborhood, also, is one of the most miserable quarters of Zanzibar; but the missionaries convey with them the power to improve, refine and elevate, despite its extreme poverty and misery. It is all very well, we think; but if we look from the windows and examine the character of the ground into which the walls of the building have been sunk, we will see that it is a quagmire, with putrid heaps of cow dung and circular little pools of sink-water, which permeate through the corrupting soil, and heave up again in globules and bubbles, exhaling the vilest odor that ever irritated the civilized European's nose. And if what we have seen below is not enough to conjure up in the mind a dismal prospect of sickness and pain and sorrow for the unhappy missionaries who may be appointed to live here, the view of the long and broad stretch of black mud, which the shallow waters of the Malagash leave behind them for hours night and day, will certainly do it. It would require the treasury of a government to redeem the ground from its present uninhabitable state. All I can say, however, is that I can only hope that the dismal future suggested by the scenes near the mission building may never be realized, and that the worthy missionaries may be prosperous in the new field before them.

Dr. Steere,[39] lately consecrated Bishop of Central Africa, is about

38. Likmidas Ladha, the son of Ladha Damji, succeeded to the direction of his father's business after his death, thus becoming local representative of the firm of Jairam Sewji and the customs master of Zanzibar. New, *Life, Wanderings, and Labours in Eastern Africa*, 37.

39. Edward Steere (1828–1882) went to Central Africa with the Universities Mission in 1862, and then went to Zanzibar in 1864. He succeeded Tozer as bishop in 1874. Steere gave vital direction to the mission, returning it once more to the Nyasa region. He is perhaps best remembered today for his pioneering studies of the Swahili language. Heanley, *A Memoir of Bishop Steere;* Whiteley, "Swahili and the Classical Tradition," 215–16, for some notes on his language work. For the almost universally high opinion of Steere in East Africa, see Kirk to Hill, Aug. 29, 1882, FO 84/1619, PRO.

to arrive here, as successor of Bishop Tozer. If report speaks correctly he is about to establish mission buildings near Lake Nyassa, in which case he will have the hearty sympathy and support of every good man; and, did Livingstone live, Bishop Steere would depart with his blessings and best wishes for success. The very name of Bishop Steere suggests success. He is a practical and an indefatigably industrious man. He is devoid of bigotry, but while devoted to his Church he does not neglect the great fact that conversion of the heathen means more than the mere teaching of the formula of the Church of England. In short, he is a fit leader, because of his plain, practical good sense, his industry, his intellectual acquirements and religion for the new Christian mission, and I heartily congratulate the Board of the Church Mission for their selection and choice of such a man. While we are almost certain that Bishop Steere will be able to show results worthy of him, it is absolutely necessary for the cause of religion throughout Africa that he should be properly supported by his friends at home. There must be no niggard supplies sent to him, for the establishment of such a mission as will insure success requires considerable resources, and the Church Mission should this time make a supreme effort worthy of their great Church.

From the English Mission to the country is but a step, and before closing this letter we should like to ask the reader to accompany us as far as the ridges of Elaysu.[40] The path which we choose lies through cultivated tracts and groves of fruit trees which stretch on either side of it, thickening as they recede, and growing intensely deep and umbrageous, even to the depth and intensity of a forest. We note the sad effects of the hurricane in the prostrate and fast rotting trunks of the cocoanut palm, and the vast number of palms which lean from the perpendicular, and threaten before long to also fall. We note these things with a good deal of pity for the country, the people and the poor, unfortunate Prince, and we also think what a beautiful and happy isle this Isle of Zanzibar might be made under a wise and cultivated ruler. If such a change as is now visible in Mauritius, with all its peaks and mountains and miles of rugged ground, can be made, what might not be made of Zanzibar, where there are no mountains nor peaks nor rugged ground, but gentle undulations and low ridges eternally clothed in summer green verdure. At every point, at every spot you see something improvable, something that might be made very much better than it now is. And so we ride on with such reflections, which reflections are somewhat

40. Welezo, a ridge to the west of Zanzibar town. See the map in Baumann, *Der Sansibar-Archipel. II,* and Cave, *Three Journeys,* 79.

assisted, no doubt, by the ever-crooked path which darts toward all points of the compass in sudden and abrupt crookedness. But the land and the trees are always beautiful and always tropical. Palms and orange trees are everywhere, with a large number of plaintains, mangoes and jack fruit trees; the sugar cane neighbor, the Indian corn, the cassava, is side by side with the holcus sorghum, and there is a profusion of verdure and fruit and grain wherever we turn our eyes. And shortly we arrive at the most picturesque spot on the island of Zanzibar—Elaysu, or Ulayzu—as some call it—every inch of which, if the island were in the possession of the white man, would be worth a hundred times more than it is now, from its commanding elevation, from the charming views of sea and land and town its summit presents, for its healthiness, its neighborhood to town, for it is but five or six miles off. What cosy, lovable, pretty cottages might be built on the ridge of Elaysu, amid palms and never-sere foliage, amid flowers and carol of birds, amid shades of orange and mango trees! How white men and white women would love to dream on verandas, with open eyes, of their far away homes, made far pleasanter by distance and memory, while palms waved and rustled to gentle evening breezes, and the sun descended to the west amid clouds of all colors. Yes, Elaysu is beautiful and the receding ridges, with their precipitous ravines, fringed with trees and vegatation, are extremely picturesque, and some short bits of scenery which we view across the white glaring bars of sunlight are perfectly idyllic in their modest beauty. But much as I would be pleased to dilate on this and that view to you, with all the varying tints and shadows, gleaming brightness, and soft twilight, of unsurpassed tropical scenes and continuous groves of trees, I am constrained for want of space to refuse. As we turn our horses' heads around to return, we view the town and harbor of Zanzibar charmingly somnolent in the pale gray haze through which they are seen, representing but too fitly, in that dreamy state in which we imagine them, the lassitude and indifference of the people of Zanzibar.

17

District of Mpwapwa, Country of Usagara
Dec. 13, 1874 [1]

Uncouth as the name of the district and the cluster of villages whence I date my letter may appear in writing, it is not at all dis-

1. *NYH*, March 1, 1875. Stanley was now about half-way to Unyanyembe.

cordant to the ear. Nay, the sweet voice of an Msagara damsel can even give it a pleasant sound, and, as near as I can make it, it ought to be written Mbambwa. I can hardly describe my feelings as I revisited this spot after an absence of two years. I first experienced a sharp throb of regret as I recollected that it was the scene of the death of my Scotch assistant, William Farquhar, who perished here in 1871, and as I cast my eyes toward the west over the sere expanse and autumnal leafage of miles and miles of undulating plain. I verily believe that my next feeling was one of sorrowful foreboding at the momentary suggestion that perhaps one, if not all, of the white men on this expedition might find similar unhonored graves in this strange land. These feelings were not of long duration, however, for the cheery voices of the guides were heard loudly proclaiming that we were approaching Mpwapwa, and the view of high towering mountains, slopes all green with wide shadowing mimosa and tamarind, hollows dark with the verdant globes of foliage of sycamores, and the broad bed of the Mpwapwa stream, washed with crystal water, dispelled evil presentiments and all melancholy prognostigations. Thoughts of misfortune and dark days to come fled like a sick man's fancies before the spring coloring of noble mountains and the refreshing verdure of well watered slopes.[2]

Honestly, no man has less right to begin a letter in this strain than I have; for no man, however lucky his star may be, has more right to be proud and happy and cheerful than I have this day. For I have had an unprecedentedly successful march from the Indian Ocean, and surprisingly favorable influences have attended the expedition ever since we left Zanzibar. Nothing of the blight and misfortune that I predicted in my last letter from Zanzibar, nothing whatever of the vexatious delays, frequent desertions, half-hearted conduct of the armed escort, and various annoyances I surmised would befall us. On the contrary, we have arrived at the "half-way house" to Unyamwezi in an incredibly short time, as I will presently show you. We have suffered less sickness, less trouble, and, altogether, have had more good fortune than any expedition which ever came into Africa.

The expedition left Bagamoyo on the 17th of November and arrived here yesterday, the 12th day of December, which makes a period of only twenty-five days! This fact, stated thus briefly, might not surprise those uninitiated with the usual time required for this

2. A later visitor would consider Mpwapwa "not quite so inviting" as Stanley described it. *Report of the Rev. R. Price of his Visit to Zanzibar and the Coast of Eastern Africa,* 35–36.

march; but if I state that on my expedition in search of Livingstone the same march occupied me fifty-seven days, and that it occupied Lieutenant Cameron's party four months, even the most superficial reader will not fail to perceive that I have every reason to be devoutly grateful and extremely cheerful. And, while considering this rate of speedy marching, it must be remembered that this is a very large expedition, bearing such cumbersome things as the pontoon *Livingstone* and the cedar boat *Lady Alice,* and that since leaving the coast we have been travelling along an entirely new route, much north of any yet adopted.

Though I may look now with pleased expression on the distance traversed so speedily, as auguring well for the further prosecution of the march to the unknown lands north, and thence to the Nile sources, the day we left Zanzibar, with its wild disorder, did not promise much success. Nearly every member of the expeditionary force was either drunk, tipsy or elevated, or, as some would say, "a little the 'better' for the liquor." Many were absent from muster, and a few had deserted with their advance. I consoled myself with thinking, as I noticed the confusion and insolence of some of the most inebriated, "All right, my sable gentlemen; to-day is your day; to-morrow the reign of discipline and order begins."

After disembarking at Bagamoyo matters were not mended. The men had not as yet expended all their advance, and the consequence was that they betook themselves into the vile liquor shops of the Goanese at Bagamoyo, and after brutalizing themselves with the fire-water retailed there they took to swaggering through the streets, proclaiming that they were white men's soldiers, maltreating women, breaking into shops and smashing crockery, some even drawing knives on the peaceable citizens, and in other ways indulging their worst passions.

Of course, as long as I remained at Bagamoyo this state of things would continue; a few might be arrested and severely punished, but it would be too great a task to watch about 300 such men scattered among the houses of so large a town as Bagamoyo.[3] I was so engrossed with the novel duties of supressing turbulence and debauchery that I had not much time left for anything else. On the fifth day, however, after arriving at Bagamoyo, the bugle announced the march, and although we had some trouble in collecting the laggards, by nine A.M. the last man had left the town.

At Shamba Gonera, my former first camp, the men manifested a

---

3. For notes on the development of this most important center, Leue, "Bagamoyo."

disposition to stop, in order to make "one more night of it" at Bagamoyo; but by this time, as you may imagine, I had had enough of such scenes, and they were bodily driven on by the armed guard, not without considerable violence. Arriving at the Kingani River, the sections of the *Lady Alice* were screwed together, and her powers of transportation and efficiency here were well tested. I ascertained that the utmost she could bear in ferrying across the river were thirty men and thirty bales of cloth, or the weight of three tons, which was perfectly satisfactory to me. The *Livingstone* pontoon was not uncovered, as the *Lady Alice* proved expeditious enough in transporting the force across the river. When the ferriage was completed we resumed the journey, and long before sunset we encamped at Kikoka.

The intense heat of the Kingani Plains lying on either side told severely on those men who were unaccustomed to travelling in Africa, and who had indulged their vicious propensities at Zanzibar and Bagamoyo before departure, which compelled us to remain a day at Kikoka. I had, however, taken the precaution to leave a strong guard at the river to prevent the men from returning to Bagamoyo, and another on the hills between Bagamoyo and the Kingani Plain, on the eastern side of the river, for a similar purpose.

During the afternoon of this day, as I was preparing my last letters, I was rather surprised at a visit paid me in my camp from a party of the Sultan's soldiers, the chief of whom bore a letter from the Governor of Bagamoyo,[4] wherein he complained that my people had induced about fifteen women to abandon their masters.

On mustering the people and inquiring into their domestic affairs it was discovered that a large number of women had indeed joined the expedition during the night. Most of them, however, bore free papers accorded to them by the political agent at Zanzibar; but eleven[5] were, by their own confessions, runaway slaves. After being hospitably received by the Sultan of Zanzibar and the Arabs it was no part of a stranger's duty, unless authorized by some government likely to abide by its agent's actions, to countenance such a novel mode of liberating the slaves. The order was, therefore, given that these women should return with the Sultan's soldiers; but, as this did not agree with either the views of the women themselves or their abductors, the females set up a determined defiance to the order, and the males seized their Snider rifles, vowing that they should not return. As such a disposition and demonstration of hos-

4. Mansur bin Suliman. *TDC,* I, 74.
5. *Ibid.*, 86, says nine.

tility was not politic nor calculated to deserve my esteem, or to win for me the Arab's good will, this disposition was summarily suppressed and the women returned to their masters.

The first victim on this expedition has been the noble mastiff Castor, presented to me by the Baroness Burdett Coutts,[6] who died between the Kingani and Kikoka, from heat apoplexy. The second was the mastiff dog Captain—a very fine though ferocious animal —who died a few ways after. I still have three dogs—the retriever Nero, the undaunted bulldog Bull and a well-bred bull terrier Jack, who so far have borne the fatigues of the march very well, though the latter is considerably exercised in his mind by the numbers of grasshoppers he meets in the country while en route.

Our course since leaving Rosako has been mainly west-northwest, until approaching Mpwapwa we travelled due west. For several days we journeyed along the southern bank of the Wami River, making the discovery that the Wami can never be navigable during the dry season, as its channel for many miles is choked with granite boulders. During the rainy season very large craft could ascend as far as the Usagara Mountains; there is a rise of over sixteen feet in the river. On crossing the Wami we entered Nguru,[7] which is north of Useguhha—a country studded with tall peaks and mountains, the highest of which is a truncated cone, Mount Kidudwe, having an altitude of about 12,000 feet above the sea. As we journeyed through Nguru we crossed the several tributaries of the Wami, which are the Mwehweh, the Mkindo, the Mvomero, the Usingwe, the Rudewa and Mukondokwa.[8]

From Nguru we entered Northern Usagara, over ground which the aneroids indicated was 4,475 feet above sea level. Then we descended into lower ground about 3,400 feet above sea level until we came to Mpwapwa, which, I have ascertained, has an altitude, according to boiling point and two barometers, of 3,575 feet. Three days from here we crossed three tributaries of some river flowing east north of the Wami, which may probably be the Pangani.[9] The most ex-

6. Angela Burdett-Coutts (1814–1906), one of the richest women of her time, was a supporter of many philanthropic causes. To Stanley she was, according to his biographer, "an ever faithful friend and admirer." Patterson, *Angela Burdett-Coutts and the Victorians;* Hird, *Stanley,* 278.

7. The home of the Ngulu people, a group closely related to the Zigula. Last to Wigram, June 2, 1879, C.A6/014, CMS; Beidelman, *Matrilineal Peoples of Eastern Tanzania,* 57–66.

8. For Stanley and the Wami system, see document 12, note 4.

9. For the general altitudes of the region, Maurette, *Afrique Equatoriale, Orientale et Australe,* 88ff., and Moffett, *Handbook of Tanganyika, passim.* Mpwapwa is 3,700 feet above sea level. *Ibid.,* 542. Stanley was not near any of the tributaries of the Pangani River.

treme north which we reached on our journey here from the coast has been south latitude 5 deg. 49 min., which I ascertained by taking double altitudes. This was at the village of Kitangeh.

We intend to prosecute our journey to-morrow, but before leaving the Unyanyembe road for the land of discoveries and the sources of the Nile, which I am eager to reach, I will drop you a short letter informing you of our march through inhospitable Ugogo.

P.S. I have omitted to state that the white men, Edward and Francis Pocock and Fred Barker, are enjoying excellent health and spirits. The three have gone through their seasoning fevers without much trouble.

18

Village of Kagehyi, District of Uchambi, Usukuma, on the Victoria Niyanza
March 1, 1875 [1]

The second part of the programme laid before me as Commander of the Anglo-American Press Expedition to perform, ended successfully at noon on the 27th February, 1875. The great lake first discovered by Captain Speke—the Victoria Niyanza—was sighted and reached by us on that day; and it is with the feeling of the most devout gratitude to Almighty God for preserving us, amid manifold perils, that I write these lines.

It seems an age since we departed from Mpwapwa, Usagara, whence I despatched my last letter to you. We have experienced so much, seen and suffered so much, that I have to recapitulate carefully in my memory and turn to my note book often to refresh my recollections of even the principal events of this most long, arduous and eventful march to the Victoria Niyanza.

I promised you in my last letter that I would depart as soon as practicable from the old route to Unyanyembe, which is now so well known, and would, like the patriarch Livingstone, strike out a new line to unknown lands. I did so, but in our adventurous journey north I imperilled the expedition and almost brought it to an untimely

1. *NYH*, Oct. 11, 1875. Kageyi is located in Busukuma chiefdom, southeast of the lake-shore settlement of Kayenzi.

end, but which, happily for me, for you and for geographers, a kindly Providence averted.

On leaving Mpwapwa we edged northward across the Desert of the Marenga Mkali,[2] or the Bilber Water, leaving the vain chief of Mbumi far to the south, and traversed Northern Ugogo with the usual success attending travellers in Southern Ugogo. The chiefs practised the usual arts to fleece us of property and blackmailed us at every opportunity. Now, we met chiefs more amiably disposed toward strangers to pay heavier tribute in other chiefs' lands. We crossed broad and bleak plains, where food was scarce and cloth vanished fast, to enter hilly districts where food was abundant, the people civil and the chiefs kind. We traversed troublesome districts, where wars and rumors of wars were rife, the people treacherous and hostile, to enter countries lying at the mercy of the ferocious Wahumba[3] on the north, and the Wahehe to the south. Thus good and evil fortune alternated during our travels through Ugogo—an epitome in brief of our after experiences. Furious rainy tempests accompanied us each day, and some days both nature and man warred against us, while on other days both seemed combined to bless us. Under our adverse fates the expedition seemed to melt away; men died from fatigue and famine, many were left behind sick, while many, again, deserted. Promises of reward, kindness, threats, punishments, had no effect. The expedition seemed doomed.

The white men, though selected out of the ordinary class of Englishmen, did their work bravely—nay, I may say heroically. Though suffering from fever and dysentery, insulted by natives, marching under the heat and equatorial rain-storms, they at all times proved themselves of noble, manful natures, stout hearted, brave men, and —better than all—true Christians. Unrepining they bore their hard fate and worse fare; resignedly they endured their arduous troubles, cheerfully performed their allotted duties, and at all times commended themselves to my good opinion.

The western frontier of Ugogo was reached on the last day of 1874. We rested two days, and thence struck direct north, along an almost level plain, which some said extended as far as Niyanza. We found by questioning the natives that we were also travelling along the

2. ". . . a flat jungle-covered plain between thirty and forty miles wide, without a single drop of water or a single human habitation." Wilson and Felkin, *Uganda and the Egyptian Sudan*, I, 57.

3. The Baraguyu, the southernmost Nilo-Hamitic group in Africa. See Biedelman, "The Baraguyu," 245–78.

western extremity of Uhumba, which we were glad to hear, as we fondly hoped that our march would be less molested.

Two days' march north brought us to the confines of Usandawi,[4] a country famous for elephants; but here our route inclined northwest, and we entered Ukimbu, or Uyanzi, at its northeastern extremity.

We had hired guides in Ugogo to take us as far as Iramba,[5] but at Muhalala, in Ukimbu, they deserted. Fresh guides were engaged at Muhalala, who took us one day's march farther northwest, but at night they also deserted, and in the morning we were left on the edge of a wide wilderness without a guide. On the roads the previous day the guides had informed us that three days' march would bring us to Urimi,[6] and relying on the truth of the report I had purchased two days' provisions, so that this second desertion did not much disconcert us nor raise any suspicion, though it elicited many unpleasant remarks about the treachery of the Wagogo. We therefore continued our march, but on the morning of the second day the narrow, ill-defined track which we had followed became lost in a labyrinth of elephant and rhinoceros trails. The best men were despatched in all directions to seek out the lost road, but they were all unsuccessful, and we had no resource left but the compass. The day brought us into a dense jungle of acacias and euphorbia, through which we had literally to push our way through by scrambling, crawling along the ground under natural tunnels of embracing shrubbery, cutting the convulvulvi and creepers, thrusting aside stout, thorny bushes, and, by various detours, taking advantage of every slight opening the jungle afforded, which naturally lengthened our journey and protracted our stay in the wilderness. On the evening of the third day the first death in the wilderness occurred.

The fourth day's march lasted nearly the whole day, though we made but fourteen miles, and was threefold more arduous than that of the preceding day. Not a drop of water was discovered during the march, and the weaker people, laboring under their loads, hun-

4. The Sandawi of the Kondoa Irangi area; they have physical and linguistic similarities with the Hottentots. Trevor, "The Physical Characteristics of the Sandawe"; Huntingford, *Southern Nilo-Hamites*, 135–39.

5. The Iramba people live in the area of the Iramba plateau, the Wembere steppe, and the Dulumo valley. Moffett, *Handbook of Tanganyika*, 158. For a description, Reche, *Zur Ethnographie das abflusslosen Gebietes Deutsch-Ostafrikas*, 92–100.

6. The Rima, or Nyaturu, of the Singida region. *Ibid.*, 31–68; see below, note 13.

ger and thirst, lagged behind the vanguard many miles, which caused the rear guard, under two of the white men, much suffering. As the rear guard advanced they shouldered the loads of the weaker men, and endeavored to encourage them to resume the march. Some of these men were enabled to reach the camp, where their necessities were relieved by medicine and restoratives. But five men strayed from the path which the passing expedition had made, and were never seen alive again. Scouts sent out to explore the woods found one dead about a mile from our road; the others must have hopelessly wandered on until they also fell down and died.

The fifth day brought us to a small village, lately erected, called Uveriveri, the population of which consisted of four men, their wives and little ones. These people had not a grain of food to spare. Most of the men of our expedition were unable to move for hunger and fatigue. In this dire extremity I ordered a halt and selected twenty[7] of the strongest men to proceed to Suna, twenty-nine miles northwest from Uveriveri, to purchase food. In the interval I explored the woods in search of game, but the search was fruitless, though one of my men discovered a lion's den and brought me two young lions, which I killed and skinned.

Returning to camp from my fruitless hunt I was so struck with the pinched faces of my poor people that I could have wept heartily could I have done so without exciting fear of our fate in their minds, but I resolved to do something toward relieving the pressing needs of fierce hunger.

To effect this a sheet iron trunk was emptied of its contents, and being filled with water, was placed on the fire. I then broke open our medical stores and took five pounds of Scotch oatmeal and three tins of revalenta arabica, with which I made gruel to feed over 220 men. Oh, it was a rare sight to see these poor famine stricken people hasten to that torquay dress trunk and assist me to cook that huge pot of gruel, to see them fan the fire to a fiercer heat, and, with their gourds full of water, stand by to cool the foaming liquid when it threatened to overflow, and it was a still more rare sight to watch the pleasure steal over their faces as they drank the generous food. The sick and weaker ones received a larger portion near my tent, and another tin of oatmeal was opened for their supper and breakfast. But a long time must elapse before I shall have the courage to describe my feelings during the interval

7. *TDC,* I, 110, gives forty; *Diary,* 43, twenty.

I waited for the return of my people from Suna with food, and fruitless would be the attempt to describe the anxiety with which I listened for the musketry announcing their success.

After forty-eight hours' waiting we heard the joyful sounds, which woke us all into new life and vigor. The food was most greedily seized by the hungry people, and so animating was the report of the food purveyors that the soldiers, one and all, clamored to be led away that afternoon. Nowise loath myself to march away from this fatal jungle, I assented; but two more poor fellows breathed their last before we left camp. We camped that night at the base of a rocky hill, overlooking a broad plain, which, after the intense gloom and confined atmosphere of the jungle, was a great pleasure to us, and, next day, striking north along this plain, after a long march, under a fervid sun, of twenty miles, reached the district of Suna, in Urimi.

In Urimi, at Suna, we discovered a people remarkable for their manly beauty, noble proportions and nakedness. Neither man nor boy had either cloth or skins to cover his nudity; the women bearing children only boasted of goat skins. With all their physical beauty and fine proportions they were the most suspicious people we had yet seen. It required great tact and patience to induce them to part with food for our cloth and beads. They owned no chief, but respected the injunctions of their elders, with whom I treated for permission to pass through their land. The permission was reluctantly given, and food was begrudgingly sold, but we bore with this silent hostility patiently, and I took great care that no overt act on the part of the expedition should change this suspicion into hatred.

Our people were so worn out with fatigue that six more poor fellows died here, and the sick list numbered thirty. Here also Edward Pocock fell seriously ill of typhoid fever. For his sake, as well as for the other sufferers, I halted in Suna four days; but it was too evident that the longer we stayed in their country the natives regarded us with less favor, and it was incumbent on us to move, though much against my inclination. There were many grave reasons why we should have halted several days longer, for Edward Pocock was daily getting worse and the sick list increased alarmingly; dysentery, diarrhoea, chest diseases, sore feet, tasked my medical knowledge to the utmost; but prudence forbade it. The rearguard and captains of the expedition were therefore compelled to do the work of carriers, and every soldier for the time being was converted into a *pagazi*, or porter. Pocock was put into a hammock, the sick and weakly were encouraged to do their utmost to move on with the expedition to more auspicious lands, where the natives were less suspicious, where food was more abundant, and where cattle were numerous. Imbued with this hope, the expedition resumed its march across the clear, open and well cultivated country of Urimi.

We reached Chiwyu about ten o'clock, after a short march, and here the young Englishman Edward Pocock breathed his last, to the great grief of us all. According to two rated pedometers we had finished the 400th mile of our march from the sea, and had reached the base of the watershed whence the trickling streams and infant waters begin to flow Nileward, when this noble young man died. We buried him at night, and a cross cut deep into a tree marks his last resting place at Chiwyu.

The farther we traveled north we became still more assured that we had arrived in the dewy land whence the extreme southern springs, rivulets and streams discharge their waters into the Nile. From a high ridge overlooking a vast extent of country the story of their course was plainly written in the deep depressions and hollows trending northward and northwestward, and as we noted these signs of the incipient Nile we cherished the darling hope that before long we should gaze with gladdened eyes on the mighty reservoir which collected these waters which purled and rippled at our feet, into its broad bosom, to discharge them in one vast body into the White Nile.

From Chiwyu we journeyed two days through Urimi to Mangara, where Kaif Halleck—the carrier of Kirk's letter bag to Livingstone, whom I compelled to accompany me to Ujiji in 1871—was brutally murdered. He had been suffering from asthma, and I had permitted him to follow the expedition slowly, the rear guard being all employed as carriers because of the heavy sick list, when he was waylaid by the natives and hacked to pieces.[8] This was the first overt act of hostility on the part of the Warimi. Unable to fix the crime on any particular village, we resumed our journey, and entered Ituru, a district of Northern Urimi, on the 21st day of January.

The village near which we camped was called Vinyata, and was situated in a broad and populous valley, containing, probably, some 2,000 or 3,000 souls. Here we discovered the river which received all the streams that flowed between Vinyata and Chiwyu. It is called here Leewumbu,[9] and its flow from this valley was west. Even in the dry season it is a considerable stream, some twenty feet in

8. *TDC*, I, 122–23, gives a slightly different sequence of events.
9. See below, note 17.

width and about two feet deep, but in the rainy season it becomes a deep and formidable river.

The natives received us coldly, but as we were but two days' journey from Iramba I redoubled my exertions to conciliate the surly suspicious people, and that evening my efforts seemed crowned with success, for they brought milk, eggs and chickens to me for sale, for which I parted freely with cloth. The fame of my liberality reached the ears of the great man of the valley, the magic doctor, who, in the absence of a recognized king, is treated with the deference and respect due to royalty by the natives. This important personage brought me a fat ox on the second day of my arrival at Vinyata, and in exchange received double its value in cloth and beads, and a rich present was bestowed upon his brother and his son. The great man begged for the heart of the slaughtered ox, which was freely given him, and other requests were likewise honored by prompt gifts.

We had been compelled to take advantage of the fine sun which shone this day to dry the bales and goods, and I noticed, though without misgiving, that the natives eyed them greedily. The morning of the third day the magic doctor returned again to camp to beg for some more beads to make brotherhood with him. To this, after some slight show of reluctance to give too much, I assented, and he departed apparently pleased.

Half an hour afterward the war cry of the Waturu was heard resounding through each of the 200 villages of the valley of the Leewumbu. The war cry was similar to that of the Wagogo, and phonetically it might be spelt "Hehu, A Hehu," the latter syllables drawn out in a prolonged cry, thrilling and loud. As we had heard the Wagogo sound the war notes upon every slight apparition of strangers we imagined that the warriors of Ituru were summoned to contend against some marauders like the warlike Mirambo or some other malcontent neighbors, and, nothing disturbed by it, we pursued our various avocations, like peaceful beings, fresh from our new brotherhood with the elders of Ituru. Some of our men were gone out to the neighboring pool to draw water for their respective messes, others were gone to cut wood, others were about starting to purchase food, when suddenly we saw the outskirts of the camp darkened by about 100 natives in full war costume. Feathers of the bustard, the eagle and the kite waved above their heads, or the mane of the zebra and the giraffe encircled their brows; their left hands held their bows and arrows, while their right bore their spears.

This hostile presence naturally alarmed us, for what had we done to occasion disturbance or war? Remembering the pacific bearing of Livingstone when he and I were menaced by the cannibal Wabembe,[10] I gave orders that none should leave camp until we should ascertain what this warlike appearance meant, and that none should, by any demonstration, provoke the natives. While we waited to see what the Waturu intended to do, their numbers increased tenfold, and every bush and tree hid a warrior.

Our camp was situated on the edge of a broad wilderness, which extended westward many days' march; but to the north, east and south, nothing was seen but villages and cultivated ground, which, with the careless mode of agriculture in vogue among savages, contained acres of dwarf shrubbery; but I doubt whether throughout this valley a better locality for a camp could have been selected than the one we had chosen. Fifty or sixty yards around us was open ground, so that we had the advantage of light to prevent the approach of an enemy unseen. A slight fence of bush served to screen our numbers from those without the camp, but, having had no occasion to suspect hostilities, it was but ill adapted to shield us from attack.

When the Waturu were so numerous in our vicinity that it was no longer doubtful that they were summoned to fight us, I despatched a young man who knew their language to ascertain their intention. As he advanced toward them six or seven warriors drew near to talk with him. When he returned he informed us that one of our men had stolen some milk and butter from a small village and that we must pay for it in cloth. The messenger was sent back to tell them that white men did not come to their country to rob or quarrel; that they had but to name the price of what was stolen to be paid at once, and that not one grain of corn or milletseed should be appropriated by us wrongfully. Upon this the principal warriors drew nearer, until we could hear their voices plainly, though we did not understand the nature of the conversation. The messenger informed us that the elders demanded four yards of sheeting, which was about six times the value of the stolen articles; but at such a time it was useless to haggle over such a demand, and the cloth was paid. When it was given to them the elders said they were satisfied, and withdrew.

But it was evident that though the elders were satisfied the warriors were not, as they could be seen hurrying by scores from all

10. See *HIFL*, 511–14.

parts of the valley and gesticulating violently in crowds. Still we waited patiently, hoping that if the elders and principal warriors were really amicably disposed toward us, their voices would prevail, and that they would be able to assuage the wild passions which now seemed to animate the others. As we watched them we noted that about 200 detached themselves from the gesticulating crowds east of the camp and were hurrying to the thick bush west of us. Soon afterward one of my men returned from that direction bleeding profusely from the face and arm, and reported that he and a youth named Sulieman were out collecting firewood when they were attacked by a large crowd of savages, who were hidden in the bush. A knobstick had crushed his nose and a spear had severely wounded him in the arm, but he had managed to escape, while Sulieman was killed, a dozen spears having been plunged into his back.

This report and the appearance of the bleeding youth so excited the soldiers of the expedition that they were only with the utmost difficulty restrained from beginning a battle at once. Even yet I hoped that war might be prevented by a little diplomacy, while I did not forget to open the ammunition boxes and prepare for the worst. But much was to be done. The enclosure of the camp required to be built up, and something of a fortification was needed to repel the attack of such a large force. While we were thus preparing without ostentation to defend ourselves from what I conceived to be an imminent attack, the Waturu, now a declared enemy, advanced upon the camp, and a shower of arrows fell all around us. Sixty soldiers, held in readiness, were at once ordered to deploy in front of the camp, fifty yards off, and the Wangwana, or freemen of Zanzibar, obedient to the command, rushed out of the camp, and the battle commenced.

Immediately after this sixty men, with axes, were ordered to cut bushes and raise a high fence of thorn around the camp, while twenty more were ordered to raise lofty platforms like towers within, for sharpshooters. We busied ourselves in bringing the sections of the *Lady Alice* to make a central camp for a last resistance, and otherwise strengthening the defences. Every one worked with a will, and while the firing of the skirmishers, growing more distant, announced that the enemy was withdrawing from the attack, we were left to work unmolested. When the camp was prepared I ordered the bugler to sound the retreat, in order that the savages might have time to consider whether it was politic for them to renew the fight.

When the skirmishers returned they announced that fifteen of the enemy were killed, while a great many more were wounded and borne off by their friends. They had all distinguished themselves —even "Bull," the British bulldog, had seized one of the Watura by the leg and had given him a taste of the power of the English canines of his breed before the poor savage was mercifully despatched by a Snider bullet.

We rested that day from further trouble, and the next morning we waited events until nine o'clock, when the enemy appeared in greater force than ever, having summoned their neighbors all about them to assist them (I felt assured now) in our ruin. But, though we were slow to war upon people whom I thought might be made friends the previous day, we were not slow to continue fighting if the natives were determined to fight. Accordingly I selected four experienced men to lead four several detachments, and gave orders that they should march in different directions through the valley and meet at some high rocks distant five miles off; that they should seize upon all cattle and burn every village as soon as taken. Obedient to the command they sallied out of the camp and began the second day's fight.

They were soon vigorously engaged with the enemy, who fled fast and furious before them to an open plain on the banks of the Leewumbu. The detachment under Farjalla Christie[11] became too excited, and because the enemy ran, imagined that they had but to show themselves to cause the natives to fly; but once on the plain —having drawn them away isolated miles from any succor—they turned upon them and slaughtered the detachment to a man, except the messenger, who had been detailed to accompany the detachment to report success or failure. I had taken the precaution to send one swift-footed man to accompany each detachment for this purpose. This messenger came from Farjalla to procure assistance, which was at once despatched, though too late to aid the unfortunate men, but not too late to save the second detachment from a like fate, as the victorious enemy, after slaughtering the first detachment, had turned upon the second with the evident intention to cut the entire force opposed to them in detail. When the support arrived they found the second detachment all but lost. Two soldiers were killed. The captain, Ferahan, had a deep spear wound in his side. The others were hemmed in on all sides. A volley was poured into the

11. Farjalla Christie had previously served with Livingstone and the missionary, New. New, "Journey from Pangani," 414; Gray, "Livingstone's Muganda Servant," 128.

rear of the astonished enemy, and the detachment was saved. With their combined forces our people poured a second volley, and continued their march almost unopposed to the northern and eastern extremity of the valley. Meanwhile, smoke was seen issuing from the south and the southeast, informing us that the third and fourth detachments were pursuing their way victoriously, and soon a score or more villages were enwrapped in dense volumes of smoke. Even at a distance of eight miles we beheld burning villages, and shortly after fired settlements to the north and east announced our victory on all sides.

Toward evening the soldiers returned, bringing cattle and an abundance of grain to the camp; but when the muster-roll was called I found I had lost twenty-one men, who had been killed, while thirty-five deaths of the enemy were reported.

The third day we began the battle with sixty good men, who received instructions to proceed to the extreme length of the valley and burn what had been left the previous day.[12] These came to a strong and large village to the northeast, which, after a slight resistance, they entered, loaded themselves with grain and set on fire. Long before noon it was clearly seen that the savages had had enough of war and were demoralized, and our people returned through the now silent and blackened valley without molestation.

Just before daybreak on the fourth day we left our camp and continued our journey northwest, with provisions sufficient to last us six days, leaving the people of Ituru to ponder on the harsh fate they had drawn on themselves by their greed, treachery and wanton murder, and attack on peaceful strangers.[13]

We are still a formidable force, strong in numbers, guns and property, though, for an expedition destined to explore so many thousands of miles of new countries, we had suffered severely. I had left the coast with over 300 men; but when I numbered the expedition at Mgongo Tembo, in Iramba, which we reached three days after departing from the scene of our war, I found that I had but 194 men left. Thus, in less than three months, I had lost by

12. *TDC*, I, 128, says the enemy appeared again; *Diary*, 50–51, says none came.

13. On his return to Britain, Stanley, in reply to critics of his proceedings in Africa, boldly asserted, "I am happy to say we did not leave that place until we had perfectly sickened them." Stanley, "On His Recent Explorations and Discoveries in Central Africa," 151. The Swiss trader Broyon asserted these hostilities opened up the region to Nyamwezi caravans, but the area remained in general hostile to visitors, at least to Arabs and Europeans. De Freycinet to MAE, Sept. 14, 1878, CCZ, IV; Baumann, *Durch Masailand*, 110ff. For another view of the hostilities, see document 21.

dysentery, famine, heart disease, desertion and war, over 125 men natives of Africa and one European.[14]

I have not time—for my work is but beginning—to relate a tithe of our adventures, or how we suffered. You can better imagine our perils, our novel and strange fortunes, if you reflect on the loss of 126 men out of such an expedition. Such a loss even in a strong regiment would be deemed almost a calamity. What name will you give such a loss when you cannot recruit your numbers, where every man that dies is a loss that cannot be repaired; when your work, which is to last years, is but beginning; where each morning you say to yourself, "This day may be your last?"

On entering Iramba we found that the natives called out against all strangers, "Mirambo and his robbers are coming." But a vast amount of patience and suave language saved us from the doom that threatens this now famous chieftain. Despite, however, all medicines and magic arts that have been made and practised as yet, Mirambo lives. He seems to make war upon all mankind in this portion of the African interior, and appears to be possessed of ubiquitous powers. We heard of him advancing upon the natives in Northern Ugogo, Ukimbu was terror-stricken at his name, the people at Unyanyembe were still fighting him, and here in Iramba he has been met and fought, and is again daily expected.

As we journeyed on through Iramba and entered Usukuma his fame increased, for we were now drawing near some of the scenes of his exploits. When we approached the Victoria Niyanza he was actually fighting, but a day's march from us, with the people of Usanda and Masari, and a score of times we came near being plunged into wars because the natives mistook our Expedition for Mirambo's force; but our color always saved us before we became actually engaged in conflict.

Various were our fortunes in our travels between Mgongo Tembo, in Iramba, and the Niyanza. We traversed the whole length of Usukuma, through the districts of Mombiti, Usiha, Mondo, Sengerema and Marya, and, passing through Usmaow, re-entered Usukuma by Uchambi, and arrived at the lake after a march of 720 miles.[15]

As far as Western Ugogo I may pass over without attempting to describe the country, as readers may obtain a detailed account of it

14. There are different figures in *Diary*, 53.

15. Busanda, Busiha, Mondo, Sengerema, and Busmao are Sukuma chiefdoms. Mombiti, Masari, and Marya (Malya) are Sukuma settlements. Malcolm, *Sukumaland*, 2, 9–10; Cory, *Sukuma Law and Custom*, 170–71; *TDC*, I, 134.

from *How I Found Livingstone*. Thence north is a new country to all, and a brief description of it may be interesting to students of African geography.

North of Mizanza a level plain extends as far as the frontier of Usandawi, a distance of thirty-five miles (English). At Mukondoku the altitude, as indicated by two first rate aneroids, was 2,800 feet. At Mtiwi, twenty miles north, the altitude was 2,825 feet. Diverging west and northwest, we ascend the slope of a lengthy mountain wall, apparently, but which, upon arriving at the summit we ascertain to be a wide plateau, covered with forest. This plateau has an altitude of 3,800 feet at its eastern extremity; but as it extends westward it rises to a height of 4,500 feet. It embraces all Uyanzi, Unyanyembe, Usukuma, Urimi and Iramba—in short, all that part of Central Africa lying between the valley of the Rufiji south and the Victoria Niyanza north, and the mean altitude of this broad upland cannot exceed 4,500 feet. From Mizanza to the Niyanza is a distance of nearly 300 geographical miles, yet at no part of this long journey did the aneroids indicate a higher altitude than 5,100 feet above the sea.[16]

As far as Urimi, from the eastern edge of the plateau, the land is covered with a dense jungle of acacias, which, by its density, strangles all other species of vegetation. Here and there, only in the cleft of a rock, a giant euphorbia may be seen, sole lord of its sterile domain. The soil is shallow, and consists of vegetable mould mixed largely with sand and detritus of the bare rocks, which crown each knoll and ridge, and which testify too plainly to the violence of the periodical rains.

In the basin of Matongo, in Southern Urimi, we were instructed by the ruins of hills and ridges, relics of a loftier upland, of what has been effected by nature in the course of long ages. No learned geological savant need ever expound to the traveller who views these rocky ruins the geological history of this country. From a distance we viewed the glistening, naked and riven rocks as a singular scene; but when we stood among them, and noted the appearance of the rocky fragments of granite, gneiss and prophyry, peeled, as it were, rind after rind, or leaf after leaf, like an artichoke, until the rock was wasted away, it seemed as if Dame Nature had left these relics, these hilly skeletons, to demonstrate her laws and career. It seemed to me as if she said, "Lo and behold this broad basin of Matongo, with its teeming village and herds of cattle and

16. Mizanza is on the border region of Ugogo. *TDC,* I, 102–04. For the area Stanley refers to, Moffett, *Handbook of Tanganyika,* 151–64, and the map opposite p. 151.

fields of corn, surrounded by these bare rocks—in primeval time this land was covered with water, it was the bed of a vast sea. The waters were dried, leaving a wide expanse of level land, upon which I caused heavy rains to fall five months out of each year during all the ages that have elapsed since first the hot sunshine fell upon the soil. These rains washed away the loose sand and made deep furrows in course of time, until at certain places the rocky kernel under the soil began to appear. The furrows became enlarged, the water frittered away their banks and conveyed the earth away to lower levels, through which it wore away a channel first through the soil and lastly through the rock itself, which you may see if you but walk to the bottom of that basin. You will there behold a channel worn through the solid rock some fifty feet in depth; and as you look on that you will have an idea of the power and force of tropical rains. It is through that channel that the soil robbed from these rocks has been carried away towards the Niyanza to fill its depths and in time make dry land of it. Now, you may ask how came these once solid rocks, which are now but skeletons of hills and stony heaps, to be thus split into so many fragments? Have you never seen the effect of water thrown upon lime? The solid rocks have been broken and peeled in an almost similar manner. The tropic sun heated the surface of these rocks to an intense heat, and the cold rain falling upon the heated surface caused them to split and peel as you now see them."

This is really the geological history of this country simply told. Ridge after ridge, basin after basin, from Western Ugogo to the Niyanza, tells the same tale; but it is not until we enter Central Urimi that we begin to marvel at the violence of the process by which Nature has transformed the face of the land. For here the perennial springs and rivulets begin to unite and form rivers, after collecting and absorbing the moisture from the watershed; and these rivers, though but gentle streams during the dry season, become formidable during the rains. It is in Central Irimi that the Nile first begins to levy tribute upon Equatorial Africa, and if you look upon the map and draw a line east from the latitude of Ujiji to longitude thirty-five degrees you will strike upon the sources of the Leewumbu, which is the extreme southern feeder of the Victoria N'yanza.

In Iramba, between Mgongo Tembo and Mombiti we came upon what must have been in former times an arm of the Victoria Niyanza. It is called the Luwamberri Plain, after a river of that name, and is about forty miles in width. Its altitude is 3,775 feet above the sea and but a few feet above the Victoria Niyanza. We were fortunate in crossing the broad, shallow stream in the dry season, for during the *masika,* or rainy season, the plain is converted into a wide lake.

The Leewumbu River, after a course of 170 miles, becomes known in Usukuma as the Monangah River. After another run of 100 miles it is converted into Shimeeyu, under which name it enters the Victoria east of this port of Kagehyi. Roughly the Shimeeyu may be said to have a length of 350 miles.[17]

After penetrating the forest and jungle west of the Luwamberri we enter Usukuma—a country thickly peopled and rich in cattle. It is a series of rolling plains, with here and there, far apart, a chain of jagged hills. The descent to the lake is so gradual that I expect to find upon sounding it, as I intend to do, that, though it covers a vast area, it is very shallow.

Now, after our long journey, the Expedition is halted a hundred yards from the lake, and as I look upon its dancing waters I long to launch the *Lady Alice* and venture out to explore its mysteries. Though on its shore, I am as ignorant of its configuration and extent as any man in England or America. I have questioned the natives of Uchambi closely upon the subject at issue, but no one can tell me positively whether the lake is one or more. I hear a multitude of strange names, but whether they are of countries or lakes it is impossible to divine, their knowledge of it being very superficial. My impression, however, is that Speke, in his bold sketch and imagined outline, is nearer the truth than Livingstone, who reported of it upon hearsay at a great distance from its shores; but as soon as I can finish my letters to you and my friends the sections of the *Lady Alice* will be screwed together, and the first English boat that ever sailed on the African lakes shall venture upon her mission of thoroughly exploring every nook and cranny of the shores of the Victoria. It is with great pride and pleasure I think of our success in conveying such a large boat safely through the hundreds of miles of jungle which we traversed, and just now I feel as though the entire wealth of the universe could not bribe me to turn back from my work. Indeed, it is with the utmost impatience that I think of the task of writing my letters before starting upon the more pleasant work of exploring, but I remember the precept, "Duty before pleasure."

I hear of strange tales about the countries on the shores of this

17. The Simiyu is a relatively unimportant river flowing into Lake Victoria. The rivers Stanley claimed were connected with the Simiyu from the south actually flowed into lakes Eyasi and Kitangiri. Baumann, *Durch Masailand*, 66ff.; Johnston, *Nile Quest*, 267. See document 19.

lake, which make me still more eager to start. One man reports a country peopled with dwarfs, another with giants, and another is said to possess a breed of such large dogs that even my mastiffs are said to have been small compared to them. All these may be idle romance, and I lay no stress on anything reported to me, as I hope to be enabled to see with my own eyes all the wonders of these unknown countries.

It is unfortunate that I have not Speke's book with me; but a map of Central Africa which I have with me contains the statement, in brackets, that the Victoria Niyanza has an altitude of only 3,308 feet above the ocean. If this statement is on Speke's authority, either he or I am wrong, for my two aneroids, almost fresh from England, make it much higher. One ranges from 3,550 to 3,650 feet; the other from 3,575 to 3,675 feet. I have not boiled my thermometers yet, but intend doing so before starting on the work of exploring the lake. I have no reason to suspect that the aneroids are at fault, as they are both first class, and have been carefully carried with the chronometers.[18]

With regard to Speke's position of Muanza, I incline to think that he is right, but as I have not visited Muanza I cannot tell. The natives point it out westward of Kagehyi and but a short distance off. The position of the port of Kagehyi is south latitude 2 deg. 31 min., east longitude 33 deg. 13 min.

I mustered the men of the expedition yesterday and ascertained it to consist of three white men and 166 Wanguana soldiers and carriers, twenty-eight having died since leaving Ituru thirty days ago. Over one-half of our force has thus been lost by desertion and deaths. This is terrible, but I hope that their long rest here will revive the weak and strengthen the strong. The dreadful scourge of the expedition has been dysentery and I can boast of but few men cured of it by medicine, though it was freely given, as we were possessed of abundance of medical stores. A great drawback to their cure has been the necessity of moving on, whereas a few days' rest, in a country blessed with good water and food, would have restored many of them to health; but good water and good food could not be procured anywhere together except here. The Arabs would have taken nine months or a year to march this long distance, while we have performed it in only 103 days, including halts. As I vaccinated every member of the expedition on the coast, I am happy to say that not one fell a victim to smallpox.

18. Speke gave Lake Victoria an altitude of 3,740 feet on his first visit and of 3,306 feet on his second. Speke, "Upper Basin of the Nile," 325, 332. The actual height of the lake is 3,720 feet.

I leave this letter in the hands of Sungoro,[19] a Msawahili trader, who resides here, in the hope that he will be enabled shortly to send it to Unyanyembe, as he frequently sends caravans there with ivory; but a copy of it I shall take with me to Uganda, and deliver it to Mtesa, the King, to be conveyed, if possible, to Colonel Gordon. Since leaving Mpwapwa I have not met one caravan bound for Zanzibar; and after leaving Ugogo it was impossible to meet one, or to despatch couriers through such dangerous countries as we have traversed. The letters containing the account of our explorations of the Victoria Niyanza and our subsequent march to the Albert Niyanza I hope to be able to deliver personally into the hands of Colonel Gordon.

P.S. You may have observed that I have differed from Captain Speke in spelling Nyanza, as he calls it. I have taken the liberty of writing it as it is actually pronounced by both Arabs and natives, Ni-yanza or Nee-yanza.[20]

March 5. The boiling point observed by one of Negretti & Zambra's apparatus this day was 205 degrees 6 minutes; temperature of air, 82 degrees Fahrenheit. The boiling point observed by another instrument by a different maker was 205 degrees 5 minutes; temperature of air, 81 degrees Fahrenheit. The barometer at the same time indicated 26.90 inches. The mean of the barometrical observations at Zanzibar was 30.048. The mean of the barometrical observations during seven days' residence here has been 26.138.

19

Kagehyi, on the Victoria Niyanza
March 4, 1875 [1]

Dear Sir.[2] A most unpleasant, because sad, task devolves upon me, for I have the misfortune to have to report to you the death of your son Edward of typhoid fever. His service with me was brief, but it was

19. Sungoro Tarib; he was killed in a quarrel with Lukonge of Ukerewe in 1877. See Gray, "Arabs on Lake Victoria. Some Revisions," 76–78; Hartwig, "Bukerebe, the Church Missionary Society and East African Politics, 1877–1878."

20. Burton commented that Stanley, "although strong in the vernacular, proved in his first work . . . that he ignored the minutiae of speech, and that his ear must not be relied upon." Burton's letter of Oct. 19, 1875, 354. On his return from Africa, Stanley affirmed he would not use his proposed new spelling out of respect for the memory of Speke. *TDC*, I, 162.

1. *NYH*, Oct. 11, 1875. As recounted in the following despatches, Stanley and part of his expedition set off to explore Lake Victoria in the *Lady Alice*. Barker and F. Pocock remained behind.

2. Edward Pocock's father, Henry J. Pocock.

long enough for me to know the greatness of your loss, for I doubt that few fathers can boast of such sons as yours. Both Frank and Ted proved themselves sterling men, noble and brave hearts and faithful servants. Ted had endeared himself to the members of the expedition by his amiable nature, his cheerfulness, and by various qualifications which brought him into high favor with the native soldiers of this force. Before daybreak we were accustomed to hear the cheery notes of his bugle, which woke us to a fresh day's labors; at night, around the camp fires, we were charmed with his sweet, simple songs, of which he had an inexhaustible *répertoire*. When tired also with marching it was his task to announce to the fatigued people the arrival of the vanguard at camp, so that he had become quite a treasure to us all; and I must say that I have never known men who could bear what your sons have borne on this expedition so patiently and uncomplainingly. I never heard one grumble either from Frank or Ted; have never heard them utter an illiberal remark, or express any wish that the expedition had never set foot in Africa, as many men would have done in their situation; so that you may well imagine that, if the loss of one of your sons causes grief to your paternal heart, it has been no less a grief to us, as we were all, as it were, one family, surrounded as we are by so much that is dark and forbidding.

On arriving at Suna, in Urimi, Ted came to me, after a very long march, complaining of pain in his limbs and loins. I did not think it was serious at all, nor anything uncommon after walking twenty miles, but told him to go and lie down, that he would be better on the morrow, as it was very probably fatigue. The next morning I visited him and he again complained of pains in the knees and back, at which I ascribed it to rheumatism and treated him accordingly. The third day he complained of pain in the chest, difficulty of breathing and sleeplessness, by which I perceived that he was suffering from some other malady than rheumatism, but what it could be I could not divine. He was a little feverish, so I gave him a mustard plaster and some aperient medicine. Toward night he began to wander in his head, and on examining his tongue I found it almost black, and coated with dark gray fur. At these symptoms I thought that he had a severe attack of remittent fever, from which I suffered in Ujiji in 1871, and, therefore, I watched for an opportunity to administer quinine—that is, when the fever would abate a little. But on the fourth day, the patient still wandering in his mind, I suggested to Frank, that he should sponge him with cold water, and change his clothing, during which operation I noticed that the chest of the patient was covered with spots like pimples or smallpox pustules, which perplexed me greatly. He could not have caught the smallpox, and what the disease was I could not imagine; but, in turning to my medical books, I saw that your son was suffering from typhoid, the description of which was too clear to be longer mistaken, and both Frank and I devoted our attention to him. He was nourished with arrowroot and brandy, and everything that was in our power to do was done; but it was very evident that the case was serious, though I hoped that his constitution would brave it out.

On the fifth day we were compelled to resume our journey, after a rest of four days. Ted was put in a hammock and carried on the shoulders of four men. At ten o'clock on the 17 of January we halted at Chiwyu, and the minute that he was laid down in the camp he breathed his last. Our companion was dead.

We buried him that night under a tree, on which his brother Frank had cut a deep cross, and read the beautiful service of the Church of England over him as we laid the poor wornout body in its final resting place.

Peace be to his ashes! Poor Ted deserved a better fate than dying in Africa, but it was impossible that he could have died easier. I wish that my end may be as peaceful and painless as his. He was saved the stormy scenes we went through shortly after in our war with the Waturu; and who knows how much he has been saved from? But I know that he would have rejoiced to be with us at this hour of our triumph, gazing on the laughing waters of the vast fountain of old Nile. None of us would have been more elated at the prospect before us than he, for he was a true sailor and loved the sight of water. Yet again I say, peace be to his ashes; be consoled, for Frank still lives, and from present appearance is likely to come home to you with honor and glory such as he and you may well be proud of.

20

Ulagalla, Mtesa's Capital, Uganda
E. Lon. 32 Deg. 49 Min. 45 Sec., N. Lat. 0 Deg. 32 Min.
April 12, 1875 [1]

I write this letter in a hurry, as it is the mere record of a work begun and not ended—I mean the exploration of the Victoria Niyanza. But brief as it necessarily must be, I am sure it will interest thousands of your readers, for it solves the great question, "Is the

1. *NYH*, Nov. 29, 1875.

Victoria Niyanza one lake, or does it consist of a group of lakes?" such as Livingstone reported it to be.[2] In answer to the query, I will begin by stating that I have explored, by means of the *Lady Alice,* the southern, eastern, and northeastern shores of the Victoria Niyanza, have penetrated into every bay, inlet and creek that indent its shores, and have taken thirty-seven observations, so that I feel competent to decide upon the question at issue, without bias or prejudice to any hypothesis. I have a mass of notes relating to the countries I visited, and ample means of making a proper chart at my camp at Usukuma, but I have neither paper, parallel rules nor any instrument whatever to lay down the positions I have taken, with me at present. I merely took an artificial horizon, sextant, chronometer, two aneroids, boiling point apparatus, sounding line, a few guns, ammunition and some provisions, as I wished to make the boat as light as possible, that she might work easily in the storms of the Niyanza. But when I reach camp I propose to draw a correct chart of the Niyanza and write such notes upon the several countries I have visited as will amply repay perusal and study.

I have already informed you that our camp at Kagehyi, in Usukuma, is situated in longitude 33 deg. 13 min. east and latitude 2 deg. 31 min. south. Before starting on the exploration of the lake I ascertained that Muanza was situated a few miles west, almost on the same parallel of latitude as Kagehyi. Now Muanza is the point whence Speke observed the Victoria Niyanza and where he drew his imaginary sketch of the lake from information given to him by the natives. If you will look at Speke's map you will find that it contains two islands—Ukerewe and Maziti. Looking at the same objects from Kagehyi, I would have concluded that they were islands myself; but a faithful exploration of the lake has proved that they are not islands, but a lengthy promontory of land extending from longitude 34 deg. 45¼ min. east, to longitude 32 deg. 40 min. 15 sec. east.[3] That part of the lake that Speke observed from Muanza

2. The postulation that Lake Victoria was in reality a group of lakes was advanced by Burton in a volume originally published in 1864. See Burton and Macqueen, *The Nile Basin and Captain Speke's Discovery of the Source of the Nile.*

3. The Majita peninsula. See Speke, *What Led to the Discovery,* 306, 310. Burton, "Lake Regions," 274, helps to explain the confusion by pointing out that the Arab word for both island and peninsula is the same. The inhabitants, the Jita, are classed as part of the Shashi group by Murdock, *Africa,* 348, while Gulliver, "Tribal Map of Tanganyika," 72, affirms they are closely related to the Kerewe. For the Jita region, "Einem Berichte des Lieutenants d. R. Meyer über seine Expedition nach Kavirondo," 517–18; Baumann, *Durch Masailand,* 51ff.; Spring, *Ostafrika,* 121–23. Stanley missed the bay to the south of the peninsula; Baumann visited it in 1892 and later in the year Spring named it Baumann Gulf.

is merely a huge gulf, about twenty-five miles wide by sixty-five miles long. To the noble Lake Niyanza Speke loyally added that of Victoria, as a tribute to his sovereign, which let no man take away; but in order to connect forever Speke's name to the lake which he discovered I have thought it but simple justice to the gallant explorer to call this immense gulf Speke Gulf. If you look again on Speke's map you will observe how boldly he has sketched the Niyanza stretching eastward and northeastward. Considering that he drew it from mere native report, which never yet was exact or clear, I must say that I do not think any other man could have arrived so near the truth. I must confess that I could not have done it myself, for I could make nothing of the vague and mythical reports of the natives of Kagehyi.

Proceeding eastward to the unknown and fabulous distance in the *Lady Alice*, with a picked crew of eleven men and a guide, I coasted along the southern coast of the lake, round many a noble bay, until we came to the mouth of the Shimeeyu, in longitude 33 deg. 33 min. east, latitude 2 deg. 35 min. south—by far the noblest river that empties into the lake that we have yet seen. The Shimeeyu has a length of 370 miles, and is the extreme southern source of the Nile. Before emptying into the lake it unites with the Luamberri River, whence it issues in a majestic flood to Lake Victoria Niyanza. At the mouth it is a mile wide, but contracts as we proceed up the river to 400 yards. Even by itself it would make no insignificant White Nile. By accident our route through Ituru took us from its birthplace, a month's march from the lake, and along many a mile of its crooked course, until by means of the *Lady Alice* we were enabled to see it enter the Niyanza, a river of considerable magnitude.

Between the mouth of the Shimeeyu and Kagehyi were two countries—Sima and Magu—of the same nature as Usukuma, and inhabited by peoples speaking the same dialect. On the eastern side of the river is Mazanza, and beyond Manasa. Coasting still along the southern shore of the lake, beyond Manasa, we come to Ututwa, inhabited by a people speaking a different language, namely that of the Wajika, as the Wamasai are called here, a people slender and tall, carrying formidably long knives and terrible and portentous spears.[4]

In longitude 33 deg. 45 min. 45 sec. east we came to the extreme

4. Sima, Magu, Nasa, and Masanza are Sukuma chiefdoms. Cora, *Sukuma Law and Custom,* 170–71. Ututwa was a Sukuma district, but it had a mixed population, including Sukuma and Shashi. Peters, *Das Deutsch-Ostafrikanische Schutzgebiet,* 179–81. Stanley also called the Wajika the Wirigedi. *TDC,* I, 159.

end of Speke Gulf, and then turned northward as far as latitude 2 deg. 5 min. south, whence we proceeded westward almost in a straight line along Shashi and Iramba,[5] in Ukerewe. In longitude 33 deg. 26 min. east, we came to a strait—the Rugeji strait—which separates one-half of Ukerewe from the other half, and by which there is a direct means of communication from Speke Gulf with the countries lying north of Ukerewe. We did not pass through, but proceeded still westward, hugging the bold shores of that part of Ukerewe which is an island, as far as longitude 32 deg. 40 min. 15 sec. east, whence, following the land, we turned northwest, thence north, until in latitude 1 deg. 53 min. south we turned east again, coasting along the northern shores of Ukerewe Island until we came to the tabular-topped bluff of Majita (Speke miscalled this Mazita, or Maziti, and termed it an island),[6] in longitude 33 deg. 9 min. 45 sec. east, and latitude 1 deg. 50 min. south, whence the land begins to trend northward of east. North of Kashizu in Ukerewe lies the large island of Ukara, which gives its name with some natives to that part of the lake lying between it and Ukerewe.[7] It is about eighteen miles long by twelve wide, and is inhabited by a people strong in charms and magic medicine. From Majita we pass on again to the north shore of Shashi, whose south coast is bounded by Speke Gulf, and beyond Shashi we come to the first district in Ururi.

Ururi[8] extends from Shashi in latitude 1 deg. 50 min. south, to latitude 0 deg. 40 min. 0 sec. south, and embraces the districts of

5. The Shashi, a mixed group of Sukuma origin. For visits to their territory, Baumann, *Durch Masailand*, 196–203; Kollmann, *Auf deutschen Boden in Afrika*, 279–90; Kollmann, *The Victoria Nyanza*, chap. 8; Moffet, *Handbook of Tanganyika*, 189. Iramba is a part of the Bukerewe chiefdom on the mainland. Cory and Masalu, "Place Names in the Lake Province," 71.

6. See document 20, note 2.

7. Ukara Island; its inhabitants call themselves Baregi and their island Buregi, but they are generally known as the Kara. Swahili traders had brought news of the island to the coast and referred to this area of Lake Victoria as the Ukara Lake. The Kara were consistently hostile to outsiders and drove a series of visitors from their shores—one observer not inappropriately called the island "the Malta of the Nyanza." Paterson, "Ukara Island"; Wakefield, "Routes of Native Caravans," 309; Wilson and Felkin, *Uganda and the Egyptian Sudan,* I, 189; Baumann, *Durch Masailand,* 47–50; Schweinitz, *Deutsch-Ost-Afrika,* 168–71; Spring, *Ostafrika,* 118–20; Brard, "Der Victoria-Nyansa," 79. One disgruntled German official could only say of them: "No other people in East Africa is capable of such perfidy." From a speech of Schweinitz, in *DKZ* 6 (1893), 86.

8. The Ruri are part of the Shashi group. The area Stanley describes contained also, in the north, Gusii, Suba, and Luo. See the maps in Murdock, *Africa,* and Gulliver, "Tribal Map of Tanganyika." See also Scholbach, "Die Volksstämme der deutschen Ostküste des Victoria-Nyansa," 184–89; Neumann, "Bericht über seine Reisen in Ost-und Central-Afrika," 284–86. Neuman in 1893 reported that the Ruri had been overrun by the Luo.

Wye, Iriene, Urieri, Igengi, Kutiri, Shirati and Mohuru. Its coast is indented most remarkably with bays and creeks, which extend far inland. East of the immediate coast line the country is a level plain, which is drained by an important river called Shirati. All other streams which issue into the lake along the coast of Ururi are insignificant.

North of Shirati, the most northern district of Ururi, begins the country of Ugeyeya,[9] whose bold and mountainous shores form a strong contrast to the flats of Shirati and Mohuru. Here are mountains rising abruptly from the lake to a height of 3,000 feet and more. This coast is also very crooked and irregular, requiring patient and laborious rowing to investigate its many bends and curves. The people are a timid and suspicious race, much vexed by their neighbors, the Waruri, south, and Wamasai, east and are loath to talk to strangers, as the Arab slave dealers of Pangani have not taught them to love people carrying guns.[10]

The Wageyeya, having been troubled by the Waruri, have left many miles of wilderness between their country and that of their fierce neighbors uninhabited. But Sungoro, the agent of Mse Saba,[11] who prompted the Waruri to many a devilish act, and has purchased the human spoils, is constructing in Ukerewe a dhow of twenty or thirty tons burden, with which he intends to prosecute more actively his nefarious trade. Nothing would have pleased me better than to have been commissioned by some government to hang all such wretches wherever found; and, if ever a pirate deserved death for inhuman crimes, Sungoro, the slave trader, deserves death. Kagehyi, in Usukuma, has become the seat of the inhuman slave trade. To this part they are collected from Sima, Magu, Ukerewe, Ururi and Ugeyeya; and when Sungoro has floated his dhow and hoisted his blood-stained ensign the great sin will increase tenfold, and the caravan road to Unyanyembe will become hell's highway.

On the coast of Ugeyeya I expected to discover a channel to another lake, as there might be a grain of truth in what the Wanguana reported to Livingstone; but I found nothing of the sort, except

9. The country of the Luo and Gaya. See Evans-Pritchard, *The Position of Women in Primitive Societies and Other Essays in Social Anthropology*, 205–27; Southall, *Lineage Formation among the Luo*; Fischer, "Vorläufiger Bericht über die Expedition zur Auffindung Dr. Junkers," 367; Ogot, *History of the Southern Luo*, 127ff.

10. For the Pangani traders to Lake Victoria, Fischer, "Bericht über die im Auftrage der Geographischen Gesellschaft in Hamburg unternommene Reise in das Masai-Land," 38ff.

11. In *Diary*, 63, Stanley says "Sungoro, or Mse Saba."

unusually deep bends in the shore, which led nowhere. The streams were insignificant and undeserving the name of rivers.

A few miles from the Equator I discovered two islands formed of basaltic rock and overgrown with a dense growth of tropical vegetation. One had a natural bridge of rock thirty feet long and fifteen feet wide; the other had a small cave. In longitude 34 deg. 49 min. east, at Nakidimo, Ugeyeya, we came to the furthest point east of the Victoria Niyanza.[12]

North of Ugeyeya begins Baringo,[13] a small country, extending over about fifteen miles of latitude. Its coast is also remarkable for deep indentations and noble bays, some of which are almost entirely closed by land and might well be called lakes by uncultivated Wanguana. Large islands are also numerous, some of which lie so close to the mainland that if we had not hugged its shore closely we should have mistaken them for portions of the mainland. North of Baringo the land is again distinguished by lofty hills, cones and plateaus which sink eastward into plains, and here a new country commences—Unyara,[14] the language of whose people is totally distinct from that of Usukuma, and approaches to that of Uganda and Usoga.[15]

Unyara occupies the northeastern coast of the Victoria Niyanza, and by observation the extreme northeastern point of the Niyanza ends in longitude 34 deg. 35 min. east and latitude 33 min. 43 sec. north. As I intend to send you a chart of the Niyanza, it is needless here to enter into minor details, but I may as well mention here that a large portion of the northeastern end of the lake is almost

12. Stanley had missed finding the Kavirondo Gulf which is shielded from Lake Victoria by an island. Thomson in 1883 reached its eastern shores, but the exact configuration of the gulf was not ascertained until a detailed survey was made of the lake in 1898–1899. Thomson, *Masailand*, 484; Whitehouse, "To the Victoria Nyanza by the Uganda Railway," 229–41. See document 23, note 14.

13. Stanley refers to Nduru, or Baringo, a part of Gaya territory. Reports referring to the Lake Baringo had been current since at least the 1840's— through Krapf, Rebmann, Speke, Wakefield—but it was not proved a separate lake until visited by Thomson in 1884. Thomson, *Masailand*, 529–36; Gregory, "Contributions to the Physical Geography of British East Africa," 311; Johnston, *Nile Quest*, 113, 162.

14. The Luhya, or Bantu Kavirondo, occupy this region. Stanley, perhaps, had heard the name of one of their divisions, Nyala. See Wagner, *The Bantu of North Kavirondo;* see also Osogo, *Life in Kenya in the Olden Days: The Baluyia*, 32.

15. The Soga inhabited a number of small independent states in an area bordered by Lake Kyoga, the Victoria Nile, Lake Victoria, and the Mpologoma River. See Fallers, *Eastern Lacustrine Bantu;* Fallers, *Bantu Bureaucracy;* Luboga, *A History of Busoga.*

entirely closed in by the shores of Ugana and of two islands, Chaga and Usuguru, the latter of which is one of the largest in the Niyanza.

While Unyara occupies the northeastern coast of Niyanza, Ugana commences the northern coast of the lake from the east, and, running southwest a few miles, forms here a large bay. It then trends westward, and the island of Chaga runs directly north and south for eight miles at a distance of twelve miles from the opposite coast of Unyara. With but a narrow channel between, Usuguru island runs from the southern extremity of Chaga, in a south-southeasterly direction, to within six miles from the eastern shore of the mainland. Thus almost a lake is formed separate from the Niyanza.[16]

North of Chaga Island Usoga begins with the large district of Usowa, where we met with the first hostile intention—though not act, as the act was checked by show of superior weapons—on the part of the natives. Thence, as we proceed westward, the districts of Ugamba, Uvira, Usamu and Utamba line the coast of Usoga.

Where Utama begins, large islands again become frequent, the principal of which is Uvuma,[17] an independent country and the largest in the Victoria Niyanza. At Uvuma we experienced treachery and hostility on the part of the natives. By show of friendship on their part we were induced to sail within a few yards of the shore, while a mass of natives were hid in ambush behind the trees. While sailing quietly by, exchanging friendly greetings with them, we were suddenly attacked with a shower of large rocks, several of which struck the boat; but the helm being quickly put "hard up," we sheered from shore to a safer distance, but not before one of the rascals was laid dead by a shot from one of my revolvers.

After proceeding some miles we entered a channel between the islands of Uvuma and Bugeyeya, but close to the shore of Uvuma. Here we discovered a fleet of large canoes—thirteen in number—carrying over a hundred warriors, armed with shields and spears and slings. The foremost canoe contained baskets of sweet potatoes, which the people held up as if they were desirous to trade. I ordered

16. Shagga (Chaga) is a promontory on Bugana Island. Usuguru is Sigula Island. See the notes by Thomas, "Captain Eric Smith's Expedition to Lake Victoria in 1891," 151.

17. The Buvuma Islands around the entrance of Napoleon Gulf. See J. F. Cunningham, *Uganda and Its Peoples*, 129–41. For a brief historical account, Ashe, *Chronicles of Uganda*, 386–90. Buvuma later lost many of its inhabitants through the ravages of sleeping sickness. Fishbourne, "Lake Kioga (Ibrahim) Exploratory Survey, 1907–1908," 194.

my people to cease rowing, and as there was but a slight breeze we still held on with the sail and permitted the canoe to approach.

While we were bargaining for potatoes with this canoe the other canoes came up and blocked the boat, while the people began to lay hands on everything; but we found their purpose out, and I warned the canoes away with my gun. They jeered at this and immediately seized their spears and shields, while one canoe hastened away with some beads they had stolen, and which a man insolently held up to my view, and invited us to catch him. At sight of this I fired, and the man fell dead in his canoe. The others prepared to launch their spears, but the repeating rifle was too much for the crowd of warriors who had hastened like pirates to rob us. Three were shot dead, and as they retreated my elephant rifle smashed their canoes, the result of which we saw in the confusion attending each shot. After a few shots from the big gun we continued on our way, still hugging the shore of Uvuma, for it was unnecessary to fly after such an exhibition of inglorious conduct on the part of thirteen canoes, containing in the aggregate over one hundred men.[18]

In the evening we anchored in the channel between Uvuma and Usoga, in east long. 33 deg. 40 min. 15 sec., and north lat. 0 deg. 30 min. 9 sec. Next morning the current perceptibly growing stronger as we advanced north, we entered the Napoleon Channel [19] that separates Usoga from Uganda, and then sailed across to the Uganda shore. Having arrived close to the land, we pulled down sail and rowed towards the Ripon Falls, the noise of whose rushing waters sounded loud and clear in our ears. The lake shoaled rapidly, and we halted to survey the scene at a spot half a mile from the first mass of foam caused by the escaping waters. Speke has been most accurate in his description of the outflowing river, and his pencil has done fair justice to it. The scenery around, on the Usoga and Uganda side, had nothing of the sublime about it, but it is picturesque and well worth a visit. A few small islands dot the channel and lie close ashore; while at the entrance of the main channel,

18. This account of the fight essentially agrees with *Diary*, 69, but in *TDC*, I, 179–81, Stanley, perhaps influenced by criticisms on his return to Europe, asserts he first fired over the heads of the Africans before firing at them in earnest.

19. Named by Speke after Napoleon III (1808–1873) "in token of respect" for the award of a medal by the Société de Géographie for Speke's discovery of Lake Victoria. Speke, *Journal of the Discovery*, 469. It became known as Napoleon Gulf from the 1890's. Thomas and Dale, "Uganda Place Names: Some European Eponyms," 117.

looking south, the large islands of Uziri and Wanzi stretch obliquely, or southwest, toward Uvuma. But the eye of the observer is more fascinated by the ranks of swelling foam and leaping waters than by the uneven contour of the land; and the ear is attracted by the rough music of their play, despite the terrors which the imagination paints to us, and it absorbs all our attention to watch the smooth, flowing surface of the lake, suddenly broken by the rocks of gneiss and hematite which protrude, white and ruddy, above the water, and which threaten instant doom to the unlucky navigator who would be drifted among them. There is a charm in the scene that belongs to few such, for this outflowing river, which the Great Victoria Niyanza discharges from its bosom, becomes known to the world as the White Nile. Though born amid the mountains of Ituru, Kargue and Ugeyeya it emerges from the womb of the Niyanza the perfect Nile which annually resuscitates parched Egypt.[20]

From the Ripon Falls we proceeded along the coast of Ikira southwest until, gaining the shore opposite Uziri, we coasted westerly along the irregular shore of Uganda. Arriving at the isle of Kriva we secured guides, who voluntarily offered to conduct us as far as Mtesa's capital. Halting a short time at the island of Kibibi, we proceeded to Ukafu, where a snug horseshoe-shaped bay was discovered. From Ukafu we dispatched messengers to Mtesa to announce the arrival of a white visitor in Uganda, after being most hospitably received with fair words but with empty hands along the coast of Uganda.[21]

I was anxious to discover the entrance of the Luajerri, and questioned the natives long and frequently about it, until, securing an interpreter who understood the Kiswahili, we ascertained that there was no such river as the Luajerri, that Luaserri meant still water, applicable to any of the many lengthy creeks or narrow inlets which indent the coasts of Uganda and Usoga, from which I conclude that Speke was misinformed, and that his "Luajerri" is Luaserri, or still water.[22] At least, we discovered no such river, either sluggish or quick, flowing northwards; while in the neighborhood of

20. Stanley probably means Karagwe instead of Kargue.
21. A clear sketch of Bugaia and the other islands is given in Carpenter, *A Naturalist on Lake Victoria*, map opposite p. 322.
22. Speke described it as "a huge rush-drain three miles broad," but he said it "scarcely deserves the name of a river." From African information it was said to be a river rising in Lake Victoria and flowing into the Nile. Stanley named it Grant Bay after Speke's companion, but the name did not stick. Speke, *Journal of the Discovery*, 459, 472; Speke, "Upper Basin of the Nile," 330; *TDC*, I, 299; Thomas and Dale, "Uganda Place Names," 112.

"Murchison Creek" I did discover a long and crooked inlet called Mwrau—a Luaserri, or still water—which penetrated several miles inland, the termination of which we saw. I noticed a positive tide here during the morning. For two hours the water of this creek flowed north, subsequently for two hours it flowed south, and on asking the people if it were a usual sight they said it was, and was visible in all of the inlets on the coast of Uganda.

Arriving at Beya, we were welcomed by a fleet of canoes sent by Mtesa to conduct us to Murchison Creek. On the 4th of April I landed amid a concourse of 2,000 people, who saluted me with a deafening volley of musketry and waving of flags. Katakiro,[23] the chief Mukungu, or officer in Uganda, then conducted me to comfortable quarters, to which shortly afterward were brought sixteen goats, ten oxen, an immense quantity of bananas, plantains, sweet potatoes, besides eggs, chickens, milk, rice, ghee and butter. After such a royal and bountiful gift I felt more curiosity than ever to see the generous monarch.

In the afternoon, Mtesa, having prepared beforehand for my reception, sent to say that he was ready to receive me. Issuing out of my quarters I found myself in a broad street eighty feet wide and half a mile long, which was lined by his personal guards and attendants, his captains and their respective retinues, to the number of about 3,000. At the extreme end of this street and fronting it was the King's audience house, in whose shadow I saw dimly the figure of the King sitting in a chair.

As I advanced toward him the soldiers continued to fire their guns. The drums, sixteen in number, beat a fearful tempest of sound, and the flags[24] waved, until I became conscious that all this display was far beyond my merits, and consequently felt greatly embarrassed by so flattering a reception. Arrived before the audience house the King rose—a tall and slender figure, dressed in Arab costume —approached me a few paces, held out his hand mutely, while the drums continued their terrible noise, and we stood silently gazing

23. Mukasa, the *Katikkiro,* held that office from about 1872; he continued in power under Mutesa's successor, Mwanga, until 1888, when Mwanga was deposed. Mukasa was killed during the disorders of 1889. The missionary Ashe described him as "one of the most remarkable Africans I have met." Faupel, *African Holocaust,* 5–6, 69ff.; Rowe, "The Purge of Christians at Mwanga's Court," 65–70; Ashe, *Chronicles of Uganda,* 133–34. For the functions of the *Katikkiro,* Roscoe, *The Baganda,* 234ff.

24. The Baganda flag was then described as having "a white ground of 12 inches wide from the staff, 36 inches red, bordered with three pendant strips of monkey skin, of long hair." Alpers, "Charles Chaille-Long's Mission to Mutesa of Buganda," 7.

at each other a few minutes, I, indeed, more embarrassed than ever. But soon, relieved from the oppressive noise of the huge drums and violence of the many screaming, discordant fifes, I was invited to sit, Mtesa first showing the example, followed by his great captains, about one hundred in number.

More at ease, I surveyed the figure and features of this powerful monarch. Mtesa is about thirty-four years old, and tall and slender in build, as I have already stated, but with broad shoulders. His face is very agreeable and pleasant, and indicates intelligence and mildness. His eyes are large, his nose and mouth are a great improvement upon those of the common type of negro, and approach to that of the Muscat Arab slightly tainted with negro blood. His teeth are splendid, and gleaming white.

As soon as Mtesa began to speak I became captivated by his manner, for there was much of the polish of a true gentleman about it —it was at once amiable, graceful and friendly. It assured me that in Mtesa I had found a friend, a generous King, and an intelligent ruler. He is infinitely superior to Seyd Burghash, the Arab Sultan of Zanzibar, and he appears to me like a colored gentleman who has visited European courts, whence he has caught a certain polish and ease of manner and a vast amount of information which he has collected for the improvement of his race. If you will recollect that Mtesa is a native of Central Africa, and that he had seen but three white men until I came,[25] you will, perhaps, be as much astonished at this as I was. And if you will but think of the enormous extent of country he rules, extending from east longitude 34 to east longitude 31, and from north latitude 1 to south latitude 3.30, you will perceive the immense influence he could wield toward the civilization of Africa.[26] Indeed, I could not regard this King or look at him in any other light than the Augustus by whose means the light of the Gospel will be brought to benighted Middle Africa.

Undoubtedly the Mtesa of to-day is vastly superior to the vain youth whom Speke and Grant saw. There is no butchery of men or women; seldom one suffers the extreme punishment. Speke and Grant left him a raw, vain youth, and a heathen. He is now a gentleman, and, professing Islamism,[27] submits to other laws than his own erratic will, which, we are told, led to severe and fatal consequences. All his captains and chief officers profess the same

25. Speke, Grant, and the American , Chaillé-Long.
26. See below, note 32.
27. Mutesa, although sympathetic to Islam at this time, was not, of course, a convert. See Katumba and Welbourn, "Muslim Martyrs of Buganda," 151–58.

creed, dress in Arab costume and in other ways affect Arab custom. He has a guard of 200 men—renegades from Baker's expedition, Zanzibar defalcators, a few Omani and the elect of Uganda.[28]

Behind his throne, an armchair of native manufacture, the royal shieldbearers, lancebearers and gunbearers stand erect and staid. On either side of him are his grand chiefs and courtiers, sons of governors of his provinces, chiefs of districts, &c. Outside the audience house the lengthy lines of warriors begin with the chief drummer and noisy goma beaters.[29] Next come the screaming fifers, the flag and banner bearers, the fusilliers, and so on seemingly *ad infinitum* with spearmen.

Mtesa asked a number of questions about various things, thereby showing a vast amount of curiosity and great intelligence.

The King had arrived at this camp—Usavara—fourteen days before my arrival, with this immense army of followers, for the purpose of shooting birds. He now proposed to return, after two or three days' rest, to his capital at Ulagalla, or Uragara.[30] Each day of my stay at Usavara was a scene of gayety and rejoicing. On the first after my arrival we beheld a grand naval review—eighty-four canoes, each manned by from thirty to forty men, containing in the aggregate a force of about 2,500 men. We had excellent races and witnessed various manoeuvres by water. Each admiral vied with the other in extolling aloud the glory of their monarch, or in exciting admiration from the hundreds of spectators on shore. The King's three hundred wives were present *en grande tenue,* and were not the least important of those on shore.

The second day the King led his fleet in person to show me his prowess in shooting birds. We rowed, or were rather paddled, up "Murchison Creek," visiting *en route* a dhow he is building for the navigation of the lake, his place of residence, and his former capital, Banda, where Speke and Grant found him.

En passant, I may remark that Speke could not possibly have

28. The egotistical Baker objected to this remark. He affirmed that he had never lost any men by desertion and that the "renegades" were probably slave-dealers who had suffered from his activities. Baker, who greatly overestimated his work against the slave trade in the Sudan, went on to say that Stanley had been received in such a friendly manner because of "orders" he sent to Mutesa regarding any Europeans who might arrive at his court. Baker's remarks in a discussion of Nov. 29, 1875, *PRGS* 20 (1875–1876), 48–49. See below, note 36.

29. Drum—*ngoma.* For the role of drums in Buganda, Roscoe, *Baganda,* 25ff.

30. For the Ganda ruler's capital, or *Kibuga,* which Stanley found at Rubaga, Gutkind, *The Royal Capital of Buganda.*

seen the whole of the immense bay he has denominated creek. It is true that from a short distance west of Dwaga, his Ramazan palace, up to Mngono, the extremity of the bay, a distance of about eight miles, it might be termed a creek, but this distance does not approach to one-half of the bay. I respectfully request geographers, Messrs. Keith Johnston and Stanford [31] especially, to change the name of Murchison Creek to Murchison Bay, as more worthy of the large area of water now known by the former inappreciative title. Murchison Bay extends from north latitude 15 deg. to north latitude 27 deg., and from east longitude 32 deg. 53 min. to 32 deg. 38 min. in extreme length. At the mouth the bay contracts to a width of four miles, but within its greatest breadth is twelve miles. Surely such a body of water—as terms go—deserves the more appropriate name of bay, but I leave it to fair judging geographers to decide. [32] For the position of Mtesa's capital I have taken three observations, three different days. My longitude agrees pretty closely with that of Speke's, while there is but four miles difference of latitude.

The third day the troops of Mtesa were exercised at target practice, and on the fourth day we all marched for the Grand Capital, the Kibuga of Uganda, Ulagalla or Uragara. Mutesa is a great King. He is a monarch who would delight the soul of any intelligent European, as he would see in Mtesa the hope of Central Africa. He is King of Karagwe, Uganda, Unyoro, Usoga and Usui. [33] Each day I saw something which increased my esteem and respect for him. He is fond of imitating Europeans and great kings, which trait, with a little tuition, would be of immense benefit to his country. He has prepared broad highways in the neighborhood of his capital for the good time that is coming when some charitable European will send him any kind of a wheeled vehicle. As we approached the capital the highway from Usavara increased in width from 20 feet to 150 feet. When we arrived at this magnificent breadth we viewed the capital crowning an eminence commanding a most extensive view of a picturesque and rich country teeming with gardens of plantains and bananas, and beautiful pasture land. Of course huts,

31. Edward Stanford (c. 1827–1904), head of a prominent cartographic firm and publisher of the journals of the Royal Geographical Society. *GJ* 24 (1904), 686–87; Marston, "Edward Stanford. A Personal Reminiscence."

32. Stanley's suggestion was accepted. Thomas and Dale, "Uganda Place Names," 116.

33. Mutesa ruled only his own state; he had influence of varying strengths in other neighboring states. Low, "Northern Interior," 336–37. For Usui, a Zinza chiefdom, see document 23, note 7.

however large, lend but little attraction to a scene, but a tall flag-staff and an immense flag proved a feature in the landscape.

Arrived at the capital I found that the vast collection of huts crowning the eminence were the Royal Quarters, around which ran five several palisades and circular courts, between which and the city was a circular road, ranging from 100 to 200 feet in width, from which radiated six or seven magnificent avenues, lined with gardens and huts.

The next day after arrival I was introduced to the Royal Palace in great state. None of the primitive scenes visible in Speke's book were visible here. The guards, clothed in white cotton dresses, were by no means comical. The chiefs were very respectable looking people, dressed richly in the Arab costume. The palace was a huge and lofty structure, well built of grass and cane, while tall trunks of trees upheld the roof, which was covered with cloth sheeting inside.

On the fourth day after my arrival news came that another white man was approaching the capital from the direction of Unyoro, and on the fifth day I had the extreme pleasure of greeting Colonel Linant de Bellefonds, of the Egyptian service, who had been des-patched by Colonel Gordon to Mtesa, to make a treaty of commerce between him and the Egyptian government.[34] The meeting, though not so exciting as my former meeting with the venerable David Livingstone, at Ujiji, in November, 1871, still may be said to be singular and fortunate for all concerned. In Colonel Bellefonds I met a gentleman extremely well informed, energetic and a great traveller. His knowledge of the countries between Uganda and Khartoum was most minute and accurate, from which I conclude that but little of the geography of Central Africa between the cataracts of the Nile and Uganda is unknown. To which store of valuable geographical acquisitions must now be added my exploration of the Nile sources, which pour into the Niyanza and the new countries I have visited between the Niyanza and the Unyanyembe road. In Colonel Belle-fonds I also perceived great good fortune, for I now had the means to despatch my reports of geographical discoveries and my long delayed letters.

34. Ernest Linant de Bellefonds; he was killed fighting the Bari in 1875 after his return to Gordon's headquarters. Thomas, "Ernest Linant de Bellefonds and Stanley's Letter to the 'Daily Telegraph' "; Gray, "Ernest Linant de Belle-fonds." Bellefonds' own account of the visit is given in his "Itinéraire et Notes. Voyage de Service fait entre le poste militaire de Fatiko et la Capitale de M'tesa, roi d'Uganda. Février-Juin 1875."

The day after to-morrow I intend to return to Usukuma, prosecuting my geographical researches along the western shores of the Victoria Niyanza. After which I propose to march the expedition to the Katonga Valley,[35] and thence, after another visit to Mtesa, march directly west for Lake Albert Niyanza, where I hope to meet with some more of the gallant subordinates of Colonel Gordon, by whom I shall be able, through their courtesy, to send several more letters descriptive of discoveries and adventures.

I might protract this letter indefinitely by dwelling upon the value of the service rendered to science and the world by Ismael Pacha,[36] but time will not allow me, nor, indeed, is it necessary, as I dare say by this time you have had ample proofs of what has been done by Gordon. Baker, unfortunately, appears to be in bad odor with all I meet. His severity and other acts receive universal condemnation; but far be it from me to add to the ill report, and so I leave what I have heard untold.[37]

Then, briefly, thus much remains to be said. Livingstone, in his report of the Niyanza consisting of five lakes, was wrong. Speke, in his statement that the Niyanza was but one lake, was quite correct. But I believe that east of the Niyanza, or rather northeast of the Niyanza, there are other lakes, though they have no connection whatever with the Niyanza; nor do I suppose they are of any great magnitude or extend south of the Equator. If you ask me why, I can only answer that in my opinion the rivers entering the Niyanza on the northeastern shore do not sufficiently drain the vast area of country lying between the Niyanza and the western versant of the Eastern African mountain range. From the volume of the Niyanza feeders on the northeastern side I cannot think that they extend further than longitude 36 deg. east, which leaves a large tract of country east to be drained by other means than the Niyanza. But this means may very probably be the Jub, which empties its waters into the Indian Ocean. The Sobat cannot possibly approach near the Equator. This, however, will be decided definitively by Gordon's officers. Colonel Bellefonds informs me that the Assua, or Asha, is a mere torrent.[38]

When you see my chart, which will trace the course of the Luam-

35. See Hurst, *Nile,* 155, 219.

36. Isma'il Pasha (1830–1895), Khedive of Egypt from 1863 to 1879. His ventures in Central Africa entrusted to Baker and Gordon added to the debt burden of Egypt which led to his deposition in 1879. Hill, *Biographical Dictionary,* 182–83.

37. Baker countered by asserting that the bad reputation was due to his actions against the slave trade. *PRGS* 20 (1875–1876), 48–49. Hill, *Egypt in the Sudan 1820–1881,* 135–36, puts this issue in perspective.

38. The Aswa. See Hurst, *Nile,* 120.

berri and the Shimeeyu, the rivers which drain the whole of the south and southeast countries of the Niyanza, you will be better able to judge of their importance and magnitude as sources of the Nile. I expect to discover a considerable river southwest; but all of this will be best told in my next letter.[39]

P.S. I had almost forgotten to state that the greatest depth of the Niyanza as yet ascertained by me is 275 feet. I have not yet sounded the center of the lake; this I intend to do on my return to Usukuma South.

21

Mtesa's Capital, Uganda
April 14, 1875 [1]

I had almost neglected to inform you and your readers of one very interesting subject connected with Mtesa which will gratify many a philanthropic European and American.

I have already told you that Mtesa and the whole of his Court profess Islamism. A long time ago, some four or five years, Khamis Bin Abdullah (the only Arab who remained with me three years ago, as a rearguard, when the Arabs disgracefully fled from Mirambo) came to Uganda. He was wealthy, of noble descent, had a fine, magnificent personal appearance, and brought with him many a rich present, such as few Arabs could afford, for Mtesa. The King became immediately fascinated with him, and really few white men could be long with the son of Abdullah without being charmed by his presence, his handsome, proud features, his rich olive complexion and his liberality. I confess I never saw an Arab or Mussulman who attracted me so much as Khamis Bin Abdullah, and it is no wonder that Mtesa, meeting a kindred spirit in the noble Arab of Muscat, amazed at the magnificent figure, the splendor of his apparel, the display of his wealth and the number of his slaves fell in love with him. Khamis stayed with Mtesa a full year, during which time the King became a convert to the creed of Khamis—namely, Mohammedanism. The Arab clothed Mtesa in the best that his wardrobe offered. He gave him gold embroidered jackets, fine white

39. See also Stanley's letter to Arnold, Appendix L.
1. *NYH*, Nov. 29, 1875.

shirts, crimson slippers, swords, silk sashes, daggers and a revolving rifle, so that Speke's and Grant's presents seemed quite insignificant.[2]

Until I arrived at Mtesa's Court the King delighted in the idea that he was a follower of Islam; but by one conversation I flatter myself that I have tumbled the newly raised religious fabric to the ground, and, if it were only followed by the arrival of a Christian mission here, the conversion of Mtesa and his Court to Christianity would be complete. I have undermined Islamism so much here that Mtesa has determined henceforth, until he is better informed, to observe the Christian Sabbath as well as the Moslem Sabbath, and the great captains have unanimously consented to it. He has caused the ten commandments of Moses to be written on a board for his daily perusal, as Mtesa can read Arabic, as well as the Lord's Prayer and the golden commandment of our Saviour, "Thou shalt love thy neighbor as thyself." This is great progress for the few days that I have remained with him, and, though I am no missionary, I shall begin to think that I shall become one if such success is so feasible.

But, O that some pious, practical missionary would come here! What a field and a harvest ripe for the sickle of the Gospel! Mtesa would give him anything he desired—houses, lands, cattle, ivory, &c. He might call a province his own in one day. It is not the mere preacher that is wanted here. The bishops of all Great Britain collected, with all the classic youth of Oxford and Cambridge, would effect nothing here with the intelligent people of Uganda. It is the practical Christian tutor, who can teach people how to become Christians, cure their diseases, construct dwellings, understands agriculture and can turn his hand to anything, like a sailor—this is the man that is wanted here. Such a man, if he can be found, would become the saviour of Africa. He must be tied to no Church or sect, but profess God and His Son, and live a blameless Christian, be inspired by liberal principles, charity to all men and devout faith in God. He must belong to no nation in particular, but the entire white race. Such a man or men Mtesa, King of Uganda, Usoga, Unyoro and Karagwe—a Kingdom 360 geographical miles in length by fifty in breadth—invites to come to him. He has begged me to tell the white men that if they will only come to him he will give them all they want.[3]

2. There is a reference to Khamis bin Abdullah at the court in Welbourn, "Speke and Stanley at the Court of Mutesa," 223. Stanley does not mention Khamis' role in *TDC*. See document 3, note 50.

3. As Gray observed, Stanley had been "splendidly duped" by Mutesa, who

Now where is there in all the pagan world a more promising field for a mission than Uganda? Colonel Linant de Bellefonds is my witness that I speak the truth, and I know he will corroborate all I say. The Colonel, though a Frenchman, is a Calvinist, and has become as ardent a well-wisher for the Waganda as I am.

Then why further spend needlessly vast sums upon black pagans of Africa who have no example of their own people becoming Christians before them? I speak to the Universities Mission at Zanzibar and to the Free Methodists at Mombasa,[4] to the leading philanthropists and the pious people of England. Here, gentlemen, is your opportunity—embrace it! The people on the shores of the Niyanza call upon you. Obey your own generous instincts, and listen to them, and I assure you that in one year you will have more converts to Christianity than all other missionaries united can number. The population of Mtesa's kingdom is most dense. I estimate the number of his subjects at 2,000,000.[5] You need not fear to spend money upon such a mission, as Mtesa is sole ruler, and will repay its cost tenfold with ivory, coffee, otter skins[6] of a very fine quality, or in cattle, for the wealth of this country in all these products is immense. The road here is by the Nile, or via Zanzibar, Ugogo and Unyanyembe. The former route, so long as Colonel Gordon governs the countries of the Upper Nile, is the most feasible.

With permission I would suggest that the mission should bring to Mtesa as present three or four suits of military clothes, decorated freely with gold embroidery, with half a dozen French *képis,* a sabre, a brace of pistols and suitable ammunition; a good fowling piece and rifle of good quality, as the King is not a barbarian; a cheap dinner service of Britannia ware, an iron bedstead and counterpanes, a few pieces of cotton print, boots, &c. For trade it should

---

was seeking outside support because of pressure in the north from Egypt. Chaillé-Long agreed in a contemporary judgment that Stanley had been the "dupe of the artful savage." Stanley reacted against such criticism when his book appeared by stating "I cannot hide from myself the fact that the conversion is only nominal," but naturally without admitting he had been "Mtesa's dupe." Gray, "Mutesa of Buganda"; Chaillé Long, *Central Africa,* 310; *TDC,* I, 195, 405.

4. See New, *Life, Wanderings, and Labours,* and Wakefield, *Thomas Wakefield,* for this mission.

5. *TDC,* I, 401, gives a figure of 2,750,000. The figure is for the whole area Stanley asserted to be under Mutesa's rule. He gave 750,000 for Buganda alone. See document 36, note 3.

6. There are several varieties of the otter in the region. See Thomas and Scott, *Uganda,* 184; Moffett, *Handbook of Tanganyika,* 417, 487.

bring the blue, black and gray woolen cloths, a quantity of military buttons, gold braid and cord, silk cord of different colors, as well as binding, linen and sheeting for shirts, fine red blankets and a quantity of red cloth, a few chairs and tables. The profit arising from the sale of these things would be enormous.

For the mission's use it should bring with it a supply of hammers, saws, augers, chisels, axes, hatchets, adzes, carpenters' and black-smiths' tools, as the Waganda are apt pupils; iron drills and powder for blasting purposes, trowels, a couple of good sized anvils, a forge and bellows, an assortment of nails and tacks, a plough, spades, shovels, pickaxes and a couple of light buggies as specimens, and such other small things as their own common sense would suggest. Most desirable would be an assortment of garden seed and grain; also white lead, linseed oil, brushes, a few volumes of illustrated journals, gaudy prints, a magic lantern, rockets and a photograph apparatus. The total cost of the whole need not exceed £5,000.[7]

22

Village of Kagehyi, District of Uchambi, Usukuma, Central Africa
May 15, 1875 [1]

Mrs. Charlotte Barker: Dear Mrs. Barker—I grieve to have to write you on such a sad topic as this letter must contain. I would that some one else had undertaken the task or that Francis Pocock, your son's companion, had fulfilled before his departure from here what I had expressly ordered him to do.

But that I wish to save you from a too sudden blow I would have delayed writing until Pocock had written his report to me of the manner how or when of your poor son's last hours, for you must know that your son, Frederick Barker, is gone to his eternal rest.

I was absent on an exploring expedition of Lake Victoria, having left Francis Pocock and Frederick Barker in charge of my camp. Altogether I was absent fifty-eight days. When I returned, hoping that I would find that all had gone well, I was struck with the

7. The mission reaction to this letter is given in Oliver, *Missionary Factor in East Africa*, 39ff.; Low, *Religion and Society in Buganda 1875–1900*. Stanley commented on the later troubles of the missionaries: "Africans, however, would be less than men if they did not struggle, as the ancient Romans did, against the advances of Christianity." Stanley, *My African Travels*, 17.

1. *NYH*, Oct. 11, 1875.

grievous news that your son had died twelve days before of an intermittent fever.

What little I have been able to learn of your son's death amounts to this: On April 22 he went out to the lake with Pocock to shoot hippopotami, and all day enjoyed himself. On the morning of the 23d he went out for a little walk, had his tea and some pancakes, washed himself, and then suddenly said he felt ill and lay down in bed. He called for a hot stone to be applied to his feet; brandy was given him, blankets were heaped on him; but he felt such cold in his extremities that nothing availed to restore the heat in his body. His blood seems to have become congealed. At eight A.M., an hour after he lay down, he was dead. Such is what I have been able to glean from Pocock of the manner of his death, but by our next letter-carrier Pocock shall send you a complete account.

His clothes and effects shall be sold at auction in this camp, and whatever they produce, with such money as may be due to him for wages, shall be rendered to you. His papers, photos and Testament I shall keep until I have an opportunity to send them to you.

Dear Mrs. Barker, you may believe me as you may, but in Fred Barker I have lost one of as much value to me as he was dear to you. He was such a clever, quick, intelligent servant that had he lived to reach home, and I had lived to see him there, his future need never have been a source of anxiety to him. Indeed, there is no doubt he before long would have ranked high in the estimation of worthy men, and become a most useful member of intelligent society. Gentlemanliness, honesty and politeness were his special characteristics. I had such confidence in him that I had placed him in charge of all my stores, and, during my absence on the lake, appointed him half share in the command of 166 soldiers.

From the coast to this lake, a distance of 720 miles, he trudged it afoot like a hero. When sick, of course he rode one of our animals. Whatever I told him became so impressed on his memory that I need never repeat the order or complain of its neglect. Whatever I advised him to do became with him a law, whatever I suggested to him immediately was obeyed, as though it were a command. He was a rare young man, mettlesome, manly, and thoroughly English in his good qualities. It is then to be grieved that you have lost such a hopeful son, I such a true servant, and his country such a promising character. I sympathize with you deeply—not I alone, we all of us in this camp, for we have lost one such that his place cannot be filled.

God's comfort be with you in this distress . . .

23

Village of Kagehyi, District of Uchambi, Country of Usukuma
May 15, 1875 [1]

By the aid of the enclosed map you will be able to understand
the positions and places of the countries mentioned in my last [2] and
of some I shall be obliged to describe in this letter. It is needless
to go over the same ground I described in my letter from Uganda;
but, since I send you a map,[3] it will be but charity to again briefly
sketch the characteristics of the countries lying east between Usukuma and Uganda.

Between the district of Uchambi, which is in Usukuma, and the
Shimeeyu River, the principal affluent of the Niyanza, lie the pretty
districts of Sima and Magu, governed by independent chiefs. On
the eastern side of the Shimeeyu is Masanza, a rugged and hilly
country, thinly populated and the resort of the elephant hunters.
Beyond Masanza the coast is formed by Manasa and the country
is similar in feature to Masanza, abounding in elephants. This extends to the eastern extremity of Speke Gulf, when we behold a
complete change in the landscape. The land suddenly sinks down
into a flat, marshy country, as if Speke Gulf formerly had extended
many miles inland, as I have no doubt, but rather feel convinced,
it did.

This country is called Wirigedi,[4] peopled by savages, who have
little or no intercourse with Usukuma, but are mostly exclusive and
disposed to take advantage of their strength to rob strangers who
visit them. Urrigedi is drained by the Ruana, which discharges itself
into Speke Gulf by two mouths. It is a powerful stream, conveying
a vast quantity of water to Speke Gulf, but in importance not to
be mentioned in the same category as the Shimeeyu and the Kagera,
the two principal affluents of Lake Victoria.

Speke Gulf at its eastern extremity is about twelve miles in width.
Opposed to the hilly ranges of Manasa and Masanza are the sterile
naked mountains and plains of Shashi, Uramba and Urirwi.[5] The
plains which separate each country from the other are as devoid of
vegetation as the Isthmus of Suez. A thin line only, bordering the
lake, is green with bush and cane. The gulf, as we proceed west

1. *NYH*, Oct. 12, 1875.
2. Letter of April 12, 1875, document 20.
3. See Map II.
4. See document 20, note 3.
5. See *TDC*, I, 141.

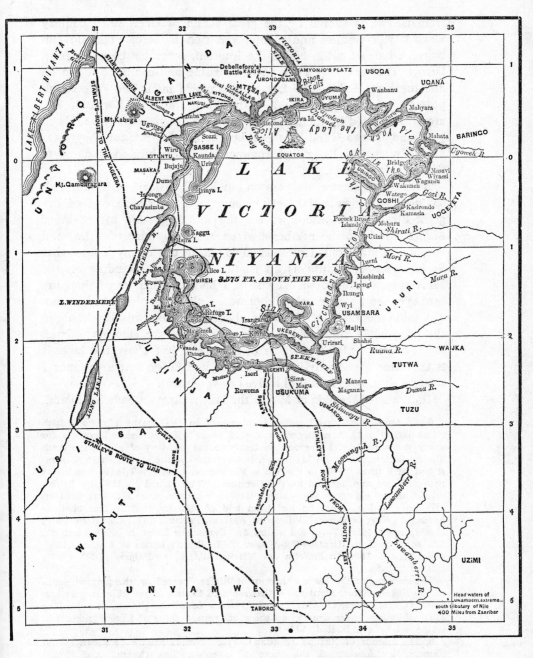

Map II. Stanley's early sketch map of Lake Victoria (from *NYH*, Oct. 12, 1875)

from Urirwi, is shored by the great island of Ukerewe, a country blessed with verdure and plenty, and rich in herds of cattle and ivory. A narrow strait, called the Rugeshi, separates Ukerewe from Urirwi. The Wakereweh are an enterprising and commercial people, and the King, Lukongeh,[6] is a most amiable man. The Wakereweh possess numerous islands—Nifuah, Wezi, Iraugara, Kamassi, &c., are all inhabited by them. Their canoes are seen in Ugeyeya, Usongora and Uzinza;[7] and to the tribes in the far interior they have given, by their activity and commercial fellowship, their name to the Victoria Niyanza.

Rounding Ukerewe, we pass on our left the Island of Ukara, and, sailing past Shizu and Kiveru,[8] come to the northern end of Rugeshi Strait, from where we see the towering table mountain of Majita a little to the northeast of us, the mountains of Urimi and Uramba in our front. I mentioned to you in one of my letters[9] that Speke described Majita as an island, and that I, standing on the same spot, would do so likewise if I had no other proof than my own eyes. As we approach Majita we see the reason of this delusion. The table mountain of Majita is about 3,000 feet in altitude above the lake, while on all sides of it, except the lake side at its base, are low brown plains, which rise but a few feet above the lake. It is the same case with Urirwi, Uramba and Shashi. At a distance I thought them islands, until I arrived close to them.

On the northern side of Majita the brown plain extends far inland,

6. Rukonge (Lukongeh), after involvement in the deaths of two British missionaries in 1877, managed to live in peace with European intruders for many years. In 1892 he agreed by treaty to the building of a German Anti-Slavery Society station on his island, but he attacked the station in 1895, after it had been turned over to the White Fathers, and destroyed it. Rukonge was then defeated and deposed by the Germans. When visited in 1877 by British missionaries, Rukonge spoke against Stanley; they claimed he was very unfavorably impressed by what he had been told of Americans—"the fact of their having no King or Queen." Wilson to Wigram, Feb. 22, 1877, C.A6/025, CMS; *Mackey of Uganda*, 77–78; Kollmann, *Auf Deutschen Boden in Afrika*, 240–41, 273–74; Schweinitz, *Deutsch-Ost-Afrika*, 162ff.; Brard's letters of Aug. 17, 1895, and March 6, 1896, in *Bulletin des Missions d'Afrique (d'Alger)* (1895–1897), 279–80, 351–53.

7. Usongora, or the Haya chiefdom of Kiziba, located on the plateau south of the Kagera River. Stanley, "A Geographical Sketch of the Nile and Livingstone (Congo) Basins," 393; Taylor, *Western Lacustrine Bantu*, 132–44. The Zinza chiefdoms were situated on the southwestern shore of Lake Victoria and on the nearby islands. *Ibid.*, 144–48.

8. The islands of Nafuba (Nifuah), Vesi (Wezi), Irugwa (Iraugara), and Kamassi are located off the shore of Ukerewe. Sizu (Shizu) and Kweru (Kiveru) islands lie between Ukerewe and Ukara.

9. Letter of April 12, 1875, document 20.

and I do believe a great plain or a series of plains bounds the lake countries east, for we have views distant or near everywhere. In endeavoring to measure the extent of this plain I am compelled to think of Ugogo, for, as we traversed its northern frontier we saw each day stretching north the barren, thorn-covered plain of Uhumba. On leaving Iramba we came again in view of a portion of it, more recently covered with water, under the name of the Luwamberri Plain. As we journey through Usmaow we saw from many a ridge the plain extending north. That part of the plain lying between Urimi and the lake is, of course, drained by the Luwamberri, the Mwaru and the Duma rivers, and discharged into the Niyanza under the name of the Shimeeyu. But northeast of the Shimeeyu's mouth imagine the land heaved into a low, broad and lengthy ridge, forming another basin drained by the Ruana, and still another drained by the Mara, and again another by the Mori, &c. If we ask the natives what lies beyond the immediate lake lands we are assured briefly, "Mbuiga tu," "Only a plain."

From Majita north we sail along the coast of Ururi, a country remarkable for its wealth of cattle and fine pastoral lands. It is divided into several districts whose names you will find marked on the map. Mohuru and Shirati, low, flat and wooded districts of Ururi separate this country from Ugeyeya, the land of so many fables and wonders, the El Dorado of ivory seekers and the source of wealth for slave hunters.

Our first view of it while we cross the Bay of Kavirondo[10] is of a series of tall mountains, and of a mountainous projection, which latter from a distance we take to be a promontory, but which on a nearer view turns out to be an island, bearing a tall mountain on its back. At the northeastern extremity of this bay is Gori River, which rises northeast near Kavi—no important stream, but one that grows duruing the rainy season to large breadth and depth. Far east beyond the Niyanza for twenty-five days' march the country is one continuous plain, low hills rising here and there dotting the surface, a scrubby land, though well adapted for pasture and cattle, of which the natives have vast herds. About fifteen days' march east the people report a land wherein low hills spout smoke, and sometimes fire. This wonderful district is called Susa, and is situated in the Masai Land. All combine in saying that no stream runs north, but that all waters come into the Niyanza—for at least twenty

10. Stanley was mistaken about Kavirondo Bay; see document 20, note 11.

days' march. Beyond this distance the natives report a small lake, from which issues a stream flowing toward the Pangani.[11]

Continuing on our way north we pass between the Island Ugingo and the gigantic mountains of Ugeyeya, at whose base the *Lady Alice* seems to crawl like a mite in a huge cheese, while we on board admire the stupendous height and wonder at the deathly silence which prevails in this solitude, where the boisterous winds are hushed and the turbulent waves are as tranquil as a summer's dream. The natives as they pass regard this spot with superstition, as well they might, for the silent majesty of these dumb tall mounts awe the very storms to peace. Let the tempests bluster as they may on the spacious main beyond this cape, in this nook, sheltered by tall Ugingo isle and lofty Goshi on the mainland, they inspire no fear. It is this refuge which Goshi promises the distressed canoe men that causes them to sing praises of Goshi, and to cheer one another when wearied and benighted that Goshi is near to protect them.[12]

Sailing between and out from among the clustering islands, we leave Wategi behind, and sail towards two low isolated islands not far from the mainland, for a quiet night's rest, and under the overspreading branches of a mangrove tree we dream of unquiet waters and angry surfs and threatening rocks, to find ourselves next morning tied to an island which, from its peculiarity, I have named Bridge Island, though its native name is Kihwa. While seeking a road to ascend the island to take bearings, I discovered a natural bridge of basalt, about twenty feet in length by twelve in breadth, under which one might repose comfortably, and from one side see the waves lashed to fury and spend their strength on the stubborn rocks which form the foundation of the arch, while from the other he could see his boat, secure under the lee of the island, resting on a serene and placid surface, and shaded by mangrove branches from the hot sun of the Equator. Its neighborhood is remarkable only for a small cave, the haunt of fishermen.[13]

11. There were tales on the coast in the 1860's of a volcano on the route to Lake Victoria. Perhaps the travelers referred to the extinct volcano of Suswa, near Lake Naivasha. See Christie, *Cholera Epidemics*, ix, 22–23, 225; Pringle, "With the Railway Survey to Victoria Nyanza," 125; Sadler, "Notes on the Geography of British East Africa," 175–76.

12. Stanley was passing territory then described as Gaya. See Meyer, "Berichte," 519; "Von der wissenschaftlichen Expedition Oskar Neumanns," 423. See also Naval Intelligence, *Handbook of Kenya*, 69, for a mountain, Gwashi, south of the Kavirondo Gulf.

13. See Whitehouse, "To the Victoria Nyanza," 234; he visited, in 1899, Bridge Island and confirmed Stanley's description.

From the summit of Bridge Island the view eastward takes in all Masari as far as Nakidimo, and discovers only a flat and slightly wooded district, varied at intervals by isolated cones, and northward, at the distance of twenty miles or so, finds the land makes a bold and long stretch eastward. Knowing, however, by experience that the appearance of the land is deceptive, we hoist our sail and scud merrily before a freshening breeze, hugging the coast, lest it should rob us of some rarity or wonder.

At noon I found myself under the Equator, and four miles north I came to discolored water and a slight current flowing to the south-west. Seeing a small bay of sufficient breadth to make a good river, and no land at its eastern extremity, I made sure I had discovered a river, which would rival the Shimeeyu; but within an hour land all round revealed the limit and extent of the Bay of Nakidimo. We anchored close to a village and began to court the attention of some wild looking fishermen, but the nude barbarians merely stared at us from under penthouses of hair, and hastily stole away to tell their wives and relatives of how an apparition in the shape of a boat with white wings to it had suddenly come before them, bearing strange men with red caps on their heads, except one—a red man, clad in white, whose face was as red as blood, who, jabbering something unintelligible, so frightened them that they ran away. This will become a pleasant tradition, one added to the many wonders now told in Ugeyeya, which, with the art of embellishment inherent in the tongue of the wondering, awe-struck savage, may become in time the most wonderful of all wonders.

Perceiving that our proffered courtesies were thus rudely rejected, we also stole out of the snug bay and passed round to another much larger and more important. At its extremity a river issued into the bay, which, by long and patient talk with the timid natives, we ascertained to be the Ugoweh.[14] In this the hippos were as bold as the human savages were timid, and to a couple of the amphibious monsters we had to induce the *Lady Alice* to show a swifter pace in retreat than the savages of Nakidimo had shown to us. These hippopotami would afford rare sport in a boat specially built for killing them; then they might splinter her sides with their tusks, and bellow and kick to their utmost; but the *Lady Alice,* if I can help it, with her delicate skin of cedar and ribs of slender hickory, shall never come in close contact with the iron-hard ivory of the hippopotamus, for she would be splintered into matches and crushed like an egg

14. Later search proved Ugoweh to be the name of a village in Kadimu; Stanley placed Ugoweh Bay in the location of Kavirondo Gulf. *Ibid.,* 229–41.

before one could say "Jack Robinson," and then the hungry crocodiles would leisurely digest us. The explorer's task, to my mind, is
a far nobler one than hunting hippos, and our gallant cedar boat
has many a thousand miles to travel yet before she has performed
her task.

The yet unknown expanse of the Victoria Niyanza, northward and
westward and southwestward, invites us to view it delights and
wonders of nature. The stormy Lake Albert and the stormier Tanganyika, though yet distant, woo us to ride on their waves; and
far Bangweolo, Moero and Kamolondo and the Lincoln Lakes promise us fair prospects and as rich rewards if we can only bide the
buffets of the tempests, and the brunt of savage hostility and
ignorance till then. Shall we forego the vantage of all this ripe
harvest and acquisition of knowledge for an hour's fierce pleasure
with the simple but full-muscled hippopotamus? Not by my election
or consent. Let the admirers of the *Field, Bell's Life* and the *Spirit
of the Times*[15] call it faintheartedness, or even a harsher name, if
they will. I call it prudence. But I have an adventure with a hippo
—a cowardly, dull-witted, fat-brained hippo—(I can abuse him savagely in your columns, for his brothers in Europe, thank fortune,
do not read the *Telegraph* or the HERALD without fear of a civil
or criminal suit for libel)—to tell some day, when I have no higher
things to write of, which will warm all your young bloods; and I
have had another with a lion, or I should say a herd of lions, just
as exciting. But these must remain until I camp under the palms
of Ujiji again, with half my work done, and my other half still undone. Let us pass on, however, to our subject, and the place where
I left off—namely, cowardlike, running away from a pair of bull
hippos. I am not sure they were bulls either, though they were hippopotami, sure enough.

We flew away with a bellying sail along the coast of Maheta,
where we saw such a dense population and clusters of large villages
as we had not seen elsewhere. We thought we would make one
more effort to learn of the natives the names of some of these
villages, and for that purpose steered for a cove on the western
shore of Maheta. We anchored within fifty yards of the shore, and
so lengthened our cable that but a few feet of deep water separated
us from the shore. Some half-a-dozen men wearing small land
shells above their elbows and a circle round their heads, came to

15. Possibly the London periodicals *The Field* and *Bell's Weekly Messenger*,
and the New York *Spirit of the Times*.

the beach. With these we opened a friendly conversation, during which they disclosed the name of the country as Maheta in Ugeyeya; more they would not communicate until we should land. We prepared to do this, but the numbers on the shore increased so fast that we were compelled to pull off again until they should moderate their excitement and talk. They seemed to think that we were about to pull off altogether, for suddenly appeared out of the bush on each side of the spot we had intended to land such a host of spears that we hoisted our sail and left them to whet their treachery on some other boat or canoe more imprudent than ours. The discomfited people were seen to consult together on a small ridge behind the bush lining the lake, and, no doubt, they thought we were about to pass close to a small point at the north end of the cone, shouting gleefully at the prospect of a prize; but, lowering the sail, we pulled to windward, far out of the reach of bow or sling, and at dusk made for a small island, to which we tied our boat, and where we camped in security.

Next day we continued on our course, and coasted along Nduru and Wangano, and sailed into the bay which forms the northeastern extremity of Lake Victoria Niyanza. Manyara, on the eastern side of the bay, is a land of bold hills and ridges, while the very northeastern end, through which issues the Yagama River into the Niyanza, is flat. The opposite coast to Manyara is that of Muwanda and the promontory of Chaga, while the great slug-like island of Usuguru, standing from west to east across the mouth of the bay, shuts the bay almost entirely in.[16]

At Muwanda we again trusted our fortunes with the natives, and were this time not deceived, so that we were enabled to lay in quite a stock of vegetables and provisions at a cheap rate. They gave us all the information we desired. Baringo, they said, is the name applied by the people of Ugana to Nduru, a district of Ugeyeya, and the bay on which our boat rode the extreme end of the lake, nor did they know or had they heard of any lake, large or small, other than the Niyanza.[17]

I described the coast from Muwanda to Uganda, and my visit to Mtesa, with my happy encounter with Colonel Linant de Bellefonds, of Gordon's staff, at some length, so I need not go over the same ground. The day after my last letter was written I made arrangements with the King of Uganda, by which he agreed to lend me

16. See *TDC*, I, 365.
17. See document 20, note 12.

thirty canoes and some 500 men, to convey the expedition from Usukuma to the Katonga River. With this promise, and ten large canoes as an earnest of it, I started from Murchison Bay on April 17. We kept company as far as the Katonga River, but here the chief captain of the Waganda said that he should have to cross over to Sesse, distant twelve miles from the mainland, and the largest island in the Lake Niyanza, to procure the remaining twenty canoes promised by Mtesa.[18] The chief gave me two canoes to accompany me, promising that I should be overtaken by the entire fleet before many days. I was impatient to continue my survey of the lake and to reach Usukuma, having been so long absent from the expedition, during which time many things contrary to my success and peace of mind might have occurred.

I took my observations twice a day with a sea horizon—one at noon for latitude, and one in the afternoon for longitude—and I am sorry to say that, if I am right, Speke is about fourteen miles wrong in his latitude along the whole coast of Uganda. The mouth of the Katonga River, for instance, according to his map, is a little south of the Equator. I have made it by meridian altitude, observed April 20, to be in latitude 0 deg. 16 min. 0 secs. north. Thus it is nearly with all his latitudes. His longitudes and mine vary but little; but this is easily accounted for. The longitude of any position can be taken with a chronometer, sextant, and artificial horizon with the same accuracy on land as on sea. If there is any difference it is very likely to exist in the error of the chronometers. What instruments Speke possessed to obtain his latitudes I know not, but if he found the altitude of the sun ascending about 65 deg. he could never obtain it with an ordinary sextant except by double altitude, and that method is not so exact as taking a simple meridian on a quiet lake, with an ample horizon of water. But there are various methods of determining one's latitude, and Speke was familiar with many. My positions all round the lake have been determined with a sea horizon. When near noon my plan was, if the lake was rough to seek the nearest island or a quiet cape at the extremity of a bay, and there take my observations as deliberately as though my life depended on their accuracy.

But this task was, indeed, a work of pleasure for me, and I have found a rich reward for most of my pains and stormy life on this

18. For the Sesse and their role as builders and users of canoes, Roscoe, *The Baganda*, 383–91. Stanley described them as "the most skillful canoe-builders in the world." Stanley, "Geographical Sketch of the Nile," 392.

lake in looking at the fair extent of white on my map, with all its bends, curves, inlets, creeks, bays, capes, debouchures of rivers, &c., known by the name of Victoria Niyanza. Any errors which may have crept into my calculations will be determined by competent authorities on my return from Africa, or on the arrival of my papers in Europe. Meantime I send my map as I have made it.

The Katonga is not a large river, and has but one mouth. The Amionzi River empties itself into the Niaynza about eight miles W.S.W. of the Katonga. Uganda stretches to the Kagerah,[19] situated in S. lat. 0 deg. 40 min. On the south side of the river begins Usongora, extending to S. lat. 1 deg. South of 1 deg. is Kamiru,[20] extending to S. lat. 1 deg. 15 min.

Thence is Uwya,[21] a country similar in enterprise to Ukerewe's people. Beyond Uwya is Uzinja or Uzinza, called by the Wanyamwezi Mweri. Uzinja continues as far south as Jordan's Nullah, and east of it is Usukuma again, and one day's sail from Jordan's Nullah[22] we pass Muanza, which Speke reached in 1858, and brings us home to Kagehyi, and to our camp, where we are greeted joyfully by such as live to mourn the poor fellows who, in my absence, have been hurried by disease to untimely graves.

I must be brief in what I have to say now. I did think to make this a long letter, but Sungoro's slave, who carries this, is in a hurry to go, as his caravan has already started. My next letter must continue this from the Kagera River, called in Karagwe the Kitangule, and it shall describe some foul adventures that we went through, which caused us to appear in a wretched condition to our expedition. Though our condition was so wretched, it was not half so bad as it would have been had we returned two days later, for I doubt much whether I should have had an expedition at all. I had been absent too long, and our fight with the Wavuma had been magnified and enlarged by native rumor to such a pitch that Wolseley's[23] victory at Ardahsu was as nothing to ours, for it had been said that we

19. See document 30, note 14.
20. Probably a reference to Bwogi IV Kamiro of the Haya Bukara chiefdom. Cory, *History of the Bukoba District*, 63–67; Mors, "Geschichte der Bahinda des alten Kyamtwara-Reiches am Victoria-Nyanza-See," 711.
21. In *TDC*, I, 250, Stanley gives this as a former name for the Haya chiefdom of Ihangiro.
22. Named by Speke after his family home in Somerset. Speke described a "nullah" as "a watercourse that only runs in wet weather." It is an Indian word. Speke, *What Led to the Discovery*, 299; Johnston, *Nile Quest*, 120.
23. Garnet Wolseley (1833–1913) led the British forces in the 1873–1874 campaign against the Ashanti. *DNB. Twentieth Century 1912–1921*, 587–91.

had destroyed a whole fleet of canoes, not one of which had escaped, and that some other tribe or tribes had collected a force, overtaken us, and destroyed us in like manner—an incredible story, which had so won upon a faction of the soldiers that they had determined to return to Unyanyembe, and thence to Zanzibar. But God has been with us here, and on the lake, and, though we have suffered some misfortune, He has protected us from greater ones. We had been absent from camp fifty-eight days, during which we had surveyed in our brave little boat over 1,000 miles of lake shores; but a part of the south-west coast has yet to be explored. We shall not leave the Niyanza, however, until we have thoroughly done our work.

I returned to find also that one of the white men, Frederick Barker, of the Langham Hotel, London, had died on the 23d of April, twelve days before I reappeared at Kagehyi. His disease was, as near as I can make it out from Frank Pocock's description, a congestive chill—that is the term applied to it in the States. Pocock calls it "cold fits," a term every whit, I believe, as appropriate. I have known several die of these "cold fits," or aguish attacks—the preliminary symptoms of severe attacks of the intermittent fever. These aguish attacks, however, sometimes end the patient before the fever arrives which generally follows the ague. The lips become blue, the face bears the appearance of one who is frozen, the blood becomes, as it were, congealed, the pulse stops and death ensues. There are various methods of quickening the blood and reviving the patient. However, a common one is to plunge him into a vapor or hot water and mustard bath and apply restoratives—brandy, hot tea, &c., but Pocock was not experienced in this case, though he gave Barker some brandy after he lay down, from feeling a slight nausea and chill. It appears by his companion's report that he did not live an hour. Frederick Barker suffered from one of these severe aguish attacks in Urimi, but brandy and hot tea quickly given to him soon brought him to that state which promises recovery.

Thus two out of four white men are dead. I wonder who next? Death cries, Who next? and perhaps our several friends ask Who next? No matter who it is. We could not better ourselves by attempting to fly from the fatal land; for between us and the sea are seven hundred miles of as sickly a country as any in Africa. The prospect is fairer in front, though there are some three thousand miles more to march. We have new and wonderful lands before us, whose wonders and mysteries shall be a medicine which shall make us laugh at fever and death.

24

Mahyiga Island, Three Miles from Bumbireh Island, Lake Victoria
Niyanza
July 29, 1875 [1]

This expedition which you have intrusted to me seems destined
to meet with adventures more than enough. When a boy I loved to
read books of adventure and travel, especially of the Mayne Reid [2]
type, and followed their several heroes with breathless interest
through all their varied fortunes; but since I have been compelled
lately to act the hero of the adventure oftener than is consistent
with peace of mind and a comfortable night's rest, however glorious a thing it may appear on paper, you may take my word for it
I would much rather read of the adventure than be an actor in it.
As I compare my former trip to Ujiji with this journey I am forced
to admit that the former was mere child's play. The adventures we
have gone through already, if faithfully related, would fill a good
sized volume, while, I may say, we have but begun our journey
as yet.

Continuing my narrative of our journey from Uganda to Usukuma
by the western shore of Lake Niyanza, I resume it from the point I
left off in my last letter—viz., the Kagera River or the Kitangule.

We had two canoes belonging to Mtesa accompanying our boat as
an escort, until the dilatory Grand Admiral Magassa[3] should overtake us with his fleet of thirty canoes, and the day we left the
Kagera River we rested at night on a smooth, sandy beach at the
foot of the Usongoro plateau, at a point called Kagya. The natives
were friendly and disposed to be hospitable, so that we argued well
for our reception during our travels along the coast of Usongora.

The next afternoon we camped at Makongo, and received an apparently friendly welcome by the natives, each of whom was engaged as we landed in the grave occupation of imbibing pombe or
beer by means of long straw pipes, exactly as we take a "sherry
cobbler" or a "mint julep" in the United States. The chief slightly
reeled as he came forward to salute me, and his eyes had that un-

1. *NYH*, Aug. 9, 1876.
2. Thomas Mayne Reid (1818–1883), a prolific writer of adventure stories
that took place in all parts of the globe. *DNB*, XVI, 875–76.
3. The *Gabunga,* or admiral, of the Ganda fleet; for his functions, Roscoe,
The Baganda, 254. He died in 1884. O'Flaherty to Wigram, April 1, 1884,
G3.A6/01, CMS. Stanley correctly refers to the admiral as the *Gabunga* in *Diary*,
98, and *TDC*, I, 212.

certain gaze which seemed to hint that he saw double, or two white men when there was only one. However, he and his people were good natured—and contented with our arrival.

About ten P.M. we were all awakened from sleep by a furious drumming, accompanied now and then by shrill yells. The Waganda said that this drumming and yelling was in welcome to the white stranger. I did not believe them, and therefore put my people on their guard, ordered them to load their guns and place them under their sleeping mats and arranged all my own in a handy and safe position. Except the continued drumming and yelling, nothing occurred during the night, but at daybreak we found ourselves in presence of about 500 warriors, armed with bow, shield and spear, who had crept quietly near the camp, and then had stood up in a semicircle, preventing all escape save by water. I was so astonished by this sudden apparition of such a large body of armed men that I could barely believe that we were still in Mtesa's territory.

There was also something very curious in their demeanor. For there was no shouting, yelling or frantic behavior, as we had several times witnessed on the part of savages when about to commit themselves by a desperate deed. They all wore a composed though a stern and determined aspect. It was a terrible moment to us. We knew not what to make of these hundreds of armed savages, who persisted in being silent and gave no hint as to their intentions, unless the forest of spears might be taken as a clear, unmistakable and explicit hint that their object was a bloody one. We feared to make a movement lest it might precipitate a catastrophe which might possibly be averted; so we remained a few minutes silently surveying each other.

The silence was soon broken, however, by the appearance of the chief who had welcomed us (though he was then inebriated) the evening before. He had a long stick in his hand, which he flourished before the faces of the savages, and by this means drove them several paces backward. He then came forward, and, striking the boat, ordered us to get off, and he himself lent a hand to shove the boat into the lake.

As the boat glided into the water another chief came forward and asked us what we meant by drawing our boat up so far on their beach. We replied that we had done it to protect the boat from the surf, and were about to add more reasons when the first chief cut the matter short by ordering us to shove off and go and camp on Musira Island, distant four miles, whither he would follow us with food.

We were nothing loath to obey such good counsel, and soon put a distance of 100 yards between ourselves and the hostile beach. As the Waganda were not yet out of danger, we prepared our guns to sweep the beach. So dense was the crowd of armed men near the water line that we might have taken a fearful revenge had we been so vengefully disposed, or had the necessity of saving the Waganda compelled us to fire. Happily though, our friends, not without loud remonstrance and much wordy altercation, embarked in safety and followed us to Musira Island. Here the chief came, and, learning our wants and our objects, sent off three bunches of bananas which he presented to us, and then left us to our fate.[4]

In the afternoon we sighted our Grand Admiral Magassa, with a large fleet of canoes, paddling slowly to a neighboring island, where he camped for the night. Desirous of quickening his movements I sailed from Musira Island for Alice Island, distant thirty-five miles. The two chiefs of our escorting canoes accompanied us a mile or two, and then, alarmed by the aspect of the weather, turned back, shouting to us at the same time that as soon as the wind moderated they would follow us. It was near midnight when we arrived at Alice Island, and by steering for a light on shore we fortunately found a snug, well-sheltered cove. The light we discovered was that of a fire made by some Bumbireh fishermen curing fish. My men were so hungry that they resolved to seize this food to the great alarm and terror of its owners. I restrained my people and quieted the fears of the fishermen by paying a double price for a quantity of fish sufficient for a day's provisions for the boat's crew.[5]

When daylight came we found ourselves at the foot of a huge beetling cliff, and discovered that we had taken shelter near a kind of penthouse formed by overhanging rocks, which were now blackened with the smoke of many fires. The natives of the island came down to visit us, holding out wisps of green grass as a sign of peace and friendliness. But though they were friendly enough they were so extortionate in their demands that we gained nothing by their friendship, and were compelled to depart at noon, with every pros-

4. *TDC*, I, 216–19, has a few minor variations of detail for this episode. Busira Island was used for the interment of the corpses of chiefs and important men. Stanley, in the account given in *ibid.*, 218–24, did not realize this. Werner, "The Native Races of German East Africa," 60.

5. Alice Island is probably Kerebe Island. Fitzner, *Der Kagera-Nil*, 17. The island and the *Lady Alice* were probably named after Alice Pike of New York. Luwel, "Considérations sur quelques livres récents ayant trait à Henry Morton Stanley," 537. See also the suggestions in Shann, "Tanganyika Place Names of European Origin," 84; Matson, "A Note on Non-Native Vessels on Lake Victoria," 225.

pect of starvation before us, unless Bumbireh Island (a large and populous island lying southwest of Alice Island about twenty-five miles), to which I determined to sail, furnished us with food.

Amid rain, thunder, lightning and a sounding surf on all sides, we dropped anchor under the lee of Pocock's Island [6] about midnight. It rained and thundered throughout the night, and we had much trouble to keep our boat afloat by constant bailing. At daybreak we hurried away from our dangerous anchorage before a steady strong breeze from the northeast, and within three hours drew near the comfortable little cove near the village of Kajuri, at the southeastern extremity of Bumbireh Island. As we looked on the plenty which green slopes, garnished with large groves of bananas and dotted with herds of fat cattle, promised, we anticipated an abundance of good food, ripe bananas, a fat goat, a large supply of milk and other things good for famishing men. But we were disappointed to hear the large number of people on the plateau above the village shouting their war cry.

Still we pressed nearer the beach; hunger gave us much confidence, and a rich tribute, we were sure, would pacify the most belligerent chief. Perceiving that we persisted in approaching their shore the people rushed down the slope of the plateau toward us. Prudence whispered to me to at least get ready our guns, which I accordingly did, and then rowed slowly toward the beach, certain that, if hostilities began, indications of such would appear in time to enable us to withdraw from the shore.

We halted at the distance of twenty yards from the shore, and I observed that the wild behavior of the natives changed, as they approached nearer, to affability and friendliness. We exchanged the usual friendly greetings, and were invited to come ashore in such tones as dissipated the least suspicion from our minds. No sooner, however, had the keel of the boat grounded than the apparently friendly natives rushed in a body and seized the boat and dragged her high and dry on land, with all on board. The reader may imagine the number of natives required to perform this feat when I state the boat, baggage and crew weighed nearly 4,000 pounds.

Twice I raised my revolvers to kill and be killed, but the crew restrained me, saying it was premature to fight, as these people were friends, and all would be right. Accordingly I sat down in the stern sheets and waited patiently for the decisive moment. The savages fast increased in numbers, and the hubbub grew greater. Violent language and more violent action we received without com-

6. *TDC*, I, 226, and *Diary*, 75, call it Barker's Island.

ment or word on our part. Spears were held in their hands as if on the launch, arrows were drawn to the head and pointed at each of us with frenzied looks and eyes almost bursting out of their sockets.

The apparently friendly savages seemed to be now personified furies. Throughout all the scenes of civilized and savage life which I have witnessed I never saw mad rage or wild fury painted so truly before on human features. It led them to the verge of absurdity even. They struck the ground and the boat, stamped, foamed at the mouth, gnashed their teeth, slashed the air with their spears, but they shed no blood. The chief Shekka prevented this, reserving that pleasure, I presume, for a more opportune time, when a new excitement would be required.

Our interpreters, in the meantime, were by no means idle; they employed to the utmost whatever gifts of persuasion nature had endowed them with and fear created in them, without, however, exhibiting any servility or meanness. Indeed, I was struck to admiration by the manly way in which they stated our objects and purposes in travelling on the Niyanza, and by the composure of their bearing. The savages themselves observed this, and commented on it with surprise. This calm behavior of the crew and interpreters acted as a sedative on the turbulence and ranting violence of the savages, though it broke out now and then, sputtering fitfully with the wildest of gestures and most murderous demonstrations.

For three hours I sat in the stern sheets of the boat observing all these preliminaries of a tragedy which I felt sure was about to be enacted, silent, except now and then communicating a suggestion to the interpreters, and seemingly an unconcerned spectator. But I was not idle. I wished to impose on the savages by my behavior. I was busily planning a resistance and an escape. As we were in their power it only remained for us to be quiet until they proceeded to acts of violence, and in the meantime endeavor to purchase peace, or at least postpone the strife.

Comformably with these ideas the interpreters were instructed to offer cloths and beads to the chief Shekka, who appeared to have despotic authority over all, judging from the reverential and ready obedience paid to his commands. Shekka demanded four cloths and ten necklaces of large beads as his price for permitting us to depart in peace. They were paid to him. Having secured them, he ordered his people to seize our oars, which was done before we understood what they were about. This was the second time that Shekka had acted cunningly and treacherously, and a loud jeering laugh from his people showed him how much they appreciated his wit.

After seizing the oars Shekka and his people slowly went to their village to eat their noon meal, and to discuss what other measures should be adopted toward the strangers. A woman came near us, and told us to eat honey with Shekka, as it was the only way to save our lives, for Shekka and his people had determined to kill us and take everything we had. The coxswain of the boat was sent to proffer terms of brotherhood to Shekka. The coxswain was told to be at ease, no harm was intended us, and on the next day Shekka promised he and his people should eat honey and make lasting and sure brotherhood with us.

The coxswain returned to us with triumphant looks, and he speedily communicated his own assurances to the crew. But I checked this over-confidence and trustfulness in such cunning and treacherous people, and told them to trust in nothing save our own wit, and by no means to leave the neighborhood of the boat, for their next act would be to seize the guns in the same manner as they seized the oars. Immediately the crew saw the truth of this suggestion, and I had no reason to complain that they paid no heed to my words.

At three P.M. the natives began to assemble on the ridge of a low hill about a hundred yards from the boat, and presently drums were heard beating the call to war until within half an hour about 500 warriors had gathered around Shekka, who was sitting down addressing his people. When he had done about fifty rushed down and took our drum, and kindly told us to get our guns ready for fight, as they were coming presently to cut our throats.

As soon as I saw the savages had arrived in the presence of Shekka with our drum, I shouted to my men to push the boat into the water. With one desperate effort my crew of eleven men seized the boat as if she had been a mere toy and shot her into the water. The impetus they had given her caused her to drag them all into deep water. In the meantime the savages, uttering a furious howl of disappointment and baffled rage, came rushing like a whirlwind toward the water's edge.

I discharged my elephant rifle, with its two large conical balls, into their midst; and then, assisting one of the crew into the boat, told him to help his fellows in while I continued to fight. My double-barrelled shotgun, loaded with buckshot, was next discharged with terrible effect; for, without drawing a single bow or launching a single spear, they retreated up the slope of the hill, leaving us to exert our wits to get the boat out of the cove before the enemy should decide to man their canoes.

The crew was composed of picked men, and in this dire emergency they did ample justice to my choice. Though we were without oars the men were at no loss for a substitute. As soon as they found themselves in the boat they tore up the seats and footboards and began to paddle the boat out as though she were a canoe, while I was left to single out with my rifles the most prominent and boldest of the enemy.

Twice in succession I succeeded in dropping men determined on launching the canoes, and seeing the sub-chief who had commanded the party that took the drum I took deliberate aim with my elephant rifle at him. That bullet, as I have since been told, killed the chief and his wife and infant, who happened to be standing a few paces behind him, and the extraordinary result had more effect on the superstitious minds of the natives than all previous or subsequent shots.

On getting out of the cove we saw two canoes loaded with men coming out in pursuit from another small cove. I permitted them to come within 100 yards of us, and this time I used the elephant rifle with explosive balls. Four shots killed five men and sank the canoes. This decisive affair disheartened the enemy, and we were left to pursue our way unmolested, not, however, without hearing a ringing voice shouting out to us, "Go and die in the Niyanza!"

When the savages counted their losses they found fourteen dead and eight wounded with buckshot, which I consider to be very dear payment for the robbery of eight ash oars and a drum, though barely equivalent, in our estimation, to the intended massacre of ourselves.[7]

Favored by a slight breeze from the land we hoisted our sail, and by night were eight miles southeast of Bumbireh. A little after dusk the breeze died, and we continued on our course paddling. All night I kept the men hard at work, making, however, but little progress through the water. At sunrise we were about twenty miles southeast of Bumbireh, and by noon were about twenty-five miles off. At this time we had a strong breeze from the northwest, and we sped before it at the rate of five knots an hour. At sunset we were about twelve miles northeast of Sosua or Gosua Island,[8] and if the breeze continued favorable we hoped to be able to make a haven

7. For the implications of this encounter with the Haya of Bumbire, and of hostilities there, see the Introduction. Stanley gives a more elaborate account in *TDC*, I, 227–37, of this first episode, but there are no significant differences from the despatch to the *Herald* and *Telegraph*. *Diary*, 75–76, offers a very brief description that again is in agreement.

8. The Sosswa islands are located to the southeast of Bumbire.

some time before midnight. But the breeze, about eight P.M., rose to a fierce gale, and, owing to the loss of our oars, we could not keep the boat before the wind.

As we were swept by the island we made frantic efforts to get to leeward, but it was to no purpose; we therefore resigned ourselves to the wind and waves, the furious rain and the horror of the tempest. Most of your readers, no doubt, have experienced a gale of wind at sea; few, however, can have witnessed it in a small boat. But our situation was more dangerous even than the latter. We had rocks and unknown islands in our neighborhood, and a few miles further a mainland peopled by savages, who would have no scruple in putting us all to death or making slaves of us. If our boat capsized the crocodiles of the lake would make short work of us; if we were driven on an uninhabited island death by starvation awaited us. Yet with all these terrors we were so worn out with hunger, fatigue and anxiety that, excepting the watchman, we all fell asleep, though awakened now and then by his voice calling the men to bale the boat out.

At daybreak the tempest and high waves subsided, and we perceived we had drifted eight miles westward of Sosua and to within six miles of the large island of Mysomeh. We had not a morsel of food in the boat; I had but a little ground coffee, and we had tasted nothing else for forty-eight hours; yet the crew, when called to resume their rough paddles, cheerfully responded and did their duty manfully. A gentle breeze set in from the westward, which bore us quickly east of Sosua, and carried us by two P.M. to an island which I have distinguished by the name of Refuge Island.

On exploring this island we found it to be about two miles in circumference, to have been formerly inhabited and cultivated, and, to our great joy, we found an abundance of green bananas, and of a small ripe fruit resembling cherries in appearance and size, but having the taste of dates. To add to this bounty I succeeded in shooting two brace of large fat ducks, and when night closed in on us, in our snug and secure camp close by a strip of sandy beach, few people that night blessed God more fervently than we did.

We rested a day on Refuge Island, during which time we made amends for the scarcity we had suffered, then, feeling on the second day somewhat recovered, we set sail for Singo Island. We imagined we were near enough to Usukuma to venture to visit Ito Island, situated a mile south of Singo, whose slopes were verdant with the frondage of banana and plantain, but, on attempting to land, were met by a force of natives who rudely repulsed us with stones shot from slings. Our cartridges being all spoiled by the late rainy weather we were unable to do more than hoist sail and speed away to more kindly shores.

Two days afterward our boat rounded the southwestern extremity of Wiro, a peninsula of Ukerewe, and rode on the gray waters of Speke Gulf, the distant shore line of Usukuma bounding the view south about twenty-two miles off. A strong head wind rising we turned into a small bay in Wiro Peninsula, where we purchased meat, potatoes, milk, honey, ripe and green bananas, eggs and poultry; and, while our boat was at anchor, cooked these delicacies on board and ate with such relish and appetite as only starving men can properly appreciate, grateful to Providence and kindly disposed to all men.

At midnight, taking advantage of a favorable wind, we set sail for Usukuma. About three A.M. we were nearly in mid-gulf, and here the fickle wind failed us; and then, as if resolved we should taste to the utmost all its power, it met us with a tempest of hailstones as large as filberts from the north-north-east. The sky was robed in inky blackness, not a star was visible, vivid lightnings, accompanied by loud thunder crashes, and waves which tossed us up and down as though we were imprisoned in a gourd, lent their terrors to this fearful night. Again we let the boat drift whither it might, as all our efforts to keep on our course were useless and vain. Indeed, we began to think that the curse of the people of Bumbireh, "Go and die in the Niyanza," might be realized after all, though I had much faith in the staunch boat which Messenger, of Teddington, so conscientiously built.

A gray, cheerless raw morning dawned at last, and we discovered ourselves to be ten miles north of Ruwoma,[9] and twenty miles northwest of Kagehyi, at which latter place my camp was situated. We put forth our best efforts, hoisted sail, and though the wind was but little in our favor at first it soon rewarded our perseverance, and merrily rushing tall waves came booming astern of us, so that we sailed in triumph along the well known shores of Usukuma straight to camp. Shouts of welcome greeted us from shore, when even many miles away; but as we drew near the shouts changed to volleys of musketry and waving of flags, and the land seemed alive with

9. Rwoma ruled the Zinza state of Bukara from 1864 to 1895, when he was killed fighting the Germans. For his turbulent career, van Thiel, "Businza unter der Dynastie der Bahinda," 512; Schweinitz, *Deutsch-Ost-Afrika*, 154–61; Langheld, *Zwanzig Jahre in deutschen Kolonien*, 101ff.

leaping forms of glad-hearted men, for we had been fifty-seven days absent from our people, and many a false rumor of our death, strengthened each day as our absence grew longer, was now dissipated by the appearance of the *Lady Alice*, sailing joyously to the port of Kagehyi.

As the keel grounded over fifty men bounded to the water, dragged me from the boat and danced me round camp on their shoulders, amid much laughter, clapping of hands, grotesque wriggling of human forms and Saxon Hurrahing. Having vented their joy they set me down and all formed a circle, many men deep, to hear the news, which was given with less detail than I have the honor to write to you. So ended our exploration of Lake Victoria Niyanza.

25

Port of Dumo, Southwestern Uganda
August 15, 1875 [1]

The Anglo-American Expedition has arrived at last in Uganda, but it remains to inform you how we came here, which will make a letter second in interest to none I have yet despatched from Africa. I closed my last letter with a description of our reception at camp by the soldiers and porters of the expedition. When I had given briefly the news of our adventurous exploration I demanded the report of Frank Pocock of what had occurred in camp during my long absence.

The principal items of this report were a rumor that had obtained considerable credence in camp of the boat having been forcibly seized by the natives of Magu two days after we had left camp, upon which day soldiers had been despatched to effect our release, peaceably if possible, forcibly if necessary. This rumor was, of course, false, nothing of the kind having transpired anywhere near any part of the coast washed by the waters of Speke Gulf. The second item was a report of our fight with the Wavuma, considerably exaggerated, and in the main false, because it described the manner of our deaths and the force that attacked us. The third item was the discovery of a conspiracy to attack our camp and capture the goods of the expedition. The conspirators were Kipingiri, Prince of Lutari; Kurrereh, Prince of Kayenzi, and the chief of Igusa. The plot, however, was discovered to the captains of the camp by Ka-

1. *NYH*, Aug. 10, 1876.

duma, the prince in whose village of Kagehyi the expedition was encamped. The captains took immediate measures to meet the conspirators, distributed ammunition to the soldiers and sent out spies. The conspiracy, however, was nipped by the death of the chief of Igusa and the continuancy of Kurrereh.[2]

The fourth item was a meeting held by the soldiers and porters of the expedition, at which it was determined that if the "Bana Mkuba" (the Great Master) did not return within fifteen days from that date or the beginning of the new moon they would strike camp and march for Unyanyembe. I arrived at camp the last day of the old moon, within one day of the intended departure. The fifth item was the death of Frederick Barker, ten days before my arrival. Besides Barker, six stout fellows had died of dysentery and fever. Young Barker's death saddened me very much, as he was a promising young man, with sufficient intelligence to appreciate the work of exploration and likely to continue in it out of mere love for it. I left him enjoying excellent health and to all appearance happy. On my return I found a mound of stones, which his companion, Pocock, pointed out as Barker's grave.

I could not help contrasting the color of my features with those of my European attendant, Pocock. The latter's complexion, from living much indoors, was of the color of milk, while mine might be compared to a red Indian's; the equatorial sun of Africa had painted my face of an intense fiery hue, while my nose was four times peeled, and my eyes were as bloodshot as those of the most savage Andalusian *toro* ever *matador* killed.

Sweet is the Sabbath day to the toil worn laborer, happy is the long sea-tossed mariner after his arrival in port, and sweet were the days of calm rest we enjoyed after our troublous exploration of the Niyanza. The *brusque* storms, the continued rain, the cheerless gray clouds, the wild waves, the loneliness of the islands, the inhospitality of the natives, were like mere phases of a dream, were now but reminiscences of the memory—so little did we heed what was past while enjoying the luxury of a rest from our toils. Still it added to our pleasure to be able to conjure up in the mind the varied incidents of the long lake journey; they served to enliven and employ the mind while the body enjoyed repose, like condiments quickening digestion.

2. Kaduma ruled Kageyi until his death in 1882. Copplestone to Lang, April 24, 1882, G3.A6/01, CMS. For a missionary impression of him, Wilson and Felkin, *Uganda*, I, 81–85. Lutare is about two miles east southeast of Kageyi; Igusa is to the south of Lutare.

It was a pleasure to be able to map at will in the mind so many countries newly discovered—such a noble extent of fresh water explored for the first time. As the memory flew over the lengthy track of exploration how fondly it gazed upon the many picturesque bays margined by water lilies and lotus plants, or by green walls of the slender, reed-like papyrus! Enclosing an area of water whose face was as calm as a mirror, because lofty mountain ridges surround it, with what kindly recognition it roved over the little green islands in whose snug havens our boat had lain securely at anchor when the rude tempest without churned the face of Niyanza into a foamy sheet! With what curious delight it loved to survey the massive gneiss rocks as they towered one upon another in huge fragments, perpendicular and horizontal, as they were disintegrated from the parent mass by the elements!

At one place they remind us of the neighborhood of Avila and the Escurial, at another of Stonehenge; in another place they appear as if a race of Titans had collected these masses together and piled them up in their present irregular state with a view to building a regular structure which should defy time and the elements. The memory also cherishes a kindly recollection of the rich grain bearing plains of Ugeyeya, the soft outlined hills of Manyara, the tall dark woods and low shores opposite Namunji Island, as well as of the pastoral plateau and slopes of Uvuma and Bugeyeya. But most of all it clings to Uganda, the beautiful land, its intelligent and remarkable King, and no less remarkable people. Here memory received the deepest impressions; it therefore retains the fondest recollections. For in Uganda imagination, that had hitherto been hushed to somnolence by the irredeemable state of wildness and savagery witnessed between Zanzibar and Usukuma, glowed into warm life, and from the present Uganda painted a future dressed in the robe of civilization; it saw each gentle hill crowned by a happy village and spired church, from which the bells sounded the call to a Gospel feast; it saw the hill slopes prolific with the fruits of horticulture, and the valleys waving fields of grain; it saw the land smiling in affluence and plenty; its bays crowded with the dark hulls of trading vessels; it heard the sounds of craftsmen at their work, the roar of manufactories and foundries and the ever buzzing noise of enterprising industry. What wonder, then, if intercourse with the King of Uganda and his people induced imagination to paint this possible, nay probable picture—that memory should have engraven deep on it the features of the land and the friendliness and hospitality of its people?

As we follow the flights of memory she reminds us also almost too vividly of the scenes of terror and misfortune we have lately gone through—of our adventure with a flotilla of canoes manned by drunken natives who persisted in following us and entertaining us at sea with their beer and intrusive hospitality; of our escape from an ambuscade of Wageyeya; of our fight with the Wavuma and battle of Kajuri;[3] of the miserable churlishness of many a tribe; of days of starvation, tempestuous nights and stormy days. These and a hundred others, now happily past, treasured only in the memory and our journal, serve but to heighten the enjoyment of our rest and to inspire in my heart and in the hearts of my semi-barbarous comates in peril a feeling of devout thankfulness to Divine Providence for our protection.

I deemed it not only necessary, but politic, to remain inactive for some days, for I hoped that the dilatory Grand Admiral Magassa would appear with his canoes. Indeed, I could suggest no reason, despite our experience at Bumbireh, why he should not arrive. He had been to Usukuma on a visit some months previous to my advent in the country, and he was accompanied by two of my best men, who, of course, would do their utmost to stimulate him to make renewed efforts to reach our camp. But when nine days had passed and Magassa had not made it his appearance it became obvious to us all he would not come. Preparations were therefore made to march overland to Uganda along the lake shore.

As we were almost ready to start there came an embassy to camp from Ruwoma, King of Southern Uzinza or Mweri, bearing a message from him to me. The message ran, according to the interpreter, as follows: "Ruwoma sends salaams to the white man. He does not want the white man's cloth, beads or wire, but the white man must not pass through his country. Ruwoma does not want to see him, or any other man with long red hair down to his shoulders, white face, and big red eyes.[4] Ruwoma is not afraid of him, but if the white man will come near his country Ruwoma and Mirambo will fight him."

Here, indeed, was a dilemma. The lake journey to Uganda was impossible, because Magassa proved a recreant to the trust reposed in him by Mtesa; the land journey now became impossible because Ruwoma forbade it. We knew enough of Ruwoma to know that he was able to repulse two such expeditions as ours. He possessed 150

---

3. Kajuri was the battle at Bumbire Island.
4. Stanley commented: "it was probably Frank [Pocock], though a libellous caricature of him certainly." *TDC*, I, 246.

muskets of his own, and had several thousand spearmen and bowmen. Besides, Mirambo was but a day's march from Urima, and
but three days from our camp. To force a passage through Ruwoma's country was therefore out of the question. Even if the feat
were possible it would be bad policy, because the expedition would
lose too many valuable lives, without whom the expedition would
become a wreck. What was to be done, then? Turn away from the
Albert Niyanza, and direct our course for the Tanganyika, leaving
the former lake to be explored by Gordon's officers? Who, then,
would explore the debatable land lying between the Albert Niyanza
and the Tanganyika? Again the question came—What is to be done?

If canoes could be obtained anywhere else than Uganda the lake
route to Uganda would at once resolve the question. But what country or king could supply me with thirty or forty large canoes on
demand other than Uganda? I instituted inquiries respecting the
maritime power of each tribe and nation bordering on Speke Gulf,
by which I obtained some curious statistics; but the most valuable
result of my inquiries was the information that Lukongeh, King of
Ukerewe, would be the most likely person to do me the necessary
service. Falling seriously ill, the result of exposure on the lake,
added to the present anxiety, I was obliged to send Frank Pocock
and Prince Kaduma to the King of Ukerewe with a suitable gift to
request the loan of forty canoes to convey the expedition to Uganda
along the Uzinza coast.[5] After an absence of twelve days Frank
and Kaduma returned with fifty canoes and some 300 Wakerewe,
but they came according to the King's instructions to convey the
expedition to Ukerewe. The King's brother, who had charge of the
canoes, was told by me that if Lukongeh gave me all his land and
slaves and cattle the expedition should never go to Ukerewe; that
Lukongeh must lend me canoes to go by my road, and no other, and
that I was going myself to see Lukongeh, and he (the King's brother)
might return to Ukerewe as soon as he pleased.

Being sufficiently restored to health I set sail for Ukerewe, and
on the second day from Kagehyi landed near Lukongeh's capital.
Not ignorant of the importance of first impressions I was furnished
this time with proper gifts and the best apparel my wardrobe afforded, and, equipped with the best arms, the expedition possessed.
The second day after our arrival was fixed for audience day. When
the hour had come the crew of the *Lady Alice* were mustered,
dressed in their smartest, and the bugle sounded the order to march.

---

5. See Pocock's account of his trip, Appendix R.

Ten minutes brought us to a plain, on a knoll in which Lukongeh was seated in state, surrounded by hundreds of bowmen and spearmen. The King, an amiable, light-colored young man, was conspicuous from his robe of red and yellow silk damask cloth, and, though he did nothing at first but good-naturedly stare at me, I perceived that he was a man disposed to assist me.

A private message beforehand had informed him of the object of my visit, but my interpreter requested that I should be permitted to state it in person to himself and a few select chiefs. Assenting to this request, he stepped forward to a pole of stones a short distance off, whither he invited his most select chiefs and my party. Here the object was stated clearly, with everything that concerned it, the number of canoes required, the distance we had to travel and the gifts that were to be given by me to the King should he assist me. The King listened attentively, was very affable and kind, depreciated the value of his canoes, said that they were rotten, unfit for a long voyage, and he feared that if he gave them to me I should lose a great many things, and then I would certainly blame him and say, "Ah! Lukongeh is bad; he gave me rotten canoes that I might lose my people and property." I replied that if I lost people and property I might blame the canoes, but I should certainly not think of blaming him. At the end of the conference he said that he should give me as many canoes as I wanted, but in the meantime the white man's party must rest a few days and taste of Lukongeh's cheer.

It were well, perhaps, to enter here into a description of Ukerewe, its king and people, and into its history, which is very curious and instructive, and well explains the history of all the black races of Africa from Kaffraria to Nubia; but I have no time nor space to do them justice. At a future time, if nothing between happens, I promise to attempt the subject.

Lukongeh, the very amiable King of Ukerewe, was no niggard in his hospitality. Beeves and goats, chickens and milk and eggs, bananas and plantains, ripe and green, came in abundance to our camp; neither were large supplies of native beer wanting to cheer the crew during our stay in the land.

Finally, on the fifteenth day, Lukongeh came to my tent with his chief councillor and imparted to me his secret instructions and advice. He said he had ordered fifty canoes to depart with me to Usukuma, but he doubted much whether that number would leave his country, as his people had heard it reported that I was going to Uganda, to which country no one was willing to go. As he desired to assist me to the utmost of his power he had been obliged to have recourse to a little strategy. He had caused it to be reported that he had prevailed on me to come and live in his land; it was therefore necessary for me to second his strategy. On reaching Usukuma, as soon as all the canoes had been drawn on shore, I was to seize them and secure the paddles, and having rendered the Wakerewe unable to return, I was to explain to them what I wanted. Having promised that I would implicitly obey all his instructions he sent his Prime Minister and two favorites to assist me in the project, and after an earnest of what I promised was given we were permitted to depart.

On arriving at our camp in Usukuma I found only twenty-three canoes come ashore, and though these were quite inadequate to convey the expedition at one time, I resolved to make the best I could of even this small number, and accordingly whispered orders to the captains of the expedition to muster up their men and seize the canoes and paddles. This was done, and the canoes drawn far on land; but the Wakerewe, on being told why we had so acted, declared war against us, and being as strong in numbers as we were, and armed with bows and sheaves of arrows, were very likely to do some damage if I did not take energetic measures to prevent them. Accordingly every soldier of the expedition was summoned by bugle sound to prepare for battle, and having seen each one properly equipped, I drew the men in line, charged on the Wakerewe with the muzzles of our guns, and forcibly ejected them out of camp and the vicinity of the port.

A few harmless shots were fired, and the people of Lukongeh suffered no other injuries than a few sore ribs from our gun muzzles. On the third day after the bloodless affair I embarked two-thirds of the expedition and property in the canoes, and five days afterward arrived safely at Refuge Island, two days' sail from Bumbireh and half way to Uganda. The mainland was about six miles off; and as, on my solitary journey in the boat the natives of the mainland were not very friendly disposed, I built a strong camp on the rocks, taking advantage of each high rock as positions for sharpshooters, so that the camp, during my absence, would be impregnable. I then returned to Usukuma after leaving fifty soldiers to defend that island, and after an absence of fifteen days saw Kagehyi once more. I now prepared myself to defeat the projects of Kaduma, Prince of Kagehyi, who was more than half inclined to second his brother Kipingiri to seize on me and hold me as his prisoner until I should pay a heavy ransom, probably half of our entire property. I spoke Kaduma fair each day, made small presents to his favorite wife until the day came for departing, as I sincerely hoped forever, from Kagehyi and

Usukuma. On that day Kaduma and Kipingiri came to the water's edge with a strong force, but, pretending to see nothing of their evil intentions, we made merry and laughed while we loaded the canoe and embarked the men.

When the work of embarkation was nearly concluded I proceeded leisurely to the boat, and shoved off from the shore with my guns and those of the boat's crew ready. Kaduma, seeing that I had got away, left the port, leaving Kipingiri to act as he pleased; but this treacherous man, perceiving himself covered with our guns, permitted the last canoe to depart without molesting it; and, having seen all safely off, I waved the treacherous people a last farewell, and followed our miniature fleet.[6] The rotten canoes, buffeted by storms and waves, fast gave out, so that, on arriving again at Refuge Island, we only had fifteen left. Nothing had occurred on the island to mar my joy at seeing my people all safe, but much had happened to improve it. The King of Itawagumba and Kijaju, his father, Sultan of all the islands from Ukereweh to Ihangiro,[7] perceiving our island too well garrisoned and too strong for invasion, made friends with us and provided the soldiers with abundance of food at little cost. At my request also they furnished us with a guide to Ihangiro, who was to accompany us to Uganda; they also sold us three canoes. After a few days' rest on Refuge Island we proceeded once again on our voyage, and halted at Mahyiga Island, five miles south of Bumbireh, and one mile south of Iroba, which lay between Mahyiga and Bumbireh. Remembering the bitter injuries I had received from the natives of Bumbireh, the death by violence and starvation we had so narrowly escaped, I resolved, unless the natives made amends of their cruelty and treachery, to make war on them, and for this purpose I camped on Mahyiga Island and sent the canoes back for the remainder of the expedition, which in a few days safely arrived.[8]

6. There is no reference to this episode in TDC, I, 267, or Diary, 87.
7. Kyigaju, or Kijaju, was the ruler of Kome Island off the Zinza coast. Gray, "Mackay's Canoe Voyage along the Western Shore of Lake Victoria in 1883," 19; Peters, Deutsch-Ostafrikanische Schutzgebiet, 186; Cory and Masulu, "Place Names in the Lake Province," 68.
8. Stanley has several differing accounts of the following attack on Bumbire. Diary, 88–96, has important differences of detail, but agrees in the main with the newspaper recounting. In Yule and Hyndman, Stanley and the R.G.S., 36–38, there is an account taken from a speech of Stanley's where he quotes from his "private journal" to defend his actions; the sections are brief and do not agree with the events listed for the same dates in Diary. But in TDC, I, 271–94, Stanley clearly restates the affair to put his African opponents in the wrong, making his proceedings purely a consequence of their determination to block him on the way to Buganda. In the process Stanley even adds a quotation from Livingstone to uphold his conduct.

I sent a message to the natives of Bumbireh to the effect that, if they delivered their King and the two principals under him to my hands, I would make peace with them. At the same time, not trusting quite the success of this, I sent a party to invite the King of Iroba, who very willingly came, with three of his chiefs, to save his people from the horrors of war. Upon their arrival I put them in chains, and told the canoemen that the price of their freedom was the capture of the King of Bumbireh and his two principal chiefs. The natives of Bumbireh treated my message with contempt, but the next morning the people of Iroba brought the King of Bumbireh to me, who was at once chained heavily, while the King of Iroba and his people were released, with a promise that neither his island nor people would be touched by us. A message was also sent to Antari,[9] King of Ihangiro, on the mainland, to whom Bumbireh was tributary, requesting him to redeem his island from war. Antari sent his son and two chiefs to us, who told us so many falsehoods and had treachery written on their faces, to treat with us.

They brought a few bunches of bananas as an earnest of what the King intended to give; but I thought that such a bird in my hand as his son would be worth a thousand tedious promises, and accordingly his son and his two chiefs were seized as hostages for the appearance of the two chiefs of Bumbireh. In the meantime seven large canoes from Mtesa, King of Uganda, *en route* to Usukuma, to convey an Arab and his goods to Uganda, appeared at Iroba. The chief was requested not to proceed to Usukuma until we had taken our expedition to Uganda.

This chief, Sabadu,[10] informed me that Magassa, the dilatory Grand Admiral, had returned with the boat's oars to Mtesa and the news that I and my crew were dead, for which he had been chained, but subsequently released and sent by land, with a large party, to hunt up certain news of me. Sabadu was induced, after a little persuasion, to accede to my request.

Two days after his arrival Sabadu sent his Waganda to Bumbireh to procure food. The savages would not give them any, but attacked

9. Ntari II, ruler of the Haya state of Ihangiro. See Cory, *Historia ya Bukoba,* 35–51, 111–113.

10. The *ssabaddu,* Kapalaga, gave Stanley much of the information concerning Buganda in *TDC,* I, 344ff. He became *mujasi,* the commander-in-chief of the *kabaka's* permanent military force, and he played a prominent role as one of the Muslim leaders against the Ganda Christians. He was killed in the Ganda troubles of 1888. Faupel, *African Holocaust,* 69; Ashe, *Chronicles of Uganda,* 80, 112; Ashe, *Two Kings of Uganda,* 136ff. For the positions of *ssabaddu* and *mujasi,* Fallers, *Eastern Lacustrine Bantu,* 64.

them, wounding eight and killing a chief of Kattawa's,[11] a neighbor
of Antari, which gave me another strong reason why Bumbireh
should be punished. Accordingly next morning I prepared a force
of 280 men, 50 muskets, 230 spearmen, and placed them in eighteen
canoes. About noon we set off, and, as Bumbireh was eight miles
off, we did not reach the island until two P.M. The natives of Bumbireh seemed to know by instinct that this was to be a day of
trouble, for every height had its lookout ready, and when they saw
the force I had brought with me no doubt many of them regretted
that they had been so prone to attack peaceable strangers. Through
my field glass I observed messengers running fast to a plantain
grove that stood in a low hill commanding a clear open view of a
little port at the southern end of the island, from which I concluded
that the main force of the savages was hidden behind the grove.
Calling the canoes together I told the chiefs to follow my boat and
steer exactly as I steered, and by no means to attempt to land, as
I did not intend that a single soul with me should be hurt. I wished
to punish Bumbireh, not to punish myself; and if a subject of Mtesa
was lost how should I present myself to him? And I could not afford
to lose a single soldier of my own.

Accordingly I rowed straight to the port, the canoes following
closely, and we became hid from view of those in the plantain grove
and of all lookouts; then, turning west, we skirted close to the land
for a mile, until we came to a cape, after rounding which we came
in view of a noble bay, into which we steered. By this manoeuvre
I managed to come behind the enemy, who was revealed in all his
strength. Perceiving that the savages of Bumbireh were too strong
for me to attack them in the plantain grove I steered for the opposite
shore of the bay, where there were bare slopes of hills covered with
short green grass. The savages, perceiving my intention to disembark on the opposite shore, rose from their coverts and ran along
the hill slopes to meet us, which was precisely what I wished they
would do, and accordingly I ordered my force to paddle slowly so
as to give them time. In half an hour the savages were all assembled on the bare slope of a hill in knots and groups, and after approaching within 100 yards of the shore I formed my line of battle,
the American and English flags waving as our ensigns. Having anchored each canoe so as to turn its broadside to the shore I ordered

11. Stanley names him Kytawa instead of Kattawa, and refers to him as ruler
of Usongora, in *TDC*, I, 285, 376. Stanley probably refers to Kaitaba, one
of the Kiamtwara chiefs. See Cory, *Historia ya Bukoba*, 63–65; Mors, "Geschichte der Bahinda des alten Kyamtwara," 711.

a volley to be fired at one group which numbered about fifty, and the result was ten killed and thirty wounded. The savages, perceiving our aim and the danger of standing in groups, separated themselves along the lake shore, and advanced to the water's edge slinging stones and shooting arrows. I then ordered the canoes to advance within fifty yards of the shore, and to fire as if they were shooting birds. After an hour the savages saw that they could not defend themselves at the water's edge, and retreated up the hill slope, where they continued still exposed to our bullets.

Another hour was passed in this manner. I then caused the canoes to come together, and told them to advance in a body to the shore as if they were about to disembark. This caused the enemy to make an effort to repulse our landing, and, accordingly, hundreds came down with their spears ready on the launch. When they were close to the water's edge the bugle sounded a halt and another volley was fired into the dense crowd, which had such a disastrous effect on them that they retired far up the hill, and our work of punishment was consummated.

About 700 cartridges were fired, but as the savages were so exposed, on a slope covered with only short grass, and as the sun in the afternoon was directly behind us and in their faces, their loss was very great. Forty-two were counted on the field, lying dead, and over 100 were seen to retire wounded, while on our side only two men suffered contusions from stones slung at us. Thus I had not only the King and one chief of the Bumbireh in my power, but I had the son of Antari and an important chief of his also, besides punishing the natives so severely.

When our force saw that the savages were defeated the chiefs begged earnestly that I would permit them to land and destroy the people altogether; but I refused, saying that I had not come to destroy the island, but to punish them for their treachery and attempted murder of myself and the boat's crew, when we had put faith in their professed friendship. It was dark when we arrived at our camp, but at the sound of our bugle lights flew all over the island camp, where we presently arrived, and where we were received with shouts and songs of triumph.

The next morning, more canoes having arrived from Uganda, I embarked the entire expedition, and sailed from Mahyiga Island. Our fleet of canoes now numbered thirty-two, and as we steered close to Bumbireh I had an opportunity of observing the effect of the punishment on the natives, and I was gratified to see that their boldness and audacity were completely crushed, for one bullet put to flight over 100 of them, whereas the day before they had bravely stood before a volley. Others who came down to the shore begged us to go away, and not to hunt them any more, which gave me an opportunity to preach to them that they brought the punishment on their own heads for attempting the murder of peaceful strangers. In the evening we camped on the mainland, in the territory of King Kattawa, who treated us most royally for avenging the murder of his chief by the people of Bumbireh.

After stopping with him a day we camped on Msira Island, where the Waganda, under the Grand Admiral Magassa, so shamefully deserted me. This island is nearly opposite Makongo, where the natives had thought to attack us on our first journey.[12] But the fame of what I had done at Bumbireh compelled them on this occasion to bring me five cattle, four goats and 100 bunches of bananas, besides honey, milk and eggs, as a propitiatory offering. Kayozza,[13] the King of Usongora, also sent word to me that he had given his people orders to give me whatever I desired, even to 100 cattle. I told him I needed none of his cattle, but if he would lend me ten canoes to carry my people to Uganda I would consider him as a friend. Ten canoes were accordingly brought the next day to me, with their crews. Sabadu, the Waganda chief, earnestly requested that I would attack him, as Kayozza had committed several murderous acts on the Waganda; but I refused, saying that attacking black people when they desired peace was not the custom with white people, and that I would not have attacked Bumbireh had they shown that they were sorry for what they had done to me, with which Sabadu was satisfied.

Five days after leaving Bumbireh, the expedition landed and camped at Dumo, Uganda, which is two days' march north of the Kagera River and two days south of the Katonga River. This camp I selected for the expedition because it was intermediate, whence I could start on a northwest, west or southwest course for the Albert Niyanza, after ascertaining from Mtesa which was best. For between the Victoria Niyanza and the Albert Niyanza are very powerful tribes, the Wasagara,[14] Wa Ruanda, and Wasangora[15] especially, who are continually at war with Mtesa.

Our loss on the lake during our travel by water from Usukuma

12. See document 24, note 4.
13. Kahyoza was the ruler of the Haya state of Bugabo. Cory, *Historia ya Bukoba*, 131–33; Junker, *Travels in Africa during the Years 1882–1886*, 533–57.
14. The Nyankore of Western Uganda; see document 26, note 6.
15. Inhabitants of the region between lakes George and Edward; Busongora became one of the divisions of Toro. Taylor, *Western Lacustrine Bantu*, 41–71.

to Dumo, Uganda, a distance of nearly 220 miles, was six men drowned, five guns and one case of ammunition. Three of the riding asses also died from being bound in the canoes, which leaves me now but one. Ten of our canoes became wrecks also. The time occupied by the lake journey was fifty-six days; but as 200 miles of the journey were traversed three times it will be seen that we travelled in fifty-six days over 720 miles of water. During fifty-one days the corn I had brought from Usukuma in the canoes was almost entirely the means of sustaining the expedition; for though we received food from Itawagumba and Kijuju of Komeh, we received it because it was their good will that gave it us. Excepting twenty doti of cloth given to these two kings no other cloth was used, so that we lived nearly two months on the bale of cloth which purchased the corn in Usukuma. I have, therefore, every reason to feel gratified at the result of this long journey by water, though the loss of my men and guns gives me serious regret, and the loss of all the riding asses is a calamity. On the other hand, had I forced my way overland through Mirambo and Ruwoma, I should have been either dead or a ruined fugitive.

After arranging the camp I intend to visit Mtesa once more, who may be able to give me guides to the Albert Niyanza, for doubtless he has several men who have traded with the natives bordering that lake. My European servant, Frank Pocock, enjoys his health amazingly, and seems to have become acclimated to Africa.

26

Kawanga, Frontier Village, between Unyoro and Uganda, Central Africa
January 18, 1876 [1]

Six days ago the Anglo-American expedition, under my command, and 2,000 choice spearmen of Uganda under the command of "General" Samboozi,[2] were encamped at Unyampaka,[3] Unyoro, on the

1. *NYH*, Aug. 11, 1876.
2. A later visitor would call Sembuzi "one of the most intelligent of Mtesa's chiefs." Wilson and Felkin, *Uganda*, I, 103, 258. For some of his other activities, Faupel, *African Holocaust*, 106; Taylor, *The Growth of the Church in Buganda*, 34, 36, 50.
3. The Banyampaka, a Hororo group, lived in Bunyaruguru, to the east of Lake Edward. Taylor, *Western Lacustrine Bantu*, 98; Meldon, "Notes on the Bahima of Ankole," 138, 140, 245; Morris, "The Making of Ankole," 9–10.

shore of the Albert Niyanza.[4] Mtesa, Emperor of Uganda, faithfully fulfilled his promise to me so far as to furnish me with force
sufficient to pierce the hostile country of Kabba Rega[5] and to penetrate to the Albert Niyanza, near which we were encamped three
days. But though we were successful so far as to reach the lake,
drink of its waters, take a couple of astronomical observations and
procure much information respecting the contiguous countries, I
soon perceived that exploration of the lake was out of the question,
unless I then and there resolved to terminate my journey with the
exploration of the Albert. For having penetrated by force through
Kabba Rega's country, it would have been folly to expect that 2,200
men could long occupy Unyampaka in the face of the thousands
which Kabba Rega, King of Unyoro, and Mtambuko, King of Ankori,[6]
would array against them.

Ever since Sir Samuel Baker and his Egyptian force provoked the
hostility of the successor to Kamrasi,[7] Unyoro is a closed country to
any man of a pale complexion, be he Arab, Turk[8] or European. Besides, Gordon's officers in the north frequently engage the Wanyoro
wherever they are met, and thus the hate which Kabba Rega bears
to Europeans is not diminishing. South of Unyoro extends the
country of Ankori inhabited by a powerful tribe, whose numbers
have generally been found sufficient to give Mtesa measure for measure and blow for blow, and whose ferocity and singular aversion to
strangers have compelled all trading caravans to keep clear of them.

Upon considering the chances of success along the various routes
to Lake Albert it became too evident to me that, unaided by a force
of Waganda, I could not so much as reach the lake, and that even
with the Waganda, unless the Emperor assisted me with 50,000 or
60,000, it would be almost hopeless to expect that we could hold
our ground long enough to enable me to set out on a two months'
voyage of exploration, and find on my return the expedition still

4. Stanley was on the escarpment above Lake George, the small lake connected to Lake Edward by the Kazinga Channel. He was not then aware he
had reached a lake unknown to Europeans. His route there is mentioned in
Langlands, "Early Travellers in Uganda: 1860–1914," 58.

5. Cwa II Kabarega, ruler of Bunyoro from about 1870 to 1899, when he
was deposed and exiled by the British; he died in 1923. Dunbar, *A History of
Bunyoro-Kitara*, 58ff.

6. Mutambukwa, ruler of Nkore (Ankole); he died in 1878. See Low,
"Northern Interior," 336; Morris, "Making of Ankole," 4–5. For Ankole, Taylor,
Western Lacustrine Bantu, 95–114.

7. Kyebambe IV Kamurasi, ruler of Bunyoro from the early 1850's until his
death about 1869. For his career, Dunbar, *History of Bunyoro*, 51–58.

8. The usual designation for officials of the Egyptian forces to the north of
Bunyoro.

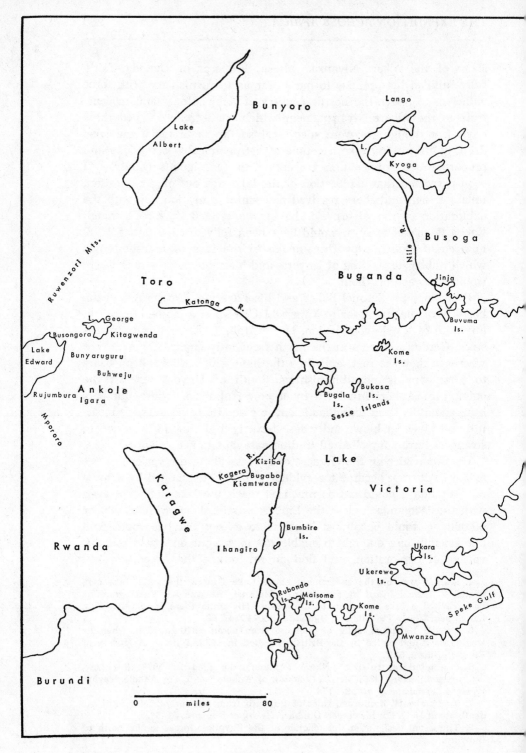

Map III. Uganda and the Victoria region

intact and safe. On representing these ideas to the Emperor he and his chiefs assured me that 2,000 men were amply sufficient, as Kabba Rega would not dare lift a spear against the Waganda, because it was he (Mtesa) who had seated Kabba Rega on the throne of Kamrasi.[9] Though not quite convinced with the assurances Mtesa gave me that there would be no trouble I entreated him no further, but accepted thankfully General Samboozi and 2,000 men as escort.

Our march across Uganda, west and northwest, was uninterrupted by any event to mar the secret joy I felt in being once more on the move to new fields of exploration. We made a brave show of spears and guns while marching across the easy swells of pastoral Western Uganda. Game was also abundant, and twenty-seven harte beests fell victims to my love of hunting and our necessities of life.

Having arrived at the frontier of Unyoro we made all warlike preparations, and on January 5 entered Kabba Rega's territory. The people fled before us, leaving their provisions in their haste behind them, of which we made free use. On the 9th we camped at the base of the tremendous mountain called Kabuga,[10] at an altitude of 5,500 feet above the sea. East of the low ridge on which we camped the Katonga River was rounding from the north to the east on its course toward Lake Victoria, and west of the camp the Rusango River boomed hoarse thunder from its many cataracts and falls as it rushed westward to Lake Albert. From one of the many spurs of Kabuga we obtained a passing glimpse of the king of mountains, Gambaragara,[11] which attains an altitude of between 13,000 and 15,000 feet above the ocean. Snow is frequently seen, though not perpetual. On its summit dwell the chief medicine men of Kabba Rega, a people of European complexion.

Some half dozen of these people[12] I have seen, and at sight of

9. There was no foundation to this story. Dunbar, *History of Bunyoro*, 58.

10. Kabuga Hill in Toro. Stanley gave it the name Mt. Edwin Arnold after the editor of the *Daily Telegraph*, but the name did not last. *TDC*, I, 432 (where Stanley gives the height as 9,000 feet); Thomas and Dale, "Uganda Place Names," 109.

11. A Baganda name for the Ruwenzori mountains; the highest peak, Mt. Stanley, reaches 16,794 feet. Stanley named the peak he saw Mt. Gordon Bennett, but the location he gives does not fit any of the Ruwenzori group. *Ibid.*, 111; *TDC*, I, 431; Bere, "Exploration of the Ruwenzori." See Appendix T, note 3. Another report concerning the summit of Gambaragara held that a deity resided there; offerings were made to it during smallpox epidemics. Felkin, "Notes on the Waganda Tribe of Central Africa," 704; Wilson, "Uganda et Lac Victoria," 22.

12. Bahuma, or Bahima, pastoralists. Their position in the various entities of this area is discussed in Taylor, *Western Lacustrine Bantu*, *passim*. Johnston said of the Ankole Bahima, "I have seen some men and women so light in complexion that I actually thought they were some of Emin Pasha's refugee Egyptians." Johnston, "The Uganda Protectorate, Ruwenzori, and the Semliki

them I was reminded of what Mukamba, King of Uzige, told Livingstone and myself respecting white people who live far north of his country. They are a handsome race, and some of the women are singularly beautiful. Their hair is kinky, but inclined to brown in color. Their features are regular, lips thin, but their noses, though well shaped, are somewhat thick at the point. Several of their descendants are scattered throughout Unyoro, Ankori and Ruanda, and the royal family of the latter powerful country are distinguished, I am told, by their pale complexions. The Queen of Sasua Islands, in the Victoria Niyanza, is a descendant of this tribe.

Whence came this singular people I have had no means of ascertaining except from the Waganda, who say the first King of Unyoro gave them the land around the base of Gambaragara Mountain, wherein through many vicissitudes they have continued to reside for centuries. On the approach of an invading host they retreat to the summit of the mountain, the intense cold of which defies the most determined of their enemies. Two years ago Emperor Mtesa despatched his Prime Minister with about 100,000 men to Gambaragara and Usongora; but though the great General of Uganda occupied the slopes and ascended a great height in pursuit, he was compelled by inclement climate to descend without having captured more than few black slaves, the pale-faced tribe having retreated to their impregnable fortress at the summit.

The mountain, it appears, is an extinct volcano, for on the summit is a crystal clear lake, about 500 yards in length, from the centre of which rises a column-like rock to a great height. A rim of firm rock, like a wall, surrounds the summit, within which are several villages, where the principal medicine man and his people reside.

Two men of this tribe, who might be taken at first glance for Greeks in white shirts, accompanied Sekajugu, a sub chief under Samboozi, and our expedition to Lake Albert and back to Uganda, but they were extremely uncommunicative, and nothing of the history of their tribe could I obtain from them. Their diet consists of milk and bananas, and they were the only men of rank in the entire force under Samboozi who possessed more than two milch cows to supply them with milk while on the march. Sekajugu, to whom they were friendly and under whom they had enrolled themselves, states that they rebelled against Kabba Rega, and, to avoid his vengeance, sought refuge with him.

Forest," 25. Stories of these "whites" were of course common throughout East Africa. See for example M. W. Shepard's account in Bennett and Brooks, *New England Merchants,* 263.

Another specimen of this tribe of white complexioned people I saw at the Court of Mtesa in the person of Prince Namionju, the brother of the reigning King Nyika of Gambaragara.[13] When I first saw him I took him for a young Arab of Cairo, who had taken up his residence in Uganda for some unknown reason, and it was not until I had seen several specimens of the same pale color that I could believe that there existed a large and numerous tribe of people of such a singular color in the heart of Africa, remote from the track of all travellers and trading caravans.

Africa is certainly the "haunt of light-headed fable," romance and superstition, but I shall believe hereafter that there exists some slight modicum of truth in all the statements and revelations of these simple people. On the shores of the Victoria, in Usukuma, I heard of a people far north possessing very large dogs, of such fierce nature that they were often taken to war against the enemies of their masters. These people I subsequently ascertained to be the Wakedi,[14] a tribe living north of Usoga. The same people also, in their various wars with Uganda, have been found wearing iron armor. About four years ago, when exploring the Tanganyika with Livingstone, I heard there existed a race of white people north of Uzige. At that time Livingstone and myself smiled at the absurdity of a white people living in the heart of Africa, and ascribed the report to the brown color of the Warundi. Now I have not only seen the country of these white people, but several specimens of themselves at different periods and in different places. Were it not for the negroid hair I should say they were Europeans or some light-colored Asiatics, such as Syrians or Armenians. Apropos of these singular people, I have heard that the first King of Kishakka,[15] a country southwest of Karagwe, was an Arab, whose scimitar is still pre-

13. Stanley apparently meant Nyaika of Toro; he died in 1878. There was then a war over the succession, with Namuyonjo, a Toro prince, winning out through Ganda aid. Low, "The Northern Interior," 344–45.

14. A popular term generally held to mean the "Naked People," or the "People of the East." It referred to the Lango and other groups to the east of Buganda and Bunyoro. Driberg, "The Lango District, Uganda Protectorate," 119; Driberg, *The Lango*, 36; LaFontaine, *The Gisu of Uganda*, 9; Hobley, "Kavirondo," 366. The tales Stanley heard about the Kedi were also reported, with some other variations, in Speke, *Journal of the Discovery*, 89–90, and Grant, "Summary of Observations on the Geography, Climate, and Natural History of the Lake Region of Equatorial Africa . . . ," 261–63.

15. Gissaka, a once independent state on the western side of the Kagera River. It was incorporated into Rwanda in the 1840's or 1850's by Mutara II Lwogera. Bourgeois, *Banyarwanda et Barundi*, I, 144, 174–75; Pagès, *Un Royaume Hamite au Centre de l'Afrique*, 149–51; Elliot, *A Naturalist in Mid-Africa*, 241, 256.

served with great reverence by the present reigning family of Kishakka.

Our further passage to Lake Albert was along the southern bank
of the Rusango River, which winds in and out among deep mountain folds, and rushes headlong on its course in roaring cataracts
and brawling rapids. Ten hours' swift marching enabled us to cross
an uninhabited tract of Ankori and emerge again in Unyoro, in the
district of Kitagwenda,[16] which is well populated and cultivated.
Our sudden appearance on the scene, with drums beating, colors
flying and bugles blowing, drove the natives in a panic from their
fields and their houses in such hot haste that many of our people
found the family porridge still cooking and great pots full of milk
standing ready for the evening meal.

It had previously been agreed upon between "General" Samboozi
and myself that if the natives chose to permit our peaceful passage
through Unyoro that no violence was to be done to any person. But
at Kitagwenda we found ourselves in possession of a populous and
thriving district, with not a single native near us to give us information. Lake Albert, on the evening of January 9, was about three
miles due west from us, and it behooved us that we might not be
surprised to obtain information as to the feelings of the natives
toward us. Samboozi was clever enough to perceive our position,
and he consented to send out 200 men next morning as scouts, and
to capture a few men through whom we could communicate with
the chief of Kitagwenda, and satisfy him that if unmolested we
had no hostile intention, and, if permitted to reside two months,
would pay him cloth, beads or wire for whatever we consumed.

The next day was a halt, and the scouts brought in five natives,
who were sent with a peaceful message to the chief. The chief did
not deign to answer us, though we knew he resided on the summit of
a mountain close by. On the 11th we moved our camp to within
one mile of the edge of the plateau, a thousand feet below which
was the Albert Niyanza. Here we constructed our camp on the morning of the 11th, and, receiving no word from the chief of the Kitagwenda or of Unyampaka, sent 500 Waganda and fifty of the Anglo-
American Expedition to seek out a locality for a fenced camp, and
to seize upon all canoes along the coast at the base of the plateau
on which we were camped. In about three hours the reconnoitering
party returned, bringing information that they had only succeeded
in securing five small canoes, too small to be of any service to us,

16. A Lacustrine state located to the east of Lake George. It became part of
Toro during the period of British rule in Uganda. Lugard, *The Rise of Our
East African Empire*, II, 262; Taylor, *Western Lacustrine Bantu*, 20, 97.

and that the alarm had already spread far along the coast that a large force of strangers had arrived at the lake for war purposes.

The 12th was spent by me in endeavoring to induce Samboozi to move to the lake, that we might build a fortified camp and put the boat *Lady Alice* together, but it was in vain. The natives had by this time recovered their wits, and, strongly reinforced from the neighboring districts, they were preparing themselves for an effort to punish us for our temerity, and, by the impunity they enjoyed from attack, they occupied all the heights and villages east of our camp. Once we sallied out of our camp for a battle; but the natives, while withdrawing, told us to keep our strength for the next day. Unable to persuade Samboozi to move his camp or stay longer than the next day, there remained for us only to return with them to Uganda, for among such people it was useless to think for a moment that a peaceable residence would be permitted. Besides the country was Unyoro and Kabba Rega, the enemy of the Europeans at Gondokoro was the King. Therefore a peaceful solution of our difficulty was out of the question. Accordingly, on the night of the 12th it was resolved to return and try to discover some other country where the expedition could camp in safety while I explored the lake in the *Lady Alice*.

On the morning of the 13th we set out on our return from the lake in order of battle, 500 spearmen in front, 500 spearmen for rear guard, 1,000 spearmen and the expedition in the centre. Whether it was our compact column that prevented an attack or not I cannot say. We were, however, permitted to leave the country of Kitagwenda unmolested, the natives merely closing in on our rear to snatch stragglers. On the 14th our expedition comprised the rear guard, and as we entered Benga, in Unyoro, the natives rushed from some woods to attack us, but a few rounds of ball cartridge dispersed them. On the 18th we re-entered Uganda.[17]

However slightly your readers may think of our trip to the Albert, honestly I do not suppose I have been guilty of such a harebrained attempt as this before. Looking calmly at it now, I regard it as great folly, but the success of having penetrated through Unyoro and reached the Albert redeemed it somewhat from absurdity. I sometimes think, though it would have been entirely contrary to orders, that, having reached the Albert, it would have been better to have launched the boat and explore the lake, leaving the expedi-

17. A historian of Bunyoro indicates that Kabarega opposed the progress of the expedition since the Ganda with Stanley had ruined the country passed through, but that since the expedition left quickly they were not opposed. Dunbar, *History of Bunyoro*, 63.

tion to take care of itself, to perish or survive my absence. But I thought it too great a pity that a first class expedition, in first class order should terminate on the shore of the Albert, and if one road was closed there might probably be others open; and after much deliberation with myself I resolved to return and endeavor to discover countries more amenable to reason and open to friendly gifts than hostile Unyoro or incorrigible Ankori.

Though we made strict inquiries we could discover no news of Gordon or his steamers. The natives of Unyampaka had never heard of a ship or any vessel larger than a canoe; and it is impossible that a vessel so singular as a steamer could approach near Usongora without the news of so singular an apparition becoming notorious.

The geographical knowledge we have been able to acquire by our forcible push to the Albert Niyanza is considerable. The lay of the plateau separating the great reservoirs of the Nile, the Victoria and Albert Niyanzas, the structure of the mountains and ridges, and the course of the watersheds, and the course of the rivers Katonga and Rusango have been revealed. The great mountain Gambaragara and its singular people have been discovered, besides a portion of a gulf of the Albert, which I have taken the liberty to call, in honor of Her Royal Highness Princess Beatrice, Beatrice Gulf.[18]

This gulf, almost a lake of itself, is formed by the promontory of Usongora, which runs southwest some thirty miles from a point ten geographical miles north of Unyampaka. The eastern coast of the Gulf is formed by the countries of Irangara, Unyampaka, Buhuju and Mpororo, which coast line runs a nearly south-southwest course.[19] Between Mpororo and Usongora extend the islands of the maritime State of Utumbi.[20] West of Usongora is Ukonju, on the western coast of Lake Albert, reputed to be peopled by cannibals.[21] North of Ukonju is the great country of Ulegga.[22]

18. Beatrice (1857–1944), a daughter of Queen Victoria. She had been present at Stanley's meeting with Victoria in 1872. The name, given of course to a part of Lake George, did not last. Thomas and Dale, "Uganda Place Names," 107–08; *Autobiography*, 290.

19. Igara (or Irangara) and Buhweju (or Buhuju) were independent states until absorbed into Ankole. Mpororo, also formerly an independent state, once comprised territory now in Ankole, Rwanda, and Kigezi. Morris, *A History of Ankole;* Taylor, *Western Lacustrine Bantu*, 14, 96–99.

20. The area to the south of Lake Edward; probably the state of Rujumbura. *Ibid.*, 114–32; Stuhlmann, *Mit Emin Pascha*, 250ff.

21. The Konjo live on and around the Ruwenzori Mountains. Taylor, *Western Lacustrine Bantu*, 89–95. See Roscoe, *The Bagesu*, 140, on their cannibalism.

22. The Lendu are often termed the Lega. Murdock, *Africa*, 226. See Baxter and Butt, *The Azande and Related Peoples of the Anglo-Egyptian Sudan and*

Coming to the eastern coast of Lake Albert we have Ruanda running from Mpororo on the east to Ukonju on the west, occupying the whole of the south and southeast coast of Lake Albert. North of Unyampaka, on the east side, is Irangara and north of Irangara the district of Toro.[23] Unyoro occupies the whole of the east side from the Murchison Falls of the Victoria Nile to Mpororo, for Unyampaka, Toro, Buhuju and Irangara are merely districts of Unyoro. The great promontory of Usongora, which half shuts in Beatrice Gulf, is tributary to Kabba Rega, though governed by Nyika, King of Gambaragara.

Usongora is the great salt field whence all the surrounding countries obtain their salt.[24] It is, from all accounts, a very land of wonders, but the traveller desirous of exploring it should have a thousand Sniders to protect him, for the natives, like those of Ankori, care for nothing but milk and goatskins. Among the wonders credited to it are a mountain emitting "fire and stones," a salt lake of considerable extent, several hills of rock salt, a large plain encrusted thickly with salt and alkali, a breed of very large dogs of extraordinary ferocity, and a race of such long-legged natives that ordinary mortals regard them with surprise and awe. The Waganda, who have invaded their country for the sake of booty, ascribe a cool courage to them, against which all their numbers and well known expertness with shield and spear were of little avail. They are, besides, extremely clannish, and allow none of their tribe to intermarry with strangers, and their diet consists solely of milk. Their sole occupation consists in watching their cows, of which they have an immense number; and it was to capture some of those herds that the Emperor of Uganda sent 100,000 men under his Prime Minister to Usongora. The expedition was successful, for by all accounts the Waganda returned to their country with about 20,000; but so dearly were they purchased with the loss of human life that it is doubtful whether such a raid will again be attempted to Usongora.

Belgian Congo, 125–27; Maes and Boone, Peuplades du Congo Belge, 95–98; Struck, "On the Ethnographic Nomenclature of the Uganda-Congo Border," 283–84.

23. The Lacustrine state of Toro located on the plateau to the east of the Ruwenzori Mountains. Toro had broken away from Bunyoro in the 1830's, but at about this time was to suffer heavily from the efforts of Kabarega to reconquer it. Taylor, Western Lacustrine Bantu, 41–71; Low, "Northern Interior," 344–45.

24. See the descriptions in Roscoe, The Bagesu, 156–58; Lugard, "Travels from the East Coast to Uganda, Lake Albert Edward, and Lake Albert," 835.

I propose to rest here a couple of days and then proceed to Karagwe to discover another road to Lake Albert.

P.S. Our camp on Lake Albert in Unyampaka was situated in longitude 31 deg. 24 min. 30 sec. by observation and latitude 25 min. by account. The promontory of Usongora, due west, was about fifteen miles.

27

Kafurro, Arab Depot, near Rumanika's Capital, Karagwe, Central Africa
March 26, 1876 [1]

Before parting with "General" Samboozi I received some more unkindness from him, which made another cause of complaint to add to his refusal to assist building a fenced camp on Lake Albert. The "General," no doubt perceiving that his hopes of reward from me were very slim, undertook to reward himself and accordingly refused to return three porters' loads of beads given him for carriage, and appropriated them for his own benefit. By such a proceeding he became guilty of theft, and, what is worse in Uganda, of disrespect and misbehavior to the Emperor's guest, and laid himself open to the severest penalties. My letter of complaint was no sooner received by the Emperor than a force of musketeers were despatched under Saruti,[2] their chief, who despoiled "General" Samboozi of cattle, wives, children, slaves and every article he possessed, and the "General" himself was seized, bound and carried in chains to the Emperor, whose influence must be used to save even his head.

Mtesa also sent a series of messages after me, imploring me to return, and promising me Sekibobo[3] with 50,000 men and Mquenda[4] with 40,000 men to escort me back again to Lake Albert, and giving me the solemn assurance that these chiefs should defend the camp until I returned from my voyage of exploration. But, though I almost wept from sheer vexation, and was extremely sorry

1. *NYH*, Aug. 11, 1876. The Arab trading center of Kafuro went into decline after the death of Rumanika. See Stuhlmann, *Mit Emin Pascha*, 224–25.

2. The title of a court official, the brewer. Speke, *Journal of Discovery*, 255. See also Wilson and Felkin, *Uganda*, I, 104.

3. The *Sekibobo* was the *ssaza* chief of Kyagwe; he was in charge of relations with Busoga. Roscoe, *The Baganda*, 233, 250–51.

4. The *Mukwenda* was the *ssaza* chief of Singo; he acted as the official shield bearer. *Ibid.*, 233, 249–50.

to refuse such a generous offer, I respectfully declined relying upon Waganda any more; and wrote him to that effect as fast as each message came from him. Besides, I was too far south, being encamped on the north banks of the Kagera River when I first learned Mtesa's intentions, and to return from the Kagera to the Katonga and march back again to Lake Albert would have occupied three months, and should Sekibobo and Mquenda prove as faithless as Samboozi I should find, on my return to Unyampaka from the lake, that the Waganda and the expedition were flown. I had many other strong reasons for persisting in my refusal to return; and, though I prosecuted my march to Karagwe, it was with a sad heart I bade farewell to my hopes of exploring Lake Albert from the East side.

Until I arrived at Karagwe I was daily encouraged with the reports of simple natives that a country lay behind Mpororo where we would be received as friends; but on inquiry of the gentle, sweet tempered Pagan Rumanika, I was informed that the friendly country was Utumbi, but was inaccessible, owing to the people of Mpororo, who would not even let his own people enter their territory. On asking if Ruanda was accessible to travellers I was informed that at five different times Arabs had endeavored to open intercourse with them, but each time had been repulsed, and some had been murdered by the treacherous people.[5] I then inquired if there was no road between Ruanda and Urundi by which I could reach Uzige. The old King smiled at the question, and said the Warundi were worse than the natives of Ruanda. Not quite satisfied with his replies, I questioned Hamed Ibrahim,[6] an Arab gentleman, who has done business in Karagwe twelve years. As to the possibility of penetrating anywhere westward from any point near Karagwe, his replies, though more definite and explicit, swept away almost all hope of ever again reaching Lake Albert from the east side.

To test Rumanika's friendship I requested he would permit me to explore the frontier of Karagwe as far north as Mpororo, and south to Ugufu,[7] a distance of eighty geographical miles, and that he

5. For the attitude of Rwanda and Burundi to foreign traders and raiders, Meyer, Die Barundi, 71ff.; Pagès, Un Royaume Hamite, 161–64.

6. Ahmed bin Ibrahim (c. 1820/25–c. 1885). His story is told in Gray, "Ahmed bin Ibrahim—the First Arab to Reach Buganda"; see also Gray, "Trading Expeditions from the Coast to Lakes Tanganyika and Victoria Before 1857," 237.

7. The Gufi are Rundi living now in the northwest region of Tanzania; they are known at present as the Hangaza. They broke away from Burundi during the second half of the nineteenth century. Hall and Cory, "A Study of Land Tenure in Bugufi"; Cory, "The People of the Lake Victoria Region," 24; Westermann, Geschichte Afrikas, 343.

would lend me guides and a native escort. To my surprise the gentle old King not only gave me guides and escort, but canoes and the freedom of Karagwe, or, in other words, he promised that so long as I explored I and my people should have subsistence gratis! Thus I was assisted a second time by African monarchs in the cause of geography.

I lost no time, you may rest assured, in getting ready. The boat *Lady Alice* was conveyed to Speke's Lake Windermere[8] and the sections screwed together, and the next day, convoyed by six of Rumanika's canoes, manned by Wanyambu (natives of Karagwe),[9] we set out for another exploring trip. After circumnavigating Lake Windermere we entered the Kagera River, and almost immediately it flashed on my mind that I had made another grand discovery, that I had discovered, in fact, the true parent of the Victoria Nile.

If you glance at Speke's map, you will perceive that he calls this river the Kitangule River, and that he has two tributaries running to it, called respectively the Luchuro and the Ingezi. Speke, so wonderfully correct, with a mind which grasped geographical knowledge with great acuteness, and arranged the details with clever precision and accuracy, is seriously in error in calling this noble river Kitangule. Neither Waganda nor Wanyamba know it by that name, but they all know the Kagera River, which flows near Kitangule. From its mouth to Urundi it is known by the natives on both banks as the Kagera River. The Luchuro, or rather Lukaro, means "higher up," but is no name of any river. Of the Ingezi I shall have occasion to speak further on.[10]

While exploring the Victoria Lake I ascended a few miles up the Kagera, and was then struck with its great volume and depth—so much so as to rank it as the principal affluent of the Victoria Lake. But in coming south, and crossing it at Kitangule, I sounded it and found fourteen fathoms of water, or eighty-four feet deep, and 120 yards wide. This fact, added to the determined opinion of the natives that the Kagera was an arm of the Albert Niyanza, caused me to think the river worth exploring. I knew, as all know who know anything of African geography, that the Kagera could not be an

8. Lake Ruanyara; Speke named it Windermere because it reminded his companion, Grant, of the English lake. Speke, *Journal of Discovery*, 220; Stuhlmann, *Mit Emin Pascha*, 228. There is some confusion about Windermere because the African lake has several names.

9. The non-Hima population was referred to as Nyambo. Grant, "Stanley's Exploration of Victoria," 25; Burton, "Lake Regions," 286.

10. *Rukaro*, or *lukaro*, does mean "higher up." *Ngezi* means river, or current. My thanks to Israel Katoke for this information.

effluent of Lake Albert, but their repeated statements to that effect caused me to suspect that such a great body of water could not be created by the drainage of Ruanda and Karagwe—that it ought to have its source much further, or from some lake situate between Lakes Albert and Tanganyika.

When I explored Lake Windermere I discovered, by sounding, that it had an average depth of forty feet, and that it was fed and drained by the Kagera. On entering the Kagera I stated that it flashed on my mind that the Kagera was the real parent of the Victoria Nile; by sounding I found fifty-two feet of water in a river fifty yards wide. I proceeded on my voyage three days up the river, and came to another lake about nine miles long and a mile in width, situate on the right hand of the stream. At the southern end of the lake, and after working our way through two miles of papyrus, we came to the island of Unyamubi, a mile and a half in length. Ascending the highest point on the island the secret of the Ingezi or Kagera was revealed. Standing in the middle of the island I perceived it was about three miles from the coast of Karagwe and three miles from the coast of Kishakka west, so that the width of the Ingezi at this point was about six miles, and north it stretched away broader, and beyond the horizon green papyri mixed with broad gray gleams of water. I discovered, after further exploration, that the expanses of papyri floated over a depth of from nine to fourteen feet of water; that the papyri, in fact, covered a large portion of a long, shallow lake; that the river, though apparently a mere swift, flowing body of water, confined apparently within proper banks by dense, tall fields of papyri, was a mere current, and that underneath the papyri it supplied a lake, varying from five to fourteen miles in width and about eighty geographical miles in length.

Descending the Kagera again, some five miles from Unyamubi, the boat entered a large lake on the left side, which, when explored, proved to be thirteen geographical miles in length by eight in breadth. From its extreme western side to the mainland of Karagwe east was fourteen miles, eight of which was clear, open water; the other six were covered by floating fields of papyri, large masses or islands of which drift to and fro daily. By following this lake to its southern extremity I penetrated between Ruanda and Kishakka. I attempted to land in Ruanda, but was driven back to the boat by war cries, which the natives sounded shrill and loud.[11]

11. Stanley was on Lake Ihema; he had tried to land without success on the Mubari coast. Bourgeois, *Banyarwanda et Barundi*, 167. Stanley below writes "Muvari" for "Mubari."

Throughout the entire length (eighty miles) the Kagera maintains almost the same volume and almost the same width, discharging its surplus waters to the right and to the left as it flows on, feeding, by means of the underground channels, what might be called by an observer on land seventeen separate lakes, but which are in reality one lake, connected together underneath the fields of papyri, and by lagoon-like channels meandering tortuously enough between detached fields of the most prolific reed. The open expanses of water are called by the natives so many "rwerus" or lakes; the lagoons connecting them and the reed-covered water are known by the name of "Ingezi." What Speke has styled Lake Windermere is one of these rwerus, and is nine miles in extreme length and from one to three miles in width. By boiling point I ascertained it to be at an altitude of 3,760 feet above the ocean and about 320 feet above Lake Victoria. The extreme north point of this singular lake is north by east from Uhimba south; [12] its extreme southern point, Karagwe, occupies the whole of its eastern side. Southwest it is bounded by Kishakka, west by Muvari, in Ruanda, northwest by Mpororo and northeast by Ankori. At the point where Ankori faces Karagwe the lake contracts, becomes a tumultuous noisy river, creates whirlpools and dashes itself madly into foam and spray against opposing rocks, and finally rolls over a wall of rock ten or twelve feet deep with a tremendous uproar—for which the natives call it Morongo, or the Noisy Falls.

On returning from my voyage of exploration—during which time I was most hospitably entertained, so powerful was the name of the gentle pagan Rumanika—I requested guides to take me overland to the hot springs of Mtagata,[13] which have obtained such renown throughout all the neighboring countries for their healing properties. Two days' severe marching toward the north brought us to a deep wooded gorge wherein the hot springs are situated. I discovered a most astonishing variety of plants, herbs, trees and bushes; for here Nature was in her most prolific mood. She shot forth her products with such vigor that each plant seemed to strangle the others for lack of room. They so clambered over one another that small hills of brush were formed, the lowest in the heap stifled by the uppermost, and through the heaps thus formed tall mvules shot forth

12. Uhimba was "debateable land" between Karagwe and the Zinza. It was held by Karagwe at this time. Ford and Hall, "The History of Karagwe (Bukoba District)," 8; *TDC*, I, 478.

13. For other visits and information, Grant, "The Hot Springs of Mtagata ('Boiling Water') North Western Tanganyika Territory"; Kollmann, *Victoria Nyanza,* 62–63; Langheld, *Zwanzig Jahre in deutschen Kolonien,* 160.

an arrow's flight into the upper air, with globes of radiant, green foliage upon their stem-like crowns.

The springs were visited at this time by numbers of diseased persons. Male and female were seen lying promiscuously in the hot pools half asleep, while their itchy and ulcerous bodies were being half cooked. The hottest issued in streams from the base of a rocky hill, and when Fahrenheit's thermometer was placed in the water the mercury rose to 129 degrees. Four springs bubbled upward from the ground through a depth of dark, muddy sediment, and had a temperature of 110 degrees. These were the most favored by the natives, and the curative reputation of the springs was based on the properties of this water.

I camped at the springs three days, and made free use of a reserved spring; but, excepting unusual cleanliness, I cannot say I enjoyed any benefit from the water. I drank about a gallon of the potent liquid, and can say this much, that it has no laxative effect on the system. A bottleful of the purest water I took away with me, in the hope that some day it may be analyzed by professionals in Europe.[14]

I but yesterday returned from the hot springs, and, having seen all worth seeing in Karagwe, and having as yet discovered no road westward, I propose the day after to-morrow to march along the eastern shore of the lake, south or south-west, as far as practicable, with the view to follow up the interesting discoveries I have made.

28

Ubagwe, Western Unyamwezi, Central Africa
April 24, 1876 [1]

We departed from the capital of Karagwe with very brave intentions and high aspirations. We had discovered that the Kagera River formed a great lake about eighty miles in length and from five to fourteen miles in breadth, and that at Kishakka the Kagera was still a powerful, deep-flowing river, and curious reports from natives and Arabs had created curious ideas within our minds as to the source of this noble river. Imbued with the thought that by journeying a sufficient distance along its right bank we might discover this

14. For the analysis, *TDC*, I, 467.
1. *NYH*, Aug. 12, 1876.

Map IV. Stanley's later sketch map of Lake Victoria (from *NYH*, Aug. 12, 1876)

source, we made ample preparations for the crossing of a wide wilderness, packed ten days' provisions of grain on the shoulders of each man of the expedition, and on the 27th of March set out for the uninhabited land.

On the second day of our departure from the Karagwe capital we came to the east side of a lake, a long, narrow, winding body of water. We marched along its eastern shore for three days, a distance of thirty-six miles; on the fourth day and fifth day an obstructing ridge shut it from our view while marching, but by occasionally surmounting the ridge I managed to obtain views of its stream-like water, still extending south and southwest. On the sixth day we came to Uhimba, the frontier of Karagwe, where, behind a ridge, which extends between Uhimba and the lake, we saw the extreme south end of the lake we had so long followed.

From a point of observation near Uhimba we saw also a decided change in the formation of the broad valley of the Kagera. The mountainous ridges bounding the western shore of the Kagera, which, extending from Mpororo south, continue on a south by west course, became broken and confused in Southern Kishakka, and were penetrated from the northwest by a wide valley, through which issued into the Kagera a lake-like river called Akanyaru.[2] Southwest was seen the course of the Kagera, which, above the confluence of the Akanyaru with it, was only a swift flowing river of no very great depth or breadth. Such a river I thought might well be created by the drainage of Eastern Urundi and Western Uhha. My attention was drawn from the Kagera to the lake-like stream of Akanyaru, and several natives stated to me while looking toward it that it was an effluent of the Kagera, and that it emptied into the Albert Niyanza. Such an extraordinary statement as this could not be received and transmitted from me to you as a fact without being able to corroborate it on my own authority. Exploration of the mouth of the Akanyaru proves that the Akanyaru is not an effluent, but is an affluent of the Kagera.

Beyond the mouth of the Akanyaru I dared not go, as the natives of Kishakka on the left bank, and Ugufu on the right bank, are too wild altogether. I find the long-legged race inhabiting the countries west of Uganda, Karagwe and Usui[3] have a deadly aversion to strangers. The sight of a strange dog seems sufficient to send them to mad rage and paroxysms of spear shaking and bow bending. They are all kin to the long-legged mortals of Bumbireh, who sounded the war cry at the mere sight of our inoffensive exploring boat floating on the Victoria Lake. They are so dreadfully afraid of losing

2. The unnamed lake Stanley had marched alongside of was Lake Burigi. For Akanyaru, see below, note 7.

3. The Zinza state of Rusubi; see Thiel, "Businza unter der Dynastie der Bahinda," 507–09. Stanley avoided visiting Rusubi due to the heavy demands for *hongo*. TDC, I, 478–80.

their cattle that if one cow dies from sickness the whole country is searched to discover the stranger who has bewitched the cow to death, for whose loss, if one is found, his life is forfeit to the purblind, small brained natives.

Human beings frequently astonish one another in all countries by their hobbies, and by showing excessive fondness for gold, horses, dogs, cats, clothes, birds, &c., but the love which the Wasongora, Wanyankori, Wa-Ruanda, Wa-Kishakka, Wagufu, Wanyamba and Watusi exhibit for their cattle is an extreme, selfish and miser-like affection. A stranger might die in any of those countries for lack of one drop of milk. Generous and sweet-tempered as Rumanika proved himself, he never offered to give me even one teaspoonful of milk during the time I was with him, and had he given me a milk can his people would have torn him limb from limb. From this excessive love for their cattle springs their hostility to strangers, and this hostility arises from a dread of evil or fear of danger. By maintaining a strict quarantine and a system of exclusiveness they hope to ward off all evil and sudden disaster to their cattle, which are their sole means of subsistence.[4]

By comparing the information derived from natives of Uhimba, Ugufu, Kishakka, Urundi and Ruanda I am able to give you additional details of the source and course of the Kagera River, and I hold out to myself some small hope that in a few months from the present date I may be able to explore from another quarter a tract of country which, hypothetically, I believe contains the extreme sources of this river. Until that period let the following stand for the utmost of our knowledge of it.

From a ridge near Mtagata Hot Springs, having an altitude of 6,500 feet above the ocean I obtained a view of Ufumbiro Mountains, which have a height of about 12,000 feet.[5] This group consists of two sugar loaf cones and a lumpy mass, and is situate about forty geographical miles west-northwest from Mtagata, and form a barrier at that spot between Mpororo and Ruanda.

The course of all the main ridges and valleys from Ruanda to the Victoria Niyanza appear to be south by west. Nay, you may say that from Alexandria to the Nyassa Lake, the central portion of

4. For a recent statement on this "cattle complex," Herskovits, *The Human Factor in Changing Africa*, 63–68.

5. The Birunga, or Virunga, mountains, a volcanic chain on the Congo-Uganda border. See Moore, *To the Mountains of the Moon*, 189ff.; Philipps, " 'Mufúmbiro': The Birunga Volcanoes of Kigezi-Ruanda-Kivu." Their highest peak is about 14,780 feet.

Africa appears to be formed into ridges, deep troughs or basins, or valleys, whose length is from north by east to south by west, or from northeast to southwest. Regard the course of the Nile from Lake Albert to Alexandria, the position of Lakes Albert, Tanganyika and Nyassa, as well as the Victoria Lake. Follow the course of the Mokattem range of mountains through Nubia, Abyssinia, Galla, Masai and Usagara; trace the plateau of Masai, Unyamwezi, Urori, Ubisa, south to the Bechuana country, and you will perceive that the general lay of almost all rivers, lakes, mountains, basins and plateaus is from northeasterly to southwesterly. On a reduced scale it is even so with all the mountain ridges and valleys between the Lakes Victoria and Albert. It seems as if the throes which Africa suffered during that grand convulsion which tore her asunder heaved up these stupendous ridges and sunk those capacious basins now filled with lengthy and broad expanses of crystal-clear water were keenest and severest about these lake regions; for here the mountains are higher, the valleys deeper and narrower. We have no longer the wide, billowy plateau, whose successive swells make travel and exploration tedious, but lengthy lines of mountains of enormous frame, separated from each other by deep, narrow valleys, with a hundred and many wonders presented to the view at a glance.[6]

From Mtagata Mountain, while looking toward the Ufumbiro cones, there were visible three lofty ridges, separated by as many broad valleys. First was the Ishango and Muvari ridge, west of the Kagera Lake and valley, and west of this were two ridges, with the valley of Muvari between the two easternmost and a valley of Ruanda between the two westernmost. The two latter ridges appear to run parallel with each other from east and west of Ufumbiro Mountains, and shut in the valley of the Ni-Nawarango or Nawarongo River, which, rising in Ufumbiro Mountains, flows south by west between Muvari and Ruanda, and enters Akanyaru Lake, thirty by twenty miles in extent. From Akanyaru Lake issues Akanyaru River, between Ugufu and Kishakka, into the Kagera. The Kagera proper, coming from the southwest, also enters Akanyaru Lake, but leaves the lake south of Ugufu and takes a curve northeasterly between Ugufu and Western Usui.

West of Akanyaru I could get no certain intelligence. I have heard of another large lake lying west, but what connection it has with the Kagera, or whether it has any, I cannot learn definitely. One says

6. For the Rift Valley, *East African Rift System;* for historical notes on explorers and the Rift, Bridges, "British Exploration of East Africa," 424.

that is is an arm of Luta Nzige or Lake Albert, another declares it to be a separate lake. Whatever it be I believe I will be able to discover at a later period.[7]

With the best intentions to prosecute my explorations along the Kagera I was paralyzed by famine in Usui and the hostility of the Warundi, and was obliged to abandon exploration from this side of the Tanganyika. Summing up all the chances remaining for me to do good work without expending vainly my goods and the health and energy left in me, I saw it was useless to sit down and launch invectives against the intractable natives, and that it was far better and more manly to hurry on to other regions and try Lake Albert by another route from the opposite quarter.

You will perceive by this letter that I am now in Western Unyamwezi, about fifteen days journey from Ujiji. What I propose doing now is to proceed quickly to Ujiji, then explore the Tanganyika in my boat, and from Uzige strike north to the Albert, and if that road be not open to cross the Tanganyika and travel north by a circuitous course to effect the exploration of the Albert. It may not be actually necessary to explore that lake, for Gordon or some of his officers may have accomplished that work, but I have no means of knowing whether they have done so or not; it therefore remains for me, if the feat is possible, to circumnavigate it. If it is not I shall strike out for other regions and continue exploration elsewhere, until my poverty of goods warns me to return.

By the same bearer which conveys this letter to the coast I send four others, which have been kept by me until I had an opportunity to send them. Three at least I expected to put in person into the hands of one of Gordon's officers; but it was not fated to be so. From Ujiji I shall send the duplicates of these letters to the coast, and before I quite leave that port I expect to possess other geographical items to transmit to you.

Gordon PACHA was kind enough to send me a *Daily Telegraph* of December 24, 1874, and a *Pall Mall Gazette* of the same month, which I received in Uganda just before starting for the Albert Nyanza. In the *Telegraph* I saw a short letter from Cameron, dated

7. The Niavarongo rises in the high area southeast of Lake Kivu; it is joined by the Mukungwa which rises near the eastern end of the Mufumbiro Mountains. The joint river, the Naiavarongo, is joined by the Akanyaru, which comes from the south. The Akanyaru is a swampy river. Hurst, *Nile*, 160–61. The lake to the west was Kivu. It had been represented on maps from the time of Speke, but it was not visited by a European until von Götzen's arrival in 1894. *GJ* 5 (1895), 78; Götzen, *Durch Afrika von Ost nach West*, 218ff.

May 3, 1873, wherein he says he has discovered the outlet of the Tanganyika to be the Lukuga. Cameron has been fortunate and energetic, and deserves credit for the discovery. But he says he has not quite circumnavigated the Tanganyika because he did not think it worth while after discovering the Lukuga.[8] It may be Cameron, by this omission, has left me something to discover in the Tanganyika, but whether or not, the *Lady Alice* shall not quit the waters of that lake until I have finished the two-thirds left unvisited by me on my first expedition.

In the *Pall Mall Gazette* I read a more startling statement which deserves from me a flat contradiction, as no doubt it received from Colonel Grant. The article stated that Colonel Long, of the Egyptian service, declared that he had just returned from a visit to the King of Uganda, and he had discovered, to his surprise, that Lake Victoria was a body of water about twelve miles in width![9] Now, I do know it as a fact that Colonel Long, or Long Bey, was in Uganda in July, 1873; but if he states that the Victoria Niyanza is only twelve miles in width he states what every snub-nosed urchin in Uganda would declare to be most astounding nonsense. The width of twelve miles is what I would give Murchison Bay, a portion of which bay is visible from Kibuga, one of the Emperor's capitals. If M. Linant de Bellefonds, of the Egyptian service, who discovered me in Uganda, is now in Europe, he is requested to publish his opinion of Lake Victoria, even from what he saw of it from Usavara.

The *Pall Mall Gazette* adds that it was always the opinion of Captain Burton that Speke had exaggerated the extent of Lake Victoria. Last year I sent you a map of the southern, eastern, northern and northwest coasts of Lake Victoria. Enclosed in this package you will find a sketch map of the southwest coast, with which you may compare Speke's hypothetical outline of the Victoria Lake and judge for yourselves whether Speke has been guilty of much exaggeration.[10]

8. See Cameron's letter of May 9, 1874, in PRGS 19 (1874–1875), 75–77, and "Lieutenant Cameron's Diary," 223–25.

9. Charles Chaillé-Long (1842–1917), a former officer of the American army then in Egyptian service. DAB, III, 591–92. He visited Buganda in June and July 1874. For his visit, Chaillé-Long, *Central Africa*, especially 140. His somewhat untruthful character is analyzed in Alpers, "Chaillé-Long's Mission to Mutesa," 1–11. See also the harsh comments in Pritchard, "Zande Cannibalism," 243.

10. See Map IV. The able German explorer, Stuhlmann, later praised Stanley for his accuracy in mapping the places which he had actually visited. Stuhlmann, *Mit Emin Pacha*, 727. But see the criticisms in Mackay, "Boat Voyage along the western shores of Lake Victoria . . . ," 283; Blohm, *Die Nyamwezi. Land und Wirtschaft*, 2.

29

Ujiji
August 7, 1876 [1]

Lake Tanganyika, despite its extreme length, is to be subject no more to doubts and fanciful hypotheses, for it has been circumnavigated and measured and its enormous coast line laid down and fixed as accurately as a pretty good chronometer and solar observations will admit. Captain Burton's discovery is now a completed whole, with no corner indefinite, no indentation unknown. We must banish from our charts Mr. Cooley's grand United Tanganyika and Nyassa,[2] and Sir Samuel Baker's no less grander idea of Upper and Lower Tanganyika, as also Livingstone's United Lake Liemba and Lake Tanganyika. Its total circumnavigation dispels all erratic ideas and illusions respecting its length and breadth, and furnishes us with a complete knowledge, as far as our present necessities require, of its affluents and effluents.

I write this letter, however, to explain the problem of the Tanganyika, which has puzzled Livingstone and so many explorers, and induced so many able cartographers to publish wild conjectures instead of solid facts and truths, and I take for my texts once more certain items from Lieutenant Verney Cameron's letter to the Geographical Society, dated May 9, 1874:

> I have been fortunate enough to discover the outlet of the Tanganyika. The current is small (1.2 knots), as might be expected from the levels. It is believed to flow into the Lualaba, between the Lakes Moero and Kamarondo. I went four or five miles down it, when my further progress was stopped by the floating grass and enormous rushes. The river, the Lukuga, is about twenty-five miles south of the group of islands Captain Speke explored.[3]

It is not fair to criticise such a brief letter as this, evidently written hastily after the discoverer's arrival in Ujiji, nor have I any

1. *NYH,* March 26, 1877.
2. William D. Cooley (?–1883), the classic "armchair geographer" of his era, who would arouse many explorers and geographers because of the tenacity of his opinions—even when the facts proved them wrong. Despite all the adverse criticism directed against Cooley he did, however, do much to stimulate the progress of African exploration. See the sympathetic obituary notice in *The Athenaeum* 1 (1883), 315, and the remarks in Bridges, "Speke and the R.G.S.," 25–26. For his theory on the central African lakes, Cooley, *Inner Africa Laid Open,* 72ff.
3. The letter is in *PRGS* 19 (1874–1875), 75–77.

CENTRAL AFRICA.

Stanley's Survey of the Lukuga Creek—
Lake Tanganyika.

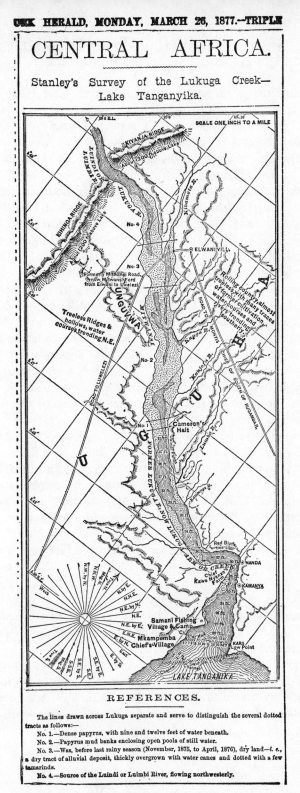

REFERENCES.

The lines drawn across Lukuga separate and serve to distinguish the several dotted tracts as follows:—

No. 1.—Dense papyrus, with nine and twelve feet of water beneath.

No. 2.—Papyrus mud banks enclosing open pools of still water.

No. 3.—Was, before last rainy season (November, 1875, to April, 1876), dry land—i. e., a dry tract of alluvial deposit, thickly overgrown with water canes and dotted with a few tamarinds.

No. 4.—Source of the Luindi or Luimbi River, flowing northwesterly.

Map V. Stanley's sketch map of the Lukuga region
(from *NYH*, March 26, 1877)

such intention; but it serves as a preface to what I am about to say, and it serves in a measure to mark the boundaries of difference between Lieutenant Cameron and myself. I send you a chart of the Lukuga Creek,[4] to enable your readers to understand clearly one of Nature's secrets in Central Africa. I shall briefly remark upon the above statements.

Lieutenant Cameron says he has been "fortunate enough to discover the outlet of the Tanganyika." He certainly has discovered Lukuga Creek, and, as I entertain friendship toward the gallant gentleman, I will admit that he has discovered what has never been the outlet, what is not the outlet, but what will be within a few years the outlet of the Tanganyika, for as yet there is no outlet, as we understand the term, for an outflowing river or effluent.

"The current is small (1.2 knots), as might be expected from the levels." Having differed with the first I must differ with the second statement, though reluctantly; but I impute the cause to his over-hurry and imperfect levels. The chief who accompanied Cameron says that he stayed but a short time, and such a current as he mentioned might well be caused by the monsoon wind blowing up the creek, but for more details and experiments testing this current I must refer you below.

"It is believed to flow into the Lualaba, between the Lakes Moero and Kamarondo." More about the flow below, but Moero is pronounced "Meveru" by all men, natives or Arabs, and of Kamarondo "Lake" I can hear nothing except a distinct and emphatic denial of there being such a lake; but all who know anything of it say there is a river called the Kamalondo, or Kamarondo, a large tributary of the Lualaba, or Ugarowa.

"I went four or five miles down it, when my further progress was stopped by the floating grass and enormous rushes." Lieutenant Cameron proceeded about three miles, and made his experiments at Lumba. His progress was stopped by the papyrus, which perhaps belongs to the species of grass, but all the specimens of pure grass seen in the Lukuga Creek at present may be eaten by a healthy ass in fifteen minutes.

"The river, the Lukuga, is about twenty-five miles south of the groups of islands Captain Speke explored." The entrance to the Lukuga Creek is situated in latitude 5 deg. 49 min. 30 sec. south, while Kasenge Island [5] is in latitude 5 deg. 35 min. 30 sec. south, making

4. See Map V.
5. Kasenge Island, off the Guha coast. See *LLJ*, II, 19–20.

the Lukuga just fourteen geographical miles south of Kasenge, discovered by Speke.

Beyond these few points I have no cause to differ with Lieutenant Cameron. To him alone belongs the credit and honor of the discovery of the Lukuga Creek, the future outlet of Lake Tanganyika. I followed his course inch by inch, marked each of his camps and employed the same guides. Where he cut across deep bays, and finally cut across Tanganyika Lake without reaching the south end by nineteen geographical miles, I diverged from his track and completed what he had left undone, in the hope, since I was on the lake and captain of my own boat, to find him in error, but after all my trouble I only came to the Lukuga Creek to discover that he is entitled to the honor of the discovery of the future outlet of the Tanganyika.[6] Imagining that because there was not at present what can be called an outflowing river visible at Lukuga Creek, I explored after Cameron as far as Kasenge, whence Cameron returned to Ujiji, leaving the northern half unexplored, and then continued the exploration along the coasts of Uguhha, Goma, Kavunvweh, Karamba, Ubwari, Masansi[7]—all new ground, unvisited by any white man —and came to the point where Livingstone and myself left off in 1871; thence to Ujiji, after having explored every corner and river mouth, bay, and creek in search of the present outlet, or, if the Lukuga must needs be called an outlet, in search of another outlet. A distance of over 800 geographical miles has been traversed by me; but though I have made several interesting discoveries during the long voyage none of them deserves our attention like the Lukuga Creek.

I hope none of Lieutenant Cameron's friends will take offence because I have found errors in his statements. Differences do not always imply errors. In this case his errors have arisen from haste and an imperfect examination of the Lukuga Creek. He is not de-

6. Stanley's conviction was confirmed in 1878 when Lake Tanganyika rose to a level that swept the Lukuga outlet clear. For a discussion of the factors involved in the fluctuations of the level of the lake, and of its eventual outflow, Devroey: *Le Problème de la Lukuga*, and *A Propos de la Stabilisation du Niveau du Lac Tanganyika*.

7. The Goma lived on the western coast of Lake Tanganyika along latitude 5° South. They were reputed to be the best canoe builders on the lake—Hore called their vessels "triumphs of African art." Kavunvweh was located by Stanley to the north of Ugoma. The Bwire occupied the Ubwari peninsula and the territory behind it. Karamba was located at the base of the Ubwari peninsula. Maes and Boone, *Peuplades du Congo Belge*, 326–27, 331–32; Hore, "Twelve Tribes of Tanganyika," 13–14; Jacques and Storms, "Notes sur l'Ethnographie de la Partie Orientale de l'Afrique Equatoriale," 190; "Lettre du R. P. Guillemé"; *TDC*, II, 56; Vansina, *Introduction à l'Ethnographie Congo*, chap. 7.

prived of the credit of the discovery of the Lukuga, nor of the credit of having gone through much trouble and hardship in his Tanganyika voyage. It is difficult for one man to be perfectly exact. One explorer loses a date, and having no means to right his error or take lunars is corrected by the next; one explorer regards an object one way, another regards it in quite an opposite way; one traveller hears one statement and obtains one version of a thing directly the reverse of his successor; one traveller contents himself with merely hearing of a fact, another is not content until he has explored it for himself, which makes a vast difference. There are more errors in the English Admiralty chart of the East African coast than there are in all the maps of the Central African travellers' routes. I have found no such absurd error in Burton's, Speke's, or Grant's or Livingstone's maps, as I found in the Admiralty chart, where Kissomang Point stands for Kisima Mafia (or Mafia's well). Let Cameron's friends, then, rest content, for in this letter I shall have to correct myself, Livingstone and Burton.

I begin, after this lengthy preamble, with tradition, the mother of history. The Wajiji, a tribe now occupying a small country near the centre of the eastern coast of the Tanganyika, immigrants long since from Urundi,[8] have two interesting traditions respecting the origin of Lake Tanganyika.

The first relates that the portion of this continent now occupied by the Great Lake was a plain "years and years and years ago;" that on this plain was a large town, near where is not known. In this town lived a man and his wife, with an inclosure round their dwelling, which contained a remarkably deep well or fountain, whence an abundant supply of fresh fish was obtained for their wants. The existence of the fountain and its treasure was kept a profound secret from all their neighbors, as the revelation of its existence had been strictly prohibited by father to son for many generations within this particular family, lest some heavy calamity dimly foretold would happen if the prohibition was not strictly respected; and, remembering the injunction, the owners of the fountain lived long and happily, and fresh fish formed their main food each day. The wife, however, was not very virtuous, for she permitted another man in secret to share the love which should have been solely bestowed on her proper husband, and, among other favors, she frequently gave to her lover some of the fresh fish, a kind of delicious meat he had

8. There had been a migration of Tusi from Rwanda-Burundi into the Ha area; they became the ruling class. Scherer, "Ha of Tanganyika," 841ff.

never before tasted, and which aroused his utmost curiosity to ascertain whence she obtained it. For a long time he ceased not to ask, which the woman steadily refused to tell.

One day the husband was compelled to begin a journey to Uvinza, but before departure he strictly enjoined his wife to look after his house closely, to admit no gossips within his doors, and, above all, not to show the fountain. This African Eve solemnly promised to comply with his instructions, though secretly she rejoiced at the prospect of his absence. A few hours after her husband's departure she left her house to seek her lover, and when she found him she said to him, "You have for a long time demanded to know whence I obtained that delicious meat you have so often praised. Come with me, and I will show you." African Eve then took him to her house, in opposition to her husband's commands; but as with a view to enhance the glories of the fountain and the pleasure of viewing the fish sportfully displaying their silver sides in the water she first entertained her lover with the fish cooked in various ways, nor was she neglectful to satisfy his thirst with wine of her own manufacture. Then, when her lover began to be impatient at the delay, and having no other cause to postpone the exhibition, she invited him to follow her. A fence of water cane plastered over with mud enclosed the wondrous fountain, within whose crystal depths he saw the fish. For some time he gazed on the brilliant creatures with admiration; then, seized with a desire to handle one of them and regard them more closely, he put his hand within the water to catch one of them, when suddenly the well burst forth, the earth opened her womb and soon an enormous lake replaced the plain.

Within a few days the husband, returning from Uvinza, approached Ujiji, and saw to his astonishment a large lake where once a plain and many towns stood, and he knew then that his wife had revealed the secret of the mysterious fountain and that punishment had fallen upon her and her neighbors because of her sin.

The other tradition imparted to me by the ancients of Ujiji relates that a long time ago—how long no one can tell—the Luwegeri, a river near Urimba,[9] flowing westward into a valley, was met by the Lukuga, flowing eastward, and its waters, driven backward by

9. The Luegeri River flows into the eastern side of Lake Tanganyika; it is roughly opposite present-day Albertville. For Urimba, TDC, II, 21. The legend recounted by Stanley, along with other of his accounts, was incorporated into a volume of poetry. Solon Doggett said that his Tanganyika and other Idyls (n.p., 1881) had been inspired by Stanley's ventures on the lake. It contains such lines as: "In Uganda's darkened solitudes, the Lu-a-laba flows" (p. 6).

the easterly flowing river, spread over the valley and formed the Tanganyika. Hence the Luwegeri is termed the mother of the Lukuga.

The Waguhha have also their tradition, which is that a long time ago, near Urungu, there was a small hill, hollow within and very deep, full of water. This hill one day burst, and the water spread over the land and became a lake.

The chief at the mouth of the Lukuga says that formerly the Lukuga was a small river flowing into the Tanganyika, receiving many others as it descended toward the lake, but the Tanganyika, filling up, "swallowed" the Lukuga and made a small lake or an arm of the Tanganyika, which until two years ago during the rainy season discharged its surplus water into the Tanganyika. The last two years, however, the Tanganyika has risen so high that the neutral ground last rainy season, between the Tanganyika's Lukuga and the Lukuga flowing to Rua, has been inundated, and the two Lukugas have become one. So much for traditions and native information.

From traditions we proceed to hypotheses, which, as will be seen, have been as wild as the above traditions. Mr. Cooley, a member of the Geographical Society, on the strength of an acquaintance with a half caste Arab, who had traded to certain parts in Central Africa, wrote the results of what he had gathered in *Inner Africa Laid Open,* wherein those who run may read and find much unwisdom, as has since been conclusively proved.[10] The Tanganyika, according to Mr. Cooley, is connected with Nyassa. Livingstone, also, the first of African explorers, was greatly misled and greatly in error about the Tanganyika. He said he tested a current three months by means of water plants, which kept continually drifting northward. Misled by these drifting water plants he constantly wrote and spoke about Upper and Lower Tanganyika. The Upper was supposed to be the Albert Niyanza; the Lower, Burton's Tanganyika. So certain was he of

10. The Arab was Khamis bin Uthman. His varied career included a period as British agent at Zanzibar, 1827–1831, and a visit to Britain in the 1830's when he passed himself off fraudulently as an agent of the Sultan of Zanzibar. One British official described him as "a rogue in every way," but Cooley defended him, and indirectly himself, against the strictures brought by Burton and others. The French naval explorer Guillain also praised Khamis' abilities. Burton, "Lake Regions," 232; Hamerton to the Private Secretary Gov. Mauritius, in Hamerton to Willoughby, Oct. 5, 1841, Enclosures, SLRB, 44; Colonial Secretary Mauritius to Hamerton, Feb. 19, 1842, E-3, ZA; Norsworthy to Newman Hunt and Co., June 27, 1834, and enclosures, F-11, *ibid.;* Burton, *Zanzibar,* I, 301, II, 286–87; Guillain, *Documents sur l'Histoire, la Géographie et le Commerce de l'Afrique Orientale,* II, 34–36; Cooley, "Capt. Burton and the Land of the Moon, or the Lake Regions," 510.

this that when he and I proceeded to explore North Tanganyika he spoke to me about continuing down the river as far as the Albert Niyanza. Since this circumnavigating voyage of mine I do not wonder at all that Livingstone was so firm in his belief, for at the extreme south end and far up the west coast I find he had made diligent search for the outlet. On foot he trudged from Cazembe's country to the frontier of Uguhha, and only took boat then to proceed by water to Ujiji. On his last march I also find that he made direct way to the Tanganyika. I have not seen his journals, though no doubt they have been published by this. From Ponda's village, as far as Ukituta, I find he has coasted along the lake.[11] Camp after camp was shown to me, and it appears to me that he only desisted from the search when he had united his last route to his former one. From which it is apparent that he made strenuous efforts to discover the lake's outlet, though, unfortunately the more the pity after such courageous striving—unsuccessfully. I never looked at the grim heights of Fipa, as I sat in my boat, without wondering how the aged traveller was able to hold out so long after such tall climbing. My men also assisted my admiration by pointing out some tremendous mountain which had occupied them an entire day to climb.

I recollect also attending the Geographical Soirée of 1874, which was held at Willis' Rooms, and seeing pendant from top to bottom of the wall an enormous map, illustrating broadly enough the "Hypothesis of Sir Samuel Baker," which was an hypothetic marriage of the Albert Niyanza with the Tanganyika.[12] Heedless of the obstacles that hinder the explorer in Africa, with one dab of a paint brush he had annihilated Ruanda, Mkinyaga, Unyambenya, Chamali, Nashi and Uzige,[13] and a broad, winding, river-like lake nearly eight hundred geographical miles in length, astonished the scientific and unscientific world.

On reading over the duplicates of my letters, sent some months ago to the coast, I proudly perceive that I have cause to congratulate myself for having approached pretty near the truth; but it must be admitted that my conjectures were not broached until I had paid a second visit to Lake Tanganyika, and had viewed with surprise the great rise of the lake which had taken place during an interval

11. Ponda, or Chata, was a Bende chief. See Cameron, *Across Africa*, I, 262–63; Avon "Vie Sociale des Wabende," 110–12. Ukituta is at the southern end of Lake Tanganyika.

12. See the map in Baker, *Ismaïlia*.

13. Mukinyaga and Bunyabungu (probably Stanley's Unyambenya) were provinces of Rwanda. Czekanowski, *Forschungen im Nil-Kongo-Zwischengebiet*, 102–07.

of five years. In my letters I ask, "Can it be possible that Lake Tanganyika is filling up, and that the Lukuga is but a partial affluence?" Now that traditions, hypotheses and conjectures must give way before the light thrown upon the subject by careful and exact exploration, it will be seen that my conjectures were not unfounded.

I forget who it was who said that the word Tanganyika was derived from the Kiswahili words Kuchanganya or Kuchanganika, which means in English to mix. Whether it was Mr. Cooley or Captain Burton, it must be admitted to have been a most ingenious explanation; but the word has the fatal objection of having been borrowed from a foreign language, because it has an accidental similarity with a Kijiji term. Whether Kiswahili or some other more northern language must be taken, for the mother language cannot be settled for some centuries yet; and, until it is definitely known by a comparison of languages and dialects and a knowledge of the course of ancient immigration, it is greatly to be doubted whether the interpretation should be admitted as the correct one.[14]

Among the inquiries made by me around this lake has been the signification of the word Tanganyika, which I discover to be only adopted by the Wajiji, Warundi, Wazige, Wavira and Wagoma, which united inhabit about a third of the shores of the lake. The Wawendi, Wafipa, Warungu and Wawemba,[15] who inhabit the southern third, call it Jemba, or Riemba, or Liemba—The Lake. It will be remembered that among some of the discoveries Livingstone said he had made was that of Lake Liemba, or Lake Lake. No doubt Livingstone asked often enough of the natives of Urmya, probably in Kibisa or Kibisa-Kiswahili, the name of the lake and was as often told it was Jemba or Liemba. Hence Livingstone wrote that he had "discovered another lake, not very large, with two islands in it. Four rivers discharged into the lake. Lake shores very pretty, romantic," &c. And in a subsequent letter said, "I find that this Lake Liemba is joined to Lake Tanganyika." Imperfect investigation also, it seems, does not exempt Livingstone from committing mistakes. Exploration of this part of Lake Tanganyika (the south end) discovers the south end tallying with the above description of Liemba. Sakarabwe village, where he was brought to by one of the chiefs of Kitumkuru as he came from Kabwire, and where he halted some time, was shown to me. The "two islands" are Ntondwe and Muri-

14. Burton, "Lake Regions," 234, suggested this; Cameron, *Across Africa*, II, 304, agreed. Schmitz, *Baholoholo*, 565, supports them.
15. The Bemba.

kwa; the four rivers are the Wizi, the Kitoke, Kapata and Mtombwa.[16]

The natives of Marungu and Uguhha occupy the western third, called Tanganyika-Kimana, from which it is evident that had Burton and Speke, the discoverers of this lake, happened to have first marched to Fipa and had not been informed about the Tanganyika, we should probably have heard of this lake as Lake Liemba or Riemba. Or had they journeyed from westward to Lake Tanganyika it is to be doubted much whether we should have heard of Lake Tanganyika at all. Undoubtedly they would have enlarged upon the vast length, sea-like expanse and romantic shores of Lake Kimana. In the same manner as all large lakes are spoken of by the Waganda as Niyanzas, so the Wajiji speak of them as Tanganyikas.

In my endeavors to ascertain the signification of the term Tanganyika, and in the attempts of the Wajiji to explain, I learned that they did not know themselves, unless it might be because it was large, and its surf always made a noise, and a canoe could make a long journey on it. From which I came almost to suppose that its signification was Large, Great, or Long Lake, Stormy Lake, Sounding Waters, or Great Wave Lake, &c. I also learned that there was an electric fish called Nika[17] in the lake, but then Tanga stood in the way of it being called after the fish; neither was the fish so remarkable an object as to give its name to such a vast body of water. Questioning in this manner only worried the natives, and I did not obtain a satisfactory solution of it until happening, as is my custom, to write down as many native names for objects as I can gather from all dialects for the purpose of comparing them, I came to Kitanga, a small lake, pool or pond, or a lake on which no canoes travel, and Nika, a plain. It appeared to me that the meaning of the word was satisfactorily obtained; that Tanganyika signifies the plain-like lake, as much so as from the fact that a plain is universally taken in inner Africa as a standard object for comparing or illustrating level bodies of earth or water of considerable extent, in the same manner as the word "bahr," or sea, is used by the seacoast people.

During the lake voyage to the Lukuga, Para, the chief guide of

16. For Kabwire, Thomson, "Progress of the Society's East African Expedition: Journey along the Western Side of Lake Tanganyika," 308; Colle, *Baluba*, I, 52. See also "Extracts from Letters and Despatches from Dr. Livingstone."

17. Probably *Malapterurus electricus*, the African catfish. Cunnington, "The Fauna of the African Lakes . . . ," 582; Schmitz, *Les Baholoholo*, 19.

Cameron, whom I also employed, pointed out several instances of changes that had occurred since Cameron had been on the lake. Sand beaches, which in many instances had served their canoes as a shelter from the lake waves, had become flooded with three to four feet water above; low points of land had become totally insulated, islands had been formed and others had been submerged; in the words of the guide, "The Tanganyika truly was swallowing the land very fast." But the best known change was at the mouth of the Lukuga. Two years ago—if Para and the chief at the entrance are to be believed—there stood a long beach of white sand extending from Mkampemba on one side to Kara Point on the opposite side, cut by a channel 400 or 500 yards wide, much nearer Mkampemba than Kara Point. Several Arabs, surprised at the change, confirmed Para's statement. I found, instead of this beach, a line of breakers rolling over with a depth of from two to five feet, from Mkampemba to Kara Point; and as Cameron's halting place was no longer a shelter for canoes we were compelled to proceed further in, about three-quarters of a mile.

The chief, Kawe-Nyange, who took Cameron in his canoe up the creek, was very affable, remembered the white man very well, and explained some of the wonderful things that had been shown him, and finally expressed a doubt as to whether he should permit me to ascend the Lukuga, as he feared that the other white man had thrown some medicine into the water, which had caused the Tanganyika to overflow much country. The beach between his village and Kara was covered with angry white waves, and a fishing village on the beach was destroyed, and the Mitwansi was covered with water. If one white man could make so many changes in the country, what might not two white men do? Kawe-Nyange was, after a little while, laughed out of his fears, and was encouraged with ample gifts to take his men with him to show me the land and water round about.

All I could hear about the Lukuga, whether at Ujiji or from the chief at the mouth, only added to the difficulty of comprehending the real state of things. Lieutenant Cameron stated that he had discovered the outlet of the Tanganyika, with a current of about 1.2 knots an hour! Arabs who had crossed the Lukuga scores of times said that it was not an outflowing river, but an inflowing river. Waguhha, from Monyis, said that there were two Lukugas, one flowing east and one flowing west, and a bank or ridge of dry land separated the two. Ruango,[18] one of my guides, said that he had crossed it

18. Ruango had accompanied Stanley and Livingstone to the north of the lake in 1871. *TDC*, II, 10.

five times; that it was a small river flowing into the Tanganyika; that if I found it flowed in any other direction than into the Tanganyika he would return his hire to me. Para, Cameron's chief guide, said that the white man could not have seen the water flow toward Rua, simply because it did not flow there. A native at Tembwe[19] said that last year there were two Lukugas, one flowing to Tanganyika, another to Rua; but this year's rain had joined the two rivers and made them one, flowing west. Kawe-Nyange, the chief at the entrance to the Lukuga, said that he would show me a river flowing to the Tanganyika, and above a little way a river flowing toward Rua. A subchief of his said that formerly there were two Lukugas, one flowing to the lake, another flowing toward Rua; but these last two years' rains had risen the Tanganyika so much that the lake had "swallowed" the Lukuga, flowing into it, and had become joined to the Lukuga, flowing to Rua; but that this union with the Rua Lukuga was not continual, only during the hours of the southeast monsoon (manda); that each afternoon, after the wind had calmed, the river returned as usual to the lake. Lastly, I may mention that Mr. J. F. de Bourgh, C.E. and F.R.G.S., a gentleman engaged by me to construct me a blank chart of Central Africa, has drawn, near the position occupied by the Lukuga in question, a small lake with a river flowing out of it toward the Tanganyika. I must say that, wherever the gentleman obtained his information, he has illustrated the subject exactly as it was a few years ago.

As the case stands to-day no one is exactly right or very wrong. Exploration and close investigation of this geographical phenomenon reconcile all these contrary statements; but, without the above chart illustrating the survey, I would despair of making my meaning very clear.

In company with Kawe-Nyange and some of his people we sailed up a fine open stream-like body of water, ranging in width from 90 to 450 yards of open water. From bank to bank there was a uniform width of from 400 to 600 yards, but the sheltered bends, undisturbed by the monsoon winds, nourished dense growths of papyrus. After sailing three miles before the southeast wind we halted at the place which Kawe-Nyange pointed out as the utmost limit of the ascent made by Cameron, a small bend among the papyrus plants, a few hundred yards northwest from the Lumba's mouth. As a first proof of what Kawe-Nyange had said about a Lukuga flowing into the lake and another flowing out of the lake, he pointed out the returning

19. A Holoholo village near Mpala. Maes and Boone, *Peuplades du Congo Belge,* 376. See also "Lieutenant Cameron's Diary," 219.

water bubbles, which "fought," he said, against the small waves caused by the southeast wind, for which he received an encouraging word.

After landing at Lumba all who were not required by me in the deliberate investigation I was about to make with the aid of the boat, I had a proper camp made and a quiet cove cleared, where the boat and canoe could lie close to the bank. I then proceeded further up the Lukuga. When about 100 yards higher up we arrived at the utmost limit of open water, and an apparently impenetrable mass of papyrus grew from bank to bank. Here we stopped for a short time, and with a portable level tried to detect a current. The level indicated none. We then pushed our way through about twenty yards of the papyrus plants, until we were stopped by mudbanks, black as pitch, enclosing slime and puddles pregnant with seething animal life. I caused four men to stand in the boat, and standing on their shoulders with an oar for support I tried to obtain a general view of what lay ahead and around us. I saw the bed of the creek or river choked from bank to bank with the papyrus plants, except where they enclosed small pools of still water, and about a mile or so higher up I saw trees which seemed to me to stand exactly in the bed. Descending from my uneasy perch, I caused two of my men to proceed opposite ways on the mud toward the banks. Perceiving, after watching them a short time, that the muddy ooze was not firm enough to sustain a man's weight, I recalled them, and returned to open water again.

I now began another experiment to test the existence of a current. I took a piece of board, with which I had provided myself before hand, and cut out a disk a foot in diameter. Into this disk I bored four holes, through which I rove a stout cord and suspended to it at the distance of five feet an earthenware pot, which, filled with water, and held in suspension by the board, would unmistakably mark the existence of a current. Into one side of the board I drove a long spike with a small ball of cotton tied round the head. This done I measured along a straight reach of water, 1,000 feet with a tape line, both ends of the track distinctly marked by a ribbon of sheeting tied to the papyrus. When these preparations had been completed I proceeded to the southeasternmost end, and in the centre of the creek dropped the disk and attached the pot in the water, and noted the time by chronometer, while we rowed far away from it. The monsoon wind blew very strongly at the time. The distance which the disk floated between 23h. 22m. 20s. and 24h. 22m. was 822 feet from southeast to northwest. Second attempt, afternoon, wind, becalmed, disk floated from northwest to southeast—that is, lakeward—159 feet in 19 minutes 30 seconds.

This closes our experiments for the first day. The second day, with fifteen of the expedition, accompanied by the chief and ten of his people, we started afoot northwestward. Keeping as closely as the nature of the bushes and the watercourses would permit to the Lukuga, I observed that the trend of the watercourses and streams was from northwest to south and south-southeasterly. After a march of a couple of hours we came to Elwani village, where the road from Monyis to Unguvwa and Luwelezi crossed the Lukuga.[20] At Elwani we augmented our party with two of the villagers, then descended by a gentle slope to the Mitwansi. At the base of the slope we came to the bed occupied by the Kibamba and Lukuga. The former was a small sluggish stream with a trend southeasterly. Crossing this we came to the dried bed of a periodical river; whether it should be called the Lukuga or the Kibamba it would be difficult to say. Prostrate and withered water cane showed that the flow of the water in the season was lakeward. A few yards further on we came to where this bed first became moist, with a dense growth of water cane flourishing and checking all progress, except by the well trodden path, which now ran through tunnels caused by the water canes embracing above our heads. Our way now was through what might be called a swamp, now over a firm path of dark brown clayey mud, then through shallow hollows, with water up to the ankles, which now and then deepened to the knees. Finally we arrived in the middle of the Mitwansi, and Kawe-Nyange halted to point out triumphantly the water flowing indisputably westward. The water was up to the knees and felt cold, but on putting a thermometer into it I found it to be only 68 deg. Fahrenheit, about 7 deg. cooler than the Lukuga Creek. By pressing the cane down with our feet to allow a free passage for the water, the flow perceptibly quickened. Borne by two men, I crossed over until I stood on the other bank, and observed that the cane-choked bed was very uneven. Sometimes the water was so deep that the men sank to the hips, but the average depth was about eighteen inches. Trees, now dead, in the centre of the bed, which proved the statement of the native true, that not long ago the Mitwansi tract was dry enough to nourish tamarind trees. This last rainy season has changed it now, for since its termination the tract has become inundated, and a continual waterflow has been observable. The name Lukuga clings to this bed until it passes the

20. See Stanley's map, TDC, II, 47, or Map V.

Kiganja Ridge, when it becomes known as the Luindi (some call it the Luimbi), which, flowing by Miketo's Land, passes through Kalumbi's in Rua, and empties into the Kamalondo, a tributary of the Lualaba.[21] This road or ford, as it must now be called, is daily traversed by men, women and children, who require to cross from one bank to the other, and is about three miles northwest from Lumba, or six miles from Mkampemba.

The result of four days' experiments and investigations and inquiries proves that as far as the southeast end of the Mitwansi tract, which may be called a marsh or an ooze, receiving and absorbing a large quantity of water pressed against it by the daily southeast wind, there is no current, but that, on the contrary, the surplus waters which cannot be absorbed by the already repleted ooze on the wind subsiding return to the lake; that for the space of two miles from the southeast end of the Mitwansi the entire bed from bank to bank is choked by immovable mudbanks enclosing stagnant pools and stream-like expanses of water, edged round with impenetrable growths of papyrus plants; that at the third mile, where the ancient lacustrine deposit is of a firmer quality, and water cane replaces the papyrus, there first becomes discernible an ooze, a trickle and a flow westward, which, proceeding westward at the base of the Kiyanja ridge, is attracted to one proper channel and approaches the dignity of a river, when it becomes known as the Luindi.

This Mitwansi is a tract of alluvial deposit, and is the result of the united action of the lake winds (which from the end of April to the middle of November prevail from the southeast) and the feeble current of the former affluent Lukuga. The current, as may be expected from the very limited area it drained, was met daily during nearly seven months annually by the waves of the lake, which encroached yearly nearer and nearer to its source, and the detrital matter which would have been borne into the lake by a stream of greater force was deposited amid the papyri. This plant flourishes in still water and sweet water lagoons in quiet bends of rivers, and once it has thoroughly obtained root it becomes almost as immovable as a forest. As the waters of the lake advanced with its annual rise they destroyed with each year some small portion of the force of the Lukuga current, and the water plants and other organic débris floating down the stream no sooner felt the influence of the lake wind

21. The Lukuga flows into the Lualaba. For its future exploration, Hore, "Lake Tanganyika," 12–13; Thomson, *Central African Lakes*, II, 55ff.; Delcommune, *Vingt années de Vie africaine*, II, 504ff.; Hine, *The Fall of the Congo Arabs*, 248–71; Mohun, "Sur le Congo de Kassongo au Confluent de la Lukuga."

than they were heaped up amid these papyri; other débris borne direct from the lake, such as floating canewood, earthy matter from the banks and the bar, were pressed against them, sometimes thrown among them. Soil, sand, decomposing vegetation sunk on them, bore them down with their weight, and thus the process of entombing the earlier débris created finally a tract of clayey mud and ooze, out of which a luxurant growth of papyrus shot their brush-like heads as dense as a field of corn.

While the Lukuga was a river it will be seen that there was a constant precipitation of detrital matter and as steady an accumulation of it in one locality, until the river became annihilated, and only its bed, now filled by the creek, and the small tributary streams mark its former course.

Since the Tanganyika has risen to the level of the Mitwansi—whether this year, last year or two years ago matters not much which—a change must be looked for, and with the advance of years this change will become more decided and positive. The mud and ooze with the papyrus of the Mitwansi is too feeble an obstacle to resist the rising floods received each year by the Tanganyika while there is a steep slope at the western end ready to receive the surplus water; the consequence will be that five years hence, perhaps a little later, an effluent will be formed of magnitude and force, for the fiat of Nature has gone forth to the Tanganyika, "Thus high shalt thou rise, and no higher."

In which results, so patiently attained, I see no opposition to Lieutenant Cameron's claiming the honor of the discovery, but a simple reconciliation of all apparently opposing statements. The whole was a perplexing riddle to me, which the more I thought of the more complicated it grew, and only a personal examination of the scene would ever have enabled me to understand, unless some traveller had illustrated his explorations with a chart like the above.

In the absence of the scientific geologist I must take upon myself to suggest a few thoughts to those of your readers who may become interested in this subject of the Lukuga, and who are more able to deal with it. I cannot satisfactorily account to myself for the existence of this interesting phenomenon otherwise than by supposing the formation of the extraordinarily deep depression in the bosom of the broad plateau richly filled by the waters of the Tanganyika to be postdiluvian. If the ideas of one accustomed to read geological history, and to analyze phases of the past ages from existing traces in the hard rock or mountain contour, may be permitted to see the light, I would say that subsequent to the universal deluge, or the retreat of the ocean to its present bed, the Malagarazi and Luwegeri Rivers have flowed over this present enormous gulf, and channelled their way for their exit westward, first severing the Kiyanja from the Kilunga ridge. This enormous gulf was in these days an apparently firm plateau, with the same rolling surface as Unyamwezi and Uhha now present; and the two rivers, joined by others of less magnitude, flowed on undisturbedly to the Lualaba for centuries, perhaps ages. For in what other manner could this deep break in what must evidently have been long ago one firm unbroken, compact ridge, have become so smoothly worn down, a thousand feet and more, so low as to permit the gently flowing Luindi to sweep by its base from the east? It required a mightier volume of water than the Luindi, with no other source of supply than the ooze of the Mitwansi, three miles east of Kiyanja, and until the present year such supply must have been scanty in the extreme.

If it will be granted that such was, or might have been, the condition of this region at that time, the subsequent changes which took place are easy enough to arrive at. We may imagine volcanic agency, then, as heaving up this plateau, rending up the solid earth and heaping along the edges of the deep chasms it created into lengthy lines of mountain ranges and changing its former smooth rolling surface into its present rugged and uneven aspect. The great stream which formerly drained all this section and rolled between the Kihinga and Kyanja ridges, with its ancient bed disrupted, falls abruptly into the immense gulf in several and separate courses, and a stream of short course and little volume is created, flowing from the eastern slopes of the above-named ridges southeastward, to be in due time known as the Lukuga, since which tremendous wrack of nature half of the waters with inverted courses have assisted the other half to fill up the chasm, and appear to be now on the eve of fulfilling their task.

The visible effects of this great geological change are not the same at the southern end as they are further north and about the centre; for at the southern end the plateau, with its folds upon folds and layers upon layers of firm rock, drops abruptly down to the blue-green depths of the lake, and voyagers coasting along these shores appear to be gazing at the zenith as they look up at the few shrubs and trees growing upon the edge of the tawny plateau; while at the centre, especially about Tongwe[22] on the east side and Tembwe

22. In the Bende area. Avon, "Vie sociale des Wabende," 109. The inhabitants had the reputation of being very dangerous to visitors. Ramsay, "Uber seine Expedition nach Ruanda und der Rikwa-See," 318–19.

on the west side, we appear to be in the vicinity of the origin of
this convulsion and the section whence the earth first began to feel
her throes. At Tongwe we see an aggregation of aspiring peaks and
semi-circular cones, which would, perhaps, with more exact knowledge be called closed vomitaries or craters. South of Tembwe we
see a ridge inclining northeasterly, lofty and irregular, with much
of the same structure as the rocks of Tongwe exhibit.

North of Tembwe, on the same side, is to be observed a considerable depression in the land. From a height of 4,000 feet above the
surface of the lake the land has suddenly subsided into a low, rolling
surface, the highest point of which is scarcely 1,500 feet above the
lake, with isolated domes and cones. The rock also changes in character from the basalt and trap to a decomposed felspathic kind, followed by a conglomerate and calcerous tufa, strongly impregnated
with iron, which is the character of the rocks on each side of the
Lukuga. In no other part of the lake coast have I found rock of such
soft character as at the Lukuga. This depressed country continues
as far as Goma, where we see the land upheaved highest, but with
slopes less abrupt and rugged than at the south end, and clothed
with tropical luxuriance of vegetation—mammoth trees and numberless varieties of shrubs and plants. The high altitude which marks
the verge of the Goma plateau compared to that of the plateau
lying immediately west of it inclines one to think that the volcanic
explosion tilted the whole of this northwestern coast, merely raising
higher and loosening the edges of the chasm, which has since by
action of weather and water become worn and decomposed, presenting for a breadth of from four to five miles various of these effects
in mountain scenes approaching to the sublime in character. Once
out of view of the chasm filled by the Tanganyika the plateau is
seen clearly in its original form, and has a gradual westward slope.

Between North Goma and the high mountains of Uvira there is
another remarkable depression in the land similar to that of Uguhha.
It appears as if there had been a sudden subsidence of this part and
a flow of the subterranean rock north-northeast, which afterward
was ejected bodily upward, and now forms the peninsula of Ubwari,
which is over thirty miles in length.

Burton and Speke, on their voyage from Ujiji to Uvira, sketched
Ubwari as an island, probably from the fact that the Wajiji carelessly called it "Kirira," or "island." Livingstone and myself, also, in
1871, heard of what our predecessors had called Ubwari Island as
the Island of Muzimu.[23] Here is an instance of four travellers mis-

23. See *HIFL*, 482, 493.

taken about one small section of Lake Tanganyika. The truth is we are all wrong.

Exploration has proved that the countries of Karamba and Ubwari form a long narrow peninsula, joined firmly enough to the main land by an isthmus seven miles in width, with an altitude in its centre of about 200 feet above the lake. So it will be seen that, before any of our former statements can become correct, the Tanganyika must have a further rise of 200 feet, which is impossible.

The fact that this is not an island, but a peninsula, proves that there must be a deep gulf penetrating south-southwest between Masansi and Ubwari. I have taken the liberty of calling this great arm of the lake Burton Gulf, in honor of the discoverer of the Tanganyika, as Speke Gulf distinguishes a somewhat similar formation in the southeast section of the Victoria Niyanza.[24]

From the summit of one of the Ubwari hills—I appear to be the first white man who has ever enjoyed this privilege, for there is always some trouble in Ubwari—and it being a clear day, by means of a field glass I obtained an extensive view—at some distance, it is true, of the impenetrably savage countries west of Burton Gulf. The land lies in lengthy mountain waves, with deep valleys between, for twenty and thirty miles westward, when, finally, the great table land of this part of Central Africa presents itself, and is seen to join at a cloudy distance, after a deep curve, southwest to the plateau of Goma. These valleys between the mountain waves give rise to many small rivers, all of which have their exit into the lake in the west side of Burton Gulf.

Such are some of the most remarkable effects of that grand convulsion which disparted the table land of Central Africa and formed this enormous chasm of the Tanganyika in its bosom. Nor has this convulsion occurred so very remotely but it might, in my humble opinion, be measured by years by competent scientists. It appears, also, that the agencies which produced this extraordinary change are not quite dead in this part of Central Africa, for about eighteen months ago, I hear, a mountain in Urundi was precipitated from its position and toppled over, burying several villages with all their inhabitants. This disaster occurred near Mukungu, in Urundi.[25]

About three years ago the surface of the Tanganyika Lake, in the

24. The name still stands. In *Diary*, 125–26, Stanley recounts a brief fight with the Bembe while in Burton Gulf. Four Bembe were killed. In *TDC*, II, 58–60, Stanley, however, asserts that he left the hostile Africans without firing on them.

25. The Virunga Mountains included active volcanoes. See Mecklenburg, *Heart of Africa*, 82, 111ff.; Jack, *On the Congo Frontier*, 187ff.

neighborhood of Ujiji, was observed to be blackened with large lumps and masses of some strange dark substance, which, as they were swept on the shore of Ujiji, were picked up, examined and wondered at. The Wajiji called it, and still continue firmly in the belief, the discharge of lightning. The Arabs called it pitch and collected large quantities of it. Requiring some substance to caulk my boat before setting out on the voyage of exploration I was presented with some of this "discharge of lightning," or pitch, and found it was asphaltum, which most probably escaped through some vent in the bed of the Tanganyika, as on no part of the shores could I obtain, after diligent inquiry, the slightest knowledge of its source.[26]

30

Ujiji
August 10, 1876 [1]

Ismail, Khedive of Egypt, is reported to have said that all travellers up the Nile generally returned with the statement that a new source of the Nile had been discovered. The publisher of the report, no doubt, thought that His Highness was poking sly fun at the discoverers. Whether it was the case or not, I must inform His Highness, through the columns of the NEW YORK HERALD and *Daily Telegraph,* that he can pride himself upon being a sovereign of a country whose great river's several sources have, and do still, task the best abilities and qualities of explorers to discover them; that his river has not one, but several sources; that one main source was discovered by James Bruce, and called the Blue Nile;[2] that another was discovered by Speke and Grant, and called the Victoria Niyanza, and that another was discovered by Samuel Baker and called by him the Albert Niyanza, but that these gentlemen did not, nor could, exhaust the discoveries of the sources of this noble river. Perhaps the facts which I send you of a new source will compel His Highness to exclaim, "Eh! what do I see now? Another new source? Can it be possible that the Nile has not yet been exhausted?" Could ancient Nilus reply to him I could fancy him saying, "And how many

26. Compare with Diderrich, "Au Lac Tanganika."
1. *NYH,* March 27, 1877.
2. Paez had visited the source of the Blue Nile in 1618; Bruce, who claimed its discovery, visited it in 1770. Ullendorf, "Bruce," 134–36.

of my sources did thy grim grandsire Mohammed Ali,[3] or his sons, Ibrahim and Ismail,[4] discover? And what has thou done with all thy power, who should have greatest interest in knowing whence I came and what trouble I have had to travel so far to water thy gardens and fields and sustain thee and thy people? Ingrates of Egypt! Which of ye all have thought it worth while to find out whence I came, that ye might honor me as I should be honored? If, by special favor merely, I whisper a few of my secrets to strangers from afar and permit them to view a few of my wondrous and sweet fountains and flowery beds, what is it to thee? Art thou envious of like honor? Then seek me at my many homes under the Equator."

If His Highness will accept my answer I respectfully beg him to glance over this letter, and to read these few remarks I have now the honor to make respecting the river known as the Kagera, or Ingezi, or Kitangule, or Nawarango, which, according to the natives of Karagwe and Uganda, is called the Mother of the River at Jinja, or the Victoria Nile.

People differ, it appears, as to the exact signification of the "source" of a river, and travellers jealous of their credit for discovery have sometimes assisted to make the meaning more uncertain. Stay-at-homes, on whom devolves the duty of toning down the exuberant enthusiasm of travellers, are generally agreed that it is the main head, origin, or extremity, whence the principal supply is obtained as a spring, fountain, marsh, lake; or it may be that the river is created by a series of these, or that one main tributary is followed to its extreme end, and that end, whatever it be, is called the source of the river.

Speke, if I remember rightly, asks somewhat pettishly in one of his books, "What should be called the source of a river—a lake which receives the insignificant rivers flowing into it and discharges all by one great outlet, or the tributaries which the lake collects, or the clouds which supply these tributaries with water?" In my opinion, if we go on at this rate, we might proceed still further and ask, "Or the moisture and vapors which the clouds absorb or the ocean which supplies these vapors and moistures?" If these questions are permitted, why should explorers go into such trouble to

3. Muhammad Ali Pasha (1769–1849), who arrived in Egypt to fight Napoleon and remained to become one of Egypt's most dynamic rulers. Hill, *Biographical Dictionary*, 249–50.

4. Ibrahim Pasha al Wali (1789–1848), eldest son of Muhammad Ali; he was justly famous for his military campaigns in Arabia, the Sudan, and Greece. *Ibid.*, 177. Isma'il Kamil Pasha (1795–1822), son of Muhammad Ali, was killed in the Sudan. *Ibid.*, 185–86.

discover sources of rivers when every child is perfectly well acquainted with the sources of all rivers? If we remember the true signification on "source," it is easy to understand why Bruce and Speke and Baker all returned home each with a new source of the Nile, and why I send you a description of another source of the Nile.

Speke and Baker both write about "reservoirs of the Nile" in their books. Speke discovered the Victoria Lake, and, while accompanied by Grant, discovered the Victoria Nile. The Victoria Lake is a magnificent extent of water, a chart of which, the result of our circumnavigation of it, I sent you some time ago. It is the recipient of many fine streams, two of which are very important. The Shimeeyu is 290 miles in length from its source to its exit into the lake. The Alexandra Nile[5] (as yet discovered) a length of 310 miles, and perhaps as many more. The Shimeeyu might be compared to the Thames, and drains off the water which falls into it from extensive plains, forests and slopes of plateaus; but the Alexandra Nile exceeds in volume, even in the dry season, the Thames and Severn united, and the color and purity of its water prove that it must either take its rise far to the westward of the Tanganyika or that its course is so intercepted by some lake where its waters were purified. Investigating the cause, I discovered there was a lake of considerable extent, known by diffeernt names.

Speke, after visiting the outlet of the Victoria Lake and travelling some distance down in its descent northerly and westerly, returned home, and soon after a fatal accident deprived the Geographical Society of one of the most indefatigable of explorers. Sir Samuel Baker, hearing from Speke and Grant of the existence of a lake west of Unyoro, proceeded to that field, and fortunately discovered another magnificent lake, called by the Wanyoro Luta N'zige; by the Waganda, Muta Mzige; by the Wasagara, Nyanja Unyoro; by the Wanyambu, sometimes all three; to which Baker, however, very properly gave the name Albert Niyanza.[6] In a native canoe he explored about sixty miles along the northeast coast, and discovered

5. The Kagera. Stanley named it for Alexandra (1844–1925), wife of the future Edward VII. The name did not gain acceptance. Thomas and Dale, "Uganda Place Names," 102. He also named a lake for her. See below.

6. The giving of such European names to African lakes led one German geographer, Karl Andree, to compare British explorers with the innkeepers he then held were similarly filling Europe with "Victoria Hotels." The Royal Geographical Society upheld the naming of Lake Albert, however, and did not formally pronounce against the giving of European names until the beginning of the twentieth century. Globus 8 (1865), 287; Alcock's speech of May 28, 1877, JRGS 47 (1877), cxcv–cxcvi; Thomas and Dale, "Uganda Place Names," 101.

the Victoria Nile, descending from the Lake Victoria, to be one of the affluents of the Albert Lake. A little further north the Albert Niyanza discharges all its collected affluents—the Victoria Nile being one of them—into the White Nile, which in its descent toward Egypt receives other affluents more or less important. Near Khartoum the White Nile receives an accession to its volume from the Blue Nile (discovered by James Bruce), which rises in Abyssinia.

If it be asked, "Why enter into these trite details?" I reply that I write for the readers of the NEW YORK HERALD and the *Daily Telegraph*, which number about half a million; that among this vast number a great many are perhaps a little confused about the sources of the Nile, know little of how much has been discovered or of how much remains to be discovered; and I believe it necessary for a thorough comprehension of the subject that these few remarks should be made.

After discovering a great gulf in the Albert Niyanza I travelled south from latitude 0.30 deg. north in search of the tributaries of these two great lakes—the Albert and Victoria—and perceived that the slope of the section was more to the east, toward the Victoria, and that no rivers worthy of the name, except the Rusango or Mpanga, fall into the Albert Lake from the east side. Nor can any river of importance supply the Albert from the south, because the Alexandra Niyanza occupies too large a bed, and must be fed from the section separating the Tanganika and Albert, and the Albert from the Victoria. If any important affluents supply the Albert other than the Victoria Nile they must be searched for on the southwest and west side of Lake Albert, by means of a vessel launched on its waters or by a journey overland. If an affluent is found on that side so large as to exercise an important influence on the lake, or would exercise on the While Nile itself did not Lake Albert intercept its course, it is obvious that such a river should be taken into consideration when speaking of the sources of the Nile.

Lake Albert, receiving such a grand affluent as the Victoria Nile, has been called by Baker a reservoir of the Nile; but in my opinion this noble lake deserves a yet higher title, as I shall presently show. It is proved by my explorations that Lake Victoria is also a reservoir of the Nile, and I shall prove that Lake Victoria deserves a higher title, distinct and separate from that given to Lake Albert.

Permit me to place in order a few questions and answers. What supplies the White Nile with water? Lake Albert, of course, principally. What supplies Lake Albert? The Victoria Nile, of course, principally (so far as is yet known). Whence proceeds the Victoria

Nile? From the Victoria Lake. What supplies the Victoria Lake? The Alexandra Nile, of course, principally. Whence proceeds the Alexandra Nile? From the Alexandra Lake.[7] What supplies the Alexandra Lake? The Upper Alexandra Nile and other streams not yet known.

It is clear, then, that the Egyptian Nile is the issue of the united Blue and White Niles; that the White Nile is the issue of Lake Albert; that the Victoria Nile is the issue of Lake Victoria; that the Lower Alexandra Nile is the issue of Lake Alexandra.

Thus it will be seen that I have given higher titles to these lakes than mere reservoirs; for, without the source of supply, what would the reservoir become? Indeed, in strict and sober verity, these several lakes are mere accidents of nature, intercepting the course of the river from the Alexandra Nile to Alexandria, disparting the river into several streams—the White Nile, Victoria Nile and Alexandra Nile.

A parallel case is presented by the Lualaba, discovered by Livingstone, which may be described in like manner as the above. The Chambezi feeds Lake Bemba; Lake Bemba creates the Luapula; the Luapula supplies Lake Mweru; Mweru creates Webb's Lualaba; Webb's Lualaba, supplied by other tributaries, supplies the Lower Lualaba (or, in other words, the Lower Lualaba is the issue of Webb's Lualaba); Webb's Lualaba is the issue of Lake Mweru; the Luapula is the issue of Bemba. These lakes, in like manner, are mere accidents of nature, as the Nile niyanzas, and are so many interceptions or basins in the course of the rivers.

I send you these facts not only to show the course of the Alexandra Nile, but because (if natives are to be believed) the Alexandra Lake serves a double purpose. It is a basin for the reception of many tributaries, and has three outlets—one north of Ugufu by the Ruvuvu into the lower Alexandra Nile; the second south of Ugufu into the same river by the Kagera; the third by means of a marsh or an ooze into the Kivu Lake, whence the Rusizi takes its rise, which Rusizi, of course, empties into Lake Tanganika.

Perhaps it would be asked by the curious why I have distinguished the discoveries illustrated above by the name of Alexandra. I shall forestall the curious with the following candid explanation:

7. The actual body of water referred to is unclear. A later visitor looking for the lake, and unable to find it, said, "apparently the name is applied to a papyrus fringe on the course of the Kagera proper." Elliot, *A Naturalist in Mid-Africa*, 256. Thomas and Dale, "Uganda Place Names," 106, suggest Lake Mugesera in Rwanda.

Captain John Hanning Speke and Captain James Grant, both British officers, while on their way to Uganda to search for the outlet of the Victoria Lake, crossed this very river, the Alexandra Nile. What they thought about it I do not know. I have not their books at hand; but it appears that, seeing this river flow in a contracted channel (150 yards wide of open, swift, deep water), and perhaps ignorant of its depth, and having another grand object in view, their actions governed by the sole hope of discovering the Victoria Nile, they did not pay that attention to it that they would have done were their mission of a more general character. It cannot be disputed, then, that two British officers were the first who saw this river. Had poor Speke lived I believe he would have returned to this interesting region, for I hear he had such an intention from King Rumanika.[8] Might he have been permitted to return, to round off as it were and unite the fragments of discovery he had made, the natives and his amiable friend Rumanika would have pointed out to him the "Mother of the Victoria Nile." On casting his thoughts around for a name to dignify these new discoveries, what name more graceful, more worthy for a thousand virtues, illustrious descent and position, could he have found to dignify them than that of Her Royal Highness Alexandra, Princess of Wales?

British officers first saw the river. The *Daily Telegraph,* an English journal, contributed one half of the funds by means of which these latest discoveries have been made. I, therefore, in the name of the English and American journals I represent here, appeal through your columns that the name of Her Royal Highness, the Princess of Wales, be permitted to distinguish these discoveries, worthy to stand near such honored names as Albert and Victoria.

I have been very deliberate, you will admit, in making up and sending you this letter, but I had strong reasons for it. I am too far from the telegraphic wire to correct an error, and I have no ambition to be charged with having made a rash statement, though I covered the offence with the excuse that the natives told me. I value native and Arab statements only as being an impellant motive power to the explorer, not to be understood, by any means, as conveying accurate and exact information. Even the most intelligent of Arabs, Wanguana, Waswahili and Central African natives, as if originally they were taken out of the same matrix, have a prurient palate for exaggeration. If the explorer is unable to visit personally the scene, he may then be excused—after sifting evidence, comparing infor-

8. Speke did have plans to return to Africa. See Speke to Rigby, March 30, 1863, July 4, 1863, Aug. 24, 1963, Zanzibar Museum.

mation acquired in different localities and weighing with judgment and a sense of distrust every particle of intelligence—for publishing geographical news on native authority. It is not until after marching from the confluence of the Ruvuvu and the Kagera to Ujiji, and circumnavigating the Tanganika, and hearing Wazige and Warundi bear witness to the same facts, that I found courage to publish what I had not seen personally, or, indeed, did I clearly understand them for myself. I will give you, in brief, three instances of people's mendacity, which will prove to you that the best weapon an explorer can arm himself with is distrust.

Manwa Sera, captain in the Anglo-American Expedition, during a casual talk with me, relates: "Master, when I was in Karagwe, some five or six years ago, I went to the top of a high mountain near Rumanika's, and I saw an enormous lake to the west of me. I should say it would take three days to reach it. I could not see the other side of the other lake." All this related slowly, as if he weighed well each word, with great gravity, and a certain dignity. Facts as viewed by the Explorer: Lake six or seven hours' march from Rumanika's; length of lake, thirteen miles; greatest breadth, eight miles; name of lake, Jhema Rweru.

Next, Baraka,[9] a smart young fellow, a soldier in the Anglo-American Expedition, relates as follows: "Speak of Ruanda! Do I not know Ruanda and all the countries round about? Who is he that has gone further than I have? Have I not been to Ankori? Yes; I have carried things of ornament to the King of Ankori. Ruanda is yellow and flat. It is like a plain; extends away, away westward —a plain, in truth!" Facts by Explorer: Ruanda is exactly the opposite of what Baraka says. The view of Ruanda from Karagwe is of a succession of lofty mountain ridges, separated by deep broad valleys. Explorer pointed out the strong contrast to Baraka. Baraka recklessly laughed and impudently showed his ivories.

Next: A Mgwana, a long time resident within a few hundred yards of the mouth of the Rusizi, relates to Livingstone and myself, in 1871: "White men, you want to know all about the Rusizi. I know all about it. I came from Mukamba's yesterday. This River Rusizi goes out of the lake. I tell you true, quite true." Facts by two explorers: The Rusizi flows into the Lake Tanganika, and not out, and the foolish Mgwana caused the explorers to infer that he told an unnecessary untruth, or, in other words, that he lied.

A native of Central Africa rarely, if ever, wilfully lies about a

9. Baraka died in 1884 while in service on the Congo River. Coquilhat, *Sur le Haut-Congo*, 226.

matter that does not concern his interests. Ignorance in most cases is the cause of wrong information from him, and lack of acquaintance with details gives a vagueness and uncertainty to what is told. But if half a dozen of them can be examined upon a subject the traveller can generally pick out much reliable information. The Waganda, Warundi and Wazige are very intelligent, especially the former.

A young Waganda, who had travelled in Karagwe and who went with me to the Albert Niyanza, has oftentimes astonished me by his remarks upon the Alexandra Nile, which he called the Kagera. I fancy if the Geographical Society had heard him they would have voted him a silver medal for his intelligent observations. As my conversation with him was very interesting I will give you in his own words, as nearly as I can remember, what he said about the Kagera.

"Master, Sambuzi, my chief, has sent me to you with his salaams, and he says that the best way for you to go to Muta Nzige (Albert) Niyanza is by the Kagera."

"Why," I asked, "is Kagera the best way?"

"Because," said he, "Kagera comes from Muta Nzige."

"Nonsense," I replied, "Muta Nzige is far below the Niyanza of Uganda; and how can a river ascend a hill?"

"Master, you white people know a great deal; but will you tell me where the Kagera comes from?"

"I cannot tell you, because I have not seen it yet, and I don't know anything of the river except what I have seen of it at the mouth."

"Master, there is no river like the Kagera. We Waganda call it 'the mother of the river' at Jinja (Victoria Nile). Where can the Kagera come from if it does not come from Muta Nzige? Look at its water. It is water of a Niyanza, and so much water as is in it cannot come from any mountain. Everybody says it comes from the Muta Nzige."

When I turned my back upon the Albert Niyanza I felt consoled somewhat by this young man's remarks upon the Kagera. From a score of persons, on the way to Kagera, I heard enough to create in me a keen desire to view and examine this river. I have already told you I obtained soundings of 70, 80, up to 120 feet of water in its bed, that it had a swift current and a width of from 150 to 200 yards.

From Rumanika—that gentle and most sweet pagan, whom I found more easy to convert to a geographer than to a Christian—I

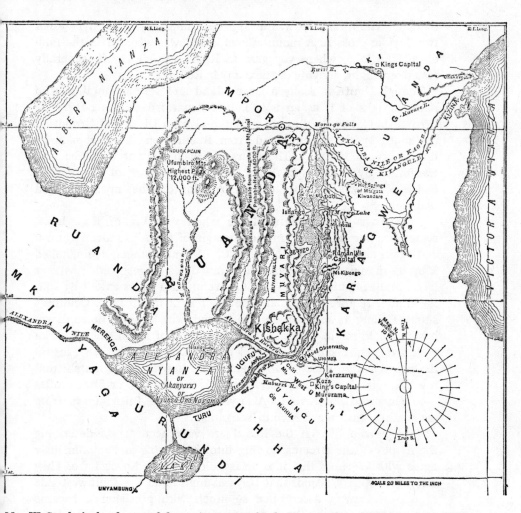

Map VI. Stanley's sketch map of the territory west of Lake Victoria (from *NYH*, March 29, 1877)

obtained every assistance, by which I was enabled to explore thoroughly the singular body of water called Ingezi, which is a shallow lake five to ten, and even fourteen miles wide, through which the Alexandra Nile continues its resistless course with a depth of from forty to sixty feet. I was enabled, after continuing my journey from Rumanika's, to obtain a pretty clear view of a good deal of the unexplored course of the Alexandra Nile. What I could not see, because of the mountains of Ugufu, was Akanyaru, or Niyanza Cha-Ngoma; but my guides assisted me to understand tolerably well the position of the lake. The Akanyaru was a large lake and very wide. It required two days to cross it. A mountainous island was situated in the middle of the lake, where voyagers to Ruanda from Ugufu generally rested one night, arriving the next day in Ruanda.

Though Ugufu is really a large island and very mountainous no native speaks of it as an island. It is separated on the north side from Kishakka by the Ruvuvu outlet, and from Uhha and Urundi on the south by the Kagera, and from Ruanda on the west side by the Alexandra Niyanza. The course of each affluent from the lake was taken by compass bearings both at the Mount of Observation and at Keza, where I obtained confirmation of what my guides had told me.

The natives much confused me when speaking of Kivu Lake, sometimes pointing it out in the direction of the Alexandra Niyanza, and again using the name Niyanza Cha-Ngoma; others, again, called it by the name of Mkinyaga. They sometimes represented it as very large, and sometimes attempted to give an idea of its extent by stating that it required so much time to cross it in a canoe. Countries situated along its shores were also named, which, being noted down, have assisted me to compare the information of natives of Kishakka with that furnished by Wazige and Warundi. Warundi on the Tanganika say that Kivu Lake is connected with Akanyaru by a marsh; that it would require a day's march along this marsh—ten or fifteen miles —to proceed from Kivu to Akanyaru; that the Rusizi flows from the southwest corner of Kivu to Tanganika.

Wazige who live on the Rusizi are very accurate in describing the names of the streams flowing into the Rusizi, and unanimously agree with Warundi that it is an issue of Kivu or Kovoe Lake. They also agree with Warundi that Unyambungu is on the southwest side of Kivu.[10] Having ascertained so much with precision it became easy then to connect the fragmentary information contained from North Uhha, West Usui and Kishakka, where the name Kivu is not generally known, and the country of Unyambungu renders the solution of the difficulty.

Mkinyaga is northwest of Unyambungu, and to a person in North Uhha, with his face turned north, Mkinyaga is said to be left of Kivu, therefore, is situated west of that lake, and, as Mkinyaga is a large country, extending to southwest Ruanda until a three days' march, would take a person to the Albert Niyanza. When hearing of

10. See document 29, note 13.

Mkinyaga Lake, we must understand it to be Akanyaru or the Alexandra Niyanza, which comprehends all the native titles of the lake.

Here, within two degrees of longitude, where seven countries meet, representatives of seven nations are unable to give a clear and connected account of this most interesting region. The cause of this ignorance arises from the peculiar character of the northern Warundi and Wa-Ruanda, who are a jealous, treacherous, and vindictive race. If an explorer could cross the country of Urundi, and enter Mkinyaga, he meets with a different race, with whom it would not be difficult to establish amicable relations; but unless he had balloons at his disposal I am unable to see how he could reach Mkinyaga from the east or the south. Were the Warundi or the Wa-Ruanda anything in disposition like the tribes or nations we have met with between here and Zanzibar, how easy a task it were to push one's way direct to the utmost reach of the Nile! We have met tribes who sternly exacted tribute, and we have paid it and passed on our way, and have met tribes who compelled us to fight our way through them; but here are two nations (not tribes) of one peculiar distinct breed, who are neither to be subject to the power of sweet suasion with gifts of sugar-candy, knick-knacks and gaudy cloths, or to be forced from the position they have assumed with a few dozen Sniders. Heaven knows the original progenitors of these fierce nations. I had half a mind once to make an alliance with the bandit Mirambo,[11] and, with the addition of a thousand Brown Besses,[12] drag the secrets of the Nile by force to the light of day. But the name of the amiable Princess of Wales could not be taken then to cover such a stain as this would have been on the source of the Nile.

No. I live in the hope that our expedition can yet reach this section without violence, from the fact, if true, that Mkinyaga can be reached from North Manyema—that the people of Mkinyaga are traders, and convey articles of trade from Manyema to Ruanda. All this, however, can only be settled at Nyangwe, whither I propose going now.

I have two reasons for going round about this way, since the direct road is closed. It has become firmly impressed on my mind that the principal river supplying the Alexandra Niyanza rises in North Manyema, northwestward of Lake Tanganika.

11. Stanley had a peaceful meeting with his former enemy, Mirambo, in April 1876, while on the way to Ujiji. *TDC*, I, 490–94.
12. Flint-lock muskets.

Secondly, I do not forget that the purpose of this enterprise of the NEW YORK HERALD and *Daily Telegraph* was to unite the fragmentary discoveries of Speke into one complete whole, to finish Baker's or Burton's discovery, and finally to take up the work left incomplete by the lamented death of Doctor Livingstone.

Lieutenant Cameron, animated by his desire to cross Africa more than to complete the discoveries of his predecessors, has crossed the Lualaba and proceeded to Lake Lincoln, thence proceeded, I am told, in a southwesterly direction with a company of Portuguese traders; probably to Ambriz or St. Paul de Loanda, by which he has left the question of the Lualaba exactly where Livingstone left it.[13] For the question in dispute was, "Is the Lualaba the Nile or the Congo?" Livingstone thought it to be the Nile; the Geographical Council thought it to be the Congo. The only way to resolve the doubt is to travel down the Lualaba along the right bank to a known point.

You will thus perceive I have two brilliant fields before me. And the prospect of entering any one of them causes me to quiver with delight, though merely anticipating what lies ahead. "Shall I search for the head of the Alexandra Nile, or shall I continue along the right bank of the Lualaba?" is a proposition which agitates the silent hours of night with me. Shall I, after arriving at Nyangwe, strike northeasterly and take this coy Nile by surprise where he first issues from the oozy womb or from the angle of some dewy valley, and trace him thence through all his sportive career, amid flower decked lakelets or the breadths of ever vernal papyrus, or where he rushes with fresh born vigor and youthful ardor by fragrant meads and forest clad slopes to the three blue Niyanzas, where he meets his kindred gathered from all points of the compass to crown him King Nilus and Lord of Floods? Or shall I worship at the shrine of the majestic Lualaba, view with awe and reverence his broad glassy bosom, watch him unfold his strength and launch himself against rocks with angry roar until the woods and valleys resound the name of this terrible monarch, behold him receiving his tribute from other potentates of less renown, and follow him through the dark unknown land to where he finally discharges his flood to the ocean? Both courses are equally enticing; both present splendid fields for geo-

13. Stanley was being rather uncharitable to Cameron, who had been blocked in his efforts to follow the Congo to the sea. Cameron later returned the compliment by affirming that a return via the Congo would have been easier than the route he followed to the coast, but that to take the river journey, "I should have had in some measure to countenance the buying and selling of slaves, and this I could not do." See Cameron's description of his expedition in Brown, *The Story of Africa and Its Explorers*, II, 266–79.

graphical research; but which I shall adopt will be best known after I reach Nyangwe.

In the meantime I lay at the feet of the mighty Princess of Wales an explorer's tribute—all that he has discovered, measured and surveyed of the Alexandra Nile—the Mother of the Victoria Nile.[14]

31

Ujiji
August 13, 1876 [1]

I must leave off writing letters and must hurry away, for times are sad, very sad, in Ujiji. A most malignant epidemic is raging here, devouring the population at the rate of from forty to seventy-five persons daily. It is a smallpox of the most fatal kind. Few attacked by it have escaped. The same evil influences which nourish this pest cause other ailments to prevail—namely, dysentery, chest diseases, typhoid fevers and agues. You may perceive by the dates of my letters to you how many days I required to write off a couple of letters and make up two surveys. I returned from the circumnavigating voyage August 1; this is now the 13th. Thirteen days to write two letters! It is true; but the time has been mostly spent fretting in bed from repeated attacks of fevers.

When I landed from my boat I received a budget of bad news only. Five deaths had already occurred in the expedition during my absence of fifty-one days; six more were down with smallpox; the

14. Stanley was roundly criticized for this despatch. Observers pointed out that Speke had visited the Kagera and had included a Lake Akanyaru on his map, thereby concluding Stanley had violated "polite usage" for naming a lake he had not visited and for changing the name of a previously discovered river. Stanley was also chided for traveling without Speke's book, the essential account of the previous visit of a European to the area. Finally, the claims Stanley made for a river and a lake he had passed earlier, and had not revisited, led to the comment that all Stanley's hypotheses were inexplicable "unless it be that each letter he sends home must contain a new discovery." Oliphant, "African Explorers," 386–391; Alcock's speech (see n. 6 above), cxcv. Despite the criticisms, Stanley was of course correct in declaring that the Kagera system is the ultimate source of the Nile. The most remote source of the Nile is the Luvironza River, rising about 25 miles from Lake Tanganyika; it feeds the Ruvuvu, which joins the Niavarongo, which joins the Kagera. Hurst, Nile, 159–60. The main exploration of the tributaries was accomplished by Kandt. See Kandt, Caput Nili, I, 237, II, 52ff.

1. NYH, March 27, 1877. See Appendix M, for another Stanley letter of Aug. 13, 1876.

fearful disease was running like wildfire through the houses of Ujiji, Arab and native. Frank Pocock had suffered severe illness three times while I had been away; an influential Arab trader died the day of my return; the Governor of Ujiji[2] and Livingstone's old friend Mohammed bin Gharib[3] had lost several children and were losing slaves each day, though their losses of slaves had been already severe. Slaves and pagazis, or porters, were fast deserting their masters for fear of this scourge. Finally, my messengers, five in number, had not yet returned from Unyanyembe, and as they have not returned up to this day I have given up all hope of them.[4] You may imagine then, the feeling which prevails in all minds at the present time in Ujiji—it is that of dismay and terror; and, as they look forward to two months more of the fatal experience they are now undergoing those who are able to quit the horrible spot should pack up at once.

When I first heard this news I was impressed with the necessity of immediate departure if I valued the welfare of the expedition; but I had also my duty to do toward you. The two letters I have written to you may, perhaps, be considered by you—if you have any inclination to be very exacting—as mere sops, but they are the best and the utmost that can be done under such aggravating circumstances. The condition of my people is really deplorable. Beside being thinned in numbers many favorites of those still living are in a bad state, and some no doubt will be taken off.

The only thing it appears to me that has saved the expedition from total wreck is vaccination. But I find when too late that many of the people lost the benefit of vaccination from sheer laziness—when summoned they would not appear.[5] My vaccine matter is all dried up now and not a particle of it can be scraped up to be of use.

2. Mwinyi Kheri. For his career, Bennett, "Mwinyi Kheri."

3. Muhammad bin Gharib, a trader resident for many years in the African interior, had been described by Livingstone "as one of the kindest and best of the Moslems in Central Africa." He was also credited with saving the missionary Hore's life. Muhammad bin Gharib died around 1886, so burdened with debts that he had been prevented from returning to Zanzibar. Burton, *Life of Burton*, I, 325; *HIFL*, 570; Hore, "Lake Tanganyika," 24; Damodar Jeram to Kirk, June 8, 1886, E-90, ZA.

4. Four of the men eventually reached Zanzibar. They claimed they had been delayed by the Mirambo wars in Tabora, but had eventually reached Nyangwe about two months after Stanley had left. After two more years' delay the men succeeded in getting to Zanzibar in a very destitute condition. Bennett, "Stanley and the American Consuls at Zanzibar," 56, 58; Tippu Tip to Taria Topan, Oct. 28, 1878, in Kirk to the Secretary of the Royal Geographical Society, June 23, 1879, unmarked volume, ZA.

5. This took place near Bagamoyo. *TDC*, II, 62.

Poor Frank Pocock has done his best for his Arab neighbors and friends, and it was very gratifying to me to hear how excellently and nobly he had behaved. He is certainly the best servant a man ever had. I would not part with him for a hundred Shaws and Farquhars. He has become a most ardent geographer, too, and, having no other companion with me, I frequently exchange views and hopes with him. He did not look very promising as a companion at first; I thought him rather slow. He has a host of virtues and not one vice, nor shadow of a vice. He is a brave, honest, manly, patient young Englishman.

I had a great many things to write about my journey round the Tanganika—it has been so very interesting. I may say it has been replete with discoveries of magnificent waterfalls, unrivalled scenery, "water hyaenas," [6] exquisitely fragrant berries, caverns and underground dwellings, the copper mines of Katanga and the mode of working them. I have heard much about the famous underground houses of Rua,[7] and have discovered what might be called a kind of religion among the tribes round the Tanganika, any of which discoveries, with abundant leisure, would furnish matter for a letter. But the necessity of immediate deaprture is too urgent, which, if I delayed, would entail the sacrifice of many valuable lives in this expedition. It will take some days to prepare, to assort and rearrange the goods after such a long stay here, and various minor matters must be attended to. I may be able to write you a small note on the day of departure to acquaint you with our position and our prospects.

32

Nyangwe
Oct. 28, 1876. [1]

The subject which I choose for this letter is one professedly of interest to a large class of Englishmen and Americans, and, I believe, to many people in Germany. It is the slave trade in the African interior and those who deal in the traffic and amass wealth out of it. In giving you an account of its nature I promise you not to indulge my personal feelings, but to be cool, precise and literal, believing

6. Otters; see document 21, note 6.
7. See document 10, note 3.
1. *NYH,* Oct. 10, 1877.

that the letter will have more effect than if it contained merely vituperations and objurgations against the slave traders.

One has to travel very far in Africa, from east toward west, before he will begin to experience that strong antipathetic feeling to the slave traders so characteristic in Livingstone; for the slave trade elsewhere is mostly confined to small private retail dealings in human flesh between Arab and Arab. Two or three, or half a dozen, or a dozen slaves are exchanged quietly between traders, as the exigencies of business or currency require. These few slaves are perhaps accepted in payment of a long standing debt, or are purchased to complete the number of domestic servants. The buying or selling of them in such a quiet, orderly manner does not strike one as being specially repulsive—rather more as an exchange from one domestic service to another.

At Unyanyembe perhaps he may see a sight once in a while to provoke indignation and disgust. To witness it daily, however, the traveller must have sharp eyes and exert himself in a hot climate a little more than is desirable or comfortable. In Uganda the trade begins to assume a wholesale character, yet it still retains a business aspect, not particularly shocking to any great extent, for the dismalities and heartrendings it provokes are all hushed up long before the slaves become the property of the Arabs. The kings and chiefs, to whose peculiar tastes such an extensive and singular trade is owing, have long ago dried the tears of the captives by searing their nerves and severing the chords of sympathy and of feeling by cruel means, so that, except in infrequent instances, there are no more tears to be shed or power of wailing left when they begin to be driven in flocks toward the Arab depots or the coast.

At Ujiji one sees a slave market established—not a central market, as at Zanzibar, but in several slave folds or slave pens, maintained by degraded half-castes or demoralized Wajiji—whence they are taken by those in need of slaves for service or for retail sale. The objects of traffic, as they are landed at the shore of Ujiji, are generally in a terrible condition, reduced by hunger to ebony skeletons —attenuated weaklings, unable to sustain their large, angular heads. Their voices have quite lost the manly ring; they are mere whines and moans of desperately sick folk. Scarcely one is able to stand upright; the back represents an unstrung bow, with something of the serrated appearance of a crocodile's chine. Every part of their frames shows the havoc of hunger, which has made them lean, wretched and infirm creatures. Just here I could, if I might, launch out into vigorous abuse of the authors of these crimes, and they deserve a thousandfold more denunciation than can be invented by me or by any humane soul in Europe; but I have promised to be cool, precise and literal. Yet I may say that all the Satanic host protects them, for it must be assuredly owing to the deep wiles of hell and its inhabitants that the people of a small island like Zanzibar are permitted to commit crimes such as no European State understands.

The living skeletons described above have all been marched from Marungu to Uguhha; thence to Ujiji they were crowded in canoes. When our expedition crossed over to Uguhha we met 800 slaves of exactly such a cast as already described, principally children and women. I do not mean to say that these 800 were all skeletonized thus by hunger. There were a few—perhaps fifty, perhaps more—who still possessed somewhat of rotundity in their forms; but these, I was told by the traders, sustained themselves by assiduous consumption of roots, berries, voided grain, &c. The canoes which brought the expedition to Uguhha returned to Ujiji with full cargoes of slaves. Frank Pocock, my European servant, had often read in English journals accounts of the treatment and condition of African slave droves, but until our arrival at Uguhha he said he never realized in his own mind what that treatment really was. Poor Frank, obliged to be sent back to Ujiji to recover some deserters, had more than enough of terrible scenes, for he was obliged to take passage in a heavily loaded slave canoe, wherein fifty little withered wretches were crowded into a mass like so many starved pigs. As the canoe was three days *en route* Frank's nerves were terribly tortured.[2]

These slaves are the profitable result of a systematic war waged upon all districts in the populous country of Marungu by banditti, supported by Arab means, directly and indirectly. Directly, because Arabs purchase the slaves taken in these wars for powder and guns, by means of which the wars are sustained; and indirectly, because there is no other market than the Arabs supply to relieve the banditti of the thousands which otherwise would have to be released from sheer want of food.

These banditti are Unyamweze, armed with guns purchased at Unyanyembe and Bagamoyo, and perfectly acquainted with Arab commerce and the most profitable wares. They band themselves for the desperate purpose of enslaving all tribes and peoples which are, from want of means and organization, too weak to resist them. No country offers such a field for these gangs of kidnappers as Marungu,

2. See Pocock's letter, Appendix U.

where every small village is independent and generally at variance with its neighbor.[3] Almost all the adult males are slain in the most cruel manner and their bodies are afterward hacked and dismembered and hung up on trees along the road, that the terror of such a fate may render villages and districts not yet attacked more submissive and unresisting. The women and youths are too valuable to slay, and the Arabs require them.

The owner of 250 of these poor, hungry, skeletonized slaves, whom we met at the Arab crossing place in Uguhha, was Said bin Salim, the Governor of Unyanyembe and the former chaperon of Burton and Speke on their journey to Ujiji in 1858–59. It was the third batch of this year, 1876, which has thus been consigned to Said bin Salim, an officer in the employ of Burghash, Prince of Zanzibar.[4] I have reflected much upon the singularity of this fact. Prince Burghash lately made a treaty with Great Britain, wherein —but you know all about it.[5] I believe it had something to do with prohibiting trade in slaves, and a promise—a written promise— from Seyed Burghash was obtained that he would do all in his power to stop the trade. Do you not think it singular that Said bin Salim, an officer of Seyed Burghash, should be engaged in this condemned traffic? I have meditated duly on the excuses which might be made for Said bin Salim, such as exigencies of business, necessities of the interior, domestic service. But, just Heavens! what can this Governor of Unyanyembe want with 500 or 600 women and children? I feel tempted to say strong things against this man, Said bin Salim, but I am restrained by my promise. This much I will say, that Said bin Salim, to the best of my knowledge and belief, is one of the principal slave traders in Africa, and Said bin Salim is an officer of Prince Burghash, and more than that, that Said bin Salim is the most trusted agent of the authorities at Zanzibar.

You will perceive this letter is dated at Nyangwe, Manyema. Many will remember that Livingstone said he was witness of some dreadful scenes enacted here, which made his "heart sore." [6] One terrible

3. For details of the Nyamwezi in this area, see the later "De Zanzibar au Katanga, Journal du Capitaine Stairs (1890–1891)," 143ff.

4. Said bin Salim later denied any connection with these slaves, attributing the report to one of his enemies. There are other proofs of his participation in the slave trade of the interior, however. Kirk passed on Stanley's report to Said bin Salim, but the British official said he would take no action. Mackay to Wigram, May 25, 1878, C.A6/016, CMS; Wilson to Wigram, Sept. 23, 1878 (addenda of Nov. 18, 1878), C.A6/025, *ibid.*; Kirk to Said bin Salim, July 28, 1878, N-25, ZA.

5. See document 16, note 22.

6. See document 7.

act he described. A half-caste, called Tagamoyo, was the principal actor. When I arrived in the same town where such a proceeding (as Livingstone wrote about) is said to have taken place, I asked if it was true. "Quite true," said a native of Zanzibar, frankly. "Ah, M'tagomoyo has no heart; his heart is very small indeed; it is as big as the end of a finger." Meaning that it was pitiless, undisturbed by compassion or feeling; for a liberal, just and kind man is said to have a big heart.

Between Bagamoyo and Unyanyembe, I said, one sees but retail sales of slaves; that in Uganda he beholds a wholesale trade without many horrors; that in Ujiji I saw large slave droves, and that in Uguhha I saw about eight hundred slaves almost too weak to stand from hunger. In Manyema I arrived on one of the fields where slaves are obtained, where it may be said they are grown, reaped and harvested, or, more correctly, where they are parked, shot or captured, as the case may be; for until slaves are needed they are permitted to thrive in their small, unprotected villages, to plant their corn, to attend their plantations and improve their dwellings, to quarrel in that soft, mild manner peculiar to simple and not over strong-minded savages, which does but little harm to anybody.

When, however, there is a growing demand for slaves, a revival in the trade, Moeni Dugambi of Nyangwe,[7] Mohammed bin Nassur of Kassessa,[8] Mohammed-bin-Said of Mama Mamba,[9] each, settled at an angle of a large triangular district, invite their friends and dependents for a few days' sport, just as an English nobleman invites his friends to grouse or deer shooting. Now, in this general battue it is understood, of course, that all men found carrying spears should be considered dangerous, and shot, to be cut to pieces afterward; but the women and children and submissive adults are prizes which belong to the victors. The murder of people on this scale is called a war and a grievance, as with your potentates—for war is soon discovered where the losses are always on the side of the simple savages. In a coarse, not always successful, manner the savages some-

7. Mwinyi Dugumbi, from Sadani, was one of the earliest Arab traders to the Congo and one of the leaders at Nyangwe; he died before 1881. Livingstone characterized him as "very friendly and a gentleman with more exploring enterprise in him than any other." Foskett, ed., *The Zambesi Doctors. David Livingstone's Letters to John Kirk 1858:1872*, 154; TDC, II, 117–18; Wissmann, *Unter deutscher Flagge quer durch Afrika von West nach Ost*, 177.

8. *LLJ*, II, 45, 178, has reference to some of his activities.

9. Muhammad bin Said, or Bwana Nzige, a relative of Tippu Tip. He would play a prominent role in the Congo as the trusted deputy of Tippu Tip. He died in Zanzibar in the early twentieth century. "Les Chefs Arabes du Haut Congo," 18; Brode, *Tippoo Tib*, 102; Coquilhat, *Haut-Congo*, 429ff.

times attempt to retaliate, and then follows another grievance and another war.

I have three little extracts from my notebook which I request you to publish, to the truth of which any Arab or Arab slave at present in Nyangwe would be quite willing to testify:

"Oct. 17. Arabs organized to-day from the three districts of Kassessa, Mwana Mamba and Nyangwe to avenge the murder and eating of Mohammed bin Soud and ten men by a tribe near Mana Mpunda, half way between Kassessa and Nyangwe. After six days' slaughter the Arabs returned with 300 slaves and 1,500 goats, besides spears, bark cloths, stools, &c.[10]

"Oct. 24. The natives of Kabanga, near Nyangwe, were sorely troubled two or three days ago by a visit paid them by some Unyamweze in the employ of Mohammed bin Said. Their insolence was so unbearable that the natives at last said, 'We will stand this no longer. They will force our wives and daughters before our eyes if we hesitate longer to kill them. Kill them! kill them! and before the Arabs come we will be off.' Unfortunately only one of the Unyamweze was killed; the others took fright and disappeared to rouse the Arabs with a new 'grievance.' To-day Mtagamoyo, whose heart is only as big as the end of one's finger, set out for the scene of action with a murderous celerity, and, besides making fifteen slaves, killed thirty, and set fire to eight villages. Mtagamoyo was said by the Arabs to have made but a 'small prize.'

"Oct. 26. The day after my arrival here has been signalled by an attack made by Mtagamoyo upon the Wagenya, or fishermen, on the left bank of the Lualaba. He departed in the night, and returned this day noon with fifty or sixty women and a few children.[11]

"'Are these wars of yours frequent?' I asked my friend Abed bin Salim.[12]

"'Frequent! Sometimes six times and ten times a month,' he re-

---

10. *Diary*, 132, does not give the same extract.

11. *Ibid.*, 133, has no entry for this date. The Genia, useful to the Arabs because of their skill as boatmen, usually lived in peace with the Arabs. See Maes and Boone, *Peuplades du Congo Belge*, 328–31; Coquilhat, *Haut-Congo*, 420; Baumann, "Die Station der Stanley-Fälle," 510–13, 647–49; Vansina, *Introduction à l'Ethnographie du Congo*, chap. 5; De Thier, *Singhitini*, passim.

12. Abed bin Salim, called Tanganyika, one of the founders of Nyangwe, was a leading Congo Arab. After about twenty-eight years in the interior, he was compelled by the pressure of debts to return to Zanzibar in 1886. He died soon afterward. Wissmann, *Durch Afrika*, 177–82; Wissmann, *My Second Journey through Equatorial Africa*, 224; W[auters]., "La Huitième Traversée de l'Afrique Centrale de Banana à Zanzibar par le Lieutenant Gleerup," 74–75; undated Stanley note in B–5, ZA.

plied. 'We cannot teach these pagans to be quiet. They are always kicking up trouble, killing some of our people whenever they can get a chance. A small force of five or ten guns dare not set out to hunt game. We are always on the lookout for trouble, and when we hear of it we all set out to punish them.'"

The method of punishment which the Arabs have adopted in Manyema means a cutthroat grab at anything or everything, from a woman to an empty gourd, from a goat or a pig to a hen's egg, and an indiscriminate shooting into anything bearing the semblance of an armed foe.

When such simple savages as these of Manyema run away half dead with fright, unnerved by the frightful noise of musketry and whistle of murderous slugs in their ears, it may well be imagined that many little things of value to Arabs and their slaves are picked up. My picture also proves how most of the miserable half-castes and Arab starvelings from Zanzibar are able to muster from 300 to 600 armed slaves each. They have but little cloth and beads to buy food for these slaves; they must therefore be sustained by the profits and loot derived from raids.

Wade Safeni,[13] one of the captains in our expedition, said to me as we marched from Mana Mamba to Nyangwe, "Master, all this plain lying between Mana Mamba and Nyangwe, when I first came here, eight years ago, was populated so thickly that we travelled through gardens and fields and villages every quarter of an hour. There were flocks of goats and droves of black pigs round every village. A bunch of bananas could be purchased for one cowrie. You can see what the country is now for yourself."

I saw an uninhabited wilderness—mostly. The country was only redeemed from utter depopulation by a small inhabited district, at intervals of six hours' march, the people of which seemed to be ever on the *qui vive* against attack. If the Arabs intended to colonize this country such reckless conduct and indiscriminate shooting of people would be deemed great folly, but the Arabs have no intention of colonizing Manyema. They are merely temporary residents in a district which up to the present time has offered golden opportunities of trade. In choosing this district the Arabs considered the character of the inhabitants, and they saw that the natives of Manyema were least able of any tribe or tribes in Central Africa to interfere with them.

As Livingstone was one of the early arrivals among the strangers

13. Wade Safeni, one of Stanley's favorite men, and his coxswain on Lake Victoria, went mad and disappeared near the end of the trip down the Congo. TDC, II, 86, 379; *Diary*, 201.

in Manyema, he was able to note and observe the first symptoms and the causes of depopulation which has been going on now for a period of eight years. Were it possible that he could rise from the dead and take a glance at the districts now depopulated, it is probable that he would be more than ever filled with sorrow at the misdoings of these traders. The Arabs have been now over eight years in Manyema, yet, though their slaves have made progress further west, they have been unable to discover a suitable locality for trade, or to secure a site for a trading depot. The natives further west appear by their reports to be extremely savage and combative. Every caravan—though one numbered 200 guns—has been compelled to turn back much reduced in numbers, with woeful tales of fighting, besieging, and suffering from want of food.

It will be thus seen that the Arab traders, having a special regard for their health, do not care to injure themselves by making raids against strong tribes; that they prefer weak, small tribes, whose want of organization and combination renders them specially powerless against a compact body of one hundred men armed with muskets. Manyema and Marungu, unfortunately for their inhabitants, offered attractive opportunities from local causes. Each small village obeyed a separate chief and their near neighborhood one to another engendered tribal jealousies and hates, so that, when the traders came, they were not only spurred to assume the offensive by their own avarice, but each chief did his best to secure their aid against his neighbor. Manyema has become a prey for the Arabs, and Marungu is being depopulated by the Uyanyamweze in Arab interests.

The Arabs buy gangs of men in the African interior, for the business of purchasing ivory necessitates a demand for human carriers, and, as hired porters are not always to be obtained, they are naturally compelled to purchase slaves to convey the precious material to the coast. Until ivory ceases to be an article of demand we ought not to blame the Arabs much for doing the best they can, consistent with the state of things, to collect it and bring it to their seaport. In the treatment of their slaves they must also be credited with not cruelly abusing their own interests. Except under very rare circumstances the condition of the slaves is not worse than when they enjoyed their savage freedom. If the Arabs contented themselves with buying slaves and were free from the charge of assisting to enslave the unfortunates we should be deprived of much right to complain of them, provided that such purchase was limited to the interior.

The charge I make against the subjects of Prince Burghash is that in Marungu, Manyema and Rua they use their power to enslave people, to capture by force thousands of men, women and children for the purpose of selling them to their countrymen for the mere sake of making money out of the sale of human beings that were forcibly and unjustly taken from their homes to feed their avarice. I charge them with being engaged in a traffic specially obnoxious to humanity—a traffic founded on violence, murder, robbery and fraud. I charge them with being engaged in a business which can be called by no other name than land piracy, and which should justly be as punishable as piracy on the high seas. That while all the nations in the world abstain from being concerned in such a trade, and generally condemn it, the subjects of Prince Burghash, equipping themselves at Zanzibar, Bagamoyo and other seaport towns, organize themselves into separate and several caravans, whose object mostly is to prosecute to the utmost of their power and vigor a system of land piracy, to attack inoffensive tribes and capture as many as they are able to for the purpose of selling them to their countrymen on the coast.

Prince Burghash, personally, I do not believe is to be blamed. It is his weakness, his inefficiency, his utter incapacity to prevent his subjects from violating all laws, human and divine, that should be shown up. We may credit him, personally, with doing all he can to prevent it, or at least with doing all he knows how to prevent the trade. But it is apparent to me and to anybody who may come to Africa that what has been done, or is doing, makes no more impression upon this appalling and desperate trade than what this letter will make.

I only write this letter because it is a part of my duty to give you such information as may come within the range of my travels; assuredly with but a faint hope that it will have a feather's weight toward checking the crying and dreadful evil. What I do trust is that, with your aid, I shall be able to cause many to reflect upon the fact that there exists one little State on this globe, which is about equal in extent to an English county, with the sole privilege of enriching itself by wholesale murder, land piracy and commerce in human beings, and that a traffic forbidden to all other nations should be permitted to be furtively monopolized by the little island of Zanzibar and by such insignificant people as the subjects of Prince Burghash.

The champions of the anti-slavery cause in England, seconded by the government, deserve great credit for having done their utmost to suppress the traffic in slaves on the high seas; but, to complete their work, it should be suggested to them that, so long as the trade is permitted in the interior, so certain is it that attempts will be made to continue it at sea. If I were to stop here I imagine very many would shrink from the appalling prospect such a project as suppressing the trade in the interior would naturally create in the mind. Many would dream of expeditions against the Arabs, of terrible expenditures of moneys, loss of life and other calamitous things; others would think such a project would call for hosts of missionaries, perhaps annexation of Zanzibar, or, at least, harsh interference with the government of an independent prince. I am no advocate for filibustering expeditions, because I think they entail as much, if not greater, evil than that which they are supposed to suppress. The heavy expense which such expeditions incur is also a drawback, besides their fruitlessness.[14]

Missionaries are also out of the question. To whom should they be sent? To scattered and stripped tribes like those of Marungu and Manyema? Even here they would be valuable, provided each mission was supported by 200 Sniders. Though, in Uganda, a missionary alone would be a boon, in Manyema, Rua and Marungu he would be impracticable. Cruel or harsh interference by a mighty Power in the affairs of a weak State is an injustice, but where the weak State is so feebly governed that its subjects riot in licentiousness and murder, and revel in the luxuries of crime unpunished, when a people convert themselves into bands of cutthroats and land pirates, undeterred by fear of God or their government, it is time, I think, for some more moral government to interfere; at least it would be desirable that such a government should interfere for the credit of humanity.

A long time ago a sentimental necessity, or what was supposed to be one, sufficed to rouse all the Christian nations of Europe, with all their magnificent force and daring; but nowadays it has become almost an article of belief that to do anything for the sake of sentiment smacks of the ridiculous, or, to use the new name for it, Quixotic. Well, I fear knightly chivalry is gone along with its burlesque. We have only the name left to remember it by. Later still Great Britain was famous for maintaining a political chivalry, which often did good service and rescued weak States from the oppressor's violence. It is sometimes called into exercise even in modern times, though now it is of milder form, and generally distinguished by the term "good offices." It is not the knightly chivalry nor the political

14. The future "filibustering" expeditions of the Belgian antislavery groups and the activities of the missionary armed forces to the east of Lake Tanganyika are discussed in Bennett's introduction to the reissue of Swann, *Fighting the Slave-Hunters in Central Africa,* forthcoming.

chivalry, but the "good offices" of England, on behalf of the African races and of Christians at large, that would be highly desirable just now at Zanzibar. Let us pray that wisdom and charity may guide England to employ her real and vast influence at once, energetically and resolutely, to rescue inland Africa, and to check these whole-sale murders of inoffensive tribes in the interior of the sad continent.

33

Nyangwe, Manyema, Central Africa
Oct. 30, 1876 [1]

In repacking my baggage and reducing it for our journey to the unknown regions west of here I came across Sir Samuel Baker's letter, given by Sir Bartle Frere to the *Times*.[2] I had forgotten all about the letter, otherwise I should have written to you long ago. But it is not yet too late, as no doubt Sir Samuel Baker has published his book and maintains the same theories divulged in this letter.[3] Perhaps absence from Africa has but deepened his impression and caused him at last to believe his theories to be facts.

You may be able to compare these remarks with such as he may have made in his book.

"Albert Niyanza. Congratulate Mr. Findlay[4] from me. His theory is correct. This lake is a simple continuation of Tanganyika. I had frequent conversations with two native merchants of Karagwe, who purchased ivory for their King Rumanika.

"These men had on several occasions arrived from Karagwe by boat via the M'wootan Nzige (Albert Niyanza). They describe the lake as immensely wide in some portions, but varying in an irregular manner. In some places it narrows suddenly and then again enlarges to a great width. For a return voyage from Masindi[5] to Karagwe by lake the merchants' route is as follows:

1. *NYH*, Oct. 9, 1877. See also Stanley's letter of Oct. 31, 1876, Appendix K.
2. In another letter Baker gave his opinion on the lakes when he heard that Livingstone was at Ujiji: "Do not come down the lake. It is now well known that the Tanganyika is the Albert Nyanza . . ." Baker to Livingstone, Feb. 10, 1873, *The Times*, Feb. 18, 1874, p. 10.
3. See Baker, *Ismaïlia*, II, 258–63.
4. Alexander G. Findlay (1812–1875), geographer and hydrographer, had written an admittedly inferential article to demonstrate that Lake Tanganyika was a reservoir of the Nile. *DNB*, XX, 23–24; Findlay, "On Dr. Livingstone's Last Journey and the Probable Ultimate Sources of the Nile."
5. In Bunyoro, near the present Masindi. Thomas and Scott, *Uganda*, 17.

"Masindi, two days' march west to Chibero,[6] on the Albert Ni-yanza. From Chibero, by boat, you pass in succession to the south Minyoro (Speke's Unyoro), Kabboyou,[7] Tambooki,[8] M'Pororo (boat stops), and in two days' overland march east you reach Karagwe, about 3 dgs. S.L., Ruanda, Baroondi (Speke's Urundi?), Chibbogora,[9] Watuta, Machoonda.[10]

"Ujiji is well known to be on the M'wootan Nzige—i.e., Albert Niyanza."

These statements would not need reply were they merely on na-tive authority instead of having the high support of Sir Samuel Baker. I remember that the first time I read the letter I felt somewhat "dashed" at the long list of native names which Sir Samuel set forth as names of stations which were said to link the two lakes—Tan-ganyika and the Albert. There were many I had never heard of, and to disprove the native evidence furnished by Baker, besides my own exploration of the north end of the Tanganyika, a better knowledge of the localities of those stations was desirable, which I am happy to say I have obtained by my late explorations in the region between Lakes Victoria and Albert.

After the names of the stations according to Sir S. Baker, he adds:

"Beyond Machoonda the merchants know nothing, except that the lake extends to the south for an unknown distance."

It was plain to me that Sir Samuel placed too much confidence in native information, for, alas! I have had a score of times such good cause to distrust all native and Arab information that I have made it a rule to take everything as doubtful.[11]

These two "merchants" had taken Sir Samuel over five lakes—the Albert, the Tanganyika, the Upper Alexandra Niyanza, the Lower Alexandra Niyanza and the Victoria. They had given the names of large countries for stations, and mixed the names of dead kings with names of insignificant stations. Let us, with the clear light thrown on this mass of error, by exploration endeavor to set things geo-

6. Kibero, in Bunyoro.

7. Kaboyo, the founder of the Toro state. Taylor, *Western Lacustrine Bantu*, 43.

8. Mutambukwa, ruler of Ankole. See document 26, note 6.

9. Stanley suggested Kibogora, ruler of Usuwi (see below). Stanley had visited him. *TDC*, I, 478–80.

10. Machunda, predecessor of Lukongeh, ruler of Ukerewe. See Burton, "Lake Regions," 270, 275; Grant, "Summary of Observations," 258.

11. Another traveler remarked that he took especial care to avoid using chief's names for territories because of Baker's errors. Emin Bey, "Journal einer Reise von Mrúli nach der Hauptstadt Unyóro's mit Bemerkungen über Land und Leute," 388.

graphically right. From Masindi, one of the capitals of Kabba Rega, King of Unyoro, it is said to be two days' march to the Albert Nianza, to a place called Chibero. Thence you are said to voyage in a boat along Unyoro, Kabboyou and Tambooki. This latter I take to mean M'tambuko, King of Ankori or Usagara, whose country, though it does not extend to Lake Albert, runs parallel with it between Southern Uganda and some small lake districts. From Tambooki, or M'tambuko's you are supposed to reach Mpororo, where the boat stops, and a two days' march overland brings you to Karagwe. The distance might probably be done in two days' march, but would strain any ordinary man's powers to perform the distance in that time, but it might be doubted whether two bodies of water, or lakes, separated by a two days' land march, could be supposed to be connected.

From Karagwe you are said to reach Ruanda. Having marched east to Karagwe, you are now compelled to go west to Ruanda, thence to Urundi South. Having gone south of Ruanda to Urundi, you must now turn about forty miles northeast to Chibbogora, which I take to mean Kibogora, King of Western Usui. From Kibogora's you proceed to "Watuta," which is not a station or a country, but a marauding tribe occupying Ugomba[12] between Unyamweze and Uhha. Finally, from "Watuta" you proceed to Machunda; that is to say, east 120 geographical miles to Machunda's, who was formerly King of Ukerewe, on Lake Victoria!

There are several other points in his letter which might be criticized, but I am perhaps "slaying the slain." I quite believe no errors would be found in the descriptions of districts and positions of localities over which Sir Samuel has personally travelled, and I believe he has done his utmost to maintain that standard of rigid accuracy which Burton, Speke, Grant, Winwood Reade[13] and Livingstone formed; but beliefs and hypotheses are perilous luxuries in Africa.

I address myself now to a more pleasant task—viz., that of giving you my glad tribute to a much younger traveller than Sir Samuel Baker—Lieutenant Cameron. Mr. Waller, of the Royal Geographical Society, is very partial to the word "pluck," it appears. He said Mr. Cameron showed great pluck in discovering the Lukuga. I do not

12. The Ngoni. See Hatchell, "The Angoni," 70. Bugomba is a village in the Ulewe chieftanship in the present Kahama district.

13. William Winwood Reade (1838–1875), traveler and novelist; he had been a fellow newspaper correspondent with Stanley during the Ashanti campaign. *DNB*, XLVII, 361–62; *JRGS* 45 (1875), cl–cli. See also Hird, *Stanley*, 106–07.

exactly know what he meant by the word in connection with the
discovery of the Lukuga, but he may use the word very properly in
connection with Cameron's march from Nyangwe to the unknown
regions southwest of here. If Arabs are to be believed, he has shown
a most brilliant example of pluck—determined courage amounting
to pure recklessness of life. I am told he had but little ammunition
left. Considering that he was in this position in the very heart of
Africa, at least six months' journey from either coast, and that he
preferred to go on thus unprepared through an unknown region, I
can only look at his feat as one of the most signal instances of high
courage and duty in the annals of African exploration. I wish the
young and gallant traveller the happiest success.

A day or two before leaving Ujiji I wrote to you to say that I was
compelled to leave off letter writing to attend to my sick people and
prepare for my journey to Manyema. I lost eight good men from
smallpox, but I suffered greater loss the day I finally set out from
Ujiji, for forty-three desertions took place. At one time I imagined
that there was a conspiracy to finish the journey at Ujiji. There was,
at least, a kind of panic among those who remained; for, as the
desertions were announced, I heard the men ask one another in fear
what it all meant, and my suspicions seemed to discover a kind of
regret in their faces that they had not deserted also. To prevent the
contagion of desertion I clapped thirty-two doubtful cases in irons,
and, after driving them into the canoes, compelled the canoes to set
off at once for Ukaranga. I believe that it is to this summary, unhesi-
tating method I owe what is left of a once powerful expedition. The
time spent by me in exploring and circumnavigating Lake Tanganyika served to demoralize the people. They were daily listening
open-mouthed to the terrible stories of the cannibals of Manyema,
and the fear of being eaten caused the simple fools to quiver with
anxiety.

Until I arrived in Uguhha, and, indeed, until I had bidden adieu to
the Tanganyika, my people made me feel as though I had become
a slave driver. The camp exhibited nothing but sadness and gloom.
The usual merriment, the broad jest and loud, reckless laugh were
wanting. Many had lost their comrades and messmates, the messes
had not yet been reorganized and the men seemed to be shy of one
another. But as we increased the distance between our camps and
the Tanganyika all this gloomy feeling wore away, and, inspired by
rapid, strenuous marching, before we reached Bambarre or Kabambarre the people had resumed their former cheery looks, and slyly

laughed at themselves for having been frightened by the stories
about the man-eaters of Manyema. I forgot to say that even Kalulu
was also one of the deserters; but he and four others were subsequently recovered. From Kabambarre we followed the Luama River
to its confluence with the Lualaba, thence followed the latter river
to Nyangwe, which place we reached in the unprecedented short
time of forty days, or twenty-eight marches from the Tanganyika.

Though I have not had the pleasure of reading Livingstone's journal you must have had. I cannot hope to add much to anything he
has said. I reserve myself for the unknown west of Nyangwe, because I shall have then something worth writing about—new, virgin
ground, of which not a whisper has reached the world outside, about
which even everybody in Nyangwe is ignorant—a region which Livingstone panted to reach, but could not, and which Cameron promised to explore, but did not. The region is all involved in mystery,
the intense superstition of the Africans has folded it with awesome
gloom.

It is peopled by their stories with terribly vicious dwarfs,[14] striped
like zebras, who deal certain death with poisoned arrows, who are
nomads and live on elephants. A great forest stretches no one knows
how far north—certainly no one has seen the end of it—through
which one may travel days and days and weeks and months without
ever seeing the sun; and the great river Lualaba continues north,
ever north; and it is possible, the Arabs and their slaves say, the
Lualaba may reach the salt sea.

After listening to the Arab [15] who has journeyed furthest north
I do not wonder at Livingstone's fixed idea that this Lualaba is the
Nile. This man, who has reached a distance of fifteen marches north
of here, through Uregga,[16] declares that he struck the Lualaba, and
at that distance the river had a decided curve, going north-northeast.
As this man's statement was corroborated by his companions I am
bound to believe him; but it suggested to my mind, not that it has
a connection with the Albert Niyanza, or the Bahr Gazelle, or with
the Nile at all, but that it continues in a northerly direction to some
point near the Equator, where it is received by an equally great

14. For accounts of Pygmies in the Congo, Turnbull, *The Forest People;*
Vansina, *Introduction à l'Ethnographie du Congo,* chap. 3.
15. Abed bin Juma. *TDC,* II, 99.
16. The Rega inhabited the great equatorial forest east of the Lualaba in
the area of the Elila and Ulindi rivers. Maes and Boone, *Peuplades du Congo
Belge,* 341–43; Delhaise, *Les Warega;* Vansina, *Introduction à l'Ethnographie
du Congo,* chap. 7.

river, having its rise in the Djebel Kumr of the Arabs, or the Lunae Montes of Ptolemy,[17] and from that point flows southwesterly into the river known as the Congo. This is my deliberate opinion at the present time, and it has caused me to make decided changes in the programme of the travels before me.

Should my opinion be confirmed I should, by following the Lualaba so far north, be taking the expedition beyond all power of aid or supplies from any quarter. Such a long distance beyond all calculation would waste every article we could possibly exchange for food. If the mere purpose of this expedition was to cross Africa, with the utmost confidence I declare to you that I could reach San Salvador[18] in six months from Nyangwe; but I should then, like Cameron, have left the question of the Lualaba just where Livingstone left it, to be discussed upon the grounds of each man's opinions. If I merely struck direct west for San Salvador, how could I prove that the Lualaba is the Congo, or that it is not the Congo, but the Nile or the Niger—whichever it may be? I should forfeit all right to be heard upon the subject or to be considered as one able to confirm any of the theories broached upon the subject. This would be lamentable.

My opinion about the Lualaba is that it cannot be the Nile, despite its northerly trend. It is too mighty a river here to be the Nile. I have crossed it, sounded it, tested its current, taken its altitude, deliberately compared it in my mind to the Nile, and my conviction is strong that there is sufficient water in it to make three rivers such as the Nile. Yet it may, though it is highly improbable, throw out a branch to the Bahr el Gazelle. It is improbable, because it would be extraordinary; yet may be so, as there are more wonders in Africa than are dreamed of in the common philosophy of geography. Instance the Tanganyika!

But, as neither conjectures, dreams, theories nor opinions will make one positive geographical fact, I propose to stick to the Lualaba, come fair or come foul, fortune or misfortune; and, that I may not be driven back by force, I have recruited the expedition to one hundred and forty rifles and muskets and seventy spears. The desertions and deaths from smallpox at Ujiji had thinned my command to such a degree that we should have been only a sop for a

17. For the uncertainty of the location of Ptolemy's Mountains of the Moon, Bridges, "The British Exploration of East Africa," 16–18. See also *TDC,* II, 276–77.

18. Mbanza Kongo, or San Salvador, capital of the former extensive Kongo state. See Cuvelier, *L'Ancien Royaume de Congo.*

ferocious tribe. Our expedition, with the late reinforcement, is now as strong as when it drove its way through Ituru and Iramba and twice crossed hostile Unyoro.

It must be a very strong tribe indeed that can drive us back now. But what savages cannot do hunger may, if the Lualaba continues running so far north of the Equator. I have ample supplies for six months. Beyond that period Heaven knows what will become of us if we find ourselves at the confluence of these two rivers, the Lualaba and the unknown river, so far out of the way of supplies, with not a single bead or cowrie to buy food! However, my naturally sanguine temperament has made me sing of the doggerel of

> Trust to luck and stare Fate in the face;
> Aisy's the heart if it's in the right place.

P.S.—I leave two letters in the hands of my friend Abed bin Salim, addressed to you. He promises to forward them to the East Coast at the earliest opportunity. I am well aware that such opportunities come very seldom, but I trust that you will receive them at least within twelve months.

34

Nyangwe, Manyema, Central Africa
Nov. 1, 1876 [1]

While in Ujiji, in 1871, Livingstone kindled in me an envious desire to see Manyema, when he permitted himself to speak about the glories of the last country he had traversed. He was truly enthusiastic about it. He spoke of gigantic, towering woods, extraordinary variety of vegetation, beautiful scenes of wooded hills and verdurous vales and basins, amiable and interesting tribes, of beautiful women, and many other things which showed that the veteran traveller had been more than ordinarily impressed. I find from diligent inquiries here that his residence, his travels hither and thither, and his journeys from and to Ujiji must have embraced a period of three years or thereabouts.[2]

1. *NYH*, Oct. 10, 1877.
2. Livingstone spent from July 1869 until October 1871 in traveling from Ujiji to Manyema and back.

The distance from Ujiji to Nyangwe is about 350 English miles, which we performed in forty days, inclusive of halts. I find he was laid up a very long time with a most painful disease of the feet at Kabambarre. From native accounts he seems to have been there from six to twelve months. It was certainly long enough for the noble old explorer to study the nature of the natives of East Manyema. I have not the slightest doubt that by the beautiful women he spoke to me about he meant the women of Kabambarre, in East Manyema. These women are, without doubt, comely, winning and most amiable compared with anything that Livingstone may have seen south of South latitude 5 deg. in Africa. But Livingstone should have visited the proud beauties of the Watusi, Wanyankore, and of the white race of Gambaragara. He would then have only remembered the women of East Manyema for their winsomeness and amiability. The traveller "Daoud," or David, is a well-remembered figure in this region between Nyangwe and the Tanganyika. He has made an impression on the people which will not be forgotten for a generation at least.

"Did you know him?" old Mwana Ngoi, of the Luama,[3] asked of me eagerly. Upon receiving an affirmative he said to his sons and brothers, "Do you hear what he says? He knew the good white man. Ah, we shall hear all about him." Then, turning to me, he asked me, "Was he not a very good man?" to which I replied, "Yes, my friend, he was good; far better than any man, white or Arab, you will ever see again."

"Ah, yes; you speak true. He has saved me from being robbed many a time by the Arabs, and he was so gentle and patient and told us such pleasant stories of the wonderful land of the white people. Hm', the aged white was a good man, indeed!"

Had old Mwana Ngoi been able to speak like an educated person I should, no doubt, have had something like a narrative of David Livingstone's virtues from him, whereas not being educated much of what he said was broken by frequent hm's and shakings of his head, as though the traveller's good qualities were beyond description or enumeration. He wisely left the rest to my imagination, and so I leave them to you.

But what has struck me, while tracing Livingstone to his utmost reach—this Arab depot of Nyangwe—revived all my grief and pity

3. The Luama River is in Bangobango, or Hombo, territory. Maes and Boone, *Peuplades du Congo Belge*, 136–37, 369. For Livingstone and Mwana Ngoi, *LLJ*, II, 26–27, 70, 73; *TDC*, II, 79–81, has minor differences in the quoted talk.

for him, more so indeed than even his own relation of sorrowful and heavy things, is that he does not seem to have been aware that he was sacrificing himself unnecessarily, nor warned of the havoc of age and that power had left him. With the weight of many years pressing on him, the shortest march wearying him, compelling him to halt many days to recover his strength, a serious attack of illness frequently prostrating him, with neither men nor means to escort and enable them to make practical progress, Livingstone was at last like a blind and infirm man, aimlessly moving about. From my conscience, with not a whit of my admiration and love for him lessened in the smallest degree, but rather increased by what I have heard from Arabs and natives, I must say I think one of his hardest taskmasters was himself.

For instance, he wants to strike the Lualaba directly west of Kabambarre. He accompanies a small caravan half way to the river, and then, finding that the caravan proceeds no further, he is compelled to come to a halt, even turn back with it to Kabambarre. Next he proceeds to Nyangwe; is about two months on the road, though the distance is only about fourteen marches; from Nyangwe he is desirous of continuing his journey and of following the Lualaba, but he has no means of purchasing canoes, neither is following the Lualaba practicable, because it is frequently interrupted by falls and rapids, and to follow it by land he has no men; while on the very first day's attempt to do it his people are driven back by overwhelming numbers. He is then compelled to come to a long halt in Nyangwe, for he cannot go anywhere. His men are not unwilling to do the best they can for him, but they and his Arab and native friends tell him that he is not strong enough to force his way; that he should have 150 or 200 guns to escort him, and abundance of beads and shells to pacify and make friends of those who could be induced to be friendly. It all ends by Livingstone sitting down at Nyangwe, waiting for an eastward-bound caravan, with which he finally departs on the road to Ujiji, a sorely tried and disappointed traveller.

Indeed, from my own experience of his terrible determination, I know how useless it would be to advise him. I slyly suggested several times to him that he should return home, to build his strength up, that he might recommence his work under better auspices. "No, no, no!" "See home, friends, country?" "No, no, no, no!" "To be knighted by the Queen and welcomed by thousands of admirers!" "Yes, but impossible! Must not, cannot, will not!"

Then how could such a determined man be persuaded or advised by his servants and his Arab friends?

I am astonished to perceive that I have written at great length about Livingstone, but the words Nyangwe, Manyema, Lualaba, cannot be dissociated from his name. Besides I am daily told something about him by my friend Abed bin Salim, and the ruins of his residence here are about thirty feet from the front door of my burzah.[4]

In his conversation with me at Ujiji Livingstone ascribed much just praise to almost all of the region west of the Goma Mountains.[5] It is a most remarkable region—more remarkable than anything I have seen in Africa. Its woods, or forests, or jungles, or bush—I do not know by what particular term to designate the crowded, tall, straight trees rising from an impenetrable undergrowth of bush, creepers, thorns, gums, palms, fronds of all forms, canes and grass—are sublime, even terrible. Indeed, nature here is either remarkably or savagely beautiful. At a distance everything looks charming. Take your stand on any eminence or coigne of vantage for view-seeing you may please, be it the crest of a ridge, the summit of a hill, the crown of a rock, and if you look around you will find yourself delighted, fascinated. A hundred or a thousand different outlines are in view of ridges and ranges, peaks and cones, the boldly waving or softly rolling, of gradual or abrupt slope, of mounds, little patches of levels, of the grand and the picturesque, in bewildering diversity of form. You will exclaim that you see the splendor of the tropics—that you have caught Nature rejoicing and happy. Overall she has flung a robe of varying green; the hills and ridges are blooming; the valleys and basins exhale perfume; the rocks wear garlands of creepers; the stems of the trees are clothed with moss; a thousand streamlets of pure cool water stray, now languid, now quick, toward the north and south and west. The whole makes a pleasing, charming illustration of the bounteousness and wild beauty of tropical Nature.

Look closer and analyze all this, that you may find how deceptive is distance. The grasses are coarse and high and thick. They form a miniature copy of an African forest. Their spear-like blades wound like knives and their points like needles; the reeds are tall and tough as bamboo; in those pretty looking bushes are thorns—truly the thorns are hooks of steel; the crown of that yonder low hill with such a gentle slope is all but inaccessible. See that glorious crop of crimson flowers on that low bush in the middle of the lawn green. Pause, my friend, before you venture to pluck them. First, that lawn is a deception; it is a forest of tall trees you see, and that beautiful,

4. See also Stanley's letter to King, Appendix K.
5. See document 29, note 7. Hore called the mountains "one of the sights of the lake." Hore, "Lake Tanganyika," 10.

gorgeous poison bush is nearly thirty feet high, and those green banks of vegetation in those hollows are almost impenetrable forest belts.

Let me show you a specimen of a forest in Manyema. You will, no doubt, remember that our friend Livingstone was enthusiastic about the woods of Manyema. You would fear to be alone in those mighty solitudes at night. I made a ramble—a very short one—into a forest once in search of a rice cane. There are plenty of canes in these woods, just like Malacca. I crawled first through something like a hazel copse, then through a brake, wherein thorns and palmettas were very conspicuous, then through a strip of morass out of which shot upward a dense growth of tall grasses and stiff water cane. Crushing my way through this obstacle I came to the edge of the forest, where lines of tall, straight young giants stood foremost, extended like skirmishers in front of the dense masses of Titans, which solemnly stood behind. The young giants offered no impediment, and I proceeded further in, feeling my eyes open wider and wider with astonishment at sight of the enormous thickness, height, number and close array of the forest monarchs.

But I went to look for canes, and after a quarter of an hour's search for one of the desired size I at last found it, and pointed it out to my gun bearer, who cut it. As I was leisurely peeling it I perceived that my mind, not satisfied with the transient impression made on it by the massiveness and great height of the trees, felt overwhelmed by the scene. It seemed to receive a solemn or pensive repose from it; and my hands, acted upon by the mind, ceased their labor, and my eyes were instantly uplifted. I gradually felt myself affected more strongly than can be described at the deathly stillness, in the middle of which appeared those majestic, lofty, naked and gray figures, like so many silent apparitions. I looked at them with the same feeling I have often felt in looking at very ancient ruins; for these were also venerable monuments, witnesses of the ancientness of time, all the more impressive because I alone was thus surrounded by them.

Looked I above or around, north or south, east or west, I saw only the silent gray shafts of these majestic trees. The atmosphere seemed weighted with an eloquent, though dumb, history, wherein I read, heard, saw and inhaled the record of lost years and lands. For the time I dropped all remembrance of self and identity—all perception of other scenes and reposes. I seemed to hear proclaimed their antiquity, their grand old age, their superiority and their imperturbability. They appeared to say: "Centuries ago were we sown. Silent, serene and undisturbed we grew. We know no strife, contention or passion of your world. Though born of the earth, fed and nourished by it, yet are we unaffected with the fate of things on the earth. We are 500 years old. Where wast thou, atom of restless humanity, when we were born? What art thou but a brief accident, slight as the dead leaves under thy feet? Go and tell your kind you have seen silence?"

But really Manyema woods are exceedingly solemn. I shall probably see more of them as I travel west. I am told by those who have penetrated some distance into them that they contain any number of sokos (gorillas).[6] Livingstone informed me that these sokos are gorillas. I have not seen any yet; I have only heard their hoarse cries in the woods; but from the descriptions given of them by the Arabs and natives I am inclined to think they are chimpanzees. Other singular creatures of these forests are said to be the dwarfs, whose heights have been variously given from thirty inches to four feet. They are evidently nomads, and they must have an exceedingly wide range. They are said to be exceedingly fond of meat, all creatures furnishing them with the means of existence, from an elephant to a rat. They are more attached to the pursuit of the elephant than any other, probably because of the abundance of meat those animals supply. Their weapons are poisoned arrows, whose deadly effect is so feared by the Wanguana that they have renounced all intention to molest them any more. While in the new region to which I am bound I shall endeavor to obtain a personal knowledge of the sokos and the dwarfs.

The name of Manyema has become very familiar to readers of late African travels. The word is pronounced in various ways—Man-yema, Manu-yema, Many-wena, but I believe Man-yema is the most popular. I take it to be a corruption of Mana, or Mwana-Yema—the son of Yema. It is rare we hear of the proper names of countries in this region. Thus we are told Kabambarri is Mwana-Kusu, Kizambala is Mwana-Ngoi, Tubanda is known to most people under the name of Mwana-Mamba. We have also Mwana-Kidenda, Mwana-Marumbu, Mwana-Melenge or Merenge, &c. It is not a very large country. It covers an area of about ten thousand square miles.[7] About half of it is spread over with dense woods; the more southern half is embraced by the broad Luama Valley and the fine open country of

6. The chimpanzee (*Pan satyrus schweinfurthi*). See Schweinfurth, *The Heart of Africa*, I, 479, 518–22; Johnston, "Livingstone as an Explorer," 439; Behm, "Livingstone's Reisen in Inner-Afrika," 174; Schmitz, *Les Baholoholo*, 18. Livingstone described the chimpanzee: "He is not handsome: a bandy-legged, pot-bellied low-browed villain, without a particle of the gentleman in him." "Dr. Livingstone's Letters to Sir Thomas Maclear," 73.

7. See Stuart, "Manyema Culture and History prior to 1894," 1–2; Cornet, *Maniema*, 11–12.

Uzura.[8] The hills are without doubt the effect of that great convulsion which formed Lake Tanganyika. In certain localities the streams run over lava beds and iron ore, which has the aspect of being smelted.

But Manyema is not so interesting nor a fourth as large as Uregga. It is difficult to enter into any details about a country as yet but partially explored, but from the descriptions given of its mountains and hills, and of the many large rivers which intersect it, I have a strong conviction Uregga would repay exploration. Uregga, like Manyema, consists of small districts governed by independent chiefs.

The "Lualaba" is an instance among many in his nomenclature I could furnish you of Livingstone's excessive partiality for the letter B. According to the natives, it should be pronounced Lu-ál-awa, not Lua-lá-ba, but foreign tongues, with their respective influences—that of the Arab slaves over the Arabs, the Arabs over the white travellers, the white traveller over his countrymen—have given us a choice of names.

When Moeni Dugumbi's slaves first entered Manyema they thought they heard the great river called U-gál-owa, whereas the natives no doubt said Lu-ál-awa or Lu-ál-uwa. The slaves, returning to their master, Dugumbi, said they had seen a sealike river called U-gá-lowa.

Dugumbi is interested at once, and repeats, interrogatively, "Ugá-rowa?" by which we find Ugalowa is changed to Ugarowa. Dugumbi writes, in his letters to his friends at Ujiji and Unyanyembe, about Ugarowa. Arab slaves convey tidings wherever they go of Ugalowa. Mohammed bin Gharib brings Livingstone with him from Ujiji, who is destined to give the river another name. On the road to Nyangwe, with interested ears, he hears the native name Lu-á'l-awa. His dislike of the Arab and the slave hunter causes him to reject, and rightly, the corrupted term Ugalawa, or Ugarowa, but he cannot resist giving the word a Livingstonian impression. We therefore heard of—not Lu-á'l-awa—but Lua-lá-ba.

If geographers left it to me to decide what name should be given it most heartily would I beseech them to let it be called Livingstone River or Livingstone's Lualaba, to commemorate his discovery of it and his heroic struggles against adversity to explore it.[9] At the pres-

8. The Wazula live in the Genia area. Maes and Boone, *Peuplades du Congo Belge*, 329.

9. Cameron had anticipated Stanley. In 1873 he said he aimed to reach the Lualaba at Nyangwe "or, as it ought to be called, the Livingstone." The Royal Geographical Society, however, demurred; its president, Alcock, said the society had "strong objection to altering a name that had been current [the Congo] for the last 300 years." Leopold II of Belgium also had no wish to

ent dry season the river here is about one thousand yards wide; during the monsoon or rainy season it extends to about two miles in width at Nyangwe.

Three days from date I propose to set out in a northerly direction, through Uregga, occasionally striking the Lualaba, to maintain an acquaintance with it, and continue northerly to the utmost of my limits, means and power.

35

Banyamboka, two marches from Emboma
August 8, 1877 [1]

Messrs. Motta Vega and J. M. Harrison, Emboma, Congo River: [2] GENTLEMEN—I have received your very welcome letter, but better than all, and more welcome, your supplies. I am unable to express, just at present, how grateful I feel. We are so overjoyed and confused at our emotions at the sight of the stores exposed to our hungry eyes, at the sight of the rice, the fish, the rum, and, for me, wheat bread, butter, sardines, jam, peaches and beer. Ye Gods! Just think, three bottles of pale ale, besides tea and sugar. We cannot restrain ourselves from falling to and enjoying the bounteous store, so that I beg you will charge our apparent want of thankfulness to our greediness. If we do not thank sufficiently in words rest assured we feel what volumes cannot describe. For the next twenty-four hours we

change the Congo's name since it would, he feared, give Britain too close an association with it. Stanley, nevertheless, continued to call it the Livingstone River for some years. Cameron to Frere, Dec. 4, 1873, in "The Livingstone East Coast Aid Expedition," 283; Alcock's words given in Stanley, "Nile and Livingstone Basin," 409–10; Roeykens, *Les débuts de l'oeuvre africaine de Léopold II (1875–1879)*, 289; Hathorne to Whitney, Dec. 11, 1879, Hathorne Papers, PM.

1. *NYH*, Oct. 12, 1877. Stanley sent a previous letter to Boma, but the *Herald* did not include it in its columns. The letter, of Aug. 5, 1877, is reproduced in de Vasconcellos, "Dois Autographos de H. M. Stanley." In the letter Stanley requested food for his starving party. The letter given here is in *TDC*, II, 459–60, but is there dated Aug. 6, 1877; it has also been rewritten somewhat. The long delay between the writing of this despatch and document 34 was due to Stanley's traveling through territories where there was no means of communicating with the outside world.

2. Motta Veiga was the chief agent of Hatton and Cookson at Boma. See Delcommune, *Vingt années de Vie africaine*, I, 61, 87–90, for Stanley's arrival there; see also de Bouveignes, "L'Arrivée de Stanley à Boma en 1877."

shall be too busy eating to think much of anything else; but I may say that the people cry out while their mouths are full of rice and fish, "Verily our master has found the sea and his brothers, but we did not believe him until he showed us the rice and rum. We did not believe there was any end to the great river (Congo); but, God be praised forever, we shall see white men to-morrow, and our wants and troubles will be over."

Dear sirs, though strangers, I hope we shall be great friends, and it will be the study of my life to remember my feelings of gratefulness when I first caught sight of your supplies, and my poor, faithful and brave people cried out, "Master, we are saved; food is coming," and the old and the young, men, women and children lifted up their wearied, wornout frames and began to chant lustily an extemporaneous song in honor of the white people by the great sea (the Atlantic) who had listened to their prayers. I had to rush to my tent to hide the tears that would flow despite all my attempts at composure.

Gentlemen, may the blessing of God attend your footsteps whithersoever you go, is the very earnest prayer of yours, very gratefully . . .

36

Kabinda, or Cabenda, West Coast of Africa, near mouth of Congo River
August 13, 1877 [1]

Mr. Thomas H. Price, of the great firm of Messrs. Hatton & Cookson, of Liverpool,[2] is about to go home to recruit his health after a protracted stay on the West Coast of Africa, and he has kindly offered his services to take to England any despatches or letters I may have for you. While I would gladly avail myself of this opportunity, still I am so prostrated just now, and, I may say, so excited at the sight of white faces, and the scores of "Welcomes" I hear, and so confused with the good things of this life they press on me, that,

1. NYH, Oct. 9, 1877.
2. Price was the Cabinda agent of Hatton and Cookson of Liverpool. TDC, II, 468. The firm was one of the earliest trading agencies in the Congo area. After 1869 the firm was directed by Edward Hatton Cookson and Thomas W. Cookson. My thanks to N. Carrick of the Liverpool Record Office, Liverpool City Libraries, for this information. See also BCB, III, 162. For some of the firm's activities, Anstey, Britain and the Congo, passim; Delcommune, Vingt années de Vie africaine, I, 43ff.; Pechuel-Loesche, "Das Kongogebiet," 259.

with the keenest desire to do my duty to you, I yet am constrained to ask you not to exact too much from your very willing servant, but to give him a week's breath. Anything very important or interesting relating to the discoveries I have made from the point where Livingstone left off (Nyangwe in Manyema), I shall defer until my nerves, strained so long, have become a little more composed.

I send you duplicates of letters written at Nyangwe, and despatched to the East Coast by couriers of Mohammed bin Said, November, 1876, just ten months ago. The originals may not have arrived in Europe, in which case you may publish the duplicates.

I cannot refrain from congratulating you upon the perfect success which has attended the explorations of the Anglo-American expedition despatched by you from Zanzibar. The instructions, though onerous, have been faithfully and literally performed. These, I must remind you, were to complete the discoveries of Captain J. Hanning Speke and Captain (now Colonel) Grant, of the sources of the Nile; to circumnavigate lakes Victoria and Tanganyika, and by the explorations of the latter lake to complete the discoveries of Captains Burton and Speke, and, lastly, to complete the discoveries of Dr. Livingstone.

With a feeling of intense gratitude to Divine Providence, who has so miraculously saved me and my people from the terrors of slavery, from the pangs of cruel death at the hands of cannibals, after five months' daily toil through fifty-seven cataracts, falls and rapids— who inspired us with manliness sufficient to oppose the hosts of savages, and, out of thirty-two battles, brought us safe across unknown Africa to the Atlantic Ocean—I inform you that the work of the Anglo-American Expedition which you commissioned me to perform has been performed to the very letter. Other explorations we imposed on ourselves, but their successful prosecution depended on your means, and the fruits of all our long labors are due to you.

Large as the number of cataracts and rapids mentioned above may be, we have discovered that the great highway of commerce to broad Africa is the Congo, and happy will that Power seem which shall secure for itself a locality for a depot at the extreme limit of the navigation of the Lower Congo, and establish there a people such as the freed slaves, to assist it in enriching itself, the poor races employed in the service, and the redemption of the splendid central basin of the continent by sound and legitimate commerce.

So far as I have been permitted to observe I find that Eastern Central Africa and Western Central Africa must be acted on by two different influences. While all Africans, naturally, as savages, would more readily appreciate the trader than the missionary, still the missionary would be the most powerful agent in East Central Africa; while in West Central Africa the trader must precede the missionary. The reasons for this are obvious at a glance.

In East Central Africa the people are gathered under powerful emperors and kings—the great Empire of Uganda, which has an estimated population of 5,000,000; the great Empire of Ruanda, with an equal estimated population; the Empire of Urundi, with about 3,000,000;[3] the Kingdoms of Usagara, the two Usuis, Unyoro, Karagwe and Usongora and Ukerewe—all of these empires and kingdoms governed despotically, subject to the will of their respective monarchs. In his worthy efforts for the moral improvement of these benighted races the missionary, using a discreet judgment, can soon secure the good will, assistance and protection of the supreme powers of these countries.

In West Central Africa, from Lake Tanganyika to the mouth of the Congo River, the peoples are gathered in small, insignificant districts, towns or villages, each governed by its respective chief. As we approach nearer the West Coast the explorer dares not begin to classify the people after the usual manner employed in Africa, as the districts are so small, the population so great, the number of villages so confusing, that there are as many kings ruling over a hundred-acre plot as there are officials in Greece, all animated by an intense thirst for trade and distinguished for their idolatry, hostility to each other and foolish pride. The love of trade and barter is, however, universal, as I shall be able to explain in a subsequent letter.

Setting aside the contributions of our expedition to geography, the grandest discovery it has made is the great field for trade it has opened to the world, especially to the English, French, Germans and Americans, the English especially, for greater attention to those fabrics and wares generally purchased by Africans on the West Coast. In round numbers—I shall be more exact in another letter—you have thrown open to commerce an area embracing over six hundred thousand square miles, which contains nearly two thousand miles of an uninterrupted course of water communication, divided among

3. Stanley here gives a figure for all the area he held to be under the sway of the Ganda ruler. His estimate for the Ganda state alone was 750,000. *TDC*, I, 401, gives 2,775,000 for the Ganda empire. Fallers, *The King's Men*, 3, 83, considers Stanley's Ganda-state estimate a good one. For statistics on Ganda population, Kuczynski, *Demographic Survey of the British Colonial Empire*, II, 235ff. Rwanda and Burundi statistics are discussed in Louis, *Ruanda-Urundi*, 107–09, where pre-World-War-I German surveys show Rwanda with a population of around 2,000,000 and Burundi with around 1,500,000. See also document 21, note 5.

the Upper Congo and its magnificent affluents. It will take a long time to make up my map, but I promise you a rough sketch of the unknown half of Africa, now revealed for the first time, and you will find that in this brief letter that I am underestimating the merits of this new field for commerce. I will show you, when I have had time to arrange my notes, how near we are to extensive gold and copper fields, and what products merchants may expect in return for their fabrics.

For those interested in geography I may say that one time I never dreamed that you could hear anything of me until some time in 1878 or 1879, for my wonderful river continued a northerly course two degrees north of the Equator, sometimes taking great bends easterly, until I thought sometimes that I should soon be in the neighborhood of Jebel Kumr (the Mountains of the Moon), in which case I should either have to resolve, after reaching five degrees north latitude, to force my way toward Gondokoro through the wild Baris who are fighting with Gordon Pacha,[4] or continue on my way north to some great lake, and ultimately perchance the Niger.

At the Equator the Lualaba turned north-northeast, as if it really had, by some unknown means—unless all aneroids and barometers were wrong—a connection with the Albert Niyanza, and I hurrahed rather prematurely for Livingstone. This north-northeast course did not last long, for the Lualaba was simply collecting its force to tilt against a mountain, where, of course, there was the wildest scene imaginable.

Now, in regard to geographical problems, I have been flattering myself that I have settled all problems that were given out in 1874, the year I left England for Africa; but I fear, unless Gordon Pacha and his subs—who, by the by, threatened to be fearfully energetic when I was in Uganda and met Colonel de Bellefonds—can resolve the question that I must indicate one more problem to be settled by those who can settle it.

North of the Equator, while we were gliding down the river very quietly indeed, close to the right bank, we suddenly came to the second greatest affluent of the Lualaba—at the mouth 2,000 yards wide—coming from a little north of east.[5]

We had good cause to remember this river, for in midstream we had the second toughest fight of all. A fleet of canoes, fifty-four in

4. See Gray, *History of the Southern Sudan*, 108–12.
5. The Aruwimi. Stanley is unreliable in his listing of the relative sizes of the affluents since he would not discover them all in his course down the Congo. See document 40, note 13.

number, came down on us with such determined ferocity that four of our canoes began to give way and run. One of the enemy's canoes contained over eighty paddlers; a platform at the bow, for the best warriors, held ten men; eight steersmen, with ten-feet paddles, steered the great war vessel, while from stem to stern there ran a broad planking, along which the principal chiefs danced up and down, giving rehearsal to what they proposed to do with us. In half an hour the fight was decided in our favor, of course, or we should not write to you to-day. This great affluent puzzles me a good deal. Can it possibly come from the Albert Niyanza? Or is that gulf I discovered in 25 min. N. lat. a separate lake,[6] giving birth to this affluent of the Lualaba? Or is it merely the Welle of Schweinfurth? [7]

The people at home can best say which it is, for I am ignorant of everything that has transpired since November, 1874. Neither letters nor newspapers have reached me, except a wreck of a few *Illustrated London News*, sent to me by Colonel Gordon, in the early part of 1875, from Ismailia;[8] but these contained no geographical news.

If Gordon Pacha and his officers have explored the Albert Niyanza, as Colonel de Bellefonds informed me they were about to do, the question is easily answered as regards the Albert Lake; but if they have not, one may build any number of hypotheses without being censured by authority. One may say that the Albert Lake is possibly not a reservoir of the Nile alone, but also of the Congo; that the Lake Victoria, on which I spent such laborious toil, not unaccompanied with frequent dangers, is also not only a reservoir of the Nile, but of the Congo; and proceed in this strain until everything is muddled with theories again. And I remember that Colonel de Bellefonds had something to say about the uncertainty—putting it mildly—of Sir Samuel Baker's discoveries. But, as I remarked before, the geographers at home can best determine all these questions, for they gather the news from all points, and the best thing an explorer can do is to leave it all to them.

Another thing I must hint to you about—for, as I told you, this is a letter or note written very hurriedly, upon a very exciting occasion; I cannot enter into details now—the incorrectness, or rather the infamous inaccuracy, of the chart of Western Africa. The chartmaker

6. Beatrice Gulf. See document 26, note 18.
7. Georg Schweinfurth (1836–1925), Riga-born explorer and naturalist, was the first European to cross the Nile-Congo watershed. He had discovered in 1870 an unknown river flowing west—the Uele. *BCB*, I, 537–41; *GJ* 62 (1926), 93–94; Beck, "Georg Schweinfurth."
8. Gondokoro.

may be to blame, after all; but if he can produce his authority and the source of his information he is saved from the serious charge of having published much of his work upon hearsay, without marking his information as "such." I dare not imagine Captain Tuckey to be responsible for these errors. I should much rather accuse Portuguese traders, who might be presumed to be very uncertain about the meaning of the words "geographical accuracy." In plainer terms, nothing that can be seen on your map of Western Africa twenty miles east of Yellala Falls is correct. It is a simple show of names that I hear nothing about and a wild wavy line marked deeply black which pretends to be the Congo. We have also just above the Falls of Yellala a sketch of a river four or five miles wide, with islands, the whole of which I shall be able to show you is sheer nonsense, and anybody who doubts it need only spend £100 to satisfy himself by a personal investigation. Besides the enormous amount of internal satisfaction he will receive he will have a pleasant five days' walk through a picturesque country.[9]

You will be surprised and grieved to hear, however, that to these errors on this map I owe the loss of one of the most gentle souls, and withal one of the bravest—Francis Pocock—along with fifteen of my people, two narrow escapes of myself, the loss of about $18,000 worth of ivory, twelve canoes, a mutiny of my command and the almost total ruin of the expedition, besides dislocated limbs, bruises without number and a wearing anxiety during five months which has made me an old man in my thirty-fifth year.

But the gracious God be thanked, who has delivered us from "the mouth of hell and the jaws of death!" We are now safe, and the merchants on the West Coast are doing their very best to make us feel at home. About sixty of my people are suffering severely from scurvy, others from dropsy, dysentery, &c. One young fellow just lived to reach the ocean. Another has gone mad for joy and has taken to the bush and become lost, and I myself am so prostrated with weakness that I must once again ask you to excuse me for a few days.

9. James Tuckey (1776–1816) of the Royal Navy; he led an expedition to the Congo River in 1816. The venture was a major disaster since sixteen Europeans died from disease, including Tuckey. BCB, IV, 889–94. Anstey, *Britain and the Congo*, 1–9; Boahen, *Britain, the Sahara, and the Western Sudan*, 37–41. The results were later published in Tuckey, *Narrative of an Expedition to Explore the River Zaire*. Stanley was severely criticized for his statement about Tuckey—"the only way to account for Mr. Stanley's extraordinary statement is that he was provided with some incorrect manuscript compilation, and that he had never seen Tuckey's map." "Mr. Stanley's Voyage Down the Congo," 319. Compare *TDC*, II, 432, 441. See also de Bouveignes, "Tuckey et Stanley."

37

Loanda
Sept. 1, 1877 [1]

For the satisfaction of those who have become interested in Francis Pocock, whose courage, many virtues and fidelity to duty have formed the subject of many a paragraph in my former letters, I cannot do better than give a slight sketch of his character as he appeared to me from our first acquaintance up to the day of his death.

For the first six months of our companionship he remained to me as an undeveloped man. There was no great demand on his active moral or mental powers. He was rather shy and reserved, and there was no call for whatever of usefulness lay concealed in him. He had simply to obey orders, and this he did without meriting much praise. He labored under the disadvantage of not understanding the language of the people over whom he was sometimes required to exercise supervision and control; but by and by he became quite a proficient in the vernacular, and it was then he began to be surprisingly useful, showing a perfect acquaintance with his duties, with a readiness to perform them and a true devotion to our mission. Hitherto he had been frequently subject to the acclimatizing fevers of Africa, which were sometimes of a very severe form; but finally his healthy constitution triumphed over all attacks of fever, and I flattered myself that I should be able to introduce to science and commerce one young Englishman who might be a great acquisition to future explorers.

During my absence with Mtesa, Emperor of Uganda, he was placed in several delicate positions, out of which he extricated himself with great credit. It was after this last three months' absence from camp that Frank began to endear himself to me. While exploring the Alexandra Nile he had another opportunity of distinguishing himself for his prudence and tact. While I explored the Tanganyika, and my people were stricken with that terrible scourge of Africa, the smallpox, he was in constant attendance on them, and by his assiduous devotion to them in their illness he quite won the love of the Wanguana and the respect of the Arabs of Ujiji. When we set out for the western half of Africa he had elevated himself, by his many good qualities and thorough appreciation of the work before us, to be my friend. From this time I never ventured on any task without first

1. *NYH,* Nov. 14, 1877.

hearing his views of it. He was a constant visitor in my tent, and I do not believe he ever quitted it without leaving me fresher, stronger and more confident.

In this manner it happened that at Nyangwe, before I made my final resolution to follow the Lualaba, Frank and I spent a long time together. The question was, Should I follow the Lualaba to the sea or should I follow it only as far as the Lowa, and then strike off for Monbuttu? [2] Indeed, there were many questions to be decided in connection with this one. Would it be possible, with twenty-three Sniders and thirty-one muskets, to defend ourselves against the cannibals, when another explorer, with forty-seven Sniders, declined attempting it? Was it right attempting a task so desperate, when all the Arabs did their utmost to show us that it was an impossible task? "Toss up," said Frank; "heads for the north, tails for the south and Katanga." The proposition was adopted; but tails won after three trials. Yet neither of us liked the idea of being thus ordered south by destiny; it was too much like poaching on known ground. Finally it was decided between us to take advantage of the Arabs' escort to get clear of Nyangwe, and then to go on alone and never to return, no matter what opposed us; but to charge with heads of steel against any and everything hostile to our arriving at the ocean. [3]

The tramp through the gloomy forests of Uzimba and Uvinza [4] wore Frank's last pair of shoes out, and mine were getting well used up also. The Arabs were tired of their bargain and wished to return, but another contract induced them to accompany us across the Lualaba and to try the left bank a short distance. They then abandoned us and we resumed our journey with our own people unsupported by any volunteer. At the several falls we were obliged to pass overland, a good deal of rough tramping through bushes and forests and over rocks, backward and forward, had to be made, and nothing that Frank or I could invent endured very long. Portmanteaus and bull hides were cut up and sewn and patched over and over, but it was useless; three or four days always sufficed to leave him as unprotected as ever.

2. The Mangbetu, an amalgam of peoples living to the south of the Uele River and along the Bomokandi River. They had been visited by Schweinfurth. Baxter and Butt, *Azande and Related Peoples*, 36–37; Maes and Boone, *Peuplades du Congo Belge*, 270–75; Vansina, *Introduction à Ethnographie du Congo*, chap. 2.

3. There is a much expanded version of this famous episode, with different details, in *TDC*, II, 109–14.

4. For the Zimba of Manyema, Maes and Boone, *Peuplades du Congo Belge*, 351–52. For Uvinza, in Manyema, *TDC*, II, 71; Cameron, *Across Africa*, I, 347–48, II, 311–12.

His feet became chafed, rocks and thorns wounded them, and at Mowa Falls, or the thirty-fifth of the lower series, he became permanently disabled from walking, being attacked with ulcers in both feet. The duty of leading the way over the rapids and selecting the best and most feasible paths for hauling boat and canoes overland devolved on myself, while his duty now was to superintend the soldiers as they carried the goods overland and distribute each day's rations; and it was in the prosecution of my dangerous labors that I had at times narrowly escaped death. Feeling almost sure that if either of us was destined to be lost it would be myself I had prepared my mind for that event, and had drawn up instructions for Frank how to proceed. At Mowa Falls, as Frank, disabled by ulcers, could neither be trusted to do duty supervising the passage of the canoes, as he was altogether too bold, and nothing but the utmost prudence could save life, nor could he proceed overland with the goods party, he was placed on the sick list along with twenty-five sick Wanguana, and obliged to wait until hammock bearers could be sent for him.

I now refer to my journal of June 3, 1877:[5] This morning the people shouldered the goods and baggage, and under Kacheche marched overland three miles to Zinga,[6] while I resolved to attempt the passage down two small falls, the Massesse and Massassa, in the boat with the boat's crew. Clinging close to the shore we rowed three-quarters of a mile or thereabouts, when we halted by a lofty cliff, by the sides of which we could proceed no further as the tide, thrust to right and left from the centre of the river by the furious waters escaping from the Mowa Falls, came running to meet us up river with many a brown wave, and heave, and dangerous whirlpool. Steering for the centre of the river, we fought sturdily on against this strong back tide, but we could make no headway. Then we thought we would attempt the central stream that rushed down river with a foamy face. We could not reach it, and fortunately, for the boat was sinking steadily under its growing weight of water, since she was very leaky, and the repairs we had made were utterly insufficient.

By observing the shores and the increasingly menacing appearance of the river I perceived that, instead of making any advance down river, we had imperceptibly drawn up toward the terrible whirling pools which almost momentarily play near the confluence of the down stream and the back tide, where the great waves, heaved upward by the raging and convulsive centre, and parting to right and

5. *Diary*, 187–92, is substantially the same.
6. Stanley has some notes on the Zinga region in Stanley, *The Congo*, I, 313–18.

left, are opposed by the back tide flowing on strong toward the fearful current. Presently, at a little distance I saw the first symptoms of a whirling vortex. There is a convulsive heave in mid-river; the waters are shot off as from the cone of a hill to all sides. This watery hill subsides quickly, and soon the returning waters begin to whirl round and round, a deep hole digs itself, faster and faster, wider and wider, until the entire river seems on the point of whirling.

This, after some dozen experiences, I recognized as a deathly snare, to escape from which I must struggle no more against the back tide, but instantly turn away from the scene. I motioned to the steersman, and shouted to leave off bailing, and do their best or die. Meantime, my own preparations were too significant not to be understood. I threw off coat and belt, shoes and stockings, for it might be that the whirling, flying pool would overtake us. My gallant crew had been too often in danger with me, and they understood me. In a short time we saw the whirlpool yawning wide a few yards from the stem of the boat; she hesitated a little on the verge of it, but a kindly wave assisted our wild efforts, and we were saved. The boat by this time was half full of water, and, finding it impossible to proceed in the leaky craft, I returned to the Mowa Falls, with the intention of proceeding, after a short rest, in a canoe; but, while talking with Frank the boat's crew scattered, and the others had not returned from Zinga. As it was necessary that one of us should hurry overland after the goods, and Frank was unable to move, for the first time I was compelled to leave the supervision of the passage of the falls in other hands; and, accordingly, I instructed Manwa Sera, my chief captain, how to proceed.

"You will first send a rescue canoe, with short ropes fastened to the sides. The crew will pick their way carefully down river until near the falls; then let the men judge for themselves whether they are able to take the canoe further. Above all things, stick to the shore and don't play with the river." I bade goodby to Frank, told him I would send his breakfast to him immediately with hammock bearers, shook hands and at once commenced to climb the 2,000 feet mountain toward camp. Breakfast had been sent to Frank, friendship and introductions had been made with the kings of Zinga, and in the afternoon, about three o'clock, I was seated on the rocks of that place, field glass in hand, looking up the terrible river, exceedingly anxious, for this was the first time I had permitted any person but myself to lead the way down its wild water.

About three o'clock something dark and long was recognized in the midst of the fierce waves of Massassa Falls, as they were tumbling into the basin of Bolo-bolo. It was a canoe capsized, and clinging to it were several men. I instantly despatched two chiefs and ten men to take position near the bend, to which I supposed the current that forced its way through the basin would take the wreck. Meanwhile, I watched the men as they were floating through Bolo-bolo Basin. I saw them struggling to right her. I saw them raise themselves on the keel, and paddling with their hands for dear life, because below them a short half mile roared the Zinga cataract. Finally, as they approached land, I saw them leap into the river and swim ashore, and presently their canoe, which they but a moment before abandoned, swept by me with the speed of an arrow over the Zinga cataract into the white waves below, into the depths of whirlpool after whirlpool, and finally away out of sight.

Bad news travels fast. Messengers, breathless with haste and livid with terror, announced that there were eleven men who had embarked in that canoe, eight of whom were saved; three men were drowned, one of whom was my brave, honest, kindly natured Frank! Francis Pocock, my faithful companion and friend! "But," I asked the coxswain Uledi, sternly, "how came Frank in that canoe? What business had he, a lame man, in the rescue canoe?"

"Ah master," said he, "we could not help it. He would not wait. He said, 'Since the canoe is going to camp I will go. I am hungry and cannot wait any longer. I cannot walk, and I don't want anybody to carry me, that the natives may all laugh at me. No; I will go with you,' and without listening to Manwa Sera, the captain, who wished to remonstrate with him, he took his seat and told us to cast off. We found no trouble in forcing the canoe against the back tide. We struck the down current, and when we were near the falls I steered her into a cove to take a good look at it first. When I had climbed over the rocks and stood over it I saw that it was a bad place, that it was useless to expect any canoe could pass it without going over, and I went to the little master and told him so. He would not believe me, but sent other men to report on it, and they returned with the same story, that the fall could not be passed by shooting over it in a canoe. Then he said to us that we were always afraid of a little water, and said we were no men. 'All right,' said I; 'if you say cast off I am ready, I am not afraid of any water, but my master will be angry with me if anything happens.'

" 'Cast off, nothing will happen,' the little master answered, 'am I not here?' You could not have counted ten, master, before we were all sorry. The cruel water caught us and tossed and whirled us round, and shot us here and shot us there, and the noise was fearful. Suddenly the little master shouted, "Look out, take hold of the ropes!" and he was tearing his shirt off when the canoe which was whirling round and round with its bow in the air, was dragged down, down, down, until I thought my chest would burst, then we were shot out into daylight again and took some breath.

"The little master and two of our people were not to be seen, but shortly I saw the little master face upward, but insensible. I instantly struck out for him to save him, but we were both taken down again, and the water seemed to be tearing my legs away; but I would not give in. I held my breath hard then, and I came to the surface, but the little master was gone forever! This is my story, master." The boat's crew, separately examined by me, indorsed Uledi's statement in all main points.

This is scarcely the place to say much of Uledi, but I cannot refrain from giving this young African, who was the coxswain of the *Lady Alice,* a meed of praise here. Uledi is a young fellow twenty-seven or twenty-eight years old, lithe and active as a leopard and brave as a lion. He is one of a hundred thousand. I doubt whether there is another in the island of Zanzibar equal to him. There are few in this expedition who are not indebted to him for life or timely rescue or brave service. He was the first in war and the most modest in peace. He was the best soldier, the best swimmer, the best carrier, the best sailor, the best workman in wood or iron, and the most faithful of the black faithfuls. He was certainly the last man in the world who should have been dared into doing a desperate act, such as shooting a cataract. But Frank was too brave also, and had a strange contempt for the terrors of the river, having been a Medway waterman from his boyhood. It is first to sheer rashness, and second to his accidentally striking his head against the canoe as he endeavored to rise to the surface, that I attributed the loss of such an expert swimmer as Frank Pocock.

As I look at his empty tent this evening and at his dejected servants, and recall to mind his many inestimable qualities, his extraordinary gentleness, his patient temper, his industry, his cheerfulness and tender love of me, I feel myself utterly unable to express my feelings or describe the vastness of my loss. Every instance of his faithful services that is recalled only intensifies my grief. The long copartnership in perils thus abruptly severed, his piety and cheerful trust in a gracious Providence, fills my heart with misery to think that he has departed this life so suddenly and unrewarded for his many manly virtues.

38

Loanda
Sept. 2, 1877 [1]

My Dear Mr. Pocock: By means of my telegrams to the *Daily Telegraph* you have, no doubt, an idea as to the reason that induces me to write to you. The subject is very serious and sad. I would to God that Frank had to write to you about my death rather than I should be compelled to write about Frank's death. The feeling is still fresh in my mind how I hankered after death—after that long, long sleep from which there is no waking, for we were passing through a most troublous period; hunger and sickness had destroyed all that enthusiastic energy with which we had rushed through the lands of the cannibals. I had lost many men in our incessant wars with the natives; sickness and despair had worried many others to their death. Still our work seemed to have no end, and we could not see one ray of hope ahead. Our sick list grew heavier and heavier, until we had but sixty-three fit for work. I had about fifteen men down from ulcers and ten men from dysentery and debility. So long, however, as I had Frank and my boat's crew I felt myself able to endure and fight it out—savages or cataracts, it mattered not much which. If there were hostile savages we felt ourselves able to cut through them; if there were forests through which roads must be made, we would make them; if we had to pull our canoes over mountains, we would pull them up. It was only a question of time. And all this time Frank cheered me on and said, with me, "We must and we will do it."

There were two series of cataracts and rapids. The upper series consisted of six separate falls; the lower series consisted of seventy-four falls, great and small rapids, fifty-seven of which only were important. Of this lower series we had already passed thirty-five separate falls and rapids, but there were only three more really dangerous. It was while passing the thirty-seventh fall—Masassa—that Frank lost his life. The truth is that Frank was lost through his own rashness and immense contempt for the water. He had been placed on the sick list, because for ten or twelve days previously he was incapacitated from duty through ulcers on both feet of a most painful kind, and a man on the sick list ought not to have assumed the responsibility of commanding "active duty" men to proceed to execute a dangerous work, and take him with them, when he could actually do nothing

1. *NYH,* Nov. 28, 1877.

to assist them or superintend them. Frank was scarcely able to stand, least of all to climb the rocks to take a good view of the dangers ahead so that he might judge of his situation.

What does Frank do? He crawls on his knees to the canoe—the rescue canoe—manned with the most daring young fellows in the expedition, headed by the most desperate and daring young fellow I ever knew,[2] and, despite all remonstrances of the crew and chief he orders them to cast off. Still Frank might have been safe if, when the last chance was given him, he would have permitted himself to reflect upon his own condition—his own distressing, pitiful condition. The chief acted prudently enough in what he did, though he would have done better and more to my satisfaction had he done exactly as I had taught him when over forty-one falls and rapids I was leader. This chief steered his canoe into a cove, just above the fall, and started to reconnoitre, to take a good look at the fall, and he came back and told Frank that it was impossible to shoot over the fall —that, in fact, it was a very bad place. Frank would not believe him, but sent the youngsters to look at the fall and report upon it. They returned with the same story—that the fall was very bad. I have no doubt that had Frank been able to view the scene himself he would have agreed with them; but Frank, seated in his canoe, unable to move, thought, as he came down the river to the cove where they were consulting, that he had seen in midriver a place clear of falling water and waves, and he of course argued with the crew upon the strength of that.

It seems that he remembered what I had told him a few days before—that whenever he was going to risk the lives of others in a dangerous undertaking it was not fair to give the final word without exposing to them all the dangers of it and asking them to give their judgment upon it, and if their judgment was against the undertaking they should not be compelled to it. Frank hinted to the crew at this time that he knew exactly who had told me of this, and therefore, lest he should be charged by me with having risked the lives of others, he would say nothing.

"But," he asked, "tell me, what am I to do? I have eaten nothing to-day, and here am I lame, unable to move. Will you leave me here to die of hunger?"

"Oh, no," said the chief. "I will send a man at once for your food, and for men to carry you, and in a couple of hours they will be here."

"Oh, very well," said Frank; "do as you please," and Frank assumed

2. Uledi.

the look of one badly and disagreeably used. And then he told them that they were always afraid of the least little wave, and other querulous things, which only a sick man would have said. Poor Frank was only pushing himself nearer and nearer to death.

The chief then said, "Little Master, we are not afraid of the river. I think I have proved I am not afraid, and, if I say the word, these boys of mine will follow me to the bottom. Master has told us not to play in the river—not to do anything foolish—and if master was here he would tell us that the fall was dangerous. But if anything should happen, if you will take the blame, I say I and my people are ready, and if we die we die, if we are saved we are saved."

"Oh, never fear; I will take the blame. Nothing will happen. Did I not see the river as we came down? Cast off, then, and let us go."

Five minutes afterward they were over the falls and in the depth of a fearful whirlpool, and out of the eleven men that went down but eight came out safe. Presently Frank was seen with his face up and the chief sprang after him, but before he could reach him they were both drawn into another whirlpool immediately, and sucked down and whirled and tossed about, and only the chief came out, faint and exhausted.

Twenty miles below Frank's body was seen floating down river, a wonder and a terror to the tribes, who could not imagine where the white man had come from, and then his remains were seen no more.

I have told you as much as I know and a good deal of what I have heard, but, as I have proposed to the commander of the *Sea Gull* [3] and the English and American Consuls[4] that they should question officially about all causes relating to Frank's death, you may hear more.

Meantime, dear Mr. Pocock, believe me when I tell you that I feel his loss as keenly as though he were my brother. Sorrow is difficult to measure and is expressed by different people in different ways. My tears are over, the indescribable grief I felt when I was assured that I should see my amiable, faithful Frank no more has lost its intensity; but even now, whenever my mind recurs to those days of danger, despair and death, I feel my heart sinking when memory recalls the day I lost Frank. My pity and sympathy are also roused each time I think of you. I had flattered myself of the pride I should

3. H.M.S. *Seagull*, Commander F.W.B. Maxwell Heron. *TDC*, II, 473; Clowes, *Royal Navy*, VII, 283.

4. The British consul was David Hopkins; the American was Robert Newton. *TDC*, II, 473; Cameron, *Across Africa*, II, 272; de Bouveignes, "Stanley à Boma," 202.

feel when I would be able to tell you that there was not a finer, braver, better young man in the world than your son Frank. Now, what is it I can show you, what can I tell you, but the sad, sad story of your son's death?

Whenever you think what a pity it is, believe me, I can echo even your very thought. Whenever you sigh for his fate believe that there is one who sighs with you. Whenever you grieve believe that I sympathize truly in your grief.

P.S. I shall take charge of the papers, letters and journal of Edward and Frank until I can send them to you safe. His more interesting papers—which, I am sure, you will be glad to see—I shall send by mail.

39

Loanda, West Coast of Africa
Sept. 5, 1877 [1]

To avoid constant explanation I will make a few remarks about the name generally given to the greatest African river and the third largest river in the world.[2] There is no such river as the Congo, properly speaking, in Africa. There is a country called Congo,[3] occupying an extensive portion of mountain lands south of the river, and running parallel with it, at a distance of five or six miles from it, in that broad mountain range which separates the West Coast land from the great plains of the interior. Following the example of the natives among whom they lived the Portuguese colonists and fathers of the fifteenth century called it the River of Congo, which was just as if the natives of Middlesex county, England, called the Thames the River of Middlesex. By the Kabindas, near the mouth of the river, it is called the "Kwango," or, if you do not like the African look of the spelling, the "Quango." The natives of the cataract region also designate the river below them as the Kwango, and those living between the Mosamba and Tala Mungongo Mountains call the Nkutu River at its source the Kwango. As Congo Land does not occupy any very

1. *NYH*, Nov. 14, 1877.
2. The Congo is considered the sixth longest river in the world. Goode, *Goode's World Atlas*, 161. It is over 2,700 miles in length.
3. The territory once under the state of Kongo, with its capital at San Salvador. See Vansina, *Introduction à l'Ethnographie du Congo*, chap. 8; Vansina, *Kingdoms of the Savanna*, 37ff.; Doutreloux, "Introduction à la culture Kongo."

great portion of the river bank it has no right to give its name to the river any more than any other of the hundred different districts by which it flows. By a small tribe near the Equator I heard it called Ikutu Ya Kongo, which, in my ignorance of the word Ikutu, I take to mean the River of Congo, but after passing that tribe the name is known no more, except in books and charts of the West Coast of Africa.[4]

Dr. Livingstone, the discoverer of the Lualaba, devoted the last years of his life to exploring the head waters of the Congo, the Chambezi and Karungwesi, which feed Lake Bemba, or Banweolo.[5] He traced the Luapula as far as Mweru Lake, but from Mweru Lake to the Luama River no European knows anything from personal observation of its course or its affluents. Striking across country from Tanganyika Lake Livingstone arrived at Nyangwe, near which Arab depot the Lualaba, by which name the Congo is known there, flows west of north with a volume of 124,000 cubic feet of water per second. Unable for want of men and means to extend his exploration, the renowned traveller left its further course to conjecture and theory.

His opinion was that the Lualaba was the Nile, he hoped it was the "grand old Nile;" he was unwilling, he said, to waste his labor on any other river than the Nile; he certainly would "not attempt the foolhardy feat of following it in canoes, and risk becoming black man's meat for the Congo." [6] He felt convinced it was the Nile, and he half convinced me that he must be right, and I wished sincerely that the good old man would prove right. Savants unbiased by sentiment declared, upon the strength of Livingstone's own letters, that such a great volume of water could not be the Nile. Not only was its enormous body against such a theory, but the altitude of the river at Nyangwe proved the irreconcilability of the theory with common sense. A great deal was written and said by eminent men just then about the Lualaba, and the belief generally prevailed at last that it must be the Congo.

While many may feel surprised that such a practical traveller was led astray the causes that blinded him are very obvious. He himself confessed to a suspicion that it was the Congo; but he had been so long absent from Europe that he was unaware of the discoveries made

4. The Kabinda, or Kakongo, live along the right bank of the lower Congo and along the coast of Cabinda. Maes and Boone, *Peuplades du Congo Belge*, 241–42. For the names of the Congo, Stanley, *The Congo*, I, 1ff.; Laman, "The Kongo," 4 (1953), 1, 10. For the Kwango and Nkutu, see note 25, below.

5. The Kalungwizi River flows into Lake Mweru on the Zambian side of the lake.

6. See *LLJ*, II, 188.

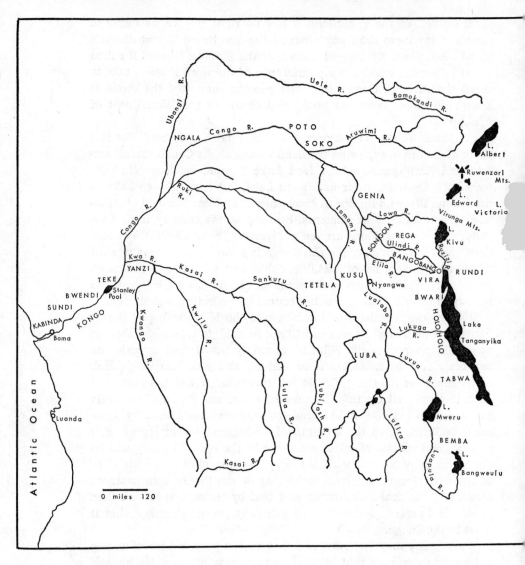

Map VII. The Congo

by Schweinfurth; he relied on Arab statements that the river flowed north a long distance; and, to tell the exact truth, I fear that his religious sentiments and his love of the Nile for its biblical and classical associations prejudiced him. To such a man what was the parvenu river, with ever so many future associations of traffic? Yet he loved Africa dearly, but unfortunately he was unaware of the vastness of his discovery, and of its future utility for the prosecution of his own views and hopes for the civilization and redemption of the continent for which he sacrificed a dear and noble life.

But before Livingstone had described the river at Nyangwe no one, scientific or unscientific, imagined that the Congo had such a great length. Though Captain Tuckey's explorations in the neighborhood of Yellala Falls, in the year 1816, furnished the elements for Dr. Behm's computation respecting the volume of the Lower Congo,[7] geographers waited for Livingstone's arrival at Nyangwe and Dr. Schweinfurth's arrival at Monbuttu[8] before they came to the idea that the Lualaba must be the Congo. Previous to this it is in the memory of many how scientists were involved in discussions and elaborate arguments to prove that the great Congo was simply the united Kaseye[9] and Quango, or Congo, which was giving it a length of but 800 miles. Ah! had Speke become interested in this river and had obtained one glance at the mouth even, and had gleaned but one or two facts from the natives, I believe that his rare and wonderful geographical instinct would have pencilled out the course of this stream somewhat nearer the truth. When Lieutenant Cameron arrived at Nyangwe he also expressed a conviction that the Lualaba must be the Congo; but, with the exception of a divergence of opinion, he threw no newer light on its real course.

Sixteen months after the Lieutenant's departure for the South I appeared at Nyangwe, and I then learned definitely that he had abandoned the project of following the Lualaba. As it seemed the most important task of exploration I resolved to attempt it. Ignorant, foolish and heathenish as Europeans may deem Arab traders and African savages to be the "Great River" has been the subject of as many hot disputes under the eaves of the mud houses of Nyangwe and the cane huts of the river fishermen as it was under the dome at Brighton or the classic roof of Burlington House,[10] and my enthusiasm for this new field of exploration—the unknown half of Africa and the mighty river that "went no man knew where"—was stimulated as

7. Ernst Behm (1830–1884), a leading German geographer; he was the founder of the *Geographisches Jahrbuch* and the chief editor of *PM* after the death of its founder. *Deutsche Rundschau für Geographie und Statistik* 6 (1884), 335, 523–25. There is an English translation of his study—"Dr. Livingstone's Exploration of the Upper Congo."

8. See document 37, note 2.

9. The Kasai River; see note 25, below.

10. The Royal Geographical Society met at Burlington House from 1858 to 1868. Markham, *The Fifty Years' Work of the Royal Geographical Society*, 113. For Stanley's experiences at the meetings of the Geographical Section of the British Association at Brighton in 1872, Anstruther, *I Presume*, 149–53.

much by the earnestness with which Arabs and natives discussed it as though each member of the Royal Geographical Society had bestowed a scientific blessing on me and unanimously wished me success.

Nyangwe is in latitude 4 deg. 16 min. south. If you follow the parallel of latitude 4 deg. east to the Indian Ocean, you will observe there are 13½ degrees of longitude or 810 geographical miles. If you will measure the distance between Nyangwe and the Atlantic, along the same parallel, you will find there are 15½ degrees of longitude, or 930 geographical miles.[11] The eastern half of Africa is generally known, but that western half was altogether unknown. To any one arriving from the East Coast with the love of exploring unknown wilds, what a field lay extended before him! The largest half of Africa one wide enormous blank—a region of fable and mystery—a continent of dwarfs and cannibals and gorillas, through which the great river flowed on its unfulfilled mission to the Atlantic! Darkness and clouds of ignorance respecting its course everywhere! What terrible dread thing is it that so pertinaciously prevents explorers from penetrating and revealing its mysteries! It struck me thus also, as though a vague indescribable something lay ahead.

I believe I was made half indifferent to life by my position; otherwise I doubt if I should have deliberately rushed upon what I was led to believe—as my predecessors were—was almost certain death. I had not anticipated hearing such forbidding things as I did hear of the regions north or meeting such obstacles as I met. Neither of my predecessors could obtain canoes at Nyangwe, nor was I more successful; and the Arabs at Nyangwe, pretending to be very solicitous about my safety, said they could not think of permitting my departure. But my fate seemed to drive me on. I listened to their stories about how many caravans attempting to open trade below had been annihilated; but I had calculated my resources, and had measured my strength and confidence, and I declared to the Arabs that I intended to try it.

I was quite prepared to hear that I should be murdered and eaten, and that my people would desert; that I would meet opposition of such a nature that I never heard of or dreamed of, and that they (the Arabs) could not listen to such a project. Being prepared, these things did not surprise me. It was perhaps time I should be murdered; it was perhaps impossible to penetrate the wild, wide land before me, but it was no reason why I should not try and put the practicability

11. Nyangwe is located on Lat. 4°15′ S. and Long. 26°14′ E. *The Times Index-Gazetteer of the World* (London, 1965), 613.

of its exploration to the test. "If you did not try it for more than a week or so, how do you know it was impossible?" people might ask me, and very rightly too. "You say there are cannibals who will eat me. It may be true; but I have one comfort, they cannot eat me before they kill me. Can they?" "No, certainly not." "You say they will fight me. I have had wars enough already on this expedition, and I should not like to have another war; but what can I do if savages will attack me? I have a few young men who are aware of what we can do in the way of fighting, and we do not propose to sleep, or let any man draw his knife across our throats without remonstrating in a most energetic manner. Granted that we shall have fighting to do, what else is there to fear?" "Oh, plenty of things; but you will see." We did see, it is true; but I reserve that story for another letter.

The journey over the hitherto unknown half of Africa now being finished, the difficulties and terrors, wars after wars, troubles after troubles, toil upon toil, the dismay and despair being ended, it cannot be wondered that we breathe a little freer and feel more relief now than when we were about to begin the journey. Our experiences have been very sad and dreadful, and we have paid dearly for the temerity and obstinacy with which we held on. You might cull all the terrible experiences that African travellers relate in their books, and united they would scarcely present such a list of difficulties as we could show. Our losses, nevertheless, have not been so great comparatively. Our journey's length from Nyangwe is nearly one thousand eight hundred miles; our losses in men are one European and thirty-four Wanguana. Captain Tuckey lost eighteen Europeans and eleven colored men in about three months. Mungo Park[12] lost his own life and the lives of all his people, and out of Peddie's Niger expedition[13] the commander and all the principal officers lost their lives and the expedition was broken up. Much earnest effort was necessary to break through, and there is no doubt that if we had not made it some explorer with a little more determination and less nonsense in him would have done it, and his troubles would have been much the same.

But I have paid for my triumph with one of my band whose loss almost causes me to regret that I also did not permit myself to be dissuaded from entering the unknown regions. Though born in an humble sphere of life Francis Pocock was an extraordinary man; a

12. Hallett, *The Penetration of Africa*, 227ff., gives an account of the explorations of Mungo Park (1771–1806).

13. For John Peddie's unsuccessful expedition, Newbury, *British Policy towards West Africa, Select Documents 1786–1874*, 6, 44; Boahen, *Britain, The Sahara, and The Western Sudan*, 37–42.

man to make himself respected and beloved; a man of many fine qualities, of cool, steadfast courage, that knew no quailing; of great manliness, a cheerful, amiable companion; a gentle, pious soul, and a staunch friend in trouble. One instance of his courage is worth relating. The natives of Ibaka[14] prepared to attack us and advanced on us for that purpose. I stood up in the boat to speak to them, and while engaged in conversation with one of the chiefs a canoe crept up near Frank's and Frank was made aware that he was a target for two or three guns, and lifted his gun to fire or to threaten them. Seeing this, that it would precipitate us into another fight, before exhausting all endeavors, for peace, I cried out to Frank to drop his gun. He instantly obeyed, and permitted them to approach within thirty yards of him without making the least motion, though every one was exceedingly anxious. Finding that his eyes were fastened on them two of the savages that were aiming at Frank suddenly changed their minds, and gave my boat's crew the benefit of their attentions, firing among us, wounding four of my best men, though fortunately not fatally, and the third emptied his gun among Frank's people, wounding one. He then received permission to avenge himself, which he did in an effective manner.

It has been a custom from a remote period, with merchants and European travellers desirous of penetrating inland from the West Coast, to give "rum dashes." Rum is an article unknown on the East Coast, and I cannot but think that it acts perniciously on the insignificant chiefs of small villages.[15] We found them exceedingly bumptious, and not easily mollified without rum. Having almost crossed Africa we could not gratify their demands for rum, and had to stand firm and resolute in our determination to pass through these small tribes; and, though we were not compelled to use force, there was frequently a disposition among them to oppose by arms our journey. Neither had we the gaudy uniform coats of a bygone century to gratify their love of tinsel and finery.

Still, there was here no rupture of the peace. We were allowed to proceed without violence, more as strange curiosities than anything else, I believe, and as people who had come from wild lands whither the white people had never ventured before. Possibly on that account there may have been a small feeling of respect mingled with their jealous regard of us. I speak, of course, about the people called

14. In the Yanzi area. See Stanley, *The Congo*, I, 561ff. and *passim*. See also Johnston, *The River Congo*, 232–42, and note 23, below.

15. The problem was less acute in East Africa, but by the 1880's would begin to be of more concern. Bennett, "Edward D. Ropes, Jr."

Basundi and those inhabiting Eastern Mbinda.[16] The tribes above the
Babwende and Bateke were more kindly disposed.[17] I am indebted
to them for many a laborious service performed for very little pay,
and during five months our intercourse with them was of the most
amicable kind. Those on the south side vied with those of the north
side of the river in the cataract districts to assist us. Food was generally more plentiful on the south side, and, in many instances, the
natives were more friendly.

The entire area the Congo drains embraces about 860,000 square
miles. Its source is in that high plateau south of Lake Tanganyika,
in a country called Bisa, or Ubisa, by the Arabs. The principal tributary feeding Bemba Lake is the Chambezi, a broad, deep river, whose
extreme sources must be placed about longitude 33 deg. east. Bemba
Lake, called Bangweolo by Livingstone, its discoverer, is a large body
of shallow water, about 8,400 square miles in extent. It is the resi-
duum of an enormous lake that in very ancient times must have
occupied an area of 500,000 square miles, until by some great convulsion the western maritime mountain chain was riven asunder, and
the Congo began to roar through the fracture. Issuing from Bemba
Lake, the Congo is known under the name of Luapula, which, after
a course of nearly two hundred miles, empties into Lake Mweru, a
body of water occupying an area of about one thousand eight hundred
square miles. Falling from Mweru, it receives the name of Lualaba from
the natives of Rua. In Northern Rua it receives an important affluent
called the Kamalondo. Flowing in a direction north by west, it sweeps
with a breadth of about one thousand four hundred yards by Nyangwe, Manyema, in latitude 4 deg. 15 min. 45 sec. south, longitude
26 deg. 5 min. east, and has an altitude of about fourteen hundred
and fifty feet above the ocean. Livingstone, having lost two weeks
in his dates, appears, according to Stanford's map of 1874, to have
placed Nyangwe in latitude 4 deg. 1 min. south, longitude 24 deg.
16 min. east, but this wide difference may be due to the carelessness
of the draughtsman. Those who feel interested in it should compare
it with the latest map issued by Stanford or the map published with

16. The Sundi, one of the Kongo group; they lived upriver from Isangila
on the right bank. Maes and Boone, *Peuplades du Congo Belge*, 176–81; Soret,
Les Kongo Nord-Occidentaux; Laman, "The Kongo." Mbinda was near Isangila.
TDC, II, 440–44.

17. The Bwendi lived along the Congo to the south of Stanley Pool. Teke
was a general name for the populations north of Stanley Pool on both sides
of the Congo. Maes and Boone, *Peuplades du Congo Belge*, 48–50, 180–85;
Soret, *Les Kongo, passim;* Vansina, *Kingdoms of the Savanna,* 102–09; Vansina,
Introduction à l'Ethnographie du Congo, chap. 9.

the traveller's last journals. The distance the Congo has flowed from its extreme source in Eastern Bisa to Nyangwe, Manyema, is about eleven hundred miles. Lake Ulenge I inquired very industriously for, but I am unable to confirm what Livingstone appears to have heard from Abed-bin-Salim and Mohammed-bin-Said, his informants. Kamalondo River, which runs through Rua to the Lualaba, is a lacustrine river, and I am told it has several small lakes in its course. Probably Ulenge may be a name given to one of these small lakes.[18]

At Nyangwe, Manyema, the Congo is distinguished by various names. The Arabs and Wanguana call it the Ugarowa, the Waguhha carriers pronounce the name Luálaba, emphasizing the second syllable. The natives of Nyangwe, also emphasizing the second syllable, call it Lu-álawa, while the Northern Wagenya distinctly pronounce the name as Ru-árowa. To prevent confusion, however, it is best to adopt the spelling given by the European discoverer of the river—viz., Lualaba. A few hours north of Nyangwe the Lualaba inclines east of north. It meets impediments. High spurs from the Uregga Hills bristle across the river and wild scenes of falls and foamy water meet the eye. Near these cataracts very impracticable savages are found, who resent in a ferocious manner the appearance of strangers. Arabs have paid terribly for their intrusion.

Along the river banks on both sides dwell the fishermen, called Wagenya by the Arabs, and Wenya—pronounced Wainya by themselves—a most singular tribe, singularly cowardly, but also singularly treacherous and crafty, and utterly impenetrable to the usual "soft soap," "sugar and honey" style. North of Uvinza is a powerful tribe of another kind, of superior mettle; but habitually cannibalistic, but very aggressive. Each time Arabs have ventured to enter their region they have met with decided repulse. This tribe is called by the Arabs Wasongora Meno, by themselves Wabwire.[19] They inhabit a large extent of country on the right bank. On the left bank are still the Wagenya, which, as you proceed west, introduce you to the warlike Bakusu,[20] where, at all hours, the traveller must be a man of action. Upon these gentry the approaches of a whole congress of bishops and missionaries could have no effect, except as native "roast beef." The Lualaba you hear now in plain accents called Ruwárowa. It

18. The Congo drains an area of 1,425,000 square miles. The Chambezi, rising in Zambia between lakes Nyasa and Tanganyika, is considered its source. The river leaving Lake Mweru is the Luvua; it joins the Lualaba. *Encyclopedia Britannica* (Chicago, 1964), VI, 318–21.

19. The Songola. Maes and Boone, *Peuplades du Congo Belge*, 348–50.

20. The Kusu. *Ibid.*, 87–90; see also 147–49, 185–88; Verhulpen, *Baluba et Balubaïsés,* 65; Vansina, *Introduction à l'Ethnographie du Congo,* chap. 5.

still clings to longitude 26 deg. east. It begins to receive great affluents, the principal of which along the right bank are the Lira, Urmeli or Ilindi, the Lowa and the Kankora. On the left bank are the
Ruiki, the Kasuka and the Lumami, though there are scores of
creeks and streams constantly visible as you proceed down river from
either bank.[21]

For a thorough comprehension of the subject, without fatigue of
study, you must understand that from the moment the Congo issues
from Lake Bemba, or Bangweolo, it skirts, at a distance of two hundred miles or so, the mountain chain which shuts in the Tanganyika
on the west, and—as if its bed was related to the same system by
which the great lakes, Nyassa, Tanganyika and the Albert, are disposed
—it still clings to the base of that extraordinary mountain region
long after it has left the parallel of latitude of the north end of
Lake Tanganyika. By a series of powerful affluents it drains the entire western versant of the lake regions as far north as 4 deg. north
latitude, while along the counterslope torrents and unimportant
streams find their steep course to the lakes Albert, Kivu and Tanganyika.

At the Equator the great river which has been the immediate recipient of all tributaries from the east, and has skirted the western
base of the lake mountain region between east longitudes 25 deg.
and 26 deg. sinks into a lower bed and turns northwest, having
reached the great plains which extend between the maritime mountain region and the lake mountain region.

The service the great river hitherto performed for itself—viz., to
receive the northern tributaries discharged down the western versant
of the lake mountain region now devolves uopn the Aruwimi—the
Welle of Schweinfurth (?)—the second affluent of the Congo, which,
no doubt, at a future time will prove of immense value, as it is open
to any vessel that may be successfully launched on the Upper
Congo.[22] Below the junction of the Aruwimi our intercourse with
the cannibals of these lands was of so precarious a nature that we
dared not continue our exploration along the banks, because they
involved us in conflicts of the most desperate nature with powerful

21. Stanley names the Elila River the Lira; the Ulindi, the Urmeli or Ilindi.
The Kankora is probably the Maiko. The confusion over the Lomami, or Lu-
mami, probably came from Livingstone who thought a river—he called it the
"Lake River Young"—joined the main Lualaba in this region. Stanley realized
his error on his return to the Congo. *TDC*, II, 213–25; Stanley, *The Congo*,
II, 359; *LLJ*, II, 65–66. See the maps in Maes and Boone, *Peuplades du Congo
Belge*, 330, 334.
22. The Uele River flows into the Ubangi. See document 36, note 7.

tribes. For this reason I have no doubt we passed a great many important tributaries. Besides, it spread over such an enormously wide bed, with sometimes a dozen channels, that though I frequently passed what appeared to me to be new rivers, I preferred to construct my chart free from hypothetical streams. An almost certain guide to me as I journeyed down river along one of the many broad channels in distinguishing the main from the islands was that the former was inhabited, the islands below the Aruwimi very rarely.

When forced by famine to risk an encounter with the ferocious savages I made for the right bank, and opportunities were then given me to explore. But the interests of humanity and the interests of geography were ever at variance in this region. The natives had never heard of white men; they had never seen strangers boldly penetrating their region, neither could they possibly understand what advantage white men or black men could gain by attempting to begin an acquaintance. It is the custom for no tribe to penetrate below or above the district of any other tribe. Trade has hitherto been conducted from hand to hand, tribe to tribe, country to country; and, as the balance of power is pretty fairly maintained, only three tribes have as yet been able to overcome opposition. These are the Warunga, Wa-Mangala and the Wyzanzi.[23]

After our battle with Mangala we showed a preference for the left bank and soon after discovered the greatest affluent of the Congo, the Ikelemba, which I take to be the Kas-sye, the last syllable pronounced like "eye," "bye," &c.[24] It is nearly as important as the main river itself. The peculiar color of its water, which is like that of tea, does not commingle with the silvery water of the Congo until after a distance of 130 miles below the confluence of the two great streams. It is the union of these two rivers which gives its light brown color to the Lower Congo.

A little after passing longitude 18 deg. east we come to the river called by Europeans, on their vague charts of the Congo region, the "Kwango," a deep stream, about five hundred yards wide, entering the Congo through lines of hills which, receding from the neighbor-

23. The Bangala, or the "Gens d'Eau," lived in the area between the lower Ubangi and the Congo. Burssens, *Les Peuplades de l'Entre Congo-Ubangi,* 36–48. The Yanzi (Stanley's Wyzanzi) live in the Bolobo area (see above, note 14). Maes and Boone, *Peuplades du Congo Belge,* 202–07. For their peaceful meeting with Stanley, Bentley, *Pioneering on the Congo,* I, 65. The Warunga are perhaps the Rungu referred to by Johnston as living near the Ubangi River. Johnston, *George Grenfell and the Congo,* I, 107.

24. The Ruki. Stanley later discovered his error. Stanley, *The Congo,* II, 31–38; Johnston, *Grenfell,* I, 139–45; "Le Rouki, affluent du Congo." For the Kasai, see note 25, below.

hood, assume the altitude of mountains. This Kwango is known to the natives as Ibari Nkutu, or the River of Nkutu.[25] A little west of longitude 17 deg. east the great river, which spreads itself out into enormous breadths, slowly contracts, becomes interrupted by lines of rocky relics of hill points, rocky islands or bars of lava rock, and thunders down steep after steep along a distance of nearly one hundred and eighty miles to the majestic and calm Lower Congo.

In these 180 miles it has a fall of 585 feet, according to boiling point. The cataracts and rapids along this entire distance may be passed overland by a month's easy march along either the south side or the north side. We encountered no difficulty with the peoples of this region. Once the cataracts are passed the explorer may push his way to Koruru[26] or Monbuttu, I sincerely believe, or to the southern ridge of the Great Basin; and if he can find cause to quarrel with the lower tribes he must be charged with having sought it. If we take into consideration the fact that each day's march introduces one to fresh chiefs and clans, and that a cordial reception will be given to him by all, we are compelled to respect these very various people still more for their amiability and gentle manners with strangers.

The Basundis, perhaps, may give trouble to the traveller, but, being well supplied with cloth and rum and using tact and great patience, the traveller just starting from the West Coast has a better chance of ingratiating himself with them than I, who had exhausted my cloth and beads and all means to win particular favor. What we possessed were simply a few cloths and beads to purchase food from the natives on the south side. As travellers bound for the Great Basin must in future start from the West Coast, and may very probably take the Congo route—as they ought to do, for we have shown its practicability—they perhaps will pardon me if I suggest that a want of firmness and perseverance has caused most of the expeditions from the West Coast to collapse. Neither Bacongo nor Basundi, I feel convinced, will use force to oppose him, and there is no cause to feel frightened by big words. There are no martial or ferocious savages in the neighborhood of the West Coast on the north or south side of the Congo after passing Yellallas Falls. If I, with my knowl-

25. The Kasai system, the principal southern affluent of the Congo. The confluence is known as the Kwa; the Kwango is the largest river flowing into the Kasai. Stanley, *The Congo*, I, 410ff.; Johnston, *Grenfell*, I, 146ff.; Stanley, "Geographical Sketch of the Nile and Livingstone," 406. *Ibare* is the term given to any great river; the Ibare Nkutu was the Kwa. Vansina, "Long-Distance Trade-Routes in Central Africa," 378. See also Storme, "Le problème de la rivière Kasayi. Etude de géographie historique."

26. See *TDC*, II, 242.

edge of the character of the peoples of this region, were bound on an exploration of the Great Basin, I should undoubtedly prefer the south bank because of its greater supplies of food. In our descent of the lower cataracts we suffered terribly from want of food when the violence of the rapids happened to keep us on the north side.

In writing of the Lower Congo I am compelled to disclose the errors of the Congo expedition of 1816. I am well aware its principal members were scientific men. Captain Tuckey was the author of a book on maritime geography. Still, having found one cataract on his chart where there ought to have been dozens of falls, I soon discovered that his qualifications did not prevent him from going wrong. Between that position and Isangila, or Sangala, the existing map is a tissue of errors. From Sangala, or rather Isangila, Falls we travelled overland, in five easy marches, to Boma with a sick and starving expedition, a distance which the Congo expedition estimated at 100 miles in a straight line, or one hundred and thirty miles or so according to the road, to have accomplished which, though I took no observations *en route* overland, I consider would have been an impossible feat, considering the character of the country and the debility of our people. According to pedometer the distance we travelled was fifty-seven miles; geographically, forty-five miles. One of Captain Tuckey's sentences, "Terrible march; worse to us than the retreat from Moscow," and the sad general mortality in that expedition both of Europeans and negroes, I suspect may together explain the enormous discrepancy between their distances and ours. Under such physical prostration what wonder that a mile should seem a league! In such a state as the members of that unfortunate and disastrous expedition must have been I doubt whether any of them took the trouble to make astronomical observations.

In Stanford's map, which I believe to have been constructed from information obtained from Captain Tuckey's expedition, with additions from the Fathers at San Salvador, I find a great many names of countries and towns also about which no one could give me any information. "Pombo, a general name for the inland country," means nothing of the kind, but Mpumbus is the name of a great market or fair district on the south bank, inhabited by the Basesse, near longitude 16 deg. east. "Auzico," printed large and black, is unknown. "Monsol, Royal Town," unknown, may mean Mossul, or Little River, as called by the up tribes. "Concobella" may possibly be Néhuvila, "King of Nkunda, Esseno, Hondi, Canga, Dinjee, Condo Yonga, Pangwelunghi," are all unknown. "Vambre" and "Vambre River" I inquired particularly for, but did not succeed in discovering one native who had ever heard of such a name. Mosongo is, no doubt, Misongo in Uyanzi. Mopendea and Fungeno are absolutely unknown. The Bancora River is no doubt a corruption of Bangala or Bangara, a people inhabiting Mangala.[27]

As I have stated above, in rough numbers the entire area drained by the river of Congo, or the river Kwango, as it should be called, is about 860,000 square miles, 450,000 miles of which is almost taken up entirely by the great basin lying between the lake and maritime regions. The length of the Congo is about 2,900 miles, divided thus: From the source to Nyangwe, 1,100 miles; from Nyangwe to the Atlantic, nearly 1,800 miles.

My experiences of the river to date from the 1st of November, 1876 to the 11th of August, 1877, a period of over nine months. Its highest rise lasted from the 8th of May to the 22nd of May, and was caused by the periodical rains known to us on the East Coast as the Masika. While the flood is of great advantage to the navigation above the cataracts of the maritime region, where the river assumes a lacustrine breadth, it vastly increases its terrors at the cataracts, because of the trebled fury with which the swollen water sweeps down the steep incline of its bed through the rocky narrows to the sea. The depth of the rise varies naturally, owing to the great disproportion of the breadth of the stream. Up river it is about eight feet, but in the narrows it is from twenty to fifty feet. In some places of the cataract district the rise was as much as fifteen inches per diem, but then the river was at that point only 500 yards wide. Whatever efforts may be made by the explorer in future in the commercial development of this river no one need try to ascend through any part of the cataract region by means of any kind of floating vessel. It might be done, since very few things are impossibilities; but the ascent mainly must be overland, as nothing floating could climb six, ten, twenty and twenty-five foot falls. Besides, even where there are neither falls nor foaming rapids the rush of water through the rocky narrows is so great that it would be a Sisyphean labor altogether.

The Congo River is the Amazon of Africa, the Nile is the Mississippi. While the latter has greater length the Congo could furnish water to three Niles. It requires enormous breadth or great depth to restrain all this impetuosity. Though the Nile is a most valuable river for commerce the Congo is still better. The former has its

27. Some discussion of Tuckey's terms may be found in Johnston, *Grenfell,* I, 77; Burton, *Two Trips to Gorilla Land and the Cataracts of the Congo,* II, 102ff.; Johnston, *Congo,* 62ff. See also Maes and Boone, *Peuplades du Congo Belge,* 196–97, for Mpumbu, and *Diary,* 171, for Nkunda.

course frequently interrupted by cataracts, but the Congo fortunately has all its falls and rapids in two series—the upper, between east longitude 25 deg. and 26 deg., consisting of six great falls, terminating all navigation that might be established above the lower series, which consist of sixty-two important falls and rapids, though there are many minor rapids I do not think necessary to include in the list. I remember when about starting from Nyangwe I told Frank that I hoped I should find the cataracts in a "lump."

Once above the lower cataracts we have the half of Africa before us with no interruption, and not, like the Lower Nile regions, deserts of sand, but one vast, populous plain, so populous, indeed, that, excepting Ugogo, I know no part of Africa so thickly inhabited. The usual term village is a misnomer for most of the collections of dwellings; they are towns in some places two miles long, with one or more broad streets between the rows of neat, well-built houses. The houses are superior to anything in East Central Africa. The natives are different also. Every thought seems engrossed with trade, and fairs and markets are established everywhere.

There has been a suspicion generally entertained that ivory must soon become a curiosity; but I can vouch that at least it will not be so for three or four generations. This is the land of ivory "temples," or idol enclosures, where the commonest utensils for domestic use are made of ivory. The people do not seem able to comprehend why any one should take the trouble to pay for it when it is so plentiful in each village.

The entire plain is also distinguished for its groves of the oil palm. In Ukusu there are huge forests of this tree. Almost everything that Africa produces is to be obtained in the Congo Basin—cotton, india-rubber, groundnuts, sesamum, copal (red and white), palm kernels and palm oil, ivory, &c. By means of the Congo a journey to the gold and copper district of Katanga is rendered, moreover, very easy.

The Congo River gives 110 miles below and 835 miles above the cataracts of navigable water, while the great affluents north and south traversing the basin, will give over 1,200 miles, and perhaps much more. The greatest affluent, the Ikelemba, is over a thousand miles in length; the Nkutu River is over 700, the Aruwimi must be over 500, while there are four or five others which, by their breadth, I should judge to be navigable for great distances. I would not advise any solitary explorer to venture near the cannibal lands, unless he wishes trouble, but the influence of trade, once it is established on the equitable basis, will soon reduce those natives also to reason.

A trader ascending the river has a better chance of ingratiating himself with the natives than an explorer descending a river from a region whither no trading native has dared to venture. As he must halt a considerable time for business at each capital his reputation for being just and good will precede him and bring him hosts of customers. Indeed, the great difficulty will be to restrain their inordinate love of barter. The islands on the river will afford him safe camps and quiet retreats, and it will be better for the trader and the native to occupy island depots near the mainland until mutual confidence is thoroughly established.

I feel convinced that the Congo question will become a political question in time. As yet, however, no European Power seems to have the right of control. Portugal claims it because she discovered its mouth; but the great Powers—England, America and France—refuse to recognize her right, and express their determination, in plain terms, to dispute her assuming possession of the river.[28] If it were not that I fear to damp any interest you may have in Africa or in this magnificent river by the length of my letters I could show you very strong reasons why it would be a politic deed to settle this Congo question immediately.

I could prove to you that the possessor of the Congo, despite the cataracts, would absorb to himself the trade of the whole of the enormous basin behind, which extends across thirteen degrees of longitude and over fourteen degrees of latitude. The Congo is, and will be, the grand highway of commerce to West Central Africa. If so, why should it be left to dispute as to who shall rule the lower river and its banks? Why should it be left to the mercy of the piratical Mussolongos? I hear that British men-of-war have been castigating those scoundrels lately with bombshells in a more determined manner than I have been punishing the piratical cannibals on the eastern border of the Great Basin; and probably about the same period.[29]

But merely castigating these people is not enough; there should be vessels of war to prevent such deeds as the destruction of European ships; and the question is, What Power shall be deputed in the name of humanity to protect the youth of commerce in this little known world? An explorer is seldom called upon for the expression of his views, nor would I venture on this ground or meddle in the matter if I did not feel so very strong an interest in Africa. But I will present you with an example of what might come to pass if the

28. See Anstey, *Britain and the Congo, passim,* for a discussion of the political situation of the Congo.

29. The Sorongo of the Kongo group. They live along the lower Congo and on the Atlantic coast to the south of the river. Maes and Boone, *Peuplades du Congo Belge,* 294–97. See note 30, below.

question be not settled. A number of European merchants interested in African commerce construct houses and stores and depots on the Congo, say on either bank, north or south. The natives, troubled with indigestion or bad dreams, take it into their heads that it would be a fine thing to rob the white people and burn their dwellings and depots and murder them. The thing is done, pandemonium is re-enacted, the newspapers and public opinion hear the news, and expressions of "shame" on all the Powers interested are very loud and strong. British men-of-war hurry up and bombard everybody, or, to use an expressive though vulgar phrase, they "knock things into a cocked hat;" and perhaps the punishment exceeds the offence, because the innocent would be involved in the destructive fury. Or, as the case might easily be, suppose the European merchants capable of defending themselves, and that by a little strategy they capture the conspirators and doom them, one and all, without mercy, to death by chaining them in gangs, young and old, and drown them offhand in the deep water of the Congo. What would be said of this? I do not say it has or has not been done. I merely state what might happen. I put a possible case before the enlightened reader. Would you be surprised to hear that it has been done? [30] What ought, then, to be planned to prevent Mussolongos and natives, with bad dreams and deranged indigestion, from strangling lawful, legitimate and humane commerce? What ought to be done to prevent pitiless, vengeful merchants from placing themselves under the ban of Christians?

Let England arrange with Portugal at once to proclaim sovereignty over the Congo River to prevent the sensibilities of the world being shocked some day when least expected. I have hinted to you a few strong reasons why the question ought to be settled. I could say very much more, but space will not permit me, and "a word to the wise is sufficient."

40

Loanda, West Coast of Africa
Sept. 5, 1877 [1]

When the Anglo-American expedition left Zanzibar, November, 1874, Her Majesty's Consul had just received instructions from Lieu-

---

30. This episode is given in Delcommune, *Vingt années de Vie africaine*, I, 38–42, 59; Stanley, *The Congo*, I, 97–98; W[auters], "Boma"; Bentley, *Pioneering on the Congo*, I, 46–48.
1. *NYH*, Nov. 24, 1877.

tenant Cameron to forward his letters to the Falls of Yellala, as that gallant officer had announced his intention of following the Lualaba to the sea. From the day I received this information I was under the impression that the best thing for me to do was to follow to the letter my instructions, which would take me far from his field of exploration, though eventually I should have to touch at a point where his decision, as well as my own, would have to be made. Acting under that impression, after exploring Lake Victoria, I led 2,280 men across hostile Unyoro. Such a large force was necessary to pierce the country of Kabba Rega, against whom Sir Samuel Baker had warred and with whom Gordon Pacha was then fighting. Once launched on Lake Albert in my exploring boat and canoes, 2,000 men of this force were to return to the Emperor of Uganda, and I was to pursue my way across Lake Albert and penetrate the region with the view to reach Nyangwe, and then resolve on the next course.

We reached Lake Albert,[2] January, 1876, descended to the lake, took observations for latitude and longitude, took altitudes, &c., and endeavored to make arrangements for crossing the lake. We were unable to do so, and such a vast force was gathering to punish us for our temerity and to close us in that we were compelled to retreat. Returning to Uganda, I released the Uganda escort and travelled south on a road parallel with Speke's, but west of his road, to Karagwe. I devoted a month to explore the Alexandra Nile, then marched southwest to prosecute the river to its source. Famine compelled us to abandon the project I had half formed to penetrate the region south of Lake Albert and north of Lake Tanganyika, and I was obliged to move further south still, then finally came to Ujiji.

At this place I heard first that Cameron had abandoned the Lualaba, but the reports were not very clear. However, I circumnavigated the Tanganyika and afterward set off for Nyangwe, with the intention, if the above report was not confirmed, of penetrating the northern regions as far as Monbuttu, and then cutting across Africa along the watershed that separates the Niger basin from the Congo basin.

Arriving at Nyangwe, I saw the Arabs who had escorted my predecessor to Utotera, or King Kasongo's country,[3] and they gave me abundant proofs that he had proceeded south in company with Portuguese traders. The causes that led him to abandon such a great

2. Lake George; see document 26, note 4.
3. The Tetela. Cameron visited their ruler, Kasongo Kalombo (ruled c. 1865–1885), in 1875. Maes and Boone, *Peuplades du Congo Belge*, 185–88; Vansina, *Kingdoms of the Savanna*, 158, 232, 242; Cameron, *Across Africa*, II, 60ff.; Verhulpen, *Baluba et Balubaïsés*, 102–03; Vansina, *Introduction à l'Ethnographie du Congo*, chap. 5.

task were, as they told me, "impossibility of getting canoes and the savage character of the river tribes below."

At first I was rather elated at being permitted to explore this important field, but my feelings of joy were somewhat dampened when I reflected, upon hearing all the Arabs had to report about it, that I should very probably pay dearly for the privilege. Frank Pocock was by this time an enthusiastic explorer. Africa agreed with him, his powers of endurance were immense, and no matter what field I proposed or what project I made I was certain of Frank's support. One night we resolved together that it was our duty to try it, and if beaten we felt that no one could blame us very much when we had over twenty illustrious examples who had from various points attempted to penetrate the unknown half of Africa, but were obliged to return unsuccessful. The reports about the savage character of the natives of the bush and their cannibalism, the ferocity of a tribe of dwarfs, &c., considerably reduced the courage of our people. So, in order to prevent their desertion, I engaged a great Arab chief [4] and his followers to escort us sixty camps along the river banks under the idea that such a distance must necessarily enable us to reach some friendly tribe either west or northeast. This addition to our force restored the confidence of my people, and on November 5 last year we left Nyangwe.

We were unable to picture to ourselves any idea of the new, strange, mysterious half of Africa on which we were now entering. Everything we heard of it only tended to dispirit us—"terrible dwarfs," "ferocious cannibals," "poisoned arrows," "treacherous natives," "an eternal forest," and a mighty river, which few believed could have an end. All we knew was that our purposes were upright, that our cause was good, that we bore malice to none, and were more than willing to be charitable and forgiving, even if hard pressed. Alas! the forest through which we travelled three weeks proved too true. Uzimba and Southern Uregga were nothing but one dense gloomy forest, infested with most uncharitable people. Each day's task was a heavy diplomatic one; we labored with might and main to preserve the peace, and, fortunately, succeeded, not because of our diplomacy alone, but rather from the fear that we might prove too powerful.

4. Tippu Tip (*c.* 1840–1905). His comments on his participation in the expedition are in *Maisha ya Tippu Tip,* 111–19. See also Becker to Strauch, Sept. 8, 1881, Storms Papers, MAC; Jameson, ed., *The Story of the Rear Column of the Emin Pasha Relief Expedition by the Late James S. Jameson,* 300. Stanley said of Tippu Tip: he was "a remarkable man—the most remarkable man I had met among Arabs, Wa-Swahili, and half-castes in Africa." *TDC,* II, 95.

The length of this forest, its density and gloom, and the fearful discomforts each day's march through the terribly doleful region provoked, proved too much for our Arab escort. It disheartened them, and they talked of returning. This plunged me into a new dilemma that I little anticipated; but, unable to withstand the temptation of the wild, unexplored region, I proposed that we should strike for the river, cross it, and try the left bank. After much deliberation and argument pro and con the proposition was accepted, and we reached the river in latitude 3 deg. 35 min. 17 sec. south, just forty-one geographical miles north of Nyangwe.

We began to put up our faithful boat, the *Lady Alice,* and in two hours she was launched for the first time on the Lualaba. My tent was pitched close to the boat, and a comfortable plot of soft young grass induced repose, where I could contemplate the calm, majestic river and my picturesque surroundings—isles of undying verdure, long, black winding walls of great trees. It was here the resolution never to abandon the Lualaba until it revealed its destination was made.

I mustered all my people and my Arab escort, and, pointing out the great river to them, I told them—for the sight of the river had warmed me to a high pitch of enthusiasm—"This great river has flowed on thus since the beginning through the dark wild lands before us, and no man, either white or black, knows whither it flows; but I tell you solemnly that I believe the one God has willed that this year it shall be opened throughout its whole length and become known to all the world. I do not know what lies before us. We may meet very bad people; we may suffer hunger; we may die. We are in the hands of God. I hope for the best. As we do not come for war we may make friends of the people; we have enough property with care to last a long while and to buy the friendship of chiefs. You, my people, will, therefore, make up your minds that I am not going to leave this river until I reach the sea. You promised at Zanzibar, two years ago, that you would follow me wherever I wanted to go for two or three years. We have still a year before us, but I promise you we shall reach the sea before the year is out. All you have to do, then, is to say, 'In the name of God,' and follow me." The young men, about fifty of them, stepped briskly up and shouted out, "In the name of God," adding, "Inshallah! Master, we will follow you and reach the sea," but the oldest had many misgivings and shook their heads gravely.[5]

5. Compare *ibid.*, 149–51, for a more elaborate version.

We soon became acquainted with the worst side of the natives of this region, and they presently demonstrated their wildness. After five or six hours' talk they agreed to make blood brotherhood with a white chief, but the white chief must proceed with only a few men to an island in the middle of the river. Frank Pocock volunteered to go through the disgusting ceremony for the benefit of all concerned. I conveyed him and ten men, armed with revolvers, to the island, as guns might arouse suspicions, and I took position on the right bank of the river with thirty armed men, to be ready should the natives intend treachery. We had not waited above an hour before we saw signs of great excitement in the neighborhood of the island, and heard violent shouts and peculiar war cries. Immediately we dashed toward the island, where we saw about thirty canoes loaded with men, some standing up in the act of launching spears. Our sudden appearance, however, scattered them, and from Frank we learned that their behavior had been anything but friendly. However, no harm was done, except that the natives, by sounding the war cries, alarmed those down river, and caused people who perhaps might have been disposed to be friendly to assume the offensive.

We were too powerful to be openly attacked, for our united forces numbered about five hundred fighting men; and so long as they contended themselves with vocal violence and some hideous gestures no one was harmed.

As we had arranged, we crossed over to the left bank and after a short stay, we moved down river in two divisions, one by land and one by water. That day we were separated; the land party were subjected to many difficulties; they lost the road, and we, ignorant of the cause of their non-appearance, floated down the Lualaba as far as the Ruiki River and camped at the confluence.[6] Two days passed by, and, as no news was heard of the land party, I ascended the Ruiki River about twenty miles, leaving my little camp in charge of twenty-five men and boys. After searching the Ruiki River banks for traces of the land party I was approaching camp when we heard musketry, and as we imagined it announced the arrival of the land party we hastened to welcome them. Our astonishment was great to perceive the narrow mouth of the Ruiki blocked with canoes loaded with savages and to hear rifles at earnest work, as if the position of the little camp and its defenders was desperate. We gave a shout to attract the attention of the savages and the effect was immediate, for the canoes at once vanished, the savages paddling down the Lualaba.

6. Stanley was in the Genia area. *Ibid.*, 156–61.

After arriving at camp we congratulated ourselves that all were safe, though their position at one time had been dangerous, as the camp party had permitted the savages to come within five paces of the camp before they resolved to fire. The spears and pointed sticks thrown into the camp made quite a bundle. This was the first fight on the Lualaba, and our first initiation to savage warfare on the great river. The savages might return in greater numbers than ever, and if they attacked us with skill and boldness it would have been our utter annihilation. It therefore behooved us to communicate with the land division, of which we had heard nothing for two days. Five of the boat's crew volunteered to set out overland in search of the missing people. After several hours' toiling through the dense bush they found a slightly used path which soon brought them face to face with the scouts of the land party, and before night we were all gladdened at their appearance.

Two days' march north of the Ruiki brought us to falls—the Falls of Ukassa. The Arabs and people were rather glad, as they seemed to think that this would certainly compel me to abandon the foolish journey, for they themselves have suffered terribly by falls. You may possibly remember that Livingstone said he had "no intention of attempting the foolhardy feat," and no desire to become "black man's meat." This sentence was written while all the Arabs at Nyangwe mourned for the loss of thirty men, three large canoes and much valuable property, which had been swept over a cataract fifteen miles below Nyangwe.

I took ten of the boat's crew and proceeded overland, and almost fell into an ambuscade. But we were also bush people and could not be caught. We explored the banks and examined the nature of the falls.[7] Returning to camp to commence the operations I was astounded to hear that two of my captains, with two soldiers, had desperately resolved to explore the falls by water, and had consequently been taken over the falls, capsized and sucked down the whirlpool, after which they had not been seen. This was terrible news. If they had escaped the whirlpool they could not escape the fleet of canoes below the falls that had been assembled to dispute our passage down the river. I instantly retraced my steps through the bush with fifty men to lend them aid,[8] and we fortunately arrived in time to save them, as they were floating down the river with the canoe

7. In *Diary*, 141–42, Stanley asserts the enemy was seen and then driven off; *TDC*, II, 162–63, agrees with the letter.
8. In *Diary*, 142, Stanley says he sent others; there is no reference to his accompanying them.

upside down—one captain defending himself and party with a revolver, for their Sniders were lost except one, which had been prudently lashed within the canoe. I thought this was exploration with a vengeance, and I informed them that the next time they disobeyed orders they would be left to their fate; but it was scarcely necessary, as the narrow escape they had had was sufficient to frighten them from exploring on their own account.

Despite the hopes of our Arab escort the Falls of Ukassa were passed without loss, by simply allowing the current to take the canoes over the falls and picking them up below. It was done so expeditiously that the natives had no time to dispute the passage, for before they had reached the falls the river division were seated in the boat and canoes and we had formed a compact line of battle, with the land division protecting our left flank. The natives did not attack us and we were allowed to pass without firing a shot, but to all attempts at reconciliation and gifts they turned deaf ears.

On the 6th of December we arrived at Usongora Meno, an extensive country, occupied by a powerful tribe. The belligerency of the natives increased. As soon as they caught sight of us on the river they came with fierce demonstrations, numbering fourteen large canoes, against our six canoes and boat *Lady Alice*. An Arab, who was passenger through illness that day, was told to speak them fair, to explain to them who we were, what we had come for, that we were rich, and that we were able and willing to pay our way. Fifteen minutes were spent in this midriver palaver. His answer was a shower of poisoned arrows, which fell a little too short of our boat. Though we had eighteen sick of smallpox lying in the canoes we charged on them and cleared a passage through. The land party was also attacked in the bush and several were wounded, for they had ventured too near the country of the warlike tribe of the Bakusu, whose trade is war on a large scale.

Smallpox began to rage in our Arab escort. There were eighteen deaths within two or three days. Dysentery attacked us, ulcers formed on the limbs of many, incapacitating a large number from marching, until boat and canoes were merely floating hospitals. In this condition we arrived at Vinya Njara,[9] 125 geographical miles north of Nyangwe. This day the river had again taken us further than the land division could possibly reach in two days.

Immediately we had arrived at Vinya Njara with our sick we were attacked; one of my people was killed; others were wounded. We

9. There are slight differences in *TDC*, II, 178–88.

had seventy-two sick with smallpox. We plunged into the bush with desperate energy, and in a short time cleared the skirts of the camp. Then returning, we at once set to work to make the place defensible, and while skirmishers lay in wait in front we cut the bush down for a distance of 200 yards. Through the night the poisoned arrows flew, and were heard tapping trees and huts most unpleasantly, and every now and then some wide awake skirmisher awoke the echoes of the night with his loud-voiced musket, but with harmless effect. Next morning we moved and occupied the town of Vinya Njara, to house our sick and wounded, and the day was spent in repelling attacks and fortifying the town. Two days and two nights we bore attacks by land and water.

The entire country was roused against us. From Usongora Meno they came in a large number of canoes; the Bakusu warriors were engaged by Vinya Njara to enter their country and eat us. These bowmen climbed tall trees, and any person showing himself in the broad street of the great town became a target at once. We were unable to bury our dead or to attend to the delirious wounded.

On the morning of the third day the land division appeared and things changed for the better; but a great force of Wasongora Meno, with forty or fifty canoes, were gathered on an island in our vicinity with the intention of possessing themselves of our boat and canoes. These it was necessary to punish, and I accordingly led a night expedition and cast all their canoes adrift. Some of the best canoes we secured. The next morning I visited the island. They had already become aware of their position, and had, by means of three or four canoes, unseen by us during the night, escaped. I next turned my attention to the Bakusu and their friends, and they were also driven from the woods, and for the next ten days there was rest, during which time the natives made proposals of peace, which we gladly accepted.

Here the Arab escort, after taking us 125 miles from Nyangwe, parted from us. They had already exacted that the natives should leave the road free for them. It was an anxious period this of our parting, for I feared that there would be a mutiny, but my young men were staunch and too well trained to desert me at this critical period. My captains were also secured and largesses given to everybody.

"The white man with the open hand was their father. He had taken them through ever so much trouble safe, and, please God, they would take him to his white brothers on the sea. They had known him now nearly seven years and his hand was always open. As they had been faithful to the aged traveller who had died in Muilala,[10] so they would be to him who led them through Turu and Unyoro and round the great lakes."

On December 28 the expedition was mustered—146 souls, men and women—and each person answered to his name.

To the sound of the thrilling farewell song of the Wanyamwezi we took our seats and formed a line in mid river, the boat in front. The influence of the song, whose notes were borne in wild and weird tones across the river, proved too much for my people. They wept as though they were nearly heart broken.

"Children of Zanzibar," I shouted to them, "lift up your heads. Cry out 'Bismillah!' and dash your paddles into the water. Let the Wanyamwezi return to Nyangwe and tell the tale to your friends what brave men those were who took the white man down the great river to the sea."

It was one of the saddest days I remember to have spent in Africa.

On January 4, 1877, we came to the first of what proved a series of cataracts, or, to use a more correct term, falls, below the confluence of the Lumami, and the Lualaba, or the Lowa, as the river was now called.[11] Our troubles began now in earnest. We were hunted like game. Night and day every nerve was strained to defend ourselves. Four times on January 4 we broke through the lines of canoes brought out against us, and finally we were halted by the Baswa Falls, in latitude 0 deg. 32 min. 36 sec. south. The savages seemed to think that we had no resource left but to surrender and be eaten at their leisure. Again and again were we compelled to repulse the furious charges that they made to drive us over the falls. The people of the Falls Islands also came up to assist the cannibals of Mwana Ntaba.[12] We were at bay, and became desperate. Return we could not, as we could not pull against stream and fight. We pulled ashore first on the right bank, then across river to the left, and made a camp in the woods, drawing our canoes and boat up after us. After constructing a fence of brush around on the forest side the best sharpshooters were placed in position for defence. After a short time the natives retired and left us to rest. For the ensuing twenty-four days we had fearful work, constructing camps by night along the line marked out during the day, cutting roads from above to below each fall, dragging our heavy canoes during the day, while

10. Livingstone died at Chitambo's village near Lake Bangweulu. Debenham, *Way to Ilala*, 326.
11. See document 39, note 21.
12. Stanley was in the Genia area. See *Diary*, 148–49; *TDC*, II, 224.

the most active of the young men—the boat's crew—repulsed the savages and foraged for food.

On January 27 we had passed in this desperate way forty-two geographical miles, by six falls, and to effect it had dragged our canoes a distance of thirteen miles by land by roads which we had cut through the forest. Our provisions in the meantime we had to procure as we best could. When we had cleared the last fall, latitude 0 deg. 14 min. 52 sec. north, we halted two days for rest, which we all very much needed. In the passage of these falls we lost five men only.

After passing this series of falls we entered upon different scenes. The river was gradually widening from the usual 1,500 to 2,000 yards breadth to two and three miles. It then began to receive grander affluents, and soon assumed a lacustrine breadth from four to ten miles. Islands also were so numerous that only once a day were we able to obtain a glimpse of the opposite bank. We had reached the great basin lying between the maritime and lake regions.

The first day we entered this region we were attacked three times by three separate tribes; the second day we maintained a running fight almost the entire day, which culminated in the grand naval fight at the confluence of the Aruwimi—the Welle (?)—with the Lualaba. As we crossed over from the current of the Lualaba to that of the Aruwimi, and had taken a glance at the breadth of the magnificent affluent, we were quite taken aback at the grand preparations for our reception. Fifty-four canoes rushing down on us with such fury that I saw I must act at once if I wished to save the expedition. Four of our canoes, in a desperate fright, became panic stricken and began to pull fast down stream, but they were soon brought back.

We dropped our stone anchors, formed a close line and calmly waited events. Down the natives came, fast and furious, but in magnificent style. Everything about them was superb. Their canoes were enormous things, one especially, a monster, eighty paddlers, forty on a side, with paddles eight feet long, spear-pointed, and really pointed with iron blades for close quarters, I presume. The top of each paddle shaft was adorned with ivory balls. The chiefs pranced up and down a planking that ran from stem to stern. On a platform near the bow were ten choice young fellows swaying their long spears ready. At the stern of this great war canoe stood eight steersmen, guiding her towards us. There were about twenty—three-fourths of her size—also fine looking, but none made such an imposing show. At a rough guess there must have been from fifteen hundred to two thousand savages within these fifty-four canoes.

I cannot think that these belonged to one power. I imagine that it was a preconcerted arrangement with neighboring tribes, got up specially for our entertainment. We had no time even to breathe a short prayer or to think of indulging in a sentimental farewell to the murderous cannibalistic world in which we found ourselves. The enemy, in full confidence of victory, was on us, and the big monster as it shot past us launched a spear—the first. We waited no longer; they came to fight. The cruel faces, the loudly triumphant drums, the deafening horns, the launched spears, the swaying bodies, all proved it; and every gun in our little fleet angrily gave response to our foes. We were in a second almost surrounded, and clouds of spears hurtled and hissed for a short time—say, ten minutes. They then gave way, and we lifted anchors and charged them, following them with fatal result. We were carried away with our feelings. We followed them to the shore, chased them on land into their villages, ten or twelve of them, and, after securing some of the abundance of food we found there, I sounded the recall.

To the victors belong the spoil—at least so thought my people— and the amount of ivory they discovered lying useless about astonished me. There was an ivory "temple," a structure of solid tusks surrounding an idol; ivory logs, which, by the marks of hatchets visible on them, they must have used to chop wood upon; ivory war horns, some of them three feet long; ivory mallets, ivory wedges to split wood, ivory pestles to grind their cassava, and before the chief's house was a veranda, or burzah, the posts of which were long tusks of ivory. There were 133 pieces of ivory, which, according to rough calculation, would realize, or ought to realize, about $18,000. These, I told the men, they must consider as their prize money. In this fight we only lost one man.[13]

Our expedition was becoming thinned in these repeated attacks made on us by these piratical cannibals. We had lost sixteen men already. There were no means to return to Nyangwe, for we had resolutely put six cataracts between us and the possibility of returning; besides, we were about three hundred and fifty miles, according to the course of the river, or 296 geographical miles, north of Nyangwe. Why should we not ascend the Welle and try by that road? I felt almost convinced I was on the Congo. I was in latitude 0 deg. 46 min. north. Look where I might on my chart I saw I was in the midst of a horrible, hateful blackness—a meaningless void. Yet to

13. The conflict was with the Soko. Maes and Boone, *Peuplades du Congo Belge*, 168–70; Stanley, *The Congo*, II, 114–33; Reid, "The River Aruwimi." Most of the booty taken here was lost before the trip was over. *Diary*, 199–200.

fight daily three or four times each day our ammunition would not last. Nature even could not sustain such a strain as we experienced. The increasing breadth of the river below this last great affluent pointed a way of escape. I would abandon the mainland and lose myself among the islands. I thus would pass by many affluents, but it could not be helped. The main thing, after all, was the Great River itself, the receiver of all affluents.

The boat led the way to the islands. The first attempt was unsuccessful, for the channels, after taking us by half a dozen islands, exposed us again to the savages, and we, of course, were again compelled to fight. After two or three attempts we learned to distinguish the mainland from the islands, and we glided down for five days without trouble, further than anxiety for food.

Driven at last by pressing hunger to risk an encounter with the savage, we came to a village[14] in latitude 1 deg. 40 min. north and longitude 23 deg. east, where the behavior of the natives was different. Three canoes advanced to meet us, and addressed some words which we did not understand. The canoes retreated, but, telling my little fleet to drop anchor, the boat floated down and anchored opposite the village, at only twenty yards from the shore. We made signs that we wanted food, showed copper bracelets, cowries, red and white necklaces, cloths and brass wire—in short, resorted to our usual way of opening friendly communications when permitted by natives disposed to be friendly. The negotiations were long—very long; but we were patient. What made us hopeful was their pacific demeanor, so opposite to those above, and at last, after five hours, we succeeded. That day, after twenty-six fights on the Great River, was hailed as the beginning of happy days. We certainly were the happiest fellows in existence.

When the old chief came to the bank to negotiate with the white stranger we lifted our anchor and steered for him. My coxswain and self sprang ashore. Our canoes were anchored 400 yards off. The kindly visage of the old chief was so different from the hateful faces we had lately seen that I almost crushed his hand, making him hop, out of pure love. My coxswain—a braver soul was never found within a black skin, but more of him by and by—hugged everybody all round, and hugging matches took place. The boat boys grew enthusiastic, and they also followed the example of Uledi, the coxswain. In

14. Rubunga village. See *TDC*, II, 281–83; *Diary*, 160; Johnston, *Grenfell*, I, 283. This probably was a Poto area. Maes and Boone, *Peuplades du Congo Belge*, 157–59; Stanley, *The Congo*, II, 98–102; Vansina, *Introduction à l'Ethnographie du Congo*, chap. 4.

the meantime the old chief drew me apart and pointed to the face of Frank, which gleamed white amid the dark skins of the soldiers in mid-river. "Ah! he is my young brother," I said. "Then he must make friends with my son," said the chief; and Frank was accordingly hailed and told to come ashore, and the solemn ceremony of brotherhood—the white man's and black man's blood were made to flow in one current, and a covenant of eternal peace and brotherhood was concluded.

"What river is this, chief?" I asked.

"The River," he replied.

"Has it no name?" I asked.

"Yes, the Great River."

"I understand; but you have a name and I have a name, your village has a name. Have you no particular name for your river?" (We spoke in bad Kikusu.)

"It is called Ikutu Ya Kongo."

The River of Congo!

There was, then, no doubt but we were still about eight hundred and fifty miles from the Atlantic Ocean and over nine hundred miles below Nyangwe, Manyema.

We spent three days at this village in marketing—an era of peace long to be remembered by us. We saw also four muskets here, and we augured from this fact that the perils of our desperate voyage were over. It was a false augury, however.

One day's run brought us to Urangi[15]—a populous country, where there was one town about two miles long—and our friends introduced us to these people. The first introduction over about one hundred large and small canoes appeared and began trading. One thing after another disappeared. A man lost his mat and clothes; my cook lost a copper plate or dish; a gun was snatched at but recovered without trouble. I arranged with the King that all trade must be done in the canoes. Everybody was contented.

The next day we began to prosecute our voyage, two native canoes leading the way to introduce us to the tribes below. The 100 canoes that were employed in doing trade and visiting the day before now contained neither women nor children, but men with muskets and spears. We, however, did not regard it as anything extraordinary, until our guides at a signal paddled fast away, and we were at once assaulted.

"Form close line!" I shouted; and "Paddle slowly down river close to the island!"

15. See *TDC*, II, 287–92; *Diary*, 162. This was also a Poto area.

The boat's crew rested on their oars, allowed all the canoes to pass by, and we followed after them. Two out of the crews of each canoe, and two out of the crew of *Lady Alice*, with myself, maintained a running fight for two hours, until another tribe joined in the chase. The pirates of Urangi returned, but the Mpakiwana[16] took the fight up and maintained it until we came to another tribe. This tribe took up the chase, charging furiously sometimes and then being repulsed endeavored with admirable pertinacity the capture of one of our canoes. Frequently were we all compelled to drop paddles and oars and defend ourselves desperately. At three P.M. the last of our enemies abandoned their designs and we steered for the islands again.

The 14th of February we lost the island channels, and we were taken—too late to return—along a channel which took us to the right bank to the powerful tribe of Mangara, or Mangala,[17] of whom we had heard so much sometimes as very bad people, at other times as great traders. The fact that they pursued trade caused us to imagine that we should be permitted to pass by quietly. We were woefully deceived. Despite the war drums and horns summoning the tribe to war, as it was near noon and a bright sun shone, and there was sufficient stretch of river to take a good observation, I would not lose such a splendid opportunity to fix the position of this important locality. I ascertained it to be latitude 1 deg. 16 min. 50 sec. north; by count, longitude 21 deg. east. I closed my sextant and put it away carefully, and then prepared to receive the natives—if they came for war, with war; if they came for peace, with gifts. We cast loose from Obs Island [18] and started down stream. Sixty-three canoes of light, even elegant make, approached. Some of the natives were gorgeous in brass decorations, and they wore headdresses of the skins of white goats, while skins of the same color hung down their shoulders like short mantles; the principal men wore robes of crimson blanket cloth.

We ceased rowing. When they were about three hundred yards off I held a crimson cloth up to view in one hand and a coil of brass wire in another, and by signs offered it to them. My answer was from three muskets, a shower of ironstone slugs, and four of my boat's crew and one in my canoes wounded. A fierce shout of exultation announced to the hundreds on the banks their first success.

16. *TDC*, II, 292, calls it a district; *Diary*, 163, "a very large village." It was a Poto area.

17. The Ngala thought the unexpected newcomers were enemies and attacked. For African accounts of the fight, Coquilhat, *Haut-Congo*, 183–85; Brom, *Sur les Traces de Stanley*, 259–60; Luwel, *Stanley*, 56.

18. Observation Island. *TDC*, II, 299.

We formed our usual close line, and allowed the canoes and boat to float down, every rifle and revolver being required here. The battle consisted of bullets against slugs. We were touched frequently, boat and canoes pitted, but not perforated through. Dead shots told in the end. Breech-loaders, double-barrelled elephant rifles and Sniders prevailed against Brown Besses, though for two hours our fate was dubious. The battle lasted from twelve o'clock to near sunset. We had floated down ten miles during that time; but we had captured two canoes, swift as they were. We had dropped anchor for an hour, protecting a storming party, which took a village and burned it. At sunset our people sung the song of triumph; the battle was over. We continued floating down in the darkness until about eight o'clock, and then camped on an island. This was the thirty-first fight and the last but one.

We clung to the island channels, for four days longer, unseen by any of the natives, for the river was very wide—between five and ten miles. At a place called Ikengo,[19] a great trading people, we found friends. We made blood brotherhood with many kings and collected a vast deal of information. This tribe was one of the cleverest and most friendly of any we had seen. We halted three days with them. We met no armed force to oppose us in the river below Ikengo, though a few canoes indulged in the customary little distractions of savage life by firing iron slugs at strangers; but, as no one was hurt, we permitted them to have their pleasures without regarding them. In the words of a dry humorist—one of our soldiers—"We ate more iron than grain."

Six miles below the confluence of the river—called the Kwango by Europeans[20]—and the Congo we had the thirty-second fight.[21] We proposed to halt in the woods and cook breakfast. We were collecting fuel to make a fire when a quick succession of shots from the bush startled us and wounded six of our people. We had not the slightest idea that any tribe lived in that vicinity, for it seemed all forest. We sprang to our arms and a regular bush fight began, and ended in a drawn battle, each side separating with a little more respect for each other. The advantage we gained was that of being permitted to stay in our camp unattacked. I have stated this was our thirty-second fight and last. So far as interchange of bullets between natives and ourselves went this is true. But we have been many a time on the verge of fighting since. However, diplomacy,

19. The Wangata, or Bolemba, occupy the left bank below the Ruki River. Maes and Boone, *Peuplades du Congo Belge*, 338–39; Murdock, *Africa*, 285; *TDC*, II, 305–08.

20. See document 39, note 25.

21. See *TDC*, II, 323–24; *Diary*, 169–70.

vast patience, tact and stern justice saved us from many a severe conflict.

Soon after quitting Nyangwe I had issued orders—knowing the propensities of many of my people to take advantage of our strength —that whoever molested a native or appropriated anything without just return would be delivered up to native law, the punishment of which would be certain death or eternal servitude. I had purchased several of my people who were guilty of theft from native power by extraordinary sacrifices of money, until we were almost bankrupts from this cause. The time came when it was necessary to place everybody on half rations from our poverty. Yet the knowledge that we should be unable to make further sacrifice to save thieves did not restrain some from committing depredations on native property. These were surrendered to native law. When five men had been thus dealt with the people began to awake to the fact that I was really in earnest, and I heard no more complaints from the natives.

A terrible crime in the eyes of many natives below the confluence of the Kwango and the Congo was taking notes. Six or seven tribes confederated together one day to destroy us, because I was "bad, very bad." I had been seen making medicine on paper—writing. Such a thing had never been heard of by the oldest inhabitant. It, therefore, must be witchcraft, and witchcraft must be punished with death. The white chief must instantly deliver his notebook (his medicine) to be burned, or there would be war on the instant.

My notebook was too valuable; it had cost too many lives and sacrifices to be consumed at the caprice of savages. What was to be done? I had a small volume of Shakespeare, Chandos edition. It had been read and reread a dozen times, it had crossed Africa, it had been my solace many a tedious hour, but it must be sacrificed. It was delivered, exposed to the view of the savage warriors. "Is it this you want?" "Yes." "Is this the medicine that you are afraid of?" "Yes; burn it, burn it. It is bad, very bad; burn it."

"Oh, my Shakespeare," I said, "farewell!" and poor Shakespeare was burnt. What a change took place in the faces of those angry, sullen natives! For a time it was like another jubilee. The country was saved; their women and little ones would not be visited by calamity. "Ah! the white chief was so good, the embodiment of goodness, the best of all men." [22]

I now come to a tragic period, before which our running the

22. *Ibid.*, 192–93, gives a different version of this much-quoted episode. Stanley said there: "I gave a sheet of paper scribbled over carelessly to satisfy them, which was torn and burnt . . ." *TDC*, II, 384–86, agrees with Stanley's despatch.

gauntlet through the cannibal lands a thousand miles seems child's play. Our days of battle and our days of hunger may be forgotten as years of peace and rest may roll over our heads, but our months of toil and wild energy in the cataracts never; for each day of that period has its own terrible tale of narrow escapes, of severe injuries, of despair and death.

Nearly fourteen hundred miles had been passed. The Congo became straitened by close-meeting aspiring banks of naked cliffs, or steep slopes of mountains shaggy with tall woods, or piles above piles of naked craggy rock, and presently swept impetuously down in serpentine curves, heaving upward in long lines of brown billows, sometimes as though ruffed by a tempest, or with a steep glassy fall, or thundering down steep after steep, tossing its waters upward in huge waves, with their crests dissolving in spray and mist, or boiling round isles of bowlders, which disparted it into two branches with fearful whirlpools, with uprising whirling caldrons, and as it varied its wild aspect so it varied its thunder, moan and plaint. At one time the rush sounded like the swash of sea waves against a ship's prow driven before a spanking breeze, at another time like a strong tide washing against piers and buttresses of bridges, at another time it overwhelmed the senses and filled the measure of a deep grief with the roar of its fury; and far up on the height of the tableland, the timorous and superstitious Basundi, straying near the cliffy verge, stopped his ears against the dreadful thunder and hurried away as from doom.

While we were fighting our tragical way over the long series of falls along a distance of over 180 miles, which occupied us five months, we lived as though we were in a tunnel, subject at intervals to the thunderous crash of passing trains.

Ah! so different from that soft, glassy flow of the river by the black forests of Uregga and Koruru, where a single tremulous wave was a rarity, when we glided day after day through the aerie wilds, in sweet, delicious musings, when our souls were thrilled at sight of the apparently impenetrable forests on either hand, when at misty morn, or humid eve, or fervid noon wild nature breathes a soft stillness.

There is no fear that any other explorer will attempt what we have done in the cataract region. It will be insanity in a successor. He may travel overland, and the native will point out the 2,000 feet altitude up which we dragged our three, four and five ton canoes. He will perhaps point out the stumps of the giant trees we cut down and from which we carved out our canoes within eight and ten days, working night and day, whereas no canoe was ever made in that region under three months. He may show him the craggy rocks over which we constructed tramways with a system of rollers. He may show him where we cut a grove of tall trees down to fill the great pits between the rocks. He may show him the scenes celebrated by dreadful tragedies, and by heroisms enacted by some of the white stranger's men. He may point out localities where the white men entered their canoes and brought their people down long foaming stretches of river, to the fright of all who saw them and against all advice. He may point out the terrible falls where the boat with the white chief and his boat's crew were swept over, and whirled round and tossed and smitten by brown waves until his native friends, who were spectators of the expected catastrophe, were in an agony of fear; and finally, with a shudder, guide him to the spot where the younger chief was carried over the falls, taken down in a whirlpool and was lost. But there is no fear of any other explorer attempting to imitate our work here.

Nor would we have ventured upon this terrible task had we the slightest idea that such fearful impediments were before us. Tuckey's map led me astray, and the natives, who seldom travel further than their own homes, assisted Tuckey to delude us. Neither Tuckey nor the natives knew any better. On Captain Tuckey's map I find east of Yellala Falls, after a very wide unnoted interval, a cataract set down in about 16 degrees of east longitude. At the same time the names of places are marked on the land as if he had left Yellala Falls and proceeded overland as far as the Kwango River. The whole is published as the map of a district well known. Need I do more than to say that below this supposed cataract are over thirty falls and rapids, and that if any part of this region had been explored such falls and rapids would be prominently set down? Our losses in valuable men should be a warning to explorers not to set down more than they actually have seen, or, if they needs must publish hearsay information, to make a difference between explored localities and what is unexplored.

My observations informed me that we were in the neighborhood of this supposed cataract of Tuckey's and believing that we should soon reach it I resolutely fought on. After passing that position the natives cheered us on by stating that there were but two more after passing those. Other natives said there were one or two more, and so on each day, until finally arriving at Isangila Falls, and hearing there were five more falls, after five months' toil and the loss of one European and fifteen soldiers in the lower cataracts, I said, "Enough," and drew my boat and canoes high upon the rocks above the Cataract of Isangila.

We came to the country where previous explorers and white merchants have pampered native kings with what is called "dashes" or rum and cloth and beads. These kings came before us to demand dashes. They said they must have "dashes" of rum and cloth.

"Dashes from us! Poor miserable creatures like us! Why, we have nothing. We have but just enough to reach the sea, and cannot spare a bead."

"Ah, but you must, or—"

"What, must again! Get out of my camp this minute, and bring the full value in food of what you desire." And they brought it, and only the value of the food did they receive. But one king resented this indignity, and brought his valorous fighters to dispute the road. The immediate disposition of our people, and a plain hint that we were quite ready to begin, however, calmed his noisy truculence, after which we made peace, exchanged gifts and passed on.

I sent messengers in advance praying for relief from any European in Emboma, or Boma, as it is called south of the cataracts. By good fortune the letter was put in the hands of the agents of Messrs. Hatton & Cookson, Liverpool merchants. The promptitude of the agents, Mr. Motta Veiga and Mr. Harrison, saved us from much misery. We were on the brink of destruction by famine. Such an abundance of luxuries was showered on us that we were almost delirious with the sudden transition from the pains of famine to the joys of plenty, and the voices that forty times had fiercely mocked the war cries of savages in war joined in an extemporaneous chant of thanksgiving and sang the praises of the white men who live by the sea.

After a day's halt to digest the good things we resumed our march toward Boma. A few miles from that place we were met by several gentlemen of the European colony with hampers of good things, with rum and champagne, port and Madeira, &c. What a difference between those cleanly, well fed and well dressed gentlemen of Boma and myself! It was as much as that which distinguished the strong, healthy bodies of their hammock bearers from the bare-ribbed, gaunt soldiers of the Anglo-American expedition.

The story is now told briefly, and, perforce, imperfectly, how we crossed the hitherto unknown half of Africa; how we journeyed 1,800 miles from Nyangwe to the ocean. You have had a prefatory glimpse of the wide wild land that lies between that Arab depot and the Atlantic.

You may now divine the nature of our struggles to gain civilization, of our desperate battles with the cannibals, of the patience required to cross the cataract districts with our fleet, of our daily terrors and griefs at the loss of dear and valued comrades during the
passage of fifty-seven falls and rapids that interrupt the flow of the
mighty river through the maritime region. I have told you nothing
about sickness, of the insalubrity of some portions we traversed, of
the intense gloom and depression we experienced in the doleful regions of Uzimba and Uvinza, and of the severe fatigues we have
undergone, which have bowed our manhood and reduced our energies; but you may imagine them.

I have endeavored to take you rapidly through a few of our thousand and one experiences as we struggled through the dense darkness
and mystery of the unknown into light. A few exciting contests I
have briefly described—contests with human demons who delighted
in craft, fraud, treachery and cruelty, who regarded us much as we
regarded the noble beasts that roved over the plains of Usukuma, as
so many heads of seasoned game to be slaughtered and carved, and
broiled and eaten. They attacked us with spears, assegays, poisoned
arrows and muskets, and at one time they actually surrounded our
camp with hidden nets. They drove poisoned sticks into the ground,
so that in the charge to scatter them from the neighborhood of our
camp our people might have their feet pierced with these instruments
of torture. On all sides death stared us in the face, cruel eyes watched
us day and night, and a thousand bloody hands were stretched out to
take advantage of the least carelessness. We defended ourselves like
men who knew that pusillanimity would be our ruin—that mercy
was unknown to these savages. Out of charity and regard for my own
people, and myself as well, on whom devolved the responsibility of
taking the expedition through these savage regions, I wished naturally
that it might have been otherwise, and looked anxiously and keenly
for any sign of forbearance and peace, as I saw my African comrades
drop one by one from my side in the oblivion of the terrible wilds.
We thank Heaven that these dark days are over.

Yet we had some briefest intervals of pleasure even during that
stormy period. One pacific tribe—the day after a desperate battle
with a martial tribe above, who, it seemed, had oppressed them
greatly—warned by the huge drums that sounded the approach of
strangers, turned out in dense crowds along the river banks, while
the boldest of their warriors manned their enormous canoes and bore
down on us, taking care, however, to cry out the magic word, "Sennené!" which caused us to drop our guns and echo the happy word

with such fervor of lungs that the thousands on the banks, who might
have been a little distrustful, instantly distinguished its hearty sincerity, and repeated it with equal fervor until for a time, even after
they had ended, the forests across the river seemed to thunder mys-
teriously, "Sennené! Sennené!" We dropped our stone anchors abreast,
and near enough to the vast crowds on the banks, and invited the
warriors in the canoes to approach.

From childish shyness they would not come nearer than fifty
yards or so, and two old women—ladies, I ought to call them—
"manned" a small canoe, and, coming straight to my boat, they
brought their tiny vessel alongside, and after an introductory laugh
offered us palm wine and a couple of chickens! Presently the warriors,
shamed out of their shyness—it was not fear—drew their canoes
alongside—great, enormous things, twice the length of our boat, and
completely hid, almost crushed, the tiny canoe of the women; but
the most pleasing sight to me, to which my eyes were constantly
attracted, was the faces of the two women, and the tiny messenger of
peace and comfort to us in the midst of our days of trial. On looking
into the great war canoes of this tribe I observed with pleasure that
there was not one spear or bow and arrow in any of them, which
caused me to confirm my opinion of their tact and delicacy, to look
more attentively at the crowds on the bank, and there was not one
weapon of war visible anywhere. Presently I observed one huge canoe
make off for the shore, load gourds of palm wine and baskets of
potatoes, and return, each man singing enthusiastically. The potatoes
were for me, the palm wine for my people.

When I asked how it happened that they were so kind to strangers
when we had fought three times the day before, they said that though
the drums above river summoned them to fight us, some of their
people had been up river fishing among the islands the day before,
and the drums had caused them to hide themselves and see what
took place. They had seen us talk to the natives, offer cloths and
beads, and had seen them refuse all proffers and fight us. "They are
always fighting us, and stealing our people, but we are not strong
enough to kill them. This morning when you left that island where
you slept last night we sent very early a canoe with two slaves—a
boy and a woman in it—with potatoes and palm wine; if you were
bad people you would have caught that canoe and made those two
slaves your own, but when you allowed it pass you, saying 'Sennené,' we knew that you were good people, and we did not beat our
drum for war, but for peace. If you had taken that little canoe this
morning you would have had to fight us now. You killed our enemies

yesterday, and you did not injure our two slaves this morning. You are our friends."

Throughout our entire journey, unless all opportunities for friendly intercourse were closed by furious onsets, and all minds were engrossed with the necessity of immediate and desperate defence, we made overtures of conciliation and friendship. I can recall many and many an instance when kindness, sociability and forgiveness won many tribes from a suspicious and menacing attitude to sincere friendship and open, candid conduct. Many tribes have, on my departure from among them, implored me to return soon, and have accompanied me long distances as though loath to part with me. Others, in their desire to see their friend again, have brought their medicines and idols before me and conjured me by their sacred character to tell their white brothers how glad they would be to see them and trade with them and make eternal friendship with them; and one king, whose friendship must be secured before any explorer can enter the Congo Basin, outdid me in generosity with such delicacy and tact that I looked upon him, and still regard him, as a phenomenon of benignity.

Appendices

A man should not swerve from his path because of the barking of dogs.
—*Autobiography*, 527.

A

STANLEY'S ARRIVAL IN ZANZIBAR, 1872 [1]

The bark *Mary A. Way*, Captain Russell, arrived at this port yesterday,[2] one hundred days from Zanzibar. The vessel had a safe and pleasant voyage all the way through, and the taut and clean appearance she presents after so long a trip speaks well of the efficiency of both officers and men. The *Mary A. Way* is the property of Thomas P. Way, of this city, and is engaged in the spice, clove and hide trade, Zanzibar being the chief port on the African coast for the purchase and sale of these commodities. The vessel has been absent for more than eight months, eighteen days of which were spent at the African port.

Captain Russell brings along with him letters and despatches to the editor and proprietor of the HERALD from Mr. Stanley, the discoverer of Livingstone, with whom he spent most of the time that the vessel was detained at the port. He also brings letters and messages from Mr. Stanley to a number of private gentlemen, old friends and acquaintances of the adventurous explorer. One passenger arrived on the vessel, Mr. Richard M. Whitney, an American, long resident at Madagascar.[3]

On yesterday a HERALD reporter boarded the bark, which is at present lying off the Battery, in search of Captain Russell and Mr. Whitney. The first object which attracted his attention on setting foot on the deck was a magnificent brown dog, larger than a lion, which was quietly sleeping on the forecastle. The mate of the vessel, Mr. Charles O. Welch, courteously received the reporter, and, noticing the look of astonishment which the latter cast at the dog, informed him that the animal was a present sent from Mr. Stanley to the editor of the HERALD. It is a mixture of the St. Bernard and some native African breed, and the mate states that the crew on the long voyage had come to regard him as a companion, and will grieve over his loss as that of a personal friend.

Captain Russell and Mr. Whitney had both left the vessel in the morning, as soon as she touched, and the mate was in sole charge.

1. *NYH*, Sept. 2, 1872.
2. New York.
3. Richard M. Whitney of Winchendon, Mass., was an agent of the Salem merchant John Bertram in Madagascar. He served at times as American vice-consul in Tamatave. Robinson to State Department, Jan. 3, 1882, Despatches from United States Consuls in Tamatave (microfilm), III, National Archives; Maude, *Five Years in Madagascar*, 169.

Though the men were busily engaged in overhauling the vessel and holystoning the deck, Mr. Welch spared time to accord a short interview to the reporter, and gave some interesting details relative to Mr. Stanley, of which the following is an abstract:

REPORTER—Did you see Mr. Stanley during your stay at Zanzibar, Mr. Welch?

MR. WELCH—See him? I should think I did. Why, he was constantly with Captain Russell during the eighteen days he remained, and, in company with the American Consul and several other residents of the port, he dined on board the vessel.

REPORTER—Was this after he had found Livingstone?

MR. WELCH—Lord, yes. He arrived from Bagamoyo two days after we did in a native dhow, as they call their boats there; drums beating and the American flag flying. I was not on shore at the time, but the captain was, and I understand there had been a great time in the city.

REPORTER—I suppose there was considerable talk among the residents about the expedition?

MR. WELCH—Talk! I should say there was. Why nothing else was talked of; even the blacks seemed to have caught the general contagion, and they were almost as excited as the white residents were. We were fortunate to arrive at the time we did to be in time for the triumphal return of the explorer, and it made us all feel good to see the American flag flying at the gaff of the dhow.

REPORTER—How did Mr. Stanley look?

MR. WELCH—Well, he looked very worn and jaded, presenting just the appearance that a man would after undergoing the terrible ordeal that he had passed through; but I tell you he looked tough, too, through all. He is a man who would not let up on any undertaking until he had carried it successfully through.

REPORTER—And yet, Mr. Welch, some of the wise men of Gotham presume to doubt the authenticity of the story he tells.

MR. WELCH—Doubt the authenticity of the story! Well, that is news to me. How people in New York presume to know more than the British Consul at Zanzibar, the residents there, Lieutenant Dawson,[4] of the English expedition, and Dr. Livingstone's son,[5] is more than I can imagine. I would stake my life on the veracity of the story. Why, Mr. Stanley was filled with anecdotes about the Doctor,

4. L. S. Dawson of the Livingstone Search Expedition. See Bridges, "Sponsorship and Financing of Livingstone's Last Journey."

5. Oswell Livingstone (1851–1892). Northcott, *Robert Moffat: Pioneer in Africa, 1817–1870*, table opposite p. 328. See Seaver, *Livingstone*, 601, for the reasons for O. Livingstone's failure to seek out his father.

and the manner in which they had spent their five months together; and the letters he brought were recognized as genuine by all who had ever been in communication with Livingstone. Doubt the truth of the story! That is a good joke. I see by the papers to-day—the first that I have seen for months—that Mr. Stanley is the lion of London society, and I know of no one more deserving of honor than he is. My intercourse with him was slight, as I had to attend to my regular duties, but the captain was constantly with him, and he will doubtless give you more information.

As the mate had his hands full of work the reporter left the vessel and departed in search of Captain Russell, whom it was rather a difficult job to find; but he was finally discovered at the house of Mr. Thomas P. Way, on Lexington avenue, whither he had went on his arrival in the city. He was delighted to see a HERALD representative and readily entered into conversation. Though a thorough sailor, Captain Russell does not look much like one of his profession, his appearance being more suggestive of a dashing cavalry officer than the captain of a merchant vessel. After some formal conversation the business of the interview was entered upon and the following is a report of the conversation:

REPORTER—I understand, captain, you are direct from Zanzibar.

CAPTAIN—Yes, sir; we are just a hundred days from the port to-day and we had a safe and pleasant voyage all the way through.

REPORTER—How long did you remain at Zanzibar?

CAPTAIN—About eighteen days altogether, during which time we transacted all our business.

REPORTER—Did you see much of Mr. Stanley?

CAPTAIN—I spent most of my spare time with him after he arrived. He did not get in until two days after us.

REPORTER—You saw him arrive then?

CAPTAIN—I did, and I shall not readily forget the excitement and interest which all classes manifested in the matter. It was a gala day in Zanzibar, and every one hurried out to receive him. His coming had been announced some time previously, but the precise date of his arrival could not be ascertained. A sharp lookout, however, was kept, and when the native dhow, with the American colors flying at the gaff, was seen coming in the wildest joy was manifested. It made us Americans proud of our country when we saw its colors associated with so noble an undertaking.

REPORTER—Had Stanley many persons with him on his return?

CAPTAIN—He had all the survivors of the expedition—Selim, the Jerusalem boy, and the other natives who had accompanied him. I suppose you are aware that the two white men had deserted him on the journey into the interior. I don't think their loss was very serious, as they did not amount to much at the best.

REPORTER—Was Stanley greatly worn?

CAPTAIN—Fearfully. His hair had turned quite gray. His body was wasted and emaciated, and he looked more like a man of forty-five than of twenty-six. When I first saw him he was suffering from an attack of fever and was very low. He, however, recruited wonderfully, and in a few days he presented a very different appearance. He was the guest of the American Consul, Mr. John F. Webb, during his stay, who was extremely proud of his countryman.

REPORTER—What was the feeling at Zanzibar?

CAPTAIN—Oh! a most extraordinary feeling. No event ever occurred at the port which produced so profound a sensation. Among the English residents in particular the interest taken in Stanley and his discoveries was great, but mingled with it was a certain amount of chagrin that an American was the first to bring relief and succor to the distinguished traveller. This very natural way of thinking was, however, thrown in the shade by the joy experienced at the intelligence that the Doctor was alive, and the honors and attentions showered upon his discoverer were given with no grudging hand. The American residents were, of course, the first to take the initiative in the matter, and I myself had the honor of entertaining Mr. Stanley at a dinner given on board my vessel, which was one of the most pleasant affairs in which I have ever participated. Mr. Stanley was the life of the party, and the stories and anecdotes he told were listened to with breathless attention by all present. The Sultan of Zanzibar also gave a grand *fête* in honor of Stanley, at which I was present. It was a very grand affair, the Sultan exerting himself to the utmost to make it a success.

REPORTER—Had the English expedition arrived by this time?

CAPTAIN—Oh, yes. Lieutenant Dawson was there before we came, and was a guest at my table. He is a perfect specimen of a gentleman, and was one of the first to welcome and congratulate Stanley. When he saw the proofs that Stanley brought he knew that his mission was at an end, and being convinced that it was useless for him to penetrate further into the interior, the purpose for which he had been sent having been accomplished, he resigned the command of the expedition to the second officer,[6] who in turn surrendered it to

6. T. R. Henn. See his letter explaining his course of action in this affair in *NYH,* Aug. 23, 1872.

young Livingstone, and he finally broke it up, after taking such supplies as he thought his father would require.

REPORTER—Did young Livingstone want to go on to the interior?

CAPTAIN—No, he did not. He is not of a very adventurous turn of mind, and the prospect of the journey frightened him, though Stanley urged him to go in my presence. He did not, however, think it necessary to do so, and when Dawson gave up the command he thought it better not to go. Stanley did not advise Lieutenant Dawson to pursue any particular course. Dawson acted on his own responsibility, and he considered his action was the most judicious course he could adopt under the circumstances. I took the Lieutenant as far as St. Helena on my return, where I left him, he remaining to take the first steamer for England.

REPORTER—Did you see Dr. Kirk, the British Consul?

CAPTAIN—I saw him, but had no talk with him about the expedition. The letters he received from the Doctor, I was told, however, gave him great pleasure, and he was deeply grateful to Stanley for having brought them. He had been the only correspondent the Doctor had in Zanzibar, and the sight of the familiar handwriting was a great relief and removed the painful suspense under which he had so long labored. The style of the composition, too, was very reassuring, the contents of the letters presenting all the Doctor's peculiarities, and he regarded the discovery as one of the greatest achievements of the age.

REPORTER—Did you hear anything of the complaints the Doctor made about the treatment he had received from Kirk?

CAPTAIN—I heard Stanley speak about it, but I did not pay much attention to the matter. I believe it was some neglect in the forwarding of stores that was complained of. He cannot, though, complain of any lack of supplies for some years to come, as Stanley left him sufficient to last for five years; and not content with this, he was personally superintending the caravan which was to be forwarded to him immediately that it could be got in readiness. Stanley's attachment to the Doctor is very strong, and his knowledge of the interior convinced him that if any green hand would arrange the supplies the affair would be bungled. So, in order that there might be no mistake, he fixed everything himself. It is not, I suppose, necessary to give you any particulars of the journey into the interior. You have already received all these points from Stanley himself. He is firmly persuaded that Livingstone will successfully accomplish the great mission he has undertaken and is convinced that he is perfectly safe from all danger. So thoroughly is the Doctor wrapped up in his work that he sent letters to various persons in Zanzibar requesting that no further expedition would be sent after him, as he has everything he requires and wishes to prosecute his work undisturbed.

REPORTER—Did you leave Mr. Stanley behind?

CAPTAIN—Yes; I left him waiting to catch the first steamer for Bombay; and as one was expected to sail in a week I suppose he left Zanzibar on it.[7] I took Lieutenant Dawson and let him off at St. Helena, as I said before.

This terminated our conversation, and thanking Captain Russell for his valuable information, the reporter withdrew. The letters and dog the Captain will deliver in person, according to a promise made to Stanley.

B

AN INTERVIEW WITH RICHARD M. WHITNEY [1]

As stated in yesterday's HERALD,[2] a single passenger, Mr. Richard M. Whitney, arrived in the *Mary A. Way* on Sunday, direct from Zanzibar. Mr. Whitney has been seven years a resident in Madagascar, where he was engaged in mercantile business; and it was on his return voyage to his own city that he visited Zanzibar. He was formerly engaged in business in this city, and was widely known through his connection with the large commission house of Belt & Cilley. His character for truthfulness and reliability is highly spoken of among his friends, who assert that he would make no statement that would not be literally correct.

A HERALD reporter called on Mr. Whitney yesterday to get some particulars relative to the Livingstone Expedition, which were readily given to him, and their interest may be learned by the fact that Mr. Whitney arrived in Zanzibar just one day previous to the return of Mr. Stanley from the interior, after his great discovery. Mr. Whitney's residence in Madagascar has somewhat browned his complexion, but he states that the climate is very healthy, although the local society is by no means desirable. The following is the report of

7. Stanley left Zanzibar on May 29, 1872 on the steamer *Africa*, belonging to the Hamburg firm of O'Swald, for the Seychelle Islands; from the latter place he went on to Bombay. *HIFL*, 677–79.

1. *NYH*, Sept. 3, 1872.

2. See the preceding document.

the interview: REPORTER—I have called, Mr. Whitney, to get some account of your stay in Zanzibar and your acquaintance with Mr. Stanley.

MR. WHITNEY—Well, sir, I shall be happy to afford you all the information I possess, and as I have a sincere admiration for Mr. Stanley and thoroughly appreciate the work he has done I shall be all the more willing to answer any question relative to him.

REPORTER—How did you come to touch at Zanzibar?

MR. WHITNEY—The vessel I was coming home on had some business at the port, there being a considerable amount of trade carried on at the place. I had heard very little of Stanley or the Livingstone expedition before we came to Zanzibar; in fact, I may say nothing, and I was no little astonished when the American Consul informed me that the correspondent of a New York paper had found the long lost traveller. Mr. Stanley was hourly expected at the time, the American Consul having received intelligence that he was coming.

REPORTER—How did he receive the intelligence?

MR. WHITNEY—From part of Stanley's cavalcade which preceded him. A number of the natives attached to the expedition had come in a day or two previous, with the intelligence that Dr. Livingstone had been found and that Mr. Stanley would immediately return. Dr. Kirk, who speaks the language of the country, interviewed them, and they gave a straightforward account of the expedition and its results, fully confirming the intelligence that Mr. Stanley very soon after brought. After they arrived we were all on the *qui vive* watching for the first approach of the explorer.

REPORTER—Did you see Mr. Stanley come in?

MR. WHITNEY—I did; and it certainly was a great sight. When the dhow neared Zanzibar the gun fired and the American colors were soon visible, proudly flying from the gaff. The beach was lined with people, native and white, who testified their delight by an unceasing discharge of small arms. The guns in the Sultan's batteries fired repeated salutes, and, in fact, the enthusiasm was something unparalleled. There was certainly never anything seen like it in Zanzibar, and the Americans in particular were joyful in the extreme. The intelligent native merchants were loud in their praises of the great explorer, as they called Stanley, and looked upon his exploit as marvellous. The Americans and the English were equally demonstrative in their praises only that the English were somewhat chagrined that the Americans had carried off the honors attached to the discovery. They would have preferred to have found him themselves, but did not know what way they should go about it. I saw an absurd statement in an English paper at St. Helena, claiming that Mr. Bennett should have informed the Geographical Society, in England, previous to taking any steps, that he was about to send an expedition to Africa. I think it would be very foolish to do anything of the kind, as it might have hindered the work.

REPORTER—Did you see Mr. Stanley soon after his arrival?

MR. WHITNEY—Mr. Stanley arrived about twelve o'clock in the forenoon, and I was introduced to him the next morning at the house of the American Consul, Mr. Webb, with whom he was staying as a guest. All the American residents in Zanzibar were present at the time, and it was a scene of general rejoicing.

REPORTER—How did Mr. Stanley look?

MR. WHITNEY—He looked just as a man would who had experienced the hardship of a ten-hundred-mile journey into the interior of Africa. I tell you it is a tremendous thing to go through such a journey, and only that Mr. Stanley is a man of iron he never would have survived. When he came in he was suffering from fever, but, under the hospitable roof of the American Consul, he soon recovered and regained his strength.

REPORTER—Were there any doubts entertained at Zanzibar of the authenticity of the letters and the genuineness of the discovery?

MR. WHITNEY—Why, no; and I am perfectly astonished to find on my return home that any such doubts exist. I cannot see that any grounds exist for such doubts. Why, the proofs Mr. Stanley brought to Zanzibar were of the most convincing kind, and the shadow of an objection to them was never raised. A great many questions were asked of the native followers of Stanley relative to Dr. Livingstone and his habits, but it never entered into the mind of any individual to question the truth of his discovery. Lieutenant Dawson, of the English expedition, was so thoroughly satisfied that there was no occasion for him to go on that he resigned his command to Lieutenant Henn, who, in turn, resigned it to Mr. Oswell Livingstone. Oswell considered the matter carefully over, and, on his own responsibility, decided that he would not go on, and came to the conclusion of sending on all the stores to his father and returning to England. Mr. Stanley supervised the arrangement of the caravan, his knowledge of the interior leading him to believe that it would be better to see to the matter himself.

REPORTER—Were you present at the *fête* the Sultan of Zanzibar gave in honour of Mr. Stanley?

MR. WHITNEY—I was not, and cannot tell much about it, but I know it came off, and was pronounced to be a grand success. I was present at a dinner given by the American Consul, to which all the Americans were invited, as well as the members of the English expedition, and Mr. Oswell Livingstone. It is scarcely necessary to say that Mr. Stanley was the soul of the party, and sat on the right hand of the host. The dinner was a very pleasant affair and the best of feeling prevailed. Mr. Stanley subsequently dined on board the *Mary A. Way* with Captain Russell.

REPORTER—Did you hear young Livingstone talk about the letters he received from his father?

MR. WHITNEY—There was a conversation took place one morning at a breakfast, or tiffin, at the American Consul's, at which Captain Russell, Lieutenant Dawson, young Livingstone, the Consul, Mr. Stanley and myself were present. We were talking of the letters of the Doctor, and as near as I can recollect Oswell communicated the contents of the letters he received, which were of public interest to the company, but stated that there were some private matters spoken of in the letters which were known only to, and concerned no other persons than his father, and himself. I have seen Dr. Kirk, but had no conversation with him relative to the letters he received, but heard from other sources that he was perfectly satisfied that they were authentic. Indeed, he never doubted that they were so, nor did any one else in Zanzibar. I have spoken frequently to Lieutenant Dawson about the expedition, as he was my fellow passenger to St. Helena, and he never had any doubt about the matter; and I may say here that, next to the discovery being made by an American, I know of no one whom I would rather see accomplish the undertaking than Lieutenant Dawson. I see he has brought additional confirmation, if any were needed, to England. The impression I formed of Mr. Stanley was that he was an honest man, and that every word he said could be implicitly relied on. His appearance thoroughly coincided with this, and I was no little astonished, as I said before, to find that his integrity has been questioned. Why, if he has hoaxed the public, he would be the greatest genius that ever lived; but it was impossible for him to do so, and I am as sure that he has found Livingstone as that I am now talking to you.

REPORTER—You left Mr. Stanley behind?

MR. WHITNEY—I did to my great regret, and I shall esteem the fact of our meeting the pleasantest episode of my life. I did not think on reaching Zanzibar that I would find a countryman so famous, and I am delighted to find that the English people so thoroughly appreciate his enterprise and daring. I know of no one who is so richly deserving of honors and rewards.

This terminated the interview, and bidding Mr. Whitney good evening, the reporter withdrew.

C

LEWIS NOE TO THE EDITOR OF THE SUN

Sayville, L.I.
August 16, 1872 [1]

Sir: Permit me to express a little incredulity in reference to the story of Henry Stanley, Dr. Livingstone's alleged discoverer. I know the man. I know his fertile powers of invention, and more than once I have seen his ingenuity impose upon men and impose most successfully. But, as I do not desire to throw discredit upon his alleged discoveries without at least showing a fair reason for my convictions, I will tell his story as I heard it from his own lips, from the lips of his relatives, and from irrefragable proofs which shall be forthcoming when desired.

Near the close of the late civil war, when a boy of fifteen, I enlisted in the navy, and was soon afterward assigned to the United States frigate *Minnesota,* Commodore Joseph Lanman, lying at Hampton Roads, Va., where I was employed as Commodore's messenger. A young man calling himself Henry Stanley was one of the crew. Though he had enlisted as a landsman, I believe he was, by reason of his marked ability, intelligence, and skill as a penman made ship's clerk. He was full of aspirations for adventure; told marvellous tales of foreign countries, and he urged that when we should leave the service I should accompany him on a proposed tour in Southern Europe. Being of a romantic turn of mind, I was pleased at the suggestion.

To hasten the opportunity of our departure, he planned our desertion from the navy, secured my acquiescence in it, and by his ingenuity it was accomplished at Portsmouth, N.H., when the frigate had gone to the navy yard for repairs. Soon after our arrival there, early in February, 1865, when I had been eight months in the service, Stanley forged a pass, affixing the Commodore's name to it, permitting Stanley and myself to pass the gate of the navy yard. Once without the gate, we took off our sailor clothing, under which we wore suits of citizens' clothes, that had been procured through the aid of carpenters who were at work in the navy yard. We were now free to go where we pleased.[2]

1. *The Sun,* Aug. 24, 1872.
2. Stanley had enlisted in the navy on July 19, 1864, for a three-year term. He became a petty officer on the *Minnesota.* The desertion took place at Portsmouth on February 10, 1865. Farwell, *Man Who Presumed,* 28–30.

We came directly to New York. The next day I returned to my home on Long Island, to the astonishment of my parents, who, directly they were informed of my desertion, sent me back to New York to proceed as quickly as possible to the ship. This was my purpose, but on arriving at New York I met Stanley, and he dissuaded me from it, telling me that disgrace and punishment awaited me if I should go back. He then unfolded to me a plan for raising the means necessary for us to proceed on our travels. It was for him to enlist me in the army, he taking the bounty money; then through his aid and connivance for me to desert, to reinlist and secure more bounty, to again desert, and so repeat this process until he had the money secured to enable us to go in search of adventure. But I was too strongly burdened by a sense of guilt for my own desertion to desire to add to it a repetition of the offence, and I declined to acquiesce in his plan. He was angry at me for my refusal, and finding that neither persuasion nor scolding would swerve me from my resolution, he set to work to procure employment. At his suggestion I made the same effort in my own behalf. He was more successful than I. His pleasing address, engaging manners, neat penmanship, and with all, his intelligent conversation and air of confidence enabled him to get a position, I believe in a law office.[3]

After a few days of unsuccessful effort to obtain employment, I left New York without his knowledge and worked for a week with a farmer, Mr. Joshua Hubbs of Hicksville, L.I. I then returned to the city, where I enlisted as a private under the name of Lewis Morton, in the Eighth New York Mounted Volunteers, Col. Pope, and continued in the service until after the close of the war, when I received an honorable discharge.

Meantime Stanley made efforts in New York to learn my whereabouts. Failing in this, he called on my parents, who informed him that I was in the army. He at once commenced a correspondence with me, in which he opened up a scheme of travel to the Rocky Mountains. He urged me to join it. To enable me to do so, he again proposed desertion. To assist me in this he promised to meet me at some point with a suit of citizens' clothes. As I declined to act upon his suggestion he went to Colorado alone, where he remained until the spring of 1866, continuing his correspondence with me, and keeping alive the interest he had early inspired in me in reference to travel in foreign lands. On his return, he visited my parents, and

3. *Autobiography*, 221, makes no reference to Stanley's working in a law office. Hird, *Stanley*, 45, assumes Stanley worked for a newspaper. See also Appendix E.

urged them to allow me to accompany him. His winning manners, gentlemanly bearing, and his seeming attachment for me impressed them so favorably that they were inclined to look upon his previous conduct in deserting as an indiscretion for which there were palliating circumstances. Of his efforts to graduate me as a bounty jumper I had not informed them.

My admiration of Stanley amounted to a youthful enthusiasm, and I longed to go with him in search of romance and adventure. He told my parents that he desired to educate me and give me the polish that could be best obtained by intercourse with the world. He told of diamonds, and rubies, and precious stones, and rich India shawls and other fabrics in Central Asia, the real value of which the natives knew scarce anything, which could be procured by us for insignificant sums of money, and could be sold at an enormous profit. He professed to have acquired abundant means in Colorado, and was willing to pay all my expenses for the pleasure of my companionship. My parents were in humble circumstances, and naturally they desired to promote the welfare of their son, and they gave their consent.

About the first of July, 1866, we left for New York, where he met a gentleman named Cook whose acquaintance he had formed in the Rocky Mountains, and who was to accompany us on our travels.[4] Stanley introduced me to Cook as his half-brother. This part I was compelled to play on our travels abroad, whenever Stanley's caprice suggested it. We proceeded to Boston. About the middle of July we embarked on the bark *E. H. Yarrington* for Smyrna.[5]

Just before the vessel quit her moorings I confess I was a little surprised, after the rose colored prospects Stanley had held out to me, when he expressed a wish for me to work my passage on the vessel, for which he stated he had made arrangements, because of a special object he had in view, the nature of which he would explain to me on our arrival at our destination. My faith was so unbounded in his wisdom, his integrity, and his love for me, that I readily acquiesced. With my previous experience at sea, I was enabled to make myself serviceable on the voyage.

After sixty days voyage we arrived at Smyrna and to my further surprise I found that the exchecquer of the expedition was not of the large proportions I had supposed from Stanley's representation. His purpose was a prolonged tour through Asia Minor and Persia into the heart of Asia, and thence to the coast of India, through

4. See Appendix E.
5. The *E. H. Yarrington,* Captain Mayo, cleared from Boston on July 10, 1866, for Smyrna. *Boston Evening Transcript,* July 10, 1866.

Thibet. With what little means he and Mr. Cook had they purchased a couple of sorry horses, a few cheap cooking utensils, and other things to make up a meagre outfit. This being accomplished, the whole amount of money left did not exceed the value of $5 in gold. The two horses, such as they were, were used by Stanley and Mr. Cook. Instead of the finely-equipped Arab horse which I was to have to ride I was compelled to trudge along on foot, on a projected journey of thousands of miles, through barbarous, or, at best, semi-civilized countries. A hundred dollars in gold would have purchased everything we had in the way of an outfit—horses, arms, ammunition, utensils, and camp equippage.

With no more means left than I have stated, Stanley, with an effrontery unexceeded negotiated with a man at Smyrna to accompany us as a guide to a certain point, offering him, if I recollect aright, equivalent to $60 a month and his expenses! The bargain was concluded, but the day before our departure from Smyrna, the man sensibly concluded not to proceed, and we started on our tour without him.

I asked Stanley what he meant by engaging a man for this service when he knew he would be without the means to pay him when we arrived at the point to which the guide was to leave us, and what he would do if the guide insisted upon payment. His reply was characteristic: "I would tie him to a tree and blow his brains out, as I don't intend to have any man go back to Smyrna and let them know how we travel."

On our second day from Smyrna, while we were at rest, and Mr. Cook was seated by a bunch of bushes, half asleep, in boyish sport I set fire to the bushes to give him a scare. He was scared, and Stanley and I had our laugh on him; but the flames went further than I had intended. They spread into a briar hedge and soon burned it. The inhabitants became much excited, and four or five men, evidently invested with some kind of police authority, came up, and after some resistance arrested Stanley and Cook. During the struggle that occurred, I escaped and made my way to Smyrna on foot, a distance of ten or twelve miles.

That same afternoon Stanley came back to Smyrna in search of me, and stated that after I left he and Mr. Cook were taken to a guard house, where their papers were examined, and after some little delay they were released. By flattering words and professions of love he reassured me, and I consented to go on with him again.

Soon I learned what I had dimly suspected before leaving Smyrna —the real character of the men I had confided in. Instead of being a traveling companion, I found that I was to be a slave and a beggar, and a slave too of a remorseless master. My duties were soon taught me. They were simple; to perform any menial service he directed and to procure the necessaries of life—black Turkish bread and fruit —and any articles of camp equippage to add to our scanty stock by begging, or, failing in this, by theft. The latter was not unfrequently resorted to. Indeed, all the food we used on our route for many weeks was what I obtained in these disreputable ways under the guidance of my new instructor in morals. I was taught the next day after my escape by an impressive lesson that my own will must be subjected to his. Soon after our departure from Smyrna he said to me in the severest tones, "Remember you are here to do my bidding. If I tell you to cut a man's throat, you do it."

I was not long in learning that there was no mistaking the significance of these words. My attempt to escape was an assertion of the independence of my own will, and a violation of that duty which he had laid out for me, and he could not let it pass unpunished. Without giving me notice of his intention he asked me into a pomegranate forest off the travelled road. He seized me, tied my hands together around a tree, stripped my clothing from my back, and on my bare skin scourged me with a whip which he cut from the trees, and on which he left the sharp knots, until the blood ran from my wounds. Stanley understands the refinement of cruelty in whipping. Each blow caused the most excruciating agony, which continued for hours. While he was tying me he looked significantly at his revolver, which was lying on the ground, and said he wished me to understand that I was in his power. Before he commenced his whipping he asked me if I knew what he was going to do. I told him I did not. Said he, "I am going to give you the d—dest thrashing you ever had."

I then asked him what I had done to deserve a whipping. He said that "whipping does boys good, whether they have done anything or not."

During the scourging, as he rested between the blows, he recalled to me facts in our past intercourse in the navy and in New York when I had offended him, and particularly my leaving him in New York, and enlisting in the army without his knowledge. When he had concluded, he comforted me by saying: "I think you are a good boy, just the one I want for a companion. We will let the matter drop, for I am satisfied."

Two or three days afterward he asked me if I recollected what he had told me on our voyage from Boston to Smyrna, that he was going to give me a severe trial, and one which would convince him whether I was the companion he wanted or not.

I told him I did. He added, "You now see what I meant. It is the way you stood that whipping that has convinced me I made a correct choice."

About five days after the whipping, as he was removing the scabs from the wounds, he made a further comforting statement that "I was a very healthy boy, or else the wounds would not heal so rapidly."

Each day Stanley made new revelations of his character. They convinced me that he was capable, if a sufficient inducement existed, of any crime. Having been blessed with moral and religious training in my youth it was hard for me to believe that one who could speak in such pleasant tones as he had been wont to before the departure could consent to commit the crimes he did, and make a young boy who had confided in him as the soul of honor accessory to them. Abhorring his character as soon as I comprehended it, my thoughts were again on escape. But escape in such a country, from such a man, for a boy of seventeen, penniless and friendless, ignorant of the language, manners, and customs of the people, seemed like an impossibility. He had taken from me my arms before whipping me, and had not returned them. I had tried to escape once, and quick upon that effort I had been most infamously scourged. After this he had frequently given me the kind assurance that if I attempted to escape again, he would shoot me down like a dog. I was convinced that he meant what he said and I made up my mind to continue on the travel until some deliverance should be vouchsafed to me.

It came in an unexpected manner. When we were some fifteen miles distant from Chihisar, a squalid mountain hamlet about 300 miles from Smyrna, Stanley remarked, as he had frequently done before, that their cheap horses would not hold out for their journey much further, and to make better progress we must have new horses. Knowing he had no means, I asked him how he was going to obtain them. His reply was, "I will show you how."

He did so, and in a brief time convinced me that his genius was equal to highway robbery. Perceiving a Turk in advance of us in possession of two horses, he said to me, "I am going to have those horses, and to help me to get them I want you to do as I tell you."

Mr. Cook was at this time some distance in the rear and not within sight. We accelerated our pace and overtook the Turk, who was leisurely riding one horse and leading the other. Stanley, who had learned some of the language from a phrase book, soon engaged the Turk in conversation, the nature of which I did not then understand, though he told me afterward. As he related it to me he had asked the Turk if he didn't want to buy a girl, and represented to him that I, though dressed in boy's clothing, was really a girl. The

Turk was incredulous, but Stanley insisted upon it, and finally said that the Turk might inspect my person and satisfy himself. Both then dismounted, and the Turk approached me with smiles, apparently with the hope of finding a girl in breeches, and Stanley following him, seized a favorable opportunity, raised his sabre, and, with all the force he could muster, struck the Turk a blow on the head which I thought would kill him. Fortunately, the poor fellow had within the fez he wore a kind of thick pasteboard stiffening, which stopped the force of the descending sabre sufficiently to prevent it proving fatal.

The Turk was staggered by the blow, but did not fall. Two other strokes followed in quick succession, which I think he warded off, and then they closed, seemingly for a death struggle. The Turk fought with the desperation of a man who knew that his life was at stake. With a drawn dagger he tried to reach the heart of his antagonist, and soon seemed about to obtain a mastery over him. Stanley struggled to free himself, but finding he could not, he called out to me, "Shoot him, Lewis; shoot him, or he'll kill me."

My experience with Stanley had taught me the prudence of obeying orders. I raised the gun, levelled it at the breast of the poor Turk, and pulled the trigger. The rifle failed in its intended work. That morning, after shooting at a mark, Stanley had failed to reload it, and by this fortunate omission I was spared the guilt of shedding an innocent fellow being's blood. Stanley continued to cry out "Kill him! kill him!" and then as the only resort I approached them, clubbed the Turk with the butt of the rifle, and Stanley again was free. The whole conflict was quicker than I can narrate it, and was as desperate as a death struggle between two powerful men.

With Stanley free, and I there to assist him, the Turk was at a disadvantage. He retreated back in the direction from which we had come. Stanley's fingers were cut inside by grasping the Turk's dagger while in the midst of the struggle, and were bleeding profusely. But to allow the Turk to escape might hazard our own safety, and Stanley rushed to his saddle bags, took out his revolver and fired two successive shots at the retreating Turk, then two or three rods distant. He missed his mark, and the Turk continued his retreat to the top of a small hill some forty rods distant. By the escape of the Turk, the anxiety of Stanley was increased, for he saw that he must himself be a fugitive. His effort was to secure his immediate escape. He mounted one of the Turk's horses, and was about to start when he found that the horse's feet were entangled in the bridle of the other. To disengage him, I had to cut the bridle reins and also rope by which one horse was attached to the other. He very hurriedly directed me to gather up our blankets and utensils and to follow him.

Just at that moment Mr. Cook came up, and with a cry, "Ho, for the mountains," Stanley galloped off, Mr. Cook following. As quick as possible, I gathered up what few things I could and mounted the remaining horse. It was with difficulty that I could get him to move, for the Turk kept calling to him from the hill and he seemed resolute in going the other way. It was only by means of striking him with a sabre that I finally got him under control. I galloped off after Stanley and Cook who had left the highway and moved to the south toward the mountains. We ran our horses a distance of fifteen miles, when they were exhausted and we were compelled to encamp for the night.

But in the meantime the Turk had not been idle. He collected a force of eight or ten men and started in hot pursuit of us; and just before dark, when Stanley thought that all was safe, we were startled by the yells of the Turks, who captured us, bound us with lariets, conveyed us to Chihissar, and there held us prisoners for four or five days, during which we were subjected to cruel torture.

Each day we were drawn up over the limbs of trees by ropes and lariets around our necks to compel us to give them money. At other times they laid our heads on blocks and sharpened knives before us and by signs made us understand that we must give them money or they would cut our throats. But, as we were penniless, of course we could not accede to their demands. They refused to believe we were without means because it was usual for foreign travellers to be abundantly provided.

The first night of our imprisonment I was taken out by three of the Turks and treated in a shocking manner. At last, tired themselves of thus torturing us to no purpose, the band took us to Afium-Kara-Hissar, a city about four hours' travel from Chihisar, where we were again imprisoned, and a charge of highway robbery was preferred against us before the Cadi.

But, fortunately, the excesses of our captors in committing outrages upon us and robbing us of what little we had—our arms, our passports and blankets, and our few extra garments—opened an avenue for our escape, and Stanley's genius was quick to take advantage of it. As he himself expressed, "Boys, I've got you in this scrape, and I'll get you out of it."

He did it most ingeniously. When we were accused of robbery, Stanley, in a spirit of injured innocence, made a counter accusation, and said that we not only had not robbed, but that we had ourselves been robbed, and that the truth of his statement could be verified by examining the persons of our accusers. Sure enough, underneath their garments were found our papers and property, and the Cadi was convinced that Stanley's story was true. At once they were put under arrest and afterwards conveyed to Broussa, a provincial city, nearly a day's journey from Constantinople, where, after some delay and many adjournments, the Turks were convicted of robbing us of our valuables and a large amount of money which we never possessed. Our stories were dictated by Stanley. They were consistent with the circumstances, as they were proven, and everybody seemed convinced that we were wholly guiltless and our captors wholly guilty.

My own testimony was directed, if I recollect aright, wholly to the outrage committed on me personally. So far as I concealed a part of the fact of Stanley having been the original aggressor, I have this to say in extenuation; I was but a boy of seventeen, friendless, in a strange land, destitute of means and almost of clothing. I had been deceived, wronged, and had been subjected to a course of abuse and outrage by Stanley to teach me that he was my master, and fear so operated upon my mind that I dared not disobey his orders or directions. Another consideration that influenced me was that if I told the truth, I, as well as Stanley, would be subjected to trial and punishment, unless, in the mean time, I was assassinated for betraying him. At my present age, and with more experience, I probably should have had the courage to tell the whole truth.

While the trial was pending at Broussa, we went two or three times to Constantinople, reaching there at first destitute of means, ragged and forlorn. But Stanley's brilliant genius was equal to the financial emergency. He appealed to the Hon. E. Joy Morris, American Minister to Turkey, and so fully did he enlist the sympathies of the gentleman in our behalf, and so plausible a story did he tell, that Mr. Morris advanced from his private funds an amount equal to several hundred dollars, Stanley giving therefore a draft for the amount on his father, whom he represented was a wealthy merchant in New York. The draft was forwarded for collection only to be returned protested, and with the intelligence that no such man as Henry Stanley's father could be found.[6]

In Stanley's interviews with Mr. Morris I was studiously kept in the background, and I had no opportunity to communicate with him at all. Stanley obliged me to sign a statement that I had received one-third of the amount Mr. Morris had advanced. But my third went into Stanley's pocket, and that is the last I ever saw of it.

6. See Appendices F and G.

With a fictitious draft sent to America, Stanley felt that the air of Constantinople would not be conducive to his health. Without waiting for Mr. Cook, who was still at Broussa awaiting the termination of the trial, we, without any knowledge on the part of Mr. Morris of our intention to return to Europe, took a steamer for Marseilles, France, and thence proceeded to Liverpool. Here he left me in the house of an uncle and aunt of his people in humble circumstances, while he proceeded to Wales, where he was born and where he had always lived until at the age of fifteen years he came to America. It was from his relatives that I learned his early history, and learned, too, that he possessed the same characteristics as a boy that he has since exhibited as a man.[7]

His aunt told me that his real name was John Rowland, and he was so called by his relatives in my presence. I remained for some weeks with his uncle and aunt, and was most kindly treated by them, though they were illy able to bear the burden of my supoprt. I frequently urged Stanley by letter to send me means to reach my home, but without success, and was unable to leave Liverpool until I received means from my parents.

It was while I was at Liverpool that Stanley spoke to me of Dr. Livingstone's explorations in Africa. They seemed to be an object of great interest to him. He expressed a desire to go into Africa himself, and said he should aim to do so as a correspondent of the *Herald,* and thereby make a story and a sensation, and gain both fame and money.

The story of his travels he has told. He may have succeeded in his search. If he has, he will receive due credit for his enterprise. If he has not, he has the ingenuity to fabricate a plausible story which will gain him a passing fame. Though, as he told me himself, he never went to school a day since he was fifteen years of age, he has picked up a large fund of information. He is, as I have already stated, a ready and skillful penman, and can write in many styles, from a rapid current to an elaborate round copy hand. I have received letters before and since our eventful tour, and I have also photographs of him taken at different periods of his life. By flattery and honeyed words he has sought to prevent me from exposing him, and I have only postponed this statement until, by the prominence he should give himself, I could make the exposure more effectual.

To sum up his character, Stanley is a daring adventurer, bold and unscrupulous, but intelligent and specious. His manners are those of a quiet man. In disclosing his infamy to the world, I have but a

7. Thomas and Maria Morris. See *Autobiography,* 55–68.

single object and purpose, and that is, as far as I can, to prevent the subjection of others to the outrage and wrong I was compelled to submit to at his hands. More than once he has threatened to kill me if I exposed him. With his cruel and revengeful nature I believe he would not hesitate to carry his threat into execution, if a favorable opportunity occurred in which he could do it with impunity. And I am not without my fears of assassination. Indeed, I should confidently expect it were we to meet without the bounds of civilization or in a sparsely-settled country where crimes would not be quickly discovered or where the avenues of escape were open.

D

AN INTERVIEW WITH LEWIS NOE [1]

The remarkable disclosures of Mr. Louis H. Noe of Sayville, L.I., contained in his communication published in THE SUN of the 24th inst., determined us to send a reporter to visit Mr. Noe at his home, and have a personal interview with him. Our reporter readily found the residence of Mr. Noe's parents, which is situated in the village, and shortly after Mr. Noe himself came in. The residence is a plain and comfortable two-story house, and fairly compares with the old-fashioned Long Island homes. The reporter met with a ready welcome, and soon was engaged in conversation with Mr. Noe on the subject of his visit. Noe himself is a tall, spare young man, of about 23 years of age, with black eyes and hair, dark complexion, an aquiline nose, and a black moustache, not heavy. He is modest in demeanor, but converses freely and intelligently. While he denies having any personal animosity toward Stanley, he says that it is due to the world that the real character of the man should be known, as illustrated by conduct with which he was personally familiar. He felt confident of Stanley's identity, based upon the statements of his travels in Asia Minor, which had been incidentally alluded to in the public prints in connection with the published statements of his alleged discovery of Dr. Livingstone.

He produced a copy of *Frank Leslie's Illustrated Newspaper* of July 13, in which was contained a portrait of Stanley copied from a photograph by Abdullah Brothers, Constantinople. The reporter asked him whether the portrait resembled Stanley.

1. *The Sun,* Aug. 29, 1872.

"Yes, some," said Noe, "but I have a photograph of him taken by Abdullah Brothers which is an exact likeness."

"Let me see it," said the reporter, "and a comparison of it with the printed portrait will show whether there is any resemblance."

The photograph was produced bearing the imprint of "Abdullah Brothers, Photogrepes de sa Majesté Impériale le Sultan, Pera, Constantinople." It is an ordinary *carte de visite* of a young man in a standing position dressed in a naval officer's coat. A comparison of the picture with that published in the illustrated papers showed some points of general resemblance, but the expressions were so different that one would hardly suspect they were intended to represent the same person.

"I notice," said the reporter, "that Stanley has on a naval officer's coat; how did that happen?"

"Oh," said Noe, "that happened in this way: Stanley, as I have stated, was in the navy during the war. He was ship's clerk, and he was always inclined to put on the airs of a navy officer. On arriving at Constantinople we were ragged, and, of course, had to have some clothing as soon as we could get the means to procure it. My impression is that the means to pay for our clothing were derived from money obtained by Stanley on the fictitious draft on his supposed father in New York; and then, to make himself look as distinguished as possible, he had a naval officer's suit made. You see the gold lace on the ends of the sleeves. But when it came to the buttons he found himself embarrassed. He had no American navy buttons, and in this strait he had to use Turkish buttons. If you will look close you will see the crescent and star on the buttons."

The reporter looked closely and saw that the buttons were Turkish, as stated.

"That, however, was a kind of mild fraud," said Noe. "But I have other pictures of Stanley. Here's one sent me from—I've forgotten where—some place in or about Egypt—I think. It was sent after I had returned home, and it shows him as he appeared in his Oriental rig."

Noe produced the photograph referred to, also a *carte de visite* bearing the imprint of "Ch. Nedey." On the back is written in Stanley's handwriting, "Burburra, Soumalé Land, Jan. 1, 1869. Still your friend, Khan Bahadoor, alias Stanley." [2]

2. Stanley spent from November 1868 until February 1869 in Aden on a mission for the *Herald*. There had been rumors that Livingstone was coming out of Africa and Stanley had gone to Aden to seek news of his whereabouts. A trip to Berbera, on the Somali coast, would have been an easy venture

In this picture Stanley is in a sitting posture, with loose, baggy Turkish trowsers and a jacket. On his head is a turban, such as are commonly seen in Saracen scenes. In his mouth is a meerschaum cigar holder with a cigar. Nearly in front of Stanley is seated a little negro boy, apparently ten years old, whose only garment is a breech cloth. Behind the two is a cadaverous negro woman or man, also seated. The group makes a decidedly novel picture.

"Here's another picture," said Noe, "taken when he was a boy in Wales. I think he said he was thirteen or fourteen years old—I am not certain though. You see that at that time he evidently had not been much in society and must have been in moderate circumstances, judging from his dress."

This picture is also a *carte de visite,* and has the imprint of "J. Laing, photographer, Castle street, Shrewsbury, and at 3 Queen street, Wellington, salop." It represents an ungainly, loutish boy, seated in an awkward posture, with an evident consciousness of the awful responsibility resting upon him of having his picture taken. His garments are ill-fitted to his person, and the whole picture is suggestive of awkward uneasiness.

"Have you got any more pictures?" asked the reporter.

"Yes," said Noe, "I have one taken when he was still a young man and before we went on our tour. It shows him very much as he appeared when he was in the navy."

Noe here produced a larger photograph—a cabinet size—in which the expression of the face is much more clearly defined. It represents a young man of about twenty-one, with a manifest decision of character and firmness of purpose, and with gray eyes, having a cold, sinister, and even vicious look.[3]

"Really," said the reporter, "you have got quite a picture gallery of Stanley. You say he is a Welchman. Do you know whether he speaks the Welch tongue?"

"Oh, yes," said Noe; "he always wanted to keep from me the knowledge of the fact that he was Welsh. But after his return from Wales,

---

from Aden. Stanley apparently sent a despatch about this visit to Aden to the *Herald;* in the issue of July 2, 1872, when the *Herald* expedition after Livingstone was in the forefront of the news, a letter of Stanley's of February 9, 1869, was printed. The heading of the letter is given as the "Island of Zanzibar," a change no doubt made to stimulate its news value. The letter itself is of little interest; it merely restates what little was known of Livingstone in Africa at that date.

3. *Autobiography,* opposite pp. 69 and 167, has pictures of Stanley at ages fifteen and twenty. Farwell, *Man Who Presumed,* opposite p. 48, has Stanley at seventeen.

having learned in the mean time that I had exposed him, he commenced a tirade against me with his uncle and aunt in Welsh. This uncle spoke up, saying: 'Speak English, so that the boy (meaning me) can understand what you say. I don't want anything said so that Lewis cannot take his own part.' "

"What part of Wales was he from?" the reporter inquired.

"That I do not know," said Noe, "for I am not familiar with the geography of Wales at all. But I have two letters from him, received while I was in Liverpool with his uncle and aunt waiting an opportunity to get home, and which were written to me in Wales. Here they are. One is dated 'Denbigh, Vale street, December 20, 1866,' and the other I can't make out because a word is written across it; but as near as I can make it out it is 'Bokedelwydden Village (I am not sure about the third and fourth letters), near Saint Asaph, Dec. 25, 1866.' His uncle and aunt told me that it was a mountainous region there. In that last letter he wrote to me to come on to Wales and see his folks, and urged me strongly to do so—indeed, he insisted upon it. He had then heard through a member of his uncle's family that I had told of his conduct to me, and when I showed them his letter urging me so strongly to come to Wales, his uncle told me not to go. He said if John—that is what they always call him—if John got me in the mountains there, with his present feelings against me, I would never get out alive."

"Have you any objection to giving the names of Stanley's uncle?" asked the reporter.

"Not in the least," said Noe. "His name is Thomas Morris, and he then lived—this was in the fall of 1866—at 18 Davies street, Liverpool. Mr. Morris is a good, kind-hearted man; and I hardly know how I should have got along until I received money from home, had it not been for him and Mrs. Morris."

"You say," said the reporter, "in your letter that Stanley and yourself and his other companion, when you left Smyrna, had not more than five dollars. How did he suppose it possible that he could travel through the heart of Asia to India without any means whatever?"

"He proposed to procure means," said Noe. "He opened up his plans to me as we travelled along; and after what I have related in respect to his manner of getting horses, you will not be surprised that he should seek to procure money in an equally dishonest way. He said that we would not always have to travel in the way we were travelling; that as soon as we got to Erzeroum, a city some nine hundred miles on our route from Smyrna, he should get up a story of being robbed of a letter of credit, and get means there to go on to Tiflis in Persia, of course using fictitious drafts, I suppose, on which to negotiate the loan. By the time the fraud would be discovered, he calculated that we would be beyond the frontier of Asia Minor, too far in the interior of Persia for the banker to feel disposed to go to the expense of chasing us up."

"You say in your letter," said the reporter, "that Stanley and your party claimed to have been robbed of valuables and a large amount of money. Have you any evidence of that except your own statement?"

"Yes," said Noe: "I have here a copy of the *Levant Herald,* containing a letter written by Stanley to the editor on our arrival in Constantinople, in which he states that we were robbed of all our money, valuables and clothing to the tune of 80,000 piasters. He says, in the same letter, that when the Turks were searched, after he had accused them of robbing us, only 40 piasters were found on them. That may have belonged to the Turks themselves; but I know we had no money left at the time we were prisoners.[4] But here is a handbill he sent me, in which he tells of a still bigger story of his losses."

Noe here handed the reporter a printed handbill, in the words following:

The American Traveller,

HENRY STANLEY,

who was cruelly robbed by the Turks on September 18, 1866, and stripped, by overwhelming numbers, of his arms, passports, letter of credit, and over $4,000 in cash, will lecture on his

TRAVELS AND ADVENTURES IN TURKEY

AND

LIFE IN THE ORIENT!!

on _____ evening, at _____ in _____ the __ inst.

Doors open at 7 o'clock. Lecture commences at $7\frac{1}{2}$ o'clock.

Mr. Stanley has served in the American Navy from January, 1862, till the fall of Wilmington, at which he was present, in January 1865.

He then took a grand tour through the interior of Asia Minor, from which he has just returned.

During his lecture he will appear in the costume of a Turkish naval officer.

4. The letter from Stanley, dated Oct. 11, 1866, is reprinted in *The Sun,* Aug. 30, 1872. In addition, the *New York Times,* Feb. 5, 1867, has a despatch from its Constantinople correspondent describing the episode.

He will also show to the audience a Saracenic coat of mail, needlework by a Turkish maiden, Turkish Fez, and the elegant cap of a Greek pirate, a Turkish Chibouque, a piece of skull from the tomb of Sultan Bajozet, commonly called "Lightening" or "Thunderer," a whetstone from Mount Olympus, near the ancient city of Troy, of which Homer and Virgil sung about 2,000 years ago.

There will also be on exhibition a Firman, signed by the present Sultan of Turkey, Abdul Azziz. Also, a passport signed by our Secretary of State, William H. Seward.

Mr. Stanley will repeat the Moslem call to prayer after the manner of the Muezzin, in the sacred Arabic language used by 140,000,000 people.

The lecturer will close the exercise of the evening by singing a Turkish song *à la Turque* . . .

"How did you get this?" the reporter inquired.

"Stanley sent it to me after I returned home," said Noe, "as he did his photographs. This handbill was printed in America, and was intended for use here. Here is one of the tickets to the lecture."

Noe here produced a ticket in the words following: LECTURE on TRAVELS AND ADVENTURES IN TURKEY, AND LIFE IN THE ORIENT, by HENRY STANLEY ADMIT ONE, TICKETS TWENTY-FIVE CENTS.

"You see," said Noe, "that in the handbill he speaks of his service in the navy. He don't mention the way he left the service."

"No," said the reporter, "he would hardly be apt to state that. That is a point I wanted to ask you about. You mention the desertion of Stanley and yourself from the *Minnesota* at Portsmouth, N.H. Have you any evidence of that besides your own statement?"

"Yes," replied Noe; "undoubtedly the records of the *Minnesota* will show the fact, and also the records of the Navy Department. But in addition to that, I have a letter from Stanley, in which he alludes to it."

"Have you any similar evidence to sustain the charge of his getting money from Mr. Morris, the American Minister at Constantinople, on a worthless draft on his supposed father in New York?" asked the reporter.

"Oh, yes," said Noe. "He told me so himself, and he states the fact in letters to me. Mr. Cook also knows the fact from Mr. Morris. If anybody were to ask Mr. Morris whether Stanley had borrowed money from him, giving a draft for it on his father in New York, which came back with a statement that there was no such man as

Stanley's father to be found, I think Mr. Morris would corroborate
my statement, though I never spoke to the gentleman in my life."

"What letters have you got from Stanley?" asked the reporter.

"Well, I have got a good many," said Noe. "Here is one to my
sister, Mrs. Davis, dated New York, April 19, 1865, in which he tries
to vindicate himself from an accusation which my folks made of
deceit on his part. You see, after I enlisted in the army without his
knowledge, he came to our house for the first time with an extract
cut from a newspaper, in which it was stated that a young man was
found drowned bearing my description, and the name he told me to
assume after our desertion, and he was certain it was I. My folks
told him that I was in the army and gave him my name and address
—Louis Morton, Eighth N.Y. Mounted Volunteers. That was the
name he wanted to enlist me under, when he asked me to be a
bounty jumper, and Morton is what M stands for in his middle name.
He calls himself now Henry M. Stanley.[5] My sister insinuated that
he had made up the story about the boy being found drowned and
got it printed, and this letter is a denial of the imputation. Here is
another letter to my sister dated New York, May 9, 1865.

"You will notice that they are two different handwritings, one bold
and careful as a copy hand and the other delicate and fine, more like
a lady's. The next letter is also addressed to my sister, and is dated
Black Hawk City, Colorado, Sept. 4, 1865. The next is to me from
Black Hawk City, dated Oct. 19, 1865, and encloses a long diary of
his travels from New York to Colorado, which I also have here. Then
there is one to my sister again, dated Black Hawk City, Oct. 21, 1865.
Here is one to my mother dated Black Hawk City, Jan. 26, 1866.
The next is to my sister, dated Central City, Colorado, April 29, 1866.
These are all he wrote during his absence at the West at that time.
Then he came on East, and we started on our journey to Asia Minor.
The next letter is dated Boston, Mass., July 26, 1866, just before
we sailed,[6] and is addressed to my sister. The two I find next in
date are the ones I have told you about, and were written to me from
Wales while I was in Liverpool; one is dated Denbigh, Vale street,
December 20, 1866, and the other Bokedelwydden Village, near St.
Asaph, December 25, 1866. A few days after he wrote to my mother
a long, closely-written letter from Liverpool, dated Jan. 12, 1867, in
which he gives a long account of our journey, and in it endeavors

5. In 1869, Stanley signed his name, at least in one instance, as Henry
Morelake Stanley. Balch, "American Explorers," 279, 281. In 1884 Harry John-
stone dedicated his volume, The River Congo, to "Henry Moreland Stanley."
6. But see Appendix C, note 5.

to smooth over his conduct to me. Then he writes me a letter dated on board the steamer *Damascus*, Jan. 18, 1867, off Londonderry, Ireland. He was then, I suppose, on his way to America; and that spring he was out West again, for his next letter was dated Headquarters Department of the Missouri, Cheyenne Camp, Kansas, New Mexico, April 15, 1867. The next is from the same region, though no place is mentioned, and he dated April 30, 1867. Then I have another in which he speaks of being with Hancock's command fighting Indians, but there is neither place nor date, but it was written about that time. After that he left the West, came East, and went to Europe, and my last letter from him is dated Paris, Jan. 1, 1868."

"You have quite a stock of correspondence," said the reporter.

"Yes," said Noe, "there are a good many letters, and it may be there are more I can find. I gathered these up within a few days. All his letters to me while I was in the army I destroyed, because I could not carry them around with me."

The reporter read over the letters, when the conversation was renewed.

"I notice," said the reporter, "that in many of these letters and in the diary he quotes Scripture and talks more or less of piety."

"He is excellent on that," replied Noe. "His pious talk was one of the things that gave my parents and brothers and sisters confidence in him. But he can swear and break the Commandments as easy as he can quote the Bible—in fact, a good deal better."

"But what is his object in so many of these letters in professing love and affection for you?" inquired the reporter.

"First," said Noe, "it was to induce an attachment for him so that I would accompany him on his travels; and after I had done so, knowing that his abuse of me might cause me to betray his secrets, he flattered me and praised me in the hope that I would keep my mouth shut."

"What reason have you to suppose, as you have stated in your letter, that Stanley has not found Dr. Livingstone?" inquired the reporter.

"Nothing," said Noe, "except that he told me that he meant to go to Africa as the correspondent of the HERALD, to get up a big story and make a sensation. I believe that he has imposed on the HERALD the same as he has imposed on others. He can tell the biggest stories and in the most plausible way I ever heard, and make people believe them, too."

"But," said the reporter, "the receipt of Dr. Livingstone's diary and letters have been acknowledged by his friends in England, and do you suppose they could be imposed upon by fictitious handwriting professing to be Dr. Livingstone's?"

"Yes, I do," said Noe. "Look over those letters and you can see half a dozen different handwritings, so different that you would not suspect they were written by the same man. If Stanley was able to get hold of any of Dr. Livingstone's writing, either before he went to Africa or after he got there, he could imitate so well that it would trouble anybody to detect the fraud."

"There is another point I wish to get a little further information on," said the reporter. "You say that at Constantinople Stanley made you sign a statement that you had received one third of the money he had got from Mr. Morris, the Minister to Turkey. How was that brought about?"

"That happened in this way," said Noe. "After having got the money from Mr. Morris on the draft, Stanley was very much agitated, and at night he could not sleep. I retired and was soon in a sound sleep. Stanley, however, sat up and was writing. About midnight he woke me up and said, 'Lewis I want you to sign this paper.' He read it to me. It was a certificate that I had received one-third of the money that he had got on the draft. I replied that I had not received it yet. Being within the bounds of civilization, I felt disposed to parley a little over the matter. His reply was, 'It don't make a d—d bit of difference whether you have or not—I want you to sign it.' My reluctance took him aback a little, in view of the promptness with which I had been accustomed to obey his commands, and there was silence for a minute or two. I then said to him that he had not made Mr. Cook sign any such paper. 'Well,' said he, 'I intend to make him.' I said I did not believe Mr. Cook would do it. He said that Cook would do it or he would blow his brains out, or any other person's who didn't do as he commanded in this regard. His pistol was then lying on the table. Then there was another interval of silence. He then jumped up and, with a look of intense rage and a voice of thunder, said, 'Louis, are you going to sign that paper?' I said, 'I will if I am obliged to.' Then he said, 'I command you to do it; if you don't, I'll serve you as I would Cook.' I arose, and after reading it over myself I signed it. "There was one mistake," Noe added, "in the printing of my letter in THE SUN. I am made to say that Stanley had the manners of a 'quiet man.' It should read 'gentleman.' "

Much more was said in the conversation with Mr. Noe in reference to the details of his acquaintance with Stanley, but they are hardly of sufficient importance to print. The reporter left Mr. Noe and his family most favorably impressed with their respectability, honesty, and candor.

E

AN INTERVIEW WITH HARLOW COOK [1]

Dr. Livingstone has, undoubtedly, had more than one man's share of the public attention. He has been buried and resurrected time and again. He has furnished a small mouthful for the gentle crocodile, and many columns for the capacious newspapers. One day the world has had him chopped into fine bits by ebon-hued barbarians; the next, paddling up the Nile in his little canoe. One thing and another has he been doing for years, till at last the people were contented to have him resting by the banks of the river for whose sources he had so long sought. Then Stanley, the adventurous, made a $50,000 voyage, at *The Herald's* expense, to stir up the bones of the oft-buried explorer, and share with him popular notice and the honor of being an Africa penetrator.

Now that Stanley has been in full measure successful, at least of gaining notoriety, lo! forth steps an overgrown boy, who blubbers out a tale of personal grievances, and seeks to give his own name eminence by casting mud at that of *The Herald* reporter.

This person's name is Lewis H. Noe, of Saybrook, L.I., and a considerable part of his story was given in THE TIMES of Tuesday, creating no little excitement inasmuch as it boldly charged Stanley with committing many crimes, and with showing a disposition to commit the rest, under favorable circumstances. The New York *Sun* gave birth to the article. Why, it is needless to say, since the friendly fellow-feeling existing between that sheet and *The Herald* is too well known. Of course the *Sun* was not, as Noe undoubtedly was, jealous.

A TIMES reporter, on reading the startling and unequivocal utterances, was profoundly moved with contempt for the writer, and disbelief in his words. What should one think of a creature who says: "And I have only postponed this statement until, by the prominence he should give himself, I could make the exposure more effectual."

The reporter was also moved with a desire to prove whether the Long Islander was a liar or Noe. He sat down to commune with himself, and argued in this wise:

There were but three persons in the party, of which Noe was one. The others were Stanley and "a gentleman named Cook." Stanley was in England. Noe was on Long Island or in *The Sun* office. Therefore, Cook must be in the neighborhood of Chicago. Therefore, because the reporter well knew there could be no three great travelers

1. *The Chicago Times,* Aug. 31, 1872.

or three great anythings, but at least one of them might be found
hard by the great city of the west.

Patient inquiry proved his reasoning entirely correct, and without
loss of time he was seated in a Chicago, Burlington and Quincy
coach, whirling along toward Yorkville, a suburban village about 50
miles to the southwest. A train off the track, and vexatious delay
subsequent therefrom, served but to give relish to the chase, and in
high spirits the reporter ascended the rickety stairs leading to the
sanctum of the Yorkville *News,* and softly entered.

At the table sat a gentleman of some 30 years, bearing so strong
a resemblance to the great Dickens that the reporter started with
surprise as he looked up.

"Is the editor, Mr. Springer, to be seen?"

"No, sir; he has gone to Bristol."

"Is Mr. Cook now connected with *The News?*"

"My name, sir, is Cook."

Very good. Better than seeing the editor, since Mr. Cook was the
very individual whom the reporter wished to chat with, as he took
occasion to inform him.

Reporter—You have seen the letter of one Noe, regarding Stanley,
have you not?

Cook—Yes; I read it in THE TIMES on yesterday.

R.—And you are the person referred to as the gentleman met in
New York?

Cook—Yes, I suppose I am.

R.—Good. If you will believe it, I have come all the way from
Chicago hither to talk with you confidentially on that very letter.
When I read it, I didn't believe it. And I don't now. Do you?

A look of surprise, but no quick answer.

R.—And knowing that you could settle the doubts in my mind,
I came straight to you. You were with Stanley a considerable time,
were you not?

Cook (musingly)—Yes; a considerable time.

R.—Of course knew him intimately, traveling so far together?

Cook—Like a brother.

R.—Then can my soul bide in peace; for you can tell me all about
it, and whether Noe has said the truth or a lie, and—

Cook—Yes; but—

R.—And I shall be satisfied at last.

Cook—But I don't exactly—

R.—Did Stanley ever do all those things Noe charges?

Cook—No; but (rousing more energy) who are you?

R.—Oh, me? Why, thought you knew me.

(Handed him a card, which he looked at, but without evincing decided satisfaction.)

Cook—But what is your business, I mean?

R.—My business; of course! Am a reporter on THE TIMES.

Cook (with an elevation of the eyebrows)—Ah! and THE TIMES wants to know about this thing, eh?

R.—Exactly.

Cook—Well, I must think over it.

Here Cook is quite deeply engaged in thinking. Meanwhile, the reporter learns that he does not doubt the genuineness of Stanley's discovery of Livingstone, and is quite out of sorts at Noe's "peaching," or rather lying. When he returns from the realms of thought the conversation continues:

Cook—I hardly know what I can say to you. I do not want to tell what I can at this time for more reasons than one. I have written both Stanley and Noe; the former, to see how he thinks I can best aid him by my side of the story; the latter, to find out his motive.

R.—Then you consider Stanley to have been slandered?

Cook—Basely slandered. Noe's statements are not at all in accordance with what he told me, nor with what Stanley told me.

R.—What motive could he have?

Cook—Spite, and jealousy of Stanley's good fortune. He was always envious, because Stanley, being the most gifted, took the lead in everything.

R.—These are serious charges to make for such reasons.

Cook—He had others, too. Both he and Stanley, in their letters to me since, have mentioned a quarrel they had in London, after they left me in Constantinople, and were on their way home. I forget the particulars, but Noe was very wrathy, and I suspect this is the outgrowth of that. It is too personal, and shows too much spite to be of much weight.

R.—Noe gives names of places and dates, and makes a story seemingly straight, though.

Cook—Yes, the piece is too well written for him. He is not smart enough to write in any such style. I have no doubt *The Sun* reporter got hold of him and made him say anything to suit his taste; then enlarged on the statements and made a mountain out of it. Any lie to blacken Stanley was plainly the policy of the writer.

R.—What kind of a character is Noe?

Cook—A weak, dish-water kind of a boy he was when we went abroad. No backbone to him, nor character at all.

R.—Strange that Stanley should make a companion of such a one.

Cook (with a laugh)—Companion! Stanley never did. Noe was our servant. Stanley helped him once in the navy because he knew the boy would do anything for him, and might be useful in such a voyage as he was even then contemplating. What Noe says about intimacy with Stanley is absurd. He was a chit of a boy, and with no signs of a man about him. Stanley was young but manly, and easily 50 years ahead of Noe in everything. But, as I said, I must wait till I hear from Stanley before I tell of these things. Then I may give them to you.

R.—And you may not.

Cook—There is some money in it for me, I think, and I ought to look out for it.

R.—Certainly. It is every man's duty to turn an honest penny. Now, I want you to decide just how much what you have to tell is worth to you, and then we can talk about how many honest pennies do you hope to turn? And while you are making up your mind, you can, at least, tell me if that absurd desertion business is true.

Cook (abstractedly)—Not according to what either of them told me. Stanley did not desert. I will tell you how that was, since I have begun. You see, Stanley's time was out, and he was free to leave the *Minnesota*. He wanted Noe to go with him, as he was full of his European trip, and it could not be undertaken alone. He had charge of the books on the *Minnesota*, and Noe was in arrears to the ship to the amount of $60. For this the officers were going to hold him till he worked out its equivalent. Stanley could not wait, so he fixed up the books, and got Noe off. That was all of it. I am sure there was no desertion, for Stanley immediately went to New York and entered a prominent lawyer's office, having resolved to study for the bar. He would have been more cautious if a deserter. Noe just manufactured that or the *Sun* reporter did it for him.

R.—Noe says he was introduced to you as Stanley's half brother.

Cook—A cool statement indeed, as I knew of him from Stanley long before I met him in New York. When Stanley and I made our plan to trip it around the world, Noe was counted in as a servant from the first. Stanley said he was anxious to go, as he himself afterward avowed. I never heard of the half-brother arrangement. It must have been a secret union, unknown to any but Noe.

R.—But the poor boy had to work his passage.

Cook—He worked no more than we all did. Stanley and he understood the ship, and I wanted to. So we would turn in and help once in a while for the sport of it.

R.—Pretty rough to have to foot it through a barbarous land of scorching sand.

Cook (laughing heartily)—Walk over there. He would look pretty doing it; or any other man. That is made from whole cloth. He had the same fare as the rest of us.

R.—But he makes your fare out as pretty poor. Only $5 in the crowd after buying a scant outfit. How is that?

Cook (laughing yet more)—Of the same stamp as the other. It is likely we would start around the world without any funds. It is true we meant to go as cheaply as we could with comfort; but we had enough for all our purposes as far as we could see, and we had counted the cost. I cannot see why Noe should tell so false a tale. If we had been poor, as he says, it could not reflect on Stanley's character. It shows up the weak, senseless side of Noe, that is all.

R.—Stanley's bargaining for a guide, when he had no money to pay with, how was that?

Cook—He did at first think of having a guide. But the price was too high, and Stanley too fond of doing it all himself, not the lack of money, that made us go without him.

R.—Did Stanley say that he would blow the guide's brains out?

Cook—Not to my knowledge. If he did, it was to impress Noe, who was fool enough to take down a dose of that kind.

R.—Noe says he was scourged. The lashes seem to have cut deep into his soul.

Cook—The whining little pup. It was a wonder Stanley did not whip him, for he was so impudent, and Stanley so hot-tempered. But all that is like a farce to me, who saw it. And as for his being a help-less baby of nineteen, unable to run away from us when in the midst of Asia, and being threatened with death! Ha, ha! it is too good even to deceive people who are ready to take up any evil against a man.

The interview was progressing finely. The thinking-cap, as to how much the information was worth, had not yet come off, and it would have pleased the reporter had it never come off. But the inter-viewed began to suspect he had dropped a remark or two more than he intended and suddenly became reticent, referring to the fact that he must await advice from Stanley.

In vain did the reporter try to convince him that the interest would blow over before ever Stanley would get his letter, and that, financially, the thing would be a wreck. Mr. Cook had an object or two in view, where he could use such information as he possessed. The reporter tried to get at the minor facts, but it was rather plain that a good deal had already leaked out, and mum was the word.

R.—Well, have you decided how much the facts I want are worth to you?

Cook—Yes. For a complete account of our travels, my acquaintance with Stanley, our plans, and the sudden end put to them by robbery, and so on, I should want $100.

Reporter was silent a few moments, trying to be a good judge of the value of money on one side, and foolscap sheets on the other. Were there no lower terms, or was a compromise as to the amount of information among the possibilities?

No, there was no argument allowable. To give part would be to take the freshness from the whole. As Johnny Coon might say, "one hundred or nothing" was his determination.

Reporter did not know, but would see. Where did the robbery mentioned take place?

No knowledge gained on that point. Other pleasant topics were then introduced, and at a decent suburban hour the reporter and Mr. Cook went to their respective beds, and took a good sleep over the matter.

Next morning all was fair, but reticent. To cut a long story as short as it can be properly cut, what follows is the rest of what was obtained without the desired pecuniary value to Mr. Cook. The reporter assured him, after it was done, of his sorrow to have taken the piece from his mouth unwillingly, but that he was obliged to do it, as he would not abate a jot or tittle from the original sum.

Mr. Cook welcomed him to all he had procured, perhaps not imagining how much that was, and thus freely given its use, the reporter could not fail to as freely give it to the readers of THE TIMES, who are at present interested in anything concerning Stanley. This is Mr. Cook's yarn as it was wormed out.

"Stanley's first appearance before the public was during the late war, as correspondent of *The Herald.* Though then a mere boy, his graphic descriptions of naval engagements won for him a distinguished place among the literati of the army. He was at this time clerk in one of the departments on the war ship *Minnesota,* having entered the service as a landsman. As Noe says truly, Stanley was promoted for his aptness and skill as a penman. The way he came to get on the *Minnesota* was not quite common. He was on a trip to England, during war times, and getting out of funds wanted to come back. He imposed upon the credulity of the captain of a rebel cruiser to take him to New Orleans, his wonderful memory enabling him to describe the streets and places so exactly that the captain could not doubt but he was brought up in that place. Stanley promised to play spy, to pay for his passage. The vessel anchored off Hampton Roads, and Stanley was stationed on guard to prevent anyone else from deserting. He quietly took a boat from the ship's side and sculled coolly up to a United States steamer lying near. The information he gave induced the captain to take him on board, and then began his navy career. This Stanley told me, and Noe corroborated it.

"After the war Stanley went into a law office in New York. He did not desert, nor did he try to get Noe to jump bounty, nor anything of the kind. If he had, I should have known it, for Stanley told me of all his doings. We were very intimate, naturally, being thrown together in places tending to make us closest friends.

"Well, Stanley found law too musty. He resolved on seeing the west. I was traveling in Colorado. One day, in the spring of '66, at Mohawk City, I was reading a local paper, when an article in it struck my attention. I inquired who the writer was, and found Stanley to be the author.

"I struck up an acquaintance with him, and the result was that we joined hands for a voyage round the world. This was prevented by an unforeseen circumstance, occurring after 8,000 miles of it had been made. We were not going, as *Frank Leslie's* said, to join the Cretan Insurrection, though sympathizing with the movement. Stanley had seen enough of Colorado. On the way out he had made himself notorious, and shown his character, by making a man twice his size kneel and ask his pardon for something said reflecting on his character. He was the hottest blooded man I ever saw. He never stopped for consequences. He put a pistol to the man's head, and said: Retract, d—n you, and the big fellow flopped down and retracted. After a year in Colorado we started on our memorable trip. To show our recklessness, we determined to take a skiff and row down the Platte river, the banks of which were infested with Indians, while the river itself was full of snags, eddies, and shallow spots. Several parties had gone down, but none had got through alive, they told us at Denver, the head of navigation even for canoes.

"This and other of our plans may seem quixotic. But they were not with such a man as Stanley to lead. I admired his fearlessness then, and do more admire him now, after what he has achieved.

"When we left Denver to try the perils of the Platte, we had a definite plan to go to Boston, thence to Smyrna, going overland through Asia, and passing through Turkey, Armenia, Georgia, Cashmere, Bokhara and other countries. Our objects were experience and information for writing a book, comprehending our travels, and giving those facts hitherto unknown to civilization. Our idea of writing the book is now postponed indefinitely.

"It was on the 6th of May, '66, that we started from Denver for the Missouri, *via* the dangerous Platte. The mountain snows had melted and swollen the river, and the prospect was not promising. But we argued that if we could not go down the Platte we could not go through Asia, and our career had better find its end in American waters than on barbarian soil. Our skiff was flat, and drew but eight inches of water, many places in the bed being not six inches deep. After upsets and mishaps enough we reached a station of United States troops, and were taken for deserters from Fort Laramie. I never saw Stanley come out as he did then. He walked toward the door of the hut we were in, together with the commander of the post and others, and motioned me to follow. Commander said;

" 'Shall I put you under arrest?'

" 'Yes,' said Stanley promptly, while his hand was on his revolver, 'if you have men enough to take me.' The glance of his eye cowed the commander, and we passed on. We got to St. Louis all right, and then went east. Noe joined us, and we set sail for Smyrna. After a 51 days' voyage we reached there. Noe's account of our outfit and doings is not at all true. We had everything provided for our comfort. Noe never complained when we were together. Then we were robbed by a band of stragglers, but after a tedious confinement, when they found we could get no ransom money, were released, though stripped of everything. This compelled us to give up the rest of the trip. I staid in Constantinople, while Stanley and Noe started for England. There they quarreled.

"This attack is a malicious thing, and I shall take measures to refute it; as I said before, when I hear from Stanley. Whether Noe will answer my letter I can not tell.

"As for Stanley's character I can vouch. I knew him intimately a year and a half, and men who were side by side in the face of death are wont to know each other well. I found nothing to justify the words of Noe. His story is 'too thin,' as they say. Stanley is short and quick and not easy to forget an enemy, but he is also firm and true as a friend."

It was time for the reporter to take the return train to Chicago. Mr. Cook drove him to the depot, and was greeted by his friends with queries:

"Seen that piece in THE TIMES on Stanley?"

"How is it that air feller that went with you, Harlow?"

"Is that true about the man you traveled with?" etc. To all of which he was obliged to give answer.

So the reporter was satisfied. The word of Mr. Cook, who is a gentleman, and of unblemished reputation, can surely outweigh the evidence extorted from a weak-minded, envious, spiteful, untruthful boy by an unscrupulous and jealous New York journal.

Chicago, through THE TIMES, submits these facts to the consideration of the easterners in particular. If they want to know something responsible on subjects of interest, let them come to Chicago.

F

INTERVIEW WITH EDWARD JOY MORRIS [1]

Atlantic City, N.J., August 31, 1872

Among the many prominent Philadelphians who own summer cottages at this charming seaside suburb of the Quaker City is Mr. E. Joy Morris, ex-United States Minister to the Sultan of Turkey. After a long period of honorable service he now lives here in quiet retirement, failing health having compelled him to remove from the active sphere of public life, with which he has been for many years associated. As his name has been mixed up with the marvellous fabrication which the long-haired Long Island philosopher and inventor, Louis Noe, has given to the world, I called upon him this morning to ascertain what he knew about the case, and was most cordially received.

Mr. Morris is small in stature and slight in frame; but the delicate face and the high, open brow give evidence of a rare intellect and a keen perception of human nature in all its phases. His cottage fronts on the sea; and when I arrived I found the ex-minister reading a copy of the HERALD containing the account of the search expedition to sleepy Sayville, and he was laughing heartily at the narrative.[2] I explained to him the purpose of my visit, and he readily consented to give me all the information he possessed relative to Mr. Stanley and his false friend Noe. Sitting on the veranda of the

1. *NYH*, Sept. 7, 1872. Edward Joy Morris (1815–1881) of Pennsylvania, American Congressman, diplomat and author. He was minister to Turkey from 1861 to 1870. *DAB*, XIII, 206.

2. See *NYH*, Aug. 29, 1872. The account is devoted to poking fun at Noe and contains little of value relating to Stanley.

cottage, with the roar of the breakers ringing in our ears, a tale was unfolded of travel and adventure, "hair-breadth escapes," "moving accidents by flood and field" and desperate undertakings in which the hero of the Livingstone expedition was the leading, and indeed it may be said, the only character. Pictures of Oriental life and romantic journeyings into unexplored countries made the narrative seem almost like a fable, but Mr. Morris certifies that every particular of the story which he tells is true to the smallest detail.

Before commencing Mr. Morris expressed his regret and indignation at the occurrence of the circumstances which made my visit necessary, saying, "My God, sir, I am shocked that any attempt has been made to diminish the laurels Mr. Stanley has so justly earned, and I exceedingly regret that my name has in any way been connected with the story. It has been used without authority from me, for I would be the last man to attempt to cast any stigma upon the man I am proud to call my friend, and whom I would defend to the last, with all my influence and power. There have been private dealings between Mr. Stanley and myself, which concerned only ourselves, and I do not see why outside parties have interfered with the business of two gentlemen, for the purpose of hashing up a sensation. Mr. Stanley is not here to defend himself, being absent, receiving the honors which he has so justly earned; and the attempts to injure him behind his back are, to say the least of it, malicious and cowardly. Now, sir, after this expression of opinion I am ready to answer any questions.

REPORTER—You have read the story of Louis Noe, Mr. Morris. I would like to know how far your knowledge of circumstances will substantiate him, and, in beginning, I would ask, when did you first meet Mr. Stanley?

MR. MORRIS—I first met Mr. Stanley, or at least heard of him, in October, 1866. I was then at my country residence in Bujukdere, on the Bosphorus, and while there I received intelligence from Constantinople stating that three American travellers, named Stanley, Noe and Cook, had been barbarously and cruelly treated and robbed of all their effects by a band of Turks in Asia Minor. In the advance of the arrival of the travellers at the Turkish capital Stanley sent an account of the occurence to the *Levant Herald*, a paper published in English, in which the particulars of the attack, the capture, the robbery and the outrages which succeeded were all fully narrated. I lost no time in taking the necessary steps, when the tidings reached me, for the protection and relief of my countrymen when they should arrive. I forgot to state that in the meantime the Turks who were the perpetrators of the outrage had been captured and conveyed, strongly guarded, to Broussa, a small town near the Sea of Marmora.

REPORTER—Did you see the Americans on their arrival?

MR. MORRIS—I did; the American Consul General and myself were both waiting to receive them when they arrived, and of course they immediately repaired to the Embassy when they got into the city.

REPORTER—What appearance did they present?

MR. MORRIS—A most miserable appearance, sir. If ever the condition of men presented the traces of cruel treatment theirs did. Mr. Stanley's own plight fully corroborated his story. He had been stripped of all his clothing, and though he had been enabled to procure some outside covering by the generosity of Mr. L. E. Pelesa, agent of the Ottoman Bank at Afiund-Karahissar, he had neither shirt nor stockings on when he came to me, and he showed other evidences of great suffering. I relieved his more pressing necessities and advanced him a loan of money to procure an outfit for himself and his companions. I considered it to be my duty to do this, both as American Minister and as an American who was bound by the tie of nationality to stand by my countrymen in distress. I gave Mr. Stanley a check on my banker and he drew the money—£150. The first thing he did was to repay the agent of the Ottoman Bank the amount advanced by him, and then he took his companions to a clothing bazaar, and both he and they procured the clothing of which they were so much in need.

REPORTER—What security had you for your loan?

MR. MORRIS—I had no security, nor did I ask any. The money was advanced without condition of any kind. I see it has been stated by Noe that the amount was given in consequence of a draft which Stanley offered, payable by a person in New York. This is false; no draft was given to me at that time, nor was any promise of a repayment made until subsequently. I advanced the money as a loan, asked for no security, nor was there any offered. Some time after Mr. Stanley inconsiderately did give me a draft, but I looked upon this as altogether superfluous, and did not attach much value to the act, though it may have been well meant. The draft proved valueless, but it is unnecessary to enter into details of a transaction which has been long satisfactorily settled between Mr. Stanley and myself, and which does not, as I said before, concern any persons outside ourselves. I may state, however, that the action of Mr. Stanley was superfluous in another way, as Mr. Cook, Stanley's fellow traveller, came to me after the money had been sent and assumed all responsibility connected with the loan, stating that if the money was not recovered from the Turkish government he would personally indemnify me, giving me his American address.

REPORTER—Had you in any of those transactions seen or spoken to the young man, Noe? He states that he has never spoken to you?

MR. MORRIS—I have certainly seen him, and spoken to him as well, though he was not so conspicuous as the others during the time they remained.

REPORTER—What impression did you form about Mr. Stanley at the time?

MR. MORRIS—I regarded him as a young man of great courage and determination; his countenance showed this, it being stern, almost to serenity, but with nothing sinister about it.

REPORTER—Did Noe, at any time during the stay, bring any charges of cruelty against Stanley.

MR. MORRIS—None that I recollect of, though he was at perfect liberty to do so. The statements he makes about his being in dread of assassination from the hands of Stanley, while in Constantinople, are entirely too absurd to be believed. He was as safe in Constantinople and as much his own master as he is now at Sayville.

REPORTER—Was the story of Stanley, which Noe now asserts to be false, found to be true?

MR. MORRIS:Wait a moment, we are coming to that. As stated before, the Turkish outlaws were taken to Broussa, on the Sea of Marmora, and after some time had elapsed they were placed up on trial. As there was no American Consul at the place, I obtained from Lord Lyons a promise that the British Consul, Mr. Sandison, should watch the trial and attend to the interests of my clients, Stanley, Cook and Noe, who were all present as witnesses at Broussa.

REPORTER—Was Noe a witness?

MR. MORRIS—Certainly; he appeared in common with the others. The Turks were placed upon trial and attempted to defend themselves, but the evidence against them was overpowering. Some of the effects of Stanley and his party were found upon their persons, including $300 which the party carried, and they were convicted and sentenced to various terms of imprisonment.

REPORTER—Did Noe swear to all the facts?

MR. MORRIS—*He did; and his sworn statement will, if I mistake not, be found in the archives of the State Department. I never was more astonished in my life than I was when I heard that he now states that everything he related at Broussa, while under oath, was entirely false.*

REPORTER—Probably Louis does not scruple to add perjury to the long list of other offences of which he is guilty, according to his own confession.

MR. MORRIS—You may call it anything you please, but he certainly testified to the narration of Stanley, in common with Cook, and upon the strength of that evidence the Turks were convicted.

REPORTER—Were any counter charges brought by the Turks?

MR. MORRIS—I do not recollect any. If any such attempts were made the evidence to the contrary was too strong and they were abandoned.

REPORTER—What steps did you institute in the meantime to obtain restitution from the Turkish government?

MR. MORRIS—I had Stanley and the others draw up an inventory of the effects which had been lost, and they attested to the losses upon oath as being in every instance correct. I then forwarded the claim to the Turkish Minister, including the money advanced by myself, which of course was included among the losses. The entire amount, as near as I can recollect, was about twelve hundred dollars, and the claim was prosecuted on our part with the greatest vigor and pertinacity.

REPORTER—Did Stanley and his friends remain in Constantinople after the trial?

MR. MORRIS—Not long. Stanley and Noe left for England, and Cook remained some time behind settling affairs. Before separating an agreement was entered into between them and me that if I recovered any money it was to be sent to Cook, as, I believe, it was he that bore the expenses of the journey to Smyrna. Soon after Cook left also. I urged the claim time after time upon the Turkish government, but did not meet with much success, as there was no disposition shown to pay, and at length I was about to abandon the prosecution of the claim in despair when the Turkish Minister of Foreign Affairs, Saferet Pacha, called upon me at my residence and offered to compromise the case by giving a smaller amount, alleging that the Sultan did not wish the shadow of a difference to exist with the United States over the affair. I had some conversation with the Grand Vizier, Ali Pacha, about the same time and to the same effect, and I accepted the proposition in the amicable spirit in which it was offered. The money was paid, and I first took out of it the £150 which I had lent. According to my agreement, I was to have deducted interest, but I did not do so, merely taking the exact sum. The balance of the money I sent to Cook. I forgot to say that when I thought the money could not be recovered, I sent instructions to my lawyer in Philadelphia to communicate with Cook and remind him of his promise to repay. This was done, and Cook acknowledged his indebtedness, but at the same time, stated that he wished to know if I had exhausted all reasonable efforts to recover from the Turkish government. Of course, when the claim was allowed, no repayment on his part was necessary.

REPORTER—Did any of the money go to Stanley?

MR. MORRIS—Not a cent. I received a letter from Noe, in which he desired to have a part, but as I did not wish to be dealing with too many parties I sent the money, as I said, to Cook; but Stanley did not finger any of it, and if Noe was treated with any injustice Cook was the person he had got to look to, not to Stanley or me. This closed the transaction at the time, and I heard nothing more of the parties for some years.

REPORTER—When did you see Mr. Stanley again?

MR. MORRIS—During the last year of my official residence in Turkey.

REPORTER—Would you please state under what circumstances?

MR. MORRIS—In that year a distinguished American clergyman[3] called upon me at the Embassy and asked me did I remember anything about a person named Stanley. I answered in the affirmative, and he then stated that Mr. Stanley had desired him to call relative to a long-standing debt of £150, which, he believed, was owing to me, which had never been settled and which he was desirous to pay. I told the clergyman (who is now, I think, a professor in Dickinson College) that the matter had been long settled and that I had been paid. The gentleman further stated that Mr. Stanley desired to call upon me, and I replied that he was at perfect liberty to do so. The same evening Mr. Stanley and the clergyman, who were both stopping at the Hotel de Byzants, called and by invitation remained to dinner. The two gentlemen had come on from Egypt together, and the clergyman had an admiration which almost amounted to veneration for the character of the HERALD correspondent.

REPORTER—Was Mr. Stanley much changed in his appearance and manner?

MR. MORRIS—Wonderfully. The uncouth young man whom I first knew had grown into a perfect man of the world, possessing the appearance, the manners and the attributes of a perfect gentleman. The story of the adventures which he had gone through and the dangers he had passed during his absence were perfectly marvellous,

3. Probably Henry Harman, Professor of Greek and Hebrew at Dickinson College, 1870–1896. Morgan, *Dickinson College 1783–1933*, 329; *Autobiography*, 246.

and he became the lion of our little circle. Scarcely a day passed but he was a guest at my table, and no one was more welcome, for I insensibly grew to have a strong admiration and felt an attachment for him myself. Instead of thinking he was a young man who had barely seen twenty-six summers you would imagine that he was thirty-five or forty years age, so cultured and learned was he in all the ways of life. He possessed a thorough acquaintance with most of the eastern countries, and, as I took an interest in all that related to Oriental life, we had many a talk about what he had seen and what I longed to see. He stated to me that he had a sort of roving commission for the HERALD, but that he had exhausted all known countries and was at a loss to understand where he should go next.[4]

REPORTER—Did you help to enlighten him?

MR. MORRIS—I think I did. I said to him, "Stanley, what do you think of trying Persia? That is an unexplored country, and would well repay a visit if you could get back with your life; but as I know you do not fear danger no consideration of personal peril would, I think, deter you." Stanley thought over the proposal, and rapidly came to the conclusion he would go. I busied myself in procuring him letters of introduction to the Russian authorities in the Caucasus, in Georgia and in other countries through which he would have to pass. He saw the Russian Ambassador at Constantinople in person, who was so well impressed with him that he made extra exertions to facilitate his progress to the mysterious home of the Grand Llama.[5] I had some time previous to this had a Henry rifle sent me from a friend in New York, as a specimen of American art, and this I presented to Stanley, with my best wishes for the success of his undertaking.[6] He started on the desperate enterprise some time after, and my table thereby lost one of its most entertaining guests. When I say desperate enterprise I mean it, for Persia is to a European a practically unexplored country; and, in consequence of its weak government and the marauders with which it abounds, a journey to Zanzibar or Unyanyembe would be a safe trip compared to it. How Mr. Stanley accomplished the task he undertook the columns of the HERALD will tell. I received a letter from him, while on the way, narrating the hospitable manner in which he had been entertained by the Russian authorities, and the way in which he had astonished them by the performances of his Henry rifle. His journey through the Caucasus and Georgia was a sort of triumphal march, though he was looked upon as a lost man by all who knew anything of the East.

---

4. Stanley was, of course, concealing his mission.
5. Stanley never visited Tibet.
6. *HIFL*, 79, calls the gift a Winchester rifle.

The route he took was an entirely new one, as he went in a kind of zigzag way to Thibet, and he must have a charmed life to have come through so much peril in completely safety. After this affair I returned home, and I did not hear of Mr. Stanley again until I heard of him as the discoverer of Livingstone.

REPORTER—Were you astonished at hearing of the latter fact?

MR. MORRIS—Not in the slightest. I would be astonished at no feat in the line of travel that he would accomplish. He is a born traveller, and I used to say to myself at my table in Constantinople, "Here is a man who will yet achieve greatness, and leave his mark behind him in the world." He has all the qualities which the great explorers possessed—Mungo Park, Humboldt [7] and Livingstone himself—a hardy frame, unflinching courage and inflexible perseverance. If such a thing were possible that I were forced to become a member of a band to undertake some forlorn hope, some desperate enterprise, I know of no one whom I would so readily select as the leader of such an undertaking as Henry Stanley. I receive his narrative of the discovery of Livingstone with implicit faith, and from my knowledge of him and his character I am lost in wonder that his story should be for an instant doubted. That he has found Livingstone is, in my opinion, as great a certainty as that you are now in Atlantic City. The perils of a journey into the interior of Africa would have no terrors for him, as he, like Nelson, does not know fear in the ordinary acceptation of the term.

REPORTER—Then your knowledge of the antecedents of Stanley leads you to believe in the truth of his story?

MR. MORRIS—Most undoubtedly, and I may again say that Mr. Stanley is my friend, and any testimony I can offer in his favor will be gladly given.

Thanking Mr. Morris for his courtesy the reporter withdrew, more than ever impressed with the opinion that Noe is not, nor ever has been, anything but a fraud, a traitor and a liar.

G

INTERVIEW WITH EDWARD JOY MORRIS [1]

The story of Lewis H. Noe in reference to the antecedents of Henry Stanley was one so detailed and circumstantial that it could

7. Alexander von Humboldt (1769–1859), naturalist and explorer in South America and Asia. See Schultze, *Alexander von Humboldt; JRGS* 29 (1859), cii–cxii.

1. *The Sun*, Sept. 5, 1872.

be easily disproved if not true. In respect to the giving of the fictitious draft to the Hon. E. Joy Morris, late United States Minister to Turkey, it was suggested by two or three journals the statement of Noe could be refuted, if not true, by an inquiry of Mr. Morris. And to settle any doubt on the question, a reporter of THE SUN paid a visit to Atlantic City, N.J., where Mr. Morris has been passing the summer with his family. He found Mr. Morris residing in a tasty cottage in Pacific Avenue, but a short distance from the beach. The reporter was shown into the library. On the table were copies of newspapers published in modern Greek, and several works in the Turkish, Persian and Arabic languages. Evidently Mr. Morris is a student in fields unusual for an American. Soon the gentleman entered. He is about medium height, rather spare in form. He appears to be about fifty years of age. His hair, side whiskers, and moustache are blonde, his nose aquiline, and his eyes a light blue. He has broad, high, and full forehead, and impresses one as a gentleman of large culture, extensive reading, and close observation. An extreme prominence of what the phrenologists call the organ of ideality would indicate that Mr. Morris is a gentleman whose tastes are aesthetic, and that many of his highest pleasures are derived from walks among poetry and the fine arts, and a contemplation of the beautiful in nature.

Mr. Morris received the representative of THE SUN with urbanity and politeness. He stated that he was exceedingly sorry that the controversy in reference to Mr. Stanley had arisen, as the fact stated by Noe, which brought his own name forward, was one which he had regarded as settled long since, and so far as he was concerned was never intended to be mentioned again.

"But," continued Mr. Morris, "as silence on my part when asked in reference to the matter would be construed unfavorably to Mr. Stanley, I may as well tell the affair, and then state what I regard as extenuating circumstances in his favor."

"But," said Mr. Morris, "I presume that all I shall tell you will be published before you return. A Gentleman from the *Herald* visited me on Thursday on a similar mission, and I gave him a full account of my acquaintance with Mr. Stanley."

"There has nothing appeared as yet," said the SUN reporter, "and as the *Herald* is generally prompt to publish anything it learns in reference to Mr. Stanley, I presume the reporter must have lost his notes." [2]

"Another point that the gentleman wished to be informed on," said Mr. Morris, "was the residence of Mr. Cooke, who accompanied

2. See the preceding document.

Stanley and Noe in the Asia Minor tour. He said they desired to visit him."

"If they had inquired at the SUN office," said the reporter, "they could have got the information, as we have several letters in the handwriting of Mr. Cooke."

"Well," said Mr. Morris, "to begin at the beginning. In the summer and fall of 1866 I was residing at Bu-Yukdere, the summer residence of the diplomatic corps, about fourteen miles distant from Constantinople, on the Bosphorus. In the fall of that year Mr. Stanley presented himself at my house, and there recounted the story of the robbery of himself and companions. He said that they had lost all their means, travelling equipage, clothing, &c., and that they were in great destitution. The fact was apparent, for Mr. Stanley had no shirt and no collar, and nothing but his outer garments (for I don't think he had any socks), and he looked more like a beggar than a foreign traveller. He passed the night at my house, and I gave him some clothing. In the course of our conversation I questioned him about the necessities of himself and companions, and in the morning, without his naming any sum himself, I gave him an order on my banker, Mr. Azarian of Constantinople, for 150 English pounds. Stanley made no particular promise of repayment, and I gave him the money as a matter of charity, trusting that some time he would repay me.

"He then voluntarily offered to give me a draft for the amount on his father, who, he said, was a lawyer at 20 Liberty St., New York. He made it out and handed it to me. He then went to Constantinople.

"Were Cooke and Noe present at this interview?" asked the reporter.

"No," said Mr. Morris, "they were not with him at that time. With this money, as I understood, they bought some clothing, for when I saw Stanley next at Constantinople he was well dressed."

"In a navy uniform," asked the reporter.

"Yes," said Mr. Morris, "a kind of semi-navy officer's coat and vest, with gold lace on the sleeves, and Turkish buttons, the same as seen in the picture. I understood from Stanley that it was his intention to return direct to America. He left Constantinople unexpectedly to me, and without calling and taking leave. I thought it rather strange in view of the manner in which I had befriended him, that he should not at least come and announce his intended departure and take leave; but on further consideration I did not think it was remarkable, in view of the general traits I had observed in him. He was brusque and even rude in his manners, and I came to regard his abrupt departure without calling on me as wholly consistent with his odd ways. Noe went with him. Mr. Cooke remained behind, as his presence was necessary at Broussa to give further evidence at the trial of the Turks, who were charged by them with the robbery."

"What amount did Stanley tell you they had been robbed of?" asked the reporter.

"While he remained in Constantinople," said Mr. Morris, "I told him that he must make out a statement of their losses on paper, naming each article separately, and carrying out its approximate value, which statement he must deliver to the Secretary of Legation, and must make an affidavit of its correctness, and that the statement must be made in duplicate. All this was done. Mr. Brown is since dead, and, by the way, I will say that he always suspected Stanley, and had no confidence in him whatever."

"Do you recollect what Stanley said he had lost—what amounts of money and what articles of property?" inquired the reporter.

"Yes, generally," said Mr. Morris, "there were various articles of clothing, guns, &c. Then I recollect particularly he stated that they had three cartridges boxes in which they had $300 in American gold —each box holding $100. I thought it very strange that they should be traveling in Asia Minor with American coin."

"Did he say anything about a letter of credit?" asked the reporter.

"Oh, yes," said Mr. Morris; "that was a matter that seemed rather strange also. He spoke about a draft that he had on a merchant in Tiflis, in Persia, of which he had been robbed. I asked the particulars about it and he said that it was a draft drawn in his favor by a correspondent or merchant in Maiden Lane, New York, having relations with a Tiflis house. I suggested that as the draft had not been recovered from the robbers, he had better write to Tiflis and inform the party on whom it was drawn of its loss, and thus prevent the person who had possession of it from collecting it through somebody who should personate Stanley. I thought it a rather remarkable circumstance that a New York house should have commercial relations with Tiflis, and was only able to account for it upon the supposition that there were large exports of wool from Pote on the Black Sea, which came from Caucassus and Georgia, and thought it not improbable that through this trade to the United States commercial relations might exist between an extensive New York house and a concern as far distant as Tiflis. The fact of these wool exportations gave color to his statement."

"Do you recollect the amount of the draft?" asked the reporter.

"I know it was a very large sum," said Mr. Morris—"over a thousand dollars, considerably, and I don't know but two or three thousand. The way the conversation arose about the draft was this: He told me of the $300 in American gold that they had lost, and I remarked that they had not money enough to more than carry them to Tiflis. He then said that they had provided for that contingency by this draft, upon which they were to realize when they reached there."

"Can you recall the amount of the losses as claimed by Stanley?" asked the reporter.

"My impression," said Morris, "is that the amount collected was equal to $1,200 or $1,500. Stanley, as the representative of the party, made out this detailed statement, as I have mentioned before, and signed it. I don't know whether Cooke and Noe signed it or not. I will not say positively that it was verified under oath, but I feel confident that the verification was in the nature of an affidavit. I know that my instructions to the Secretary of Legation were to take the statement and have it properly authenticated. Cooke remained for two or three weeks, if I recollect aright, after Stanley and Noe had gone, and with a knowledge of the claim that I was to make on the Turkish Government for the losses they had sustained, as stated in Stanley's statement. Cooke never intimated that the statement was not correct, and never until Noe's statement did I suppose there was the least question as to the claim having been made in good faith. Indeed, I can hardly believe now that it was a fraud, and I will explain why. First let me say that Cooke told me that in case Stanley did not repay the loan I had made he would pay it. I suppose that he, knowing that Stanley had committed a wrong in giving the draft to me on his father, felt conscience-stricken, he being a recipient of a portion of the money, and that knowing that the draft was worthless, he was in duty bound to see that I was reimbursed. My impressions of Cooke were that he was an honorable and trustworthy man, but possessing rather negative traits of character. It was generally understood that he was the treasurer, and bore the expenses of the party. Soon after the robbery a Rev. Mr. Van Lennep, residing at Smyrna, wrote to me about it. The trial of the Turks on the charge of robbery took place at Broussa, and the proceedings confirmed Stanley's story. Through the courtesy of the British Ambassador, Lord Lyons, the British Consul at Broussa, Mr. Sandison, who had resided in Turkey perhaps twenty-five years, at my request attended the trial. He was conversant with such proceedings, and my impression is he speaks the Turkish language fluently. I believe that the Rev. Mr. French, an American missionary, was also present at the trial, which resulted in the conviction and sentence of the Turks. This result fortified Stanley's statement, and it seems to me to be almost impossible that Noe's charge of highway robbery against Stanley can be true without the fact having been brought out on the trial. At any rate, I put in a claim in their behalf against the Turkish Government, and it was for some time discussed between me and the authorities, off and on, until somewhere about the month of August, 1867, when the then acting Minister of Foreign Affairs, Safvet Pasha, came to me and said that they did not wish to have a shadow of difficulty with the American Legation, and in a spirit of amity they were willing to settle this claim if I would consent to a reduction, and he offered, I think, 20,000 or 30,000 Turkish piasters less than the original claim. Safvet Pasha and I were personal friends, and he was a strong friend of mine in the Ministry. Liking the spirit in which he had approached me on this subject, I said that in the same spirit I would reciprocate the friendly feeling he had shown, and I accepted the offer. He told me that in a few days he would give me a draft on the Ottoman Bank for the money."

"Stanley in his letter to the *Levant Herald* stated that their loss was 80,000 piasters," said the reporter.

"I don't think the claim presented amounted to so much as that," said Mr. Morris. "Twenty-three Turkish piasters are equivalent to an American dollar. Eighty thousand piasters would be considerably over $3,000. Allowing for the reduction, I think the amount received from the Government was equal to $1,200 to $1,500."

"What was the result of the draft for £150 that Stanley gave you?" asked the reporter.

"That," said Mr. Morris, "I sent to Mr. Perkins of Philadelphia, who had the care of my property interests during my absence. He sent it to New York for collection, and it came back protested, with the statement that no such man as the drawer could be found. Before Stanley left he directed me, if I succeeded in recovering anything from the Turkish Government, to send it to Mr. Cooke, whose address he gave me. Mr. Cooke asked me to reimburse myself for the loan and interest out of the money collected, or in case of Stanley's failing to pay or my inability to collect anything, he would himself pay me. When I got the money I took out the £150 and the loss by exchange, charging no interest, and sent the residue of the amount collected to Mr. Cooke. My directions were for him to aportion it among the party as it should be, as I didn't want to deal with more than one person in reference to it. I subsequently got a letter from him acknowledging the receipt of the money."

"When did you next hear from Stanley?" inquired the reporter.

"I never heard anything of him," said Mr. Morris, "until one day— I don't recollect the year, but I think 1869 or 1870—I know it was after the Abyssinian war—a gentleman, Prof. Herrman or Harriman of Dickinson College, called upon me at the legation, and after some conversation, he stated that he had been travelling with a gentleman named Stanley, who had confided to him the fact that I had once done him a great kindness, which he had requited in a most discreditable manner, and Mr. Stanley had requested him to call upon me and pay the amount I had loaned him, with interest in full. I told the gentleman that was all settled—that I had collected the amount of their losses from the Turkish Government and had reimbursed myself. He was surprised to learn it after what Mr. Stanley had stated to him, and then he said that Mr. Stanley was desirous of having an interview with me to make personal apology, and he asked me if I had any objection to seeing him. I said I had not, and I would be glad to see him. Mr. Stanley at that time was stopping at the Hotel de Bysance. He called on me and after some pleasant conversation he asked me if I still had the draft. I told him that I believed I had. I regarded it as so much waste paper, and did not know but I had thrown it in the waste basket; but on looking in my secretary drawer, I discovered it among some loose papers. I told him also that I had paid myself out of the amount I had received from the Turkish Government. He asked me if I had any objection to his destroying it. I told him I had not and he took the draft and tore it up.

"He said in extenuation of his act that he was at the time in a state of destitution, and did not know what to do. He asked me if I had spoken of the matter to the people. I did not care to tell him much about the currency which the fact had obtained, but it was pretty well known in Constantinople. I think he asked me then if I would give him a writing stating that he was not liable to me in any way, and was satisfied with his conduct. I told him I had no objection, and I did give him some kind of writing, and very likely it may be produced some time. I will say that I found Mr. Stanley then a changed man, much more frank and loyal in his bearing. He was changed in his manner and was riper in his mind and character, and I became very favorably impressed with him. He was at my home frequently, and was very entertaining in his accounts of Abyssinia."

"You say," said the reporter, "that Stanley sent Prof. Herrman to you after the Abyssinian war with the statement that Stanley had authorized him to pay you the amount of the draft. That must have been as late as 1869. Here is a letter from Stanley to Noe, dated April 30, 1867, in which he says, 'Full compensation has been awarded us for goods received and for the abominable outrage on you.' "

"It is possible," said Mr. Morris, "that Stanley knew I had been paid when he sent Prof. Herrman to me. After that I got him letters from the Russian Ambassador, Gen. Ignatiff, to the civil and military authorities of Caucasus, and to the members of the diplomatic corps at Tehehran, in Persia. He subsequently went on a tour into Caucasus, Georgia, and Persia, and wrote very interesting letters. I was sorry to have heard these accusations against him, for I felt that if he had succeeded in finding Dr. Livingstone—I was in doubt at first whether he had—his antecedent career ought to be forgotten. As for myself, I have none but the kindest feelings toward him, and never had, though, of course, I was disappointed when I learned from America that he had given me a worthless draft, and particularly as I had not asked him for a draft at all."

The reporter thanked Mr. Morris for the statement he had made, and with a polite good-by took his departure.

H

STANLEY TO JAMES GORDON BENNETT
NO. 8 DUCHESS STREET, PORTLAND PLACE, LONDON
SEPT. 13, 1872 [1]

Dear Sir—Your agent in this city to-day kindly sent me three copies of a newspaper published in the city of New York, bearing the dates respectively of the 24th, 30th and 31st of August of the present year.[2] It would be a difficult matter for me to describe the conflicting emotions I felt during the perusal of certain articles found therein. My first feelings were those of profound astonishment at the discovery of so debased a character as this wretched young man, Noe, turns out to be. He proclaims himself the victim of a foul and unnatural outrage, gives his name in full, with his present address; he dwells

1. *NYH*, Sept. 26, 1872.
2. *The Sun* of Aug. 24, 1872 contained the letter of Noe of Aug. 16; *The Sun* of Aug. 30 and 31 contained editorials and other information against the character of Stanley and his meeting with Livingstone.

fondly on the disgusting details which unmanned him; offers himself up voluntarily to public scorn and contempt, and deliberately stamps himself as the greatest moral idiot in existence. I then felt regret at discovering the fact that there was a newspaper in the city of New York which could lend itself for the publication of such a disgusting, immoral letter as the one purporting to be written by Lewis H. Noe, and exhibit a morbid delight in every circumstance and detail of this most shameless story.

To enter upon a detailed refutation of the various charges and accusations falsely levelled at me by this eccentric youth would be undignified and unworthy of me; it would but serve to bring the contemptible newspaper and its unmanly correspondent into greater prominence than they deserve. I content myself with simply asserting that the statements of this man Noe, in so far as they refer to me, consist of a series of the most atrocious falsehoods that the most imaginative villain could have devised to the detriment of any one man's reputation.

They are oft-recurring questions to me, "Wherein have I incurred any man's hostility? Why should people attack my private character? How have I injured any person so much as to induce him to villify me in this manner?" It is with the utmost confidence that I can reply that, intentionally, I have never injured any living man.

In the summer of 1866 I took this boy as a kind of companion, who was to make himself generally useful. A few miles east of Smyrna the young rascal set fire to a valuable grove belonging to some Turks, who were so enraged at the incendiary act that myself and companions were in danger of our lives; upon which, after mollifying the anger of the natives, I punished the young villain with a few strokes of a switch, a far lighter punishment than he deserved, as any sensible man will at once admit. Near Chihissar the chief of a gang of brigands which infested the environs of Ofium-Karahissar insulted him, upon which, in my indignation, I struck him with my sword. He immediately raised such an outcry that I was compelled to order my companions to mount and hurry away; but, in our ignorance of the country, we rode direct into the neighborhood of the robbers' den, and were consequently captured without much trouble. The indignities and outrages which the ruffians subsequently visited upon a member of our party need not be repeated here, but I may mention that I was the one who was instrumental in relieving my party from all apprehensions of a worse fate. Now possibly this boy —now a man in years at least—remembers the slight flogging I administered to him, and, stung by the memory of it, has proposed to himself that the author of it, having in some way distinguished himself by the discovery of Dr. Livingstone, might now be made to feel his resentment, and proceeds to do so by investing him with a Satanic character; with all the attributes of a "bold and unscrupulous, daring, but intelligent and specious adventurer." Positively, if I thought the young wretch who wantonly set fire to the Turk's grove near Smyrna and endangered his own and our lives was insane, I think him ten times more so now by hurrying into print, to glory in his shamelessness and make public what the most debased courtesan in any great city would never have published. But enough of this abominable fraud, with his series of absurd fictions. Let me dilate a little on the accusations levelled at me.

About the Livingstone letters you know yourself, sir, as well as your former agent, that I was utterly ignorant of the commission you gave me at the Grand Hotel in Paris before you delivered to me instructions regarding it. Captain Francis R. Webb, late Consul at Zanzibar, now residing at Salem, can tell you, as an impartial witness, how I set about the work you requested me to perform. Mr. Spalding and Mr. Morse, both of whom are at this present moment in New York, can also add their testimony to it. Mr. John Bertram, the great merchant at Salem, can also inform you, whether or not he honored the drafts I drew on you. Dr. Kirk, also—with whom I have at present an unpleasant difference about the aid he says he freely gave Dr. Livingstone, but which I say that he did not give so freely as is generally believed—can inform you whether or not he saw me at Bagamoyo preparatory to marching for the interior. Also the *Journal des Débats* of Paris states that Mr. de Vienne, then Consul of France at Zanzibar, acknowledges to have seen me on that island preparing my expedition. Apropos of Mr. de Vienne, it is said that this gentleman "described me as rather eccentric in my way of doing things; that I refused everybody's advice and was consequently reduced to my own resources." This gentleman unconsciously gives me high praise by saying so; for it seems to me that I thus avoided the rock upon which the English Livingstone Search Expedition split. Lieutenant Dawson had too many advisers, and therefore failed. Had he not acted according to the advice of Dr. Kirk, Lieutenant Dawson had surely succeeded. When Mr. de Vienne says that I refused everybody's advice he refers to my having refused Dr. Kirk's advice to go up the Rufiji River, which was a round-about way of going after Dr. Livingstone, which no sane man would have adopted.[3]

3. Stanley was in the midst of his quarrel with Kirk.

I have stated that I found Livingstone in Ujiji, just returned from
the Lualaba; that I obtained two letters from him, one addressed to
"James Gordon Bennett, Esq., Junior," and the other addressed to
"James Gordon Bennett, Esq., New York Herald;"[4] that to neither of
these letters have I put pen or pencil; that I neither interpolated nor
suggested one word, phrase or quotation to Dr. Livingstone while he
was writing them; that I knew not what he had written until he had
finished writing them and handed them to me, asking me, "Will
those do?" That I delivered them to your agent, whom I met at Mar-
sailles, precisely as the letters were written by Dr. Livingstone. What
I have stated above I will adhere to until Dr. Livingstone shall himself
come to England and publicly proclaim the fact himself. As for the
authenticity of the other letters which I brought with me Lord Granville, of the Foreign Office;[5] J. B. Braithwaite, Livingstone's Solici-
tor;[6] Thomas Steele Livingstone, the Doctor's eldest son;[7] Miss
Janet Livingstone, the Doctor's sister;[8] Miss Agnes Livingstone,[9] Captain Black, of the Peninsula and Oriental Company,[10] Mr. James
Young, of Durris House, near Aberdeen;[11] Dr. John Kirk, Her Brit-
tanic Majesty's Consul at Zanzibar; Rev. Horace Waller, the Doctor's
friend, have one and all come forward to testify to their authenticity.
In the letters to his children Dr. Livingstone speaks of things with
which no living person, least of all an American newspaper correspondent, could possibly be cognizant of. In his letter to the Foreign
Office the Doctor writes of countries that were wholly unknown to
any one east of the Lake Tanganyika, that no fancy, however fertile,
could have imagined. Again, the Queen of England advised by her
Ministers, has signified her approbation of my conduct by sending

4. The letters are given in NYH, July 26, 1872, July 27, 1872, Aug. 24, 1872.
5. Earl Granville (1815–1891). See Fitzmaurice, The Life of Granville George
Leveson Gower Second Earl Granville.
6. J. Bevan Braithwaite (1818–1905), a Quaker friend of Livingstone. J.
Bevan Braithwaite. A Friend of the Nineteenth Century (by his Children),
especially 193–99, 222.
7. Thomas S. Livingstone (1849–1876). Northcott, Moffat, table opposite p.
328; Seaver, Livingstone, 115, 468.
8. Janet Livingstone (d. 1895). See Fraser, Livingstone and Newstead,
179; Seaver, Livingstone, 16, 36.
9. Agnes Livingstone Bruce (1848–1912), Livingstone's daughter. See Bartholomew, "Mrs. Livingstone Bruce and the Scottish Geographical Society."
10. Thomas O. Black, an agent in India for the Peninsula and Oriental
Line. LLJ, II, 6.
11. James Young (1811–1883), manufacturer and inventor. He was an old
friend of Livingstone and used his wealth to aid the explorer. Boase, Modern
English Biography, III, 1,574–1,575; Seaver, Livingstone, 25, 466; PRGS 5
(1883), 354.

me a gold snuff box enriched with over sixty diamonds,[12] and a letter of thanks, signed by Lord Granville; she has also received me most graciously at Dunrobin Castle, the seat of the Duke of Sutherland, and has taken the opportunity of thanking me in person. Now, is it possible that the British Ministers could be so thoroughly deluded as to advise Queen Victoria to send me such a testimonial, or to receive me in person through any appearances whatever other than genuine? Can any imposture, however consummate, however daring, hope for such success?

I might ask, also, how was it possible that I could have obtained the "Lett's Diary," full of observations and geographical notes, which I delivered over to Miss Agnes Livingstone, and which precious property lies now in the strong room of a Glasgow bank? How come I possessed of the Doctor's chronometers and watches, for which I have the receipt from Admiral Richards,[13] of the Hydrographic office, London.

But if, after the receipt of this letter, there may be unbelievers still, my advice to them is to form another expedition for Central Africa and find· out from Livingstone himself whether the letters I brought are genuine or not. Then, perhaps, if they live to come back to tell their story, they must bear witness to my veracity at least, if to nothing else. In the meantime, sir, I would ask whether you ever found cause to repent of your confidence in me, or had reason to suspect in the least my truthfulness and integrity? If you can conscientiously answer "No!" I shall feel amply rewarded and need no more.

P.S. I have omitted to mention the fact that I have seen in an American newspaper some account of an article which has appeared in an Omaha paper derogatory to me. This Omaha paper can only be the Omaha *Herald*,[14] whose local editor—"Little Mac" by name —I kicked publicly for slander and threats.[15] This local editor had

12. See the amusing reference in Bennett, "Stanley and the American Consuls at Zanzibar," 57–58.
13. George H. Richards (1819–1876), hydrographer to the Admiralty. Boase, *Modern English Biography*, III, 138–39; Clowes, *Royal Navy*, VII, 564–67, 574.
14. The Omaha *Herald* denied this, affirming it had always supported Stanley. *NYH*, Oct. 1, 1872.
15. F. M. MacDonough, editor in 1872 of the *Nebraska Watchman*, replied to Stanley's charges in *The Sun*. He gave his version of the fight (see Introduction) with Stanley and went on to say he never had believed Stanley had found Livingstone since "I knew that his Colorado letters to the *Missouri Democrat* were written in a one-horse newspaper office in Omaha." *The Sun*, Oct. 21, 1872.

me brought up before the Mayor, Charles Brown,[16] for assault and battery. The jury returned a verdict of "Not guilty," and "Little Mac," besides suffering the indignity of a vigorous kicking in his rearward parts, was compelled to pay "costs." If any one doubts this let him examine files of the Omaha *Republican;* let him ask Governor Butler, of Nebraska;[17] Major Balcombe,[18] Judge Strickland,[19] Mayor Brown, and he will receive a complete confirmation of the fact. It is but natural, therefore, that the Omaha *Herald* should bear me a grudge.

I

LEWIS NOE TO THE EDITOR OF *THE SUN*
Sayville, L.I., Sept. 30, 1872 [1]

Sir: The *Herald* of the 26th inst. contains a letter from Henry M. Stanley, dated the 13th, which attempts to reply to the charges made by me against him in my communication published in THE SUN of Aug. 24.[2]

"A short horse is soon curried," and I can dispose of Stanley's reply in a very brief space.

I stated in my letter referred to:

1. That Stanley was a deserter from the United States Navy in 1865, and induced me, a boy, to desert with him.

2. That he forged a pass while the frigate *Minnesota* was lying at Portsmouth, N.H., by which we were enabled to pass the gates of the navy yard.

3. That he tried to induce me to become a bounty jumper.

4. That a year afterwards he falsely represented to my parents and myself that he possessed the means to go on an extended tour in Asia, and induced my parents to consent to my accompanying him.

5. That on learning at Smyrna the desperate character of the journey he had projected—he being utterly without means—because I

---

16. Charles H. Brown, sometime mayor of Omaha. Sorenson, *Omaha,* 278–80.

17. David Butler, Governor of Nebraska, 1866–1871. Olson, *History of Nebraska,* 130–31, 150–59.

18. St. A. D. Balcombe (*d.* 1904), editor and owner of the Omaha *Republican.* Sorenson, *Omaha,* 430–31.

19. Silas A. Strickland (*d.* 1878); in 1876 he was U.S. District Attorney for Nebraska. *Ibid.,* 343–45.

1. *The Sun,* Oct. 9, 1872.

2. See the preceding letter.

attempted to leave him soon after starting, he most cruelly whipped me on my bare back.

6. That he compelled me to beg and steal the food and supplies we used during some three hundred miles of our journey.

7. That he attempted to murder an old Turk whom we overtook on the route, with a view to robbing him.

8. That though he failed to kill the Turk, he robbed him of his horses, and made me an accessory to the crime.

9. That he committed perjury at Broussa and at Constantinople.

10. That he gave a worthless draft on a supposititious father in New York to the American Minister at Constantinople, the Hon. E. Joy Morris, in exchange for money equal to several hundred dollars, which that gentleman kindly loaned him from his private means in our distress.

11. That he clandestinely left Constantinople, taking me with him, purposely avoiding to inform Mr. Morris of his intention to leave, or where we were going.

12. That he represented himself to be an American when he was a Welchman, and had always lived in Wales until he was fifteen years of age.

13. That his real name is John Rowland, and that Henry Stanley is an alias that he assumed after coming to America.

These are the baker's dozen of charges I preferred against Stanley, and I think they were sufficiently explicit. He meets them by a general denial. He says:

> The statements of this man Noe, in so far as they refer to me, consist of a series of the most atrocious falsehoods that the most imaginative villain could have devised to the detriment of anyone's reputation.

Dodging the issues I presented by a sweeping denial (except in two instances which I shall refer to further on), he attempts to distract attention from his rascality by surrounding himself with a blaze of glory for having found Dr. Livingstone. I never raised any issue on that point except upon the probabilities. I could neither positively affirm nor positively deny the success of his search because, fortunately, I did not enjoy the pleasure of accompanying him. Once such luxury is enough for a lifetime. Learned men in Europe doubted that Dr. Livingstone could have written the letters attributed to him in view of the geographical situations described therein. Others doubted because the style of language used in those letters was, in many instances, regarded as wholly unlike that which Dr. Livingstone would use. I stated facts showing Stanley to be a heartless scoundrel, with the genius to conceive and the skill to execute a gigantic fraud; and I will add that nothing which has yet been published has satisfied me that the so-called Livingstone letters are not bogus.

In respect to the first and second charges I made I have Stanley's own handwriting refering to the facts, which leave no doubt as to their truth; and undoubtedly the records of the Navy Department will furnish corroborative evidence.

As to the third I have nothing beyond my own statement, which will be reiterated under oath whenever Stanley desires to raise that issue.

The fourth can be proven by every member of my family and by his own letters in my possession.

As to the fifth charge, Stanley says in his letter to the *Herald,* speaking of me:

"The young rascal set fire to a valuable grove" and "I punished the young villain with a few strokes of a switch," &c.

The "valuable grove" was a clump of wild briars of no value and the fire did no damage, as the land surrounding it was barren and rocky. Stanley saw me set them on fire, was cognizant of my intention to do it, and he laughed heartily over the fright it caused Mr. Cooke. The "few strokes of a switch" was a merciless whipping, inflicted after he had tied me to a tree, so that I was in a condition of utter helplessness. But I thank Stanley for corroborating my charge as far as he has, though I have a letter of his in which he states as much.

The sixth charge Mr. Cooke can confirm if he will.

The seventh and eighth charges Stanley confirms in part, and a passage in one of his letters to me furnishes another link to corroborate the truth of my statement. In his letter to the *Herald* he says:

When near Chi-Hissar, the chief of a gang of brigands which infested the environs of Affium-Kara-Hissar insulted him (meaning me) upon which, in my indignation, I struck him with my sword. He immediately raised such an outcry that I was compelled to order my companions to mount and hurry away; but in our ignorance of the neighborhood, we rode right into the robber's den, and were consequently captured without much trouble.

Stanley omits to mention that in the confusion he mounted one of the Turk's horses, and ordered me to mount the other; and also that the "chief of the gang of brigands" was an ex-cadi of Affium-Kara-Hissar. But as this is the first time Stanley has ever published the fact he struck the Turk a blow with his sword, and thus caused our capture, I am much obliged for that confession in corroboration of my statement.

The ninth charge—perjury—is well sustained. Minister Morris required that Stanley make out a detailed statement of our losses, to be sworn to by him, that a claim of damages might be put in against the Turkish Government. This Stanley did, and, as appears by Mr. Morris's statement to the reporter of THE SUN, he included $300 in American gold, a draft on a mercantile house in Tiflis, and a variety of articles of value, making up some 80,000 Turkish piasters in value as the amount of our loss. When he made that affidavit Stanley knew that the gold and the draft never existed except in his imagination. He was also guilty of perjury at Affium-Kara-Hissar in suppressing the truth that he was the original robber, and that the robbery by the Turks, small as the extent was, was in retaliation.

The tenth and eleventh charges are corroborated by his own letters and also by the statement of Minister Morris, as published in THE SUN. Not only did Stanely [sic] have no father at 20 Liberty street, on whom the worthless draft was drawn by him, but I will add that he had no father anywhere; and if his uncle and aunt, Mr. and Mrs. Thomas Morris, of Davies street, Liverpool, are to be believed, he never had a father anywhere. This last fact I should not have alluded to (as I do not believe in visiting the sins of parents upon their children) but that he has chosen to characterize my statements as a "series of atrocious falsehoods."

The twelfth and thirteenth charges can be proven by Stanley's uncle and aunt, and by his own letters, which I have in my possession. They have been proven by Mr. Evans,[3] who knew John Rowland in Wales and knew Henry Stanley in Africa, and who says that they are one and the same person. And if Stanley will visit Denbigh, St. Asaph, or Bodelwydden, in Wales, the members of his family and numberous acquaintances there will be able to remove any lingering doubts which may exist in his mind as to whether he was born in Wales or America, whether his mother tongue is Welsh or English, whether his name is John Rowland or Henry Stanley; in fine, whether

3. An E. B. Evans had written to a British newspaper that Stanley's real name was Rowlands; he also gave details on his early life. Stanley called the letter "all bosh" and denied knowing Evans, concluding that his name was "plain Henry M. Stanley." *The Sun*, Sept. 2, 1872, Sept. 9, 1872.

I have written a "series of atrocious falsehoods" or whether he is a
first-class extemporaneous liar.

I trust that he will make the visit and publish the result in the
Herald.

J

STANLEY TO EDWARD KING
VILLAGE OF KAGEHYI, LAKE VICTORIA NIYANZA
May 19, [1875] [1]

Kagehyi is a straggling village of cone huts, twenty or thirty in
number, which are built somewhat in the form of a circle, hedged
round by a fence of thorn twisted between upright stakes. Sketch
such a village in your imagination, and let the centre of it be dotted
here and there with the forms of Kidlings who prank it with the
vivacity of Kidlings under a hot, glowing sun. Let a couple of warriors and a few round-bellied children be seen among them, and near
a tall hut, which is the chief's, plant a taller tree, under whose shade
sit a few elders in council with their chief. So much for the village.
I am sure you will know it if you come this way! Now outside the
village, yet touching the fence, begin to draw the form of a square
camp, about fifty yards square, each side flanked with low, square
huts, under the eaves of which place as many figures of men as you
please—for we have many—and you have the camp of the Anglo-
American expedition commanded by your friend and humble servant.
From the centre of the camp you may see the Lake Victoria, or that
portion of it I have called Speke Gulf, and twenty-five miles distant
you may see table topped Magita, the large island of Ukerewe, and
toward the northwest a clear horizon, with nothing between water
and sky to mar its level. The surface of the lake, which approaches
to within 100 yards of the camp, is much ruffled just at present with
a northwest breeze, and though the sun is glowing hot under the
shade it is agreeable enough, so that nobody perspires or is troubled
with the heat. You must understand that there is a vast difference

1. *NYH*, Aug. 12, 1876. The letter was reprinted from the *Boston Morning
Journal*. Edward King (1848–1896), an American newspaperman and author,
was an old friend of Stanley's; he had seen Stanley off in Paris in 1869 when
the explorer left on his Livingstone quest. *DAB*, X, 387–88; *HIFL*, xix–xx.
See also Edward King, "An Expedition with Stanley," *Scribner's Monthly* 5
(1872), 105–12.

between New York and Central African heat. Yours is a sweltering heat, begetting languor and thirst; ours is a dry heat, permitting activity and action without thirst or perspiration. If we exposed ourselves to the sun we would feel quite as though we were being baked.

Come with me to my lodgings now. I lodge in a hut but little inferior in size to the chiefs. In it is stored the luggage of the expedition which fills one-half. It is about six tons in weight, and consists of cloth, beads, wire, shells, ammunition, powder barrels, portmanteaus, iron trunks, photographic apparatus, scientific instruments, pontoons, sections of boat, &c., &c. The other half of the hut is my sleeping, dining and hall room. It is as dark as pitch within, for light cannot penetrate the mud with which the wood work is liberally daubed. The floor is of dried mud, thickly covered with dust, which breeds fleas and other vermin, to be a plague to me and to my poor dogs. I have four youthful Mercuries, of ebon color, attending me, who on the march carry my personal weapons of offence. I do not need so many servants to wait on me, but such is their pleasure. They find their reward in the liberal leavings of the table. Did they not minister to me they know they would have to subsist on their rations, and black youths have such capacity of distension in their stomaches that would shame the veriest glutton in Europe. If I have a goat killed for the European mess half of it suffices for two days for us. When it becomes slightly tainted my Mercuries will beg it and devour it at a single sitting. Just outside the door of my hut are about two dozen of my men, squatted in a circle and stringing beads. A necklace of beads is each man's daily sum wherewith to buy food. I have now a little over 160 men. Imagine 160 necklaces given for food each day for the last three months; in the aggregate the sum amounts to 14,400 necklaces; in a year it will amount to 58,400 necklaces. A necklace of ordinary beads is cheap enough in the States, but the expense of carriage makes a necklace here equal to about twenty-five cents in value. For a necklace I can buy a chicken or a peck of sweet potatoes or half a peck of grain. I left the coast with about 40,000 yards of cloth which, in the States, would be worth about twelve and a half cents per yard, or altogether about $5,000; the expense of porterage as far as this lake makes each yard worth about fifty cents. Two yards of cloth will purchase a goat or a sheep, thirty yards will purchase an ox, fifteen yards is enough to purchase a day's rations for the entire caravan.

These are a few of the particulars of our more domestic affairs. The expedition is now divided into eight squads of twenty men each, with an experienced man over each squad. They are all armed with

Snyder's and percussion-lock muskets. A dozen or so of the most faithful have a brace of revolvers in addition to their other arms.

We have had four battles since we left the coast. The first occurred in Ituru with a desperate set of savages, rivalling the Apaches in ferocity and determination. The battle lasted three days. I lost twenty-one men killed. Their loss was thirty-five killed and some hundred or so wounded. Twice we made a clean sweep through their country, burning and destroying everything we came across, and would have liked to exterminate the wretches had not my mission required my duty in another direction.

On water we were as successful as on land; but, as God is my judge, I would prefer paying tribute and making these savages friends rather than enemies. But some of these people are cursed with such delirious ferocity that we are compelled to defend ourselves. They attack in such numbers and so sudden that our repeating rifles and Snyders have to be handled with such nervous rapidity as will force them back before we are forced to death; for if we allow them to come within forty yards their spears are as fatal as bullets. Just think, I had twenty-one men killed in one day and but one wounded! The spear makes a frightful wound, while their contemptible looking arrows are deadly weapons. I have for the sake of experiment sent an arrow almost clean through a bullock at twenty yards, and the arrow head is so barbed and gashed that if a man is wounded a large piece of tortured flesh must be cut out ere it is extracted. We had a narrow escape lately. We were but twelve in our boat's crew, the savages several hundreds. As they came down to attack I ordered the boat to be shoved off, which was done so rapidly that with the impetus they had given it they were themselves carried into deep water, and only myself in the boat. I had to keep the beach clear of the rascals, and I emptied my elephant rifle, double barreled shot gun and re-volvers at them, while the men swam with the boat off shore in a water infested with crocodiles. None of us, thank fortune, were in-jured, but each of us had some narrow escape to relate from whizzing spears and arrows.

Since I left Zanzibar I have travelled 720 miles by land and 1,004 miles (by computation) by water. This in six months is good work. Over 100 positions settled by astronomical observations—for you must know that from the very day I got my commission I strenu-ously prepared to fit myself for geographical work, in order that I might be able to complete Speke, Burton, Baker and Livingstone's labors, which they left undone. Now Speke's work is done. What he commenced I have finished. I do not know whether you comprehend the drift of this expedition, but I will explain.

You must know that Speke, in 1858, came to the southwest end of Lake Victoria, and from a hill near the lake he discovered the vast body of fresh water. Having gazed his fill he returned to England and was commissioned to find its outlet. In 1861 and 1862 he marched from Zanzibar to Uganda,[2] when he saw the lake again. At the Ripon Falls he saw the lake discharge itself into the Victoria Nile, and went home again imagining that he had done his work. If his work was merely to find the outlet of Lake Victoria he completed his task, but if his task was to discover the sources of the Nile he had but begun his work. He went away without discovering the feeders of Lake Victoria, which in reality are the Nile's sources. Extreme southern sources, I mean. Then Baker came to Central Africa and discovered Lake Albert. He voyaged sixty miles on the lake, and he ran home also without knowing everything of the lake's sources. Burton went to Tanganyika, saw it, and returned home without knowing its extent, outlet or affluents. Livingstone came next to the chain of lakes west of Tanganika, and died nobly in harness. Well, we are sent to complete what these several travellers have begun. While they are content with having discovered lakes, I must be content with exploring these lakes and discovering their sources, and unravelling the complications of geographers at home. It is a mighty work, but a fourth of that work is already done. Until I can say I have done the half, I bid you farewell.

K

STANLEY TO EDWARD KING
NYANGWE, MANYEMA
Oct. 31, 1876 [1]

Just recall to mind the time when I related in your ears what Livingstone spoke of Nyangwe. Just think, if you can, of what I gave you as my opinion of that old, brave explorer, and glance at the

2. The test reads Ugawa.
1. NYH, Oct. 14, 1877. The letter is reprinted from the Boston Morning Journal. The original of the letter is in the Houghton Library, Harvard University—bMS Am 1518 (2077).

name of the town or depot at which I write from. It is in east longitude 26 deg. odd and south latitude 4 deg. 16 min. It is not far from the ocean, east and west of this sable continent. Well, two or three days ago I reached here after a quick march of forty days. Livingstone took a much longer time to reach it, but what of that; I do not wonder at it at all. He was aged and broken-hearted, but though my hair is fast turning gray I am young. I have been all the time I have been here reminded of the old man Livingstone, and I wonder more than ever as I begin to grasp in my mind the difficulties he labored under, at the terrible determination which animated him. Pity, not unmixed with admiration, is the prominent feeling in my mind. Poor Livingstone! I wish I had the power of some perfect master of the English language to describe what I do feel about him. I wish I could say verbatim what the Arabs say of him, and tell you of the anxious looks the amiable natives of this region cast toward the road leading from the Indian Ocean, looking wistfully for news of him. But he will never return to be greeted by his dark children of Manyema.

Do you know, King, that I have a faint idea people in England and America did not quite understand the man? Of course, they have not said in plain terms that the man was a "humbug," but it is strongly impressed on me, somehow, that they think he did not write as he really felt—which must be, that they felt, in plain English, that he was something of an old hypocrite. God forgive them for such vile thoughts. In this prosaic age I have not heard of or seen a man more worthy of honor from his white brothers, and I am certain I will die in that opinion. Perhaps you are also of the above number, and therefore I will stop; only I will say this much: Were you in my place to-day I think you would entertain the same high opinion of this matchless man as I have.

This place is the farthest reach of Livingstone; it is also the place whence Cameron struck southwest in company with some Portuguese traders. They were both eager to follow this river, but circumstances opposed them. I have discovered what these were, and I am fully resolved to take advantage of my discovery, to settle this question of the Lualaba forever. If I do settle it, there should be no blame attached to either Livingstone or Cameron that they left the task for me to do. Indeed, I feel rather grateful to Cameron, for if he had followed this great river to the ocean I should be inclined to ask him, should I ever meet him, like Baker asked Speke—"Why was this laurel wreath not left for me to pluck?"

If I fail and am driven back I have some comfort, and I may ask, "Why they blame me and not blame my predecessors?" But don't imagine I am going to be driven back. I can die, but I will not go back. I anticipate trouble and many disagreeable things—possibly the digestion of myself in some cannibal's stomach—but I cannot picture to myself the idea of me standing, hat in hand, explaining personally to the proprietor of the NEW YORK HERALD why I came back without fulfilling my promise. There is one thing which I must tell you of. I have not boasted of what I was going to do. I remember distinctly to have written from Ujiji—"I do not know what is left for me to do. I shall be better able to tell you when I reach Nyangwe." Meaning, of course—if you don't know it—that whatever task Cameron had left me to do I would try to do, for until I came here I was sure a gallant fellow like him would do his very best to follow the river.

Should I live to reach the ocean I cannot imagine what part of it I shall come out at. This Lualaba is not the Nile. I will stake every hope on that. It has not such an altitude as Livingstone gave it by 1,000 feet. I can only make it out 1,454 feet above sea level. Livingstone has got it somewhere about 2,300 or 2,400 feet, which is a wide difference. It is the same way with the Tanganika and Lake Victoria. Speke and I agree pretty nearly. Granted that it is not the Nile, what river is it? It may be the Niger; if not the Niger then certainly the Congo. Suppose the former, when do you think I could reach the western ocean? In 1879 or 1880, unless it was clear sailing down the river? Mungo Park, I know, lost his life on that famous river and Stanley may lose his. I hope not, but I am quite ready for anything.

It is a curious thing how the climate of Africa so tries the temper of a man that he does not care very much what will become of him. He is so worried and tortured and annoyed that he begins to feel by and by, after some months of it, that the best thing for him would be eternal, dreamless rest. I dare say, if I could fly over to New York and enjoy one good meal, that I would instantly abandon such melancholy ideas, but as I must "bore through," like an auger, before I can enjoy that satisfactory meal, and as I must "bore through" for many months to come, I find myself dwelling on such melancholy things oftener than is consistent with courage or manliness.

Let us drop the subject. The event or result will decide all. The unknown half of Africa lies before me, involved in mystery. It is useless to imagine what it may contain, what I may see, what wonders may be unfolded. I am eager for it. I feel myself straining like on a leash. I have solemnly told my people that "God has written that this year the great Lualaba and the unknown half of Africa shall be revealed." I am a prophet—at least I am imbued with a vast amount of enthusiasm just now—but I cannot tell whether I shall be able to reveal it in person or whether it will be left to my dark followers.

In three or four days we shall begin the great struggle with this mystery, but first I thought it would be a relief to me if I could sit down and begin telling you a few of my thoughts and shake hands, mentally, across the great gulf which separates the friend of my soul from me. God bless us all.

L

STANLEY TO EDWIN ARNOLD
Undated [1]

You may lay as much stress as you please upon the fact of having discovered the Shimeeyu, the extreme southern source of the Nile so far ascertained. The Thames approaches to the Shimeeyu in volume, breadth & length. Even should the Albert extend 1° S of Equator it cannot have a feeder extending any distance South as the Tanganika is in the way.

Extreme reach of the Shimeeyu is in S. Lat 5°13′ which is nearly the paralel of Ujiji.

I have discovered a group of Islands—uninhabited—which I have called Telegraph Islands, the principal of which is Levy Island, about 12 miles from Bennett Island, Lat 2° South.

Fortune so far has followed me. Pray dear Sir that it continues . . .

P.S. What was it the *D.T.* said long ago about my meeting with Gordon's people—the singular meeting—four or five days apart—one from Egypt—the other from the far South-East—flush of valuable discoveries which he sends home to the dear *D.T.*

Bellefonds is my courier.

I am in perfect health thank God. The Nile Source atmosphere makes me more strong & increases my energy.

En Avant Gentlemen.

1. PM. Edwin Arnold (1832–1904) was chief editor of the *Daily Telegraph* at this time. *DNB*, XXIII, 58–60.

M

STANLEY TO EDWARD LEVY
UJIJI
August 13, 1876 [1]

I must congratulate you and Mr. Bennett upon the Success which has hitherto attended your Joint Expedition. The Discoveries made by it begin to crowd on you, because we have lately been in the midst of a region where they might have been looked for.

Your leaderwriter on the subject of the Alexandra Nile need have no fear or hesitation, but boldly assert & declare so far as is consistent with the Contents of my letter, and in my opinion he cannot do better than—for his own satisfaction—imagine those Nyanzas out of the way altogether, and the several Niles then would be one great continuous river taking its *principal rise* a little West of Southwest of the position given to Alexandra Nyanza.

This is no sensation, nor Nile madness, for I assure you I do not care so much about the sentimental glory of discovering the Nile, except as it conduces to the glory of those who sent me. I am clear-headed enough to perceive that of all previous travellers I have gained supreme vantage, and authority by my systematic & exact explorations. I do not—like Speke, Baker or Livingstone—rush into interesting corners, but I soberly begin at the extreme South source, the Shimeeyu, & follow it from its natal marsh to the Lake Victoria.

I then circumnavigate this recipient of sources and search for the river which supplies it principally. I discover it to be the Kagera & explore it up from the Lake, following its course, sounding & measuring it, with all its erratic water basins, and after about 200 miles of its course have been thoroughly examined during which it does not appear to lose any great quantity of its volume, I set on foot systematic inquiry, which lasts over an interval of five months and find it creates Lakes above still higher and that a very large river comes to the Alexandra from the W.S.W. direction.

Very well—I do not then rush away home to tell the news, but I continue South to find out where the Tanganika's waters flow to, because if by accident my predecessors were wrong in the altitude of the Lake, it might be that the Tanganika supplied with its efflux an affluent to the Nile of greater importance than the Alexandra Nile even.

1. PM. Edward Levy-Lawson (1833–1916), son of Joseph Moses Levy, owner of the *Daily Telegraph*, and later owner himself. *DNB*, XXIV, 331–33.

But what is the result? The Tanganika has no outlet as yet (strictly) and its altitude is too low to have connection with the Nile. I thus have cut off conjectures & their cause—by this rounding these lakes overland & by water—for nothing can come from South of Tanganika.

To complete my right and title what have I still to do? I must cross Tanganika to Manyema—and from Nyangwe take an E.N.E. course to hit and cut off all water supply to that intermediate region lying between the north of Tanganika and the south of Albert Nyanza. If at some distance from the spot I discover the watershed separating what the Lualaba basin receives and what must be received by a river lying East—that river must be an affluent of the Nile waters. If this Nile affluent has a general course in the direction of the region between Tanganika and Albert—that such an affluent is the Alexandra Nile.

Ask yourselves which would you do were you in my place—follow the Lualaba to a known point & complete Livingstone, or strike up towards this interesting point, & discover the Nile source? One road only can be taken for the goods will not last longer. Then which?

I will tell you a secret idea of mine—judge for yourselves whether it be a good one.

I think that were I to strike from Nyangwe on a N E by N course, to Munza's discovered by the German *Schweinfurth,* I would resolve both Nile and Lualaba, for as I travelled North all streams to my right must be received by the Nile, all to the left by the Lualaba. The distance is only 540 geog[raphical] miles, and according to my rate of travel could be traveled in 5 months—provided there are no *obstacles* of a serious nature.

It is time that another difficulty would present itself then. We should be far from aid, with diminished resources, and my home & my people's home lie opposite ways. My people would wish to return, I should want to go on North to join Gordon.

By going down the Lualaba along the right bank I should be completing Livingstone, & settling the Nile so far as this river has any relation to it. I should be going towards home and the Falls of Yellala are 660 miles from Nyangwe. On reaching the Falls I should have to equip my men anew for their return journey to Zanzibar, or take them down the Congo to be sent round the Cape or through the Mediterranean to Zanzibar. An expensive job.

Or I could travel down the Lualaba to Fungeno, a known point, 360 miles in 110 days, then return to Nyangwe, Ujiji and Zanzibar in person—saving expenses—but considerably tasking my own strength.

However I have to look cheerfully forward to Nyangwe and at that spot I shall consider all these things and resolve on the best course. I hope that five months from Nyangwe in any direction will be able to settle everything & finish our journey of Exploration with honor & credit to all concerned.

P.S.

We have obtained a signal triumph over Cameron, the Protégé of the R.G.S., whose attainments were said to be vastly superior to those of Burton, Speke or Livingstone & Baker—if Markham[2] was to be believed. At the Lukuga, he simply sounded the water at the end, and then vanished from the scene only taking the Chief's word that the "River went to Rua." Possibly he would have been more careful had he suspected a "damned penny a liner" for a successor in that locality.

By crossing the Lualaba and striking off in a wrong direction he has left the question of the Lualaba where Livingstone left it.

N

EDWARD POCOCK TO HIS PARENTS
ZANZIBAR
Sept. 24, 1874 [1]

I hope this will find you in good health, as it leaves us all in the best of health at present. We arrived here yesterday, after a fine passage. This place is much better than Aden. It is beautiful weather, something like England in summer, if you wasn't to see the blacks. There is plenty of oranges and all fruits. We are staying at the American Consul's. Plenty of good grub—good beef. I expect we shall be here about a week and then we shall start for the river[2] and try it, and then back to Zanzibar again, so we can write again. Africa is not half so bad as people make out—it is most beautiful; you can walk about with a jacket on and don't sweat. I have just enjoyed myself with a piece of sugarcane. We have nothing to do whatever —get coolies to wait on us for everything we want. The place is swarmed with cocoanut trees. We will send our photographs next letter. All you want here is to keep steady and not drink; you can then get along all right.

[P.S.] Direction of meals: Coffee at six A.M.; breakfast, ten; tiffin, two; dinner, five; tea, half-past six. All teetotalers.

2. Clements R. Markham.
1. *NYH*, Jan. 7, 1875.
2. The Rufiji, see Stanley's despatches, documents 12 through 14.

O

EDWARD POCOCK TO HIS PARENTS
ZANZIBAR, EAST COAST OF AFRICA
Oct. 22, 1874 [1]

We had fifteen days' cruise in the boat up the River Rufiji, about
200 miles along the coast. The boat handles first rate, and Mr. Stanley is very pleased with us and her and the way we sail her. The
first morning we were out Ted had the fever. He was taken in a
minute, and laid down about one hour and a half; he got up as fresh
as ever. It is just the same as the ague. I have not had a pain since
I left home. We sailed up the coast and anchored at Darra Salaam
on the 2d.

3d. Started at daybreak up coast.

4th. Started at daybreak; anchored at Rawley Island.

5th, Sunday. Arived in mouth of River Rufiji; anchored at Sani-
zore.

6th. Started at seven A.M. up river. Fresh water four miles up;
hippopotamus and alligators in great abundance; thickly populated
with good-tempered people, most of whom ridiculed the idea of us
wanting to see the river. The chiefs came off to barter for physic;
they are Arabs, the men which buy and sell the slaves; they thought
first we were English men-of-war's men. We passed thirty villages in
one day. Chief Jumbe came to see us; his tribe is called Mtupe.

7th. Went up so far that the river was like a ditch at the foot of
the mountain. We soon went back with the tide, which is a very
strong ebb-tide; no flood-tide. About ten miles up the river is very
much like Burham reeds, very high, where the native people came
to look. Anchored at the island of Similine.

8th. Started anchor at seven A.M. Chased from three to five miles
by a hippopotamus.

9th. From the river went to the isle of Konde, in another part,
which is haunted with wild boar; a beautiful place, like a prairie.

10th. Left Simbo; wind south-southeast, light. There are several
ways into this river; one is about half a mile wide; channel deep.

11th. Visited Choguin, a little island; plenty of wild chicken; enormous turtle.

12th. Started at eight A.M. toward Mafia Island; got milk, eggs, and
fowl, then proceeded to Choguin; anchored at sunset; went on shore
to bathe.

1. *NYH,* Jan. 7, 1875. Pocock gives Lufiji in place of Rufiji in his letters.

13th. Mr. Stanley went on shore to sketch the place, and then we got under way to go home; wind southwest by south; under way all night. Came to anchor off Burgamoya.[2] Layed all night; this place is opposite Zanzibar, on the mainland; it is about thirty miles. Thank the Lord, the river is done! Although a fine place, it is very unhealthy about the many marshy parts; but we have no more to do and we have our health first rate. Me and Ted have to take the boat with goods and people a distance of thirty miles. Mr. Stanley is so pleased to think he can trust us. I pay the slaves we have to work for us cleaning the boat out or anything else that is to be done. The men work all day very hard for twelve pice, that is three annas—four and a half pence. The people here are all fasting for fourteen days on account of the new moon. I cannot say if we shall go away before the next mail. If so the letters will be forwarded over to us. We shall stop on the mainland three weeks before going in the interior.

P

FRANCIS POCOCK TO HIS BROTHER
ZANZIBAR, EAST OF AFRICA
Oct. 22, 1874 [1]

I write with a light heart to send you good news, and that is we are enjoying the best of health, and I hope this will find you all the same. We arrived here on the 21st of September. Since then we have had a cruise of fifteen days to the River Rufuji, which is 200 miles south of Zanzibar. I cannot tell you all that occured in the river; but we went about 120 miles up to the foot of a mountain. It took us three days to get there. We were ten miles farther up the first day than other white men had been. On the second day Chief Jumbe (his tribe called Mtupe) came to barter, brought chicken and rice, plenty of cocoanut, eggs, goats and fruit, and plenty of fights, too. There were thousands to see us, with spears and arrows. One of the chiefs was coming off in our small boat, and Ted sounded the bugle. He jumped overboard flying, afraid of it, but there were thousands looking through the reeds, all ready for a spring had we not hoisted the flag. There is a great deal of slave trade done here, and the Arab masters thought we were an English man-of-war boat. We were six

2. Bagamoyo.
1. *NYH*, Jan. 7, 1875. F. Pocock also writes Lufiji for Rufiji.

days on the river, which is thickly populated with a good sort of people at the lower part, and all of whom ridiculed the idea of our wishing to see the river. We were chased from four to five miles by an hippopotamus—a very large one. It was a hot chase. We fired two bullets at him, which glided off him. He seemed to come on top of the water like a leopard on shore. When he got close enough we put two bullets in his breast, which made him turn. They are very numerous in the Rufiji, as well as alligators. After we had explored the river we went to several islands along the coast. Further south, one we went to was strewn with wild chickens and enormous turtles; another with goats; another with coral and crabs. It is very dangerous on the coast, so many reefs and sands. Me and Ted take the boat to the mainland, a distance of thirty miles, with goods and people for the journey.

Mr. Stanley is much pleased with us in the way we handle the boat. He is a good man to be away with. We share just as he does in everything. We get on proper here. Ted blew the bugle to the Sultan of Zanzibar. He was very much pleased. We went to an evening party on Monday evening, and shall go to-night on board Her Majesty's ship *Thetis*,[2] where Ted will perform. We have plenty of everything. We have just the same as Her Majesty's service and the American Consulate, where we are staying.

Q

FRANCIS POCOCK TO HIS PARENTS
SECOMIA
May 15, 1875 [1]

I told you I think it will be December before we reach Ujiji, because Colonel Gordon is going to lend us a steamer as far as she is any use, and some men as far as Ujiji. The weather on the road was very changeable, which is the cause of so much illness. You think it thunders very heavy in England, but it is nothing to this. It shakes everything fearfully, and when it rains it is a complete deluge. It is now the wet season. Between the showers the sun is enough to burn the hair off your head; but we don't have to be out. I have had

2. H.M.S. *Thetis*, Captain Thomas Ward, was active against the slave trade in East African waters from 1873 to 1877. Clowes, *Royal Navy*, VII, 264, 278–79.
1. *NYH*, Aug. 14, 1876. The expedition was then at Kagehyi.

three months' rest, with the best of food; but it is not like the food in England. Rice is a great luxury. There is plenty of meat—goats, sheep and bullocks—but it does not do to eat too much meat. You can buy two sheep for a piece of cloth six feet by three. The cloth is sheeting. Money is of no use—beads, cloth and shells. For one strand of beads, which cost one farthing at home, will get about one gallon of sweet potatoes. Bananas are not very plentiful here. We get plenty of good fish. The natives of this part do nothing but lie and walk about all day. The women till the ground. The men wear strings of shells around their arms, and brass wire around their legs, and beads around their waists, and a goatskin slung across their shoulders. That is a fine dress; but most of them are quite naked, but none without a weapon of defence. They dance and sing, and get drunk on their beer, called pomby. This village belongs to the Sultan of Zanzibar, and there is one man, a slave of his, called Songoria.[2] During the time Mr. Stanley was away I had several presents, such as rice and sheep. I took food with him, which is a great honor to a black man to feed with the Mosonga, or white man.

I can't get on with the language much. Mr. Stanley can speak it as well as he can English; but there is a fresh lingo about every twenty miles, which all our men cannot understand. The captain of our men can talk all of them.[3] He is such a nice man; he is like a father. When we were in a desert he went twelve miles among wild beasts for water for the white men, a turn I shall never forget. I dreamed the other night that I was at home eating fine things, but I awoke and found myself in Central Africa. We have been 4,975 feet above the sea. We are now 1,308. That is the position of the lake.[4] It is splendid water here, which is very healthy. This is an awful country to forget; you lose all understanding. If you want to remember anything you must write it down. I am sure poor Ted's death was not in my mind one hour. It is the way with everybody. Of course a thought crossed my mind very often, but not to think of it. The Lord gave me strength to bear with it. There is so many changes that you can't think of everything. My dear parents, I am not certain of this letter reaching you from here, so that I will not write to any one else until we get to Uganda. If this should get home first, you must send it round to the family. If I write to one and not the other, it will not be right; but I will write again when there is better conveyance. The letters that go from Uganda go down the Nile

2. Sungoro Tarib.
3. Manwa Sera.
4. Lake Victoria is 3,720 feet above sea level.

and through Egypt, so that I shall be sure of them going home. When you write send long letters, for only a few words would come very acceptable. I have not seen or heard a white man since we left the coast. That was on the 1st of November. Give my love to all. Kiss all the children for me. I will write more next time. Tell Harry to save me a piece of cake. I have no more to say just now, so I must conclude with love to all. I am your affectionate and loving son.

R

FRANCIS POCOCK TO HIS PARENTS
LAKE VICTORIA NIYANZA
undated [1]

I dare say you think it strange not hearing anything of me. I am afraid you will hear too soon of my dear brother. I will not enter upon that, as you will know all about it. We received your letters the day after we left the coast, and were very glad to hear such news. Since then I have seen some changes, I can tell you. Sometimes without food, sometimes with plenty; sometimes wet weather, at other times dry, it is a feast or a famine with everything. I have had the fever about twelve times; but, thank God, I have got over it. I have not had it now for two months. I am now more used to the country. I have good health now to what I did.

We had rough times of it after poor Ted's death. What with fighting and long marching, it almost turned me up. We arrived here on February 27, after a journey of 103 days from the coast. When I saw the lake my heart leaped within me at the sight of the water. We were coming over a large hill, and one of the natives ran back to me and said, "Bana! bana!" (which is "Sir") "margey! (water) margey!" [2] The master was behind, so that I saw it before him. I am the third white man that ever saw the inland sea,[3] it is 1,026 miles around it, plenty of fish and crocodiles, hippopotami and birds on the shores. Plenty of islands. Me and Ted had one each, Barker one and many others, which will be on the map when issued.[4] Mr. Stanley was fifty-seven days gone in the boat to find the source of the Nile. He has been successful in his undertaking. Where Ted died

1. *NYH*, Aug. 14, 1876. Pocock was at Kagehyi.
2. *Bwana. Maji.*
3. Pocock was the fourth European—after Speke, Grant and Chaillé-Long.
4. See Map II and *TDC*, I, 226.

was the very spot where the Nile flows from. It was strange that he should say what he did. In about fifteen days after that we crossed the south arm of the Nile in the boat—the first English boat ever there. When the natives at the lake saw the boat and three white men they were surprised. They are quite wild; they are naked, but civil. We travelled 170 miles where no other white man ever was. That was where we had to fight. You will hear of it in the papers.

Dear parents, after we leave here we go to a beautiful country called Uganda. Mr. Stanley stayed fifteen days with the King while going round the lake. In fact, all the countries are healthy we are going to. We have a steamer waiting for us, with Mr. Gordon, at Lake Albert Niyanza. Our work is over one-third done; the worst is over; all the countries we go to now have plenty of food, cheap. I have plenty to tell you when I come home, if God spares me to come, which I hope He will. Frederick Barker died on April 25. I was left with 166 men. I was in charge all the time Mr. Stanley was away, but when he was gone I had no one to talk to or to ask advice. When Mr. Stanley came back he was very much pleased the way I had discharged my duty. He told me all about the trip in the boat, and many other things. He says we shall be home in about eighteen months. All the letters you or anyone else has sent will be forwarded on to Ujiji, so that I shall get them there, but that will not be before December. Dear parents, wait with patience, and you will see me come home with honor. I expect it seems a long time to you, but it seems like yesterday to me. I am in good health and happy. My thoughts are ever on you all, and my prayers are for you. I have had trouble, but I have borne up against it. Mr. Stanley says: "Frank, you are the coolest man and the happiest I ever saw." I don't know the exact time we shall leave here, but the King of Uganda has sent eighty canoes and 500 men to take us to his country. He is a Christian. Mr. Stanley said he was sorry to leave him; he is so fond of a white man. There is a French officer at his place, and Colonel Gordon further on, with several white men with him.

My dear parents, were you to see the hut I am now sitting in writing this you would say, How can you live there? but to-morrow we shall leave here, perhaps for no house at all. I have just had my evening meal of tea, boiled beef and banana. In my hut there are no less than nine black boys around me, asking me questions about England, and the boy that held Dr. Livingstone's hand is my servant and is as faithful as any Christian,[5] and a little boy, a slave, but now free. As

5. Majwara. See Gray, "Livingstone's Muganda Servant," 119–29; H. B. Thomas, "Livingstone's Muganda Servant—A Postscript."

soon as he came with me I set him free. I saw him pulled from his mother. He is about nine years old, quick and honest. His name is Benjamin.

My dear parents, keep my dog, Sailor, and I will pay for him when I come home. I should like to have him here to keep the natives away. They are afraid of the white man's dogs, but all our dogs are dead. I dare say you think it unkind of me not to say anything about my dear brother; but God's will be done, and I hope he is at rest. What can I say or think? All I can think I wish he was with me now.

I cannot explain to you all just now; but I hope to tell you in person some day. Mr. Stanley has made some great discoveries. I can tell you it is not all pleasure in Africa, but I hope it will soon be over, and we shall return. Remember me to everybody, and look for me in May, 1877.

P.S. My dear parents, I thought when I wrote the other sheets they would be on their way by this time, but the letters only go when there is a caravan going to Unyanyembe with ivory, so I can't say when this letter will reach you. Since I wrote the other I have had a trip of twelve days [in] the boat with ten men, to get canoes to convey our caravan by water to Uganda, which is only five days, and by land twenty. I went to an island called Ukereweway,[6] about 120 miles round it. The King is very great. I went to him. When I went near the natives were surprised to see a boat. There were thousands who never saw a white man or a boat. I was the first white man ever there. I was followed everywhere by hundreds of them. They were around the boat all day, and if I wanted them to move away I only had to get out of her. Men, women and children are very near all naked. They are a fine race of people—the King as fine a looking man as I have seen in Africa. When I went to him he sat on a large stone with, I should say, 2,000 people around him, all armed with something. I went with nothing in my hands nor my men, so that he should think we were friends. He had me to sit down beside him and my boy to speak at our feet. He looked at me and smiled; he touched my hair, and then wanted me to show it all.

When I took off my hat the people all laughed, but I did not mind that, as it would not do to get out of temper. Then he looked at my shoes, which surprised him very much. He laughed and talked about my dress. He had about twenty fathoms of light brass wire round his legs and large rings on his arms, beads on his neck and a

6. Ukerewe.

fine cloth—nothing on his head—that is the custom. A fine made man; he stands six feet or more. His name is Lukongu. He and his people are very kind. As soon as I asked him about the canoes he said I should have fifty the next day, but I had to stop six days for them to be repaired. He gave me two fine bullocks; he sent me milk night and morning (it was fine milk) eggs and bananas, which are very plentiful; for miles it is nothing but banana trees. The women brought me flour, but not like that at home; sweet potatoes and tobacco. I gave him presents—a gold ring and an Albert chain, a black necklace and some cloth. I gave him a rug—one color one side and another the other. That surprised him more than all. When I returned I had forty-seven canoes, but they went back the next day and the master with them. Dear parents, I have no more to say about the King. I remain your affectionate son.

S

FRANCIS POCOCK TO HIS PARENTS
UGANDA, LAKE VICTORIA NIYANZA, CENTRAL AFRICA
August 14, 1875 [1]

I dare say you think the time long since we left home. Twelve months yesterday we left our native land. I wrote a letter two months ago, but I cannot say which will be home first. We have crossed the great lake in canoes to escape a savage country. We arrived at the lake on February 27, 1875, and did not leave until June 19. We then conveyed some goods and men to an island in the sea uninhabited, where I was left in charge again until the remainder of the men came. We then worked from one island to another until we fell in with some Uganda canoes that was sent to find the white man during the time Mr. Stanley was surveying the lake, and he went to an island to buy food. They took the oars out of the boat and told him to perish in the Niyanza. With our canoes and the Uganda we went there to fight, and killed about forty or more, and not one of us got a scratch. We returned to camp, on a small island near it, with joy. Our comrades had made ready with songs and shouts. The next day we went to the main land, where food was abundant. Bananas are the main food of the natives. They keep cattle, but seldom kill one, because they are their riches. They brought the

1. *NYH,* Aug. 14, 1876.

white men milk, eggs, coffee, &c. As soon as we landed the natives all ran away.

The King of Uganda is a fine man. Mr. S. and Robert,[2] his boy, brought up in the mission at Zanzibar, almost made him a Christian. Mr. S. leaves me here to-morrow to visit him—five days' journey. I have lent Robert my Bible to read to him. My dear parents, you would like to see our camp. It is built like a street through the forest of banana trees. There is hardly anything else here but them and tobacco, which serves for grass. If Africa were all like this I could live in it for years. Our food for the white men comes from the King. Some parts of the country grows sweet potatoes and other things which are very nice. I never ate fruit in England so nice as bananas. Eat as many as you like, they never hurt anyone. All our men live on them. I weigh nearly twelve stone; my health is good; I am strong and fat. If you were to see me now you would say I was a negro. I have not had fever since April, and then very slight. I can speak a little of the lingo, and I have better health than Mr. Stanley. There is not one man in the caravan but will do anything for me, through not beating them, and not playing with them, but keeping them in their place. If a man steals I punish him accordingly—that is when I am in charge; but when the great master, as he is called, is in camp, he does as he likes. As soon as Mr. S. returns from the King we shall travel across to the other lake—Albert Niyanza—eight day's journey; and if the steamers belonging to Colonel Gordon are not finished their work and taken to pieces we shall make good way on our journey. I long to get to Ujiji to hear from you, and if the Almighty spares me to come home, I can tell you plenty I have seen —men of all colors, some savage, others more quiet. The people of Uganda go on their knees to us. They bring food for nothing. Dear parents, you must tell all the people the news.

Tell Harry and all that are not married, if they got spliced while I am away, to save me a piece of cake, and to find me a wife. Tell the people all round that I send my respects. I cannot write, as I have no more paper or envelopes. I hope to spend a better Christmas than last, for I never saw it rain so hard as it did on the eve. We lay in camp on Christmas Day, but that made no difference. All day we were drying clothes. Plain rice—we had not meat for six days—for dinner.

2. Robert Feruzi. Feruzi later served with Stanley in the Congo. On his return to Zanzibar he became one of the principal Africans in the service of the Universities' Mission. See Jones-Bateman, "Our Work in Zanzibar Town," 41; *Central Africa* 4 (1886), 190; Maurice, *Stanley's Letters*, 141.

That was in the country of Ugogo. Don't forget to make some wine, if possible. We expect to be home about Christmas, 1876. My thoughts are ever on you all. Brothers and sisters, remember me always as I do you all. Pray for me that I may come home and reap the harvest of hard marches, lonely nights and hot days, savage tribes and hard beds. Dear parents, I thought of sending some money, but I find it will not pay. If you could find a friend to lend you a few pounds, my money shall pay it back. If I do not come, you will have the money that is due to me. George sent me a beautiful letter. You must tell him to give my respects to all friends. I remain your loving and affectionate son.

T

FRANCIS POCOCK TO HIS PARENTS
ANGLO-AMERICAN EXPEDITION, CENTRAL AFRICA
April 18, 1876[1]

My heart yearns to you and home. It is now one year and five months since I heard a single word from you. I received your letters the day we left the Coast. Since then Mr. Stanley received some papers from Colonel Gordon at Gondokoro, in Egypt, and that is all we know about our homes. God only knows what has happened. There is no one knows the Pococks here or Cookham Woods. I wrote a letter to you and Bill when we arrived in Uganda. Mr. Stanley was gone to the Sultan. Three months I was left alone with the goods. We were in Uganda five months—a land flowing with milk and honey. We then went to the Albert Niyanza through Unyoro, escorted by 2,000 Waganda sent by the Sultan. We thought of seeing some white men at the Albert Niyanza; we reached there and saw the lake, but had to retreat in great haste. We marched for sixteen days from two o'clock in the morning until sunset—hungry and thirsty, weary, foot-sore; and when we halted we had no bed, but lay on the ground. I became very sick from fever, which I thought would have carried me off. But my time was not come. On the road we passed a fine mountain crowned with snow,[2] and many beautiful streams feeding the Niyanza.

1. *NYH*, Aug. 14, 1876. The expedition was in Sukuma territory.
2. Gray points out that Stanley may have missed seeing the snow of the Ruwenzori; in *TDC*, I, 427, Stanley does not use Pocock's information. John Gray's letter in *UJ* 18 (1954), 77.

I cannot say anything about the people. All I know, they are bad. They train large dogs to fight like tigers. We left Uganda on January 1, 1876, and returned to Uganda on the 17th. When we reached Uganda the Waganda left us and we travelled on to Karagwe. We crossed the Kagera River, the main source of the Nile, and drank of its waters. When we reached Karagwe we fell in with some Arabs —a lucky hit. We discovered a lake here eighty miles by thirty. There are also hot water springs near the fall of the Kagera River, the springs, six in number, boiling. We left Karagwe in March for the Wilderness of Nine Days. While we were at Karagwe I visited the King, to show him the boat. He asked me was we English? I said, "Yes." He said, "Speke was English, and he was a good man; so you must be good also." Speke travelled here fifteen years ago; his name is all the rage in Uganda and Karagwe. We are now in the country of Usambiro—good people and plenty of food.[3] We have been nearly a month in Wilderness, with but little food. An Arab has travelled with us to here; he leaves us here for Unyanyembe, and we go to Ujiji—about one month's march. The Arab will bring our letters to the Coast. I hope when we reach Ujiji to find some letters and papers from home. I am sometimes lonely. I have no one to talk to but black people. Although I can talk Swahili nearly as well as English, I can't find anything in their company to amuse me. There is no comfort in this part of the globe—hot sun and cold nights. We have crossed rivers and swamps, up to our waists in mud and water, for days and days. Then, when we reach camp, there is no kind sister to make your bed; but a nigger would throw down a lump of grass as you would to a pig. Then our food is like cattle food in England. It consists of dried beans and peas, and Matama corn, such as donkeys eat. What would I give now for an old crust such as you give to sailors or some pudding, properly cooked. But no one knows about that here. If you cannot eat, go without.

But, thank God, I enjoy good health. It is now three months since I had fever. I am strong and fat. In some places white men are thought cattle, in another they are great. There are many tribes of fine men, dressed in embogu bark cloth.[4] Many are naked; many are dressed in skins put about their shoulders. Many have long hair, others plait it in a thousand plaits, with beads sewn on; while the people of Uganda shave all off, and carry two spears and one shield, and the people of Karagwe use bows and arrows, and the people of

3. Busambiro, a Sukuma chiefdom.
4. *Mbugu.* See Roscoe, *The Baganda,* 403; Felkin, "Notes on the Waganda," 729.

Usui use one spear with which they spear a man or an ox—they don't throw it—while the people here use guns.

My dear parents, I have no doubt you think me lost; but no, I am still alive and hope to see you all. I can not write to all, and you are at the head, so you must cuppa salaam ymugo[5]—that is, give my love to all the family. Kiss the children and give them my blessing. Names are too numerous to mention.

My dear parents, be comforted and fret not for me, for I have a good Providence over head, in which I put my whole trust. No one knows of going to church here—every day is alike. The natives lay about all day and at night sit by a great fire. Some houses are grass, some are mud, with sticks. I often think, Are all well? Yes, they can't get ill in such a country. There is plenty of food, plenty of doctors and medicine. Here there is nothing but wild people, bad food and an unhealthy country, hard marching through mud and water or hot sand. Are all well in grain at Ashford? I remain your loving and affectionate son.

U

FRANCIS POCOCK TO HIS BROTHER
UJIJI, LAKE TANGANYIKA, CENTRAL AFRICA
July 20, 1876 [1]

It is a long time since I received your interesting letter. I was glad to find and to hear I had such friends that took such an interest in my welfare. Your letter contained words that at the time my tongue could not thank enough. I handed the letter to Ted without saying one word—my heart was full—and Ted handed it back to me with tears of joy in his eyes, and said, "Brother, we are not forgotten." We were then in the bush, and all the letters received there were good letters of comfort and joy. But since then I know nothing. That was in November, 1874.

The countries we have travelled through contain some curious people. About five or six days after Ted's death we had a fight in the country of Uturu—the people, a fine race of men and women, entirely naked. We arrived in camp in the afternoon. The natives brought food to barter for beads. We and our men made trade with them,

5. *Wape salaam zangu.*
1. *NYH*, May 7, 1877.

and our guide from the neighboring tribe made brotherhood with
the Sultan, and all went on well. One of our men was left in the
road, sick. He had a small piece of red cloth on, through which
he lost his life at sunset that evening. The next morning men were
sent back to seek him. The next day they returned and reported that
they saw where he was murdered, the footprints of the people in
the struggle and a piece of the red cloth. We decided on marching
the next morning, but, persuaded by the chief, we stopped. The people
were very kind and brought a bullock. It was killed and eaten before
we knew their custom. This is to make friends by giving the animal,
and if certain parts of this are not returned they fight.[2] But nothing
seemed wrong until one of our men was shot in the arm with an
arrow, and another was run through with a spear and killed. Their
arrows were coming in the camp. It was time to defend ourselves.

For four days we were fighting; we lost twenty-three men and ten
muskets. But the loss on their side was great; they had no guns, but,
brave fellows, they fought well for three days; then it grew too warm
for them. They were to be seen running to their villages among rocks,
while a few hung about close to our camp. Our men were very excited, and began setting fire to their villages, looting their stores.
Parties were sent to plunder and set fire to the houses; they did so,
too, for our camp was soon loaded with food, such as matama, peas,
beans, ground nuts, millet, maize, chickens, eggs, goats, sheep and
two bullocks, pomby (beer made of matama), honey, matama flour,
bows, arrows and spears. On the fourth day, in the evening, there
was none to be seen—not a man! At the first of the fight the savages
were as thick as bees in a hive, and as fast as they were shot down
they were carried away. On the morning of the fifth day, about two
o'clock, we mustered the men and crept away through bush and
swamp and encamped in a fort constructed by nature as if for shelter
for us. The massive heaps of granite stone on all sides protected our
weary bodies from the cold east wind, and all fear was gone.

We had found a good harbor. The next day we entirely lost the
savages, or they had lost us. Soon after leaving camp Mr. Stanley
saw a road, and this was the very road we wanted; but the natives
would not disclose the secret of this road from the first. In an hour
after finding the road we came to a river—an arm of the Nile, with
a current like a sluice, but narrow and deep. We put two sections of
the boat together after getting a rope across. This was done by a
man going far above the crossing place; he thus managed to reach

2. Compare this with Stanley's account, document 18.

the other side with a small line. We bent on the boat cable, rove through a coil of wire, and in three hours the whole caravan was on the other side, and in three days more we reached Magonga Tembo (Elephant Back)—for such is the name of the village, also of the prince, and these few lines are all I can say at present about the skirmish with the Uturu. I am no penman to explain anything with pen and ink, therefore I hope you will excuse me for this attempt. If I have the good fortune to come back I can tell you more.

Mr. Stanley left here on the 11th of June to explore the lake, and has not returned yet.

I have been sorry a thousand times I could not see you before leaving home, but I hope to see you on some fine day in May, 1877. I little thought of having such a journey as this when you left us at the factory. I little thought that Ted said "Goodby," then, for the last time; but God's will be done! I have no doubt his death was felt at home very much by all; but what must I have felt to leave a brother in such a country that we dare not say our heads were our own for an hour?

The natives were around us like wolves the night he died, thinking something was amiss; but they could not find out his grave. We had to bury him in the dark under a mambu tree[3] in the camp; Mr. Stanley performed the service, with the Wanguana kneeling around him. But the next morning we heard no more the sound of Ted's bugle—it was gone, and that was very sad. Our people were awakened to a fresh day's toil and trouble by a native's muffled drum instead. In the time of "Mabruki"—such was my brother's African name—his morning bugle call was always loud and strong, and many smiles from the Wanguana greeted him, for he was the favorite of all in camp. Even now I often hear the people of an evening, sitting around the camp fire, talk of "Bana Mabruki," what a merry fellow he was.

If Harry is married I hope he won't forget this poor castaway; truly castaway we are from the world. No white face to be seen, but all black and savage.

My dear brother, I hope you are not at a loss for some one to make your street lively at night. There is plenty of noise here at night, though different from the noise at home. Here I hear always the roar of the sea on the shore of wild Tanganika, or some poor wretch screaming for mercy who is being beaten by a slave dealer.

In my opinion they think it a fine deed to beat a poor, ill-fed

3. Perhaps a misprint of mango, or of *mbuyu* (the baobab).

woman, with a child sucking at her breast. The cruelty carried on here is dreadful to look at and to hear of. The Wali of Ujiji[4] only a few days ago put a poor creature to death for staying in the fields after work was over. He thought that she wanted to desert. He only thought so.

The Arabs come to our house and ask me all sorts of things about the slave trade, and want to know why do the English try to put down the slave trade. "They say why don't you buy and sell slaves, and make yourselves rich, as we do?" I told them English people had a better way of getting rich than buying and selling people like goats and cows. I asked, "Was man made to be bought and sold in that way, and was man made to toil in chains, carry donkeys' loads, sleep in the open air like dogs, to be lashed like horses, while you sit inside and receive the worth of their labor, and not return enough food for them to eat—no, not half enough?" They say, "English people are good, but why should they stop the slave trade and ruin us" (the Arabs)? If I offend or please by my plain speech I don't know, but I am English, and you know an Englishman's blood is not quiet at slavery; therefore he cannot help saying what he thinks, and in such a country as this it makes him feel proud he has such a home as England to boast of. But, my dear brother, we will return to another subject.

We left Karagwe on March 25, and arrived here on May 27—a very long march, with but a short time to do it in. Where we shall go to from here I must inform you in another letter, but we hope to reach one coast or the other very soon. On arriving here I was seized with dysentery. I got over that and I was then seized with fever, which nearly ended my days; but no, my time was not come; for by the hand of Providence I got well, and here I am, without hardly a shoe in which to tread the scorched, burning soil of Africa. But I hope to pull through and reach home in about May, 1877, and then if the cottage has some liquor we can drink health to the Stanley Expedition. Are all well at home? I often think of you all, and that is the most I can do. There are no merry fellows here, none of those laughing faces I have so often seen, no kind mother or father, or sister or brother.

But all is for the best. I wish not to return until enough work is done to repay our toils and troubles and those who sent us.

The slaves in Ujiji are the most degraded class and the most wretched I have seen in Africa. They are ill-fed and beaten, eaten up

4. Mwinyi Kheri.

alive with itch and scurvy, and they are driven like cattle to work in the fields and to build houses. If such work does not want help from the English it is not wanted at the coast or anywhere. Then, again, the barbarous deeds carried on with the natives.

If a fine lad or a fine young woman dies someone is supposed to have bewitched him or her. The tribe is mustered amid clouds of smoke from a wood fire under a large tree, then an old wizard man comes to the crowd, who has just emerged from the thickets of some hill, where he says he has had communication with the Sun or Moon. All are seated on the ground and silent. The old man is dressed in a fine tiger's skin, with the teeth hung on his neck, which they say contain his power of witchcraft. He mixes a certain kind of herb, and they all drink, and he goes off in a swoon. When he recovers all look eager on him to see who killed their son or daughter. By this time the witch tea, as I call it, takes effect, and whoever this affects most is the culprit, and is despatched with knives into eternity.[5] Do these people not need some light? "For all the land is foul with monstrous wrong and desolation of the sons of hell."

Then, again, the Wanguana—meaning free people—are, half of them, slaves of Arabs. Although they know white men, and know there is a God, and know and have seen the coast, ships and different things, yet they are nearly as wicked and ignorant as man can be.

They believe in all kinds of witchcraft, buy and sell slaves, and many of them are slaves themselves. In the evening one will assert he knows of a village in such a country where a man can turn himself into a tiger, and kill all the people that make great medicine so as he should be the great doctor. Such is the talk around the camp fire. We left the Victoria Niyanza and travelled through Uganda, and on January 1, 1876, we entered the country of Unyoro, totally unknown to any European eye. We travelled on for several days, not seeing a single person. They had gone to earth, for they are like rabbits, and they live chiefly underground. In time of war they put their cattle and women underground while the men fight. They have large dogs, which they train to fight. They also dig elephant pits, and holes to catch men. Several of our men were caught in them and went out of sight, but by screaming loud were heard and pulled out.

On the 11th day we reached within sight of the beautiful Albert Niyanza.[6] Here I was taken with a severe fever. We had travelled with an escort of 2,000 men, sent by Mtesa, King of Uganda, and if

5. Compare with d'Hertefeldt *et al., Les Anciens Royaumes,* 214–15. The "tiger" skin was probably a leopard.

6. Lake George.

they could have found a peaceable district for us to build our camp we should have waited for the other white men; but there was no place to build, as we did at the Victoria Niyanza while Mr. Stanley explored the lake. On the 12th men were sent in all directions to find a camp and report. In the evening they returned and told us that there was no peaceable place to be found and that the villages all around were full of armed men.

The Unyoro came to the Waganda camp (just within hearing) and asked, "What do you want here? Why have you brought the white men here for, but to kill us? To-morrow we will fight." There were many thousands about us waiting for us to go down to the lake and then come down on us. We saw the Waganda would desert us, therefore if we did not agree with them we should have perished by the hands of the Unyoro, so we returned to Uganda and from there to Karagwe.

My dear brother, I cannot explain all this with pen and ink. My words are all huddled together, so that I don't know which is put down first; but I must tell you in person when I come home. I can assure you I am longing to see you all. You must tell all and show them the letter. I cannot write to all. Tell *** and all the girls not to be down-hearted, for I am coming when little expected, and if the cottage is still in the wood we will give it a good African warming. I remain your loving and affectionate brother.

V

STANLEY'S DESPATCHES IN PUBLICATION ORDER

Part I. In Search of Livingstone

Document	Date Written	From	Date Published
1.	July 4, 1871	Kwihara	December 22, 1871
2.	September 20, 1871	Kwihara	July 15, 1872
4.	November 10, 1871	Ujiji	July 15, 1872
6.	December 23, 1871	Ujiji	July 15, 1872
8.	February 21, 1872	Kwihara	July 15, 1872
9.	March 1, 1872	Kwihara	July 15, 1872
10.	March 12, 1872	Kwihara	July 15, 1872
3.	September 21, 1871	Kwihara	August 9, 1872
5.	November 23, 1871	Ujiji	August 10, 1872
7.	December 26, 1871	Ujiji	August 15, 1872

Part II. The Expedition across Africa

12.	October 19, 1874	Zanzibar	December 2, 1874
13.	October 21, 1874	Zanzibar	December 3, 1874
14.	October 23, 1874	Zanzibar	December 4, 1874
15.	November 12, 1874	Zanzibar	December 24, 1874
16.	November 15, 1874	Zanzibar	December 26, 1874
17.	December 13, 1874	Mpwapwa	March 1, 1875
18.	March 1, 1875	Kagehyi, Usukuma	October 11, 1875
19.	March 4, 1875	Kagehyi	October 11, 1875
22.	May 15, 1875	Kagehyi	October 11, 1875
23.	May 15, 1875	Kagehyi	October 12, 1875
20.	April 12, 1875	Ulagalla, Uganda	November 29, 1875
21.	April 14, 1875	Mtesa's Capital, Uganda	November 29, 1875
24.	July 29, 1875	Mahyiga Island, Lake Victoria	August 9, 1876
25.	August 15, 1875	Dumo, Uganda	August 10, 1876
26.	January 18, 1876	Village between Unyoro and Uganda	August 11, 1876
27.	March 26, 1876	Arab Depot, near Karagwe	August 11, 1876
28.	April 24, 1876	Ubagwe, Western Unyamwezi	August 12, 1876
29.	August 7, 1876	Ujiji	March 26, 1877
30.	August 10, 1876	Ujiji	March 27, 1877
31.	August 13, 1876	Ujiji	March 27, 1877
33.	October 30, 1876	Nyangwe	October 9, 1877
36.	August 13, 1877	Kabinda	October 9, 1877
32.	October 28, 1876	Nyangwe	October 10, 1877

34.	November 1, 1876	Nyangwe	October 10, 1877
35.	August 8, 1877	Banyamboka	October 12, 1877
37.	September 1, 1877	Loanda	November 14, 1877
39.	September 5, 1877	Loanda	November 14, 1877
40.	September 5, 1877	Loanda	November 24, 1877
38.	September 2, 1877	Loanda	November 28, 1877

Bibliography

I. ARCHIVES

Archives des Affaires Etrangères, Paris.
Church Missionary Society Archives, London.
India Office Archives, London.
London Missionary Society Archives, London.
Musée de l'Afrique Centrale, Tervuren, Belgium.
Public Record Office, London.
National Archives, Washington, D.C.
Peabody Museum, Salem, Massachusetts.
Universities Mission to Central Africa Archives, London.
Zanzibar Archives.

II. PERIODICALS AND NEWSPAPERS

Annales de la Propagation de la Foi.
The Athenaeum.
Boston Evening Transcript.
Bulletin des Missions d'Afrique (d'Alger).
Bulletin Général de la Congrégation du St. Espirit et du Imé. Coeur de Marie.
Central Africa.
Chicago Times.
Chronicle of the London Missionary Society.
Deutsche Rundschau für Geographie und Statistik.
Geographical Journal.
Geographical Magazine.
Globus.
Home and Foreign Missionary Record of the Free Church of Scotland.
Journal of the Manchester Geographical Society.
Journal of the Royal Geographical Society.
Les Missions Catholiques.
Mittheilungen der Afrikanischen Gesellschaft in Deutschland.
Nautical Magazine.
New York Evening Mail.
New York Herald.
New York Times.
New York Tribune.
Proceedings of the Royal Geographical Society.
Sun (New York).

Sunday Mercury (New York).
Times (London).

III. BOOKS AND ARTICLES

Abrahams, R. G. *The Peoples of Greater Unyamwezi, Tanzania (Nyamwezi, Sukuma, Sumbwa, Kimbu, Konongo).* London, 1967.
———. *The Political Organization of Unyamwezi.* Cambridge, 1967.
Alpers, Edward A. "Charles Chaillé-Long's Mission to Mutesa of Buganda." *UJ* 29(1965), 1–11.
Anderson, Roy. *White Star.* Prescot, Lancs, 1964.
Anon. "Les Arabes du Haut Congo." *Le Congo Illustré* 1(1892), 130–131.
———. *A l'Assaut des Pays Nègres. Journal des Missionaires d'Alger dans l'Afrique Equatoriale.* Paris, 1884.
———. "Les Chefs Arabes du Haut Congo." *Le Congo Illustré* 3(1894), 17–20.
———. *East African Rift System.* Upper Mantle Committee—UNESCO Seminar, Nairobi, April 1965.
———. *A Guide to Zanzibar.* Zanzibar, 1939.
———. *Henry M. Stanley's American Lectures on the Discovery of Dr. Livingstone.* New York, 1872.
———. *The History of Smith, Mackenzie and Company, Ltd.* London, 1938.
———. *J. Bevan Braithwaite. A Friend of the Nineteenth Century,* by his children. London, 1909.
———. *Life & Finding of Dr. Livingstone.* London, 1874.
———. "The Livingstone East Coast Aid Expedition." *PRGS* 18(1873–74), 281–283.
———. "Mr. Stanley's Proceedings in the Lake Regions of Central Africa." *Geographical Magazine* 3(1876), 245–247.
———. "Mr. Stanley's Voyage Down the Congo." *Geographical Magazine* 4(1877), 318–319.
———. *The P. & O. Pocket Book.* London, 1926.
———. *Près des Grands Lacs.* Lyon et Paris, 1885.
———. "Le Rouki, affluent du Congo." *Le Mouvement Géographique* 1(1884), 62.
———. "Sewa Hadji." *DKB* 8(1897), 206–207.
———. *A Standard Swahili-English Dictionary.* Oxford, 1955.
———. *Who Was Who 1897–1915.* London, 1929.
Anstey, Roger. *Britain and the Congo in the Nineteenth Century.* Oxford, 1962.
Anstruther, Ian. *I Presume. Stanley's Triumph and Disaster.* London, 1956.
Arnold, Julian B. *Giants in a Dressing Gown.* Chicago, 1942.
Ashe, R. P. *Chronicles of Uganda.* London, 1894.
———. *Two Kings of Uganda.* London, 1889.
Association Internationale Africaine. *Rapports sur les Marches de la Première Expédition.* Bruxelles, 1879.
Avon, R. P. "Vie sociale des Wabende au Tanganika." *Anthropos* 10–11 (1915–1916), 98–113.
Baker, J. N. L. "Sir Richard Burton and the Nile Sources." *English Historical Review* 59(1944), 49–61.
Baker, Samuel White. *The Albert N'yanza.* 2 vols. London, 1866.
———. *Exploration of the Nile Tributaries of Abyssinia.* Hartford, 1868.
———. *Ismaïlia.* 2 vols. London, 1874.
Balch, Edwin Swift. "American Explorers of Africa." *Geographical Review* 5(1918), 274–281.
Barker, R. de la B. "Some Rivers of Southern Tanganyika." *TNR* 24(1947), 66–68.
———. "The Rufiji River." *TNR* 4(1937), 10–16.
Barnes, J. A. *Politics in a Changing Society. A Political History of the Fort Jameson Ngoni.* London, 1954.

Bartholomew, J. G. "Mrs. Livingstone Bruce and the Scottish Geographical Society." *SGM* 38(1912), 312–334.

Baumann, H., and Westermann, D. *Les Peuplades et les Civilisations de l'Afrique.* Paris, 1948.

Baumann, Oscar. *Der Sansibar-Archipel. I. Die Insel Mafia und Ihre Kleineren Nachbarinseln.* Leipzig, 1896.

———. *Der Sansibar-Archipel. II. Die Insel Sansibar und ihre Kleineren Nachbarinseln.* Leipzig, 1897.

———. *Der Sansibar-Archipel. III. Die Insel Pemba und Ihre Kleineren Nachbarinseln.* Leipzig, 1897.

———. *Durch Masailand.* Berlin, 1894.

———. "Die Station der Stanley-Fälle." *Mittheilungen der kais. und kön. geographischen Gesellschaft in Wien* 29(1886), 504–513, 647–656, 30(1887), 65–69.

———. *Usambara und seine Nachbargebiete.* Berlin, 1891.

Baur and Le Roy, PP. *A Travers le Zanquebar.* Tours, 1899.

Baxter, P. T. W., and Audrey Butt. *The Azande and Related Peoples of the Anglo-Egyptian Sudan and Belgian Congo.* London, 1953.

Beachey, R. W. "The Arms Trade in East Africa in the Late Nineteenth Century." *JAH* 3(1962), 451–467.

Beardall, William. "Exploration of the Rufiji River under the Orders of the Sultan of Zanzibar." *PRGS* 3(1881), 641–656.

Beattie, J. H. M. "Bunyoro: An African Feudality?" *JAH* 5(1964), 25–35.

———. *Bunyoro: An African Kingdom.* New York, 1960.

Beck, Walter G. "Georg Schweinfurth." *Paideuma* 1(1938/40), 285–302.

Becker, Jerome. *La Troisième Expédition Belge.* Bruxelles, n.d.

———. *La Vie en Afrique.* 2 vols. Bruxelles, 1887.

Beckingham, C. F., ed. *Travels to Discover the Source of the Nile by James Bruce.* Edinburgh, 1964.

Behm, Ernst. "Dr. Livingstone's Exploration of the Upper Congo." *PRGS* 17(1872–73), 21-33.

———. "Livingstone's Reisen in Inner-Afrika." *PM* 21(1875), 81–104, 162–193.

Behr, H. F. von. *Kriegsbilder aus dem Araberaufstand in Deutsch-Ostafrika.* Leipzig, 1891.

———. "Am Rufigi." *DKZ* 5 (1892), 139–143.

Beidelman, Thomas O. "The Baraguyu." *TNR* 55(1960), 245–278.

———. "Hyena and Rabbit: A Kaguru Representation of Matrilineal Relations." *Africa* 31(1961), 61–74.

———. "A History of Ukaguru: 1857–1916." *TNR* 58 and 59 (1962), 11–39.

———. *The Matrilineal Peoples of Eastern Tanzania (Zaramo, Luguru, Kaguru, Ngulu, etc.).* London, 1967.

Bellefonds, Ernest Linant de. "Itinéraire et Notes. Voyage de Service fait entre le poste militaire de Fatiko et la Capitale de M'tesa, roi d'Uganda. Février-Juin 1875." *Bulletin Trimestriel de la Société Khédiviale de Géographie du Caire* 1(1875-1876), 1–104.

Bellenger, H. *Lettres de H. M. Stanley.* Bruxelles, 1947.

Bennett, Norman R. "Charles de Vienne and the Frere Mission to Zanzibar." *Boston University Papers on Africa* 2(1966), 109–221.

———. "The Church Missionary Society at Mombasa, 1873–1894." *Boston University Papers in African History* 1(1964), 159–194.

———. "Edward D. Ropes, Jr., Salem Merchant at Zanzibar." Unpublished paper.

———. "Introduction," to Alfred J. Swann, *Fighting the Slave-Hunters in Central Africa.* Forthcoming.

———. "Mwinyi Kheri." In Norman R. Bennett, ed., *Leadership in Eastern Africa: Six Political Biographies.* Boston, 1968, 139–164.

————. "Some Notes on Two Early Novels concerning Tanzania." Unpublished study.

————. "Stanley and the American Consuls at Zanzibar." *EIHC* 100(1964), 41–58.

————. *Studies in East African History*. Boston, 1963.

————. and Brooks, George E. Jr., eds. *New England Merchants in Africa*. Boston, 1965.

Bentley, W. Holman. *Pioneering on the Congo*. 2 vols. Oxford, 1900.

Bere, R. M. "Exploration of the Ruwenzori." *UJ* 19(1955), 121–136.

Berger, M. "Oral Traditions in Karagwe." *Proceedings of the East African Institute of Social Research Conference, June, 1963*.

Blohm, Wilhelm. *Die Nyamwezi. Gesellschaft und Weltbild*. Hamburg, 1933.

————. *Die Nyamwezi. Land und Wirtschaft*. Hamburg, 1931.

Boahen, A. Adu. *Britain, the Sahara, and the Western Sudan, 1788–1861*. Oxford, 1964.

Boase, Frederick. *Modern English Biography*. 6 vols. London, 1965.

Böhm, Richard. *Von Sansibar zum Tanganjika*. Leipzig, 1888.

Bojarski, Edmund A. "The Last of the Cannibals in Tanganyika." *TNR* 51(1958), 227–231.

Bontinck, François. *Aux Origines de l'Etat Indépendant du Congo*. Louvain and Paris, 1966.

Boone, O. "Carte Ethnique du Congo Belge et du Ruanda-Urundi." *Zaïre* 8(1954), 451–465.

Bösch, Fr. *Les Banyamwezi*. Munster i. W., 1930.

Bourgeois, R. *Banyarwanda et Burundi*. 2 vols. Bruxelles, 1957.

Bourne, H. R. Fox. *The Other Side of the Emin Pasha Relief Expedition*. London, 1891.

Bouveignes, Olivier de. "L'Arrivée de Stanley à Boma en 1877." *La Revue Colonial Belge* 36(1 Avril 1947), 200–204.

————. "Deux lettres inédites de Stanley sur le façon dont il découvert Livingstone dans l'Afrique Centrale." *Brousse* 1–2(1947), 9–40.

————. "Tuckey et Stanley." *Zaïre* 5(1951), 31–44.

Brain, J. L. "The Kwere of the Eastern Province." *TNR* 58 and 59(1962), 231–241.

————. Letter on the Doe. *TNR* 57(1961), 238.

Brard, Pater. "Der Victoria-Nyansa." *PM* 43(1897), 77–80.

Bridges, R. C. "The British Exploration of East Africa, 1788–1885, with Special Reference to the Activities of the Royal Geographical Society." Unpublished Ph.D. dissertation, University of London, 1963.

————. "The Sponsorship and Financing of Livingstone's Last Journey." *African Historical Studies* 1 (1968), 79–104.

————. "John Hanning Speke and the Royal Geographical Society." *UJ* 26(1962), 25–43.

————. "The R. G. S. and the African Exploration Fund, 1876–80." *GJ* 129(1963), 25–35.

Brode, Heinrich. *Tippoo Tib*. London, 1907.

Brodie, Fawn M. *The Devil Drives. A Life of Sir Richard Burton*. New York, 1967.

Brom, John L. *Sur les Traces de Stanley*. Paris, 1958.

Brown, G. Gordon, and Hutt, A. McD. Bruce. *Anthropology in Action*. London, 1935.

Brown, Robert. *The Story of Africa and Its Explorers*. 4 vols. London, 1892–1895.

Broyon-Mirambo, Phil. "Note sur l'Ouniamouézi." *Bulletin de la Société de Géographie de Marseille* 1(1877), 254–263.

Brunschwig, Henri. *L'Avènement de l'Afrique Noire du XIXe siècle à nos jours*. Paris, 1963.

Bunyan, John. *The Pilgrim's Progress,* Edited by James Blanton Wharey; second edition revised by Roger Sharrock. Oxford, 1960.

Burdo, Adolphe. *Les Arabes dans l'Afrique Centrale.* Paris, 1885.

————. *Les Belges dans l'Afrique Centrale. De Zanzibar au Lac Tanganika.* Bruxelles, 1886.

Burssens, H. *Les Peuplades de l'Entre Congo-Ubangi.* London, 1958.

Burton, Isabel. *The Life of Captain Sir Richd F. Burton.* 2 vols. London, 1893.

Burton, Richard F. *The Lake Regions of Central Africa.* 2 vols. London, 1860.

————. "The Lake Regions of Central Equatorial Africa . . ." *JRGS* 29(1859), 1–454.

————. *Two Trips to Gorilla Land and the Cataracts of the Congo.* 2 vols. London, 1876.

————. *Zanzibar,* 2 vols. London, 1872.

————. Letter of Oct. 19, 1875. *Geographical Magazine* 2(1875), 354–355.

————, and Macqueen, James. *The Nile Basin and Captain Speke's Discovery of the Source of the Nile.* New Introduction by Robert O. Collins. New York, 1967.

Cairns, H. Alan C. *Prelude to Imperialism. British Reactions to Central African Society 1840–1890.* London, 1965.

Cable, Boyd [Ernest Andrew Ewart]. *A Hundred Year History of the P. & O.* London, 1937.

C. A. M. "Sketches from Egypt. No. I. The Dahabiah." *Frazer's Magazine* 58(1858), 266–270.

Cameron, Verney Lovett. *Across Africa.* 2 vols. London, 1877.

————. "Lieutenant Cameron's Diary." *JRGS* 45(1875), 197–228.

————. "Journal of Lieutenant V. L. Cameron." *PRGS* 18(1873–74), 136–155.

————. "On the Anthropology of Africa." *JRAI* 6(1876), 167–181.

Carpenter, G. Hale. *A Naturalist on Lake Victoria.* New York, 1920.

Cary, M., *et al. The Oxford Classical Dictionary.* Oxford, 1950.

Cave, Viscountess. *Three Journeys.* London, 1928.

Cerckel, Léon. "Les Galeries Souterraines de Mokana (Monts Mitumba)." *Le Mouvement Géographique* 15(1898), 1–6.

Ceulemans, P. *La question arabe et le Congo (1883–1892).* Bruxelles, 1959.

Chacker, Eunice. "The Kerewe. Aspects of Their Nineteenth Century History." *TNR,* in press.

Chadwick, Owen. *Mackenzie's Grave.* London, 1959.

Chaillé Long, C. *Central Africa.* London, 1876.

Chamberlin, David, ed. *Some Letters from Livingstone 1840–1872.* London, 1940.

Christie, James. *Cholera Epidemics in East Africa.* London, 1875.

Clark, J. Desmond. *The Prehistory of Southern Africa.* Penguin Books, 1959.

Claus, Heinrich. *Die Wagogo.* Leipzig und Berlin, 1911.

Clendenen, Clarence; Collins, Robert; and Duignan, Peter. *Americans in Africa 1865–1900.* The Hoover Institution on War, Revolution, and Peace, Stanford University, 1966.

Clowes, Wm. Laird, *et al. The Royal Navy.* 7 vols. London, 1897–1903.

Clyde, David F. *History of the Medical Services of Tanganyika.* Dar es Salaam, 1962.

Colle, Le R. P. *Les Baluba.* 2 vols. Bruxelles, 1913.

Cooley, W. D. "Capt. Burton and the Land of the Moon, or the Lake Regions." *The Athenaeum* 1(1864), 510–511.

————. *Inner Africa Laid Open.* London, 1852.

Coquilhat, Camille. *Sur le Haut-Congo.* Paris, 1888.

Cornet, René J. *Maniema.* 2nd ed. Bruxelles, 1955.

Cory, Hans. *History of the Bukoba District.* Mwanza, n.d.

————. "The People of the Lake Victoria Region." *TNR* 33(1952), 23–29.

————. *Sukuma Law and Custom*. London, 1953.

Cory, H. and Masalu, M. M. "Place Names in the Lake Province." *TNR* 30(1951), 53–72.

Coulbois, François. *Dix Années au Tanganyika*. Limoges, 1901.

Coupland, Reginald. *The British Anti-Slavery Movement*. 2nd ed. London, 1964.

————. *The Exploitation of East Africa 1856–1890*. London, 1939.

————. *Livingstone's Last Journey*. London, 1945.

Cross-Upcott, A. R. W. "Social Aspects of Ngindo Bee-Keeping." *JRAI* 86(1956), 81–84.

Culwick, A. T. "Ngindo Honey-Hunters." *Man* 36(1936), 73–74.

Culwick, A. T. and G. M. *Ubena of the Rivers*. London, 1935.

Cunningham, J. F. *Uganda and Its Peoples*. London, 1905.

Cunnington, William A. "The Fauna of the African Lakes . . ." *Proceedings of the Zoological Society of London* (1920), 507–622.

Cunnison, Ian. "Kazembe and the Arabs to 1870." In Eric Stokes and Richard Brown, eds., *The Zambesian Past. Studies in Central African History*. Manchester, 1966, 226–237.

————. "Kazembe and the Portuguese, 1798–1832." *JAH* 2(1961), 61–76.

————. *The Luapula Peoples of Northern Rhodesia*. Manchester, 1959.

————. "The Reigns of the Kazembes." *Northern Rhodesian Journal* 3(1956), 131–138.

Cuvelier, J. *L'Ancien Royaume de Congo*. Paris, 1946.

Czekanowski, Jan. *Forschungen im Nil-Kongo-Zwischengebiet*. Leipzig, 1917.

Dahl, Edmund. *Nyamwezi-Wörterbuch*. Hamburg, 1915.

Dale, Ivan R., and Greenway, P. J. *Kenya Trees & Shrubs*. Nairobi, 1961.

Debenham, Frank. *The Way to Ilala*. London, 1955.

De Horsey, Algernon F. R. *The African Pilot*. London, 1864.

Delcommune, Alex. *Vingt années de Vie africaine*. 2 vols. Bruxelles, 1922.

Delhaise, Commandant. *Les Warega*. Bruxelles, 1909.

Depage, H. "Notes au sujet de Documents inédits à deux expéditions de H. M. Stanley." *Bulletin de l'Institut Royal Colonial Belge* 25(1954), 130–152.

De Thier, F. M. *Singhitini, la Stanleyville Musulmane*. Bruxelles, 1963.

Devroey, E. *Le Problème de la Lukuga*. Bruxelles, 1938.

————. *A Propos de la Stabilisation du Niveau du Lac Tanganyika*. Bruxelles, 1949.

Diderrich, N. "Au Lac Tanganika." *Le Mouvement Géographique* 11(1894), 23–24.

Divine, David. *These Splendid Ships. The Story of the Peninsula and Oriental Line*. London, 1960.

Doggett, Solon. *Tanganika and other Idyls*. n.p. 1881.

Doutreloux, A. "Introduction à la culture Kongo." In L. De Sousberghe et al., *Miscellania Ethnographica*. Tervuren, 1963.

Driberg, J. H. *The Lango*. London, 1923.

————. "The Lango District, Uganda Protectorate." *GJ* 58(1921), 119–133.

Duffy, James. *Portuguese Africa*. Cambridge, 1959.

Dunbar, A. R. *A History of Bunyoro-Kitara*. Nairobi, 1965.

Dundas, F. G. "Expedition up the Jub River through Somaliland, East Africa." *GJ* 1(1893), 209–223.

Elliot, G. F. Scott. *A Naturalist in Mid-Africa*. London, 1896.

Elton, J. Frederick. "On the Coast Country of East Africa, South of Zanzibar." *JRGS* 44(1874), 230–235.

————. *Travels and Researches among the Lakes and Mountains of Eastern and Central Africa*, H. B. Cotterill, ed. London, 1879.

Emin Bey. "Journal einer Reise von Mrúli nach der Haupstadt Unyóro's mit Bemerkungen über Land und Leute." *PM* 25(1879), 179–187, 220–224, 388–397.

Erhardt, J. *Vocabulary of the Enguduk Iloigob*. Ludwigsburg, 1857.

Evans-Pritchard, E. E. *The Position of Women in Primitive Societies and Other Essays in Social Anthropology*. London, 1965.

————. "Zande Cannibalism." *JRAI* 90(1960), 238–258.

Fallers, Lloyd A. *Bantu Bureaucracy*. Cambridge, 1956.

————. ed. *The King's Men*. London, 1964.

Fallers, Margaret Chase. *The Eastern Lacustrine Bantu (Ganda and Soga)*. London, 1960.

Farwell, Byron. *The Man Who Presumed. A Biography of Henry M. Stanley*. London, 1957.

Faupel, J. F. *African Holocaust*. New York, 1962.

Felkin, Robert W. "Notes on the Waganda Tribe of Central Africa." *Proceedings of the Royal Society of Edinburgh* 13(1884–1886), 699–770.

Findlay, Alex. Geo. "On Dr. Livingstone's Last Journey and the Probable Ultimate Sources of the Nile." *JRGS* 37(1867), 193–212.

Fischer, G. A. "Bericht über die im Auftrage der Geographischen Gesellschaft in Hamburg unternommene Reise in das Masai-Land." *Mittheilungen der Geographischen Gesellschaft in Hamburg* 5(1882–1883), 36–100, 189–279.

————. "Einige Worte über den augenblicklichen Stand der Sklaverei in Ostafrika. Brieflich an Dr. Reichenow von Dr. med. G. Fischer in Zanzibar." *ZGEB* 17(1882), 70–75.

————. "Vorläufiger Bericht über die Expedition zur Auffindung Dr. Junkers." *PM* 32(1886), 363–369.

Fishbourne, C. E. "Lake Kioga (Ibrahim) Exploratory Survey, 1907–1908." *GJ* 33(1909), 192–195.

Fitzmaurice, Edmond. *The Life of Granville George Leveson Gower Second Earl Granville*. 2 vols. London, 1905.

Fitzner, Rudolf. *Der Kagera-Nil*. Halle, 1899.

Ford, J., and Hall, R. de Z. "The History of Karagwe (Bukoba District)." *TNR* 24(1947), 3–27.

Foskett, Reginald, ed. *The Zambesi Journals and Letters of Dr. John Kirk 1858–63*. 2 vols. London and Edinburgh, 1965.

————. ed. *The Zambesi Doctors. David Livingstone's Letters to John Kirk 1858: 1872*. Edinburgh, 1964.

Fox, A. H. Lane. "Report of the Committee . . . appointed for the purpose of preparing and publishing brief forms of Instructions for Travellers, Ethnologists, and other Anthropological Observers." In *Report of the Forty-Third Meeting of the British Association for the Advancement of Science*. London, 1874, 482–488.

Fraser, A. Z. *Livingstone and Newstead*. London, 1913.

Fraser, H. A., Bishop Tozer, and Christie, James. *The East African Slave Trade*. London, 1871.

Fuchs, V. E. "The Lake Rukwa Expedition." *GJ* 94(1939), 368–387.

Garstin, William. "Fifty Years of Nile Exploration, and Some of its Results." *GJ* 23(1909), 117–152.

Gavin, R. J. "The Bartle Frere Mission to Zanzibar." *Historical Journal* 5(1962), 122–148.

————. "Sayyid Sa'id." *Tarikh* 1(1965), 16–29.

Geikie, Archibald. *Life of Sir Roderick I. Murchison*. 2 vols. London, 1875.

Gibbons, A. St. Hill, "British East African Plateau Land and its Economic Conditions." *GJ* 27(1906), 242–259.

Glover, Lady. *Life of Sir John Hawley Glover*, Richard Temple, ed. London, 1897.

Goode, J. Paul. *Goode's World Atlas*. Chicago, 1957.

Götzen, G. A. Graf von. *Durch Afrika von Ost nach West*. Berlin, 1895.

Grant, C. H. B. "The Hot Springs of Mtagata ('Boiling Water') North Western Tanganyika Territory." *TNR* 24(1947), 47–48.

Grant, D. K. S. "Mangrove Woods of Tanganyika Territory, their Silviculture and Dependent Industries." *TNR* 5(1938), 5–16.

Grant, J. A. "On Mr. H. M. Stanley's Exploration of the Victoria Nyanza." *JRGS* 46(1876), 10–34.

––––––. "Summary of Observations on the Geography, Climate, and Natural History of the Lake Region of Equatorial Africa . . ." *JRGS* 42(1872), 243–342.

Gray, John Milner. "Ahmed bin Ibrahim—the First Arab to Reach Buganda." *UJ* 11(1947), 80–97.

––––––. "Arabs on Lake Victoria. Some Revisions." *UJ* 22(1958), 76–81.

––––––. "Ernest Linant de Bellefonds." *UJ* 28(1964), 31–54.

––––––. *History of Zanzibar.* London, 1962.

––––––. "Livingstone's Muganda Servant." *UJ* 13(1949), 119–129.

––––––. "Mackay's Canoe Voyage along the Western Shore of Lake Victoria in 1883." *UJ* 18(1954), 13–20.

––––––. "Mutesa of Buganda." *UJ* 1(1934), 22–50.

––––––. "Speke and Grant." *UJ* 17(1953), 146–160.

––––––. "Trading Expeditions from the Coast to Lakes Tanganyika and Victoria Before 1857." *TNR* 49(1957), 226–246.

––––––. Letter on Ruwenzori. *UJ* 18(1954), 77–78.

Gray, Richard. *A History of the Southern Sudan 1838–1889.* Oxford, 1961.

Gregory, J. W. "Contributions to the Physical Geography of British East Africa." *GJ* 4(1894), 289–315.

Guillain, M. *Documents sur l'Histoire, la Géographie et le Commerce de l'Afrique Orientale.* 3 vols. Paris, 1856.

Guillemé, P. "Lettre du R. P. Guillemé." *Annales de la Propagation de la Foi* 60(1888), 230–258.

Gulliver, P. H. "A Tribal Map of Tanganyika." *TNR* 52(1959), 61–74.

Gunn, D. L. "A History of Lake Rukwa and the Red Locust." *TNR* 42(1956), 1–18.

Gutkind, Peter C. W. *The Royal Capital of Buganda.* The Hague, 1963.

Haberland, Eike. *Galla Süd-Äthiopiens.* Stuttgart, 1963.

Hall, R. de Z., and Cory, H. "A Study of Land Tenure in Bugufi." *TNR* 24(1947), 28–45.

Hallett, Robin. *The Penetration of Africa.* New York, 1965.

Harding, J. R. "Nineteenth-Century Trade Beads in Tanganyika." *Man* 62(1962), 104–106.

Hart, James D. *The Oxford Companion to American Literature.* 4th ed. New York, 1965.

Hartwig, Gerald W. "Bukerebe, the Church Missionary Society and East African Politics, 1877–1878." *African Historical Studies,* in press.

Hatchell, G. W. "The Angoni of Tanganyika Territory." *Man* 35(1935), 69–71.

Hava, J. G. *Arabic-English Dictionary.* Beirut, 1951.

Heanley, R. M. *A Memoir of Bishop Steere.* London, 1890.

Heese, Missionar. "Sitte und Brauch der Sango." *Archiv für Anthropologie* 12(1913), 134–146.

Herodotus. *The Histories.* Translated with an Introduction by Aubrey de Selincourt. Baltimore, 1960.

Herskovits, Melville. *The Human Factor in Changing Africa.* New York, 1962.

Hertefeldt, M. d'; Trouwborst, A.; and Scherer, J. *Les Anciens Royaumes de la Zone Interlacustrine Meridionale.* London, 1962.

Heudebert, Lucien. *La Découverte du Congo.* Paris, n.d.

––––––. *Vers les Grands Lacs de l'Afrique Orientale.* Paris, 1900.

Hill, Clement H. "Boat Journey up the Wami River." *PRGS* 17(1872–73), 337–340.

Hill, George Birkbeck, ed. *Colonel Gordon in Central Africa, 1874–1879*. London, 1881.

Hill, Richard. *A Biographical Dictionary of the Anglo-Egyptian Sudan*. Oxford, 1951.

———. *Egypt in the Sudan 1820–1881*. London, 1959.

Hine, Sidney Langford. *The Fall of the Congo Arabs*. London, 1897.

Hird, Frank. *H. M. Stanley. The Authorized Life*. London, 1935.

Historical Commission of the Akademie der Wissenschaften. *Allgemeine Deutsche Biographie*. 56 vols. Leipzig, 1875–1912.

Hobley, C. W. "Kavirondo." *GJ* 12(1898), 361–372.

Hoffman, William. *With Stanley in Africa*. London, 1938.

Holmwood, Frederick. "On the River Kingani in East Africa." *Report of the Forty-Seventh Meeting of the British Association for the Advancement of Science* (London, 1878), 144–145.

———. "The Trade between India and the East Coast of Africa." *Journal of the Society of Arts* 33(1884–85), 417–429.

Hore, Edward Coode. "Lake Tanganyika." *PRGS* 4(1882), 1–28.

———. "On the Twelve Tribes of Tanganyika." *JRAI* 12(1882), 2–21.

———. *Tanganyika*. London, 1892.

Horsburgh, James. *The India Directory*. 6th ed. London, 1852.

Huntingford, G. W. B. "The Distribution of Certain Culture Elements in East Africa." *JRAI* 91(1961), 251–295.

———. *The Southern Nilo-Hamites*. London, 1953.

Hurst, H. E. *The Nile*. London, 1952.

Hyndman, Henry Mayers. *The Record of an Adventurous Life*. New York, 1911.

Ingrams, W. H. *Chronology & Genealogies of Zanzibar Rulers*. Zanzibar, 1926.

Jack, E. M. *On the Congo Frontier*. London, 1914.

Jackson, Frederick. *Early Days in East Africa*. London, 1930.

———. "On Honey Guides." *The Journal of the East Africa and Uganda Natural History Society* 4(1913–14), 78–79.

Jackson, Peggy Hervey. *Meteor Out of Africa*. London, 1962.

Jacques, V., and Storms, E. "Notes sur l'Ethnographie de la Partie Orientale de l'Afrique Equatoriale." *Bulletin de la Société d'Anthropologie de Bruxelles* 5(1886–87), 91–202.

Jameson, Mrs. James S., ed. *The Story of the Rear Column of the Emin Pasha Relief Expedition by the Late James S. Jameson*. New York, n.d.

Johnson, Allen, and Malone, Dumas, eds. *Dictionary of American Biography*. 22 vols. New York, 1922–1958.

Johnston, Harry H. *A Comparative Study of the Bantu and Semi-Bantu Languages*. 2 vols. London, 1912–1922.

———. *George Grenfell and the Congo*. 2 vols. London, 1908.

———. *Livingstone and the Exploration of Central Africa*. London, 1891.

———. "Livingstone as an Explorer." *GJ* 41(1913), 423–448.

———. *The Nile Quest*. New York, 1903.

———. *The River Congo*. London, 1884.

———. "Stanley: A Biographical Note." *JAS* 3(1903–1904), 449–463.

———. "The Uganda Protectorate, Ruwenzori, and the Semliki Forest." *GJ* 19(1902), 1–51.

Jones-Bateman, P. L. "Our Work in Zanzibar Town." *Central Africa* 2(1884), 37–44.

Junker, Wilhelm. *Travels in Africa during the Years 1882–1886*, trans. by A. H. Keane. London, 1892.

Kabeya, John B. *Mtemi Mirambo*. Nairobi, Dar es Salaam, and Kampala, 1966.

Kandt, Richard. *Caput Nili*. 2 vols. Berlin, 1914.

Katumba, Ahmed and Welbourn, F. B. "Muslim Martyrs of Buganda." *UJ* 28(1964), 151–163.

Ker, David. "Africa's Cortez." In J. Scott Keltie, ed., *The Story of Emin's Rescue as Told in Stanley's Letters.* Boston, 1890.

Kerfyser, Ed. *Henry M. Stanley.* Bruxelles, 1890.

Kiewiet, Marie J. de. "History of the Imperial British East African Company 1876–1895." Unpublished Ph.D. thesis, University of London, 1955.

King, Edward. "An Expedition with Stanley." *Scribner's Monthly* 5(1872), 105–112.

Kirk, J. "Examination of the Lufigi River Delta, East Africa." *PRGS* 13(1873–74), 74–76.

———. "On Recent Surveys of the East Coast of Africa." *PRGS* 22(1877–78), 453–455.

Kollmann, Paul. *Auf deutschen Boden in Afrika.* Berlin, n.d.

———. *The Victoria Nyanza.* London, 1899.

Kuczynski, R. R. *Demographic Survey of the British Colonial Empire.* 3 vols. London, 1948–1953.

Lacy, George. "A Century of Exploration in South Africa." *JAS* 1(1901–1902), 215–235.

LaFontaine, J. S. *The Gisu of Uganda.* London, 1959.

Laman, Karl. "The Kongo." *Studia Ethnographica Upsaliensia* 4(1953), 8(1957), 12(1962).

Lamden, S. C. "Some Aspects of Porterage in East Africa." *TNR* 61(1963), 155–164.

Landen, Robert Geran. *Oman since 1856. Disruptive Modernization in a Traditional Arab Society.* Princeton, 1967.

Langheld, Wilhelm. *Zwanzig Jahre in deutschen Kolonien.* Berlin, 1909.

Langlands, B. W. "Concepts of the Nile." *UJ* 26(1962), 1–22.

———. "Early Travellers in Uganda: 1860–1914." *UJ* 26(1962), 55–71.

Last, J. T. *Polyglotta Africana Orientalis.* London, n.d.

Leroy, Pierre. "Stanley et Livingstone en Urundi." *Lovania,* 15e année, N. 43(1957), 23–44.

Letroye, A. "Trace des itinéraires des premiers explorateurs en Afrique centrale." *Belgique d'Outremer* 263 (1957), 45–48.

Leue, A. "Bagamoyo." *Beiträge zur Kolonialpolitik und Kolonialwirtschaft* 2(1900–1901), 11–31.

———. *Dar-es-Salaam.* Berlin, 1903.

Lewis, I. M. *The Modern History of Somaliland.* London, 1965.

Livingstone, David. "Extracts from Letters and Despatches from Dr. Livingstone." *PRGS* 14(1869–70), 8–18.

———. "Dr. Livingstone's Letters to Sir Thomas Maclear." *PRGS* 17(1872–73), 67–73.

———. *Missionary Travels and Researches in South Africa.* New York, 1868.

Livingstone, David and Charles. *Narrative of an Expedition to the Zambesi.* New York, 1866.

Longland, F. "A Note on the Tembe at Kwihara, Tabora." *TNR* 1(1936), 84–86.

Louis, Wm. Roger. *Ruanda-Urundi.* Oxford, 1963.

Low, D. A. "The Northern Interior, 1840–84." In Roland Oliver and Gervase Mathew, eds., *History of East Africa,* Vol. I. Oxford, 1963.

———. *Religion and Society in Buganda 1875–1900.* East African Studies No. 8, East African Institute of Social Research. Kampala, n.d.

Luboga, Y. K. *A History of Busoga.* n.p., 1960.

Lugard, F. D. *The Rise of Our East African Empire.* 2 vols. Edinburgh and London, 1893.

———. "Travels from the East Coast to Uganda, Lake Albert Edward, and Lake Albert." *PRGS* 14(1892), 817–841.

Luwel, Marcel, *Stanley.* Bruxelles, 1959.

———. "Considérations sur quelques livres récents ayant trait à Henry Morton

Stanley." *Bulletin. Academie Royale de Sciences d'Outre-Mer* 8(1962), 536–540.

Macdonald, E. A. *The Story of Stanley.* 3rd ed. Edinburgh and London, n.d.

Macgregor, R. *The Rob Roy on the Jordan.* New York, 1870.

McIntyre, W. D. "Commander Glover and the Colony of Lagos, 1861–1873." *JAH* 4(1963), 57–79.

Mackay, A. M. "Boat Voyage along the western shores of Lake Victoria . . ." *PRGS* 6(1884), 273–283.

——. *A. M. Mackay.* By his sister, London, 1890.

Maes, J., and Boone, O. *Les Peuplades du Congo Belge.* Bruxelles, 1935.

Mahy, François de. *Autour de l'île Bourbon et Madagascar.* Paris, 1891.

Malcolm, Capt. "Der ostafrikanischen Fluss Wami. Aus einem Briefe des Capt. Malcolm, Commander des Briton, Brit. R. N., d.d. Zanzibar, 13. Februar. 1873." *ZGEB* 8(1873), 217–219.

Malcolm, D. W. *Sukumaland.* London, 1953.

Markham, Albert H. *The Life of Sir Clements R. Markham.* London, 1917.

Markham, Clements R. *The Fifty Years' Work of the Royal Geographical Society.* London, 1881.

Marston, Edward. "Edward Stanford. A Personal Reminiscence." *The Publisher's Circular* 81(1904), 581.

Marston, Thomas E. *Britain's Imperial Role in the Red Sea Area. 1800–1878.* Hamden, Conn., 1961.

Martineau, John. *The Life and Correspondence of Sir Bartle Frere.* 2 vols. London, 1895.

Mathew, Gervase, "The East African Coast until the Coming of the Portuguese." In Roland Oliver and Gervase Mathew, *History of East Africa,* Vol. I. Oxford, 1963.

Matson, A. T. "A Note on Non-Native Vessels on Lake Victoria." *TNR* 58 and 59 (1962), 225–226.

——. "Sewa Haji: A Note," *TNR* 65(1966), 91–94.

Maude, Francis Cornwallis. *Five Years in Madagascar.* London, 1895.

Maurette, Fernand. *Afrique Equatoriale, Orientale et Australe.* Paris, 1938.

Maurice, Albert. *H. M. Stanley: Unpublished Letters.* London and Edinburgh, 1957.

Mecklenburg, Duke Adolphus Frederick of. *In the Heart of Africa,* G. E. Maberly-Oppler, trans. London, 1910.

Meldon, J. A. "Notes on the Bahima of Ankole." *JAS* 6(1906–1907), 136–153, 234–249.

Meyer, Hans. *Die Barundi.* Leipzig, 1916.

——. *Das Deutsche Kolonialreich.* Leipzig and Wien, 1909.

Meyer, R. "Einem Berichte des Lieutenants d. R. Meyer über seine Expedition nach Kavirondo." *DKB* 4(1893), 517–521.

Miles, S. B. *The Countries and Tribes of the Persian Gulf.* 2 vols. London, 1919.

Mill, Robert Hugh, *The Record of the Royal Geographical Society 1830–1930.* London, 1930.

Mitchell, J. C. "The Yao of Southern Nyasaland." In Elizabeth Colson and Max Gluckman, eds., *Seven Tribes of British Central Africa.* Manchester, 1959.

Moffett, J. P., ed. *Handbook of Tanganyika.* 2nd ed. Dar es Salaam, 1958.

Mohun, M. [R. D.]. "Sur le Congo de Kassongo au Confluent de la Lukuga." *Le Mouvement Géographique* 11(1894), 84–85.

Moir, Frederick L. Maitland. "Eastern Route to Central Africa." *SGM* 1(1885), 95–112.

Moore, J. E. S. *To the Mountains of the Moon.* London, 1901.

Morgan, J. H. *Dickinson College 1783–1933.* Carlisle, Pa., 1933.

Morris, H. F. *A History of Ankole.* Nairobi, 1962.

——. "The Making of Ankole." *UJ* 21(1957), 1–15.

Mors, Otto. "Geschichte der Bahinda des alten Kyamtwara-Reiches am Victoria-Nyanza-See." *Anthropos* 50(1955), 702–714.

Mumford, W. Bryant. "The Hehe-Bena-Sangu Peoples of East Africa." *American Anthropologist* 36(1934), 203–222.

Murdock, George Peter. *Africa. Its Peoples and their Culture History.* New York, 1959.

Naval Staff Intelligence Division. *A Handbook of Kenya Colony (British East Africa) and the Kenya Protectorate (Protectorate of Zanzibar).* London, 1920.

Neumann, Oskar. "Bericht über seine Reisen in Ost-und Central-Afrika." *VGEB* 22(1895), 270–295.

——. "Von der wissenschaftlichen Expedition Oskar Neumanns." *DKB* 5(1894), 421–424.

New, Charles. "Journey from The Pangani, viâ Usambara to Mombasa." *JRGS* 45(1875), 414–420.

——. *Life, Wanderings, and Labours in Eastern Africa.* London, 1873.

Newbury, C. W. *British Policy towards West Africa. Select Documents 1786–1874.* Oxford, 1965.

——, ed. *A Mission to Gelele King of Dahome by Sir Richard Burton.* London, 1966.

Nigmann, E. *Die Wahehe.* Berlin, 1908.

Northcott, Cecil. *Robert Moffat: Pioneer in Africa 1817–1870.* London, 1961.

Ogot, Bethwell A. *History of the Southern Luo, Migration and Settlement 1500–1900.* Nairobi, 1967.

Oliphant, Laurence. "African Explorers." *The North American Review* 124(1877), 383–403.

Oliver, Roland. "Discernible Developments in the Interior, *c.* 1500–1840." In Roland Oliver and Gervase Mathew, eds., *History of East Africa,* Vol. I. Oxford, 1963.

——. *The Missionary Factor in East Africa.* 2nd ed. London, 1965.

Olson, James C. *History of Nebraska.* Lincoln, 1955.

Osogo, John. *Life in Kenya in the Olden Days: The Baluyia.* Nairobi, 1965.

Oswell, W. Edward. *William Cotton Oswell.* 2 vols. London, 1900.

Pagès, R. P. *Un Royaume Hamite au Centre de l'Afrique.* Bruxelles, 1933.

Paterson, R. L. "Ukara Island." *TNR* 44(1956), 54–62.

Patterson, Clara Burdett. *Angela Burdett-Coutts and the Victorians.* London, 1953.

Pechuel-Loesche, Dr. "Das Kongogebiet." *DKZ* 1(1884), 257–264.

Perham, Margery, ed. *The Diaries of Lord Lugard.* 4 vols. London, 1959–1963.

Petermann, A. "Henry M. Stanley's Reise durch Afrika, 1874/7." *PM* 23(1877), 466–474.

Peters, Carl. *Das Deutsch-Ostafrikanische Schutzgebiet.* München und Leipzig, 1895.

——. *Wie Deutsch-Ostafrika entstand!* Leipzig, 1940.

Petherick, Mr. and Mrs. *Travels in Central Africa and Explorations of the Western Nile Tributaries.* 2 vols. London, 1869.

Pfeil, Joachim Graf v. *Die Erwerbung von Deutsch-Ostafrika.* Berlin, n.d.

Philipps, J. E. T. " 'Mufúmbiro': The Birunga Volcanoes of Kigezi-Ruanda-Kivu." *GJ* 61(1923), 233–258.

Picarda, P. "Autour de Mandéra." *Les Missions Catholiques* 18(1886), 184ff.

Pierce, Richard A. *Russian Central Asia.* Berkeley and Los Angeles, 1960.

Price, R. *Report of the Rev. R. Price of his Visit to Zanzibar and the Coast of Eastern Africa.* London, 1876.

Price, T. "Portuguese Relations with David Livingstone." *SGM* 71(1958), 138–146.

Pringle, J. W. "With the Railway Survey to Victoria Nyanza." *GJ* 2(1893), 112–139.

Prins, A. H. J. *Sailing from Lamu*. Assen, 1965.

Putman, George Granville. "Salem Vessels and their Voyages." *EIHC* 60(1924), 17–45.

Ramsay, Hauptman. "Uber seine Expedition nach Ruanda und dem Rikwa-See." *VGEB* 25(1898), 303–323.

Ravenstein, E. G. "Henry M. Stanley." *GJ* 24(1904), 103–106.

Reche, Otto. *Zur Ethnographie des abflusslosen Gebietes Deutsch-Ostafrikas*. Hamburg, 1914.

Reichard, Paul. "Das afrikanische Elfenbein und sein Handel." *Deutsche Geographische Blatter* 12(1889), 132–168.

————. *Deutsch-Ostafrika*. Leipzig, 1892.

————. *Stanley*. Berlin, 1897.

————. "Die Unruhen in Unjanjembe." *DKZ* 5(1892), 103.

————. "Die Wanjamuesi." *Zeitschrift der Gesellschaft für Erdkunde zu Berlin* 24(1889), 246–260, 304–331.

————. "Die Wanjamuezi." *DKZ* 3(1890), 228–230, 263–265.

Reid, Robert L. "The River Aruwimi." *GJ* 38(1911), 29–34.

Richards, Audrey I. "The Bemba of North-Eastern Rhodesia." In Elizabeth Colson and Max Gluckman, eds., *Seven Tribes of British Central Africa*. Manchester, 1959.

Ricklin, L. A. *La Mission Catholique du Zanguebar. Travaux et Voyages du R. P. Horner*. Paris, 1880.

Rigby, Peter. "Dual Symbolic Classification among the Gogo of Central Tanzania." *Africa* 36(1966), 1–17.

————. "Sociological Factors in the Contact of the Gogo of Central Tanzania with Islam." In I. M. Lewis, ed., *Islam in Tropical Africa*. London, 1966.

Roeykens, P. A. *Les débuts de l'oeuvre africaine de Léopold II (1875–1879)*. Bruxelles, 1955.

————. *Léopold et l'Afrique 1855–1880*. Bruxelles, 1958.

Roscoe, John. *The Baganda*. London, 1911.

————. *The Bagesu*. Cambridge, 1924.

Rowe, J. A. "The Purge of Christians at Mwanga's Court." *JAH* 5(1964), 55–71.

Sadler, E. H. "Notes on the Geography of British East Africa." *JAS* 11(1911–12), 173–186.

Said bin Habib. "Narrative of Said bin Habeeb, an Arab Inhabitant of Zanzibar." *Transactions of the Bombay Geographical Society* 15(1860), 146–148.

Sanderson, G. N. *England, Europe and the Upper Nile*. Edinburgh, 1965.

Schapera, I., ed. *David Livingstone. Family Letters 1841–1856*. 2 vols. London, 1959.

————, ed. *Livingstone's African Journal 1853–1856*. 2 vols. London, 1963.

————, ed. *Livingstone's Missionary Correspondence 1841–1856*. London, 1961.

————, ed. *Livingstone's Private Journals 1851–1853*. London, 1960.

Scherer, J. H. "The Ha of Tanganyika." *Anthropos* 54(1959), 841–904.

Schmidt, Rochus. "Die Bedeutung Hermann von Wissmann's in der Entdeckungsgeschichte Afrikas und in Deutschlands Kolonialgeschichte." *Zeitschrift für Kolonialpolitik, Kolonialrecht und Kolonialwirtschaft* 8(1906), 354–374.

Schmitz, Robert. *Les Baholoholo*. Bruxelles, 1912.

Schneider, Karl-Günther. *Dar Es Salaam. Stadtentwicklung unter dem Einfluss der Araber und Inder*. Wiesbaden, 1965.

Scholbach, Hauptmann. "Die Volksstämme der deutschen Ostküste des Victoria-Nyansa." *MFGDS* 14(1901), 183–193.

Schultze, Joachim, ed. *Alexander von Humboldt*. Berlin, 1959.

Schweinfurth, Georg. *The Heart of Africa*, Ellen E. Frewer, trans. 2 vols. New York, 1874.

Schweinitz, H. Hermann Graf von. *Deutsch-Ost-Afrika in Krieg und Frieden.* Berlin, 1894.

Schynse, Père. *A Travers l'Afrique avec Stanley et Emin-Pacha.* Paris, 1890.

Seaver, George. *David Livingstone.* New York, 1957.

Seitz, Don C. *The James Gordon Bennetts.* Indianapolis, 1928.

Seltzer, Leon E., ed. *The Columbia Lippincott Gazetteer of the World.* New York, 1952.

Shann, G. N. "Tanganyika Place Names of European Origin." *TNR* 54(1960), 79–88.

Shepperson, George, ed. *David Livingstone and the Rovuma.* Edinburgh, 1965.

Shorter, Aylward. "Nyungu-Ya-Mawe." *JAH*, in press.

Simpson, D. H. "A Bibliography of Emin Pasha." *UJ* 24(1960), 138–165.

Slade, Ruth M. *English-Speaking Missions in the Congo Independent State (1878–1908).* Bruxelles, 1959.

———. *King Leopold's Congo.* London, 1962.

Smith, George. *The Life of John Wilson.* London, 1878.

Sorenson, Alfred. *The Story of Omaha.* Omaha, 1923.

Soret, Marcel. *Les Kongo Nord-Occidentaux.* Paris, 1959.

Southall, A. *Lineage Formation among the Luo.* International African Institute Memorandum XXVI, London, 1952.

Southworth, Alvan S. *Four Thousand Miles of African Travel.* New York, 1875.

Speke, John Hanning. "Captain J. H. Speke's Discovery of the Victoria Nyanza Lake, the Supposed Source of the Nile. From his Journal." *Blackwood's Edinburgh Magazine* 86(1859), 391–419, 565–582.

———. "Journal of a Cruise on the Tanganyika Lake, Central Africa." *Blackwood's Edinburgh Magazine* 86(1859), 339–357.

———. *Journal of the Discovery of the Source of the Nile,* London, 1863.

———. "The Upper Basin of the Nile, from Inspection and Information." *JRGS* 33(1863), 322–334.

———. *What Led to the Discovery of the Source of the Nile.* London, 1864.

Spellig, Fritz, "Die Wanjamwesi." *Zeitschrift für Ethnologie* 59(1927), 201–252.

Spring, Kapitan. *Selbsterlebtes in Ostafrika.* Dresden und Leipzig, n.d.

Stairs, Capitaine. "De Zanzibar au Katanga, Journal du Capitaine Stairs (1890–1891)," Alph. de Hautville, trans. *Le Congo Illustré* 2(1893), 5ff.

Stanley, Dorothy, ed. *The Autobiography of Sir Henry Morton Stanley.* Boston and New York, 1909.

Stanley, Henry M. "Central Africa and the Congo Basin." *Journal of the Manchester Geographical Society* 1(1885), 6–25.

———. *The Congo and the Founding of its Free State.* 2 vols. London, 1885.

———. *Coomassie and Magdala.* New York, 1874.

———. "A Geographical Sketch of the Nile and Livingstone (Congo) Basins." *PRGS* 22(1877–78), 382–410.

———. *In Darkest Africa.* 2 vols. New York, 1890.

———. *My African Travels.* London, 1886.

———. *My Early Travels in America and Asia.* 2 vols. London, 1895.

———. *My Kalulu.* London, 1873.

———. "On His Recent Explorations and Discoveries in Central Africa." *PRGS* 22(1877–78), 144–166.

———. "Twenty-Five Years' Progress in Equatorial Africa." *Atlantic Monthly* 80(1897), 471–484.

Stanley, Richard, and Alan Neame, eds. *The Exploration Diaries of H. M. Stanley.* London, 1961.

Steere, Edward. *Short Specimens of the Vocabularies of Three Unpublished African Languages (Gindo, Zaramo, and Angazidja).* London, 1869.

Stephens, Leslie, and Lee, Sidney, eds. *Dictionary of National Biography.* 28 vols. London, 1921–1959.

Stock, Eugene. *The History of the Church Missionary Society.* 3 vols. London, 1899.

Storme, M. "Le problème de la rivière Kasayi. Etude de géographie historique." *Zaïre* 11(1957), 227–262.

Storms, Capitaine. "L'Esclavage entre le Tanganika et la Côte Est." *Le Mouvement Antiesclavagiste* 1(1888–89), 14–18.

Struck, Bernhard. "On the Ethnographic nomenclature of the Uganda-Congo Border." *JAS* 9(1909–10), 275–288.

Stuart, Charles H. "Manyema Culture and History prior to 1894." Unpublished paper.

Stuhlmann, Franz, ed. *Die Tagebücher von Dr. Emin Pascha.* 6 vols. Hamburg, 1916–1927.

———. *Mit Emin Pascha ins Herz von Afrika.* Berlin, 1894.

Taylor, Brian K. *The Western Lacustrine Bantu.* London, 1962.

Taylor, John. *The Growth of the Church in Buganda.* London, 1958.

Tew, Mary. *Peoples of the Lake Nyasa Region.* London, 1950.

Thiel, P. H. van. "Businza unter der Dynastie der Bahinda." *Anthropos* 6(1911), 497–520.

Thomas, H. B. "Captain Eric Smith's Expedition to Lake Victoria in 1891." *UJ* 23(1959), 134–152.

———. "The Death of Dr. Livingstone: Cyrus Farrar's Narrative." *UJ* 14(1950), 115–28.

———. "Ernest Linant de Bellefonds and Stanley's Letter to the 'Daily Telegraph'." *UJ* 2(1934–35), 7–13.

———. "Livingstone's Muganda Servant—A Postscript." *UJ* 28(1964), 99–100.

Thomas, H. B., and Dale, Ivan R. "Uganda Place Names: Some European Eponyms." *UJ* 17(1953), 101–123.

Thomas, H. B., and Scott, Robert. *Uganda.* 2nd impression. London, 1949.

Thomson, Joseph. "Progress of the Society's East African Expedition: Journey along the Western Side of Lake Tanganyika." *PRGS* 2(1880), 306–309.

———. *Through Masailand.* London, 1885.

———. *To the Central African Lakes and Back.* 2 vols. London, 1881.

Tippu Tip. *Maisha ya Hamed bin Muhammed el Murjebi yaani Tippu Tip.* Historical Introduction by Alison Smith. Translation by W. H. Whitely. Supplement to East African Swahili Committee Journals, No. 28/2, July 1958 and No. 29/1, Jan. 1959. Nairobi.

Trevor, J. C. "The Physical Characteristics of the Sandawe." *JRAI* 77(1947), 61–78.

Tuckey, J. K. *Narrative of an Expedition to Explore the River Zaire.* London, 1818.

Turnbull, Colin M. *The Forest People.* Garden City, N.Y., 1962.

Tweedie, Ann. "Towards a History of the Bemba from Oral Tradition." In Eric Stokes and Richard Brown, eds., *The Zambesian Past. Studies in Central African History.* Manchester, 1966.

Ullendorf, Edward. "James Bruce of Kinnaird." *The Scottish Historical Review* (1953), 128–143.

Vansina, Jan. *Introduction à l'Ethnographie du Congo.* Bruxelles, 1966.

———. *Kingdoms of the Savanna.* Madison, 1966.

———. "Long-Distance Trade-Routes in Central Africa." *JAH* 3(1962), 375–390.

———. "Notes sur l'Histoire du Burundi." *Aequatoria* 24(1961), 1–10.

Vasconcellos, Ernesto de. "Dois Autographos de H. M. Stanley." *Boletim da Sociedade de Geographia de Lisboa* (1904), 217–220.

Velten, C. *Schilderungen der Suaheli.* Göttingen, 1901.

Verhulpen, Edmond. *Baluba et Balubaïses du Katanga.* Bruxelles, 1936.

Vienne, Ch. de. "De Zanzibar à l'Oukami." *Bulletin de la Société de Géographie* 14(1872), 356–369.

Villiers, Alan. *Sons of Sinbad.* New York, 1940.

Wagner, Günter. *The Bantu of North Kavirondo.* 2 vols. London, 1949–1956.

Wakefield, E. S. *Thomas Wakefield.* London, 1904.

Wakefield, T. "Routes of Native Caravans from the Coast to the Interior of Eastern Africa, chiefly from information given by Sádí Bin Ahédi . . ." *JRGS* 40(1870), 303–339.

Waller, Horace, ed. *The Last Journals of David Livingstone.* 2 vols. London, 1874.

Wallis, J. P. R., ed. *The Zambezi Expedition of David Livingstone 1858–1863.* 2 vols. London, 1956.

Ward, Gertrude, ed. *Letters of Bishop Tozer.* London, 1902.

Ward, Herbert. *A Voice from the Congo.* New York, 1910.

Ward, J. Paul. "H. M. Stanley's View of the Sixth Ashanti War through his Dispatches to *The New York Herald.*" Unpublished paper.

Waterfield, Gordon, ed. *First Footsteps in East Africa by Sir Richard Burton.* London, 1966.

W[auters], A.-J. "Boma." *Le Mouvement Géographique* 4(1887), 99–100.

———. "La Huitième Traversée de l'Afrique Centrale de Banana à Zanzibar par le Lieutenant Gleerup." *Le Mouvement Géographique* 3(1886), 73–75.

Welbourn, F. B. "Speke and Stanley at the Court of Mutesa." *UJ* 25(1961), 220–223.

Werner, A. "The Native Races of German East Africa." *JAS* 10(1910–1911), 53–63.

Westermann, Diedrich. *Geschichte Afrikas.* Köln, 1952.

Wheeler, Douglas L. "Henry M. Stanley's Letters to the *Missouri Democrat.*" *Missouri Historical Society Bulletin* 17(1961), 269–286.

Whitehouse, B. "To the Victoria Nyanza by the Uganda Railway." *Journal of the Society of Arts* 50(1901–1902), 229–241.

Whiteley, Wilfred. *Bemba and Related Peoples of Northern Rhodesia.* London, 1950.

———. "Swahili and the Classical Tradition." *TNR* 53(1959), 214–223.

Wilkins, W. H. *The Romance of Isabel Lady Burton.* 2 vols. New York, 1897.

Williams, John G. *A Field Guide to the Birds of East and Central Africa.* London, 1963.

Williams, Watkin Wynn. *The Life of General Sir Charles Warren.* Oxford, 1941.

Willis, Roy G. *The Fipa and Related Peoples of South-West Tanzania and North-East Zambia.* London, 1966.

Wilson, C. T. "Uganda et Lac Victoria." *Bulletin de la Société Khédiviale de Géographie du Caire* 9–10 (1880), 17–28.

Wilson, C. T., and Felkin, R. W. *Uganda and the Egyptian Sudan.* 2 vols. London, 1882.

Wilson, James Harrison. *The Life of Charles A. Dana.* New York, 1907.

Winans, Edgar V. *Shambala.* London, 1962.

Wissmann, Hermann von. *My Second Journey through Equatorial Africa,* Minna J. A. Bergmann, trans. London, 1891.

———. *Unter deutscher Flagge quer durch Afrika von West nach Ost.* Berlin, 1889.

Young, E. D. *Nyassa.* London, 1877.

Young, Roland, and Fosbrooke, Henry. *Smoke in the Hills.* Evanston, 1960.

Yule, Henry, and Hyndman, H. M. *Mr. Henry M. Stanley and the Royal Geographical Society; Being the Record of a Protest.* London, 1878.

Yule, Mary. *Mackay of Uganda.* London, n.d.

Index